Data Science and Data Analytics

Data Science and Data Analytics
Opportunities and Challenges

Edited by
Amit Kumar Tyagi
School of Computer Science and
Engineering Vellore Institute of Technology

CRC Press
Taylor & Francis Group
Boca Raton London New York

CRC Press is an imprint of the
Taylor & Francis Group, an **informa** business

A CHAPMAN & HALL BOOK

First edition published 2022
by CRC Press
6000 Broken Sound Parkway NW, Suite 300, Boca Raton, FL 33487-2742

and by CRC Press
2 Park Square, Milton Park, Abingdon, Oxon, OX14 4RN

© 2022 selection and editorial matter, Amit Kumar Tyagi individual chapters, the contributors

CRC Press is an imprint of Taylor & Francis Group, LLC

Library of Congress Cataloging-in-Publication Data
Names: Tyagi, Amit Kumar, 1988-editor.
Title: Data science and data analytics: opportunities 1/10 and challenges/edited by Amit Kumar Tyagi (School of Computer Science and Engineering, Vellore Institute of Technology).
Description: First edition. | Boca Raton: C&H\CRC Press, 2021. | Includes bibliographical references and index.
Identifiers: LCCN 2021007674 (print) | LCCN 2021007675 (ebook) | ISBN 9780367628826 (hbk) | ISBN 9780367628888 (pbk) | ISBN 9781003111290 (ebk)
Subjects: LCSH: Big data.
Classification: LCC QA76.9.B45 D396 2021 (print) | LCC QA76.9.B45 (ebook) | DDC 005.7--dc23
LC record available at https://lccn.loc.gov/2021007674
LC ebook record available at https://lccn.loc.gov/2021007675

ISBN: 978-0-367-62882-6 (hbk)
ISBN: 978-0-367-62888-8 (pbk)
ISBN: 978-1-003-11129-0 (ebk)

Typeset in Times
by MPS Limited, Dehradun

Contents

Section I Introduction about Data Science and Data Analytics

Section II Algorithms, Methods, and Tools for Data Science and Data Analytics

Section III Applications of Data Science and Data Analytics

Section IV Issue and Challenges in Data Science and Data Analytics

Section V Future Research Opportunities towards Data Science and Data Analytics

Preface

Data science is a multi-disciplinary field that uses scientific methods, processes, algorithms, and systems to extract knowledge and insights from structured (labeled) and unstructured (unlabeled) data. It is the future of Artificial Intelligence (AI) and the necessity of the future to make things easier and more productive. In simple terms, data science is the discovery of data or uncovering hidden patterns (like complex behaviors, trends, and inferences) from data. Moreover this, big data analytics/data analytics are the analysis mechanism used in data science by a data scientist. Several tools like Hadoop, R, etc., are being used to analyze this large amount of data that can be used in predicting the valuable information/making decisions. Note that structured data can be easily analyzed by efficient (available) business intelligence tools, while most of the data (80% of data by 2020) is in unstructured form that requires advanced analytics tools. But while analyzing, we face several concerns like complexity, scalability, privacy leaks, and trust issues. Data science helps us in extracting meaningful information (or insights) from the unstructured or complex or large amount of data (available or stored around us virtually on the cloud). Here, we get a big question: "Where do we fit in data science in the near future with this large amount of data?" In continuation to this, data is everywhere and expansive. A variety of terms related to mining, cleaning, analyzing, and interpreting data are often used interchangeably, but they can actually involve different skill sets and complexity of data. Also, several positions like data scientist (coined in 2008), data analysis, data engineer, etc., are the result of data science. Hence, this book will cover all possible areas, applications with arising serious concerns, and challenges towards this emerging area/field in detail (with a comparative analysis/taxonomy).

In this book, five tracks have been created which explain possible topics related to data science and data analytics. Further, this book provides several possible opportunities for analysis algorithms/statistical analysis in 21st century (towards data science and data analytics). This book presents several trending technologies in the current smart era like cloud computing, fog computing, edge computing, blockchain, AI for cyber security, AI for the cloud, AI for software development, blockchain for the cloud, etc. This book also discusses several myths about these trending technologies in this smart era. Lastly, several opportunities and possibilities (a way forward towards future) with current trending technologies are discussed in this book. I hope that this book will help future readers, researchers, and scientists to get in-depth information regarding terms such as data science and data analytics

Amit Kumar Tyagi

Editor

Amit Kumar Tyagi is an Assistant Professor (senior grade) and Senior Researcher at the Vellore Institute of Technology (VIT), Chennai Campus, India. He earned a PhD in 2018 at Pondicherry Central University, India. He joined the Lord Krishna College of Engineering, Ghaziabad (LKCE) for the periods of 2009–2010 and 2012–2013. He was an assistant professor and head of research at Lingaya's Vidyapeeth (formerly known as Lingaya's University), Faridabad, Haryana, India, in 2018–2019. His research focuses on machine learning with big data, blockchain technology, data science, cyber physical systems, smart and secure computing, and privacy. He has contributed to several projects such as AARIN and P3-Block to address some of the open issues related to the privacy breaches in vehicular applications (such as parking) and medical cyber physical systems (MCPS). Also, he has published more than 12 patents in the areas of deep learning, Internet of Things, cyber physical systems, and computer vision. Recently, he has awarded the best paper award for a paper titled "A Novel Feature Extractor Based on the Modified Approach of Histogram of Oriented Gradient," ICCSA 2020, Italy (Europe). He is a regular member of the ACM, IEEE, MIRLabs, Ramanujan Mathematical Society, Cryptology Research Society, and Universal Scientific Education and Research Network, CSI, and ISTE.

Contributors

Ashwani Kumar Aggarwal
Department of Electrical and Instrumentation
    Engineering
Sant Longowal Institute of Engineering and
    Technology
Longowal, India

Aishwarya
Department of Computer Science and Engineering
Nitte Mahalinga Adyanthaya Memorial Institute of
    Technology
Karnataka, India

Felix Albu
Department of Electronics
Valahia University of Targoviste
Targoviste, Romania

Paul Anand
University of Florida
Gainesville, Florida, USA

Arunakumari B.N.
BMS Institute of Technology and Management
Bengaluru, India

Nebojsa Bacanin
Singidunum University
Belgrade, Serbia

Zubair Baig
School of Information Technology
Faculty of Science
Engineering and Built Environment
Deakin University, Australia

Raswitha Bandi
Vallurupalli Nageswara Rao Vignana Jyothi Institute
    of Engineering and Technology
Hyderabad, India

Aruna Pavate
Department of Information Technology
Thakur College of Engineering
Mumbai University
Mumbai, India

Kanchipuram BasavaRaju
Sreenidhi Institute of Science and Technology
Hyderabad, India

Sumita Basu
Department of Mathematics
Bethune College
Kolkata, India

Elizabeth Behrman
Department of Physics and Mathematics
Wichita State University
Wichita, Kansas, USA

Timea Bezdan
Singidunum University
Belgrade, Serbia

Pulak Kanti Bhowmick
Mawlana Bhashani Science and Technology
    University
Santosh, Bangladesh

S. Kumar Chandar
School of Business and Management
CHRIST (Deemed to be University)
Bangalore, India

A. Chandrasekar
Department of Computer Science Engineering
St. Joseph's College of Engineering
Chennai, India

Sumika Chauhan
Department of Electrical and Instrumentation
    Engineering
Sant Longowal Institute of Engineering and
    Technology
Longowal, India

Niranjan N. Chiplunkar
Department of Computer Science and Engineering
Nitte Mahalinga Adyanthaya Memorial Institute of
    Technology
Karnataka, India

Aleksa Cuk
Singidunum University
Belgrade, Serbia

Soumi Dutta
Institute of Engineering and Management
Kolkata, India

Roshan Fernandes
Department of Computer Science and Engineering
Nitte Mahalinga Adyanthaya Memorial Institute of
    Technology
Karnataka, India

R. Gayathri
Department of Electronics and Communication
    Engineering
Bannari Amman Institute of Technology
Tamilnadu, India

Arijit Ghosal
St. Thomas' College of Engineering and Technology
Kolkata, India

Sreeya Ghosh
Department of Applied Mathematics
University of Calcutta
Kolkata, India

Shreyas Hingmire
Department of Information Technology
Atharva College of Engineering
Mumbai, India

Nazrul Islam
Mawlana Bhashani Science and Technology
    University
Santosh, Bangladesh

Nazura Javed
St. Francis College
Bangalore Central University
Bengaluru, India

S. Jeyanthi
Vellore Institute of Technology
Chennai, India

V. Kakulapati
Sreenidhi Institute of Science and Technology
Hyderabad, India

P. Shiva Kalyan
Accenture
Hyderabad, India

Jawwad Khan
Department of Information Technology
Atharva College of Engineering
Mumbai, India

Md. Saikat Islam Khan
Mawlana Bhashani Science and Technology
    University
Santosh, Bangladesh

Farhan Hai Khan
Department of Electrical Engineering
Institute of Engineering and Management
Kolkata, India

Abhishek Krishnaswami
Vellore Institute of Technology
Chennai, India

Sanjay Kumar
National Institute of Technology, Raipur
Raipur, India

Yuvaraj L.
Vellore Institute of Technology
Chennai, India

Pradeep M.
Vellore Institute of Technology
Chennai, India

Bijoy Kumar Mandal
NSHM Knowledge Campus
Durgapur, India

Joyston Menezes
Department of Computer Science and Engineering
Nitte Mahalinga Adyanthaya Memorial Institute of
    Technology
Karnataka, India

Aparna Mohan
Vellore Institute of Technology
Chennai, India

Sudhir Kumar Mohapatra
Gandhi Institute of Technological Advancements
(GITA), Bhubaneswar
Bhubaneswar, India

M. Leeban Moses
Department of Electronics and Communication
Engineering
Bannari Amman Institute of Technology
Tamilnadu, India

Jehan Murugadhas
Information Technology Department
University of Technology and Applied Sciences
Nizwa, Oman

Mostofa Kamal Nasir
Mawlana Bhashani Science and Technology
University
Santosh, Bangladesh

Sarat Chandra Nayak
CMR College of Engineering and Technology
(UGC Autonomous)
Hyderabad, India

Vijaya Padmanabha
Department of Mathematics and Computer Science
Modern College of Business and Science
Muscat, Oman

Tannistha Pal
Department of Electronics and Communication
Engineering
Institute of Engineering and Management
Kolkata, India

Ashutosh Pandey
Department of Information Technology
Atharva College of Engineering
Mumbai, India

Aruna Pavate
Department of Information Technology
Thakur College of Engineering
Mumbai University
and
Department of Information Technology
Atharva College of Engineering
Mumbai, India

T. Perarasi
Department of Electronics and Communication
Engineering
Bannari Amman Institute of Technology
Tamilnadu, India

Srinivas Prasad
Gandhi Institute of Technology and Management
Visakhapatnam, India

Appiah Prince
ITMO University
St. Petersburg, Russia

Hitesh Punjabi
K.J. Somaiya Institute of Management and Research
Mumbai, India

Maheswari R.
Vellore Institute of Technology
Chennai, India

Shashidhar R.
JSS Science and Technology University
Mysuru, India

Rejimol Robinson R.R.
Sree Chitra Thirunal College of Engineering
Trivandrum, India

S. Radhika
School of Electrical and Electronics Engineering
Sathyabama Institute of Science and Technology
Chennai, India

Molla Ramizur Rahman
Vinod Gupta School of Management
Indian Institute of Technology
Kharagpur, India

Aman Rai
BMS Institute of Technology and Management
Bengaluru, India

Ratnavel Rajalakshmi
Vellore Institute of Technology
Chennai, India

Tarik A. Rashid
Computer Science and Engineering Department
University of Kurdistan Hewler
Erbil, Iraq

D. Anantha Reddy
National Institute of Technology, Raipur
Raipur, India

Bapuji Rao
CSEA
Indira Gandhi Institute of Technology, Sarang
Dhenkanal, India

Anisha P. Rodrigues
Department of Computer Science and Engineering
Nitte Mahalinga Adyanthaya Memorial Institute of
 Technology
Karnataka, India

Prantik Roy
St. Thomas' College of Engineering and Technology
Kolkata, India

Jeyakrishna S.
Vellore Institute of Technology
Chennai, India

Sophia S.
Sri Krishna College of Engineering and Technology
Coimbatore, India

Boselin Prabhu S.R.
Surya Engineering College
Mettukadai, India

Arijit Santra
St. Thomas' College of Engineering and Technology
Kolkata, India

Niloy Sarkar
The Neotia University
Kolkata, India

Siladitya Sarkar
St. Thomas' College of Engineering and Technology
Kolkata, India

Mahesh Kumar Sharda
School of Business and Management
CHRIST (Deemed to be University)
Bangalore, India

Manmohan Singh
Department of Electrical and Instrumentation
 Engineering
Sant Longowal Institute of Engineering and
 Technology
Longowal, India

G. Suganya
School of Computer Science and Engineering
Vellore Institute of Technology
Chennai, India

K. Tejaswini
Vallurupalli Nageswara Rao Vignana Jyothi Institute
 of Engineering and Technology
Hyderabad, India

P. Thamaraiselvi
School of Management
Sri Krishna College of Engineering and
 Technology
Coimbatore, India

Ciza Thomas
Directorate of Technical Education
Government of Kerala, India
Kerala, India

Rakesh Tripathi
National Institute of Technology, Raipur
Raipur, India

Sridevi U.K.
PSG College of Technology
Coimbatore, India

Jia Uddin
Technology Studies Department
Endicott College
Woosong University
Daejeon, South Korea

Kanchana Devi V.
School of Computer Science and Engineering
Vellore Institute of Technology, Chennai
Chennai, India

K. Venkatachalam
School of Computer Science and Engineering
VIT Bhopal University
Bhopal, India

B. Vignesh
School of Computer Science and Engineering
Vellore Institute of Technology
Chennai, India

B. Vinoth
National Taiwan Normal University
Taipei, Taiwan

Ritika Yadav
St. Thomas' College of Engineering and Technology
Kolkata, India

Miodrag Zivkovic
Singidunum University
Belgrade, Serbia

Section I

Introduction about Data Science and Data Analytics

1

Data Science and Data Analytics: Artificial Intelligence and Machine Learning Integrated Based Approach

Sumika Chauhan, Manmohan Singh, and Ashwani Kumar Aggarwal

CONTENTS

1.1 Introduction

In the previous few decades, all companies have produced data in large amounts from different sources. It can be from business applications of their own, social media or other web outlets, from smartphones, and client computing devices or from the Internet of Things sensors and software. This knowledge is highly useful for companies that have resources in place to build on it. The overall toolbox for these methods is called data analytics.

Data analytics is used to represent those methods that provide an essential arrangement of the data. It can be classified into four categories, including descriptive, predictive, diagnostic, and prescriptive data analytics. Out of these methods, predictive analytics is the most dynamic approach for data analytics that involves an advanced statistical approach, Artificial Intelligence–based algorithms. Predictive analytics (PA) is the member of advanced analytics that is broadly utilized in the prediction of uncertain future events. A variety of data analysis, statistical modeling, and theoretical approaches are used to bring management, information technology, and business process forecasting together to forecast these predictive events. To define threats and possibilities in the future, the trends contained in historical and transactional data may be used. PA models may track relationships with a complex set of conditions to distribute a score or weighting among several variables to determine risk.

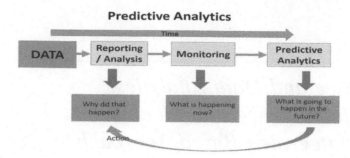

FIGURE 1.1 Predictive analytics value chain.

Predictive analytics helps companies to anticipate, construct, and focus on the evidence and not on a hunch or expectations, forecasting findings and actions. The value chain of predictive analytics is seen in Figure 1.1.

1.2 Artificial Intelligence

Artificial Intelligence (AI) invokes the simulation of computers based on human intelligence that is designed to think and imitate their behavior like humans. The word can also be extended to any system that shows features similar to a human mind, such as understanding and diagnostic. AI has an outstanding feature that is its capability to rationalize and perform decisions that have the greatest chance of fulfilling a specific target [1].

The principle idea behind AI is that it is vital to interpret human intelligence in a manner that a machine can effectively imitate and perform functioning from the easiest to those that are much more complex. The purpose of AI involves comprehension, logic, and interpretation. AI is based on the scenic concept that originally burst, followed later by Machine Learning (ML), and eventually, Deep Learning (DL) that continues to accelerate developments of AI to another level.

From Figure 1.2 it is observed that there are three concentric circles, DL is a subspace of ML, which is also a subspace of AI.

1.3 Machine Learning (ML)

ML is based on the AI that equips systems with the learning ability and upgrades from experience without being programmed directly. It can be categorized in supervised learning, unsupervised learning, and reinforcement.

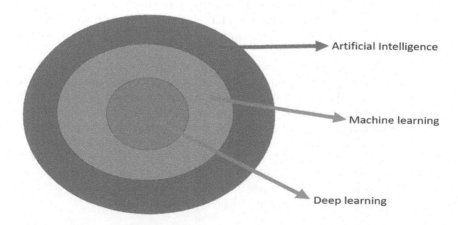

FIGURE 1.2 Distinction between AI, machine learning, and deep learning.

Supervised learning is the assignment for ML to learn an operation that outlines a vector input to an output vector, based on the I/O relationship. Classification is the method of foreseeing the class or labels of given datasets. Classification forecast methodology is the duty of estimating mapping operation from input variables to distinct output variables. Basically, the methods for supervised learning are classified into two categories: regression and classification.

1.3.1 Regression

Regression is the most powerful statistical method in data analytics that pursues to describe the power and aspects of the relationship between one dependent variable to a series of other independent variables. Various types of regression are available in the literature [2]. A few of them are discussed as follows.

1.3.1.1 Linear Regression

It attempts to relate the two features by fitting a linear relation with corresponding estimated regression parameters. One variable is taken as an explanatory vector, and the second one is considered as a vulnerable vector. The linear regression is used in cost prediction and estimation of some data analysis in the data analytics. Let us consider a sample of N objects with m variables, which can be represented as $N \times m$ matrix X and the predicted output is a vector $Y^T = (y_1, y_2, ..., y_m)$. For a particular individual i, let $X_i = (x_{i1}, x_{i2}, ..., x_{im})$, which indicates the covariate vector. The output is a continuous variable denoted by Y_i. Mathematically linear regression is given as

$$\hat{y}_i = \beta_0 + \sum_{j=1}^{m} x_{ij}\beta_j \tag{1.1}$$

The β_0 indicates the intercept and is also called the bias in machine learning, and $\beta^T = (\beta_1, \beta_2, ..., \beta_m)$ is the coefficient vector. The values of all input variates should be numeric for the feasible computation of the covariate values. The equation can be rewritten as

$$\hat{Y} = X^T\hat{\beta} \tag{1.2}$$

Parameter estimation is considered as minimization of loss function over a dataset in the supervised learning. The least-squares approach is the commonly used technique for an appropriate regression line. In this method, the calculation of the best-fitting line is accomplished using observed data to minimize the sum of the square of the vertical deviations from each data point. The cost function is defined in terms of residual sum of squares, which is computed using Euclidean distance between the measured and projected outputs, $\hat{Y}$. This can be written mathematically as

$$RSS(\beta) = \sum_{i=1}^{N} (y_i - x_i^T\beta)^2 \tag{1.3}$$

$RSS(\beta)$ represent the quadratic operation of the parameters; thus, the minimum value of it is always present. The solution is easily obtained in matrix representation, written as

$$RSS(\beta) = (y - X\beta)^T(y - X\beta) \tag{1.4}$$

The minimization of the above-mentioned equation can be obtained by setting the first derivative of $RSS(\beta)$ equal to zero. Differentiating w.r.t. β, the obtained normal equation is given as

$$X^T(y - X\beta) = 0 \tag{1.5}$$

If $X^T X$ is non-singular, then a unique solution is obtained by

$$\hat{\beta} = (X^T X)^{-1} X^T y \qquad (1.6)$$

and obtained value, which is fitted at the ith input x_i, is $\hat{y}_i = \hat{y}(x_i = x_i^T \hat{\beta})$. At an arbitrary input x_0, the prediction is $\hat{y}(x_0) = x_0^T \hat{\beta}$.

1.3.1.2 Logistic Regression

Logistic regression searches for the relationship between an unambiguous dependent variable and a number of autonomous (explainable) variables. It is a binary classification technique. The dependent variables have only two values, such as 0 or 1, or these variables are the binary type. The probability's log-odds and feature share a linear relation. For a convinced particle $X_i = (x_{i1}, x_{i2}, ..., x_{im})$, the predicted output y_i can be labeled as either 0 or 1. The equation of the logistic regression is given as

$$log\frac{Pr(y_i = 1|X_i)}{Pr(y_i = 0|X_i)} = \sum_{k=0}^{m} x_{ik}\beta_k = X_i\beta \qquad (1.7)$$

The value of x_{i0} is 1 and β represents the intercept. As we know that in the case of two-class classification $Pr(y_i = 1|X_i) + Pr(y_i = 0|X_i) = 1$; thus, from equation (1.7) we have

$$Pr(y_i = 1|X_i) = \frac{exp(X_i\beta)}{1 + exp(X_i\beta)} \qquad (1.8)$$

The parameter estimation is accomplished by maximizing the cost function in the logistic regression models. The joint conditional probability for all N points in training data is

$$Pr(y = y_1|X_1) \cdot Pr(y = y_2|X_2) \cdot \ ..... \cdot Pr(y = y_N|X_N) = \prod_{i=1}^{N} Pr(y = y_i|X_i) \qquad (1.9)$$

where y_i; $i = 1, 2, ..., N$ is the predicted labels in the training set. The log-likelihood for N observations is

$$\mathcal{L}(\beta) = \sum_{i=1}^{N} log[(Pr(y = y_i)|X_i)] \qquad (1.10)$$

where the logit transformation of conditional probability for an individual X_i is

$$log[(Pr(y = y_i)|X_i)] = \begin{cases} X_i\beta - log[1 + exp(X_i\beta)] & : \ y_i = 1 \\ -log[1 + exp(X_i\beta)] & : \ y_i = 0 \end{cases} \qquad (1.11)$$

Hence, equation (1.10) is solved as

$$\mathcal{L}(\beta) = \sum_{i=1}^{N} \{X_i\beta \cdot y_i - log[1 + exp(X_i\beta)]\} \qquad (1.12)$$

Generally, the Newton-Raphson method is utilized for maximizing this log-likelihood, where the coefficient vector is modernize as

$$\beta^{(t+1)} = \beta^{(t)} - \left[\frac{\partial^2 \mathcal{L}(\beta)}{\partial\beta\partial\beta^T}\right]^{-1} \frac{\partial\mathcal{L}(\beta)}{\partial\beta} \tag{1.13}$$

where

$$\frac{\partial\mathcal{L}(\beta)}{\partial\beta} = \sum_{i=1}^{N} X_i\left(y_i - \frac{exp(X_i\beta)}{1 + exp(X_i\beta)}\right) \tag{1.14}$$

$$\frac{\partial^2\mathcal{L}(\beta)}{\partial\beta\partial\beta^T} = -\sum_{i=1}^{N} X_i X_i^T \frac{exp(X_i\beta)}{[1 + exp(X_i\beta)]^2} \tag{1.15}$$

The initial value is $\beta = 0$ [3].

Multi-class Logistic Regression

The conditional probability for a specific variable X_i is given as

$$Pr(y_i = j|X_i) = \frac{exp(X_i\beta_j)}{\sum_{k\neq j} exp(X_i\beta_j)} \tag{1.16}$$

where $j, k\epsilon L$ and L is the label index. Therefore, the log-likelihood for N observations can be written as

$$\mathcal{L}(\beta) = \sum_{i=1}^{N}\left[X_i\beta_j - log\left(\sum_{k\neq j} exp(X_i\beta_j)\right)\right] \tag{1.17}$$

This problem is minimized by the Broyden-Fletcher-Goldfarb-Shanno (BFGS) algorithm.

Polytomous Logistic Regression

It is used when the groups of the resultant variables are trivial; that is, they have no normal structure. This is the modified version of the basic logistic regression and used to deal with multi-class datasets. Let us consider the two-class logistic regression problem. For a C-class question, $C - 1$ binary logistic regression will be fitted. Consider a case when the last group (C^{th} class) is taken as the reference, the model is given by

$$log\frac{Pr(y=1|X_i)}{Pr(y=C|X_i)} = X_i\beta_1$$
$$log\frac{Pr(y=2|X_i)}{Pr(y=C|X_i)} = X_i\beta_2$$
$$\vdots \tag{1.18}$$
$$log\frac{Pr(y=C-1|X_i)}{Pr(y=C|X_i)} = X_i\beta_{C-1}$$

It should be noted that for particle X_i the addition of all Derrirer probabilities is equal to 1. Therefore, each possible outcome will be

$$Pr(y=k|X_i) = \frac{exp(X_i\beta_k)}{1+\sum_{j=1}^{C-1} exp(X_i\beta_k)}, \quad k = 1, 2, ..., C - 1$$
$$Pr(y=C|X_i) = \frac{1}{1+\sum_{j=1}^{C-1} exp(X_i\beta_k)} \tag{1.19}$$

The model can be learned by maximum a posteriori (MAP) [3].

1.3.2 Support Vector Machine (SVM)

SVM is a multivariate statistical approach used in the problems related to regression and classification. The minimization of structural risk is the principle used in SVM. The SVM technique have non-linear charaterics, hence it is also applicable to huge amount of data. The aim of the SVM method is to classify datasets into two categories with the application of hyper-plane. This hyper-plane calculates the distance between support vectors. The SVM classifier needs binary dataset $X_{m \times n}$ with labels y_i for classification. The representation for binary classes is accomplished using -1 and 1 entities like $y_i \epsilon [-1,1]$. For optimum hyper-plane, the distance should be maximum [4]. To obtain the solution for the optimization problem for generalized separating optimum hyper-plane, the following equation is used:

$$\text{Minimize} \quad \frac{1}{2}\|\omega\|^2 + C\sum_{k=1}^{m}\xi_i$$
$$\text{subjected to} \quad y_i(\langle \omega, x_i \rangle + b) \geq 1 - \xi_i \quad ; \quad \xi_i \geq 0, \quad i = 1, 2, \ldots, m \tag{1.20}$$

The ω represents the vector for dimension m, and b is the bias value. C indicates the penalty for the error. ξ_i represents the slack variable, which is calculates the distance of hyper-plane and misclassified data points. The considered constraints for this equation are given as

$$\iota(\omega, b, \xi, \alpha, \gamma) = \frac{1}{2}\|\omega\|^2 + C\sum_{k=1}^{m}\xi_i - \sum_{i=1}^{m}\alpha_i\left[y_i(\langle \omega, x_i \rangle + b) - 1 + \xi_i\right] - \sum_{i=1}^{n}\gamma_i\xi_i \tag{1.21}$$

To satisfy the KKT conditions and to minimize ι, equation (1.21) is converted in the dual quadratic equation described as

$$\max \quad \omega(\alpha) = \max\left\{-\frac{1}{2}\sum_{i=1}^{m}\sum_{j=1}^{m}\alpha_i\alpha_j y_i y_j \langle x_i, x_j \rangle + \sum_{k=1}^{m}\alpha_k\right\}$$
$$s.t. \quad 0 \leq \alpha_i \leq C; \quad i = 1, 2, \ldots, m \tag{1.22}$$

$$\sum_{i=1}^{m}\alpha_i y_i = 0 \tag{1.23}$$

For optimal separating hyper-plane, this equation is rewritten as

$$f(x) = sgn\left(\sum_{i,j=1}^{m}\alpha_i y_i \langle x_i, x_j \rangle + b\right) \tag{1.24}$$

1.4 Deep Learning (DL)

DL is a subset of AI; the working principle is based on the behavior of the human brain when it processes the data and generates patterns to make decisions. DL is a subspace of ML in AI that has networks that are able to learn unsupervized from the unstructured or unlabeled dataset. There are numerous DL architectures including recurrent, deep, and convolutional neural networks (CNNs), etc. have been applied to various areas like machine vision, speech recognition, natural language processing, and computer vision.

1.4.1 Methods for Deep Learning

DL methods compose four elements: the dataset, a cost function to be learned, a model, and a training technique. To solve a problem using DL, the correct combination of these four elements is essential. The building blocks of DL models are briefly discussed in this section. The fundamental component of deep neural networks is artificial neurons. A number of artificial neurons are used to generate a layer, and by combining multiple such layers, a feed-forward neural network is composed. By the application of these layers and sharing parameters, we introduce a convolutional neural network, which is perfectly applicable to data having sequential and spatial correlation.

1.4.1.1 Convolutional Neural Networks (CNNs)

CNNs are also known as ConvNet. They carry deep feed-forward architecture. It has amazing quality to generalize in an improved manner in comparison to fully connected layers. Its operation is based on DL models to deals with grid pattern-based data. CNNs are constructed with the ability to have flexible learning of spatial chain of features ranking from lower to higher patterns. The consideration of CNN over other classical DL methods is as given: (i) due to the weight sharing in CNN, it requires few parameters for training given enhanced generalization. Also, as the parameter requirement for training is reduced, the problem of overfitting is solved. (ii) The learning process is implemented in both feature extraction and classification. (iii) It is easy to perform large network operations using CNNs over other ANNs. The mathematical modeling of CNN is accomplished using the following layer or components: convolution, pooling, and fully connected layers.

General Model of Convolutional Neural Network

The basic building blocks of CNN comprise three layers: viz input, hidden layer, and output layer. The input vector X is given to a distinct neuron and obtain an output Y from it using an operation F given as

$$F(X, W) = Y \tag{1.25}$$

Here, W represents the weighting factor that explains the interconnected frequency of a neighboring neuron's layer; it is used in image classification problems. The CNN's hidden layer consists of the following elements shown in Figure 1.3 and named as convolution layer, pooling layer, and fully connected layer [5]. In standard architecture, the initial convolution layer is employed followed by the pooling layer. The fully connected layers form the architecture between different layers as an ANN structure. This layer is finally connected to the output layer.

Feed propagation is accomplished by converting input data into output data using these layers. The working procedure of each element is discussed here.

Convolution Layer

The basic element of CNN architecture is a convolution layer to extract the features, carrying a set of linear and nonlinear functions known as convolution and activation functions, respectively. In convolution, a kernel (i.e., array of number) is applied to an input (tensor).

An element-wise dot multiplication is performed between kernel elements and input tensor elements and integrated to achieve the output in corresponding space in output tensor, termed a feature map, as shown in Figure 1.4. The same process is repeated in order to generate unlimited feature maps representing characteristics of different input tensors such that each kernel can be viewed as an extractor of features. The size and number of kernels are two primary parameters that describe the convolution operation.

Weight sharing in the convolution process produces the following characteristics: (i) allowing local feature patterns derived by kernel translation-invariant to move through all image positions and recognize local learned patterns; (ii) by down sampling in combination with a pooling operation, studying spatial hierarchies of feature configurations, resulting in an exponentially wider field of view being collected; and (iii) the model reliability can be learned by diminishing the number of parameters relative to fully connected neural networks. The convolution operation is performed using

$$a_{ij} = \sigma((W * X)_{ij} + b) \tag{1.26}$$

Here, X is the input given to the layer, kernel that slides over input is W, and b represent bias.

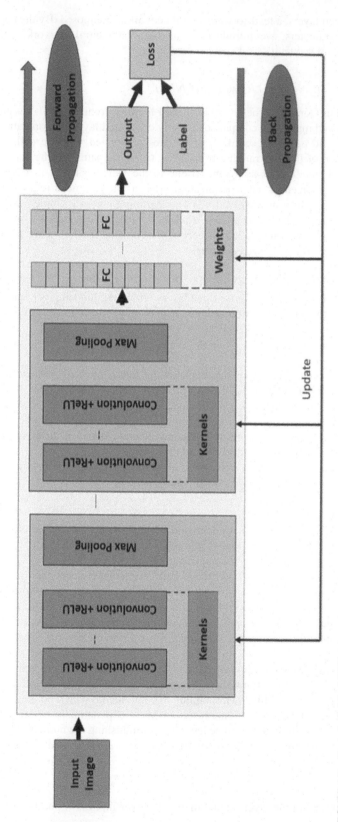

FIGURE 1.3   General model of CNN.

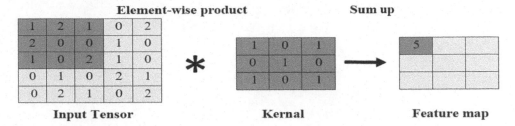

FIGURE 1.4   Procedure to perform convolution.

Nonlinear Activation Function

The activation function with nonlinear characteristics is then transferred through the outputs of convolution. Smooth, nonlinear functions including sigmoid or hyperbolic tangent functions are also available with the mathematical behavior of a biological neuron, as shown in Figure 1.5.

The rectified linear unit (ReLU) is the most widely used nonlinear activation function for two reasons: first, it is simple to determine the partial derivative of ReLU. Second, when one of the variables is training time, the saturating nonlinearities such as sigmoid are slower than non-saturating nonlinearities such as ReLU. The ReLU is mathematically described as

$$f(x) = max(0, x) \qquad (1.27)$$

Third, ReLU does not enable the absence of gradients. The considerable value of gradients in the network decreases the efficacy of ReLU, which updates the weight parameter due to which neurons do not get activated. This resembles the dying ReLU problem. This is addressed by utilizing leaky ReLU conditions:

if $x > 0$, the function activates resemble $f(x) = x$, but

if $x < 0$, the function activates as αx, where α is a constant with a small value.

Pooling Layer

In pooling, translation invariance is added to minor shifts and transformations. The number of corresponding learnable parameters is also reduced by the down-sampling procedure that decreases the in-plane dimensionality of the function maps. For this purpose, a window is chosen that executes the pooling operations and pooling function transferred input item lying in that window. Max pooling and global average pooling are widely used pooling strategies [5,6].

Max pooling – It is a widely used approach that extracts the patches from the input feature map and eliminates all other values to get the full value from each patch as an output. It reduces map size very significantly.

Global average pooling – It conducts down-sampling of a feature map into a 1 × 1 array by taking the average of all the elements present in each feature map, keeping depth its constant.

Fully Connected Layer

This layer in the general model is equivalent to a fully connected layer. The output from the first phase (i.e., convolution and pooling) is applied to a fully connected layer. The dot product is taken between weight and input vectors to achieve final output. Offline algorithm or batch mode learning is the other name for gradient descent. It decreases the value of fitness function through evaluating the fitness over full training dataset, and all values of parameters are updated after one epoch. One epoch is corresponding to the whole dataset. This provides the global optimum solution, but for the training of the larger dataset through the network, it requires a huge amount of time.

Last Layer Activation Function

A SoftMax function applies the activation function in classification problems to activate neurons that normalize all values between 0 and 1 and sum for all values is 1.

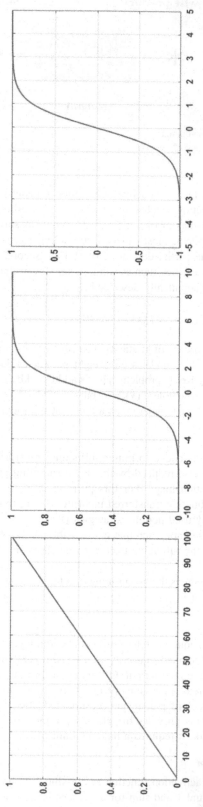

FIGURE 1.5 Activation functions for NNs: a) ReLU, b) sigmoid, and c) tanh.

1.4.1.2 Extreme Learning Machine

In previous decades, ANNs have been gaining the attention of researchers in different research areas such as DSP (digital signal processing), precise forecast, and pattern recognition. Single-hidden-layer-feed-forward-neural-network (SFLN) is the most adopted form of ANN. G. Huang et al. presented an extreme learning machine (ELM) in 2006 to provide good generalization performance and extremely fast learning speed. ELM does not require gradient-based backpropagation to work [7]. It uses the Moore-Penrose generalized inverse to set its weights.

A standard learning algorithm for the neural network is required to define all parameters of training randomly and use repetitive methods to refine the parameters. It is also possible to produce the optimum answer locally. But in the ELM, the weight and bias of hidden neurons are needed to set randomly. These weights are calculated by the Moore-Penrose rule under the criterion of least squares.

ELM is based on SFLNs, and comprises input, output, and hidden layers in its architecture. In the algorithm of ELM, only a number of hidden neurons are required to set. The value of weight used in the input and output layer and bias are generated randomly in the ELM. The calculation of the matrix for the hidden layer is also performed by it. The next step is to update the weight using the Moore-Penrose pseudoinverse. ELM has a fast learning speed because of its straightforward architecture and requirement of few parameters in calculations. ELM architecture is given in Figure 1.6.

Consider N arbitrary sample $(X_j, t_j) \in R^n X R^m$ with SLFN, having L hidden nodes which approximates these N samples with zero error. The activation function $G(\alpha_i, \beta_i, X_i)$ is mathematically modeled as

$$f_L(X_j) = \sum_{i=1}^{L} \beta_i G(\alpha_i. X_j + b_i) = t_j, \qquad j = 1, \ldots, N. \tag{1.28}$$

Here, α_i and b_i are learning parameters of hidden nodes, out of which α_i connects the input weight vector of input nodes to ith hidden node and b_i denotes the threshold of the ith hidden node. β_i and t_j represent output weight and test points, whereas activation function $G(\alpha_i, \beta_i, X_i)$ gives output for the ith hidden node. The equation is given as

$$H\beta = T \tag{1.29}$$

where $H = (\alpha_1, \ldots, \alpha_L, b_1, \ldots, b_L, X_1, \ldots, X_N) = \begin{bmatrix} G(\alpha_1, \beta_1, X_1) & \ldots & G(\alpha_L, \beta_L, X_1) \\ \vdots & \ldots & \vdots \\ G(\alpha_1, \beta_1, X_N) & \ldots & G(\alpha_L, \beta_L, X_N) \end{bmatrix}_{NXL}$

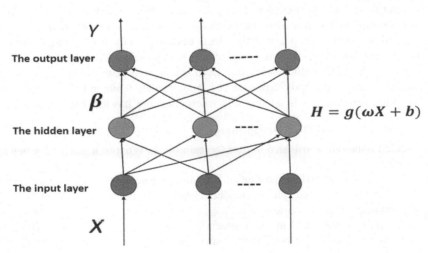

FIGURE 1.6   The extreme learning machine structure.

$$\beta = \begin{bmatrix} \beta_1^T \\ \vdots \\ \beta_L^T \end{bmatrix}, \ T = \begin{bmatrix} T_1^T \\ \vdots \\ T_N^T \end{bmatrix}$$

As per ELM theories, the values of α_i and b_i are randomly generated. The solution of the equation is given in the following way:

$$\beta = H^*T \tag{1.30}$$

H^* is inverse for the output matrix H. The Moore-Penrose generalized inverse is utilized for this purpose.

To obtain an enhanced and stable result from this network, a regularization term is added to the β [8]. If hidden layer neurons are less as compared to training samples, β can be represented as

$$\beta = \left(\frac{1}{\lambda} + H^*H \right)^{-1} H^*T \tag{1.31}$$

If nodes in hidden layers are more compared to training samples, β can be expressed as

$$\beta = H^* \left(\frac{1}{\lambda} + HH^* \right)^{-1} T \tag{1.32}$$

1.4.1.3 Transfer Learning (TL)

The basic requirement of any AI-based algorithm is that the training and target data must be of identical functional space with the same distribution. This assumption does not apply, however, in certain real-life implementations. In this case, the efficient transfer of information will significantly boost learning efficacy by preventing wasteful data-labeling attempts. If the space of features and/or the distribution of data varies, a new model must be created. Whenever it receives a new dataset, it becomes costly to generate a new model from the ground up. So, the need and efforts to remember the vast volumes of training data are minimized by TL. Transfer learning includes the method of transmitting and using information gained in one or more background assignments to facilitate the learning of a relevant target task [9–11].

Traditional algorithms for data mining and deep learning render forecasts for future data utilizing models based on statistics. These models are trained on classified or unlabeled training data that is previously obtained. The aim of TL is to take the benefit of data from the first set to gain knowledge that might help in the second set when there is a requirement to make a prediction directly. The distinction between conventional learning methods and conversion strategies is seen in Figure 1.7.

Standard machine learning methods learn each task from scratch, while in transfer learning it utilizes information from the previous task to a target task where the latter has less high-quality training data.

Important Considerations for Transfer Learning

Three main research issues are considered in transfer learning: 1) What to transfer, 2) when to transfer, and 3) how to transfer.

"What to transfer" questions which portion of the information between the source and the target activity should be moved. Some knowledge may be unique to particular domains or tasks, and some knowledge may be universal across various domains, so that the output of the target domain or task may be enhanced. "When to transfer" asks in which situations transferring skills should be done. We should not attempt to incorporate transfer learning if the source and goal domains are not at all connected. The

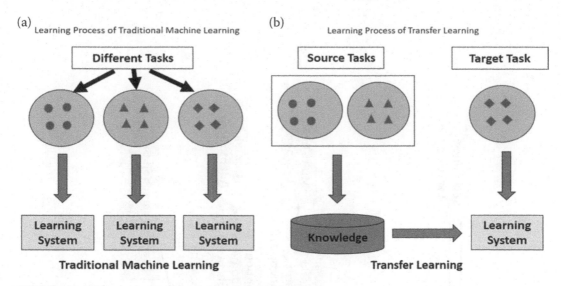

FIGURE 1.7 Difference in standard training and transfer learning.

efficiency of learning in the target domain will be harmed. This is termed negative learning. "How to transfer" describes various methods for implementing transfer learning as associated with the source and goal domain/task.

Types of Transfer Learning

Transfer learning is classified into three classes: inductive, transductive, and unsupervised transfer learning as summarized in Figure 1.8.

Transfer learning methods in three different contexts can be divided into four groups on the basis of "What to transfer." The first group uses some part source domain data which that can be utilized for learning the target domain [12,13]. In this case, instance reweighting and significance sampling techniques are used.

The second category is the feature-representation-transfer approach [14–17]. The concept used for this method is to learn a successful target domain representation of features. The information used to pass between domains in this group is encoded into the acquired function representation, which is supposed to dramatically increase the efficiency of the target task.

The third category is the parameter-transfer approach [18,19], in which certain parameters of the models are distributed between source and target tasks. In the mutual parameters or prior, the transmitted information is encoded. Finally, the last category is relational-knowledge-transfer approach, which manages relations between different domains.

1.5 Bio-inspired Algorithms for Data Analytics

An innovative approach based on the concepts and motivation of the biological evaluation of nature to create modern and efficient computational techniques is bio-inspired computational optimization algorithms. These algorithms for data analytics can be categorized as follows: swarm intelligence-based, evolutionary algorithms, and ecological-based algorithms. These algorithms are summarized in Table 1.1 [23,24].

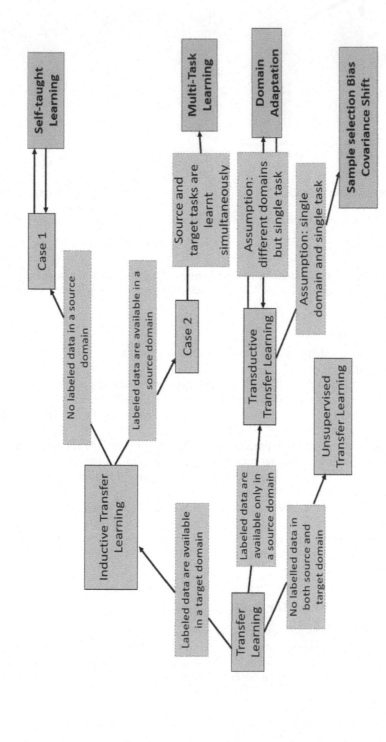

FIGURE 1.8 Relationship between the various environments of transfer learning.

TABLE 1.1

Bio-inspired Algorithms for Data Analytics

Swarm Intelligence Based	Evolutionary	Ecological
Salp swarm algorithm and its variants [20,21] Slime mold algorithm [22] Particle swarm optimization (PSO) and its variants [23] Coral reef optimizer (CRO) Artificial bee colony (ABC) [24] Squirrel search algorithm [25] Whale optimization and its variants [26,27] Grey wolf optimizer (GWO) and its variants [28] Crow search algorithm [29] Boosting salp swarm Firefly swarm optimization Cat swarm optimization (CSO) [30] Ant colony optimization (ACO) [31]	Genetic algorithm and its variants [32,33] Simulated annealing [34] Cuckoo search algorithm Evolutionary strategy Genetic programming Differential Evolution (DE) [35]	Biogeography-based optimization (BBO) [36] Artificial ecosystem-based optimization (AEO) Invasive weed colony (IWC) Multi-species optimizer (PS2O)

1.6 Conclusion

The transformation of data obtained through numerous organizations into practical knowledge is accomplished by data analytics. In data analytics, artificial intelligence has a huge scope to process and analyze the data. The advantages of artificial intelligence in data analytics are given as follows: (i) automation becomes easy with the application of AI; (ii) progressive learning; AI algorithms can train the machine to perform any desired operation; and (iii) neural networks make it easy to train the machines because networks learn from its input data, analyze it, and identify the correct dataset. Optimization algorithms are also the part of AI and very useful to obtain enhanced results for different applications such as in the field of biomedical signal processing, in the fault diagnosis of machines to identify and predict the faults.

REFERENCES

[1] S. J. Russell and P. Norvig, *Artificial Intelligence: A Modern Approach*. Englewood Cliffs, New Jersey: Alan Apt, 1995.

[2] T. Hastie, R. Tibshirani, and J. Friedman, *The Elements of Statistical Learning: Data Mining, Interface, and Prediction*, Second Edi. Springer Series in Statistics, 2009.

[3] V. Kumar, *Healthcare Data Analytics*. Taylor & Francis, 2015.

[4] A. Kumar and R. Kumar, "Time-frequency analysis and support vector machine in automatic detection of defect from vibration signal of centrifugal pump," *Meas. J. Int. Meas. Confed.*, vol. 108, no. April, pp. 119–133, 2017, doi: 10.1016/j.measurement.2017.04.041.

[5] R. Yamashita, M. Nishio, R. Kinh, G. Do, and K. Togashi, "Convolutional neural networks: An overview and application in radiology," *Insights Imaging*, vol. 9, pp. 611–629, 2018.

[6] S. Indolia, A. Kumar Goswami, S. P. Mishra, and P. Asopa, "Conceptual understanding of convolutional neural network – A deep learning approach," *Procedia Comput. Sci.*, vol. 132, pp. 679–688, 2018, doi: 10.1016/j.procs.2018.05.069.

[7] G. Huang, Q. Zhu, and C. Siew, "Extreme learning machine: Theory and applications," *Neurocomputing*, vol. 70, pp. 489–501, 2006, doi: 10.1016/j.neucom.2005.12.126.

[8] D. Xiao, B. Li, and Y. Mao, "A multiple hidden layers extreme learning machine method and its application," *Math. Probl. Eng.*, vol. 2017, pp 1–10, 2017.

[9] S. J. Pan and Q. Yang, "A survey on transfer learning," *IEEE Trans. Knowl. Data Eng.*, vol. 22, no. 10, pp. 1345–1359, 2010, doi: 10.1109/TKDE.2009.191.

[10] M. Kaboli, A review of transfer learning algorithms. Diss. Technische Universität München, 2017.

[11] D. Sarkar, R. Bali, and T. Ghosh, *Hands-On Transfer Learning with Python: Implement Advanced Deep Learning and Neural Network Models Using Tensor Flow and Keras.* Packt Publishing Ltd, 2018.

[12] W. Dai, Q. Yang, and G.-R. Xue, "Boosting for transfer learning," *Proc. 24th Int. Conf. Mach. Learn.*, pp. 93–200, 2007.

[13] W. Dai, G.-R. Xue, Q. Yang, and Y. Yu, "Transferring naive Bayes classifiers for text classification," *Proceedings – 22nd Assoc. Adv. Artif. Intell.*, pp. 540–545, 2007.

[14] A. Argyriou, T. Evgeniou, and M. Pontil, "Multi-task feature learning,"*Adv. Neural Inf. Syst.*, vol. 19, 41, pp. 41–48, 2007.

[15] S. I. Lee, V. Chatalbashev, D. Vickrey, and D. Koller, "Learning a meta-level prior for feature relevance from multiple related tasks," *Proc. 24th Int. Conf. Mach. Learn.*, pp. 489–496, 2007.

[16] T. Jebara, "Multi-task feature and kernel selection for SVMs," *Proc. 21st Int. Conf. Mach. Learn.*, p. 55, 2004.

[17] C. Wang and S. Mahadevan, "Manifold alignment using Procrustes analysis," *Proc. 25th Int. Conf. Mach. Learn.*, pp. 1120–1127, 2008.

[18] E. V. Bonilla, K. M. A. Chai, and C. K. I. Williams, "Multi-task Gaussian process prediction," *Adv. Neural Inf. Process. Syst.*, pp. 153–160, 2008.

[19] N. D. Lawrence and J. C. Platt, "Learning to Learn with the informative vector machine," *Proc. 21st Int. Conf. Mach. Learn.*, p. 65, 2004.

[20] S. J. Pan and Q. Yang "A survey on transfer learning," *IEEE Trans. Knowl. Data Eng.*, vol. 22, pp. 1345–1359, 2009.

[21] R. K. Ando and T. Zhang, "A framework for learning predictive structures from multiple tasks and unlabeled data," *J. Mach. Learn. Res.*, vol. 6, pp. 1817–1853, 2005.

[22] J. Holland, "Adaption in natural and artificial systems," *An Introductory Analysis with Applications to Biology, Control, and Artificial Intelligence*, Massachusetts, USA: MIT Press, 1975.

[23] S. Chauhan, M. Singh, and A. K. Aggarwal, "Diversity driven multi-parent evolutionary algorithm with adaptive non-uniform mutation," *J. Exp. Theor. Artif. Intell.*, no. 2020, pp. 1–32, 2020.

[24] S. Zhao and P. N. Suganthan, "Empirical investigations into the exponential crossover of differential evolutions," *Swarm Evol. Comput.*, vol. 9, pp. 27–36, 2013, doi: 10.1016/j.swevo.2012.09.004.

2

IoT Analytics/Data Science for IoT

T. Perarasi, R. Gayathri, M. Leeban Moses, and B. Vinoth

CONTENTS

2.1 Preface

A multifaceted development is data science to extract information from various data templates. Data science is defined as "unifying information, data processing, machine learning, sphere knowledge and interrelated techniques" to "comprehend and evaluate real phenomena" by knowledge. It's a "fourth paradigm" of science and argued that due to the effects of information technology and the data deluge, all about science is changing as imagined by Jim Gray.

Big data is becoming a critical instrument for corporations and enterprises of each and every size quite rapidly. Big data availability and interpretation have transformed the company representation of existing industries that have allowed new ones to be developed. The different technologies and techniques that can rely on the application are worn for data science. The strategies are as follows:

- Regression-linear and Logistics.
- Vector Machine (SVM) support.
- Clustering is a method used to group knowledge together.
- Dimensionality reduction is used to decrease data computation complications so that it can be done faster.
- Machine learning is a method for supposition patterns from data to perform tasks.

Data science offers meaningful knowledge on vast quantities of complicated data. This method blends various fields of work to analyze data for decision-making purposes in statistics and computation. Information from all the sources are collected and stored as datasets. The quantity rises with existing data leads to a new area of research of focus on big data in all sectors. Due to advances in technology and collection methods, increasing access to data is possible. Nonetheless, for productive dynamic, the ever-expanding information is unstructured and includes parsing. For organizations, this technique is confounded and tedious, henceforth the ascent of information science. So as to gather an illuminating index, cycle, and draw an insight from the set, and interpret it for investigation, information science coordinates assets from different orders. Mining, measurements, AI, examination, and programming structure make up the information science under the disciplinary fields.

To disentangle valuable and suitable information from the set, information mining applies calculations to the confounding informational collection. This removed information is utilized through factual measures or prescient investigation to ensure functions happened before. AI is an instrument of man-made consciousness that measures immense data that an individual won't have the option to measure.

Utilizing investigation, the information expert gathers and cycles the organized information, utilizing calculations from the machine learning level. The investigator deciphers, interprets, and sums up the information into a lucid jargon that can be deciphered by the dynamic group. Information science is pertinent to essentially all unique situations, and the order will expand to incorporate information design, information designing, and information organization as the part of the information researcher develops (Figure 2.1).

2.1.1 Data Science Components

As we are aware, data science is the most important unit in statistics. In order to get valuable insights, it is the process or science of gathering and analyzing numerical data in vast quantities. Visualization methodology lets you access massive amounts of data in images that are easy to interpret and digestible. Machine learning explores analysis of algorithm creations that learn to make unforeseen/future data predictions. The deep learning approach is new research in machine learning where the algorithm selects the model of study, as shown in Figure 2.2.

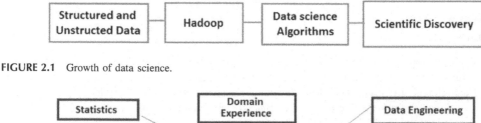

FIGURE 2.1 Growth of data science.

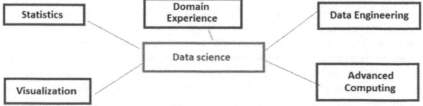

FIGURE 2.2 Data science elements.

2.1.2 Method for Data Science

The data science process is defined in Figure 2.3, which includes six stages of name discovery, data preparation, model planning, model building, activity, and results communication.

In this step, the method and technique for drawing the relationship between input variables must be determined. By using various mathematical formulas and visualisation tools, planning for a model is carried out.

Stage 1: Discovery: The phase of discovery involves collecting knowledge from all the internal and external sources known that allows you to address the business query. The data may be web server logs, social media data collected, census datasets, or online source data streamed using APIs.

Step 2: Preparation of Data: Data may have several inconsistencies, such as missing value, blank columns, and incorrect format of data that needs to be cleaned. Prior to modeling, you need to store, explore, and condition data. The cleaner your data is, the better your forecasts.

Step 3: Planning of Models: In this step, the method and technique for drawing the relationship between input variables must be determined. By using various mathematical formulas and visualization tools, planning for a model is carried out. Some of the methods used for this function are SQL review services, R, and SAS/access.

Step 4: Constructing Models: The actual model-building process begins in this phase. Here, data scientists distribute educational and research datasets. For the training data collection, techniques such as association, grouping, and clustering are applied. The model is checked against the" testing "dataset until prepared.

Step 5: Operationalize: You deliver the final baseline model with reports, code, and technical documents at this level. The model is implemented after rigorous testing in a real-time production environment.

Step 6: Communication results: The main results are conveyed to all stakeholders in this process. This helps you to determine if the project outcomes are a success or a failure based on the model inputs.

2.1.3 The Internet of Stuff

The Internet of Things represents an object network, each of which has a different IP address and can connect to the web. These things may include people, pets, and everyday appliances such as refrigerators and coffee machines. These things can connect to the web (and to one another) via this network and communicate with each other in ways not previously considered.

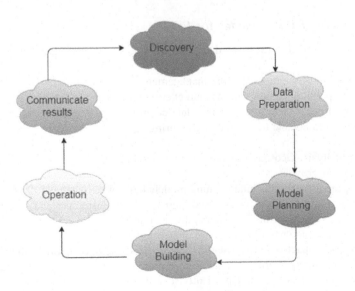

FIGURE 2.3   Step by step of data science.

Imagine a future in which your coffee maker, fridge, window, heating systems, watering equipment, weight scale, your car, mobile phone, watch, TV, wardrobe, cleaning machines for your house are all in the same network, all connect and communicate with one another, and every little object in your home is linked to the Internet and communicates with one another.

If it reminds you the *Transformers* movie scene, it's not! This is closer to reality than you can imagine.

There is no clause that defines what these devices can or cannot do.

Therefore, it is very open to the imaginations of designers and manufacturers. However, here are some obvious things to keep in mind:

- These devices will, as appropriate, interact with humans or other machines.
- Such systems will have data collection sensors that could be your pulse, your temperature, or the traffic in front of the vehicle.
- Such machines will be capable of computing. Driverless cars will all do the route planning and avoidance of accidents on their own.
- Data storage.
- To turn stuff on and off, these would have embedded controllers.

2.1.3.1 Difficulties in the Comprehension of Stuff on the Internet

Before reaching the IoT, there are a few critical difficulties to resolve.

- Communication regimes and design requirements: The scenarios for using these devices are also enormous, while the applications are huge. Each scenario requires a different style of communication: various latencies, unique frequencies, and various lengths of data. For instance, once in a while, the data needs to be transmitted by a sensor measuring human body temperature. Self-driving cars have to be supplied with electricity each second!
- Consumer privacy: Consumer privacy advocates would scream at the top of their lungs at this stage. The IoT will reveal privacy that is still open today, both at the personal and industrial level.
- Information protection: Each of these devices has its own security problems. Even after years of effort, our PCs, laptops, and cell phones still have security issues. This challenge is now going to a new level, with more devices coming on the Internet.

2.1.3.2 Sub-domain of Data Science for IoT

Real-time applications linked to real-time data and data science computing advances are based on the following.

Cognitive computing: An approach to the management of regions that have not been easy to enter through increasingly popular gadgets such as market comprehension and estimates. The processing data involves a non-stop process of information and data creation. Real-time analysis and analytics of data enables an association to be able to move quickly during those periods where acting within seconds or minutes is enormous.

Geospatial data analysis: Geospatial data science meets numerous important challenges of growing creativity and financial growth.

Deep learning: Conventional machine learning models have always been at the forefront of working with structured data and have been widely used, depending on customers and so on. The manual assembly of highlights is time-consuming, fragile, and technically not scalable to unstructured data such as photos, content, and voice records.

Sensor combination capacity in IoT: Sensor combination includes coordinating information from different sensors and sources so the subsequent information has less vulnerability than would be possible if these sources were utilized independently. For this situation, the words "decrease of vulnerability" may mean more exact, all the fuller, or more solid, or allude to the result of an advancing perspective dependent on the joined information. Sensor combination in applications, for example, aviation, has consistently assumed a key job.

Accelerometers and spinners are regularly joined into an Inertial Measurement Unit (IMU) in aviation applications, which estimates direction, characterized as Degrees of Freedom (DOF), in view of various sensor inputs. Because of severe precision and float resistances, just as high unwavering quality, however progressively, inertial route frameworks (INS) for shuttles and airplanes will cost a large number of dollars for a sensor combination in self-driving vehicles and robots where contributions from numerous sensors can be consolidated to construe more functions.

Continuous computation and IoT: Both quick and large information is associated with IoT. A characteristic collaboration with IoT is accordingly given by real-time applications. In light of both quick and wide information streaming, numerous IoT applications, for example, armada the board, savvy network, Twitter stream preparing and so forth have explicit investigation necessities. They include real-time labeling: The best way to extricate the sign from commotion is to recognize the information as it shows up, as unstructured information streams from various sources.

- a. Real-time Collection: You do continuous total on the off chance that you total and process information along a sliding time window. Over the most recent 5 seconds, discover a client movement logging example and contrast it with the most recent 5 years to recognize deviation.
- b. Real-time transient connection: Example, an area base and time-sensitive identification of rising functions, constant function relationship from a huge scope online media streaming information (above adjusted from log trust).
- c. IoT security, protection, and square chain: You reserve the option to know every sensor that tracks you when you arrive at another climate and to specifically turn it on or off too. This may sound outrageous; however, it shows the Boolean (On or Off) mindset that today rules a significant part of the talk on security. Future IoT security conversations, in any case, are probably going to be undeniably more muddled, particularly if protection and square chain are viewed as together.
- d. Edge computing: Edge computing insinuates the estimation in a machine map around the corner or edge. For the affiliations, edge figuring is additionally useful as it permits them to reduce down expenses that were recently procured on the sharing of informational collections over a framework.

2.1.3.3 IoT and Relationship with Data

Each of the IoT data is connecting IoT and data processing. The range of data accumulation takes care of and alters various types and arrangements that can be organized, formless or semi-organized of information generated from various IoT devices and sensors. The IoT-initiated monstrous amount of data is swallowed and put aside the "volume" of stacking data [1–7]. The continuous, secure planning and survey of massive IoT data is conducted in a favorable manner through the "pace" of the Big Data review [8]. The knowledge about IoT artifacts is also validated and expanded by the trust of data. In Figure 2.4, the equivalent is represented.

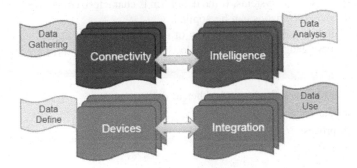

FIGURE 2.4 Illustrate the IoT-data relationship.

2.1.3.4 IoT Applications in Data Science Challenges

The "assortment" takes care of and alters various styles and ordering of data generated from various IoT devices and sensors. The continuous close planning and investigation of gigantic IoT data is carried out in a timely manner "pace" of data science analysis [9]. Similarly, the appreciation of data identifies and extends the information and the knowledge of smart IoT artefacts.

Data storage and analysis: The first problem is bulk media and higher data or yield velocity due to the staggering cost of capacity [10–14].

- Awareness discovery and computational complexities: Representation of learning is a primary problem in large data and involves a few elective fields, such as confirmation, recording, organization, conservation, retrieval, and representation of knowledge. The current tools may not be successful in processing this data for useful information due to the expansion in data size [15].
- Data scalability and visualization: Adaptability and protection is the most important test for data science approaches. In recent decades, researchers have concentrated on speeding up data processing and speeding up planning. For some associations managing dangerous datasets, data adaptability has proven to be critical, certainly when execution problems occur. The goal of data description is to show the data in a progressively correct way, using a few practical hypothesis approaches [16].
- Poor quality of data: If conceivable, it is important to uphold a deliberate distance from the manual data portion. One method to computerizing information and reducing extending typographic errors, and human gestures is application mix tools. Additionally, time spent "preparing results" prevents re-doing. Unchanging data is secure, it is not appropriate to bother to begin removing the data. This is an essential advance in ensuring the eminence of data, which leads us to challenge number two [17].
- Data structures: Most sensors relay data is exhausted for a large part of the time with nothing occurring. Although static edge-dependent cautions are a good starting stage for examining this data, they cannot allow us to advance to prescriptive phases.
- Multiple data formats together: Though time arrangement data has defined processes and procedures for commerce with it, the interactions that would be really valuable will not emerge from sensor data alone.
- Balance size and speed: Much of the actual IoT investigation will take place because of the circumstances involving the progressive handling of a lot of information [18] (Table 2.1).

2.1.3.5 Ways to Distribute Algorithms in Computer Science to IoT Data

The enhancement of the human way of life has been one of the main points of innovation and it is moving closer to achievement with the IoT. In any event, IoT needs knowledge to give enhanced rendezvous or find enormous methods in order to fully understand this aim. Data Science and Machine Learning are enthusiastic about this place. Data types [19] would have to be characterised in order to allow proper use of data science systems. If the data form is characterized, the right measurement lies in line with evident data characteristics can be applied.

The Internet of Things is a one-of-a-kind array of objects that can be connected to the Internet [20].

In any case, what these gadgets can or cannot do is not detailed. Below [2] are a few contemplations of such gadgets.

- Will work with people and with each other to deliver
- Designed for data collection
- The ability to process
- Storage of data

These tools have controls to turn items ON or OFF.

TABLE 2.1

IoT Applications and Challenges in Data Science

Challenges	Actions
Data management and analysis	Data storage and data analysis; hard drives used for data storage
Credited with a good set of data	Data warehouses and data centers; charge of extracting the data attained from the working frameworks; multi-faceted computational design, susceptibility; information discovery and computational complexities
Scalability and Visualization of data	Adaptability and protection of data scalability and visualization; proven to be necessary for handling certain dangerous datasets, certainly when execution problems occur
Poor data quality	Poor data quality requires the use of highly established industry principles and the detection of ceaseless irregularities
Too much data	Too much data overload will potentially create a large number of problems that counteract substantial progress
Data structures	Data structures relations between pieces of information collected at explicit intervals of time
Multiple data formats together	Knowledge on time arrangements has developed protocols and procedures for coping with experiences and experiences
Balance scale and speed	It may not be suitable for circumstances needing a lot of knowledge to be managed gradually, and adaptability of the cloud

i. The essence with IoT: As opposed to big data, the IoT scan is gaining traction. Numerous shopper instances and new apps alter the environment functions and converse for it. An advertisement loop must break down [21] in order to see how IoT has progressed after some time.

ii. IoT problems: There are a number of difficulties with IoT identification: Inspire devices from different manufacturers to talk to one another.

- Prerequisites and communication routines of design
- Information confidentiality

There is a test in the approval of relevant IoT applications with the advancement of the IoT-based framework, which integrates its assistance for enormous applications [22–24]. Figure 2.5 demonstrates the effect of data science on the IoT.

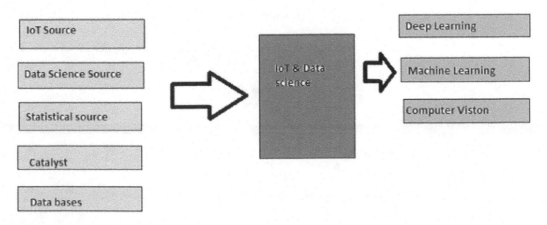

FIGURE 2.5 IoT on data science.

2.2 Computational Methodology-IoT Science for Data Science

Via several "layers" of neural network algorithms, deep learning algorithms scuttle data, each of which convey a basic illustration of the records to the next layer on datasets that have up to a few hundred elements, or columns. The most common deep learning algorithms are Convolutionary Neural Network (CNNs). It is a detachment of machine learning where, from immense quantities of data. Below is a five-step method that you should adopt to produce above-average performance on predictive modeling issues consistently:

> Stage 1: Describe the problem you have. How to describe the problem with machine learning.
> Stage 2: Get your data ready.
> Stage 3: Algorithms for spot-check.
> Stage 4: Outcomes change.
> Stage 5: Current outcomes.

On datasets that have up to a few hundred elements, or columns, most machine learning algorithms work well. However, an unstructured dataset has such a large number of characteristics, like one from an image. A conventional machine learning algorithm is to be managed by a single 800-by-1000-pixel image has 2.4 million features for RGB color. Due to an increase in layers of the neural network, deep learning algorithms picture increases as it goes through. Features are incorporated from the existing layers and applications like edges in a holistic way. A middle layer in the network analyze the parts of an object in any sort of pictures but the deep learning method is used to detect the entire object by observing the shapes of the same.

When doing with unorganized data, the ability to progression large numbers of features make deep culture very efficient. For a lesser amount of complex issue, however, deep learning algorithms may be overloaded since they need admittance to large data to be successful.

It is very possible for a deep learning model to over-fit and fail to generalize well to new data if the data is too basic or incomplete. For most realistic business problems like customer satisfaction, identifying fault transactions and the deep learning models are not as successful as others in practice. Deep learning can function with smaller, organized datasets in some contexts, such as multiclass classification.

2.2.1 Regression

The most famous model is regression, used to estimate the relationships between variables, whereas classification models belong to the group on observation, as in Figure 2.6. These systems range from linear regression (simple) to more complex techniques including gradient boosting and neural networks.

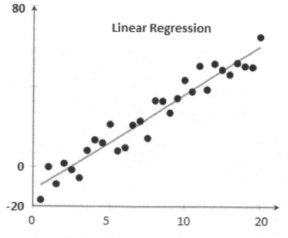

FIGURE 2.6 Regression for weather analysis.

Continuous numbers involve any machine learning problem that also includes a wide range of real-life applications; regression is essential:

- Forecasting time sequence
- Financial forecasting, such as stock prices or housing prediction
- Weather analysis
- Automotive research

Training and validation is the first step in creating a machine learning model. You must first divide your dataset to train and validate a model, which includes selecting what percentage of your data to use for the training, validation, and holdout sets. A dataset with 64% training data, 16% validation data, and 20% holdout data is shown in the following example.

2.2.2 Set of Trainings

A training set is the subsection of a dataset from which relationships between the features and the goal variable are discovered or "learned" by the machine learning algorithm. During supervised machine learning, the training data is labeled with known results in Figure 2.7.

The machine learning algorithm is applied to another subset of the input data and validates the collection and also checks the correlations between the known results for the characteristics of the dataset and other goal variable. This is referred to as the process of 'testing' data, where the data sets have been trained and validated. The performance of the machine learning model provides a final approximation of a holdout subset that should never be used to determine which algorithms to use or tuned or should be improved. Partitioning the sequences into training, validation, and holdout sets models helps you to construct the more highly precise models that are suitable to gather the information in future. A real sense of the preciseness of the model would be obtained by training the data, validating it, and checking it on the holdout collection that may lead to better decisions and trust in the precision of designed model.

2.2.3 Pre-processing

Data pre-processing is an umbrella concept that encompasses a number of operations that can be used by data scientists to bring their data into a more fitting shape for what they want to do with it. In a void, however, pre-processing data would not occur. Pre-processing provides an easy and simple solution as can be seen; there are best practices and build an intuition, and pre-processing is normally important to determine its output in context. Scale is our respective data, for each of us, this function will be the same.

Figure 2.8 Sensory information is obtained from one's surroundings (vision, sound, smell, taste, and touch) and passes to the brain for processing and reaction via the peripheral nervous system. Sensor fusion takes the simultaneous input from several sensors when integrating all of these technologies, processes the input, and produces an output that is greater than the sum of its parts (i.e., sensor fusion removes the shortcomings of each individual sensor by using special algorithms and filtering techniques, similar to how the human body works as mentioned previously).

FIGURE 2.7 Education and validation.

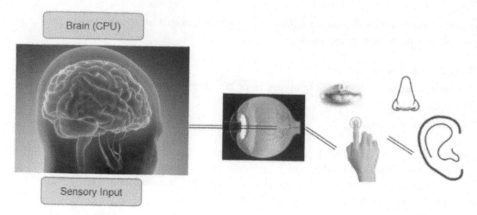

FIGURE 2.8 Sensoratory information.

Sensor fusion offers a variety of features that simplify our lives and allow us to leverage these features in a variety of services. Sensor fusion also applies to a combination of 3D accelerometers, 3D gyros, and 3D magnetometers. This configuration is called a 9-axis system and provides the user with 9 degrees of freedom (9-DoF). Freescale released the Extrinsic 12-axis sensor platform for Windows 8 in 2012, which provides a fusion solution for 12-DoF sensors. This is done by including the features of a barometer sensor, a thermometer sensor, and ambient light detection.

2.2.4 Sensor Fusion Leverage for the Internet of Things

The IoT involves many cases of usage, from connected homes and communities to connected cars and roads to devices that monitor the actions of a person and use the data collected for "push" services. The IoT is a kind of "world neural network in the sky" universal that will affect every part of our lives. The IoT is described from a technical point of view as smart machines that connect and communicate with other machines, artifacts, environments, and infrastructures, resulting in volumes of data generated and processed into useful behavior that can command and control things and make human beings' lives much easier.

2.3 Methodology-IoT Mechanism of Privacy

By applying CCs to devices that do not yet possess them, the privacy protecting IoT can be easily extended. A privacy policy exchange session will also be needed for any additional computer so fitted. A data security team is used for procedures and philosophies used for data, information, and system security. Ensuring the means of preventing unauthorized entry, use, and disruption with regard to information security, disruption, discovery, alteration, or death. Data security has three primary laws that you might think about: confidentiality, availability, and honesty. Accountability has proved to be a more important standard and is included in the three ideas of security organizations some of the time.

2.3.1 Principles for IoT Security

Protection allows an information system to ensure the availability, integrity, and confidentiality of resources to protect the objectives. There are several key goals in the network for protecting IoT devices and the framework is projected.

Confidentiality: Defending permitted data limits, including the safeguarding of individual privacy data. Lost privacy is the unauthorized revelation of knowledge.

Integrity: Preservation of despicable alteration or misfortune of data, including ensuring non-renouncement and validity of data. Lost honesty is the unauthorized alteration or loss of knowledge.

- Authenticity: The property of being true and having the right to be confident in the authenticity of a transmission, a letter, and confirmed confirmation. This means verifying that consumers are who they claim they are and that a trustworthy source is the source of any input that comes to the system.
- Availability: Ensuring that data is obtained and used in an appropriate and solid manner. Missing availability is the intrusion of data access or use.
- Accountability: The security objective which creates the requirement that an entity's activities be pursued in an interesting manner by that entity. Non-repudiation, deterrent, identification, and avoidance of intrusion, fault isolation, and recovery after intervention and legal action are assisted.

2.3.2 IoT Architecture Offline

This postulation will divide the architecture of IoT security into two forms: the offline architecture and the online architecture. As part of the IoT framework, the offline architecture is mostly made up of standard gadgets. The online architecture is related to the IoT framework, which consists primarily of clever gadgets.

2.3.3 Offline IoT Architecture

Figure 2.9 shows that the stuff (recognition gadgets) only imparts and exchanges data with data accepting gadgets in the offline IoT architecture. In offline architecture, the validation and key understanding are divided into two sections: one is the validation and key understanding between the items and the gadgets that are accepted; the other is between the requestors and the data structures of administration.

The accepting gadget would also influence the accuracy of the information investigation in subsequent IoT applications with regard to the products, verification, and information communication protection between them, from one point of view; then, again, raising new security needs.

2.3.4 Online IoT Architecture

Figure 2.10 shows that stuff can set up end-to-end correspondence connections in the online IoT architectures to get to requesters via the Internet or IoT passage. Coordinate device associations are not set

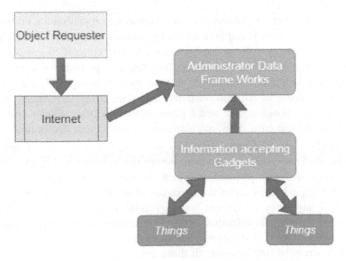

FIGURE 2.9 IoT architecture offline.

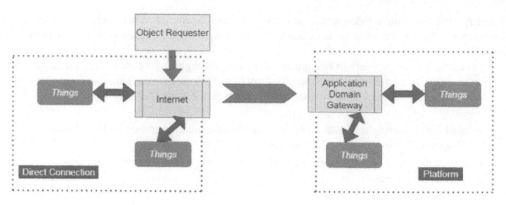

FIGURE 2.10 IoT architecture online

up by access requestors and the objects. The application domain gateway will complete the verification of the requestor and monitor it in different layers.

Since the end-to-end correspondence connects between items at the stage of IoT design applications and gets to requesters, the use procedure needs a lot of accessible name material. In addition, the size of things and question name assets of two kinds of IoT architecture applications are examined in order to promote the analysis of things, tending to protect in later sections.

2.3.5 IoT Security Issues

As opposed to the conventional model, there are many safety problems in the IoT system.

- Built to run in the field independently without a reinforcement network if the connection is lost.
- Scalability and management in the IoT of billions of individuals.
- Identifying end-focuses in a flexible way is an uncommon test like Individual Party.
  a. Capacities for small calculations
  b. Encryption calculations require a higher asset and high-power calculation
  c. Low cycles of the CPU for good encryption 20

2.3.6 Applications

- Applications for consumers: It detects your presence as you approach the door of your house, and unlocks itself automatically. It requires all energy units in the home (lights, heaters, stoves, refrigerators) to enter energy storage mode as soon as you close it to get out of the home. The opposite occurs when you come back. When you fall asleep, your wrist band detects and automatically asks your headphones and lights in your room to turn off. The sensors in your garden soil calculate the amount of soil moisture and adjust watering accordingly. Unit-efficient plant watering! Health care: imagine your watch periodically checks your heart rate and notifies you of any irregularity in the first case. You may also give a letter to your doctor and to a hospital nearby.
- Commercial applications: Computer life: Imagine a train and its track filled with sensors that control its wear and tear continuously. And before the train reaches its destination, you will be aware of the required repairs and improvements. Similarly, in order to replace them, you do not rely on the generic guidelines about the existence of tracks. The term refers to aircraft engines, wind turbines, or any heavy equipment you may think of. Smart cities: What about designing a city to make decisions on its infrastructure, which thrives on this data? What roads should be enlarged? To ease traffic, which routes need alternatives? What is the correct hospital location? What should its strengths be? Imagine all these decisions on data.

2.4 Consummation

Data science is a field of study that involves extracting information from vast amounts of data using a variety of scientific methods, algorithms, and processes. This upcoming sector in industry and education has plenty of applications and benefits. When this data science is incorporated with the Internet of things, then the world becomes simple in all sorts of technologies. This sort of analytics will improve the technology at a global level.

REFERENCES

[1] Abu-Elkheir, M., Hayajneh, M., Ali, N. A.: Data management for the internet of things: design primitives and solution. *Sensors* **13**(11), 15582–15612 (2013).

[2] Riggins, F. J., Wamba, S.F.: Research directions on the adoption, usage, and impact of the internet of things through the use of big data analytics. In: Proceedings of 48th Hawaii International Conference on System Sciences (HICSS'15), pp. 1531–1540. IEEE (2015).

[3] Cheng, B., Papageorgiou, A., Cirillo, F., Kovacs, E.: Geelytics: geo-distributed edge analytics for large scale IoT systems based on dynamic topology. In: 2015 IEEE 2nd World Forum on Internet of Things (WF-IoT), pp. 565–570. IEEE (2015).

[4] Fang, H.: Managing data lakes in big data era: what's a data lake and why has it become popular in data management ecosystem. In: 2015 IEEE International Conference on Cyber Technology in Automation, Control, and Intelligent Systems (CYBER), pp. 820–824. IEEE (2015).

[5] Desai, P., Sheth, A., Anantharam, P.: Semantic gateway as a service architecture for IoT inter-operability. In: 2015 IEEE International Conference on Mobile Services (MS), pp. 313–319. IEEE (2015).

[6] Hu, S.: Research on data fusion of the internet of things. In: 2015 International Conference on Logistics, Informatics and Service Sciences (LISS), pp. 1–5. IEEE (2015) Google Scholar.

[7] Schmidhuber, J.: Deep learning in neural networks: an overview. *Neural Netw.* **61**, 85–117 (2015).

[8] Tsai, C.-W., Lai, C.-F., Chiang, M.-C., Yang, L.T.: Data mining for internet of things: a survey. *IEEE Commun. Surveys Tuts.* **16**(1), 77–97 (2014).

[9] Sun, Y., et al.: Organizing and querying the big sensing data with event-linked network in the internet of things. *Int. J. Distrib. Sensor Netw.* 11, pp. 1–11, (2014) Google Scholar.

[10] Provost, F., Fawcett, T.: *Data Science for Business-What you need to Know About Data Mining and Data-Analytic Thinking.* O'Reilly (2013), ISBN 978-1-449-36132-7.

[11] Dhar, V.: Data science and prediction. *Comm. ACM* **56**(12), 64–73 (2013).

[12] Mattmann, C.A.: Computing: a vision for data science. *Nature* **493**(7433), 473–475 (2013).

[13] Tiropanis, T.: Network science web science and internet science. *Comm. ACM* **58**(8), 76–82 (2015).

[14] Tinati, R., et al.: Building a real-time web observatory. *IEEE Internet Comput.* **19**(6), 36–45 (2015).

[15] Sun, Y., Yan, H., Lu, C., Bie, R., Zhou, Z.: Constructing the web of events from raw data in the web of things. *Mobile Inf. Syst.* **10**(1), 105–125 (2014).

[16] Mehta, Brijesh, Rao, Udai Pratap: Privacy preserving unstructured big data analytics: issues and challenges. *Procedia Comput. Sci.* **78**, 120–124 (2016).

[17] Al-Fuqaha, A., Guizani, M., Mohammadi, M., Aledhari, M., Ayyash, M.: Internet of things: a survey on enabling technologies protocols and applications. *IEEE Commun. Surveys Tuts.* **17**(4), 2347–2376 (2015).

[18] Mohammadi, M., Al-Fuqaha, A.: Enabling cognitive smart cities using big data and machine learning: approaches and challenges. *IEEE Commun. Mag.* **56**(2), 94–101 (2018).

[19] Chen, M., Mao, S., Zhang, Y., Leung, V.C.: *Big Data: Related Technologies Challenges and Future Prospects, Heidelberg.* Springer, Germany (2014).

[20] Fadlullah, Z.M., et al.: State-of-the-art deep learning: evolving machine intelligence toward tomorrow's intelligent network traffic control systems. *IEEE Commun. Surv. Tuts.* **19**(4), 2432–2455 (2017).

[21] Lee, J., Ardakani, H.D., Yang, S., Bagheri, B.: Industrial big data analytics and cyber-physical systems for future maintenance & service innovation. *Procedia CIRP* **38**, 3–7 (2015).

[22] Hu, H., Wen, Y., Chua, T.-S., Li, X.: Toward scalable systems for big data analytics: a technology tutorial. *IEEE Access* **2**, 652–687 (2014).

[23] Xia, F., Yang, L.T., Wang, L., Vinel, A.: Internet of things. *Int. J. Commun. Syst.* **25**, 1101–1109 (2012).

[24] Zaslavsky, A., Perera, C., Georgakopoulos, D.: Sensing as a service and big data. Proceedings of the International Conference on Advances in Cloud Computing (ACC) **2**, 1–8 (2013).

3

A Model to Identify Agriculture Production Using Data Science Techniques

D. Anantha Reddy, Sanjay Kumar, and Rakesh Tripathi

CONTENTS

3.1 Agriculture System Application Based on GPS/GIS Gathered Information

The different applications of GIS systems in the agriculture system has become a recent and advanced research area in agriculture science. The statistical data like exact amount of cultivated land is less available in India (e.g., approximately each person merely has 1.3 acres, which is 28% of the rest of the world). However, in agricultural industries with farming tools like planting technique, farming administrations, or any sort of other farming technique, our country is still in a lower level of developing countries. Improvement of the agriculture industry standards not only relies on total funds and manpower, but also the various advanced technologies, modern administration methods, and the type of people used for faming development.

Therefore, to develop advanced agriculture production methods, creating and implementing a resource-saving agricultural system is very important. Here we can apply GIS (Global Information System) for enhancing production farming. GIS is a specific type of spatial information system that can analyze the different types of geographical information which has different types of connotation. With the help of hardware and software systems, basic system engineering, and computer engineering, we can implement, analyze, and use this GIS data for improving our agricultural system for the right decision making, research, and programming management.

3.1.1 Important Tools Required for Developing GIS/GPS-Based Agricultural System

GPS/GIS is basically an advanced way of gathering and combining the different location current information globally with the help of technical science-based tools and technique. This GPS- (global positioning system) based advance application provides lots of support and help to its user for gathering real data from various locations.

3.1.1.1 Information (Gathered Data)

This GPS/GIS-based system collects and integrates different types of real-time data in the layered manner with the help of spatial positional system, in which a large division of data contains a geographical type of information like images, Google maps, some sort of table, Excel sheets etc.

3.1.1.2 Map

This can be defined as a collection of images. Basically, maps are defined as a geographical suitcase of different types of layered data and their interconnection. GPS maps are very handy to copy or transfer by embedding a similar application and also easily anytime and anywhere with any person accessible.

3.1.1.3 System Apps

Different types of apps designed for naïve or trained users are available in the market for giving a unique experience to the user. Now, a day's current location or information of the user plays a very important role for tracking the user activity or any type of monitoring system where these types of system apps can be used.

3.1.1.4 Data Analysis

All of the data's real-time information that is gathered must be analyzed properly so that the captured information will be become useful for the system. A specific type of analysis known as spatial-based analysis will provide you a brief evaluation to estimate, predict, interpret, and lead you to a correct decision-making path.

3.1.2 GPS/GIS in Agricultural Conditions

In any field of research, this Google tool plays a very important role. Now, a GPS-based system is mostly used in the agricultural field. Basically a GPS-based system uses satellite communication to gather information for estimating crop yields and various types of agricultural applications that lead to very fruitful profits in agricultural advancements.

3.1.2.1 GIS System in Agriculture

The exactness of cultivating can be acquired the flexibility investigation for real development in the agricultural field in different types of areas and situations, modify measurements to nearby situations, to uncover cultivating profitable possibilities to improve fields and utilize productivity of developed agricultural field. This precise cultivating master framework is the computerized reasoning master framework that plans and improves the cutting-edge agribusiness improvement request. It has a few highlights as follow: first, it consolidates the master information on cultivating space with the man-made brainpower innovation, grasps the primary issue of cultivating produce, utilizes the rich information on the master and the data-handling capacity of the PC, acquaints the high innovation with the cultivating production in an area, and is able to improve the level and impact of cultivating administration. Second, it gives a strategy to investigating correlative issues of estimating cultivating in handling partially developed areas and unstructured area issues for cultivated production. Finally, this will give spare, engendering, need, and estimation of assessing cultivating information. The master framework of information gathering especially has the capacity of savvy investigative and measures for correlative information, to give the logical figure and dynamic help for cultivating.

3.1.3 System Development Using GIS and GPS Data

Utilizing the idea of "article arranged" to build up a master information model and setting up an idea method for displaying different tools with its interconnection provides multiple options for treating crops before cultivating the winter season seed (wheat), as depicted in the diagram (Figure 3.1), and its various operations are discussed below.

Treatment before cultivating choice has two cycles:

1. Based on atmosphere, soil richness, and item condition, logical and technological levels for finding that field motive of growing are decided about the required crop.
2. Real field fertilizer requirement and usage.

3.2 Design of Interface to Extract Soil Moisture and Mineral Content in Agricultural Lands

Rapid growth of the human population has a high need and demand of food and water supplies. Along these lines, there is a basic need to improve the necessary food required for future generations. We tried to represent a procedure for detecting soil (land) moistness sensors for checking clamminess material within sand; thus, providing data of needed water resources for excellent growth of crop production, discussed in brief in Sections 3.2.1 and 3.2.2. This standard technique for estimating soil

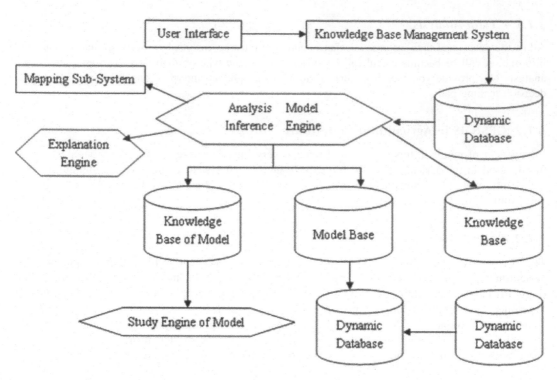

FIGURE 3.1   System design using GIS- and GPS-based expert system.

dampness content is the thermo-gravimetric strategy, which requires broiler drying of a known volume of soil at 105°C and deciding the weight reduction. This technique is tedious and dangerous to the inspected soil, implying that it can't be utilized for redundant estimations at a similar area [1]. Rapid and quick estimation methods based on utilizing some specific electronic-based sensors, for example, time-space reflectometers and impedance, provides the best solution for these types of destructive and time-consuming gravimetric measures [2]. A few different strategies were proposed to decide soil dampness [3,4]. In [5,6–13], soil dampness is checked by estimating electromagnetic radiations transmitted by soil at various temperatures. The effect of miniature waves on soil dampness is key in this technique.

3.2.1 Estimating Level of Soil Moisture and Mineral Content Using COSMIC-RAY (C-RAY) Sensing Technique

This C-RAY sensing based soil–moister level detection technique is a very advanced and advantageous method to determine the soil sogginess level. This method will detect soil soddenness with the help of unique functionalities of sensors. This method includes the specific number of neurons flowing to restrict the astronomic test rays within a moisture level of soil for rehabilitees the level of moisture in soil at various steps in agricultural growth predictions. This C-RAY sensor based method works on available water level and neutron flow in soil.

3.2.1.1 Cosmic

The connection between the deliberate neutron total count available and availability of water substance in soil can be detected with help of the COSMIC–BEAM Soil Moisture Detection physical model, known as the "COSMIC-RAY" model. Inestimable speaks to the number of quick neutrons arriving at the COSMOS near-surface estimation point cal is calculated with the help of the following equation:

as

$$s = N \int_0^\infty \left\{ A(z)[\alpha \rho_s(z) + \rho_w(z)] \right.$$
$$\left. \times \exp\left(-\left[\frac{m_s(z)}{L_1} + \frac{m_w(z)}{L_2}\right]\right) \right\} dz$$

(3.1)

Infinite discreteness of the dirt data is in 250 levels with soil data of 4 m depth. This water resource, which is in the form of different layers, has been by these C-RAY physical models. Then, the average frequently generated rate of neutrons in every layer of water source has been determined. At last, the average depth of soil dampness and its powerful detecting depthness of the C-RAY soil dampness test are likewise determined by COSMIC system.

3.2.2 Soil Moisture and Mineral Content Measurement Using Long Duration Optical Fiber Grating (LDOPG)

The LDOPG can be used as a dirt dampness sensing device. Implementation and development of this technical gadget can be used for earth and earthy soil and is uncovered an affectability to dampness layer at reach 15-half, and the outcomes were contrasted and the yield with the help of "THETA" test, the general soil dampness sensing device, which gauges the calculation of dirt. This optical-fiber-based sensing device can possibly address this, giving a moderately modest arrangement that can distinguish water over both different areas and huge spans. Such a gadget ought to be equipped for distinguishing a scope of dampness levels. Two differentiating categories of soil have been selected to examine the working condition of the sensing device. Those two categories are agrarian soil, which has a minimum salty component and can be completely depleted with a pore differential of < 3 mm, and the second one was loamy soil, which is a natural source of plantation.

3.2.3 Moisture Level and Mineral Content Detection System Using a Sensor Device

Moisture in soil available for farmland is a vital component that normally controls the large number of water cycles, evaporation level, water aspiration, and huge wastewater flow. Also, this moisture component varies with the different energy cycle of the field via transforming the present energy type in the environment and the farm field area. Basically, there are two types of moisture level detection systems available, which are completely based on a remote sensing technique as given below:

1. Active Microwave Remote Sensing Moisture Detection
2. Passive Microwave Remote Sensing Moisture Detection

3.2.4 Soil Moisture Experiment

3.2.4.1 Dataset Description

The dataset is prepared by installing a module with arduino and soil moisture sensors. The data collected had the following parameters:

timestamp, Soil humidity 1, Irrigation field 1, Soil humidity 2, Irrigation field 2, Soil humidity 3, Irrigation field 3, Soil humidity 4, Irrigation field 4, Air temperature (C), Air humidity (%), Pressure (KPa), Wind speed (Km/h), Wind gust (Km/h), Wind direction (Deg)

FIGURE 3.2   Experimental setup.

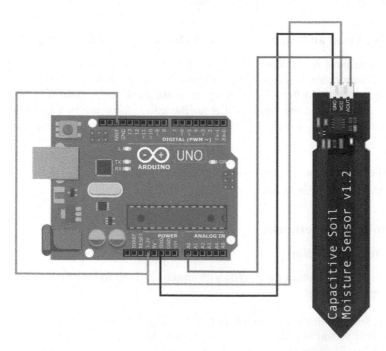

FIGURE 3.3   Circuit diagram.

Sample dataset values:

> 2020-02-23 00:00:00,67.92,0,55.72,0,1.56,1,26.57,1,19.52,55.04,101.5,2.13,6.3,225
> 2020-02-23 00:05:00,67.89,0,55.74,0,1.51,1,26.58,1,19.49,55.17,101.5,2.01,10.46,123.75
> 2020-02-23 00:10:00,67.86,0,55.77,0,1.47,1,26.59,1,19.47,55.3,101.51,1.9,14.63,22.5
> 2020-02-23 00:15:00,67.84,0,55.79,0,1.42,1,26.61,1,19.54,54.2,101.51,2.28,16.08,123.75
> 2020-02-23 00:20:00,67.81,0,55.82,0,1.38,1,26.62,1,19.61,53.09,101.51,2.66,17.52,225

3.2.5 Experimental Result

```
Soil humidity 2          1.000000
Pressure (KPa)           0.289770
Wind direction (Deg)     0.211908
Irrigation field 2       0.126485
Air temperature (C)     -0.005512
Wind gust (Km/h)        -0.114120
Wind speed (Km/h)       -0.172694
Air humidity (%)        -0.297771
```

3.3 Analysis and Guidelines for Seed Spacing

Horticultural mechanical technology is the utilization of electromechanical machines, and it is an area of expanding interest that has expected social, commercial, and financial commitments in the field [14,15]. Independent cultivating is the activity, direction, and control of independent frameworks to perform agrarian undertakings [16,17–31].

Accurate and precise farming provides the methods and techniques for effective seed planting will help to reduce the seed count per hectare. The position and distance calculations are very important to make this accurate seed spacing effective. Due to the effective and optimized implementation of the technique for seed spacing and planting, this will help to increase the wealth of farmers.

3.3.1 Correct Spacing

- One valid justification is that the right distancing (spacing) typically requires less seeds. This can save money.
- The right distancing (spacing) likewise assists crops with growing better. Plants can distinguish their nearby neighbors and adjust their development likewise.
- A few plants like to have their underlying foundations in contact. Plants can impact their neighbors by conveying substance development signals from their foundations.
- Shockingly, plants can even "speak" if nearby plants are identified with them or on the offchance that they are outsiders through root-delivered synthetic compounds! They utilize this data to modify how they develop.

3.3.2 System Components

3.3.2.1 Electronic Compass

The electronic compass is a combination of accelerometer and magnetometer. The microchip is enabled with a tri-pivot magnetometer and a tri-pivot accelerometer, which is used in our project. The module is named LSM9DS0 is utilized as an electronic compass sensor for this work. The sensor was utilized as a tilt-repaid way compass.

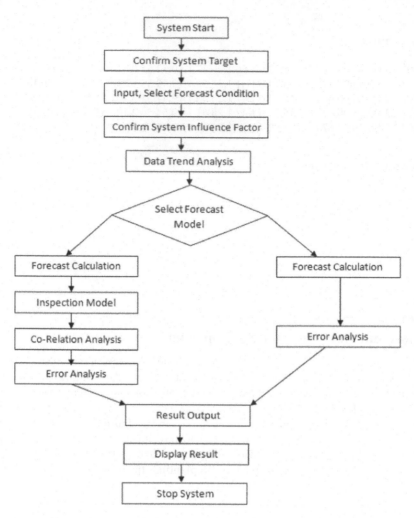

FIGURE 3.4 GIS/GPS-based seed spacing model.

3.3.2.2 Optical Flow Sensor

The optical flow sensor version V1.0 integrated with a microchip is utilized. The small camera, along with an optical sensor mouse, are a packet, called the ADNS-3080, which is used in our work. The packet is used for vehicle tracking and distance measure and to make related calculations using a track_distance () function. The return value of this function is in the form of pixel values.

3.3.2.3 Motor Driver

The motor driver use for any project was based on the type of motor used. Based on the current project, the motor driver used is VNH2SP30 (Enormous Current MD Module). The MD driver provides features like low- and high-voltage surge, sensing, analog input, thermal management, etc.

3.3.2.4 Microcontroller

The microchip provides a multi-feature microcontroller needed for the project. The microchip provides a DSPIC30F4013 microcontroller, which is a very powerful 16-bit chipset microcontroller the provides accuracy and stability to our project. This microcontroller acts as an interface between the optical flow sensor and electronic compass. The module SPI provides an interface feature between the compass and a OF sensor to collect data from it. The input to the motor driver has been provided by four pulse modulators provided by this microchip.

3.4 Analysis of Spread of Fertilizers

User fertilizer feeding and spreading is mostly inefficient and hazardous due to the inaccurate measurement, unequal spreading, and direct contact with fertilizer can be dangerous. The various experiments performed up until now provide feedback of the need of a system for better and accurate fertilizer spreading. By using this idea, a better and accurate system can improve crop yield and productivity. Thus, this operation is intended to give a basic and profitable course to farmers in order to lead fertilizer feeding and spreading measures accurately.

3.4.1 Relationship between Soil pH Value and Nutrient Availability

3.4.2 Methodology

The system methodology that is adopted in this study is the combination of Rapid Application Development (RAD) and Design Thinking (DT).

3.4.2.1 Understand Define Phase

The first and the most important phase is the understand define phase (UDP), which is the desire to understand the needs of the user of the system. This phase is to collect more and more target customer information for effective development of the system. The affectivity of this phase will help to produce correct and meaningful problem statements.

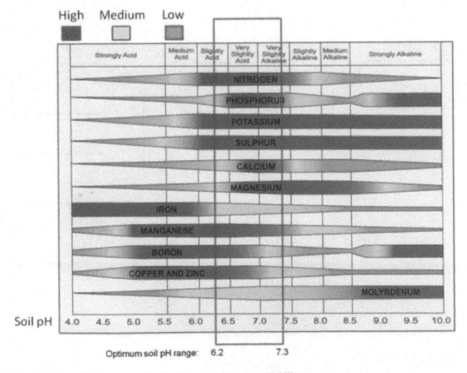

FIGURE 3.5 Relationship between soil pH value and nutrient availability.

3.4.2.2 *Analysis and Quick Design Phase*

In this phase, the major part is to investigate the user information and analyze the complete information in order to provide the correct and effective solution to the user. To collect the information online and offline, a data collection method was adopted and the feedbacks were analyzed to make a quick design phase. The design of the system architecture, along with the methodology, is finalized in this phase feedback and analysis.

3.4.2.3 *Prototype Development Phase*

Based on the system architecture and the methodology adopted in the previous phase, we have developed a prototype to represent a system. The prototype is tested by using various methods and the analysis of the testing results has been done to make the prototype effective. Then the prototype has been rebuilt to incorporate all the results obtained, after the analysis of the prototype testing.

3.4.2.4 *Testing Phase*

Input value testing and unit testing are adopted to test the working model and the testing results are analyzed to make the accuracy of the system better. The testing includes preparing the setup, conducting the testing, and presenting the outcome of testing. The complete data is then collected and analyzed for the future work.

3.4.3 System Architecture

Segments are needed to amass an equipment model. So as to collect equipment that suits client necessities, RaspberryPi-3 Model B, NodeMCU chip, Arduino UNO model, ESP-8266, pH sensor, transfer, and compost siphon are associated with one another, as shown in the schematic outline in Figure 3.6.

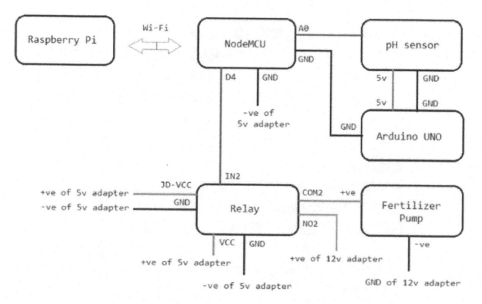

FIGURE 3.6 System architecture.

3.4.4 Experimental Setup

3.4.5 Implementation Phase

This phase will be reached when all of the above phases go well and the results of every phase back to the consecutive phases of the development stages. The correct and accurate implementation will make the deployment easy and effective.

Algorithm_path_planner

---

1 *make_dir_path:*

2 *if !(path_exists(join(*path)):*

3 *makedirs(path.join(path))*

4 *train_img_path="data/path"*

5 *train_label=listdir(train_img_path)*

6 *num_per_label=list[]*

7 *for i in train_label:*

8 *num_per_label.append(len(listdir(path.join(train_img_path,i))))*

9 *num_valid=min(num_per_label)*0.2*

10 *end for;*

11 *for i in train_label:*

12 *idx_valid = np.random.coise(listdir(path.join(train_img_path,i)),num_valid)))*

13 *make_dir([data,valid,i])*

14 *for img in idx_valid:*

15 *move(path.join(data/train,i,img),path.join('data/valid',i,img))*

16 *end for;*

17 *end for;*

FIGURE 3.7 Experimental setup.

3.4.6 Experimental Results

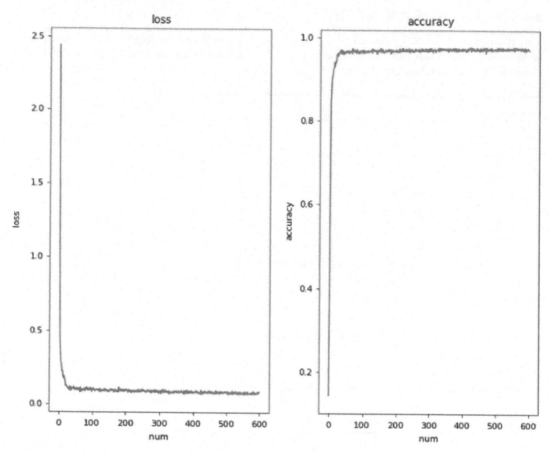

FIGURE 3.8 Experimental results.

3.5 Conclusion and Future Work

This chapter presented the detailed description on usage of Geographic Information System (GIS) and Global Positioning System (GPS) based agricultural developments, needs, and the other applications based on GIS/GPS. In the next subsection, we have presented the various models for soil moisture and mineral extraction from soil using the COSMIC-sensing technique, long duration optical fiber grating, and sensor-based systems. The experimental details, along with the experimental results, are also described and presented in this section. In the third subsection of this chapter, we have introduced the background of seed spacing, needs, and a proposed system for making the correct seed spacing. We have also presented our findings on various plants and their seed spacing required for better growth and productivity. In the next subsection, experiment setup, experimental results and analysis of spreading fertilizer has been presented, along with related technologies, current methodology adopted, and system architecture of the proposed system. This chapter can be used by any of the researchers or application developers as a baseline study material for their research and development on agricultural-based application.

The GIS- and GPS-based systems can also be used for the other applications in the field of agriculture. The inclusion of artificial intelligence can also be useful for the development of next-generation farming applications, which are helpful in achieving precision farming. Our study and experimental analysis in this field of agriculture explores the various dimensions of technology, which can be useful for making farming easy and effective. As more and more data has been generated, gathered, and available related to soil, water, and atmosphere, it is now easy to develop a system and technology based on this data along with the deep learning knowledge to make the farmer's life better.

REFERENCES

[1] P. Kumar, S. Suman, and S. Mishra, "Shortest route finding by ant system algorithm in web geographical information system-based advanced traveller information system." *The Journal of Engineering*, vol. 2014, no. 10, pp. 563–573, 2014, doi: 10.1049/joe.2014.0190.

[2] Y. Dong et al., "Automatic system for crop pest and disease dynamic monitoring and early forecasting." *IEEE Journal of Selected Topics in Applied Earth Observations and Remote Sensing*, vol. 13, pp. 4410–4418, 2020, doi: 10.1109/JSTARS.2020.3013340.

[3] C. A. Martínez Félix, G. E. Vázquez Becerra, J. R. Millán Almaraz, F. Geremia-Nievinski, J.R. Gaxiola Camacho, and Á. Melgarejo Morales, "In-field electronic based system and methodology for precision agriculture and yield prediction in seasonal maize field." *IEEE Latin America Transactions*, vol. 17, no. 10, pp. 1598–1606, Oct. 2019, doi: 10.1109/TLA.2019.8986437.

[4] E. R. Hunt, C. S. T. Daughtry, S. B. Mirsky, and W. D. Hively, "Remote sensing with simulated unmanned aircraft imagery for precision agriculture applications." *IEEE Journal of Selected Topics in Applied Earth Observations and Remote Sensing*, vol. 7, no. 11, pp. 4566–4571, Nov. 2014, doi: 10.1109/JSTARS.2014.2317876.

[5] D. Gomez-Candon et al., "Semiautomatic detection of artificial terrestrial targets for remotely sensed image georeferencing." *IEEE Geoscience and Remote Sensing Letters*, vol. 10, no. 1, pp. 184–188, Jan. 2013, doi: 10.1109/LGRS.2012.2197729.

[6] A. H. S. Solberg, T. Taxt, and A. K. Jain, "A Markov random field model for classification of multisource satellite imagery."*IEEE Transactions on Geoscience and Remote Sensing*, vol. 34, no. 1, pp. 100–113, Jan. 1996, doi: 10.1109/36.481897.

[7] H. McNairn et al., "The soil moisture active passive validation experiment 2012 (SMAPVEX12): Prelaunch calibration and validation of the SMAP soil moisture algorithms." *IEEE Transactions on Geoscience and Remote Sensing*, vol. 53, no. 5, pp. 2784–2801, May 2015, doi: 10.1109/TGRS.2014.2364913.

[8] A. Loew and W. Mauser, "On the disaggregation of passive microwave soil moisture data using a priori knowledge of temporally persistent soil moisture fields." *IEEE Transactions on Geoscience and Remote Sensing*, vol. 46, no. 3, pp. 819–834, March 2008, doi: 10.1109/TGRS.2007.914800.

[9] X. Han, R. Jin, X. Li, and S. Wang, "Soil moisture estimation using cosmic-ray soil moisture sensing at heterogeneous farmland." *IEEE Geoscience and Remote Sensing Letters*, vol. 11, no. 9, pp. 1659–1663, Sept. 2014, doi: 10.1109/LGRS.2014.2314535.

[10] M. S. Burgin et al., "A comparative study of the SMAP passive soil moisture product with existing satellite-based soil moisture products." *IEEE Transactions on Geoscience and Remote Sensing*, vol. 55, no. 5, pp. 2959–2971, May 2017, doi: 10.1109/TGRS.2017.2656859.

[11] A. Eliran, N. Goldshleger, A. Yahalom, E. Ben-Dor, and M. Agassi, "Empirical model for backscattering at millimeter-wave frequency by bare soil subsurface with varied moisture content." *IEEE Geoscience and Remote Sensing Letters*, vol. 10, no. 6, pp. 1324–1328, Nov. 2013, doi: 10.1109/ LGRS.2013.2239603.

[12] Y. Wang, S. Wang, S. Yang, L. Zhang, H. Zeng, and D. Zheng, "Using a remote sensing driven model to analyze effect of land use on soil moisture in the Weihe River Basin, China." *IEEE Journal of Selected Topics in Applied Earth Observations and Remote Sensing*, vol. 7, no. 9, pp. 3892–3902, Sept. 2014, doi: 10.1109/JSTARS.2014.2345743.

[13] K. C. Kornelsen and P. Coulibaly, "Design of an optimal soil moisture monitoring network using SMOS retrieved soil moisture." *IEEE Transactions on Geoscience and Remote Sensing*, vol. 53, no. 7, pp. 3950–3959, July 2015, doi: 10.1109/TGRS.2014.2388451.

[14] Wang Yecheng and Qiu Lichun, "Research of new type cell wheel feed precision seed-metering device." 2011 International Conference on New Technology of Agricultural, Zibo, 2011, pp. 102–105, doi: 10.1109/ICAE.2011.5943759.

[15] P. V. S. Jayakrishna, M. S. Reddy, N. J. Sai, N. Susheel, and K. P. Peeyush, "Autonomous seed sowing agricultural robot." 2018 International Conference on Advances in Computing, Communications and Informatics (ICACCI), Bangalore, 2018, pp. 2332–2336, doi: 10.1109/ICACCI. 2018.8554622.

[16] R. S. Dionido and M. C. Ramos, "Autonomous seed-planting vehicle." 2017 7th IEEE International Conference on Control System, Computing and Engineering (ICCSCE), Penang, 2017, pp. 121–126, doi: 10.1109/ICCSCE.2017.8284391.

[17] Kwok Pui Choi, Fanfan Zeng, and Louxin Zhang, "Good spaced seeds for homology search." Proceedings. Fourth IEEE Symposium on Bioinformatics and Bioengineering, Taichung, Taiwan, 2004, pp. 379–386, doi: 10.1109/BIBE.2004.1317368.

[18] K. Ramesh, K. T. Prajwal, C. Roopini, M. Gowda M.H., and V. V. S. N. S. Gupta, "Design and development of an agri-bot for automatic seeding and watering applications." 2020 2nd International Conference on Innovative Mechanisms for Industry Applications (ICIMIA), Bangalore, India, 2020, pp. 686–691, doi: 10.1109/ICIMIA48430.2020.9074856.

[19] A. I. Zainal Abidin, F. A. Fadzil, and Y. S. Peh, "Micro-controller based fertilizer dispenser control system." 2018 IEEE Conference on Wireless Sensors (ICWiSe), Langkawi, Malaysia, 2018, pp. 17–22, doi: 10.1109/ICWISE.2018.8633277.

[20] R. Eatock and M. R. Inggs, "The use of differential GPS in field data extraction and spatially variable fertilizer application." Proceedings of IGARSS '94 - 1994 IEEE International Geoscience and Remote Sensing Symposium, Pasadena, CA, USA, 1994, pp. 841–843, vol. 2, doi: 10.1109/IGARSS.1994.399280.

[21] M. S. Islam, A. Islam, M. Z. Islam, and E. Basher, "Feasibility analysis of deploying biogas plants for producing electricity and bio-fertilizer commercially at different scale of poultry farms in Bangladesh." 2014 3rd International Conference on the Developments in Renewable Energy Technology (ICDRET), Dhaka, 2014, pp. 1–6, doi: 10.1109/ICDRET.2014.6861654.

[22] S. Villette, C. Gée, E. Piron, R. Martin, D. Miclet, and M. Paindavoine, "An efficient vision system to measure granule velocity and mass flow distribution in fertiliser centrifugal spreading." 2010 2nd International Conference on Image Processing Theory, Tools and Applications, Paris, 2010, pp. 543–548, doi: 10.1109/IPTA.2010.5586738.

[23] M. Chakroun, G. Gogu, M. Pradel, F. Thirion, and S. Lacour, "Eco-design in the field of spreading technologies." 2010 IEEE Green Technologies Conference, Grapevine, TX, 2010, pp. 1–6, doi: 10.1109/GREEN.2010.5453796.

[24] K. D. Sowjanya, R. Sindhu, M. Parijatham, K. Srikanth, and P. Bhargav, "Multipurpose autonomous agricultural robot." 2017 International Conference of Electronics, Communication and Aerospace Technology (ICECA), Coimbatore, 2017, pp. 696–699, doi: 10.1109/ICECA.2017.8212756.

[25] A. K. Mariappan and J. A. Ben Das, "A paradigm for rice yield prediction in Tamilnadu." 2017 IEEE Technological Innovations in ICT for Agriculture and Rural Development (TIAR), Chennai, 2017, pp. 18–21, doi: 10.1109/TIAR.2017.8273679.

[26] A. Manjula and G. Narsimha, "XCYPF: A flexible and extensible framework for agricultural Crop Yield Prediction." 2015 IEEE 9th International Conference on Intelligent Systems and Control (ISCO), Coimbatore, 2015, pp. 1–5, doi: 10.1109/ISCO.2015.7282311.

[27] Y. Gandge and Sandhya, "A study on various data mining techniques for crop yield prediction." 2017 International Conference on Electrical, Electronics, Communication, Computer, and Optimization Techniques (ICEECCOT), Mysuru, 2017, pp. 420–423, doi: 10.1109/ICEECCOT.2017.8284541.

[28] P. S. Vijayabaskar, R. Sreemathi, and E. Keertanaa, "Crop prediction using predictive analytics." 2017 International Conference on Computation of Power, Energy Information and Commuincation (ICCPEIC), Melmaruvathur, 2017, pp. 370–373, doi: 10.1109/ICCPEIC.2017.8290395.

[29] P. S. Nishant, P. Sai Venkat, B. L. Avinash, and B. Jabber, "Crop yield prediction based on Indian agriculture using machine learning." 2020 International Conference for Emerging Technology (INCET), Belgaum, India, 2020, pp. 1–4, doi: 10.1109/INCET49848.2020.9154036.

[30] S. Bang, R. Bishnoi, A. S. Chauhan, A. K. Dixit, and I. Chawla, "Fuzzy logic based crop yield prediction using temperature and rainfall parameters predicted through ARMA, SARIMA, and ARMAX models." 2019 Twelfth International Conference on Contemporary Computing (IC3), Noida, India, 2019, pp. 1–6, doi: 10.1109/IC3.2019.8844901.

[31] R. Medar, V. S. Rajpurohit, and S. Shweta, "Crop yield prediction using machine learning techniques." 2019 IEEE 5th International Conference for Convergence in Technology (I2CT), Bombay, India, 2019, pp. 1–5, doi: 10.1109/I2CT45611.2019.9033611.

4

Identification and Classification of Paddy Crop Diseases Using Big Data Machine Learning Techniques

Anisha P. Rodrigues, Joyston Menezes, Roshan Fernandes, Aishwarya, Niranjan N. Chiplunkar, and Vijaya Padmanabha

CONTENTS

4.1 Introduction

India is a country known for agriculture in which various crops are grown in different parts of the country and often serves as a host to a multitude of emerging and invasive crop diseases [1]. Major parts of India range from tropical to subtropical and this climate is more favorable for the development of disease-causing insects and microorganisms that result in 20–30% yield losses of principal food sources; hence, prevention and early diagnosis are critical to limit the destruction caused by them [2]. *Oryza sativa* (paddy/rice) is one of the major food crops that offers more than 2.8 billion people a primary meal. Uncharted infection of a rice crop can create an immense loss of crop production that will produce fewer yields.

This chapter stresses how machine learning techniques and big data can be implemented in the identification of infection in paddy crops. The generalized architecture of crop infection detection is depicted in Figure 4.1. Important stages of image processing that need to be followed to achieve our desired results are along these lines. Existing approaches may not be reasonable due to various infections with indistinguishable infection patterns; also, these infections can widely vary with various regional conditions and numerous crop varieties.

4.1.1 Overview of Paddy Crop Diseases

This section talks about the various kinds of infection that take place in rice crops. The main purpose of this section is for better understanding for our readers as they can understand different types of disease that can affect the rice plants, along with the parameters required to be considered for diagnosing each

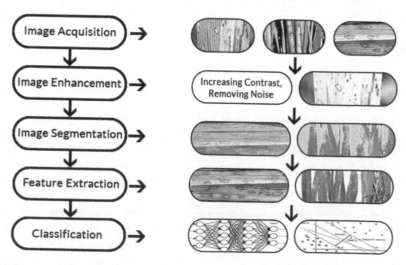

FIGURE 4.1 Overall approach of paddy crop disease detection using machine learning.

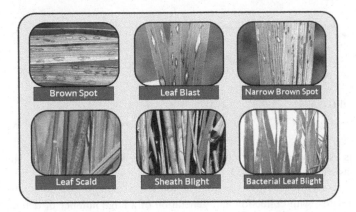

FIGURE 4.2 Various types of rice crop infection [3].

disease efficiently with appropriate image processing techniques and, hence, help the farmers with maximum yield [3]. Sample images of six commonly occurring infections are highlighted and presented below [3] in Figure 4.2.

1. Brown spot: This kind of infection arises on the leaves of the paddy crop due to fungal infection. The shape and indication of this infection are circular to elliptical form with murk brown punctures.
2. Leaf blast: This is popularly known as rice blast fungus; the peculiarities of this infection are gloom smudge to elliptical spot with a slim brownish-red border and white or ashen spot.
3. Bacterial leaf blight: This kind of disease generally is a long abrasion on the leaf end, and the abrasion gradually turns to yellow from white due to bacterial effect and are elongated.
4. Sheath blight: The indications are elliptical, brownish-red spots with gray or white or chaff-colored parts in the interior that can take place both on stems and leaf.
5. Leaf scald: These kinds of infection are tapered, brownish-red spacious stripes along with some rarely occurring lesions at the leaf border with golden and yellow borders.

4.1.2 Overview of Big Data

In the modern time, the word *big data* resembles a cluster of wide-range and composite sets of data that are hard to maintain, since the data come from various, miscellaneous, independent origins with complicated and expanding associations that continue to grow. Big data is widely categorized into three types. They are structured, semi-structured, and unstructured [4].

- Structured data: The data that might be effortlessly sorted and analyzed; for example, words and numbers. It is produced because of system sensors implanted in electric devices such as the Global Positioning System (GPS), smartphones, and similar devices.
- Semi-structured Data: This type of structured data refuses to satisfy a clear-cut and certain arrangement. The information is constitutionally self-describing and consists of markers to impose hierarchies of fields and records inside the datasets and tags.
- Unstructured data: It consists of highly complicated data; for instance videos and photos posted on social media and reviews from customers on commercial websites, likes on social media networking.

4.1.2.1 Features of Big Data

Big data comprises massive information, which is autonomous and miscellaneous in nature, has a time-factor corresponding to it. To summarize these features of big data, the well-known "3 Vs" or simple

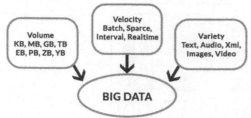

FIGURE 4.3 Features of big data.

"V3" framework is used by an international research agency known as Gartner. The 3 Vs are variety, volume, velocity, as shown in Figure 4.3.

- Volume: It relates, with collection and generation of a huge number of datasets; data size keeps increasing.
- Variety: It constitutes all kinds of datasets. Google remarks that the growth rate of unstructured data is 15 times more than structured information, which rapidly expands by 20.0% compound annual growth rate.
- Velocity: The data velocity is defined regarding the density of its production along with delivery, which is also another feature of big data.

4.1.3 Overview of Machine Learning Techniques

Machine learning algorithms have gained reasonable recognition with the plant crop disease detection to overcome the weakness of experience-based disease identification methods. The top machine learning techniques commonly used are mentioned below:

4.1.3.1 K-Nearest Neighbor

K-Nearest Neighbor (KNN) is one of the self-effacing, conservative, and non-parametric techniques for arrangement of samples. It measures the estimated distance between a range of points from the input vector, and assigns the anonymous points to the classes of its KNN [5].

4.1.3.2 Support Vector Machine

Support Vector Machine (SVM) is a prevailing supervised classification consisting of a precise learning procedure that originated in the year 1995 [6]. SVM has significantly demonstrated its effectiveness above neural networks and radial basis function classifiers. The SVM exercise is a favorable linearly separating hyper-plane tthat splits two datasets in attribute spaces.

4.1.3.3 K-Means

The K-means approach is one of the conventional clustering technique. This approach initially selects a K dataset arbitrarily as the primary cluster hub, in favor of the remaining just adjoin in the direction of clusters through the maximum resemblance stated to its space of the cluster hub, along with recalculating the cluster hub of every collection [7].

$$J_k = \sum_{k=1}^{k} \sum_{i \in C_k} (X_i - m_k)^2 \qquad (4.1)$$

In Equation (4.1), $(X_1, X_2, \cdots, Xn) = X$ is the matrix of data, along with $m_k = \Sigma_{i \in C_k} Xi/n_k$, which is the kernel of the collection C_k along with n_k at the quantity of points within C_k.

4.1.3.4 Fuzzy C-Means

Fuzzy C-Means (FCM) is among the broadly implemented clustering approaches. This method allows one portion of the dataset to fit into numerous clusters. FCM was initially developed by J. C. Dunn [8] in 1973 and enhanced afterwards by J. C. Bezdek in 1981 [9]. FCM is established on the thought of discovering cluster centroid via constantly fine-tuning its orientation; also, objective function assessment is typically determined in Equation (4.2):

$$E = \sum_{j=1}^{C} \sum_{i=1}^{N} \mu_{ij}^{k} \|X_i - C_j\|^2 \tag{4.2}$$

Here, μ_{ij} stands for fuzzy association of pixel (or model), which is X_i along with the cluster recognized through its pivot C_j, and the constant k represents the fuzziness of the resultant partition.

4.1.3.5 Decision Tree

A decision tree (DT) earns its title because it is in the shape of a tree and which are used to produce decisions. Technically, a DT is the collection of nodes with edges where each edge descends from one node to another node. These nodes symbolize the attributes measured in the assessment procedure and the edges signify the various values of an attribute. This approach is used for the effective classification of a case since it classifies an instance by ranging from the root node of the tree as well as moving throughout it until a leaf node is found [10]. Table 4.1 gives the summary of pros and cons of various crop disease analysis techniques.

TABLE 4.1

Advantages and Disadvantages of Crop Disease Analysis Techniques

Algorithm	Advantages	Disadvantages
Support Vector Machine	• Locate the finest partition hyper-plane. • Able to deal with extremely elevated data dimension. • Typically works extremely fine.	• Needs mutual negative and positive instances. • Required to choose a fine function of a kernel. • Need plenty of CPU time and memory.
K-Nearest Neighbor	• Exceptionally simple to comprehend because there are a small number of analyst variables. • Helpful for constructing models with the intention to engage substandard information types, for example texts.	• Encompass huge storage space necessities. • Responsive to the alternative of the resemblance purpose that is used to evaluate cases. • Short of an upright method to prefer K, apart from cross validation or comparable.
Fuzzy C-Mean	• It permits data points designated in numerous clusters. • Behavior of genes is represented more naturally.	• The cluster number C needs to be defined. • Membership cutoff values are needed to be determined.
K-Means	• Few complexes.	• Requirement of K specification. • Susceptible to outlier record points and noise.
Decision Tree	• Straightforward to infer and understand. • It needs modest preparation of data. • It is able to look after both categorical and mathematical data. • White box approach is used.	• The difficulty of training a finest decision tree is recognized as NP-complete beneath numerous features of easy concepts and even for optimality. • Decision tree algorithms generate trees that are overly complex.

4.1.4 Overview of Big Data Machine Learning Tools

It is not unusual to find massive sets of large objects because data expands and becomes commonly accessible. Most of these recent directions ultimately use highly complicated workflows that involve a lot of structures that are designed with the help of a mixture of modern and progressive technologies and techniques [11].

4.1.4.1 Hadoop

The term *Hadoop,* along with MapReduce, are considered synonymous by most individuals, but this is not entirely true. Initially enforced as an associate degree open-source code implementation of the MapReduce to process engines coupled to a distributed database system in 2007, since then Hadoop has developed into a colossal network of project works linked to every phase of workflow of massive sets of data consisting data collection, storage, processing, and so on [11].

4.1.4.2 Hadoop Distributed File System (HDFS)

HDFS is a file database that is configured for storage of vast volumes of information through many hardware nodes. HDFS resembles a master-slave architecture consisting of nodes that individually stores data blocks, retrieves or extracts data on request or command, and reports in return to the inventory name node that maintains records of that particular inventory and leads the traffic to the nodes upon request from the user or client.

4.1.4.3 YARN ("Yet Another Resource Negotiator")

Hadoop and MapReduce were closely coupled prior to the involvement of YARN into Hadoop project 2.0, with MapReduce completely responsible for all the clusters of resource management and processing of information. The resource management tasks have now been taken over by YARN, providing a proper distinction between infrastructure and the model for programming. Section 4.2 gives a brief, detailed review of various classifications, pre-processing, and machine learning models implemented for rice infection detection and extracts significant insights. Section 4.3 covers the proposed architecture while Section 4.4 talks about the implementation details and Section 4.5 presents results simultaneously, considering our discussions. Lastly, Section 4.6 summarizes our entire work in the form of conclusion and future work. Figure 4.4 shows the affairs among machine learning systems, processing engines, and the algorithms they implement [12].

4.2 Related Work

In this segment, we describe various works and implementations that have been previously carried out in distinct fields for instance weed recognition, fruits infection categorization, crop grading scheme, classification of rice, and so on.

4.2.1 Image Recognition/Processing

Image processing techniques are implemented on the exterior appearance of diseased crops. Du et al. [13], transformed a colored image input into a binarized picture that is used to show the layout from which they are organized, using a classifier called Move Median Centers (MMC) and extraction of two-dimensional features were performed. Nevertheless, the rate of image recognition was more or less 90% only. Y. Nam et al. [14] have proposed shape-based investigation techniques to distinguish plant infections.

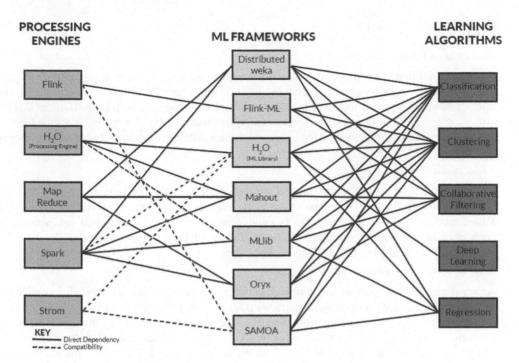

FIGURE 4.4 Associations among processing engines, machine learning frameworks, and learning algorithms.

4.2.2 Classification and Feature Extraction

The process of crop infection recognition is alienated into two segments: image processing along with machine learning techniques. The pictures that are captured from nearby crop fields are enhanced and processed using image processing methods. Feature extraction defines the behavior of an image; they are depicted in terms of storage taken, efficiency in classification, and time consumption. In general, these are the three categories that are extracted:

a. Color – It is the most significant characteristic in a picture, because it can differentiate one disease from another. Pandey et al. [15] surveyed image processing and machine learning approaches implemented in the crop grading method. Fruit quality grading is done according to texture, color, and size; calyx of fruits, stems, and sorting the fruits using shape.

b. Shape – Each infection may have a different shape; some common shape aspects are axis, angle, and area.

c. Texture – It is how patterns of color are extracted in a picture. Dhaygude S. B. et al. [16] have built a system using four stages. The initial stage is generating a RGB-altered picture. Then the transformed RGB is used to produce HIS pictures. The disadvantage of feature extraction algorithms is that their computational levels are so high; also, due to dependence on explicit facts, generalization is not easy.

4.2.3 Problems and Diseases

Crop infections are usually generated by either non-living factors, such as temperature, water, wind, soil acidity, and radiation, or by living organisms, for instance fungus and rats. Every year it is estimated that farmers lose an average of around 38% of their paddy yield to diseases and pests.

Real concerns faced by the farmers:

- Rate of crop illness and irritation:

    Precise recognition of crop quality can help enhance yield price and decrease waste. D. Nidhis et al. [17] used image-processing techniques to evaluate the percentage of the diseased area and utilize pesticides based on the severity calculated for the disease infection. Lipsa Barik et al. [18] also used image processing and machine learning approach to build a model that could detect disease and its affected region and then group them into different categories based on the severity of disease.

- Yield prediction:

    In the past, yield prediction was performed by considering farmers' experience on particular fields and crops. Burgueño et al. [19] proposed an integrated approach of factor analytic (FA) and linear mixed models to cluster environments (E) and genotypes (G) and detect their interactions. In connection to that, Burgueño et al. [20] stated that FA model can improve predictability up to 6% when there were complex G × E patterns in the data.

- Lack of continuous monitoring of the plants:

    Automation is the solution for this problem; cameras can be deployed at certain distances in the farm to capture images periodically. Anuradha Badage et al. [21] have successfully built a model using a canny edge detection algorithm and Machine Learning for training that could track the edge and get the required histogram value to predict diseases at an early stage by periodically monitoring the cultivation field. Table 4.2 shows the comparative study of segmentation techniques with complexity, segmentation effect, merit, and demerit.

4.3 Proposed Architecture

In this part, we present our projected architecture for identifying disease-infected rice leaves. In this planned approach, we aim to identify three paddy infections, specifically bacterial leaf blight, leaf blast, and brown spot. Figure 4.5 shows the block diagram of the proposed architecture. In following subsections, we talk about the dealing out stages of the proposed system. A complete discussion of different models is shown in the following segment.

4.3.1 Image Acquisition

The images of the leaves of the rice plant have been captured from the paddy fields, which is required when a dataset of images is not obtainable. The picture samples are captured from a rural community known as Belman, located in the coastal regions of Udupi district, of Karnataka state, India. All images are of jpeg format.

4.3.2 Image Enhancement

First, the RGB picture is transformed into a HSV-colored image, as shown in Figure 4.6 [22]. Since the S module does not restrain the whiteness, we extracted the S constituent of the HSV process picture. Subsequently, we removed and made all the background pixels zero by creating and using a mask.

4.3.3 Image Segmentation

The image samples are segmented by using the Spark-Based FCM Segmentation technique. We used the Apache Spark platform for implementing the Fuzzy C-Means algorithm.

TABLE 4.2

Comparison between Different Segmentation Approaches

	Techniques	Complexity	Thresholding Technique	Segmentation Technique	Segmentation Outcome	Advantages	Disadvantages
1	K-Means	Low	Local	Clustering	Precisely differentiate uninfected and infected parts of crop.	Sum of square space among object and centroid is reduced.	Complicated to forecast K with preset number of clusters.
2	Fuzzy C-Means	High	Local	Clustering	Enhanced compared to K-means and Otsu.	Partial relationship is used. Consequently, more functional in support of actual problems.	Responsive to initialization. Circumstance of the cluster center and cluster number.
3	Otsu's Method	Very High	Global	Thresholding	Good/stable	It works on real-world pictures, in spite of shape and uniformity measures.	Processing requires more time.
4	Grey-Level Thresholding	Normal	Global	Thresholding	More precise with contrast to Otsu's technique	Contrast for infection area as well as background is provided by grey-level alteration (2G-R-B).	Each instance requires selecting good threshold values for receiving improved effect in segmentation.

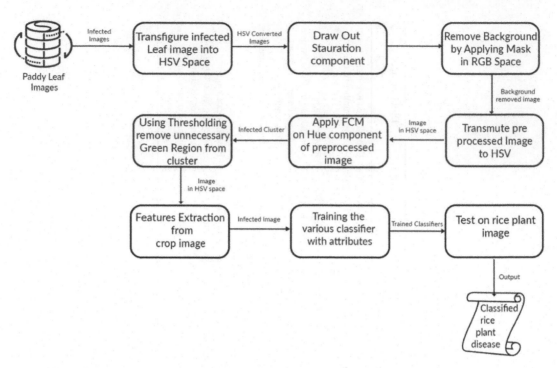

FIGURE 4.5   The block diagram of proposed architecture.

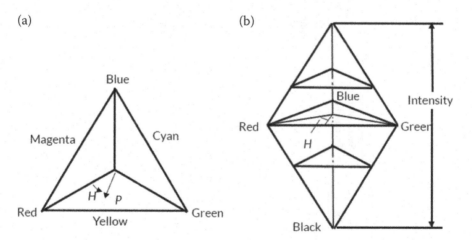

FIGURE 4.6   (a) Color triangle of HSV; (b) color solid of HSV.

4.3.4 Feature Extraction

The proposed technique distinguished one infection from another by using feature extraction. Nevertheless, appropriate interpretation and understanding of attribute values is required to select the features. The system considers the variety of features in two categories: shape feature extraction and color feature extraction.

4.3.5 Classification

The proposed system used various classification techniques, namely, Naïve Bayes, DT, SVM, and Random Forest using Spark as a cluster computing platform.

4.4 Proposed Algorithms and Implementation Details

4.4.1 Image Preprocessing

Image enhancement performs contrast adjustment and noise reduction. The acquired diseased leaf model of images in RGB color space will also convert to HSV, in addition to this intensity of the image adjusted. We have used HSV color space in the image processing because it corresponds to similar colors a human eye can read. HSI space exchange from the RGB color space picture starts by the RGB values normalization. RGB normalization is shown in Equation (4.3).

$$r = \frac{R}{R + G + B} \quad g = \frac{G}{R + G + B} \quad b = \frac{B}{R + G + B} \tag{4.3}$$

The standardized H, S, and V constituents can be acquired by using (4.4), (4.5), (4.6), and (4.7) [23–26].

$$h = \cos^{-1}\left\{ \frac{0.5[(r - g) + (r - b)]}{\sqrt{(r - g)^2 + (r - b)(g - b)}} \right\}; h \in [0, \pi] \, for \, b \le g \tag{4.4}$$

$$h = 2\pi - \cos^{-1}\left\{ \frac{0.5[(r - g) + (r - b)]}{\sqrt{(r - g)^2 + (r - b)(g - b)}} \right\}; h \in [\pi, 2\pi] \, for \, b > g \tag{4.5}$$

$$s = 1 - 3. \, min(r, g, b); \qquad s \in [0, 1] \tag{4.6}$$

$$v = \frac{R + G + B}{3.255}; v \in [0, 1] \tag{4.7}$$

Equation (4.6) is used to change HSV values to a further expedient choice of [0,360], [0,100], [0,255], respectively.

$$H = \frac{hx180}{\pi}; S = sx100; I = ix255; \tag{8}$$

Equation (4.4) is used to obtain the RGB matrix of the pictures. Figure 4.7 shows the leaf illustration of bacterial leaf blight.

Equations (4.4) to (4.8) are used to convert the RGB image into a HSV color space by enhancing the effectiveness in the image processing and minimizing calculation, which is shown in Figure 4.8.

4.4.2 Image Segmentation and the Fuzzy C-Means Model Using Spark

Apache Spark was developed at Berkeley's Algorithms, Machines and People Lab and it is based on memory computing and an open-source cluster computing platform. The Fuzzy C-Means approach is one among the finest, famous unsupervised technique for fuzzy clustering; Equation (4.9) shows the

FIGURE 4.7 Leaf sample of bacterial leaf blight.

FIGURE 4.8   Alteration of RGB image to HSV.

minimizing of the objective function J_m in the FCM approach, that accomplish fine partitioning outcome shown by searching for the finest cluster centers. An objective function, J_m, is represented in the criteria.

$$J_m (U, V, X) = \sum_{i=1}^{c} \sum_{j=1}^{n} u_{ij}^{m} d_{ij}^{2} \tag{4.9}$$

$$u_{ij} = \left[\sum_{k=1}^{c} \left(\frac{d_{ij}}{d_{kj}} \right)^{\frac{2}{m-1}} \right]^{-1} \quad 0 \le u_{ij} \le 1, \ \sum_{i=1}^{c} u_{ij} = 1 \tag{4.10}$$

$$V_i = \frac{\sum_{j=1}^{n} u_{ij}^{m} X_j}{\sum_{j=1}^{n} u_{ij}^{m} u_{ij}} \tag{4.11}$$

where $X = \{x_1, x_2, \cdots, x_n\}$ represents the datasets, along with $V = \{v_1, v_2, \cdots, v_n\}$ represents the set of clusters. m indicates the association scale of all data component to the cluster and is the real number that manages fuzziness of clustering. Generally, the value m is 2. u_{ij} is used to represent $c \times n$ size relationship matrix, where n is the size of data and c is the number of clusters. The nearness of the data constituent x_j to the center of the cluster v_i is measured by $d_{ij} = \|x_j - v_i\|^2$. The result of FCM clustering and the infected part of the rice leaf is shown in Figures 4.9 and 4.10, respectively.

4.4.3 Feature Extraction

Feature extraction plays an important responsibility in distinguishing one leaf infection from other. In our approach, we focus on the shape and color feature extraction.

FIGURE 4.9   Result of FCM clustering.

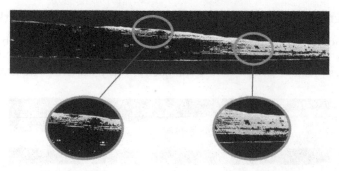

FIGURE 4.10   Infected part of the rice leaf.

I. Shape feature extraction: Shape is one of the significant frameworks of a picture. One can easily recognize and differentiate an entity by visualizing its shapes.

II. Color feature extraction: By using texture characteristics, namely skewness, cluster prominence, cluster shade, and Kurtosis. By using grey-level co-occurrence matrix, we remove the features of texture.

4.4.4 Classification

4.4.4.1 Support Vector Machine (SVM)

The proposed system uses the SVM algorithm approach, because it is known for its high precision. It has the potential to compact with elevated dimensional datasets. The SVM classification approach intends to discover a hyper-plane, which splits the facts into a distinct pre-defined quantity of classes in a manner regular with the train instances.

4.4.4.2 Naïve Bayes

This approach uses Bayes rule to formulate a forecast that it uses to calculate the probability of every attribute that belongs to a certain class. By presuming that the attributes are autonomous, the computation of probability is simplified, specified by the tag for every further attribute. For a few bigger databases, the decision tree provides better accurateness than the Naïve Bayes approach.

4.4.4.3 Decision Tree and Random Forest

The reiterative partitioning approach is used to develop a decision tree. The process called pruning is carried out once an entire tree has been constructed, and it reduces the size of the tree. The random forest consists of constructing numerous decision trees and is a packaged learning technique for regression, unpruned classifications or other jobs.

4.5 Result Analysis

In this section, we shall briefly talk about the experimental results and outcomes. Initially we shall compare speed-up and scallop performance between the Spark-based and Hadoop-based FCM algorithm of image segmentation results.

4.5.1 Comparison of Speed-up Performance between the Spark-Based and Hadoop-Based FCM Approach

In this section, we calculate the results of the Spark-based FCM algorithm using speed-up. Here, speed-up denotes how quicker a parallel algorithm is compared to equivalent serial approach. The following equation is used to define speed-up:

$$Speedup = \frac{T_1}{T_p} \tag{4.12}$$

In the above equation, T_1 refers to the implementation time of the sequential algorithm on a lone node, p refers to the number of nodes, and T_p is the execution time of the parallel algorithm. We use test images of rice leaf to validate these two Fuzzy-Means algorithms by comparing the speed-up among the Spark-based and Hadoop-based FCM approach. The results experimentation is presented in Figure 4.11 in the form of a graph that shows the overall working enhancement for the Spark-based algorithm and Hadoop-based algorithm. The following equation is used to describe the increase rate:

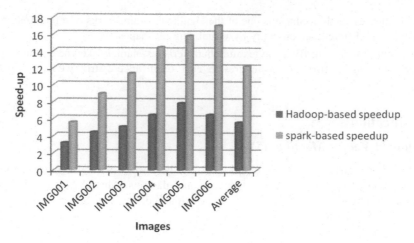

FIGURE 4.11 Comparison of the speed-up between Spark-based and Hadoop-based FCM algorithm.

TABLE 4.3

The Performance Improvement Summary

Testing Images	Hadoop-Based Speed-up	Spark-Based Speed-up	Performance Improvement
IMG001	3.16	5.58	76.53%
IMG002	4.43	8.96	102.25%
IMG003	5.06	11.34	124.11%
IMG004	6.44	14.43	124.06%
IMG005	7.82	15.78	101.98%
IMG006	6.46	17	163.15%
Average	5.56	12.18	115.32%

$$rate\_inc = \frac{Spark\_speedup - Hadoop\_speedup}{Hadoop\_speedup} \times 100\% \tag{4.13}$$

We can see that the from the Performance improvement column in Table 4.3, it is clear that the proportion enhancement changes from 76.53% to 163.15%; also, the average increase in the rate can arrive at 115.32%. These experimental outcomes specify that the Spark-based FCM approach can gain better performance improvement for all pictures compared with the Hadoop-based FCM approach.

4.5.2 Comparison of Scale-up Performance between the Spark-Based and Hadoop-Based FCM Approach

Scale-up is used to examine the scalability of the system to amplify both the dataset size and the system. It is the capability of an x-times bigger method to execute an x-time bigger work within the equal run time compared to the original approach. The following equation is used to describe the scale-up rate:

$$Scaleup(data, x) = \frac{T_1}{T_{xx}} \tag{4.14}$$

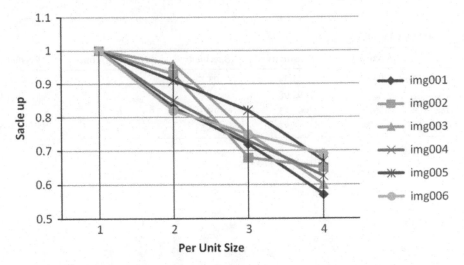

FIGURE 4.12 Comparison between scale-up between the Spark-based and Hadoop-based FCM algorithm.

Here, T_1 denotes the time of execution for processing facts on single node, and carrying out time for processing x∗ data on x computing nodes are denoted by T_{xx}. Scale-up performances of the datasets are shown in Figure 4.12. Image Img005 sustains up to 68% scalability, whereas Image Img005 also sustains up to 61% scale-up. Hence, from the following graph, we can clearly make out the Spark-based FCM approach scales just fine.

4.5.3 Result Analysis of Various Segmentation Techniques

The categorization measures have four essentials: TN, TP, FN, and FP. First, true negative (TN) is the quantity of appropriately classified standard records. Second, true positive (TP) is the amount of proper classification of attacks. Third, false negative (FN) denotes the quantity of standard records which are misclassified. Finally, false positive (FP) is the quantity of attacks which are misclassified. Hence, the following equation reflects the same:

$$Accuracy = \frac{TP + TN}{TP + TN + FP + FN} \tag{4.15}$$

Sensitivity: This is used to calculate the percentage of true positives that are properly recognized by it. It is also known as true positive rates.

$$Sensitivity = \frac{TP}{TP + FN} \tag{4.16}$$

Specificity: This is used to calculate the percentage of true negative that are properly recognized by it. It is also known as true negative rates.

$$Specificity = \frac{TN}{TN + FP} \tag{4.17}$$

In our research, we have used four eminent classifiers and compared the performance of SVM, Naïve Bayes, Random Forest, and Decision Tree with the intention of detecting the rice plant diseases. We can observe from table that sensitivity for the Random Forest classifier achieve well than all the other classifiers.

TABLE 4.4

Results of Various Classifiers

Classifiers	Accuracy	Sensitivity	Specificity	Training Time	Prediction Time
SVM	94.65	91.34	93.12	29.21	0.39
Naïve Bayes	88.32	92.98	72.45	3.20	0.15
Decision Tree	96.73	92.43	98.01	6.43	0.13
Random Forest	98.89	93.87	98.57	6.76	0.09

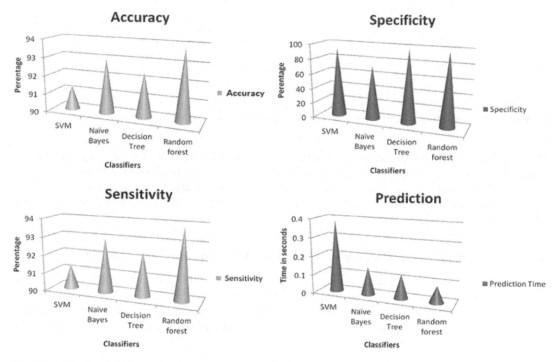

FIGURE 4.13   Result analysis of various segmentation techniques.

From Table 4.4, we can clearly see that the Decision Tree and Random Forest schemes have specificity that is approximately alike with 98.01% and 98.57%, correspondingly. However, Naïve Bayes is the least among all the algorithms when it comes to Specificity. Amongst the approaches, accuracy of the Naïve Bayes approach is less, with 72.45%. Random Forest performs well in terms of accuracy, with 98.89%. Result analysis of various segmentation techniques is shown in Figure 4.13.

4.5.4 Results of Disease Identification

Defect Rice Plant Leaf	Suggestions	Accuracy
Bacterial Leaf Blight	Switching Bacterial Leaf Blight – forbearing rice seeds such as Rc54, Rc150, and Rc170. Treating paddy seeds with zinc sulfate and calcium hypochlorite to reduce the disease.	98.49%

(Continued)

Defect Rice Plant Leaf	Suggestions	Accuracy
 Leaf Blast	Choose forbearing varieties, for instance NSIC and Rc170 PSB Rc82. Extreme exercise of fertilizer must be reduced as it leads to the occurrence of leaf blast. Remove blast-infected leaf regularly to avoid spread.	99.06%
 Brown Spot	As the fungi are transmitted through seeds, treatment of the seed using hot water (54–55°C) for 11–13 minutes may be effective prior to sowing. By doing this treatment, primary infection can be controlled at the initial stages. Appropriate managing of manure by using calcium silicate slag.	99.73%

4.6 Conclusion and Future Work

In this chapter, we have developed an approach which distinguishes the various infections present in rice crop leaf using various classification techniques coupled with image processing was productively implemented via Spark engine. Furthermore, distinctive contusions of the infected rice leaves were efficiently recognized with a correctness of 99% for the infection detection. The system was productively implemented using Spark and verified to produce a precise solution; yet, the researchers propose the subsequent suggestion to advance enhancement of the system: (1) include more varieties of rice plant disease that can be recognized using this approach; (2) consider various topological conditions and associated variety of rice plants; and (3) collect large amounts of pictures for the dataset for big data machine learning that could give a more precise outcome. In upcoming work, we would look forward to enhancing the accurateness to 100% on test photos. To be more precise, we plan to distinguish brown spot from leaf blast more accurately by using deep learning techniques to gain highly accurate results.

REFERENCES

[1] Shah, Jitesh P., Harshadkumar B. Prajapati, and Vipul K. Dabhi. "A survey on detection and classification of rice plant diseases." In *2016 IEEE International Conference on Current Trends in Advanced Computing (ICCTAC)*, pp. 1–8. IEEE, 2016.

[2] Gianessi, Leonard P. "Importance of pesticides for growing rice in South and South East Asia." *International Pesticide Benefit Case Study* 108 (2014):1–4.

[4] Buneman, Peter. "Semistructured data." [Online] Available from: http://homepages.inf.ed.ac.uk/opb/papers/PODS1997a.pdf.

[3] Sethy, Prabira Kumar, Nalini Kanta Barpanda, Amiya Kumar Rath, and Santi Kumari Behera. "Image processing techniques for diagnosing rice plant disease: A survey." *Procedia Computer Science* 167 (2020): 516–530.

[5] Suthaharan, Shan. "Big data classification: Problems and challenges in network intrusion prediction with machine learning." *ACM SIGMETRICS Performance Evaluation Review* 41, no. 4 (2014): 70–73.

[6] Manocha, S., and Mark A. Girolami. "An empirical analysis of the probabilistic K-nearest neighbour classifier." *Pattern Recognition Letters* 28, no. 13 (2007): 1818–1824.

[7] Ding, Chris, and Xiaofeng He. "K-means clustering via principal component analysis." In *Proceedings of the Twenty-first International Conference on Machine Learning*, p. 29, 2004.

[8] Dunn, Joseph C. "A fuzzy relative of the ISODATA process and its use in detecting compact well-separated clusters." *Journal of Cybernetics* 3, (1973): 32–57.

[9] Bezdek, James C. *Pattern recognition with fuzzy objective function algorithms*. Springer Science & Business Media, New York, 2013.

[10] Quinlan, J. Ross. *C4. 5: programs for machine learning*. Elsevier, USA, 2014.

[11] White, Tom. *Hadoop: The definitive guide*. O'Reilly Media, Inc., USA, 2012.

[12] Landset, Sara, Taghi M. Khoshgoftaar, Aaron N. Richter, and Tawfiq Hasanin. "A survey of open source tools for machine learning with big data in the Hadoop ecosystem." *Journal of Big Data* 2, no. 1 (2015): 24.

[13] Friis, Ib, and Henrik Balslev, eds. *Plant Diversity and Complexity Patterns: Local, Regional, and Global Dimensions*: *Proceedings of an International Symposium held at the Royal Danish Academy of Sciences and Letters in Copenhagen, Denmark, 25–28 May, 2003. Vol. 55*. Kgl. Danske Videnskabernes Selskab, 2005.

[14] Y. Nam and E. Hwang, "A representation and matching method for shape-based leaf image retrieval," *Journal of KIISE: Software and Applications* 32, no. 11 (2005): 1013–1021.

[15] Pandey, Rashmi, Sapan Naik, and Roma Marfatia. "Image processing and machine learning for automated fruit grading system: a technical review." *International Journal of Computer Applications* 81, no. 16 (2013): 29–39.

[16] Dhaygude, Sanjay B., and Nitin P. Kumbhar. "Agricultural plant leaf disease detection using image processing." *International Journal of Advanced Research in Electrical, Electronics and Instrumentation Engineering* 2, no. 1 (2013): 599–602.

[17] Nidhis, A. D., Chandrapati Naga Venkata Pardhu, K. Charishma Reddy, and K. Deepa. "Cluster based paddy leaf disease detection, classification and diagnosis in crop health monitoring unit." In *Computer Aided Intervention and Diagnostics in Clinical and Medical Images*, pp. 281–291. Springer, Cham, 2019.

[18] Barik, Lipsa. "A survey on region identification of rice disease using image processing." *International Journal of Research and Scientific Innovation* 5, no. 1 (2018).

[19] Burgueño, J., J. Crossa, P. L. Cornelius, and R.-C. Yang. "Using factor analytic models for joining environments and genotypes without crossover genotype× environment interaction." *Crop Science* 48 (2008): 1291.

[20] Burgueño, Juan, José Crossa, José Miguel Cotes, Felix San Vicente, and Biswanath Das. "Prediction assessment of linear mixed models for multienvironment trials." *Crop Science* 51, no. 3 (2011): 944–954.

[21] Badage, Anuradha. "Crop disease detection using machine learning: Indian agriculture." *International Research Journal of Engineering and Technology (IRJET)* 5, no. 9 (2018): 866–869.

[22] Orillo, John William, Jennifer Dela Cruz, Leobelle Agapito, Paul Jensen Satimbre, and Ira Valenzuela. "Identification of diseases in rice plant (oryza sativa) using back propagation Artificial Neural Network." In *2014 International Conference on Humanoid, Nanotechnology, Information Technology, Communication and Control, Environment and Management (HNICEM)*, pp. 1–6. IEEE, 2014.

[23] Orillo, John William, Jennifer Dela Cruz, Leobelle Agapito, Paul Jensen Satimbre, and Ira Valenzuela. "Identification of diseases in rice plant (oryza sativa) using back propagation Artificial Neural Network." In *2014 International Conference on Humanoid, Nanotechnology, Information Technology, Communication and Control, Environment and Management (HNICEM)*, pp. 1–6. IEEE, 2014.

[24] Gadekallu, Thippa Reddy, Neelu Khare, Sweta Bhattacharya, Saurabh Singh, Praveen Kumar Reddy Maddikunta, and Gautam Srivastava. "Deep neural networks to predict diabetic retinopathy." *Journal of Ambient Intelligence and Humanized Computing* (2020): 1–14. https://doi.org/10.1007/s12652-020-01963-7

[25] Gadekallu, Thippa Reddy, Dharmendra Singh Rajput, M. Praveen Kumar Reddy, Kuruva Lakshmanna, Sweta Bhattacharya, Saurabh Singh, Alireza Jolfaei, and Mamoun Alazab. "A novel PCA–whale optimization-based deep neural network model for classification of tomato plant diseases using GPU." *Journal of Real-Time Image Processing* (2020): 1–14. https://doi.org/10.1007/s11554-020-00987-8

[26] Reddy, G. Thippa, M. Praveen Kumar Reddy, Kuruva Lakshmanna, Rajesh Kaluri, Dharmendra Singh Rajput, Gautam Srivastava, and Thar Baker. "Analysis of dimensionality reduction techniques on big data." *IEEE Access* 8 (2020): 54776–54788.

Section II

Algorithms, Methods, and Tools for Data Science and Data Analytics

5

Crop Models and Decision Support Systems Using Machine Learning

B. Vignesh and G. Suganya

CONTENTS

5.1 Introduction

The human population throughout the world is estimated to reach around 9 billion by the year 2050 as per the prediction of the Food and Agriculture Organization (United Nations). Therefore, the demand for food and agriculture-based commodities will increase. The estimated food demand gradually increases at a rate of 2% per year, approximately. By the year 2050, the food demand will increase by 70% of the present-day food demand. Therefore the agricultural yield should be multiplied manifold to meet the increasing food demand (i.e., the food production should increase to 13.5 billion tonnes a year from the current food production, which is 8.4 billion tonnes a year) [1].

Such a huge target cannot be achieved using traditional farming methods because of the present-day challenges and environmental problems like climate change, biodiversity loss, erosion, pesticide resistance, fertilizers and eutrophication, water depletion, soil salinization, urban sprawl, pollution, and silt. Hence, traditional farming methods are unable to keep pace with the increasing food production demand [2]. Under such conditions, the increased food security threat will lead to global instability.

A sustainable and long-term solution to this problem is "smart farming," especially in countries like India that has a growing population. Smart farming is a more productive and sustainable way of farming. Smart farming maximizes the prediction of yields; reducing the resource/raw material wastage, moderate the economic and security risks so as to improve efficiency and to reduce agricultural uncertainty.

Smart farming uses intelligent and digital tools that optimize the farm operations and facilitate the use of resources in order to improve the overall quantity and quality of farm yield. The main resource for farming is land, seed, water, fertilizers, and pesticides. Thus, smart farming helps to predict and manage the imbalances between crop production, processing, and food consumption. Using smart farming technology, natural resources like water and land are effectively used, along with appropriate selection of seeds and fertilizers. This improves overall quantitative and qualitative measures involved in prediction of farm yield.

In traditional farming, the decisions about the crops and farming methods are taken based on the regional conditions, historical data, and previous experience of the farmers. The same approach is not sufficient for the present-day agriculture that faces numerous challenges. Present-day agriculture should be effective, efficient, and sustainable.

In contrast to the traditional farming, precision farming uses data from modern technologies like sensors used as part of IoT, robotics, GPS tracking, mapping tools, and data-analytics software and acts as a decision support system to provide customized solutions to each and every case. Smart farming overcomes all the challenges of traditional farming and provides effective practical solutions. Smart farming technology acts as a systematic tool that predicts and solves unforeseen problems also [3].

Moreover, precision farming increases the outcome with minimum input resources and without polluting the soil and the environment. Based on the United States Department of Agriculture (USDA) report, it is evident that the precision agriculture technology adoption increases operating profit margins, by increasing the return and crop yield [4].

In this chapter, the view of smart faming as knowledge-based agriculture is explained. It also discusses how smart farming drives agricultural productivity when data intense approach is used in collaboration with machine learning (ML) and deep learning (DL). It outlines how crop models play a potential role in increasing the quantity and quality of agricultural products.

Development of more precise, efficient, and reliable pipelines for seamless analysis of large crop model phenotyping datasets is briefed. The crop model along with DSS techniques is capable of detecting biotic and abiotic stress in plants with finite accuracy level. Hyper-spectral image (HSI) processing along with crop management is employed for the effective analysis and classification of crops based on the variety, location, and sustainable growth over a period of time. Even a small change in the crop can be recorded and processed for building an evolvable crop model. The models can be frequently improvised according to changes and increases in demand. Increases in technical processing capabilities of HSI will provide additional levers such as multidimensional hyperspectral capabilities in order to filter and process the required data precisely. Finally, the process and necessary stages for implementing a Decision Support System (DSS) for smart farming is deliberated such that it will be more useful to the farming community.

5.1.1 Decision Support System

Smart farming is empowered by a computerized decision support system (CDSS) inside which machine learning tools with its high-precision algorithms is embedded. CDSS uses real-time and historical data, along with machine learning algorithms to make specific decisions. CDSS takes the real-time data from field video cameras, sensors, and micro-meteorological data for monitoring. They analyze the collected data and give predictions and warnings about early signs of disease, weed growth, pests, and crop yield. The highly trained precision algorithms notice the changes that are not easily noticed by human beings.

The decision support systems process and convert the raw data into useful information using machine learning tools. This useful information helps in improving the precision of farming. To increase the agricultural productivity, crop models are developed and incorporated into computerized decision support systems.

5.1.2 Decision Support System for Crop Yield

To ensure higher earnings for farmers, crop yield should be higher. Only if the crop yield is higher, food security can be ensured. Decision support system aids in crop yield prediction so as to support farmers and other stakeholders for effective crop planning. Effective crop planning aids the farmers in various phases beginning from crop cultivation until marketization of crop yield.

Various existing mining techniques that predict the crop yield accuracy using a minimal dataset have lesser accuracy and are more prone to errors. To maximize the accuracy and minimize the errors, larger datasets should be processed.

Farmers can do proactive planning and get more benefit if they are provided with a decision support system that offers more accurate crop yield prediction. The following sections discuss and compare the various machine learning techniques used for the decision support systems to predict the crop yield.

The agriculture-based analytical system combines real-time sensor data and spectral images to improve farm outputs and reduce waste (Figure 5.1). The grouped dataset can be consolidated by collecting the information related to crops such as

- Crop images based on its varieties
- Crop growth over a period of time
- Required nutrients and soil quality
- Biotic and abiotic involvement for plant growth sustainability
- Climatic and weather conditions (fog, humidity, rainfall, etc.)

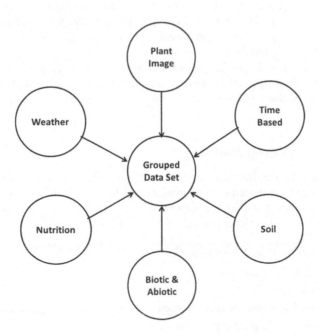

FIGURE 5.1 Grouped dataset in smart farming.

5.1.3 What Is Crop Modeling?

Crop models are useful tools in technology-based agriculture. A crop model is a representation of extracted crop features. It is a statistical representation of crop behavior. It is developed considering the conditions involved in crop management process. The process of building a crop model involves the following steps:

    i. Selection of crop
   ii. Crop data gathering (phenotype and genotype)
  iii. Extraction of attributes
   iv. Preparation of crop simulation models
    v. Breed selection with respect to environment conditions

Implementing crop models based on the crop behavioral data along with the understanding of biotic and abiotic components will impact the yield. Moreover, there are other qualified key attributes such as environment and climate conditions that enable sustainable growth that need to be included. The key benefits of data-driven agriculture are

    i. Reduce wastage of resources and raw materials
   ii. Increase productivity and crop yields
  iii. Ensure sustainability growth and revenues
   iv. Yield prediction and improved crop management life cycle
    v. Effective utilization of farmlands
   vi. Improved biomass of crop and farm components

5.1.4 Necessity of Crop Modeling

The crop behavior is represented in terms of growth and yield predictions. The predictions are based on the functions such as soil conditions, weather conditions, and integrated crop management processes. The crop models help in understanding and analyzing the perspectives for (i) enhancing the crop growth and (ii) improving the biomass of crop components. The biomass of crop components includes seed germination and harvestable product.

The crop simulation models also do predictions and selection of the crop breed, which can produce a high yield irrespective of changes in environmental conditions. The crop models assist the sessional crop management process. Such a process reduces the crop yield failures and improves the precision of farming.

5.1.5 Recent Trends in Crop Modeling

Monitoring and controlling the fundamental aspects of the field and crops such as health of crops, amount of water or fertilizer, detecting contaminants and heavy metals, and possible infections that affect the crops is an important step in precision farming. Using hyper-spectral imaging (HSI) for such monitoring gives precise results. Other benefits of crop modeling include

- Advanced and information-rich technology
- Crop- and region-specific analysis
- Agronomy-driven expertise
- Detection of complex problems such as weeds, diseases, and nutrition deficiency
- High flexibility to target specific problems

- Virtual and augmented reality is possible for remote farm inspection and identification of impediments
- Crop models can be enhanced and shared for multidisciplinary study

5.2 Methodologies

The crop models, with live data like meteorological data, soil information, and hyper-spectral images of the crops, are fed as input to the machine-learning-based Computerized Decision Support Systems (CDSS). Based on these inputs, the CDSS produces accurate analysis and precise predictions. The efficiency of the CDSS depends on how it produces sensible information from the real-time raw data. The CDSS collects the real-time data, interprets, and compares the results. Based on the comparison, it gives the predictions and thereby acts as a decision support system.

A model-based DSS can be leveraged to predict the yield. An overview of the steps involved in smart farming is shown in Figure 5.2. The agriculture-based dataset is prepared by collecting the necessary information about a crop. The crop data is enriched by preprocessing techniques along with standardization. The crop model is built over the critical attributes as a statistical function. The statistical functions can be fine-tuned by the reinforcement learning of model. Once the errors are reduced, the models are executed based on rules for effective prediction.

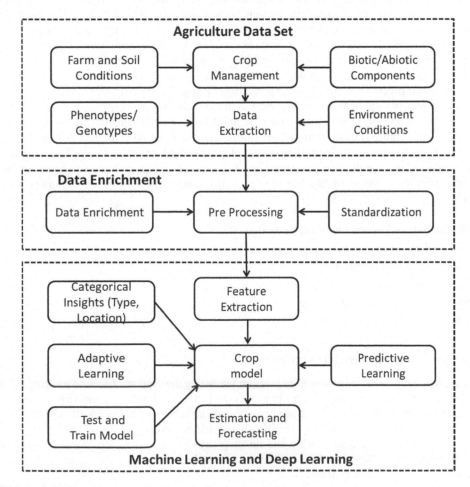

FIGURE 5.2 Overview of steps involved in smart farming.

A real-time deployable model may requires additional system capabilities such as

- Real-time data acquisition framework
- Real-time data preprocessing and enrichment
- Real-time storing and processing units
- Rule-based data model preparation and evaluation
- Real-time feedback incorporation and automated system
- Real-time testing and deployment framework such as CI/CD Pipelines
  - Continuous Integration (CI)
  - Continuous Deployment (CD)

- Generic framework for sustainability and reusability
- Adaptive and predictive learning for forecasting and estimation
- Virtual and augmented reality for remote site operations
- Data archival and deduplication of data

5.2.1 Machine-Learning-Based Techniques

Learning systems applied to agriculture is a data intensive science and non-destructive tool. Data-driven technologies provide various predictions such as assessment of crops, along with classifications and vegetation index for carrying out yield analysis and identification of a crop-specific stress and farm-specific stress. Various learning models and algorithms are applied in the area of multi-disciplinary agriculture. The possibilities of applying the learning models effectively in multi-disciplinary agriculture are plenty. Following are some of the commonly used ML-based strategies used in precision farming: (i) Application of appropriate ML techniques for farm management systems, (ii) application of ML models for developing more efficient and effective pipelines to analyze phenotyping datasets, (iii) ML models to identify the effect of plant density and yield along with multiple desired traits, (iv) implementation of ML models for predicting and decision making about crop selection etc., (v) integration and execution of a real-time artificial intelligent system in crop disease detection, and (vi) feature extraction and classification methods for smart agriculture. Some of the commonly used methods used in ML techniques are given below [5]:

- Similarity-based versus knowledge-based
- Noise-tolerant versus exact
- Top-down versus bottom-up
- Supervised versus unsupervised
- Interactive versus non-interactive
- Single- versus multi-paradigm

5.2.2 Deep-Learning-Based Techniques

More than processing an image of a crop or plant for predicting the crop attributes, leveraging the hyper-spectral images (HSIs) in agriculture helps to extract the features at different granularities such as seed, crop, and farm. The HSIs are captured in varying bandwidths and wavelengths. Recent studies show significant improvement in deploying the HSI-based methodology for agriculture. Hyper-spectral images were acquired by remote sensing and imaging devices such as handheld spectro-radiometers. The spectral data is an efficient and cost-effective method for carrying out the research in agriculture, along with a crop model that contains

- Biophysical parameters of crops and plants
  - The leaf area index (LAI) arrived for a crop [6]
  - Chlorophyll content level present in crops and plants [7,8]
  - Identification and classification of weed species specific to a crop [9,10]
  - Crop separation and classification [11–13]

- Environmental crop management and yield estimation [14]
  - Organization and planning including crop rotation
  - Crop protection from weeds depends upon the crop variety and phase of growth
  - Soil management and crop nutrition

- Precision farming and improved efficiency
  - Farming with optimum need of resources
  - Improving the efficiency of the system by minimizing waste and contingencies

5.2.3 Hyper-Spectral Imaging

The hyper-spectral data are gathered for identification and classification of crop species. Several methods are available for analyzing the hyperspectral data. The most commonly used methodologies are

- Processing the data for reducing the dimension [8]
- Discriminant analysis
- Principal components analysis
- Classification methods like partial least-squares regression
- Artificial intelligence and deep neural networks
- Image processing techniques

By using these methods the visible and near infrared spectral data are processed and models for crops are built. The wavelengths and spectral reflections vary based on the crop types, plant growth, and locations. Crop models are built for each variety of crop based on the spectral range and time (days after planting) [6]. The hyper-spectral data is collected over a period of time and a multidimensional effective crop model is built. Some of the examples of crop models built from hyper-spectral include

- Soybean, wheat, oat, and barley hyper-spectral data were extracted at 1,000–1,700 nm [15]
- Graph seed and maize in the range of 874–1,752 nm

From the hyperspectral data, a suitable bandwidth for a crop and location is identified. Over a period of time, the classification and analysis of crop models is improved and crop discrimination is empowered. Image processing and correction techniques are used to reduce the noise such as sensor calibration, platform motion, image reference with geo-position, and system calibration.

5.2.4 Popular Band Selection Techniques

Common problems involved in processing hyper-spectral images are optimal selection of bandwidth and spectrum. Key bands from hyper-spectral images can be extracted by using two techniques: supervised and unsupervised learning [16,17].

- Unsupervised learning technique employed to extract features from HSI:
  - Entropy-based method: By processing each band separately to identify the information exists for a crop model over a particular band

- Processing the first and second spectral derivative to identify the redundant data across the bands

- Supervised learning technique employed to extract features from HSI:
  - Artificial Neural Network (ANN): A multilayered ANN was used for processing the hyperspectral bands in order to identify the band sensitivity and ranked accordingly. Every band is processed such that it varied from 0.1 to 0.9 with an increment of 0.05. The band with a higher sensitivity value is ranked, along with the mean score of each band.
  - Principal Component Analysis (PCA): Identification of a principal component that shows the maximum correlation on crop data along with its dependent and independent attributes. The band with higher-order principle components were selected such that the maximum variance decreases. The lower-order principal components represent global features in the image scene rather than local features.
  - Maximum likelihood classification (MLC): MLC-based classification is widely used in image classification methods. MLC can be extended for HSI-based image classification. Gaussian probability density function is used in the MLC classification algorithm. The MLC-based methods are effective if the training dataset is larger than the features that are considered for prediction. It cannot be leveraged if the training dataset is lesser than the features that are considered for prediction. The MLC is even applicable and accurate for small number of training samples and can be extended for processing high-dimensional feature space of hyperspectral dataset. Irrespective of its limitation, generally the MLC-based techniques produce better classification accuracy.
    - Support Vector Machine (SVM): The SVM is widely used for classification of hyperspectral images and image processing systems. Compared to the other existing classification methods, SVM performs better when used in hyper-spectral remote sensing. This is because Gaussian Radial Basis kernel functions are used in SVM classification.

- Random forest (RF): The hyper-spectral data variable selection and classification can be performed using the RF algorithm. The RF algorithm creates individual decision trees based on the random sample derived from the training dataset. The least number of nodes in a sample is 1. The error handling function and node impurity can be considered a coefficient.

5.2.5 Leveraging Conventional Neural Network

The Conventional Neural Network (CNN) is used for processing and building crop models. Figure 5.3 shows the steps involved in identifying a crop from a hyper-spectral image.

The hidden layers of CNN include the following:

- Conventional layer – The images were processed with a filter known as kernel (kernel function). Simply put, the input image processed over a filter. Multiple filters are applied over the image to extract different features. The relation between the pixels was preserved by learning and can be used to perform edge detection, blur, and sharpen by different filters.
- Pooling layer – To reduce the dimension sample based on discretization process. The features are represented and tagged to related regions. Pooling is classified as min, max, average, and sum pooling.
- ReLu layer – Rectified linear unit for non-linear operation. ReLu functions are not able to differentiate during origin, softplus, and sigmoid functions were used.
- Drop-out layer – Drop-out layer is used to prevent a model from overfitting the edges. During each update of the training phases, setting the outgoing edges of hidden units to 0 randomly. (The neurons are used as a hidden layer.)
- Fully connected layer – Used to flatten the results and connected to construct the desired number of outputs.

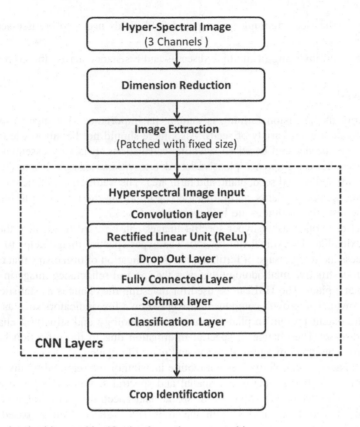

FIGURE 5.3 Steps involved in crop identification from a hyper-spectral image.

- Softmax layer – In this layer, the neural network can predict an object based on probability determination.
- Classification layer –An activation function such as logistic regression with cost functions is used to classify the image.

5.3 Role of Hyper-Spectral Data

5.3.1 Farm Based

An agricultural farm assessment can be carried out to predict the plant density and yield. A DNN model is created for HSI farm data. The model can be used to predict the key information such as [18], [27]

- Remote inspection of plots, crop density and yield, and optimize plot size for yield improvement - optimum plot size (1 × 2.4 m)
- The coefficient is 0.79 and root mean square variation up to 5.9 gm variation for a plant size of 2.5 m^2
- Improved normalized difference vegetation index (NDVI)

The model can be extended to identify further

- The effect of plant density can be studied along with high spatial resolution, in order to arrive at the yield and growth rate.

- Impact due to the side trimming for crop and field yields needs to be assessed across various varieties
- Identification and investing of multiple diseases and resistance across the crop species

5.3.2 Crop Based

In today's scenario, the precision farming is gaining its importance. The main aspect of precision farming is to cultivate a good variety of seeds. Also, there should not be any waste of resources. The need of resources can be decided based on scientific calculations. It is very essential to diagnose and classify the diseases that can impose a plant variety due to various causes. It is a challenging task to diagnosis and classify a diseased seed, plant, and farm area. The traditional methods involve destructive ways of classifying the seeds, plants, and farms thereby imposing the resources to undergo laboratory tests. Due to these tests the resources are being wasted.

The crop model developed using hyper-spectral images can be used to identify the disease, fungal infections, and toxins like deoxynivalenol (DON). The hyper-spectral image helps to improve the soil management process including usage of fertilizers and identification of organisms that cause toxins. HSI is a rapid and non-destructive methodology that uses the spectral reflectance image in order to identify the diseased crop and plant. The HSI can be used for investing the changes as statistical functions that evolve in plant growth. The growth components are based on a few indicators such as water content in plant, chlorophyll content present in plan organs, and morphology and structural changes due to the development of disease. The change in spectral information due to the reflection behavior helps to understand the problems that emerge in the crop and plant life cycle.

Hyper-spectral imagery technology does not require incision or the removal of any part of the image or spectrum. Using reflective property, the spatial and spectral features of a crop are detected and extracted using the HSI technique. Apart from spatial and spectral features of a crop, textural and contextual features of crops helps in classifying the crops. Hyper-spectral-image-based crop models are a non-invasive method that produces and processes a large data cube that can be used to extract the features required for deep learning. Deep neural network classification algorithms are applied to discern the disease area accurately. To increase the accuracy, the image needs to be preprocessed in order to avoid unwanted information and interferences.

The generalized crop classification model framework can be implemented as a two-step process.

- Step 1 – Preparation of multidimensional crop data
- Step 2 – Dimensional data structure is passed as input of conventional neural network

The effective crop model is achieved by considering all the required features that deeply elaborate the dataset properties and models characteristics. Confusion matrices and testing datasets are prepared based on the problem statements of disease classification and weed identification. The classification model should contain the hyper-spectral image pixel information that describes the problem. Several research studies substantiate that the deep neural network along with hyper-spectral imagery is an excellent path for agricultural-based technology [18,24–26].

5.3.3 Advanced HSI Processing

Hyper-spectral image classification technique is widely used across several industries in order to test and identify the quality of finished product. Some of the examples are identification of unwanted metal traces in a food processing industry and identification of leaks and cracks in machinery and storage parts. In smart farming, hyper-spectral technology is employed to drill down the level of crop and plant morphology.

Hyper-spectral imagery contains the information spread across varying bands of images. The processing and analysis of data spread across the bands is quite challenging. Also, the volume increased exponentially with respect to including the number of bands. The rich, informative bands can be classified and identified based on the spatial correlation between different bands. This will convey useful information regarding the crops and plant study.

One of the deep learning techniques, CNN, is applied for processing the spectral images. The use of CNN for HSI classification is widely emerging in recent studies [18,24–26]. Prediction using advanced HSI processing is shown in Figure 5.4.

- 1D CNN: Reflect image processing techniques based on the correlated information in order to identify the objects and pattern within the image.
- 2D CNN: The required information about the crop was retrieved from both the spatial and spectral information. The special and spectral information were highly dependent in nature. The performance of 2D CNN always depends on the spatial and spectral correlation.
- 3D CNN: Gathering of both special and spectral features from selective spectral bands. This will enable the abstract level of retrieving information from the spectral range. The processing is complex in nature.
- Hybrid Spectral CNN: The Hybrid Spectral CNN involves processing 3D CNN (Spectal – Spatial) followed by 2D CNN (spatial) [25]. The hybrid methodology reflects processing of selected spatial information along with its spectral ranges. Based on the confusion matrix and spatial correlations, the unwanted spectral-spatial information was ignored. The approach discriminates a more precise level of special and spectral representation of crop models. The crop model and computational complexity reduce to a great extent due to the nature of selected processing.

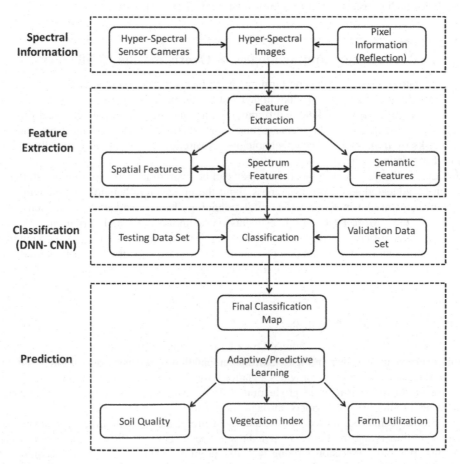

FIGURE 5.4 Prediction using advanced HSI processing.

In hybrid-spectral systems, crop models were developed by combining the 3D-CNN and 2D-CNN layers in such a way that utilizes both spectral and spatial feature maps in order to extend the high accuracy and precise information.

The HIS feature extraction techniques can be classified as manual feature extraction and deep-learning-based feature extraction techniques. Identifying the useless spectral information by computing the local covariance matrix between the spectral band helps to reduce the impact on feature extraction. A composite kernel is used to combine the HSI spatial and spectral features in order to retrieve the information properly; deep learning methodologies were applied over the combination of multiple spatial and spectral features to classify the hyper-spectral crop model information [18,26,27].

The HSI classification preformation is evaluated based on the below metrics

- Overall accuracy
- Average accuracy
- Kappa coefficient

Accuracy of model classification accuracies are measured by comparing the test and train results for specified crop variety and location information. Comparing the CNN methodologies, the time taken for training and testing of Hybrid CNN is less compared with 3D (one-third of time) [25]. The hybrid neural network with a convolutional (3D-CNN) and bidirectional recurrent layer (2D-CNN) is used to generalize the crop model [24]. Compared to CNN-based deep neural network methodologies, the hybrid model provides higher accuracy (84.6%) on validation dataset [24].

5.4 Potential Challenges and Strategies to Overcome the Challenges

The implementation phase of precision farming has to face several potential challenges and undergo initial hiccups. Major challenges are like higher initial and maintenance costs, social and economic conditions, distinctive pattern of land in different regions, unexpected pest attacks, real-time decision making, and poor infrastructure. Farmers are more worried about the safety of the crops and not ready to take up risks by implementing new technologies. Awareness about the user-friendly technologies applicable for farming is much less.

Though the challenges seem to be critical, they can be overcome using appropriate strategies. The farmers can be educated and given awareness about the prospective benefits of practicing precision farming. Government can motivate agricultural technology-based companies, announcing attractive offers and subsidies. More R&D and investments on technology-assisted agriculture should be encouraged. Transdisciplinary research by collaborating agro-chemical companies, computer technological companies, and accumulated practical knowledge of the farmers should be stimulated. Such measures will open new corridors for employment of technically skilled labor.

5.5 Current and Future Scope

According to the data from the International Labor Organization, skilled labor involved in agriculture is decreasing every year, as shown in Figure 5.5. Implementation of precision agriculture requires skilled labor. Therefore, precision farming provides a platform for skilled labor employment. Precision farming can increase productivity at reduced production costs by effectively using the natural resources. By increasing the profitability of farmers through sustainable and quality crop production, the rural economy becomes enhanced. It escalates the quality of life of the farmers. Precision faming advocates the usage of fertilizers and pesticides as per the site specifications, which strongly reduces soil and environmental pollution. Precision farming will also promote sustainable and good farming practices among the farmers. Therefore, precision farming has a bright scope in the near future. Following are the

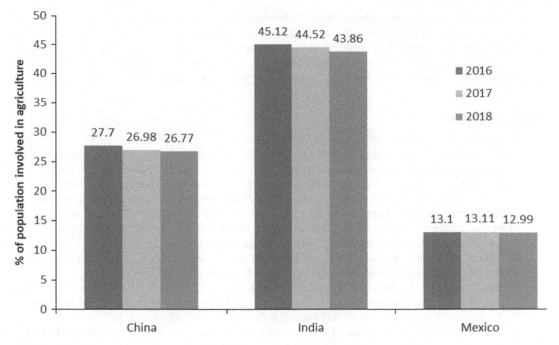

FIGURE 5.5 Percentage of population involved in agriculture over a period.

areas where agriculture-based technologies need to adopt a result-oriented approach rather than creating an analytical study:

- Enhanced productivity for socioeconomic needs and demands, effective utilization of resources such as farmland and crops with detailed index and metrics.
- Identification of use of water, fertilizers, and chemicals for crop variety based on location along with geological mapping.
- Crop model enhanced with precision farming is needed in the current economical situation in order to eliminate the poverty alleviation and to balance the quality of life and food security.
- Increased land degradation and depletion of water resources also mandate for agricultural-based technology research and developments.

5.6 Conclusion

Several unanticipated scenarios and problems may rise while applying the technology over multi-domain agriculture enrichment studies. Another problem is while applying deep learning algorithms to the real-time data in order to design and develop a new application. Once the initial hiccups and problems are covered by deep domain expertise, these precision deep learning algorithms were embedded inside the decision support system for providing more promising predictions for agricultural systems in large scale. The Convolutional Neural Network gains its significance due to a drastic increase in building a reliable crop model for agriculture-based data. The CNN-improved versions are very promising in calibrating real-time applications required for agricultural needs. The spectral information processing enables categorical identification and classification of insights. This will enable the system in the future to involve augmented and virtual reality on real-time crop classification, semantic segmentation along with object detection, disease identification, and yield prediction remotely. Evidently, a hybrid CNN is capable of providing enhanced real-time model for agricultural-based technologies.

As discussed in the previous sections, precision farming offers plenty of benefits and has a wide scope in the near present and future. Though initial glitches and challenges may come across, they can be overcome using site-specific and problem-specific strategies. Precision farming transforms the traditional farming methods into a more profitable and more productive way of farming. It also improves the economy while meeting the growing food demand with good crop quality.

REFERENCES

[1] http://www.fao.org/state-of-food-security-nutrition/en/

[2] Singh, Rinku and G.S. Singh, "Traditional agriculture: A climate-smart approach for sustainable food production." *Energ. Ecol. Environ.* 2(5) (2017): 296–316. doi: 10.1007/s40974-017-0074-7.

[3] Saiz-Rubio, Verónica and Francisco Rovira-Más, "From smart farming towards agriculture 5.0: A review on crop data management." *Agronomy* 10 (2020): 207. doi: 10.3390/agronomy10020207.

[4] Schimmelpfennig, D., "Farm profits and adoption of precision agriculture." *USDA* 217 (2016): 1–46.

[5] McQueen, Robert J., Stephen R. Gamer, Craig G. Nevill-Manning, Ian H. Witten. "Applying machine learning to agricultural data." *Comput. Electron. Agric.* 12 (1995): 275–293.

[6] Wilson, Jeffrey H., Chunhua Zhang, and John M. Kovacs. "Separating crop species in northeastern Ontario using hyperspectral data." *Remote Sens.* 6(2) (2014): 925–945.

[7] Haboudane, D., J.R. Miller, E. Pattey, P. Zarco-Tejada, I.B. Strachan "Hyperspectral vegetation indices and novel algorithms for predicting green LAI of crop canopies: Modeling and validation in the context of precision agriculture." *Remote Sens. Environ.* 90 (2004): 337–352.

[8] Thenkabail, P.S., E.A. Enclona, M.S. Ashton, B. van Der Meer. "Accuracy assessments of hyperspectral waveband performance for vegetation analysis applications." *Remote Sens. Environ.* 91 (2004): 345–376.

[9] Gray, C.J., D.R. Shaw, L.M. Bruce. "Utility of hyperspectral reflectance for differentiating soybean (Glycine max) and six weed species." *Weed Technol.* 23 (2009): 108–119.

[10] Martin, M.P., L. Barreto, D. Riano, C. Fernandez-Quintanilla, P. Vaughan. "Assessing the potential of hyperspectral remote sensing for the discrimination of grassweeds in winter cereal crops." *Int. J. Remote Sens.* 32 (2011): 49–67.

[11] Lin, W.-S., C.-M. Yang, B.-J. Kuo. "Classifying cultivars of rice (Oryza sativa L.) based on corrected canopy reflectance spectra data using the orthogonal projections to latent structures (O-PLS) method." *Chemometr. Intell. Lab. Syst.* 115 (2012): 25–36.

[12] Pena-Barragan, J.M., F. Lopez-Granados, M. Jurado-Exposito, L. Carcia-Torres. "Spectral discrimination of Ridolfia segetum and sunflower as affected by phenological stage." *Weed Res.* 46 (2006): 10–21.

[13] Zhang, H., Y. Lan, C.P. Suh, J.K. Westbrook, R. Lacey, W.C. Hoffmann. "Differentiation of cotton from other crops at different growth stages using spectral properties and discriminant analysis." *Trans. ASABE* 55 (2012): 1623–1630.

[14] Shibayama, M., and A. Tsuyoshi. "Estimating grain yield of maturing rice canopies using high spectral resolution reflectance measurements." *Remote Sens. Environ.* 36 (1991): 45–53.

[15] Caporaso, Nicola, Martin B. Whitworth, and Ian D. Fisk. "Protein content prediction in single wheat kernels using hyperspectral imaging." *Food Chem.* 240 (2018): 32–42.

[16] S.G. Bajwa, P. Bajcsy, P. Groves, L.F. Tian, "Hyperspectral image data mining for band selection in agricultural applications." *Trans. Am. Soc. Agric. Eng.* 47 (2004): 895–907.

[17] Burai, Péter, et al. "Classification of herbaceous vegetation using airborne hyperspectral imagery." *Remote Sens.* 7(2) (2015): 2046–2066.

[18] Moghimi, Ali, Ce Yang, and James A. Anderson. "Aerial hyperspectral imagery and deep neural networks for high-throughput yield phenotyping in wheat." arXiv preprint arXiv:1906.09666 (2019).

[19] Moghimi, Ali, Ce Yang, and Peter M. Marchetto. "Ensemble feature selection for plant phenotyping: A journey from hyperspectral to multispectral imaging." *IEEE Access* 6 (2018): 56870–56884.

[20] Moghimi, Ali, et al. "A novel approach to assess salt stress tolerance in wheat using hyperspectral imaging." *Front. Plant Sci.* 9 (2018): 1182.

[21] Singh, Asheesh Kumar, et al. "Deep learning for plant stress phenotyping: Trends and future perspectives." *Trends Plant Sci.* 23(10) (2018): 883–898.

[22] Fuentes, Alvaro, Sook Yoon, and Dong Sun Park. "Deep learning-based phenotyping system with glocal description of plant anomalies and symptoms." *Front. Plant Sci.*10 (2019): 1–19.

[24] Jin, Xiu, et al. "Classifying wheat hyperspectral pixels of healthy heads and Fusarium head blight disease using a deep neural network in the wild field." *Remote Sens.* 10(3) (2018): 395.

[23] Caporaso, Nicola, Martin B. Whitworth, and Ian D. Fisk. "Near-infrared spectroscopy and hyperspectral imaging for non-destructive quality assessment of cereal grains." *Appl. Spectrosc. Rev.* 53(8) (2018): 667–687.

[25] Roy, Swalpa Kumar, et al. "Hybridsn: Exploring 3-D-2-D CNN feature hierarchy for hyperspectral image classification." *IEEE Geosci. Remote Sens. Lett.*17(2) (2019): 277–281.

[26] Lowe, Amy, Nicola Harrison, and Andrew P. French. "Hyperspectral image analysis techniques for the detection and classification of the early onset of plant disease and stress." *Plant Methods* 13(1) (2017): 80.

[27] Liakos, Konstantinos G., et al. "Machine learning in agriculture: A review." *Sensors* 18(8) (2018): 2674.

6

An Ameliorated Methodology to Predict Diabetes Mellitus Using Random Forest

Arunakumari B.N., Aman Rai, and Shashidhar R.

CONTENTS

6.1 Motivation to Use the "R" Language to Predict Diabetes Mellitus?

R is the language of choice used in data analysis today. It allows for accurate statistical analysis and graphical data representation. Over the years, R has gained popularity owing to its effectiveness in data cleaning, handling, representation and analysis. Some of the primary reasons that make R preferable are:

   i. Data wrangling

      The data we encounter in real-life problems is often messy and unstructured. Data wrangling involves refining this data, which is a lengthy process. The complex data is converted into a simpler, more relevant data set which is easier to consume and analyze. Some R packages that help in this are:

      • dplyr Package – used for data exploration and transformation

      • data.table Package – allows for quick manipulation of data with less coding, thereby reducing compute times and simplifying data aggregation.

      • readr Package – helps in reading various forms of data into R language at fast speeds

ii. Popularity in academic circles

The R language is extensively used and popular among academia. Data science experimentation is carried out using the R language. Scholars and researches tend to use the R language for statistical analysis. As a consequence, there are great number of people who are proficient in the R language. Thus, since it is in use by a great many individuals since their academic years, a large set of skilled individuals capable of using R in the industry are exist. This further makes the language apt for data analysis.

iii. Effective visualization of data

Unorganized data can be put in cleaner, more structured forms and an accurate graphical representation of this data can be made using the tools provided by R language, which include the popular packages ggplot2 and ggedit. These are used in plotting of data. Ggplot2, for example, is used in data visualization itself, whereas ggedit adds to the capabilities by correcting the aesthetics of plots.

iv. Machine learning capabilities

To make predictions a possibility, it is essential to train algorithms and enable learning automation. R provides a myriad of packages focused on machine learning such as PARTY and rpart (data partitioning), MICE (missing value correction), CARET (regression, classification), and randomFOREST (decision trees). All these, and many more, make machine learning applications a real possibility using the R language.

v. Open source and freely available

R is platform independent, meaning it isn't restricted to certain operating systems. Also, it is open source, which makes it free to use. It's cost effective as it is covered under the GNU agreement. As such, the development work is continuous in the R community and it makes the language ever-expanding and improving. There various resources that aid budding programmers in learning this language as well. Hence, it is easy and not expensive to recruit and employ R developers.

The aforementioned reasons are some, among many, that endow upon R its popularity. The R language is going to expand further in the domain of statistic and graphical analysis, as well as machine learning and big data applications. It is easy to learn and ever-expanding, making it the perfect choice for data science, and in this case, prediction of diabetes.

6.2 Related Work

Extant diabetes approaches have various limitations most specifically low generalizability and poor accurateness. To overcome these shortcomings authors have developed a method using a parameter-based least-angle regression (LARS) to improve the prediction for diabetes [1,2]. The LARS technique used to measure the relationship between the individualistic and sequential features. Then weight metrics is computed for each feature using principal element investigation. It was observed that the approximation rapidity for computing dependent feature was enhanced but there are persist problems with equilibrium of the prediction model. Further, authors have made an attempt to improve the performance of prediction model by gradient enhancing procedure to contribute to the real analysis of category 2 diabetes for local and systematized treatment [3,4]. In this method, the performance and computation of the applied machine learning techniques for the problematic of diabetes diagnosis were systematically examined. However, the method fails to derive end user specific model for diabetes prediction for data collection from local sources. In addition, authors have summarized various automated diabetes mellitus detection and also their drawbacks [5]. Most notably the problems with lack of automatic optimization methods. To determine the optimum values for different deep learning architecture can be used for diabetes mellitus. However, in various cases the contextual of deep learning models is non-familiar and is hypothetical to be a black box. Also, the training with insufficient data deep learning software package usually requests a substantial amount of diabetic data for training. Researchers have used various machine learning techniques for predictive investigation [6]. The method has 77% accuracy for predicting diabetes. Nevertheless, to develop a predictive model for diabetes mellitus with 100% precision, the existing algorithms needs thousands of records with zero missing values.

In [7,8], this research shows the prediction of diabetes for cardiorespiratory data using potential of machine learning methods. The method suffers from validation results of prediction model with other related cronies. Furthermore, authors have developed a risk prediction model for category 2 diabetes based on collaborative learning technique and random forest [9–11]. The weighted attribute selection algorithm has been used for optimal attribute selection and extreme gradient enhancing classifier, hence the prediction model has better accuracy. But, to evaluate the efficacy and performance of predictive model it is necessary to take the latest hospital patient data. In artificial neural network (ANN), random forest and K-means clustering methods were realized for the early prediction of diabetes [12,13]. The technique provided a better accuracy of 75% and may be advantageous to support health experts with dealing decisions. Here, authors have considered only structured datasets but unstructured data will also be considered for prediction. A Hybrid ANN & classification and regression tree methods are implemented using a genetic algorithm to enhance the classification accuracy for finding of diabetes mellitus [14,15]. However, the performance of the proposed methods could be examined for dissimilar datasets. In this chapter we have focused on amalgamation of various methods for fine-tuning the features of models for high accuracy using R programming.

6.3 Collection of Datasets

Diabetes mellitus is a challenge in both developed and developing nations. There are 285 million diabetic individuals across the globe, according to the International Diabetes Federation. In 20 years, this number is expected to rise to 380 million. Hence, a classifier to recognize diabetes and predict it is necessary and essential in today's day and age. In this analysis, we use the Pima Indian diabetic data. The Pima Indian diabetic database is a popular choice of testing and information mining to predict diabetes. The Pima Indians are a group of Native Americans belonging to parts of Arizona, U.S.A., as well as northwestern Mexico. From this dataset, females of 21 years old or more are used to predict diabetes based on certain medical factors such as the plasma glucose levels, diastolic blood pressure, serum insulin, the thickness of triceps skin fold, BMI (body mass index), and diabetes pedigree function. After deleting for missing data, the 786 elements are reduced to 392 in this dataset. Table 6.1 shown below is the list of attributes considered in this dataset. The data can be read and then visualized as follows:

```
#LOADING THE DATASET
Dataset_pima = pd.read_csv('../input/diabetes.csv')
Dataset_pima.head()
First few rows of dataset are returned by head() function
```

The large measure of the dataset that may be greater in volume than needed is broken down via the process of information mining. This is done to segregate useful data, instrumental in making correct choices and predictive parameters. Connections between different information can also be made, and correlations derived, which ultimately help determine answers to crucial issues.

6.3.1 Implementation Methods

6.3.1.1 Decision Tree

Classification problems may be solved using supervised learning method. It breaks the given dataset in steps into two or more sets. The target variable's class value must be predicted. Data set

TABLE 6.1

List of Attributes in the Dataset

	Pregnancies	Glucose	Blood Pressure	Skin Thickness	Insulin	BMI	Diabetes Pedigree Function	Age	Outcome
0	6	148	72	35	0	33.6	0.627	50	1
1	1	85	66	29	0	26.6	0.351	31	0
2	8	183	64	0	0	23.3	0.672	32	1
3	1	89	66	23	94	28.1	0.167	21	0
4	0	137	40	35	168	43.1	2.288	33	1

segregation and the construction of the decision model to predict the unknown class. Both binary and continuous variable decision trees may be constructed as shown in Figure 6.1. The decision tree uses the highest entropy value to find the root node. Thus, they are advantageous in choosing the most consistent hypothesis. The output, a decision model, will be derived after input containing many instance values and attributes is fed to the decision tree. As the name suggests, the decision tree is of a tree structure consisting of several nodes, including the decision nodes and leaf nodes. Decision nodes may have at least 2, and can have more, branches. The very first node is referred to as the root node.

6.3.1.2 *Random Forest*

The random forest logic involves creating random sample features. What makes it different from the decision tree method is that the process of finding the root node, as well as that of splitting the feature nodes are run randomly. Random forest is a supervised learning method, utilized in both regression and classification. The steps are enlisted below:

1. The data consisting of "m" features denoting the behavior of the dataset is loaded.
2. "n" random features are selected from m features. This is known as the bootstrap or bagging algorithm/technique. It is the training algorithm for random forests. Thus, a fresh sample is trained out of the bag sample.
3. Node d is calculated using the best split, and the node is further split into sub-nodes.
4. The aforementioned steps are repeated to find n number of trees.
5. The final votes per tree for the predicting target is determined and the highest voted class is chosen as final prediction.

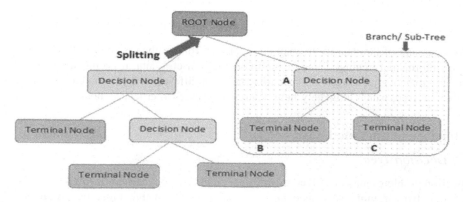

FIGURE 6.1 Decision tree.

6.3.1.3 Naïve Bayesian Algorithm

This method is based on Bayes Theorem. It performs analysis on the input dataset. The class label is predicted using Bayes' Theorem. The probability of a class in input data is calculated and, therefore, a prediction of the class of unknown data class is made. This technique is suited for large datasets. The following formula is used:

$$P(c|x) = P(x|c) \ P(c) \ P(x) \ P(c|x) = P(x|c) \ P(c) \ P(x)$$

$$P(c|X) = P(x1|c) \times P(x2|c) \times \cdots \times P(xn|c) \times P(c)P(c|X)$$
$$= P(x1|c) \times P(x2|c) \times \cdots \times P(xn|c) \times P(c)$$

where
  P(c) = given class prior probability
  P(c|x) = posterior probability of class target given predictor
  P(x|c) = predictor given class probability
  P(x) = predictor prior probability

6.3.1.4 Support Vector Machine (SVM)

The SVM model is a supervised learning and classification technique. It is useful in both classification and regression. A hyper line is found between the datasets. The logic is that the line dividing the dataset best, into two distinct classes, is the "hyper line." There are two basic steps, which include identifying the correct data space hyper line and then objects being mapped on either side of the boundary, as shown in Figure 6.2. The SVM technique helps in constructing a model that allots fresh samples to either one of the classes.

6.4 Visualization

A histogram will help visualize the range of ages. A histogram is essentially a technique to display numerical data using bars of various heights, as shown in Figure 6.3.

```
library(ggplot2)
ggplot(aes(x = Age), data=dbt) +
      geom_histogram(binwidth=1.5, color=' darkred', fill = "Red") +
      scale_x_continuous(limits=c(20,85), breaks=seq(20,80,5)) +
      xlab("Age") +
      ylab("age by no. of people")
```

In the above code, we first import the ggplot() function, which takes two arguments. The first one is the data we will work upon, which in this case is the age. The aes(x = age) part, where aes stands for aesthetic, implies the mapping of the data variables to the visual properties. The "+" is almost always used in ggplot to add extra components. The last two xlab() and ylab() methods simply impart labels to the x and y axes. The code above finally produces the following output.

Another method for visualization is a boxplot. Various entities are allotted a bar, and the size of the bar is an indication of its numeric value. The higher the bar height, the higher its value, and vice versa. We can also visualize the data using a bar plot as follows. Again the ggplot() function takes in two parameters, one for the input data, x = age_1, and dbt which stands for data build told. The geom_bar(), short for geometric bar, is another function like geom_histogram, that constructs the bar graph. In the previous exam, we used fill = 'red', which quite obviously, filled the histogram with a red color is as shown in Figure 6.3. Here we fill = "blue," hence the bar plot graphs are blue in color and as shown in Figure 6.4.

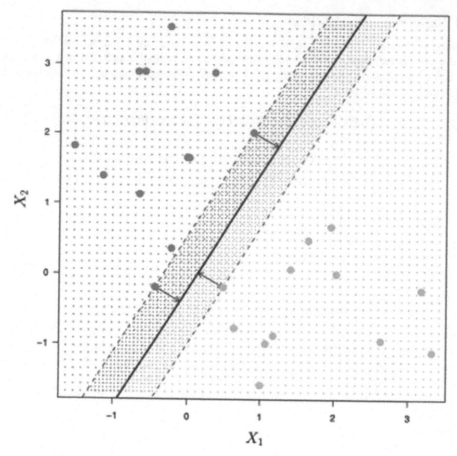

FIGURE 6.2 SVM model.

```
library(ggplot2)
ggplot(aes(x = Age_1), data = dbt) +
            geom_bar(fill='blue')
```

This is what the output will look like for the above piece of code.

Yet another visualization technique is the boxplot. It is a method to show the distribution of data over some range as shown in Figure 6.5. In the below code, we pass x- and y-axis parameters are age and BMI, respectively. Then the geom_boxplot() method is called, with an interesting new parameter, the outlier color. Outliers are certain value that lie unusually or abnormally outside the usual range of values of that parameter. They are represented by red dots in the following boxplot. The coord_cartesian() method has the ylim set as 0 to 80, implying the y-axis range to be from 0 to 80 units of BMI.

The code below produces a boxplot that plots age category on x-axis versus the BMI on y-axis for an individual.

```
ggplot(aes(x=Age_1, y = BMI ), data = dbt) +
    geom_boxplot(color='darkblue', fill = "orange", outlier.colour = "red") +
    coord_cartesian(ylim = c(0,80))
```

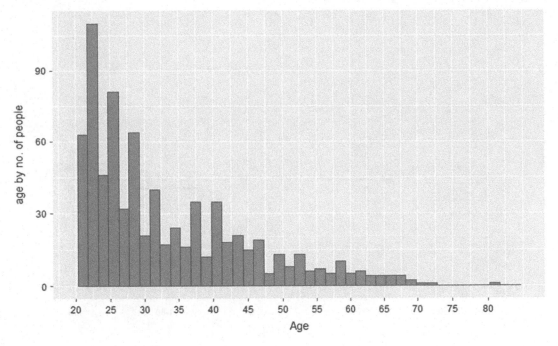

FIGURE 6.3   Histogram to visualize the range of ages.

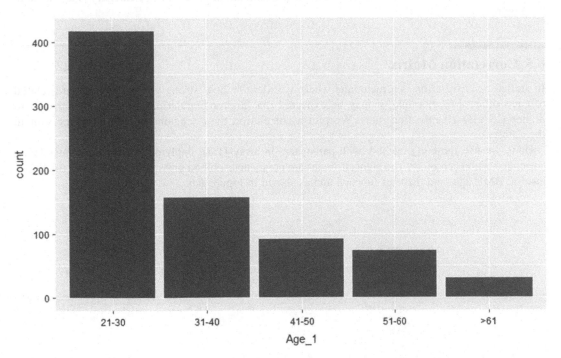

FIGURE 6.4   Visualization of data using boxplot.

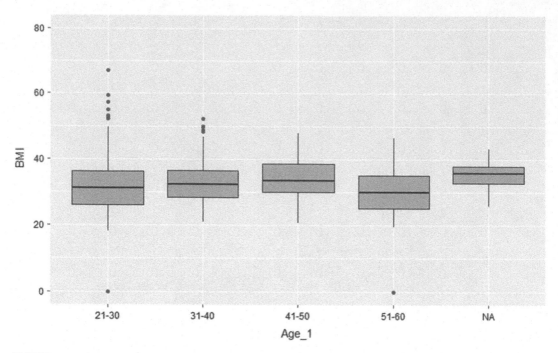

FIGURE 6.5   Visualization of distribution of data range using boxplot.

The red dots denote outliers, which are evidently maximum in the 21–30 age category is as shown in the Figure 6.5.

6.5 Correlation Matrix

In statistics, correlation is a technique where we identify how strongly two variables are related to each other. For example, it may be expected that higher population densities would lead to higher COVID-19 infection rates. We plot a correlation matrix against all variables present in the dataset.

Here, we use the cor() method, with parameters in array [1:8], implying all eight attributes being correlated with each other. The eight attributes are pregnancies, blood pressure, glucose, skin thickness, insulin, BMI, age, and diabetes function and as shown in Figure 6.6.

```
dbt_cor <- round(cor(dbt[1:8]),1)
dbt_cor
```

	Pregnancies	Glucose	BloodPressure	SkinThickness	Insulin	BMI	DiabetesPedigreeFunction	Age
Pregnancies	1.0	0.1	0.1	-0.1	-0.1	0.0	0.0	0.5
Glucose	0.1	1.0	0.2	0.1	0.3	0.2	0.1	0.3
BloodPressure	0.1	0.2	1.0	0.2	0.1	0.3	0.0	0.2
SkinThickness	-0.1	0.1	0.2	1.0	0.4	0.4	0.2	-0.1
Insulin	-0.1	0.3	0.1	0.4	1.0	0.2	0.2	0.0
BMI	0.0	0.2	0.3	0.4	0.2	1.0	0.1	0.0
DiabetesPedigreeFunction	0.0	0.1	0.0	0.2	0.2	0.1	1.0	0.0
Age	0.5	0.3	0.2	-0.1	0.0	0.0	0.0	1.0

FIGURE 6.6   Correlation matrix.

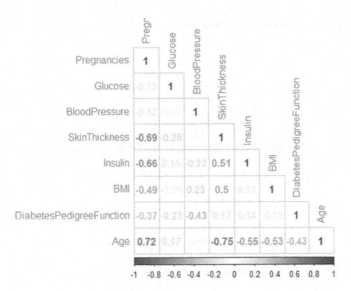

FIGURE 6.7   No inherent correlation among the variables.

The correlation matrix results help us infer that there is no inherent correlation among the variables themselves and as shown in Figure 6.7.

6.6 Training and Testing the Data

Training and then testing the data are essential components of machine learning. The training set contains the data which the algorithm uses to learn from experience. In other words, it is "trained" by feeding this data to it. Supervised learning problems consist of one or multiple input variables and an observed output variable. The test data is a dataset the is useful in determining and judging the performance of the model using some performance metric. The test and training data contain distinct elements. This means the test data may not contain the same elements as the training data, as in such a case it is hard to determine whether the trained model has simply memorized the data from the training set or actually generalized the concept. Overfitting is a concept where the model is trained with a highly complex data set, and thus ends up memorizing it. This is undesired, as such a model will fail to perform well on new examples. On the other hand, a model that generalized well is able to efficiently perform a task with new data. The goal is to balance generalization and memorization, or under-fitting and over-fitting, respectively, in any machine learning problem. Next, the caTools package is installed. It contains various utilities such as: fast calculation of AUC, LogitBoost classifier, reading and writing for GIF and ENVI binary files, and moving window statistic functions. In our case, we will call it to split the data into train and test datasets.

(installing caTools)

The dataset is split into 20% test data, and 80% training data.

```
set.seed(123)
sample = sample.split(dbt$Outcome, SplitRatio=0.80)
train = subset(dbt, sample==TRUE)
test = subset(dbt, sample==FALSE)
```

The total number of rows are found as follows.

```
nrow(dbt)
```

```
[1] 768
```

Eighty percent of this value will be the number of trained data rows, which can be affirmed in the next command.

```
nrow(train)
```

```
[1] 614
```

The remaining 20% are the test data rows.

```
nrow(test)
```

```
[1] 154
```

6.7 Model Fitting

Model fitting is essentially a measurement of the effectiveness to which a machine learning model is able to generalize to the same kind of data on which it was trained. A well-fitted model is one that produces more accurate results when run. Overfitting must be avoided as it matches the trained data more closely than desired, and an underfitted model is one that isn't close enough to the trained data set. Every machine learning algorithm tends to have certain parameters that can be varied to improve its overall accuracy. The fitting process consists of testing an algorithm over a dataset to which you already know the target variable. This is known as labeled data. Subsequently, the result is compared to real values of the target variable to determine the correctness of the algorithm. This information is useful in adjusting the parameters in order to reduce the extent of error, thus revealing relationships and patterns between the target variable and the other features. The process is repeated until valid and useful, meaningful insights are derived regarding the data. Now, we will fit our model using all independent variables.

The output shown in Figure 6.8, has a measure called AIC, which is a measure of the relative quality of the statistical models. Each model's quality can be determined this way, and hence the AIC is a good way to decide which model to choose. The lower the AIC, the better the model is.

6.8 Experimental Analysis

We predict the outcome on training datasets as follows:

```
Predict <- predict(model_1, type = "response")
summary(Predict)
```

```
   Min.  1st Qu.   Median    Mean  3rd Qu.     Max.
0.001904 0.117246 0.260366 0.348534 0.537707 0.990924
```

```
Call:
glm(formula = Outcome ~ ., family = binomial, data = train)

Deviance Residuals:
    Min       1Q    Median      3Q       Max
 -2.4548  -0.7104  -0.4188   0.7042    2.9252

Coefficients:
                          Estimate Std. Error z value Pr(>|z|)
(Intercept)               -8.202293   0.786099 -10.434  < 2e-16 ***
Pregnancies                0.133846   0.036810   3.636 0.000277 ***
Glucose                    0.036551   0.004209   8.684  < 2e-16 ***
BloodPressure             -0.016071   0.005827  -2.758 0.005816 **
SkinThickness              0.007252   0.007892   0.919 0.358146
Insulin                   -0.002382   0.001101  -2.164 0.030434 *
BMI                        0.086303   0.016810   5.134 2.84e-07 ***
DiabetesPedigreeFunction   0.681589   0.340474   2.002 0.045297 *
Age                        0.014815   0.010522   1.408 0.159132
---
Signif. codes:  0 â€˜***â€™ 0.001 â€˜**â€™ 0.01 â€˜*â€™ 0.05 â€˜.â€™ 0.1 â€˜ â€™ 1

(Dispersion parameter for binomial family taken to be 1)

    Null deviance: 793.94  on 613  degrees of freedom
Residual deviance: 575.40  on 605  degrees of freedom
AIC: 593.4

Number of Fisher Scoring iterations: 5
```

FIGURE 6.8 Measure of the relative quality of the statistical models.

Next, let's perform an operation to determine the average prediction for the two outcomes (0 and 1).

```
tapply(Predict, train$Outcome, mean)

        0           1
0.2333061  0.5639139
```

Finally, we will discuss the Receiving Operating Characteristic (ROC). In predicting binary outcomes, the Receiving Operating Characteristic is a curve to estimate the accuracy of a continuous measurement. It is a measure of how well a classification model performs at all classification thresholds.

There are two parameters – the True and False Positive Rates.

The Area Under Curve (AUC) is the 2-D area found under the ROC curve. To analyze which of the models being used predicts the classes best, we use the AUC parameter.

6.9 Results and Analysis

Finally, we are going to test and see how accurate our model is in predicting diabetes over some test datasets.

Steps: First, let us produce the ROC curve using the train data as follows.

```
# Generate ROC Curves
library(ROCR)
ROC_pred = prediction(Predict, train$Outcome)
ROC_perf = performance(ROC_pred, "tpr", "fpr")
# Adding threshold labels
plot(ROC_perf, colorize=TRUE, print.cutoffs.at = seq(0,1,0.1), text.adj = c(-0.2, 1.7))
abline(a=0, b=1)
```

The ROCR package of R helps combine up to 25 performance metrics to form a performance curve. The prediction function returns a predictor object, which is the first step in the classifier process. The parameters passed to it are the predict object, containing the predictions, and a label as the second parameter. The performance() function then takes the predictor standardized object returned in as a parameter, along with tpr and fpr which denote true and false positive rates.

Next, we will generate the AUC curve.

```
auc_train <- round(as.numeric(performance(ROC_pred, "auc")@y.values),2)
legend(.8, .2, auc_train, title = "AUC", cex=1)
```

```
# Making predictions on test set
Pred_Test <- predict(model_1, type = "response", newdata = test)
# Convert probabilities to values using the below
### Based on ROC curve above, selected a threshold of 0.5
test_tab <- table(test$Outcome, Pred_Test > 0.5)
test_tab
```

```
     FALSE TRUE
  0   84   16
  1   24   30
```

```
accuracy_test <- round(sum(diag(test_tab))/sum(test_tab),2)
sprintf("Accuracy on test set is %s", accuracy_test)
```

```
[1] "Accuracy on test set is 0.74"
```

The result is the graph shown in Figure 6.9. Seeing the AUC parameter of 0.84, we can infer that the accuracy rate is 84% on the train data. Next, we will test our model to the test data as follows. The accuracy rate is 74%, which can be improved as follows (see Figure 6.10).

```
ROCRPredTest = prediction(Pred_Test, test$Outcome)
#auc = round(as.numeric(performance(ROCRPredTest, "auc")@y.values),2)
#auc
ROC_perf2 = performance(ROCRPredTest, "tpr", "fpr")
plot(ROC_perf, colorize=TRUE, print.cutoffs.at = seq(0,1,0.1), text.adj = c(-0.2, 1.7))
abline(a=0, b=1)
```

```
auc_test <- round(as.numeric(performance(ROCRPredTest, "auc")@y.values),2)
legend(.8, .2, auc_test, title = "AUC2", cex=1)
```

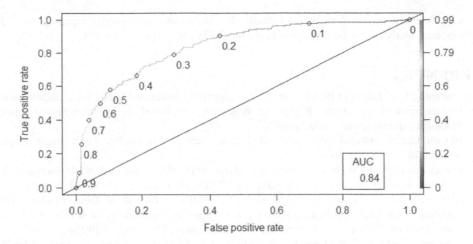

FIGURE 6.9   ROC performance curve.

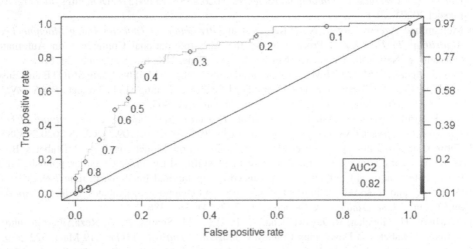

FIGURE 6.10   ROC performance curve for improved accuracy.

The final output graph is:

```
auc = round(as.numeric(performance(ROCRPredTest, "auc")@y.values),2)
auc
```

```
[1] 0.82
```

Thus, as is evident from the above result, the model is accurately able to predict if someone has diabetes or not with 82% accuracy.

6.10 Conclusion

It is evident that the R language provides many methods to accurately and quickly perform data analysis on various measures and predict the outcome, as was proved while predicting diabetes using our dataset.

There is sufficient provision for various visualization techniques to correctly represent the data. In conclusion, data analysis can be efficiently performed using R.

REFERENCES

[1] Shaoming Qiu, Jiahao Li Bo Chen et al., An Improved Prediction Method for Diabetes Based on a Feature-based Least Angle Regression Algorithm, published in Association for Computing Machinery digital library, January 2019.

[2] Hassan Uraibi, Habshah Midi, and Sohel Rana, Robust Multivariate Least Angle Regression. *ScienceAsia* 43 (2017): 56–60.

[3] Faizan Zafar, Saad Raza et al., Predictive Analytics in Healthcare for Diabetes Prediction, published in Association for Computing Machinery, ICBET '19, March 28–30, 2019, Tokyo, Japan © 2019.

[4] Abir Al-Sideiri, Zaihisma Binti Che Cob, and Sulfeeza Bte Mohd Drus, Machine Learning Algorithms for Diabetes Prediction: A Review Paper, in Proceedings of the 2019 International Conference on Artificial Intelligence, Robotics and Control December 2019 Pages 27–32.

[5] Jyotismita Chaki, S. Thillai Ganesh, S.K. Cidham et al., Machine Learning, and Artificial Intelligence Based Diabetes Mellitus Detection and Self-Management: A Systematic Review. *Journal of King Saud University – Computer and Information Sciences*, 2020. ISSN 1319-1578. DOI: https://doi.org/10.1016/j.jksuci.2020.06.013

[6] Muhammad Azeem Sarwar, Nasir Kamal et al., *Prediction of Diabetes Using Machine Learning Algorithms in Healthcare*, Proceedings of the 24th International Conference on Automation & Computing, Newcastle University, Newcastle upon Tyne, UK, 6–7 September 2018.

[7] Manal Alghamdi, Mouaz Al-Mallah et al., Predicting Diabetes Mellitus Using SMOTE and Ensemble Machine Learning Approach: The Henry Ford ExercIse Testing (FIT) Project. *PLoS ONE* 12(7) (2017):e0179805. https://doi.org/10.1371/journal.pone.0179805.

[8] Md. Kamrul Hasan, Md. Ashraful Alam et al., *Diabetes Prediction Using Ensembling of Different Machine Learning Classifiers, published in IEEE,* 2017, DOI 10.1109/ACCESS.2020.2989857.

[9] Zhongxian Xu, Zhiliang Wang et al., A Risk Prediction Model for Type 2 Diabetes Based on Weighted Feature Selection of Random Forest and XGBoost Ensemble Classifier, published in IEEE, the 11th International Conference on Advanced Computational Intelligence, June 7–9, 2019, China.

[10] W. Kerner and J. Brckel, Definition Classification and Diagnosis of Diabetes Mellitus. *Experimental and Clinical Endocrinology & Diabetes* 122(7)(2014): 384–386.

[11] A. Misra, H. Gopalan, R. Jayawardena, A. P. Hills, M. Soares, A. A. RezaAlbarrán, and K. L. Ramaiya, Diabetes in Developing Countries. *Journal of Diabetes* 11(7)(2019 Mar): 522–539.

[12] Talha Mahboob Alama, Muhammad Atif Iqbal et al., A Model for Early Prediction of Diabetes, Informatics in Medicine Unlocked 16 (2019) 100204 2352-9148/© 2019 Published by Elsevier Ltd.

[13] Hongxia Xu, Yonghui Kong, and Shaofeng Tan, Predictive Modeling of Diabetic Kidney Disease using Random Forest Algorithm along with Features Selection, Published in ISAIMS 2020. Proceedings of the 2020 International Symposium on Artificial Intelligence in Medical Sciences, September 2020 Pages 23–27.

[14] Ebru Pekel Özmen and Tuncay Özcan, Diagnosis of Diabetes Mellitus using Artificial Neural Network and Classification and Regression Tree Optimized with Genetic Algorithm. *Journal of Forecasting* 39(2020): 661–670. wileyonlinelibrary.com/journal/for © 2020 John Wiley & Sons, Ltd.

[15] N. Nai-Arun and R. Moungmai, Comparison of Classifiers for the Risk of Diabetes Prediction, *Procedia Computer Science* 69 (2015): 132–142.

7

High Dimensionality Dataset
Reduction Methodologies in Applied
Machine Learning

Farhan Hai Khan and Tannistha Pal

CONTENTS

7.1 Problems Faced with High Dimensionality Data: An Introduction

"Dimensionality Reduction leads to a comprehensive, precise & compressed depiction of the target output variables, by reducing redundant input variables."

– Farhan Khan & Tannistha Pal.

In the field of artificial intelligence, data explosion has created a plethora of input data and features to be fed into machine learning algorithms. Since most of the real-world data is multi-dimensional in nature, data scientists and data analysts require the core concepts of dimensionality reduction mechanisms for better:

i. *Data Intuition: Visualization, Outlier Detection, and Noise Reduction*
ii. *Performance Efficiency: Faster Training Intervals and Reduced Computational Processing Time*
iii. *Generalization: Prevents Overfitting (High Variance and Low Bias)*

This chapter introduces the practical working implementation of these reduction algorithms in applied machine learning.

Multiple features make it difficult to obtain valuable insights into data, as the visualization plots obtained can be 3-dimensional at most. Due to this limitation, dependent properties/operations such as Outlier Detection and Noise Removal become more and more non-intuitive to perform on these humongous datasets. Therefore, applying dimensionality reduction helps in identifying these properties more effortlessly.

Due to this reduced/compressed form of data, faster mathematical operations such as Scaling, Classification, and Regression can be performed. Also, the data is more clean and this further solves the issues of overfitting a model.

Dimensionality reduction can be broadly classified into:

i. *Feature Selection Techniques: Feature selection attempts to train the machine learning model by selectively choosing a subset of the original feature set based on some criteria. Hence, redundant and obsolete characteristics could be eliminated without much information loss. Examples – Correlation Matrix Thresholding and Chi-Squared Test Selection.*

ii. *Feature Extraction/Projection Techniques: This method projects the original input features from the high dimensional space by summarizing most statistics and removing redundant data/manipulating to create new relevant output features with reduced dimensionality (fewer dimensional space). Examples – Principle Component Analysis (PCA), Linear Discriminant Analysis (LDA), t-distributed Stochastic Neighbour Embedding (t-SNE), and Isometric Mapping (IsoMap).*

However, we have limited our discussion to Correlation Matrices, PCA, and t-SNE only, as covering all such techniques is beyond the scope of this book chapter.

7.2 Dimensionality Reduction Algorithms with Visualizations

7.2.1 Feature Selection Using Covariance Matrix

Objective: Introduce Boston Housing Dataset and use the obtained Correlation Matrix to apply Feature Selection on the strongly positive correlated data and perform regression over the selective features.

7.2.1.1 Importing the Modules

We will need three datasets for this chapter, each of which have been documented on our github repository (https://github.com/khanfarhan10/DIMENSIONALITY_REDUCTION). Hence, we will create a local copy (clone) of that repo here.

```
!git clone https://github.com/khanfarhan10/DIMENSIONALITY_REDUCTION.git
```

```
Cloning into 'DIMENSIONALITY_REDUCTION'...
remote: Enumerating objects: 14, done. [K
remote: Counting objects: 100% (14/14), done. [K
remote: Compressing objects: 100% (12/12), done. [K
remote: Total 14 (delta 1), reused 0 (delta 0), pack-reused 0 [K
Unpacking objects: 100% (14/14), done.
```

Firstly, we will import all the necessary libraries that we will be requiring for dataset reductions.

```
import numpy as np            # Mathematical Functions , Linear Algebra, Matrix Operations
import pandas as pd           # Data Manipulations,  Data Analysis/Storing/Preparation
import matplotlib.pyplot as plt # Simple Data Visualization , Basic Plotting Utilities
plt.style.use("dark_background") #just a preference of the authors, adds visual attractiveness
import seaborn as sns         # Advanced Data Visualization, High Level Figures Interfacing
%matplotlib inline
# used for Jupyter Notebook Plotting
#%matplotlib notebook          # This can be used as an alternative as the plots obtained will be
interactive in nature.
```

Initial Pseudo Random Number Generator Seeds:

In applied machine learning, it is essential to make experiments reproducible and at the same time keep weights as completely random. The Seed of a Pseudo Random Number Generator (PRNG) achieves the exact same task by initializing values with the same conditions every time a program is executed. We have used a constant value (universal seed) of 42 throughout the course of this chapter.

More info can be found on PRNGs (https://www.geeksforgeeks.org/pseudo-random-number-generator-prng/) and Seeds

(https://numpy.org/doc/stable/reference/random/generator.html).

```
univ_seed=42
np.random.seed(univ_seed)
```

7.2.1.2 The Boston Housing Dataset

The dataset is derived from information collected by the U.S. Census Service concerning housing in the area of Boston, Massachusetts. The Boston dataframe has 506 rows and 14 columns. The **MEDV** variable is the target variable (Table 7.1).

- **CRIM** – per capita crime rate by town
- **ZN** – proportion of residential land zoned for lots over 25,000 sq. ft.
- **INDUS** – proportion of non-retail business acres per town
- **CHAS** – Charles River dummy variable (= 1 if tract bounds river; 0 otherwise)
- **NOX** – nitric oxides concentration (parts per 10 million)
- **RM** – average number of rooms per dwelling
- **AGE** – proportion of owner-occupied units built prior to 1940

TABLE 7.1

The Boston Housing Dataset

	CRIM	ZN	INDUS	CHAS	NOX	RM	AGE	DIS	RAD	TAX	PTRATIO	B	LSTAT	MEDV
0	0.00632	18	2.31	0	0.538	6.575	65.2	4.09	1	296	15.3	396.9	4.98	24
1	0.02731	0	7.07	0	0.469	6.421	78.9	4.9671	2	242	17.8	396.9	9.14	21.6
2	0.02729	0	7.07	0	0.469	7.185	61.1	4.9671	2	242	17.8	392.83	4.03	34.7
3	0.03237	0	2.18	0	0.458	6.998	45.8	6.0622	3	222	18.7	394.63	2.94	33.4

- **DIS** – weighted distances to five Boston employment centres
- **RAD** – index of accessibility to radial highways
- **TAX** – full-value property-tax rate per $10,000
- **PTRATIO** – pupil-teacher ratio by town
- **B** – $1000_*(B_k - 0.63)^2$ where B_k is the proportion of blacks by town
- **LSTAT** – % lower status of the population
- **MEDV** – median value of owner-occupied homes in $1000s

```
from sklearn.datasets import load_boston        # scikit learn has an inbuilt dataset library which
includes the boston housing dataset
boston_dataset = load_boston()                   # the boston_dataset is a dictionary of values
containing the data
df = pd.DataFrame(boston_dataset.data, columns=boston_dataset.feature_names)  # creating a dataframe of
the boston_dataest
df['MEDV'] = boston_dataset.target               # adding the target variable to the dataframe
df.head(4)                                       # printing the first 4 columns of the dataframe
```

Library Information:

The variable boston_dataset is a python dictionary returned via the scikit-learn library with the following keys:

- data: The input values of the dataset.
- target: The output variable of the dataset.
- feature_names: The name of the feature variables as an array.
- DESCR: A brief description of the dataset.
- filename: Local location of the file with its full path.

You can access each key's values using boston_dataset.key_name as we used to create a pandas dataframe. You can read the official scikit learn datasets documentation (https://scikit-learn.org/stable/datasets/index.html#toy-datasets) and get to know about embedded datasets.

Alternatively:

You can also run the following alternative code, provided you have cloned our github repository (https://github.com/khanfarhan10/DIMENSIONALITY_REDUCTION).

df= pd.read_excel("/content/DIMENSIONALITY_REDUCTION/data/Boston_Data.xlsx")
df= pd.read_excel("https://raw.githubusercontent.com/khanfarhan10/DIMENSIONALITY_REDUCTION/master/data/Boston_Data.xlsx")
df= pd.read_excel("https://github.com/khanfarhan10/DIMENSIONALITY_REDUCTION/blob/master/data/Boston_Data.xlsx?raw=true")

Data Insights:

You might want to try df.isnull().sum(), df.info(), df.describe() to get the columnwise null values, dataframe information, and row-wise description, respectively. However, here the data provided is clean and free from such issues which would be needed to be processed/handled inspectionally.

7.2.1.3 Perform Basic Data Visualization

Data visualization is the key to visual data insights and can provide useful analytics about the data. Here in the following code snippet, we will find out the distribution of each columns (feature and target) in the data (Figure 7.1).

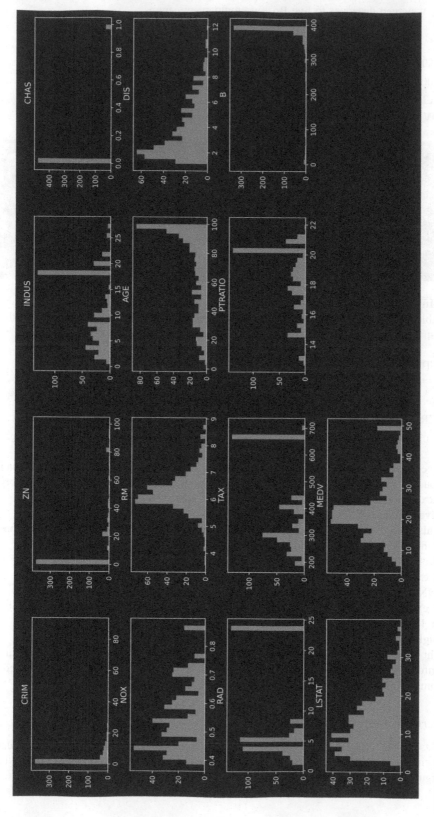

FIGURE 7.1 Frequency distribution of numerical data from the Boston Dataset

```
df.hist(bins=30,figsize=(20,10),grid=False,color="crimson"); # distribution of each column
```

Data Visualization Tips:

For more color palettes, visit Matplotlib Named Colours (https://matplotlib.org/examples/color/named_colors.html).

Almost all the visualizations used in this chapter from Pandas and Seaborn can be saved to high-quality pictures using
plt.savefig("fig_name.png",dpi=600).

7.2.1.4 Pearson Coefficient Correlation Matrix

*The **Pearson Correlation Coefficient** (also known as the Pearson R Test) is a very useful statistical formulae that measures the strength between features and relations.*

Mathematically,

$$r_{xy} = \frac{N\Sigma xy - (\Sigma x)(\Sigma y)}{\sqrt{[N\Sigma x^2 - (\Sigma x)^2][N\Sigma y^2 - (\Sigma y)^2]}}$$

where

r_{xy} = Pearson's Correlation Coefficient between variables x and y
N = number of pairs of x and y variables in the data Σxy = sum of products between x and y variables
Σy = sum of x values
Σy = sum of y values
Σx^2 = sum of squared x values
Σy^2 = sum of squared y values
For all feature variables $f_i \; \epsilon F$ arranged in any order, with $n(F) = N$
The Correlation Coefficient Matrix is $M_{N \times N}$, where

$$\mathbf{M_{ij}} = r_{ij} \; i, j \; \epsilon F$$

We will now use Pandas to get the correlation matrix and plot a heatmap using Seaborn (Figure 7.2).

```
correlation_matrix = df.corr().round(2) #default method = 'pearson', also available : 'kendall',
'spearman' correlation coefficients
plt.figure(figsize=(20,10)) #set the figure size to display
sns.heatmap(data=correlation_matrix,cmap="inferno", annot=True)  # annot = True to print the values
inside the squares
plt.savefig("Correlation_Data.png",dpi=600)
```

7.2.1.5 Detailed Correlation Matrix Analysis

The correlation coefficient ranges from −1 to 1. If the value is close to 1, it means that there is a strong positive correlation between the two variables and both increase or decrease simultaneously. When it is close to −1, the relationship between the variables is negatively correlated, or as one value increases, the other decreases.

Observations:

To fit a linear regression model, we select those features that have a high correlation with our target variable **MEDV**. By looking at the correlation matrix, we can see that RM has a strong positive correlation with **MEDV (0.7),** whereas **LSTAT (−0.74)** has a high negative correlation with **MEDV**. An

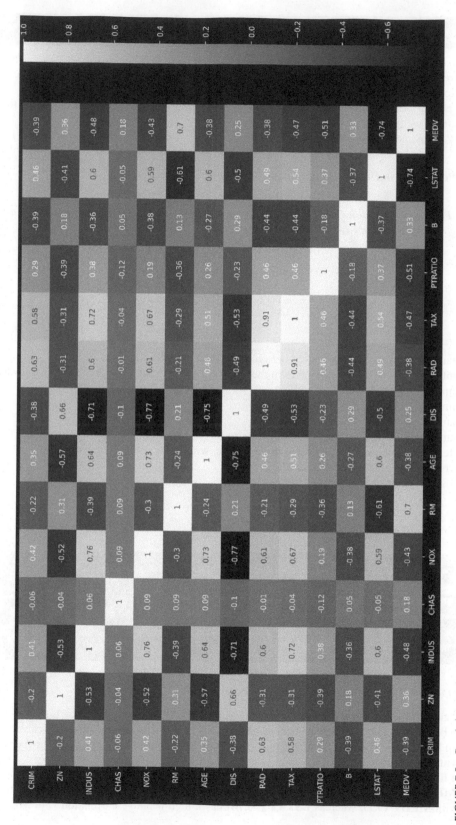

FIGURE 7.2 Correlation matrix plot from Seaborn heatmap for the Boston Dataset

important point in selecting features for a linear regression model is to check for **Multi Collinearity**: features that are strongly correlated to other features and are therefore redundant. The features **RAD** and **TAX** have a correlation of **0.91**. These feature pairs are strongly correlated to each other. We should not select both of these features together for training the model. The same goes for the features **DIS** and **AGE** which have a correlation of **-0.75**. Except for a manual analysis of the correlation, the function below computes the strongly correlated features to the target variable **MEDV**:

```python
thres_range=(-0.7,0.7) # provide the upper and lower limits for thresholding the strongly correlated
features
target_variable="MEDV"  # provide the target variable name

def get_strong_corr(correlation_matrix,target_variable,thres_range=(-0.65,0.65)):
    """
    Get the strongly positive and strongly negatively correlated components from the provided correlation
    matrix.
    Assigns values inside boundary to 0 and returns non zero entries as a Pandas Series.
    correlation_matrix : The correlation matrix obtained from the data.
    target_variable    : The name of the target variable that we need to calculate the correlation for.
    thres_range        : The thresholding range for the calculation of strongly correlated data.
    """
    thres_min,thres_max=thres_range # assign minimum and maximum values passed to threshold
    target_row=correlation_matrix[target_variable] # get the row with the target variable name
    target_row[(target_row > thres_min) & (target_row < thres_max)]=0
    # assign values out of given threshold to zero
    indices_thresholded=target_row.to_numpy().nonzero()
    # remove the zero values from the filtered target row and get indices
    strong_corr=list(correlation_matrix.columns[indices_thresholded])
    # extract feature names from their respective indices
    if target_variable in strong_corr:
        strong_corr.remove(target_variable)
        # correlation of target variable with itself is always 1, remove it.
    return target_row[strong_corr] # return the strongly correlated features with their values

strong_corr=get_strong_corr(correlation_matrix,target_variable,thres_range)
print(strong_corr)
```

```
RM       0.70
LSTAT   -0.74
Name: MEDV, dtype: float64
```

Python Code Documentation – Docstrings:

Triple quoted strings (`"""String"""`) after a function declaration in Python account for a function's documentation and are referred to as **Docstrings**. These can be retrieved later and add the advantage of asking for help towards the working of a function. Create Docstring:

def function_name(arguments): """Function Documentation"""

Retrieve Helper Docstring:

help(function_name)

For information about Docstrings, visit Docstring Conventions (https://www.python.org/dev/peps/pep-0257/). For example, you could run the following command:

help(get_strong_corr)

Based on the above observations and discussions, we will use **RM** and **LSTAT** as our features. Using a scatter plot let's see how these features vary with **MEDV** (Figure 7.3).

```python
plt.figure(figsize=(25,10))                              # initialize the figure with a figure
size

features = ['LSTAT', 'RM']                               # features to display over the dataset

for i, col in enumerate(features):                       # loop over the features with count
    plt.subplot(1, len(features) , i+1)                  # subplotting
    x = df[col]                                          # getting the column values from the
dataframe
    plt.scatter(x, target, marker='o',color="cyan")      # performing a scatterplot in matplotlib
over x & target
    plt.title("Variation of "+target_variable+" w.r.t. "+col)  # setting subplot title
    plt.xlabel(col)                                      # setting the xlabels and ylabels
    plt.ylabel(target_variable)
```

7.2.1.6 3-Dimensional Data Visualization

The added advantage of performing dimensionality reduction is that 3-D visualizations are now possible over the input features (**LSTAT** and **RM**) and the target output (**MEDV**). These visual interpretations of the data help us obtain a concise overview of the model hypothesis complexity that needs to be considered to prevent overfitting (Figure 7.4).

```python
import plotly.graph_objects as go                        # plotly provides interactive 3D plots
from plotly.graph_objs.layout.scene import XAxis, YAxis, ZAxis
df_sampled= df.sample(n = 100,random_state=univ_seed)
# use random sampling to avoid cumbersome overcrowded plots
LSTAT, RM, MEDV = df_sampled["LSTAT"], df_sampled["RM"], df_sampled["MEDV"]

# set the Plot Title , Axis Labels , Tight Layout , Theme
layout = go.Layout(
    title="Boston Dataset 3-Dimensional Visualizations",
    scene = dict( xaxis = XAxis(title='LSTAT'), yaxis = YAxis(title='RM'), zaxis = ZAxis(title='MEDV'),),
    margin=dict(l=0, r=0, b=0, t=0),
    template="plotly_dark")

# create the scatter plot with required hover information text
trace_scatter= go.Scatter3d(
    x=LSTAT,
    y=RM,
    z=MEDV,
    mode='markers',
    marker=dict(
        size=12,
        color=MEDV,
        showscale=True,          # set color to an array/list of desired values
        colorscale='inferno',    # choose a colorscale: viridis
        opacity=0.8),
    text= [f"LSTAT: {a}<br>RM: {b}<br>MEDV: {c}" for a,b,c in list(zip(LSTAT,RM,MEDV))],
    hoverinfo='text')

#get the figure using the layout on the scatter trace
fig = go.Figure(data=[trace_scatter],layout=layout)
fig.write_html("Boston_3D_Viz.html") # save the figure to html
fig.show()                           # display the figure
```

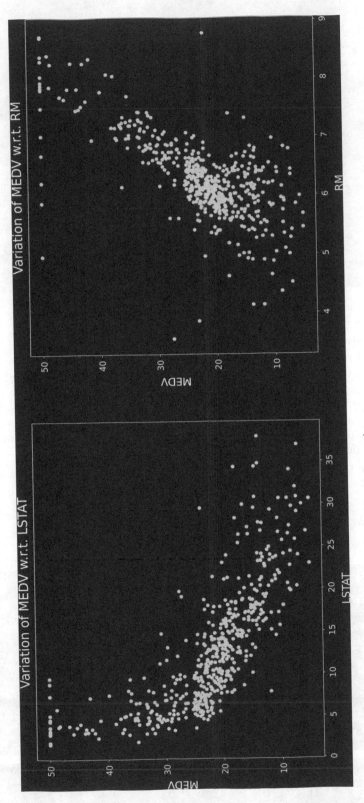

FIGURE 7.3 Variation of MEDV w.r.t. variables LSTAT and RM for the Boston dataset

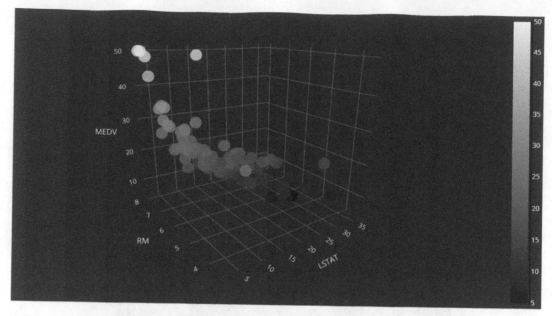

FIGURE 7.4 3-D visualizations for the Boston variables LSTAT, RM, and MEDV

Saving Interactive Plots:

To save the 3-D plots externally for future purposes use,
`fig.write_html("Boston_3D_Viz.html")`to save the interactive plots to HTML files accessible by Internet browsers.

Conclusions Based on Visual Insights:

- Home prices (**MEDV**) tend to decrease with the increase in **LSTAT**. The curve follows a linear – semi-quadratic equation in nature.
- Home prices (**MEDV**) tend to increase with the increase in **RM** linearly. There are few outliers present in the dataset as clearly portrayed by the 3-D visualization.

7.2.1.7 Extracting the Features and Target

Extract the Input Feature Variables in X and Output Target Variable in y.

```
X = pd.DataFrame(np.c_[df['LSTAT'], df['RM']], columns = ['LSTAT', 'RM']) # concatenate LSTAT and RM
columns using numpy np.c_ function
y = df['MEDV']                                                # store the target column
median value of homes (MEDV) in y
print('Dataframe Shapes : ','Shape of X : {} , Shape of y : {}'.format(X.shape,y.shape)) # print the
shapes of the Input and Output Variables
X=X.to_numpy()    # Convert the Input Feature DataFrame X to a NumPy Array
y=y.to_numpy()    # Convert the Output Target DataFrame y to a NumPy Array
y=y.reshape(-1,1) # Shorthand method to reshape numpy array to single column format
print('Array Shapes : ','Shape of X : {} , Shape of y : {}'.format(X.shape,y.shape))        # print the
shapes of the Input and Output Variables
```

```
Dataframe Shapes :  Shape of X : (506, 2) , Shape of y : (506,)
Array Shapes :  Shape of X : (506, 2) , Shape of y : (506, 1)
```

7.2.1.8 Feature Scaling

Feature scaling/standardization helps machine learning models converge faster to a global optima by transforming the data to have zero mean and a unit variance of 1, hence making the data unitless.

$$x' = \frac{x - \mu}{\sigma}$$

where
x= Input Feature Variable
x'= Standardized Value of x
μ= Mean value of x $(\bar{x})$
$\sigma = \sqrt{\frac{\Sigma (x_i - \mu)^2}{N}}$ (Standard Deviation)
x_i = Each value in x
N = No. of Observations in x (Size of x)

```
from sklearn.preprocessing import StandardScaler  # import the Scaler from the Scikit-Learn Library

scaler_x = StandardScaler()                        # initialize an instance of the StandardScaler for
Input Features (X)
X_scaled= scaler_x.fit_transform(X)                # fit the Input Features (X) to the transform

scaler_y = StandardScaler()                        # initialize another instance of the StandardScaler
for Output Target (y)
y_scaled = scaler_y.fit_transform(y)               # fit the Output Target (y) to the transform
```

7.2.1.9 Create Training and Testing Datasets

Splitting the Data into Training (70%) and Testing (30%) Sets:

```
from sklearn.model_selection import train_test_split
# import train test split functionality from the Scikit-Learn Library to perform the split

X_train, X_test, y_train, y_test = train_test_split(X_scaled, y_scaled, test_size = 0.3,
random_state=univ_seed) # print out the shapes of the Training and Testing variables

print('Shape of X_train : {} , Shape of X_test : {}'.format(X_train.shape,X_test.shape))
print('Shape of y_train : {} , Shape of y_test : {}'.format(y_train.shape,y_test.shape))
```

```
Shape of X_train : (354, 2) , Shape of X_test : (152, 2)
Shape of y_train : (354, 1) , Shape of y_test : (152, 1)
```

7.2.1.10 Training and Evaluating Regression Model with Reduced Dataset

Multivariate Linear Regression:

> *Multivariate Linear Regression is a linear approach to modelling the relationship (mapping) between various dependent input feature variables and the independent output target variable.*

Model Training – Ordinary Least Squares (OLS):

Here we will attempt to fit a linear regression model that would map the input features xi (**LSTAT** and **RM**) to y (**MEDV**). Hence, the model hypothesis:

$$h_\Theta(x) = \Theta_0 + \Theta_1 x_1 + \Theta_2 x_2$$

where

　　y = Output Target Variable **MEDV**
　　x_1 = Input Feature Variable **LSTAT**
　　x_2 = Input Feature Variable **RM**
　　Θ = Model Parameters (to obtain)
　　We perform Ordinary Least Squares (OLS) Regression using the scikit-learn library to obtain Θ_i.

```python
from sklearn.linear_model import LinearRegression
# import the Linear Regression functionality from the Scikit-Learn Library
lin_model = LinearRegression()                    # Create an Instance of LinearRegression function
lin_model.fit(X_train, y_train)                   # Fit the Linear Regression Model

points_to_round=2                                 # Number of points to round off the results

# get the list of model parameters in the theta variable

theta= list(lin_model.coef_.flatten().round(points_to_round))

theta += list(lin_model.intercept_.flatten().round(points_to_round))
print("Model Parameters Obtained : ",theta)
# merge the values of theta 1 and theta 2 (coef_) and the value of theta 0 (intercept_)
```

```
Model Parameters Obtained :  [-0.52, 0.38, 0.01]
```

```python
def get_model_params(theta,features,target_variable):
  """Pretty Print the Features with the Model Parameters"""
  text = target_variable + " = " + str(theta[0])
  for t, x in zip ( theta[1:], features) :
    text += " + "+ str(t) + " * " + str(x)
  return text
features=['LSTAT','RM'] # features names
print(get_model_params(theta,features,target_variable)) # display the features & model params
```

```
MEDV = -0.52 + 0.38 * LSTAT + 0.01 * RM
```

Model Evaluation – Regression Metrics:
We need to calculate the following values in order to evaluate our model.

* Mean Absolute Error(MAE)
* Root Mean Squared Error (RMSE)
* R-Squared Value (coefficient of determination)

```
from sklearn.metrics import mean_squared_error, mean_absolute_error, r2_score
# import necessary evaluation scores/metrics from the Scikit-Learn Library

def getevaluation(model,
  X_subset,y_subset,subset_type="Train",round_scores=None): """Get evaluation
  scores of the Train/Test values as specified""" y_subset_predict =
  model.predict(X_subset)
  rmse = (np.sqrt(mean_squared_error(y_subset,
  y_subset_predict))) r2 = r2_score(y_subset,
  y_subset_predict) mae=mean_absolute_error(y_subset,
  y_subset_predict)
  if round_scores!=None:
    rmse=round(rmse,round_scores)
    r2=round(r2,round_scores)
    mae=round(mae,round_scores)
print("Model Performance for {} subset :: RMSE: {} | R2 score: {} | MAE:
{}".format(subset_type,rmse,r2,mae))
getevaluation(model=lin_model,X_subset=X_train,y_subset=y_train,subset_type="Train",round_scores=2)
getevaluation(model=lin_model,X_subset=X_test,y_subset=y_test,subset_type="Test ",round_scores=2)
```

```
Model Performance for Train subset :: RMSE: 0.6 | R2 score: 0.65 | MAE: 0.43
Model Performance for Test  subset :: RMSE: 0.59 | R2 score: 0.6 | MAE: 0.44
```

7.2.1.11 *Limitations of the Correlation Matrix Analysis*

- Correlation coefficients are a vital parameter when applying linear regression on your datasets. However it is limited as:
- Only **LINEAR RELATIONSHIPS** are being considered as candidates for mapping of the target to the features. However, most mappings are non-linear in nature.
- Ordinary Least Squares (OLS) Regression is **SUSCEPTABLE TO OUTLIERS** and may learn an inaccurate hypothesis from the noisy data.
- There may be non-linear variables other than the ones chosen with Pearson Coefficient Correlation Thresholding, which have been discarded, but do **PARTIALLY INFLUENCE** the output variable.
- A strong correlation assumes a direct change in the input variable would reflect back immediately into the output variable, but there exist some variables that are **SELECTIVELY INDEPEND-ENT** in nature yet they provide a suitably high value of the correlation coefficient.

7.2.2 t-Distributed Stochastic Neighbor Embedding (t-SNE)

Objective: Introduce MNIST Handwritten Digits Dataset and obtain the reduced t-SNE (t-distributed Stochastic Neighbor Embedding) Features to perform k-NN (k-Nearest Neighbors) Classification over the digits.

7.2.2.1 *The MNIST Handwritten Digits Dataset*

The MNIST database (Modified National Institute of Standards and Technology Database) is a large database of handwritten digits that is used worldwide as a benchmark dataset, often used by various machine learning classifiers.

The MNIST database contains 60,000 training images and 10,000 testing images and each image size is 28x28 pixels with all images being grayscale.

Importing the dataset:

The MNIST dataset is built into scikit-learn and can be obtained from its datasets' API from OpenML (https://www.openml.org/) using the following code:

```
from sklearn.datasets import fetch_openml # to fetch the dataset
mnist = fetch_openml("mnist_784")              # get the dataset from openml.org
X = mnist.data / 255.0  # since images are in the range 0-255 , normalize the features
print("Size of Input Variable (X) : ",X.shape,"Size of Target Variable (y) : ", y.shape) # get shapes
feat_cols = [ 'pixel'+str(i) for i in range(X.shape[1]) ] # convert num to pixelnum for column names
df = pd.DataFrame(X,columns=feat_cols)                # create dataframe using variables
df['y'] = y                                          # store the target in dataframe
df['label'] = df['y'].apply(lambda i: str(i))        # convert numerical values to string literals
X, y = None, None                                    # calling destructor by reassigning, save space
print('Size of the dataframe: {}'.format(df.shape))  # get dataframe shape
```

```
Size of Input Variable (X) : (70000, 784) Size of Target Variable (y) : (70000,)
Size of the dataframe: (70000, 786)
```

7.2.2.2 Perform Exploratory Data Visualization

Since the dataframe is not human readable, we will view the rows as images from the dataset. To choose the images, we will use a random permutation (Figure 7.5).

```
rndperm = np.random.permutation(df.shape[0])         # random permutation to be used later for data viz
plt.gray()                                           # set the colormap to "gray"
fig = plt.figure( figsize=(20,9) )                   # initialize the figure with the figure size
for i in range(0,15):
# use subplots to get 3x5 matrix of random handwritten digit images
ax = fig.add_subplot(3,5,i+1, title="Digit: {}".format(str(df.loc[rndperm[i],'label'])) )
ax.matshow(df.loc[rndperm[i],feat_cols].values.reshape((28,28)).astype(float))

plt.show()                                           # display the figure
```

7.2.2.3 Random Sampling of the Large Dataset

Since the dataset is huge, we will use random sampling from the dataset to reduce computational time, keeping the dataset characteristics at the same time. The operations performed on the original dataset can now be performed on this sampled dataset with faster results and similar behavior.

```
N = 10000                                # number of rows to be sampled
df_subset = df.loc[rndperm[:N],:].copy() # generate random permutation of no of rows & copy to subset df
data_subset = df_subset[feat_cols].values # get the numpy array of this dataframe and store subset data
```

7.2.2.4 T-Distributed Stochastic Neighboring Entities (t-SNE) – An Introduction

t-SNE is a nonlinear dimensionality reduction algorithm that is commonly used to reduce complex problems with linearly nonseparable data.

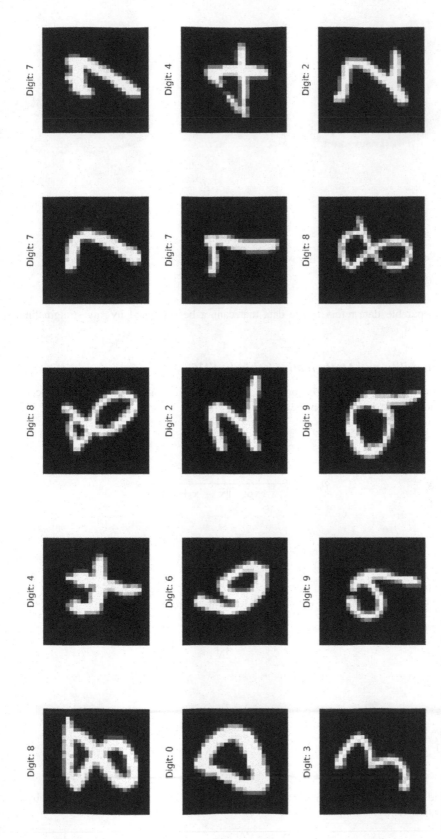

FIGURE 7.5 MNIST digits dataset visualization

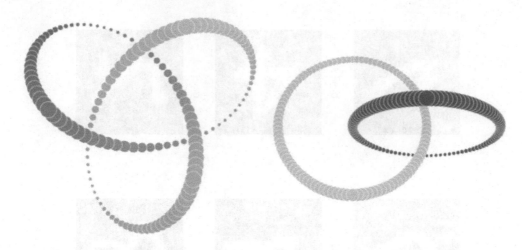

FIGURE 7.6   Few examples of nonlinearly separable datasets

Linearly nonseparable data refers to the data that cannot be separated by any straight line, such as (Figure 7.6).

7.2.2.5 *Probability and Mathematics behind t-SNE*

Provided a set of features x_i, t-SNE computes the proportional probability (p_{ij}) of object similarity between x_i and x_j using the following relation:

For $i \neq j$,

$$p_{ji} = \frac{\exp\left(-\|\mathbf{x}_i - \mathbf{x}_j\|^2 / 2\sigma_i^2\right)}{\sum_{k \neq i}\ \exp(-\|\mathbf{x}_i - \mathbf{x}_k\|^2 / 2\sigma_i^2)}$$

For $i = j$,

$$p_{i|i} = 0$$

where σ^2 is the variance.

Further, p_{ij} is calculated with the help of the bisection method:

$$p_{ij} = \frac{p_{j|i} + p_{i|j}}{2N}$$

Also notice that

- $\sum_j p_{j|i} = 1$ for all i
- $p_{ij} = p_{ji}$
- $p_{ii} = 0$
- $\sum_{i,j} p_{ij} = 1$

Also, x_i would pick x_j as its neighbor if neighbors were picked in proportion to their probability density under a Gaussian centered at x_i.

t-Distributed stochastic neighbor embedding (t-SNE) minimizes the divergence between two distributions: a distribution that measures pairwise similarities of the input objects and a distribution that measures pairwise similarities of the corresponding low-dimensional points in the embedding.

– Van der Maaten and Hinton

Hence, the t-SNE algorithm generates the reduced feature set by synchronizing the probability distributions of the original data and the best represented low dimensional data.

t-SNE Detailed Information:

For detailed visualization and hyperparameter tuning (perplexity, number of iterations) for t-SNE, visit Distill (https://distill.pub/2016/misread-tsne/)!

7.2.2.6 Implementing and Visualizing t-SNE in 2-D

Here we will obtain a 2-dimensional view of the t-SNE components after fitting to the dataset (Figure 7.7) (Table 7.2).

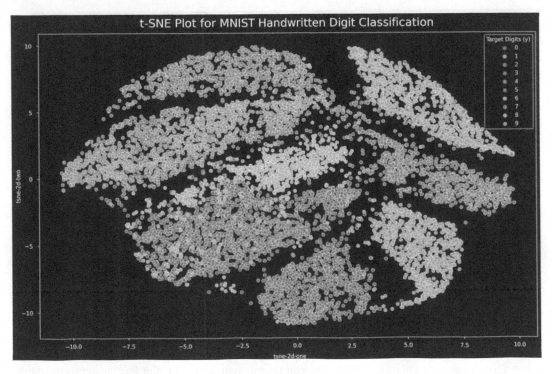

FIGURE 7.7 t-SNE plot for MNIST handwritten digit classification

TABLE 7.2

2 Components TSNE on MNIST Dataset

	y	TSNE-2d-One	TSNE-2d-Two
0	8	–1.00306	–0.128447
1	4	–4.42499	3.18461
2	8	–6.95557	–3.65212
3	7	–1.80255	7.62499

```
from sklearn.manifold import TSNE        # import TSNE functionality from the Scikit-Learn Library
tsne = TSNE(n_components=2, verbose=1, perplexity=40, n_iter=300, random_state = univ_seed)
# Instantiate the TSNE Object with Hyperparameters
tsne_results_2D = tsne.fit_transform(data_subset) # Fit the dataset to the TSNE object

[t-SNE] Computing 121 nearest neighbors...
[t-SNE] Indexed 10000 samples in 1.062s...
[t-SNE] Computed neighbors for 10000 samples in 178.446s...
[t-SNE] Computed conditional probabilities for sample 1000 / 10000
[t-SNE] Computed conditional probabilities for sample 2000 / 10000
[t-SNE] Computed conditional probabilities for sample 3000 / 10000
[t-SNE] Computed conditional probabilities for sample 4000 / 10000
[t-SNE] Computed conditional probabilities for sample 5000 / 10000
[t-SNE] Computed conditional probabilities for sample 6000 / 10000
[t-SNE] Computed conditional probabilities for sample 7000 / 10000
[t-SNE] Computed conditional probabilities for sample 8000 / 10000
[t-SNE] Computed conditional probabilities for sample 9000 / 10000
[t-SNE] Computed conditional probabilities for sample 10000 / 10000
[t-SNE] Mean sigma: 2.117975
[t-SNE] KL divergence after 250 iterations with early exaggeration: 85.793327
[t-SNE] KL divergence after 300 iterations: 2.802306
```

```
reduced_df=pd.DataFrame(np.c_[df_subset['y'] ,tsne_results_2D[:,0]],
tsne_results_2D[:,1]], columns=['y','tsne-2d-one','tsne-2d-two' ])
# store the TSNE results in a dataframe
reduced_df.head(4)  #display the first 4 rows in the saved dataframe
```

```
fig=plt.figure(figsize=(16,10)) # initialize the figure and set the figure size
reduced_df_sorted=reduced_df.sort_values(by='y', ascending=True)
# sort the dataframe by labels for better visualization results
sns.scatterplot(                          # provide the x & y dataframe columns
x="tsne-2d-one", y="tsne-2d-two",         # provide a hue column from the target variable
palette=sns.color_palette("tab10", 10),   # Color Palette for Seaborn ( Other Sets - hls, rocket,
icefire , Spectral )
data=reduced_df_sorted,                    # provide the dataframe
legend="full",                            # display the full legend
alpha=1)                                  # set the transparency of points to 0% (opaques points)
# plot the scatter plot using Seaborn with parameters

# set the plot metadata such as legend title and plot title
plt.legend(title="Target Digits (y)")
```

Color Palettes: Seaborn

For a list of color variations assigned to the plot shown, visit Seaborn Color Palettes (https://seaborn.pydata.org/tutorial/color_palettes.html).

7.2.2.7 Implementing adn Visualizing t-SNE in 3-D

Obtaining a 3-dimensional overview to t-SNE is essential for better visual observations than the 2-dimensional overview. The below code is dedicated to the better understanding of a t-SNE algorithm (Figure 7.8; Table 7.3).

```
tsne = TSNE(n_components=3, verbose=1, perplexity=40, n_iter=300, random_state = univ_seed)
# Instantiate the TSNE Object with Hyperparameters for 3D visualization
tsne_results_3D = tsne.fit_transform(data_subset) # Fit the dataset to the 3D TSNE object
```

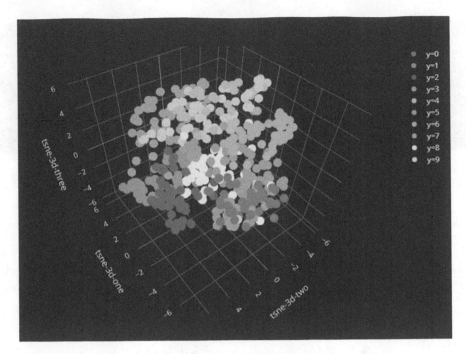

FIGURE 7.8 MNIST handwritten digits dataset of applied t-SNE 3-D visualization

TABLE 7.3

Detailed 3-Dimensional TSNE for MNIST Dataset

	y	TSNE-2d-One	TSNE-2d-Two	TSNE-3d-One	TSNE-3d-Two	TSNE-3d-Three
9996	8	−4.65108	−1.11998	0.802126	−3.5029	−2.521323
9997	3	0.219714	−4.02806	−3.190483	1.40809	−3.643212
9998	8	−0.110848	−5.17118	−2.957494	1.16458	−2.18438
9999	3	−2.01736	−2.94456	−1.057328	−0.79992	−4.963109

```
[t-SNE] Computing 121 nearest neighbors...
[t-SNE] Indexed 10000 samples in 1.027s...
[t-SNE] Computed neighbors for 10000 samples in 180.065s...
[t-SNE] Computed conditional probabilities for sample 1000 / 10000
[t-SNE] Computed conditional probabilities for sample 2000 / 10000
[t-SNE] Computed conditional probabilities for sample 3000 / 10000
[t-SNE] Computed conditional probabilities for sample 4000 / 10000
[t-SNE] Computed conditional probabilities for sample 5000 / 10000
[t-SNE] Computed conditional probabilities for sample 6000 / 10000
[t-SNE] Computed conditional probabilities for sample 7000 / 10000
[t-SNE] Computed conditional probabilities for sample 8000 / 10000
[t-SNE] Computed conditional probabilities for sample 9000 / 10000
[t-SNE] Computed conditional probabilities for sample 10000 / 10000
[t-SNE] Mean sigma: 2.117975
[t-SNE] KL divergence after 250 iterations with early exaggeration: 85.736298
[t-SNE] KL divergence after 300 iterations: 2.494533
```

```
reduced_df['tsne-3d-one']=tsne_results_3D[:,0]    # add TSNE 3D results to the dataframe
reduced_df['tsne-3d-two']=tsne_results_3D[:,1]
reduced_df['tsne-3d-three']=tsne_results_3D[:,2]
reduced_df.tail(4)                                # display the last 4 rows of the dataframe
```

```
import plotly.express as px # import express plotly for interactive visualizations
df_sampled= reduced_df.sample(n = 500,random_state=univ_seed) # perform random sampling of the dataframe
df_sampled_sorted=df_sampled.sort_values(by='y', ascending=True)
# sort the dataframe for better viz w.r.t. target variable
fig = px.scatter_3d(df_sampled_sorted, x='tsne-3d-one', y='tsne-3d-two', z='tsne-3d-three',
color='y', template="plotly_dark") # make a 3D scatterplot using plotly express
fig.write_html("MNIST_Handwritten_Digits_Dataset_tSNE_3D_Viz.html") # save the plot to interactive html
fig.show()                                           # display the figure
```

7.2.2.8 Applying k-Nearest Neighbors (k-NN) on the t-SNE MNIST Dataset

The k-Nearest Neighbors (k-NN) classifier determines the category of an observed data point by majority vote of the k closest observations around it.

The measure of this "closeness" of the data is obtained mathematically using some distance metrics. For our purpose, we will be using the Euclidean Distance (d), which is simply the length of the straight line connecting two distant points p_1 and p_2.

In one dimension, for points $p_1(x_1)$ and $p_2(x_2)$:

$$d(p_1, p_2) = \sqrt{(x_1 - x_2)^2} = |x_1 - x_2|$$

In two dimensions, for points $p_1(x_1, y_1)$ and $p_2(x_2, y_2)$:

$$d(p_1, p_2) = \sqrt{(x_1 - x_2)^2 + (y_1 - y_2)^2}$$

In three dimensions, for points $p_1(x_1, y_1, z_1)$ and $p_2(x_2, y_2, z_2)$:

$$d(p_1, p_2) = \sqrt{(x_1 - x_2)^2 + (y_1 - y_2)^2 + (z_1 - z_2)^2}$$

Based on the calculated distance with x, y, and z coordinates, the algorithm pulls out the closest k neighbors and then does a majority voting for the predictions. However, the value of k diversely affects the algorithm and is an important hyperparameter.

7.2.2.9 Data Preparation – Extracting the Features and Target

Extract the input feature variables in x and output target variables in y.

```
X=reduced_df[["tsne-2d-one", "tsne-2d-two"]].values  # extract the Generated Features with TSNE
y=reduced_df["y"].values                             # extract target values in y
print("X Shape : ", X.shape , "y Shape : ", y.shape) # display the shapes of the variables
```

```
X Shape : (10000, 2) y Shape : (10000,)
```

7.2.2.10 Create Training and Testing Dataset

Splitting the data into Training (80%) and Testing (20%) Sets:

```
X_train, X_test, y_train, y_test = train_test_split( X, y, test_size=0.2,
random_state=univ_seed) # perform the train test split
print ('Train set:', X_train.shape, y_train.shape) # get respective shapes
print ('Test set:', X_test.shape,  y_test.shape)
```

```
Train set: (8000, 2) (8000,)
Test set: (2000, 2) (2000,)
```

7.2.2.11 Choosing the k-NN hyperparameter – k

Obtaining the Predictions and Accuracy Scores for Each k:

Since the optimal value of k for the k-Nearest Neighbors Classifier is not known to us initially, we will attempt to find the value of k from a range that provides the best test set evaluation for the model. The model accuracy is the percentage score of correctly classified predictions.

```
from sklearn.neighbors import KNeighborsClassifier # import the kNN Classifier from the Scikit-Learn
Library
from sklearn import metrics                         # import the metrics from the Scikit-Learn Library

Ks = 20+1                                           # number of k values to test for
# initialize the accuracies
mean_acc = np.zeros((Ks-1))
mean_acc_train= np.zeros((Ks-1))
std_acc = np.zeros((Ks-1))
std_acc_train = np.zeros((Ks-1))
for n in range(1,Ks):

    #Train Model and Predict
    neigh = KNeighborsClassifier(n_neighbors = n).fit(X_train,y_train)
    yhat=neigh.predict(X_test)
    mean_acc[n-1] = metrics.accuracy_score(y_test, yhat)        # gets the test accuracy
    y_pred=neigh.predict(X_train)
    mean_acc_train[n-1] = metrics.accuracy_score(y_train,y_pred) # gets the train accuracy


    std_acc[n-1]=np.std(yhat==y_test)/np.sqrt(yhat.shape[0])      # compute the standard deviations
    std_acc_train[n-1]=np.std(y_pred==y_train)/np.sqrt(y_pred.shape[0])

print("MEAN ACCURACY") # print the mean training and testing accuracy
length=len(mean_acc)
for i in range(length):
test_acc='{0:.3f}'.format(round(mean_acc[i],3))
train_acc='{0:.3f}'.format(round(mean_acc_train[i],3))

    print("K=",f"{i+1:02d}"," Avg. Test Accuracy=",test_acc," Avg. Train Accuracy=",train_acc)
```

```
MEAN ACCURACY
K=    01    Avg.    Test    Accuracy=    0.827    Avg.    Train    Accuracy=    1.000
K=    02    Avg.    Test    Accuracy=    0.840    Avg.    Train    Accuracy=    0.921
K=    03    Avg.    Test    Accuracy=    0.854    Avg.    Train    Accuracy=    0.917
K=    04    Avg.    Test    Accuracy=    0.863    Avg.    Train    Accuracy=    0.902
K=    05    Avg.    Test    Accuracy=    0.870    Avg.    Train    Accuracy=    0.902
K=    06    Avg.    Test    Accuracy=    0.870    Avg.    Train    Accuracy=    0.895
K=    07    Avg.    Test    Accuracy=    0.872    Avg.    Train    Accuracy=    0.894
K=    08    Avg.    Test    Accuracy=    0.871    Avg.    Train    Accuracy=    0.890
K=    09    Avg.    Test    Accuracy=    0.866    Avg.    Train    Accuracy=    0.889
K=    10    Avg.    Test    Accuracy=    0.868    Avg.    Train    Accuracy=    0.888
K=    11    Avg.    Test    Accuracy=    0.869    Avg.    Train    Accuracy=    0.886
K=    12    Avg.    Test    Accuracy=    0.871    Avg.    Train    Accuracy=    0.885
K=    13    Avg.    Test    Accuracy=    0.871    Avg.    Train    Accuracy=    0.885
K=    14    Avg.    Test    Accuracy=    0.870    Avg.    Train    Accuracy=    0.883
K=    15    Avg.    Test    Accuracy=    0.871    Avg.    Train    Accuracy=    0.883
K=    16    Avg.    Test    Accuracy=    0.869    Avg.    Train    Accuracy=    0.881
K=    17    Avg.    Test    Accuracy=    0.870    Avg.    Train    Accuracy=    0.881
K=    18    Avg.    Test    Accuracy=    0.870    Avg.    Train    Accuracy=    0.880
K=    19    Avg.    Test    Accuracy=    0.869    Avg.    Train    Accuracy=    0.880
K=    20    Avg.    Test    Accuracy=    0.868    Avg.    Train    Accuracy=    0.878
```

Obtaining the Best Value for k:

The optimal value for k can be found graphically and analytically as shown (Figure 7.9).

```
# get the best value for k
print( "The best test accuracy was", mean_acc.max(), "with k=", mean_acc.argmax()+1)
print( "The corresponding training accuracy obtained was :",mean_acc_train[mean_acc.argmax()])

plt.figure(figsize=(15,7.5)) # set the figure size
# plot the mean accuracies and their standard deviations
plt.plot(range(1,Ks),mean_acc_train,'r',linewidth=5)

plt.plot(range(1,Ks),mean_acc,'g',linewidth=5)
plt.fill_between(range(1,Ks),mean_acc - 1 * std_acc,mean_acc + 1 * std_acc, alpha=0.10)
plt.fill_between(range(1,Ks),mean_acc_train - 1 * std_acc_train,mean_acc_train + 1 * std_acc_train,
alpha=0.10)
# plot the points for Best Test Accuracy & Corresponding Train Accuracy. plt.scatter(
mean_acc.argmax()+1,  mean_acc.max())
plt.scatter( mean_acc.argmax()+1, mean_acc_train[mean_acc.argmax()]) # set up the legend
plt.legend(('Train_Accuracy ','Test_Accuracy ', '+/3xstd_test','+/-
3xstd_train','BEST_TEST_ACC','CORRESPONDING_TRAIN_ACC'))
# set plot metadata plt.xticks(ticks=list(range(Ks)),labels=list(range(Ks)) ) plt.ylabel('Accuracy ')
plt.xlabel('Number of Neighbors (K)')
plt.title("Number of Neigbors Chosen vs Mean Training and Testing Accuracy Score",fontsize=20)

plt.tight_layout()

#this plot clearly shows that initially the model does overfit
```

```
The best test accuracy was 0.8715 with k= 7
The corresponding training accuracy obtained was : 0.893875
```

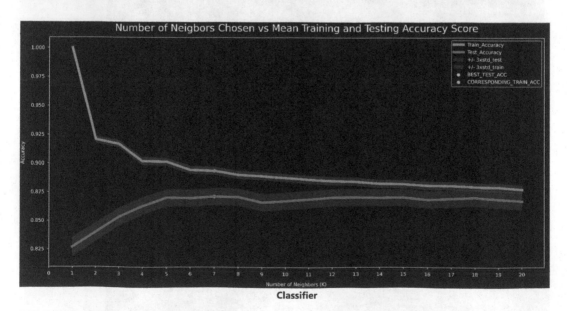

FIGURE 7.9   Number of neigbors chosen vs mean training and testing accuracy score for k-NN classifier

7.2.2.12 Model Evaluation – Jaccard Index, F1 Score, Model Accuracy, and Confusion Matrix

Model Accuracy: It measures the accuracy of the classifier based on the predicted labels and the true labels and is defined as:

$$\alpha(y, \hat{y}) = \frac{|y \cap \hat{y}|}{|\hat{y}|} = \frac{\text{No. of Correctly Classified Predictions}}{\text{Total No. of Predictions}}$$

Jaccard Index:

Given the predicted values of the target variable as $(\hat{y})$ and true/actual values as y, the Jaccard index is defined as:

$$j(y, \hat{y}) = \frac{|y \cap \hat{y}|}{|y \cup \hat{y}|} = \frac{|y \cap \hat{y}|}{|y| + |\hat{y}| - |y \cap \hat{y}|}$$

Simplifying,

$$j(y, y) = \frac{\text{No. of Correctly Classified Predictions}}{\text{No. of True Samples + No. of Predicted Samples} - \text{No. of Correctly Classified Predictions}}$$

Confusion Matrix:

The confusion matrix is used to provide information about the performance of a categorical classifier on a set of test data for which true values are known beforehand (Table 7.4).

The following information can be extracted from the confusion matrix:

- True Positive (TP): Model correctly predicted Positive cases as Positive. Disease is diagnosed as present and truly is present.
- False Positive (FP): Model incorrectly predicted Negative cases as Positive. Disease is diagnosed as present and but is actually absent. (Type I error)
- False Negative (FN): Model incorrectly predicted Positive cases as Negative. Disease is diagnosed as absent but is actually present. (Type II error)
- True Negative (TN): Model correctly predicted Negative cases as Positive. Disease is diagnosed as absent and is truly absent.

F1 Score:

The F1 score is a measure of model accuracy and is calculated based on the precision and recall of each category by obtaining the weighted average of the Precision and Sensitivity (Recall). Precision is the ratio of correctly labeled samples to all samples and recall is a measure of the frequency in which the positive predictions are taking place.

$$\text{Precision} = \frac{TP}{TP + FP}$$

TABLE 7.4

Generalized Confusion Matrix

	Actual Values	
Predicted Values	**Positive (1)**	**Negative (0)**
Positive (1)	True Positive (TP)	False Positive (FP)
Negative (0)	False Negative (FN)	True Negative (TN)

$$\text{Recall (Sensitivity)} = \frac{TP}{TP + FN}$$

$$F1 \text{ Score} = 2\left(\frac{\text{Precision} \times \text{Recall}}{\text{Precision} + \text{Recall}}\right)$$

Note to the Reader:

The implementation of the k-NN classifier over the t-SNE applied MNIST dataset has been shown only for two-component t-SNE and not for the three-component t-SNE, as the code is similar and borrowed from the former workflow. The latter code is left to the reader for implementation practice (Figure 7.10).

```python
# First,we keep a dictionary that measures all the losses/scores for our model/classifier
Test_Scores={}
Train_Scores={}


# Now evaluate the model based on metrics
# First import scoring methods
from sklearn.metrics import jaccard_similarity_score, accuracy_score, f1_score,
confusion_matrix,precision_score, recall_score


# reconstruct the best model as last model is only saved. Previous models were overwritten
best_k=mean_acc.argmax()+1  #7
neigh = KNeighborsClassifier(n_neighbors = best_k).fit(X_train,y_train)
yhat=neigh.predict(X_test)
y_pred=neigh.predict(X_train)

# training scores
Train_Scores['KNN-jaccard']=jaccard_similarity_score(y_train, y_pred)
Train_Scores['KNN-f1-score']=f1_score(y_train, y_pred, average='weighted')
Train_Scores['KNN-accuracy-score']=accuracy_score(y_train, y_pred)
Train_Scores['KNN-precision-score']=precision_score(y_train, y_pred,average='weighted')
Train_Scores['KNN-recall-score']=recall_score(y_train, y_pred,average='weighted')
print("Train Scores")
print(Train_Scores)

# testing scores
Test_Scores['KNN-jaccard']=jaccard_similarity_score(y_test, yhat)
Test_Scores['KNN-f1-score']=f1_score(y_test, yhat, average='weighted')
Test_Scores['KNN-accuracy-score']=accuracy_score(y_test, yhat)
Test_Scores['KNN-precision-score']=precision_score(y_test, yhat, average='weighted')
Test_Scores['KNN-recall-score']=recall_score(y_test, yhat, average='weighted')
print("Test Scores")
print(Test_Scores)
```

```
{'KNN-jaccard': 0.893875, 'KNN-f1-score': 0.8934953484075454, 'KNN-accuracy-score': 0.893875, 'KNN-
precision-score': 0.8941695756701838, 'KNN-recall-score':
0.893875} Test Scores
{'KNN-jaccard': 0.8715, 'KNN-f1-score': 0.8708624433676339, 'KNN-accuracy-score': 0.8715, 'KNN-
precision-score': 0.8716530002545858, 'KNN-recall-score': 0.8715}
```

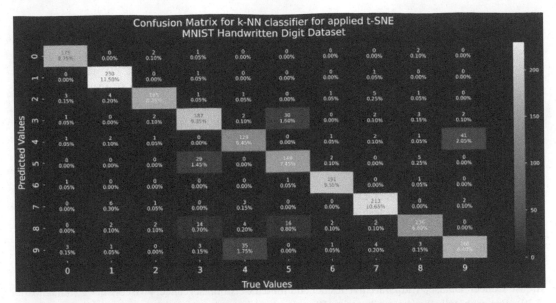

FIGURE 7.10 Confusion matrix for k-NN classification on applied t-SNE for MNIST handwritten digit dataset

```
cf_matrix=confusion_matrix(y_test, yhat) # get the confusion matrix


side_of_cm=cf_matrix.shape[0]          # get the side of the square confusion matrix


group_counts = ["{0:0.0f}".format(value) for value in cf_matrix.flatten()]
group_percentages = ["{0:.2%}".format(value) for value in cf_matrix.flatten()/np.sum(cf_matrix)]
# get the value counts and their corresponding percentages


labels = [f"{v2}\n{v3}" for v2, v3 in
zip(group_counts,group_percentages)]
# get the labels to be attached to the plot for the confusion matrix


labels = np.asarray(labels).reshape(side_of_cm,side_of_cm)
# set the figure size
fig=plt.figure(figsize=(20,8))
# seaborn plot for confusion matrix
sns.heatmap(cf_matrix, annot=labels, fmt='', cmap='inferno')
# plot metadata
plt.xlabel("True Values",fontsize=18)
plt.ylabel("Predicted Values",fontsize=18)
plt.xticks(fontsize=16)
plt.yticks(fontsize=16)
plt.title("Confusion Matrix for k-NN classifier for applied t-SNE\nMNIST Handwritten Digit
Dataset",fontsize=20)
```

7.2.2.13 Limitations of the t-SNE Algorithm

Although particularly well suited for visualization of high-dimensional dataset visualizations, there exist the following pitfalls of t-SNE:

- t-SNE scales **QUADRATICALLY** in the number of objects N and hence it is **COMPUTATIONALLY EXPENSIVE & MEMORY INEFFICIENT.**
- As compared to other dimensionality reduction algorithms, it is often very time consuming and beyond a thousand objects, it is found to be **TOO SLOW TO BE PRACTICAL.**
- Often in the case of very high dimensional data, you may need to **APPLY ANOTHER DIMENSIONALITY REDUCTION TECHNIQUE** (such as PCA for dense data or Truncated SVD for sparse data) before using t-SNE.

7.2.3 Principle Component Analysis (PCA)

Objective:

Introduce UCI Breast Cancer Dataset to perform Principal Component Analysis (PCA) and use projected features to train and test a Support Vector Machine (SVM) classifier.

7.2.3.1 The UCI Breast Cancer Dataset

This algorithms defined in this section will be based upon the University of California, Irvine (UCI) Breast Cancer Dataset (http://archive.ics.uci.edu/ml/datasets/breast+cancer+wisconsin+%28diagnostic%29). For each cell, the dataset contains 10 real valued input features.

- radius (mean of distances from center to points on the perimeter)
- texture (standard deviation of gray-scale values)
- perimeter area
- smoothness (local variation in radius lengths)
- compactness $\frac{perimeter^2}{area - 1.0}$
- concavity (severity of concave portions of the contour)
- concave points (number of concave portions of the contour)
- symmetry
- fractal dimension (coastline approximation-1.0)

The features obtained from these inputs are captured in the dataframe shown at the end of this section's code snippet.

About Breast Cancer:

Breast Cancer develops in breast cells. It can occur in both men and women, though after skin cancer it's one of the most common cancer diagnosed in females. It begins when the cells in the breast start to expand uncontrollably. Eventually these cells form tumors that can be detected via X- ray or felt as lumps near the breast area.

The main challenge is to classify these tumors into malignant (cancerous) or benign (non-cancerous). A tumor is considered as malignant if the cells expand into adjacent tissues or migrate to distant regions of the body. A benign tumor doesn't occupy any other nearby tissue or spread to other parts of the body like the way cancerous tumors can. But benign tumors may be extreme if the structure of heart muscles or neurons is pressurized.

Machine learning technique can significantly improve the level of breast cancer diagnosis. Analysis shows that skilled medical professionals can detect cancer with 79% precision, while machine learning algorithms can reach 91% (sometimes up to 97%) accuracy.

Information on Breast Cancer:

For more information, visit Wikipedia: Breast Cancer (https://en.wikipedia.org/wiki/Breast_cancer).

Importing the Dataset:

```
from sklearn.datasets import load_breast_cancer # scikit learn has an inbuilt dataset library
which includes the breast cancer dataset
cancer = load_breast_cancer()                    # load the cancer dataset form sklearn library
```

```
col_names = list(cancer.feature_names)
# create a column names of the list of all the variables and add features
col_names.append('target')   # append the target variable to column names
df = pd.DataFrame(np.c_[cancer.data, cancer.target], columns=col_names)
# concatenate the columns using the np.c_ function
```

Construct a column named **label** that contains the string values of the target mapping (Table 7.5):

- **1.0 = Benign (non-cancerous)**

- **0.0 = Malignant (cancerous)**

```
df['label'] = df['target'].map({0 :'Malignant', 1 : 'Benign'})  # mapping the numerical variables to
string target names
print("Shape of df :",df.shape)                        # display the shape of the dataframe
df.tail(4)                                             # list the last 4 rows in the dataframe
```

```
Shape of df : (569, 32)
```

Alternative:
You can also run the following code, provided you have cloned our github repository.
df= pd.read_excel("/content/DIMENSIONALITY_REDUCTION/data/UCI_Breast_Cancer_Data.xlsx")
Also, with a working internet connection, you can run:
df= pd.read_excel("https://raw.githubusercontent.com/khanfarhan10/DIMENSIONALITY_
REDUCTION/master/data/UCI_Breast_Cancer_Data.xlsx")
–OR–
df= pd.read_excel("https://github.com/khanfarhan10/DIMENSIONALITY_REDUCTION/blob/master/
data/UCI_Breast_Cancer_Data.xlsx?raw=true")

7.2.3.2 Perform Basic Data Visualization

Pair Plot:
A **pairplot** is a combinational plot of both histograms and scatterplots. A **scatterplot** is used to show the relation between different input features. In a scatterplot, every datapoint is represented by a dot. The **histograms** on the diagonal show the distribution of a single variable where the scatterplots on the upper and lower triangle show the relation between two variables (Figure 7.11).

```
sns.pairplot(df, hue='target', vars=['mean radius', 'mean texture', 'mean perimeter', 'mean area',
'mean smoothness', 'mean compactness', 'mean concavity',
'mean concave points', 'mean symmetry', 'mean fractal dimension'],
palette=sns.color_palette("tab10",2))
# create scattterplot using Seaborn
```

TABLE 7.5

UCI Breast Cancer Dataset Overview

	Mean Radius	Mean Texture	Mean Perimeter	Mean Area	Mean Smoothness	Mean Compactness	Mean Concavity	...	Worst Symmetry	Worst Fractal Dimension	Target	Label
565	20.13	28.25	131.2	1261	0.0978	0.1034	0.144	...	0.2572	0.06637	0	Malignant
566	16.6	28.08	108.3	858.1	0.08455	0.1023	0.09251	...	0.2218	0.0782	0	Malignant
567	20.6	29.33	140.1	1265	0.1178	0.277	0.3514	...	0.4087	0.124	0	Malignant
568	7.76	24.54	47.92	181	0.05263	0.04362	0	...	0.2871	0.07039	1	Benign

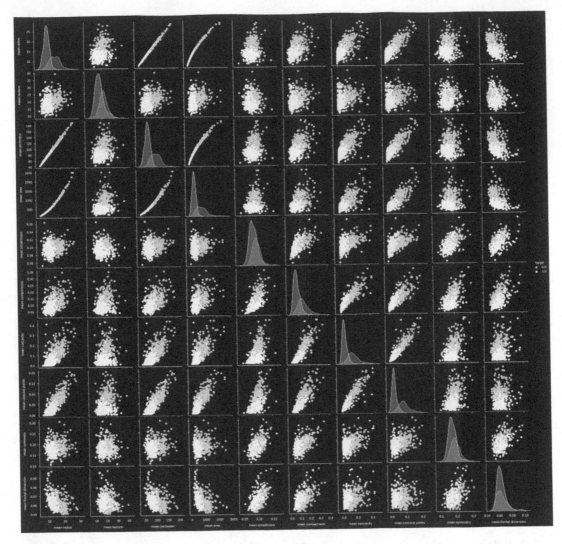

FIGURE 7.11 Seaborn pairplot for breast cancer data

Count Plot:

A **countplot** counts the number of observations for each class of target variable and shows it using bars on each categorical bin (Figure 7.12).

```
fig = plt.figure(figsize= (5,5))        # create figure with required figure size
categories=["Malignant","Benign"]       # declare the categories of the target variable
ax = sns.countplot(x='label',data=df,palette=sns.color_palette("tab10",len(categories)))
# create countplot from the Seaborn Library
# set plot metadata
plt.title('Countplot - Target UCI Breast Cancer',fontsize=20) # set the plot title
plt.xlabel('Target Categories',fontsize=16)                   # set the x labels & y labels
plt.ylabel('Frequency',fontsize=16)
for p in ax.patches:
ax.annotate('{:.1f}'.format(p.get_height()), (p.get_x()+0.3, p.get_height()+5)) #
put the counts on top of the bar plot
```

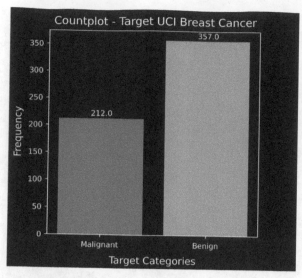

FIGURE 7.12   Seaborn countplot for UCI breast cancer – target field

7.2.3.3 Create Training and Testing Dataset

Extract the dataset into input feature variables in x and output target variables in y.

```
X = df.drop(['target','label'], axis=1)
# drop 2 colums : target is numerical (1/0) and label is string (Malignant/Benign)
y = df.target
# store the numerical target into y : 0 for Malignant and 1 for Benign
print("Shape of X :",X.shape,"Shape of y :",y.shape) # display the variable shapes
```

```
Shape of X : (569, 30) Shape of y : (569,)
```

7.2.3.4 Principal Component Analysis (PCA): An Introduction

*In higher dimensions, where it isn't possible to find out the patterns between the data points of a dataset, **Principal Component Analysis (PCA)** helps to find out the correlation and patterns between the data points of the dataset so that the data can be compressed from higher dimensional space to lower dimensional space by reducing the number of dimensions without any loss of major data.*

This algorithm helps in better data intuition and visualization and is efficient in segregating Linearly Separable Data.

Chronological Steps to Compute PCA:

* Transposing the Data for Usage into Python
* Standardization – Finding the Mean Vector
* Computing the n-dimensional Covariance Matrix
* Calculating the Eigenvalues and Eigenvectors of the Covariance Matrix
* Sorting the Eigenvalues and Corresponding Eigenvectors Obtained

- Construct Feature Matrix – Choosing the k Eigenvectors with the Largest Eigenvalues
- Transformation to New Subspace – Reducing Number of Dimensions

We will go through each step in great detail in the following sections.

7.2.3.5 Transposing the Data for Usage into Python

Interchanging the rows with columns and vice-versa is termed transposing a matrix. Mathematically,

$$X_{m \times n} = \left| a_{ij} \right|, \quad \text{for } (i, j) \epsilon \ (m, n) \ \& \ X^T_{n \times m} = \left| a_{ij} \right|, \quad for \ (i, j) \in (m, n)$$

```
X_Transposed=X.T    # create Transpose of the X matrix using numpy .T method
print("Shape of Original Data (X) :",X.shape,"Shape of Transposed Data
(X_Transposed):",X_Transposed.shape) # display shapes
```

```
Shape of Original Data (X) : (569, 30) Shape of Transposed Data (X_Transposed) : (30, 569)
```

7.2.3.6 Standardization – Finding the Mean Vector

Here we will use a slightly different approach for standardizing the dataset. By subtracting the mean from each variable value, we will have standardized all of the input features.

standardized variable value = initial variable value − mean value

Mathematically,

$$X' = X - \mu$$

```
mean_vec = np.mean(X_Transposed,axis=1).to_numpy().reshape(-1,1) # get the mean vector with
proper shape
X_std = X_Transposed - mean_vec                                  # standardize the data
print("Shape of mean vector (mean_vec) :", mean_vec.shape, "Shape of standardized vector (X_std)
:", X_std.shape) # display shapes
```

```
Shape of mean vector (mean_vec) : (30, 1) Shape of standardized vector (X_std) : (30, 569)
```

7.2.3.7 Computing the n-Dimensional Covariance Matrix

Covariance is a statistical method used to measure how two random variables vary with respect to each other and is used in n-dimensions where $n \geq 2$. In one dimension, covariance is similar to variance, where we determine single variable distributions.

For n number of features, covariance is calculated using the following formula:

$$cov(x, y) = \frac{\sum (x_i - \bar{x})(y_i - \bar{y})}{n - 1}$$

$cov(x, y)$ = covariance between variable x and y x_i = data value of x

y_i = data value of y $\bar{x}$ = mean of x

$\bar{y}$ = mean of y

n = number of data values

Note that $cov(x, y) = cov(y, x)$; hence, the covariance matrix is symmetric across the central diagonal. Also, $covariance(x, x) = variance(x)$

$$S^2 = \frac{\sum (x_i - \bar{x})^2}{n - 1}$$

where

S^2 = sample variance

x_i = the value of the one observation

$\bar{x}$ = the mean value of all observations

n = the number of observations

For 3-dimensional datasets (dimensions x, y, z), we have to calculate $cov(x, y)$, $cov(y, z)$, and $cov(x, z)$ and the covariance matrix will look like:

$$\begin{bmatrix} \text{Cov}(x, x) & \text{Cov}(x, y) & \text{Cov}(x, z) \\ \text{Cov}(y, x) & \text{Cov}(y, y) & \text{Cov}(y, z) \\ \text{Cov}(z, x) & \text{Cov}(z, y) & \text{Cov}(z, z) \end{bmatrix}$$

and similar calculations follow for higher-order datasets. For n-dimensional datasets, the number of covariance values = $\frac{n!}{2(n-2)!}$.

```
X_covariance=np.cov(X_Transposed)
# obtain the covariance matrixnusing .cov method of numpy

print("Shape of Covariance Matrix (X_covariance) :",X_covariance.shape) # display shapes
```

```
Shape of Covariance Matrix (X_covariance) : (30, 30)
```

7.2.3.8 Calculating the Eigenvalues and Eigenvectors of the Covariance Matrix

Eigenvalues:

A covariance matrix is always a square matrix, from which we calculate the eigenvalues and eigenvectors. Let covariance matrix be denoted by C, then the characteristic equation of this covariance matrix is $|C - \lambda I| = 0$ The roots (i.e., λ values) of the characteristic equation are called the eigenvalues or characteristic roots of the square matrix $C_{n\times n}$. Therefore, eigenvalues of C are roots of the characteristic polynomial $\Delta(C - \lambda I) = 0$.

Eigenvectors:

A non-zero vector X such that $(C - \lambda I)X = 0$ or $CX = \lambda X$ is called an eigenvector or characteristic vector corresponding to this lambda of matrix $C_{n\times n}$.

```
X_eigvals, X_eigvecs = np.linalg.eig(X_covariance) # Calculate the eigenvectors and eigenvalues
using numpy's linear algebra module
print("Shape of eigen values :",X_eigvals.shape,"Shape of eigen vectors :",X_eigvecs.shape) # display
shapes
```

```
Shape of eigen values : (30,) Shape of eigen vectors : (30, 30)
```

7.2.3.9 Sorting the Eigenvalues and Corresponding Eigenvectors Obtained

The eigenvector of the covariance matrix with the highest eigenvalues are to be selected for calculating the principal component of that dataset. In this way we have to find out the eigenvalues of that covariance matrix in a **DESCENDING** order. Here we will attempt to sort the eigenvalues along with their corresponding eigenvectors using a Pandas dataframe (Table 7.6).

```
eigen_df=pd.DataFrame(data=X_eigvecs,columns=X_eigvals) # create a pandas dataframe of the
eigenvalues and the eigen vectors
eigen_df_sorted = eigen_df.reindex(sorted(eigen_df.columns,reverse=True), axis=1) # sort the df
columns in a DESCENDING order
print("Shape of original eigen dataframe (eigen_df):",eigen_df.shape,
"Shape of sorted eigen dataframe (eigen_df_sorted):",eigen_df_sorted.shape) # print shapes
eigen_df_sorted.head(3) # display the first 3 rows in dataframe
```

```
Shape of original eigen dataframe (eigen_df): (30, 30) Shape of sorted eigen
dataframe (eigen_df_sorted): (30, 30)
```

7.2.3.10 Construct Feature Matrix – Choosing the k Eigenvectors with the Largest Eigenvalues

Now that we have sorted the eigenvalues, we can get a matrix that contributes to the final principal components of that dataset in the respective order of significance. The components with lesser importance (corresponding eigenvectors with lesser magnitude of eigenvalues) can be ignored. With these selected eigenvectors of the covariance matrix a feature vector is constructed. Here we will attempt to choose the top number of components (**k**) in our case number of components (**no_of_comps**) =2 (Table 7.7).

```
no_of_comps = 2 # select the number of PCA components
feature_matrix = eigen_df_sorted.iloc[:, 0 : no_of_comps] # extract first k cols from the sorted df
print("Shape of Feature Matrix (feature_matrix):",feature_matrix.shape) # get shape of feature matrix
feature_matrix.head(4) # display first 4 rows of the feature matrix
```

```
Shape of Feature Matrix (feature_matrix): (30, 2)
```

7.2.3.11 Data Transformation – Derivation of New Dataset by PCA – Reduced Number of Dimensions

The new dataset is derived simply by dot multiplication of the transposition of the standardized data on the right with the feature vector on the right.

$$\text{Final Transformed PCA Data} = \text{Data Standardized}^T \cdot \text{Feature Vector}$$

```
Final_PCA = X_std.T.dot(feature_matrix_numpy)
# perform transpose of the Standardized Data & operate dot product with feature matrix
print("Shape of Final PCA Data :",Final_PCA.shape) # display the shape of PCA
```

```
Shape of Final PCA Data : (569, 2)
```

TABLE 7.6

All Eigenvalues and Eigenvectors from the PCA Dataframe

	4.44E+05	7.31E+03	7.04E+02	5.46E+01	3.99E+01	3.00E+00	1.82E+00	...	2.85E-06	2.00E-06	7.02E-07
0	0.005086	0.009287	-0.012343	-0.034238	-0.035456	-0.131213	0.033513	...	-0.003259	0.000513	-0.000648
1	0.002197	-0.002882	-0.006355	-0.362415	0.443187	-0.213486	-0.784253	...	-0.000109	0.000129	-0.000005
2	0.035076	0.062748	-0.071669	-0.329281	-0.313383	-0.840324	0.189075	...	0.000592	-0.000283	0.000153

TABLE 7.7

Two Selected Eigenvalues and Eigenvectors from the PCA Dataframe

	443782.61	7310.1001
0	0.005086	0.009287
1	0.002197	-0.002882
2	0.035076	0.062748
3	0.516826	0.851824

7.2.3.12 PCA Using Scikit-Learn

All the tasks mentioned above can be performed using **PCA()**, which is n in-built function of scikit learn library to reduce the dimensions of a dataset.

Here we have performed PCA analysis with our data using **n_components = 2**. The n-components parameter denotes the number of principal components (components with higher significance that means these components have higher eigenvalues corresponding to its eigenvectors as performed stepwise before).

```
from sklearn.decomposition import PCA          # import the PCA algorithm from the Scikit-Learn
Library
pca = PCA(n_components= 2)                      # choose the number of components for PCA
X_PCA = pca.fit_transform(X)                    # fit the PCA algorithm
print("Shape of Scikit Learn PCA :",X_PCA.shape) # display the shapes of the PCA obtained via Scikit -
Learn
```

```
Shape of Scikit Learn PCA : (569, 2)
```

7.2.3.13 Verification of Library and Stepwise PCA

In this section, we will verify that the PCA obtained from our steps are the same as the PCA from the Scikit-Learn Library.

For this procedure, we will consider that the two PCAs are not identical but lie very close to each other, accounting for errors crept in due to rounding off (rounding errors). Hence if the true value is T and the observed value O is within the range $(T \pm \delta)$ then the observed value is considered nearly equal to the true value, where δ is the allowed tolerance value, set to a very small positive value. Mathematically, $T - \delta < O < T + \delta$ yields to true, else false. In other words, we check for: $|T - O| \leq \delta$.

We perform this verification using the all close function of numpy:

```
print(np.allclose(X_PCA, Final_PCA,rtol=0, atol=1e-08))
# use zero relative tolerance and a suitably low value of absolute tolerance to verify that the
values obtained Theoretically & Practically Match
```

```
True
```

Now we know that the value of the theoretic PCA calculated from the stepwise calculation matches the PCA from the Scikit-Learn Library. However, since there are various steps that are extensive in nature, we will now use the **SKLearn PCA** henceforth.

7.2.3.14 PCA – Captured Variance and Data Lost

Explained variance ratio is the ratio between the variance attributed by each selected principal component and the total variance. Total variance is the sum of variances of all individual principal components. Multiplying this explained variance ratio with 100%, we get the percentage of variance ascribed by each chosen principal component and subtracting the sum of variances from 1 gives us the total loss in variance.

Hence, the PCA components variance are as follows:

```
round_to=2                                          # round off values to 2
explained_variance = pca.explained_variance_ratio_   # get the explained variance ratio
# perform pretty display of ratio percentages
for i,e in enumerate(explained_variance):
print("Principal Component",i+1,"- Explained Variance Percentage :" , round(e*100,round_to))
total_variance=explained_variance.sum()             # get the total sum of the variance
ratios obtained
print("Total Variance Percentage Captured :",round(total_variance*100,round_to))
var_loss=1 - total_variance                         # calculate the loss in variance
print("Total Variance Percentage Loss :",round(var_loss*100,round_to))
```

```
Principal Component 1 - Explained Variance Percentage : 98.2
Principal Component 2 - Explained Variance Percentage : 1.62
Total Variance Percentage Captured : 99.82
Total Variance Percentage Loss : 0.18
```

Note to the Reader:
The explained variance and data loss part for three-component PCA is left as a practice activity to the reader.

7.2.3.15 PCA Visualizations

Visual insights to PCA on the Breast Cancer Dataset will help us understand breast cancer classification in a better way and is definitely an essential requirement for better data insights.

Dataframe Preparation:
First we will prepare the Pandas dataframe for visualizing the 2-D and 3-D principal components after applying PCA with the respective number of components (n_components) (Table 7.8).

```
pca_2d = PCA(n_components= 2)      # use 2-component PCA
PCA_2D = pca_2d.fit_transform(X)  # fit the 2-component PCA
pca_3d = PCA(n_components= 3)      # use 3-component PCA
PCA_3D = pca_3d.fit_transform(X)  # fit the 3-component PCA
print("Shape of PCA 2D :",PCA_2D.shape,"Shape of PCA 3D :",PCA_3D.shape) # display shapes
```

```
Shape of PCA 2D : (569, 2) Shape of PCA 3D : (569, 3)
```

```
PCA_df = pd.DataFrame(data = np.c_[PCA_2D,PCA_3D]
, columns = ['PCA-2D-one', 'PCA-2D-two','PCA-3D-one', 'PCA-3D-two','PCA-3D-three']) # create a
dataframe of the applied PCA in 2-D & 3-D
PCA_df["label"]=df["label"]                # assign label column to previously assigned labels
print("Shape of PCA dataframe",PCA_df.shape) # display shape of resulting PCA dataframe
PCA_df.tail(4)                             # display the last 4 rows in the dataframe
```

```
Shape of PCA dataframe (569, 6)
```

TABLE 7.8

Pandas PCA Dataframe Containing 2-Component and 3-Component PCA Values – An Overview

	PCA-2D-One	PCA-2D-Two	PCA-3D-One	PCA-3D-Two	PCA-3D-Three	Label
565	1045.0189	77.057589	1045.0189	77.057589	0.036669	Malignant
566	314.50176	47.553525	314.50176	47.553525	−10.44241	Malignant
567	1124.8581	34.129225	1124.8581	34.129225	−19.74209	Malignant
568	−771.5276	−88.64311	−771.5276	−88.64311	23.889032	Benign

2-Dimensional Visualizations:

We will be using the scatterplot function from the Seaborn library to get the required 2-D visualizations with some matplotlib customization (Figure 7.13).

```
plt.figure(figsize=(20,10))                                # set the size of the figure
sns.scatterplot(data=PCA_df, x="PCA-2D-one", y="PCA-2D-two", hue='label',
palette=sns.color_palette("tab10",len(categories)))

# make a scatterplot using Seaborn
plt.title("UCI Breast Cancer Dataset PCA 2-Dimensional Visualizations",fontsize=20) # set plot title
```

3-Dimensional Visualizations:

We will be using plotly to achieve interactive 3-D plotting, as shown below with some random sampling to avoid overcrowded data points (Figure 7.14).

```
import plotly.express as px  # use plotly for interactive visualizations
df_sampled= PCA_df.sample(n = 100,random_state=univ_seed)

# perform random sampling over 100 points to get a subset of the original dataset
fig = px.scatter_3d(df_sampled, x='PCA-3D-one', y='PCA-3D-two', z='PCA-3D-three',
color='label', template="plotly_dark") # chart a scatterplot

fig.write_html("UCI_Breast_Cancer_Dataset_PCA_3D_Viz.html")      # save the figure for future uses
fig.show()                                               # display the figure
```

7.2.3.16 Splitting the Data into Test and Train Sets

Before feeding data to the machine learning model, perform train(80%)-test(20%) split:

```
X_train,X_test,y_train,y_test = train_test_split(PCA_2D,PCA_df["label"],test_size=0.2)
# perform a 80%- 20% Train - Test Split
print("Shape of X_train :",X_train.shape,"Shape of y_train :",y_train.shape)
# display shapes
print("Shape of X_test :",X_test.shape,"Shape of y_test :",y_test.shape)
```

```
Shape of X_train : (455, 2) Shape of y_train : (455,)
Shape of X_test : (114, 2) Shape of y_test : (114,)
```

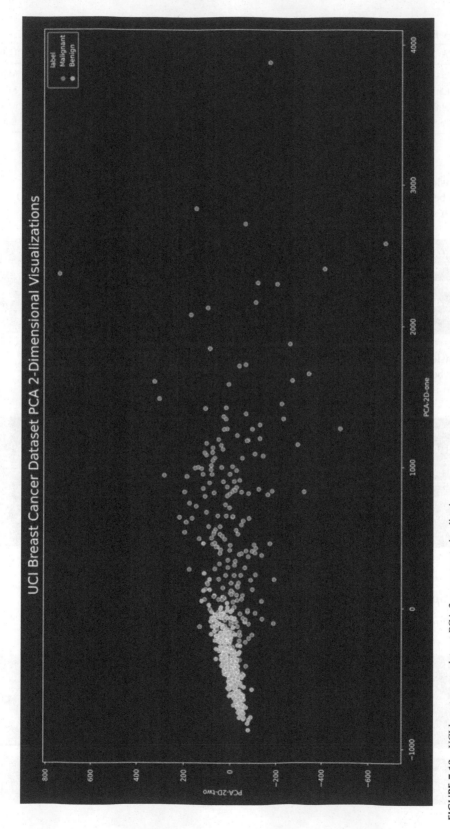

FIGURE 7.13   UCI breast cancer dataset PCA 2-component visualization

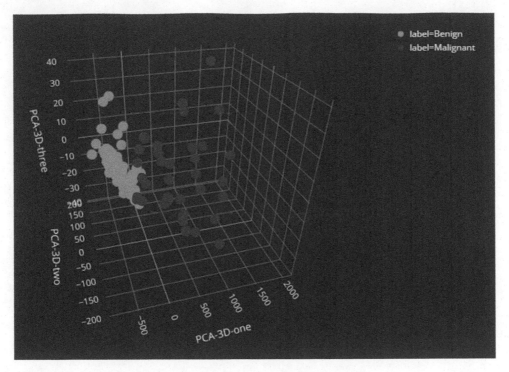

FIGURE 7.14 UCI breast cancer dataset PCA 3-component visualization

Note to the Readers:

The procedure for classification using the three-component PCA is left as a practice task for the readers.

7.2.3.17 An Introduction to Classification Modeling with Support Vector Machines (SVM)

Support Vector Machines (SVMs) are Supervised Machine Learning Algorithms that can be used for both classification and regression problems, though they are mostly used in classification problems to distinctly classify the data points.

> *The primary objective of an SVM Classifier is to find out a decision boundary in the n- dimensional space (where n is number of features) that will segregate the space into two regions where in one region the hypothesis predicts that y=1 and in another region the hypothesis predicts that y=0.*

This decision boundary is also called a **hyper-plane**. There could be many possible hyper-planes but the goal of SVM is to choose those extreme points or vectors which will help to create one hyper-plane that will have **maximum margin** i.e., maximum distance between the data points of two regions or classes. The hyper-plane with maximum margin is termed as **optimal hyper-plane**. Those extreme points or vectors are called support vectors and hence, this algorithm is termed Support Vector Machine.

Given a training data of n points: $(\overrightarrow{x_i}, y_i)$ where $y_i = 0$ or 1

The mathematical formulation,

$$min\frac{\|\overrightarrow{w}\|^2}{2}\text{such that } y_i(\overrightarrow{w}\cdot x_i + b) - 1 \geq 0 \text{ for } i = 1\dots n$$

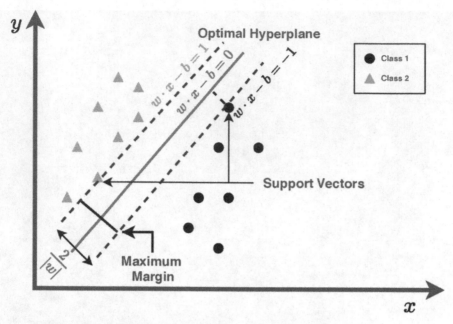

FIGURE 7.15   SVM working principle visualization in geometric coordinates

where,

$\vec{w}$ is the normal vector to the hyper-plane.

$b \geq 0$ is the distance from the origin to the plane (or line) (Figure 7.15).

7.2.3.18 Types of SVM

Linear SVM:

If all the data points in n-dimensional space can be classified into two different regions using a straight line, then such data is termed as *linearly separable data* and the classifier used is termed a*Linear SVM Classifier*. Suppose in a dataset we have only two features, G and R, which are tagged Green and Red, respectively, in a 2-dimensional space. We have to classify these two tags into two different classes. Using a simple straight line, we can easily classify these two classes in 2-D space. But they can have multiple lines competing for the classifier. Here, the SVM algorithm helps to find out the best straight line or decision boundary where the distance or margin between the support vectors and hyperplane is maximum.

Nonlinear SVM:

If all the data points in n-dimensional space can't be classified into two different regions using a straight line then such data is termed as nonlinearly separable data and the classifier used is termed a Nonlinear SVM Classifier.

The **Kernel Trick** is applied to train a linear classifier to provide predictions on a nonlinear data space. It transforms the linearly inseparable data into a linearly separable one by high-dimensional projections. Each data object is mapped using a kernel function to the original non-linear dataset that is then projected into some high dimensional set by which it becomes linearly separable.

Train and Evaluate the SVM Models:

Kernels to use in Scikit Learn SVM Classification: {"linear," "poly," "rbf," "sigmoid"}, we will try out all of these kernels sequentially computing the best test accuracy and choosing that classifier.

```
from sklearn.svm import SVC                    # import Support Vector Classifier
from sklearn import metrics                    # get the metrics used for evaluating accuracy
Kernels = ['linear', 'poly', 'rbf', 'sigmoid']  # List out all the kernels used in SVM
Ks= len(Kernels)                               # get the no of kernels we will be using
# initilaize necessary vectors for storing the metric scores
mean_acc = np.zeros((Ks))
mean_acc_train= np.zeros((Ks))
std_acc = np.zeros((Ks))
std_acc_train = np.zeros((Ks))
for n in range(Ks):
# Train Model and Predict clf =
SVC(kernel=Kernels[n])
classifier = clf.fit(X_train,y_train)
yhat=classifier.predict(X_test)
# Accumulate the scores for future use
mean_acc[n] = metrics.accuracy_score(y_test, yhat) #gets the test accuracy
y_pred=classifier.predict(X_train)
mean_acc_train[n] = metrics.accuracy_score(y_train,y_pred) #gets the train accuracy
# compute the normalized standard deviation
std_acc[n]=np.std(yhat==y_test)/np.sqrt(yhat.shape[0])
std_acc_train[n]=np.std(y_pred==y_train)/np.sqrt(y_pred.shape[0])
```

Obtain the Highest Test Accuracy Model:

Extract the best model from the list of kernel types:

```
print("MEAN ACCURACY")
length=len(mean_acc)
# get the mean accuracy for each kernel
type for i in range(length):
test_acc='{0:.3f}'.format(round(mean_acc[i],3))
train_acc='{0:.3f}'.format(round(mean_acc_train[i],3))
print("Kernel Type =",Kernels[i]," Avg. Test Accuracy=",test_acc," Avg. Train
Accuracy=",train_acc)
```

```
MEAN ACCURACY
Kernel Type = linear Avg. Test Accuracy= 0.947   Avg. Train Accuracy= 0.923
Kernel Type = poly   Avg. Test Accuracy= 0.851   Avg. Train Accuracy= 0.855
Kernel Type = rbf    Avg. Test Accuracy= 0.921   Avg. Train Accuracy= 0.919
Kernel Type = sigmoid  Avg. Test Accuracy= 0.825   Avg. Train Accuracy= 0.899
```

Visualize the Evaluation Scores:

It is necessary to visualize the accuracy as these visualizations help us know whether the model is overfitting, underfitting, or is just right (Figure 7.16).

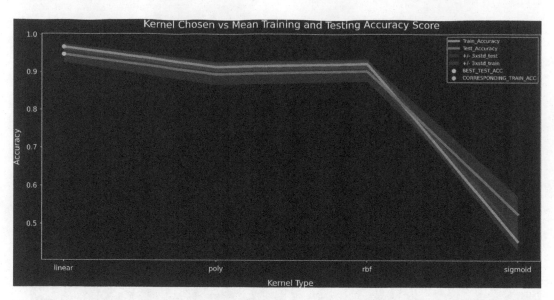

FIGURE 7.16 Kernel chosen vs mean training and testing accuracy score for support vector machine-based classification

```
imt = mean_acc.argmax() # index of maximum test accuracy
print( "The best test accuracy was", mean_acc.max(), "with Kernel=", Kernels[imt])
print( "The corresponding training accuracy obtained was :",mean_acc_train[imt])
plt.figure(figsize=(15,7.5))
# set the figure size
# plot the mean accuracies and their standard deviations
plt.plot(range(Ks),mean_acc_train,'r',linewidth=5)
plt.plot(range(Ks),mean_acc,'g',linewidth=5)
plt.fill_between(range(Ks),mean_acc - 1 * std_acc,mean_acc + 1 * std_acc, alpha=0.10)
plt.fill_between(range(Ks),mean_acc_train - 1 * std_acc_train,mean_acc_train + 1 * std_acc_train,
alpha=0.10)
# plot the points for Best Test Accuracy & Corresponding Train Accuracy.
plt.scatter( mean_acc.argmax(), mean_acc.max(), zorder=3,s=60)
plt.scatter( mean_acc.argmax(), mean_acc_train[mean_acc.argmax()],zorder=3,s=60)
# set up the legend
plt.legend(('Train_Accuracy ','Test_Accuracy ', '+/- 3xstd_test','+/-
3xstd_train','BEST_TEST_ACC','CORRESPONDING_TRAIN_ACC'))
# set plot metadata
plt.ylabel('Accuracy ',fontsize=16) # set the xlabels & ylabels
plt.xlabel('Kernel Type',fontsize=16)
plt.xticks(ticks=range(Ks),labels=Kernels,fontsize=14) # set the xticks & yticks
plt.yticks(fontsize=14)
plt.title("Kernel Chosen vs Mean Training and Testing Accuracy Score",fontsize=20)# set the plot title
plt.tight_layout() # set the tight layout for the plot
```

```
The best test accuracy was 0.9473684210526315 with Kernel= linear
The corresponding training accuracy obtained was : 0.9230769230769231
```

Metrics Report:

Get the metrics for the model as already discussed earlier: Jaccard Similarity Score, F1 Score, Accuracy, Precision and Recall (Figure 7.17).

```
First,we keep a dictionary that measures all the losses/scores for our model/classifier
Test_Scores={}
Train_Scores={}
# Now evaluate the model based on metrics , First import scoring methods
from sklearn.metrics import jaccard_similarity_score, accuracy_score, f1_score,
confusion_matrix,precision_score, recall_score
# reconstruct the best model as last model is only saved. Previous models were overwritten
best_kernel=Kernels[imt]
best_clf = SVC(kernel=best_kernel).fit(X_train,y_train)
yhat=best_clf.predict(X_test)
y_pred=best_clf.predict(X_train)
# training scores
Train_Scores['SVM-jaccard']=jaccard_similarity_score(y_train, y_pred)
Train_Scores['SVM-f1-score']=f1_score(y_train, y_pred, average='weighted')
Train_Scores['SVM-accuracy-score']=accuracy_score(y_train, y_pred)
Train_Scores['SVM-precision-score']=precision_score(y_train, y_pred,average='weighted')
Train_Scores['SVM-recall-score']=recall_score(y_train, y_pred,average='weighted')
print("Train Scores")
print(Train_Scores)
# testing scores
Test_Scores['SVM-jaccard']=jaccard_similarity_score(y_test, yhat)
Test_Scores['SVM-f1-score']=f1_score(y_test, yhat, average='weighted')
Test_Scores['SVM-accuracy-score']=accuracy_score(y_test, yhat)
Test_Scores['SVM-precision-score']=precision_score(y_test, yhat, average='weighted')
Test_Scores['SVM-recall-score']=recall_score(y_test, yhat, average='weighted')
print("Test Scores")
print(Test_Scores)
# get the confusion matrix and plot it
cm=confusion_matrix(y_test, yhat)
fig=plt.figure(figsize=(5,5))
sns.heatmap(cm, annot=True, fmt='g',cmap='inferno')
positions=np.arange(len(categories))+0.5
# set xticks & yticks
plt.xticks(ticks=positions, labels=categories)
plt.yticks(ticks=positions, labels=categories)
# set plot metadata
plt.xlabel("True Values",fontsize=12)
plt.ylabel("Predicted Values",fontsize=12)
plt.title("Confusion Matrix for SVM classifier for applied PCA\nUCI Breast Cancer Dataset",fontsize=16)
```

```
Train Scores
{'SVM-jaccard': 0.9230769230769231, 'SVM-f1-score': 0.9223163404142641, 'SVM-accuracy-score':
0.9230769230769231, 'SVM-precision-score': 0.9237428027450684, 'SVM-recall-score': 0.9230769230769231}
Test Scores
{'SVM-jaccard': 0.9473684210526315, 'SVM-f1-score': 0.9470445344129554, 'SVM-accuracy-score':
0.9473684210526315, 'SVM-precision-score': 0.9473684210526315, 'SVM-recall-score': 0.9473684210526315}
```

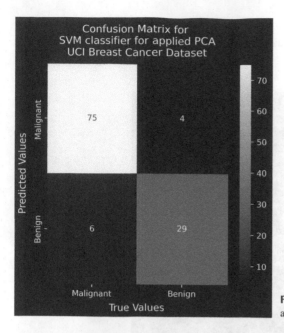

FIGURE 7.17 Confusion matrix for SVM classifier for applied PCA UCI breast cancer dataset

```
def get_SVM_params(weights,bias,features):
"""Pretty Print the Features with the Model Parameters"""
text = " "
for w, x in zip (weights, features) : text
+= " + " + str(w)+" * "+ str(x)
text += " - "+ str(float(bias)) + " = 0 "
return text


points_to_round=3                                       # points to round off to
w = best_clf.coef_.flatten().round(points_to_round)     # get the weight vector - normal vector to
the hyperplane
b = best_clf.intercept_.flatten().round(points_to_round) # get the bias vector - distance from the
origin
PCA_dim=2                                                # the PCA number of components
features=['PCA'+str(i+1) for i in range(PCA_dim) ]      # prepare labels
print(get_SVM_params(weights=w,bias=b,features=features)) # get the SVM parameters
```

```
+ 0.007 * PCA1 + -0.017 * PCA2 - 0.538 = 0
```

Finding the Optimal Model Hyperparameters:

Often machine learning engineers use search algorithms such as GridSearchCV (https://scikit-learn.org/stable/modules/generated/sklearn.model_selection.GridSearchCV.html) and RandomizedSearchCV (https://scikit-learn.org/stable/modules/generated/sklearn.model_selection.RandomizedSearchCV.html) to perform model hyperparameter fine tuning for optimal performance of the predictor. However, the implementation and detailed explanation of these algorithms are beyond the scope of this book chapter.

7.2.3.19 Limitations of PCA

Although PCA is a widely used algorithm for dimensionality reduction, it has its own limitations:

TABLE 7.9

Differences between PCA and TSNE

PCA	T-SNE
Linear Dimensionality Reduction Technique	Nonlinear Dimensionality Reduction Technique
Captures Global Structure of the Data Distribution (Covariance)	Preserves Local Structure of the Data Distribution (Cluster)
Does not generalize well as compared to t-SNE	One of the best generalized dimensionality reduction techniques
Model Hyperparameters not Involved	Model Hyperparameters – perplexity, learning rate and number of steps
Highly affected by data noise/outliers	Handle outliers efficiently
Deterministic algorithm	Non-deterministic or randomised algorithm
Rotates the vectors for preserving variance	Minimizes the distance between the points in a Gaussian distribution

- PCA is a Linear Dimensionality Reduction Algorithm and hence chooses an eigenvector with a corresponding high eigenvalue. In some cases, in the form of highly nonlinear data spaces, this approach will fail as the **NONLINEAR COMPONENTS** will be **TRUNCATED** (disregarded as noise) and will not count towards the model variance a lot. It assumes that a large variance results in a low covariance, which in turn implies high importance which may not be true 100% of the times. For this we need to shift to Kernel PCA (KPCA), which requires a lot of space.
- PCA is a **SCALE VARIANT** Algorithm, and hence any change of scale in any of the variables will affect the PCA values accordingly.
- For some data distributions, **MEAN AND COVARIANCE DESCRIPTION IS INACCURATE**. It is only true to say that for the Gaussian/Normal Data Distributions, this algorithm performs actually well, but this may not be correct for other distributions.

7.2.3.20 PCA vs. t-SNE

See Table 7.9.

Conclusion

In this chapter, we applied the concepts of dimensionality reduction in applied machine learning on various datasets. The authors recommend to try out other datasets as well to practice and get a firm understanding of the algorithms used in this chapter for reducing high dimensionality datasets.

Some reliable data sources are as follows:

- Kaggle Datasets (https://www.kaggle.com/datasets)
- Google Dataset Search (https://datasetsearch.research.google.com/)
- Github Datasets (https://github.com/awesomedata/awesome-public-datasets#machinelearning)
- UCI Machine Learning Datasets (https://archive.ics.uci.edu/ml/datasets.html)
- Socrata Finding Open Data (https://dev.socrata.com/data/)

8

Hybrid Cellular Automata Models for Discrete Dynamical Systems

Sreeya Ghosh and Sumita Basu

CONTENTS

8.1 Introduction

Dynamical system is the mathematical model for computing changes over time of any physical, biological, economic, or social phenomena [1,2]. Also, evolution of a data sequence can be viewed as an evolution of a dynamical system. Usually dynamical system is described mathematically by differential or difference equations. Another widely used computation model is Cellular Automata (CA) [3]. This model was introduced by J. von Neumann and S. Ulam in 1940 for designing self-replicating systems, which later saw applications in physics, biology, and computer science.

Neumann conceived a CA as a two-dimensional mesh of finite state machines called cells which are locally interconnected with each other. Each of the cells change their states synchronously depending on the states of some neighbouring cells (for details see [4–6] and references therein). Stephen Wolfram's work in the 1980s contributed to a systematic study of one-dimensional CA, providing the first qualitative classification of their behavior (reported in [7,8]).

A CA is capable of modeling systems where change at micro levels of each point of a surface is triggered by neighboring points [9–12,19]. Totality of these changes at micro level together generates an evolution pattern at the macro level. If the local (micro level) changes be identical, then the CA is homogeneous; otherwise the CA is hybrid. A spatially hybrid CA can be visualized to be composed of finite celled blocks where each block has a different local transition function and within any block all the cells follow same local transition function for all time-steps. And, for a temporally hybrid CA, though the transition function of the cells at a particular time maybe same, the global and local transition functions vary over different time-steps.

In this paper, we have considered only synchronous (all the cell states are updated simultaneously) CA where the underlying topology is a one-dimensional grid line which evolves over discrete time-steps [13,14].

Section 1.2 is devoted to fundamental results used in this chapter. In Section 1.3, we report our work on local and global transition function of a hybrid CA. We also discuss evolution patterns of some transition functions of a finite celled homogeneous CA with periodic boundaries which constitute a hybrid CA. Spatially and/or temporally hybrid CA models of some discrete dynamical systems have been designed in Section 1.4.

8.2 Basic Concepts

8.2.1 Cellular Automaton

Cellular Automaton (CA) is a computation model of a dynamical system where the smallest computation unit is a *finite state semi-automaton*. Thus, a CA is a finite dimensional network of finite state semi-automaton [15] known as cells.

The mathematical definition of a finite state semi-automaton is given as:

DEFINITION 1.2.1: *A **Finite State Semi-Automaton** (abbrev. **FSSA**) is a three tuple $A = \{Q, X, \mu\}$, where,*

- *Q is a finite set of memory elements sometimes referred as internal states*
- *X is the input alphabet*
- *$\mu : Q \times X \to Q$, is the rule by which an internal state on encountering an input alphabet changes to another internal state. μ is also called transition function.*

Thus, a CA is a computation model where finite/countably infinite number of cells are arranged in an ordered n-dimensional grid. Each cell receives input from the neighboring cells and changes according to the transition function. The transitions at each of the cells together induces a change of the grid pattern [16].

Here we have considered only synchronous, homogeneous one-dimensional CA. A typical one-dimensional CA is given below (Figure 8.1).

A CA does not have any external input and hence is self-evolving. However, the different possible combinations of the state of a cell at any ith grid point along with the states of its adjacent cells can be considered as inputs for the cell at the ith grid point.

Each cell works synchronously leading to evolution of the entire grid through a number of discrete time steps. If the set of memory elements of each FSSA is $\{0,1\}$, then a typical pattern evolved over time t (represented along horizontal axis) may be as shown in Table 8.1.

A formal definition of a CA [17] is given below:

DEFINITION 1.2.2: *Let Q be a finite set of memory elements; also called the **state set**. The memory elements of the cells belonging to the set Q are placed on an ordered line.*

*A **global configuration** is a mapping from the group of integers $\mathbb{Z}$ to the set Q given by $C: \mathbb{Z} \to Q$.*

The set $Q^{\mathbb{Z}}$ is the set of all global configurations where $Q^{\mathbb{Z}} = \{C | C: \mathbb{Z} \to Q\}$.

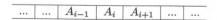

FIGURE 8.1 A typical grid of a one-dimensional CA.

TABLE 8.1

C_t Is the Configuration of the CA (Represented along Vertical Axis) at Time t

Grid Position (i) ↓\ Time →	$t = 0$	$t = 1$	$t = 2$	...
	.	.	.	.
A_{i+2}	0	0	1	...
A_{i+1}	0	1	0	...
A_i	1	0	1	...
A_{i-1}	0	1	0	...
	.	.	.	.
Configuration →	C_0	C_1	C_2	...

> A mapping $\tau: Q^{\mathbb{Z}} \to Q^{\mathbb{Z}}$ is called a **global transition function**.
>
> A **CA** (denoted by $\mathscr{C}_{\tau}^{Q}$) is a triplet $(Q, Q^{\mathbb{Z}}, \tau)$ where Q is the finite state set, $Q^{\mathbb{Z}}$ is the set of all configurations, and τ is the global transition function.

> REMARK 1: *For a particular state set Q and a particular global transition function τ, a triple $(Q, Q^{\mathbb{Z}}, \tau)$ denoted by $\mathscr{C}_{\tau}^{Q}$ defines the set of all possible cellular automata on (Q, τ). However, the evolution of a CA at times is dependent on the initial configuration (starting configuration) of the CA. A particular CA, $\mathscr{C}_{\tau}^{Q}(C_0) \in \mathscr{C}_{\tau}^{Q}$, is defined as the quadruple $(Q, Q^{\mathbb{Z}}, \tau, C_0)$ such that $C_0 \in Q^{\mathbb{Z}}$ is the initial configuration of the particular CA $\mathscr{C}_{\tau}^{Q}(C_0)$.*

At any time t, configuration $C_t \in Q^{\mathbb{Z}}$ and $\tau(C_t) = C_{t+1}$
With reference to Table 8.1,

$$C_0 = .. 001000...; \; \tau(C_0) = \tau(...0100...) = ...1010... = C_1; \; \tau(C_1) = ...0101... = C_2 \text{ etc.}$$

The CA defined above has the same global transition function $\tau: Q^{\mathbb{Z}} \to Q^{\mathbb{Z}}$ for all time t. However, there is a special class of CA called *temporally hybrid CA* where the global transition function varies over time. The formal definition is given with reference to Definition 1.2.2.

> DEFINITION 1.2.3: *A **Temporally Hybrid CA** (denoted by $\mathscr{C}_{\tau_t}^{Q}$) is a triplet $(Q, Q^{\mathbb{Z}}, \{\tau_t\})$ where Q is the finite state set, $Q^{\mathbb{Z}}$ is the set of all configurations, and τ_t is a global transition function.*

Evolution of a CA is mathematically expressed by the global transition function. However, this global transition is induced by transitions of the cells at each grid point of the CA. The transition of the state of the cell at the ith grid point of a CA at a particular time depends on the state of the ith cell $C(i)$ or c_i, and its adjacent cells. These adjacent cells constitute the neighborhood of the ith cell. The transition of the cell at each grid point is called local transition.

> DEFINITION 1.2.4: *For $i \in \mathbb{Z}$, $r \in \mathbb{N}$, let $S_i = \{i - r, ..., i - 1, i, i + 1, ..., i + r\} \subseteq \mathbb{Z}$. S_i is the neighborhood of the ith cell; r is the radius of neighborhood of a cell. It follows that $\mathbb{Z} = \cup_i S_i$.*
>
> A restriction from $\mathbb{Z}$ to S_i induces the following:

1. *Restriction of C to $\bar{c}_i$ is given by $\bar{c}_i: S_i \to Q$; and $\bar{c}_i$ may be called **local configuration** of the ith cell such that $\overline{c_i} = (c_{i-r}, ..., c_i, ..., c_{i+r})$.*
2. *Restriction of $Q^{\mathbb{Z}}$ to Q^{S_i} is given by $Q^{S_i} = \{\overline{c_i} | \overline{c_i}: S_i \to Q\}$; and Q^{S_i} may be called the **set of all local configurations** of the ith cell.*

*The mapping $\mu_i: Q^{S_i} \to Q$ is known as a **local transition function** for the ith automaton having radius r. Thus, $\forall\, i \in \mathbb{Z}, \mu_i(\overline{c_i}) \in Q$. So, if the local configuration of the ith cell at time t is denoted by $\overline{c_i}(t)$ then $\mu_i(\overline{c_i}(t)) = c_i(t+1)$.*

REMARK 2: *If $\tau(C) = C_*$, then $C_*(i) = \tau(C)(i) = \mu_i(\overline{c_i})$. So we have,*

1. $C_{t+1}(i) = \tau(C_t)(i) = \mu_i(\overline{c_i}(t)) = c_i(t+1)$
2. $\tau(C) = \tau(\ldots, c_{i-1}, c_i, c_{i+1}, \ldots) = \ldots \mu_{i-1}(\overline{c_{i-1}}).\, \mu_i(\overline{c_i}).\, \mu_{i+1}(\overline{c_{i+1}})\ldots$
3. *If all $\mu'_i\,s$ are identical, then the CA is **homogeneous**.*
4. At any time, if all $\mu'_i\,s$ are not identical, then the CA is called **spatially hybrid CA**.

DEFINITION 1.2.5: *A configuration $C \in Q^{\mathbb{Z}}$ is **k-celled repetitive block** for some finite $k \in \mathbb{N}$, if $\forall\, i \in \mathbb{Z}$*

$$C(i-k) = C(i) = C(i+k)$$

DEFINITION 1.2.6: *If for a particular CA, $|Q| = 2$ so that we can write $Q = \{0, 1\}$, then the CA is said to be a **binary CA** or a **Boolean CA**.*

DEFINITION 1.2.7: *For a binary CA, $(Q, Q^{\mathbb{Z}}, \tau)$ if $C_1, C_2 \in Q^{\mathbb{Z}}$ such that $\tau(C_1) = C_2$, where*

$$\forall\, i \in \mathbb{Z},\ C_1(i) = 0 \leftrightarrow C_2(i) = 1 \text{ and } C_1(i) = 1 \leftrightarrow C_2(i) = 0$$

*then C_1 is the complement of C_2 and vice versa. τ is said to be the **complement transition function** and is denoted by τ^c.*

DEFINITION 1.2.8: *A local transition function μ is an **identity function** denoted by μ_e if $\forall\, i \in \mathbb{Z}, \mu(\overline{c_i}) = c_i$.*

DEFINITION 1.2.9: *A local transition function μ is an **m-place left shift function** denoted by μ_{Lm} where $m \in \mathbb{N}$ is finite, if the state of the ith automaton c_i shifts m-place leftwards. So, $\forall\, i \in \mathbb{Z}, \mu_{Lm}(\overline{c_i}) = c_{i+m}$.*

DEFINITION 1.2.10: *A local transition function μ is an **m-place right shift function** denoted by μ_{Rm} where $m \in \mathbb{N}$ is finite, if the state of the ith automaton c_i shifts $m - place$ rightwards. So, $\forall\, i \in \mathbb{Z}, \mu_{Rm}(\overline{c_i}) = c_{i-m}$.*

DEFINITION 1.2.11: *A local transition function μ is a **constant function** denoted by μ_q if $\forall\, i \in \mathbb{Z}, \mu(\overline{c_i}) = q$ for a particular state $q \in Q$.*

DEFINITION 1.2.12: *Let a class of CA be given by $(Q, Q^{\mathbb{Z}}, \tau)$. Any global transition function $\tau^{-1} \in (Q^{\mathbb{Z}})^{Q^{\mathbb{Z}}}$ such that for all $C_i, C_j \in Q^{\mathbb{Z}}$,*

$$\tau(C_i) = C_j \Leftrightarrow \tau^{-1}(C_j) = C_i$$

is called the inverse of the global transition function τ.
Consequently, a CA given by $(Q, Q^{\mathbb{Z}}, \tau^{-1})$ is the inverse of the CA $(Q, Q^{\mathbb{Z}}, \tau)$ (see [17,18]).

8.3 Discussions on CA Evolutions

A homogeneous CA is a special case of hybrid CA in which all the cells follow an identical transition function.

In this section, the evolution patterns of some transition functions of homogeneous CA with periodic boundaries have been given [19].

PROPOSITION 1.3.1: *A finite celled homogeneous CA having a global transition function:*

1. τ_e *is stable from the initial step*
2. τ_q *is stable from the initial step or after the first transition step for some* $q \in Q$.

Proof.

1. From definition of τ_e, the result follows.
2. Let $C \in Q^{\mathbb{Z}}$ be such that $C(i) = q \ \forall \ i \in \mathbb{Z}$.

Then $\tau_q(C) = C$ and the CA is stable from the initial step.
Again let $C \in Q^{\mathbb{Z}}$ be such that $C(i) \neq q$ at least for some $i \in \mathbb{Z}$.
Then $\tau_q(C) = C^*$ where $C^*(i) = q \ \forall \ i \in \mathbb{Z}$ and the CA becomes stable after the first step.
Hence the proposition.

PROPOSITION 1.3.2: *An celled homogeneous CA with periodic boundaries evolving under transition function* τ_{Lm} *for some finite* $m \in \mathbb{N}$ *having initial configuration which is not block repetitive is s-periodic for* $s = \frac{n}{gcd\,(m,n)}$ *if* $m < n \in \mathbb{N}$.

Proof. Let an n-celled CA with periodic boundaries have the transition function τ_{Lm} where $m < n$. As the transition pattern continues, the cell states shift m places leftwards at each discrete time step. So, $\forall \ i \in \{1,2,\ldots n\}$,

$$\tau(C(i)) = C(i + m)$$

Let s be the smallest integer such that

$$\tau^s(C(i)) = C(i + sm) = C(i)$$

As n is finite, it will always be possible to find one such s. Since the initial configuration is not block repetitive, the initial configuration reappears at every $s = \frac{n}{gcd\,(m,n)}$ step. Hence the result follows.

PROPOSITION 1.3.3: *A countably inifinite celled or n-celled periodic boundaried homogeneous CA under transition funtion* τ_{Lm} *having k-celled repetitive block configuration for some finite* $m, k \in \mathbb{N}$ *is*

1. s-periodic where
   ◦ $s = \frac{k}{gcd\,(m,k)}$ if $m < k < n$
   ◦ $s = \frac{k}{gcd\,(m-k,k)}$ if $k < m < n$
2. stationary from initial step if $m = k < n$.

Proof. A homogeneous CA with k-celled repetitive block configuration for some finite $k \in \mathbb{N}$ can be treated as a k-celled CA with periodic boundaries having initial configuration that is not block repetitive.

1. Thus, under τ_{Lm}, the initial configuration reappears at every
   - $s = \dfrac{k}{gcd\,(m,k)}$ step if $m < k < n$
   - $s = \dfrac{k}{gcd\,(m-k,k)}$ step if $k < m < n$

2. Again, if $m = k < n$, then since the cell states shift k places leftwards at every discrete time step, the initial configuration remains stationary always.

Hence the result follows.

> REMARK 3: *Similar evolution patterns of a homogeneous CA under transition function τ_{Rm} for some finite $m \in \mathbb{N}$ can be obtained where the cell states shift m places rightwards at each discrete time step.*

8.3.1 Relation between Local and Global Transition Function of a Spatially Hybrid CA

> DEFINITION 1.3.1: *A spatially hybrid CA can be visualized to be composed of countable celled blocks where each block has a different local transition function and within any block all the cells follow the same local transition function such that each block behaves as a homogeneous CA.*

Here it is assumed that homogeneous blocks have periodic boundaries and the evolution of the blocks are independent of each other. Hence, the leftmost cell and the rightmost cell of each block are considered to be neighbors. The evolution of the hybrid CA globally depends on the evolution of the composing homogeneous blocks.

> PROPOSITION 1.3.4: *If the global transition function (τ) of a finite-celled hybrid CA with periodic boundaries composed of finite blocks is invertible, then the local transition function (μ_i) of the cells will be invertible.*
>
> *Proof.* We know that $\forall\, i \in \mathbb{Z}$, $C(i) = c_i$ and $\tau(C)(i) = \mu_i(\overline{c_i})$. If τ is invertible, then
>
> $$\tau^{-1}(\tau(C)(i)) = C(i) = c_i$$
>
> Therefore, $\exists\, \mu_i'$ such that $\forall\, i \in \mathbb{Z}$, $\mu_i'(\mu_i(\overline{c_i})) = c_i$.
> Hence the proposition follows.

> REMARK 4: *However, the converse may not be true and is justified by the following example.*

> EXAMPLE 1.3.1: ***Let us consider a hybrid CA with periodic boundaries with an initial configuration*** $C_0 = \overbrace{1010}^{B_1}\overbrace{010}^{B_2}$ *such that cells of block B_1 follow μ_{R1} and cells of B_2 follow μ_{L1}.*
>
> *Now $(\mu_{R1})^{-1} = \mu_{L1}$. But for the cells of block B_1, $\mu_{L1}(\mu_{R1}(\overline{c_i}))$ give $\overbrace{1011}^{B_1}$ and not $\overbrace{1010}^{B_1}$. Hence the CA is not invertible globally and the result follows.*

8.4 CA Modeling of Dynamical Systems

In this section, one-dimensional hybrid CA models of discrete dynamical systems representing various physical phenomena have been obtained. Let a one-dimensional linear dynamical system be represented by a first-order difference equation in variable y.

The state of the system at time $t + 1$ denoted by y_{t+1} depends on its state at the previous time step denoted by y_t and the initial configuration.

If state y_t corresponds to configuration C_t, state y_{t+1} corresponds to configuration C_{t+1} and the global transition function is τ, then

$$y_{t+1} = f(y_t) \Leftrightarrow C_{t+1} = \tau(C_t)$$

Since, $C_t \equiv (..., c_{i-2}(t), c_{i-1}(t), c_i(t), c_{i+1}(t), c_{i+2}(t), ...)$, $\forall\ i \in \mathbb{Z}$, at any particular time t, the ith cell A_i corresponds to state $c_i(t)$.

Some examples of one-dimensional discrete dynamical systems and their corresponding CA models have been depicted here.

We will restrict ourselves to the following three types of synchronous hybrid CA.

1. Spatially Hybrid CA composed of finite celled blocks of homogeneous CA which are independent of time.
2. Temporally Hybrid CA composed of countable cells evolve homogeneously for blocks of finite time intervals.
3. Hybrid CA are spatial as well as temporal in nature.

8.4.1 Spatially Hybrid CA Models

Let y_t denote the dynamical system at a particular time t.

For a spatially hybrid CA, composed of a finite number of cells $A_0, ... , A_n$, the configuration C_t at a particular time t, is

$$C_t \equiv (c_0(t), ..., c_n(t))$$

such that for $i = 0, 1, ..., n$, $c_i(t)$ is the state of the ith cell A_i at time t.

Here, the evolution of the system is independent of time and the transition function of different blocks of cells are different. Thus at any time,

$$C_{t+1} = \tau(C_t) \equiv (\mu_0(\overline{c_0}(t)), ..., \mu_i(\overline{c_i}(t)), ..., \mu_n(\overline{c_n}(t)))$$

If at a time the configuration consists of k homogeneous blocks of periods $p_1, ... \ p_k$, then the dynamical system will also be periodic with period $p = lcm(p_1, p_2 ... p_k)$.

Example 8.1: Evolution of a Binary Data Sequence Modeled by a Spatially Hybrid CA

Let y_t denote a binary data sequence of finite length at a particular time t. Each bit of this binary sequence corresponds to a cell of the CA such that the ith bit is represented by the state of the cell A_i. Let a binary sequence of length $32 - bits$ initially be

$$'11010011010101101111101100010110'$$

Let this sequence be composed of 4 blocks as follows:
Block I of length 9-bits follows 3-place right shift transition μ_{R3};
Block II of length 5-bits follows 2-place left shift transition μ_{L2};

Block III of length 8-bits follows identity transition μ_e;
Block IV of length 10-bits follows 5-place right shift transition μ_{R5}.

$$\underbrace{110100110}_{\mu_{R3}}\overset{\textit{BlockI}}{} \underbrace{10101}_{\mu_{L2}}\overset{\textit{BlockII}}{} \underbrace{10111110}_{\mu_e}\overset{\textit{BlockIII}}{} \underbrace{1100010110}_{\mu_{R5}}\overset{\textit{BlockIV}}{}$$

Clearly, Block I is periodic with $\frac{9}{gcd(3,9)}$ period, i.e., 3-period.

Block II is periodic with $\frac{5}{gcd(2,5)}$ period, i.e., 5-period.

Block III is stable from the initial step, i.e., 1-period.

Block IV is periodic with $\frac{10}{gcd(5,10)}$ period, i.e., 2-period.

Thus, the 32-bit sequence is globally periodic with $lcm(3, 5, 1, 2)$ period, i.e., 30-period.

A spatially hybrid CA model of the data sequence is shown in Table 8.2.

Example 8.2: Evolution of a DNA Sequence Modeled by a Spatially Hybrid CA

Let y_t denote a DNA sequence of finite length at a particular time t. Each nucleotide of the DNA sequence corresponds to a cell of the CA [20]. The 4 bases *Adenine, Cytosine, Guanine, and Thymine* represented by A, C, G, and T, respectively, correspond to the 4 possible states of a CA cell. Let a DNA sequence of length 33 initially be

$$'ATGGAGAGCCTTGTCCCTGGTTTCAACGAGATC'$$

Let this sequence be composed of 2 blocks as follows:

Block I of length 30-bases, follows 2-place right shift transition μ_{R2}. Therefore, at each time step, the bases of cells A_1 to A_{28} shift 2 places rightwards and the bases of the cells A_{29} and A_{30} are acquired by the first 2 cells A_1 and A_2, respectively.

Clearly, Block I is periodic with $\frac{30}{gcd(2,30)}$ period, i.e., 15-period.

Block II of length 3-bases follows identity transition μ_e. Therefore, the bases of cells A_{31}, A_{32}, and A_{33} remain the same throughout.

Thus, for the given DNA sequence of 33 bases, the initial configuration reappears after 15 time steps.

$$\underbrace{ATGGAGAGCCTTGTCCCTGGTTTCAACGAG}_{\mu_{R2}}\overset{\textit{BlockI}}{} \underbrace{ATC}_{\mu_e}\overset{\textit{BlockII}}{}$$

A spatially hybrid CA model of the evolution of the DNA sequence is shown in Table 8.3.

8.4.2 Temporally Hybrid CA Models

Let y_t denote the dynamical system at a particular time t.

For a temporally hybrid CA, composed of a finite number of cells A_0, ..., A_n, the configuration C_t at a particular time t, is

$$C_t \equiv (c_0(t), \ ..., c_n(t))$$

such that for $i=0, 1, ..., n$, $c_i(t)$ is the state of the ith cell A_i at time t.

Here, the evolution of the system is time-dependent and all the cells at a particular time t follow the same transition function $\mu^{(t)}$. Thus at time t,

TABLE 8.2

Evolution of Binary Data Sequence

Time	Block I	Block II	Block III	Block IV
$\downarrow$	$A_1 \ldots A_5 \ldots A_9$	$A_{10} \ldots A_{14}$	$A_{15} \ldots A_{18} \ldots A_{22}$	$A_{23} \ldots A_{28} \ldots A_{32}$
$t = 0$	1 1 0 1 0 0 1 1 0	1 0 1 0 1	1 0 1 1 1 1 1 0	1 1 0 0 0 1 0 1 1 0
$t = 1$	1 1 0 1 1 0 1 0 0	1 0 1 1 0	1 0 1 1 1 1 1 0	1 0 1 1 0 1 1 0 0 0
$t = 2$	1 0 0 1 1 0 1 1 0	1 1 0 1 0	1 0 1 1 1 1 1 0	1 1 0 0 0 1 0 1 1 0
$t = 3$	1 1 0 1 0 0 1 1 0	0 1 0 1 1	1 0 1 1 1 1 1 0	1 0 1 1 0 1 1 0 0 0
$t = 4$	1 1 0 1 1 0 1 0 0	0 1 1 0 1	1 0 1 1 1 1 1 0	1 1 0 0 0 1 0 1 1 0
$t = 5$	1 0 0 1 1 0 1 1 0	1 0 1 0 1	1 0 1 1 1 1 1 0	1 0 1 1 0 1 1 0 0 0
$t = 6$	1 1 0 1 0 0 1 1 0	1 0 1 1 0	1 0 1 1 1 1 1 0	1 1 0 0 0 1 0 1 1 0
$t = 7$	1 1 0 1 1 0 1 0 0	1 1 0 1 0	1 0 1 1 1 1 1 0	1 0 1 1 0 1 1 0 0 0
$t = 8$	1 0 0 1 1 0 1 1 0	0 1 0 1 1	1 0 1 1 1 1 1 0	1 1 0 0 0 1 0 1 1 0
$t = 9$	1 1 0 1 0 0 1 1 0	0 1 1 0 1	1 0 1 1 1 1 1 0	1 0 1 1 0 1 1 0 0 0
$t = 10$	1 1 0 1 1 0 1 0 0	1 0 1 0 1	1 0 1 1 1 1 1 0	1 1 0 0 0 1 0 1 1 0
$t = 11$	1 0 0 1 1 0 1 1 0	1 0 1 1 0	1 0 1 1 1 1 1 0	1 0 1 1 0 1 1 0 0 0
$t = 12$	1 1 0 1 0 0 1 1 0	1 1 0 1 0	1 0 1 1 1 1 1 0	1 1 0 0 0 1 0 1 1 0
$t = 13$	1 1 0 1 1 0 1 0 0	0 1 0 1 1	1 0 1 1 1 1 1 0	1 0 1 1 0 1 1 0 0 0
$t = 14$	1 0 0 1 1 0 1 1 0	0 1 1 0 1	1 0 1 1 1 1 1 0	1 1 0 0 0 1 0 1 1 0
$t = 15$	1 1 0 1 0 0 1 1 0	1 0 1 0 1	1 0 1 1 1 1 1 0	1 0 1 1 0 1 1 0 0 0
$t = 16$	1 1 0 1 1 0 1 0 0	1 0 1 1 0	1 0 1 1 1 1 1 0	1 1 0 0 0 1 0 1 1 0
$t = 17$	1 0 0 1 1 0 1 1 0	1 1 0 1 0	1 0 1 1 1 1 1 0	1 0 1 1 0 1 1 0 0 0
$t = 18$	1 1 0 1 0 0 1 1 0	0 1 0 1 1	1 0 1 1 1 1 1 0	1 1 0 0 0 1 0 1 1 0
$t = 19$	1 1 0 1 1 0 1 0 0	0 1 1 0 1	1 0 1 1 1 1 1 0	1 0 1 1 0 1 1 0 0 0
$t = 20$	1 0 0 1 1 0 1 1 0	1 0 1 0 1	1 0 1 1 1 1 1 0	1 1 0 0 0 1 0 1 1 0
$t = 21$	1 1 0 1 0 0 1 1 0	1 0 1 1 0	1 0 1 1 1 1 1 0	1 0 1 1 0 1 1 0 0 0
$t = 22$	1 1 0 1 1 0 1 0 0	1 1 0 1 0	1 0 1 1 1 1 1 0	1 1 0 0 0 1 0 1 1 0
$t = 23$	1 0 0 1 1 0 1 1 0	0 1 0 1 1	1 0 1 1 1 1 1 0	1 0 1 1 0 1 1 0 0 0
$t = 24$	1 1 0 1 0 0 1 1 0	0 1 1 0 1	1 0 1 1 1 1 1 0	1 1 0 0 0 1 0 1 1 0
$t = 25$	1 1 0 1 1 0 1 0 0	1 0 1 0 1	1 0 1 1 1 1 1 0	1 0 1 1 0 1 1 0 0 0
$t = 26$	1 0 0 1 1 0 1 1 0	1 0 1 1 0	1 0 1 1 1 1 1 0	1 1 0 0 0 1 0 1 1 0
$t = 27$	1 1 0 1 0 0 1 1 0	1 1 0 1 0	1 0 1 1 1 1 1 0	1 0 1 1 0 1 1 0 0 0
$t = 28$	1 1 0 1 1 0 1 0 0	0 1 0 1 1	1 0 1 1 1 1 1 0	1 1 0 0 0 1 0 1 1 0
$t = 29$	1 0 0 1 1 0 1 1 0	0 1 1 0 1	1 0 1 1 1 1 1 0	1 0 1 1 0 1 1 0 0 0
$t = 30$	1 1 0 1 0 0 1 1 0	1 0 1 0 1	1 0 1 1 1 1 1 0	1 1 0 0 0 1 0 1 1 0

$$C_{t+1} = \tau^{(t)}(C_t) \equiv \left(\mu^{(t)}(\overline{c_0}(t)), \ldots, \mu^{(t)}(\overline{c_i}(t)), \ldots, \mu^{(t)}(\overline{c_n}(t))\right)$$

However at a different time $t*$ the transition function of the cells changes to $\mu^{(t*)}$. Thus at time $t*$,

$$C_{t*+1} = \tau^{(t*)}(C_{t*}) \equiv \left(\mu^{(t*)}(\overline{c_0}(t*)), \ldots, \mu^{(t*)}(\overline{c_i}(t*)), \ldots, \mu^{(t*)}(\overline{c_n}(t*))\right)$$

Example 8.3: Trajectory of an Elevator in a Multi-Story Building Modeled by a Temporally Hybrid CA

Let y_t denote the position of the elevator at a particular time t. Each floor of the building corresponds to a cell of the CA. If at time t, the elevator is at the pth floor, then the state $c_p(t)$ of cell A_p will be **1**, while states of other cells at time t will be 0.

TABLE 8.3

Evolution of a DNA Sequence

Time	Block I	Block II
↓	$A_1 \ldots A_4 \ldots A_7 \ldots A_{10} \ldots A_{13} \ldots A_{16} \ldots A_{19} \ldots A_{22} \ldots A_{25} \ldots A_{28} \ldots A_{30}$	$A_{31} \ldots A_{33}$
$t=0$	A T G G A G A G C C T T G T C C C T G G T T T C A A C G A G	A T C
$t=1$	A G A T G G A G A G C C T T G T C C C T G G T T T C A A C G	A T C
$t=2$	C G A G A T G G A G A G C C T T G T C C C T G G T T T C A A	A T C
$t=3$	A A C G A G A T G G A G A G C C T T G T C C C T G G T T T C	A T C
$t=4$	T C A A C G A G A T G G A G A G C C T T G T C C C T G G T T	A T C
$t=5$	T T T C A A C G A G A T G G A G A G C C T T G T C C C T G G	A T C
$t=6$	G G T T T C A A C G A G A T G G A G A G C C T T G T C C C T	A T C
$t=7$	C T G G T T T C A A C G A G A T G G A G A G C C T T G T C C	A T C
$t=8$	C C C T G G T T T C A A C G A G A T G G A G A G C C T T G T	A T C
$t=9$	G T C C C T G G T T T C A A C G A G A T G G A G A G C C T T	A T C
$t=10$	T T G T C C C T G G T T T C A A C G A G A T G G A G A G C C	A T C
$t=11$	C C T T G T C C C T G G T T T C A A C G A G A T G G A G A G	A T C
$t=12$	A G C C T T G T C C C T G G T T T C A A C G A G A T G G A G	A T C
$t=13$	A G A G C C T T G T C C C T G G T T T C A A C G A G A T G G	A T C
$t=14$	G G A G A G C C T T G T C C C T G G T T T C A A C G A G A T	A T C
$t=15$	A T G G A G A G C C T T G T C C C T G G T T T C A A C G A G	A T C
⋮	⋱	⋮

Let a trajectory followed by the elevator starting from any floor and returning to that floor of an n-storey building be given as follows:

Initially the elevator is at the ith floor. During the journey, the elevator stops at each floor it passes. From the ith floor it travels up to the kth floor in m_1 time steps. At the kth floor it waits until time m_2 and then it comes down to the jth floor at time m_3. It further goes up to the lth floor at time m_4 and it comes down to the ith floor at time m_5, where $0 \le i < j < k < l \le n$ and $0 < m_1 < m_2 < m_3 < m_4 < m_5$.

This trajectory is modeled by a temporally hybrid CA with cells A_0, ..., A_n as follows: Initially cell A_i is at state 1.

For $t = 0, \ldots, m_1 - 1$, the CA follows 1-place right shift transition μ_{R1}.

For $t = m_1, \ldots, m_2 - 1$, the CA follows identity transition μ_e.

For $t = m_2, \ldots, m_3 - 1$, the CA follows 1-place left shift transition μ_{L1}.

For $t = m_3, \ldots, m_4 - 1$, the CA follows 1-place right shift transition μ_{R1}.

For $t = m_4, \ldots, m_5 - 1$, the CA follows 1-place left shift transition μ_{L1}.

A temporally hybrid CA model of the elevator's trajectory is shown in Table 8.4.

Example 8.4: Pattern of the Daily Number of COVID-19 Active Cases in India during the Month of September 2020 (as given in [21] Modeled by a Temporally Hybrid CA)

Let y_t denote the number of COVID-19 active cases on a particular day t. Each cell of the CA corresponds to a range of 10000 active cases.

Thus, cell A_0 corresponds to 0 − 9999 active cases, cell A_1 corresponds to 10000 − 19999 active cases, cell A_2 corresponds to 20000 − 29999 active cases, and so on.

On any particular day t, the number of active cases is reflected by its corresponding cell being in state **1**, while other cells having state 0 at day t.

TABLE 8.4

Trajectory of an Elevator in a Building

Time ↓	A_0	⋯	A_{i-1}		A_{i+1}	⋯	A_j	⋯	A_k	⋯	A_l	⋯	A_n
$t=0$	0	…	0	1	0	…	0	…	0	…	0	…	0
$t=1$	0	…	0	0	1	0	0	…	0	…	0	…	0
⋮	⋮	…	⋮		…	⋱	⋮	…	⋮	…	⋮	…	⋮
$t = m_1$	0	…		0	…	…	…	0	1	0	…	…	0
⋮	⋮	…		⋮	…	…	…	⋮	⋮	⋮	…	…	⋮
$t = m_2$	0	…		0	…	…	…	0	1	0	…	…	0
	0	…		0	…	…	…	1	0	0	…	…	0
	0	…		0	…	…	…		0		…	…	0
$t = m_3$	⋮	…		⋮	…	…	1	0	⋮	⋮	…	…	⋮
	0	…		0	…	…	0	1	0	0	…	…	0
	0	…		0	…	…	0	⋱	0	…	…		0
$t = m_4$	0	…		0	…	…	0	⋮	0	1	0	0	
	0	…		0	…	…	0	1	0	…	0		
	0	…		0	…	1	0	…	…	0	…		0
$t = m_5 - 1$	0	…		0	1	0	0	…	0	…	…	…	0
$t = m_5$	0	…	0	1	0	…	…	…	…	…	…	…	0

According to [21], the number of active cases on August 31st is 785127 and on September 1st is 800127. Thus, 785127 corresponds to cell A_{78} and 800127 corresponds to cell A_{80}.

If August 31st is considered to be day 0, then on day 0, cell A_{78} will have state **1** and other cells state 0. Clearly, the transition function of this CA on day 0 is 2-place right shift transition μ_{R2}, since on day 1, cell A_{80} acquires state **1** and all other cells state 0.

The number of active cases in India (from [21]) during the month of September 2020 has been given in Table 8.5.

Therefore the pattern of the active cases during September 2020 can be reflected between cells A_{78} and A_{102} of the temporally hybrid CA, as shown in Table 8.6.

> REMARK 5: *This model can also be used for modeling a continuous data set by a CA when the data can be subdivided into intervals and the dynamical system is such that the intervals evolve over time [22].*

8.4.3 Spatially and Temporally Hybrid CA Models

Let y_t denote the dynamical system at a particular time t.

For a spatially and temporally hybrid CA, composed of finite number of cells $A_0, \ldots, A_n$, the configuration C_t at a particular time t, is

$$C_t \equiv (c_0(t), \ldots, c_n(t))$$

such that for $i = 0, 1, \ldots, n$, $c_i(t)$ is the state of the ith cell A_i at time t.

Here the evolution of the system is independent of time and at a particular time t different blocks of cells follow a different transition function. Thus at time t,

TABLE 8.5

Number of COVID-19 Active Cases in India during September 2020

Date ↓	No. of Active Cases	Cell Having State 1	Transition Function
31/08/2020 (Day 0)	785127	A_{78}	μ_{R2}
01/09/2020 (Day 1)	800127	A_{80}	μ_{R1}
02/09/2020 (Day 2)	814086	A_{81}	μ_{R1}
03/09/2020 (Day 3)	829668	A_{82}	μ_{R2}
04/09/2020 (Day 4)	846092	A_{84}	μ_{R2}
05/09/2020 (Day 5)	862487	A_{86}	μ_{R2}
06/09/2020 (Day 6)	883578	A_{88}	μ_e
07/09/2020 (Day 7)	883348	A_{88}	μ_{R1}
08/09/2020 (Day 8)	897486	A_{89}	μ_{R2}
09/09/2020 (Day 9)	918790	A_{91}	μ_{R3}
10/10/2020 (Day 10)	943438	A_{94}	μ_{R1}
11/09/2020 (Day 11)	958435	A_{95}	μ_{R2}
12/09/2020 (Day 12)	973876	A_{97}	μ_{R1}
13/09/2020 (Day 13)	988205	A_{98}	μ_e
14/09/2020 (Day 14)	989860	A_{98}	μ_{R1}
15/09/2020 (Day 15)	996832	A_{99}	μ_{R2}
16/09/2020 (Day 16)	1010614	A_{101}	μ_e
17/09/2020 (Day 17)	1018454	A_{101}	μ_e
18/09/2020 (Day 18)	1014649	A_{101}	μ_e
19/09/2020 (Day 19)	1011732	A_{101}	μ_{L1}
20/09/2020 (Day 20)	1005053	A_{100}	μ_{L3}
21/09/2020 (Day 21)	976420	A_{97}	μ_{L1}
22/09/2020 (Day 22)	968655	A_{96}	μ_e
23/09/2020 (Day 23)	967161	A_{96}	μ_{R1}
24/09/2020 (Day 24)	970795	A_{97}	μ_{L1}
25/09/2020 (Day 25)	961993	A_{96}	μ_{L1}
26/09/2020 (Day 26)	957359	A_{95}	μ_{R1}
27/09/2020 (Day 27)	964407	A_{96}	μ_{L2}
28/09/2020 (Day 28)	948095	A_{94}	μ_e
29/09/2020 (Day 29)	941356	A_{94}	μ_e
30/09/2020 (Day 30)	941552	A_{94}	—

$$C_{t+1} = \tau^{(t)}(C_t) \equiv (\mu_0^{(t)}(\overline{c_0}(t)), ..., \mu_i^{(t)}(\overline{c_i}(t)), ..., \mu_n^{(t)}(\overline{c_n}(t)))$$

Moreover, at a different time $t*$ the transition function of the cells also changes. Thus at time $t*$,

$$C_{t*+1} = \tau^{(t*)}(C_{t*}) \equiv \left(\mu_0^{(t*)}(\overline{c_0}(t*)), ..., \mu_i^{(t*)}(\overline{c_i}(t*)), ..., \mu_n^{(t*)}(\overline{c_n}(t*))\right)$$

Example 8.5: Signaling System of a Toll Plaza Consisting of a Finite Row of Toll Booths, Modeled by a Hybrid CA

Let y_t denote the signaling configurations (also see [23]) of the entire row of tollbooths at a particular time t. Each tollbooth corresponds to a cell of the CA. Let the tollbooths be in one of the

TABLE 8.6

Pattern of COVID-19 Active Cases in India during September 2020

Date ↓	$...A_{77}A_{78}$ ... ... $A_{101}A_{102}...$
31/08/2020 (Day 0)	...0 1 0 0 0 0 0 0 0 0 0 0 0 0 0 0 0 0 0 0 0 0 0 0 0 ...
01/09/2020 (Day 1)	...0 0 0 1 0 0 0 0 0 0 0 0 0 0 0 0 0 0 0 0 0 0 0 0 0 ...
02/09/2020 (Day 2)	...0 0 0 0 1 0 0 0 0 0 0 0 0 0 0 0 0 0 0 0 0 0 0 0 0 ...
03/09/2020 (Day 3)	...0 0 0 0 0 1 0 0 0 0 0 0 0 0 0 0 0 0 0 0 0 0 0 0 0 ...
04/09/2020 (Day 4)	...0 0 0 0 0 0 0 1 0 0 0 0 0 0 0 0 0 0 0 0 0 0 0 0 0 ...
05/09/2020 (Day 5)	...0 0 0 0 0 0 0 0 0 1 0 0 0 0 0 0 0 0 0 0 0 0 0 0 0 ...
06/09/2020 (Day 6)	...0 0 0 0 0 0 0 0 0 0 1 0 0 0 0 0 0 0 0 0 0 0 0 0 0 ...
07/09/2020 (Day 7)	...0 0 0 0 0 0 0 0 0 0 1 0 0 0 0 0 0 0 0 0 0 0 0 0 0 ...
08/09/2020 (Day 8)	...0 0 0 0 0 0 0 0 0 0 0 1 0 0 0 0 0 0 0 0 0 0 0 0 0 ...
09/09/2020 (Day 9)	...0 0 0 0 0 0 0 0 0 0 0 0 0 1 0 0 0 0 0 0 0 0 0 0 0 ...
10/10/2020 (Day 10)	...0 0 0 0 0 0 0 0 0 0 0 0 0 0 0 1 0 0 0 0 0 0 0 0 0 ...
11/09/2020 (Day 11)	...0 0 0 0 0 0 0 0 0 0 0 0 0 0 0 0 1 0 0 0 0 0 0 0 0 ...
12/09/2020 (Day 12)	...0 0 0 0 0 0 0 0 0 0 0 0 0 0 0 0 0 0 1 0 0 0 0 0 0 ...
13/09/2020 (Day 13)	...0 0 0 0 0 0 0 0 0 0 0 0 0 0 0 0 0 0 0 1 0 0 0 0 0 ...
14/09/2020 (Day 14)	...0 0 0 0 0 0 0 0 0 0 0 0 0 0 0 0 0 0 0 1 0 0 0 0 0 ...
15/09/2020 (Day 15)	...0 0 0 0 0 0 0 0 0 0 0 0 0 0 0 0 0 0 0 0 1 0 0 0 0 ...
16/09/2020 (Day 16)	...0 0 0 0 0 0 0 0 0 0 0 0 0 0 0 0 0 0 0 0 0 0 1 0 0 ...
17/09/2020 (Day 17)	...0 0 0 0 0 0 0 0 0 0 0 0 0 0 0 0 0 0 0 0 0 0 1 0 0 ...
18/09/2020 (Day 18)	...0 0 0 0 0 0 0 0 0 0 0 0 0 0 0 0 0 0 0 0 0 0 1 0 0 ...
19/09/2020 (Day 19)	...0 0 0 0 0 0 0 0 0 0 0 0 0 0 0 0 0 0 0 0 0 0 1 0 0 ...
20/09/2020 (Day 20)	...0 0 0 0 0 0 0 0 0 0 0 0 0 0 0 0 0 0 0 0 1 0 0 0 0 ...
21/09/2020 (Day 21)	...0 0 0 0 0 0 0 0 0 0 0 0 0 0 0 0 1 0 0 0 0 0 0 0 0 ...
22/09/2020 (Day 22)	...0 0 0 0 0 0 0 0 0 0 0 0 0 0 0 1 0 0 0 0 0 0 0 0 0 ...
23/09/2020 (Day 23)	...0 0 0 0 0 0 0 0 0 0 0 0 0 0 0 1 0 0 0 0 0 0 0 0 0 ...
24/09/2020 (Day 24)	...0 0 0 0 0 0 0 0 0 0 0 0 0 0 0 0 1 0 0 0 0 0 0 0 0 ...
25/09/2020 (Day 25)	...0 0 0 0 0 0 0 0 0 0 0 0 0 0 0 0 1 0 0 0 0 0 0 0 0 ...
26/09/2020 (Day 26)	...0 0 0 0 0 0 0 0 0 0 0 0 0 0 0 1 0 0 0 0 0 0 0 0 0 ...
27/09/2020 (Day 27)	...0 0 0 0 0 0 0 0 0 0 0 0 0 0 0 1 0 0 0 0 0 0 0 0 0 ...
28/09/2020 (Day 28)	...0 0 0 0 0 0 0 0 0 0 0 0 0 0 1 0 0 0 0 0 0 0 0 0 0 ...
29/09/2020 (Day 29)	...0 0 0 0 0 0 0 0 0 0 0 0 0 1 0 0 0 0 0 0 0 0 0 0 0 ...
30/09/2020 (Day 30)	...0 0 0 0 0 0 0 0 0 0 0 0 0 1 0 0 0 0 0 0 0 0 0 0 0 ...

three signals red (denoted by R), yellow (denoted by Y), or green (denoted by G), representing Stop, Pay the toll, or Go states, respectively. At time t, the state of the signal of the ith tollbooth, corresponds to the state $c_i(t)$ of cell A_i.

The toll plaza consists of a row of 11 tollbooths initially has the signal sequence

$$R \ Y \ R \ Y \ Y \ R \ Y \ Y \ R \ R \ Y$$

At the next time step, the signal sequence changes to

$$R \ G \ R \ Y \ G \ R \ Y \ Y \ R \ R \ G$$

The entire row of tollbooths is assumed to be composed of 3 blocks with 1, 6, and 4 tollbooths as follows:

$$\overbrace{\underset{\sim}{R}}^{BlockI} \overbrace{G\ R\ Y\ G\ R\ Y}^{BlockII} \overbrace{Y\ R\ R\ G}^{BlockIII}$$

Let the configuration of the toll plaza be such that tollbooth 1 is reserved for ambulances and VIPs. Tollbooths 2 to 6 are kept for light vehicles and tollbooths 7 to 10 are for heavy vehicles. The signal of tollbooth 1 is usually red and it changes to green whenever an ambulance or VIP's vehicle passes through it. At that time, say jth time, all the other tollbooths change to the red signal to restrict general vehicular movement temporarily and ensure smooth movement of ambulances and VIPs. Again from the next time step $(j + 1)$, the initial configuration is restored.

Let a signaling system of the toll plaza be given as follows:

From time $t = 1$, Block I with 1 tollbooth follows identity transition μ_e;

Block II with 6 tollbooths follows 1-place left shift transition μ_{L1};

Block III with 4 tollbooths follows 1-place right shift transition μ_{R1}.

At time $t = j$, when an ambulance or VIP vehicle arrives, the CA follows constant transition such that, Block I has green signal i.e., cell A_1 has state G;

Block II and III have red signals i.e., cells A_2, ..., A_{10} have state R.

At time $t = j + 1$, the CA makes a transition to the initial configuration.

Henceforth the CA follows similar transition function as that for $t = 0$ to $t = j - 1$, until an ambulance or VIP vehicle arrives.

This signaling system is modeled by a hybrid CA, as shown in Table 8.7.

TABLE 8.7

Toll Plaza Signaling

Time ↓	Block I A_1	Block II $A_2A_3A_4A_5A_6A_7$	Block III $A_8A_9A_{10}A_{11}$
$t = 0$	R	Y R Y Y R Y	Y R R Y
$t = 1$	R	G R Y G R Y	Y R R G
$t = 2$	R	R Y G R Y G	G Y R R
$t = 3$	R	Y G R Y G R	R G Y R
$t = 4$	R	G R Y G R Y	R R G Y
$t = 5$	R	R Y G R Y G	Y R R G
$t = 6$	R	Y G R Y G R	G Y R R
$t = 7$	R	G R Y G R Y	R G Y R
$t = 8$	R	R Y G R Y G	R R G Y
$t = 9$	R	Y G R Y G R	Y R R G
$t = 10$	R	G R Y G R Y	G Y R R
$t = 11$	R	R Y G R Y G	R G Y R
$t = 12$	R	Y G R Y G R	R R G Y
$t = 13$	R	G R Y G R Y	Y R R G
$t = 14$	R	R Y G R Y G	G Y R R
⋮	⋮	⋮	⋮
$t = j$	G	R R R R R R	R R R R
$t = j+1$	R	Y R Y Y R Y	Y R R Y
$t = j+2$	R	G R Y G R Y	Y R R G
⋮	⋮	⋮	⋮

8.5 Conclusion

In this chapter, we have visualized a hybrid CA to be composed of finite blocks of homogeneous CA with periodic boundaries.

Evolution of binary data sequence and DNA sequence have been represented by spatially hybrid CA. Trajectory of an elevator in a building and the pattern of daily numbers of active COVID-19 cases over a month have been represented by a temporally hybrid CA. Again, a hybrid CA that is spatial as well as temporal have been used to model a signaling system at a toll plaza.

Designing CA models of two-dimensional dynamical systems may be worth attempting.

REFERENCES

[1] Meiss J. D.: *Discrete Dynamical Systems*, Dept. of Applied Maths, University of Colorado (Nov. 2008).

[2] Tabrizian P.: *Shifts as Dynamical Systems*, Expository paper, University of California, Berkeley (Dec. 2010).

[3] Knutson J. D.: *A survey of the use of cellular automata and cellular automata-like models for simulating a population of biological cells* (2011), Graduate Theses and Dissertations, Iowa State University, Paper 10133.

[4] Banks: *Cellular Automata. AI Memo 198*, MIT Artificial Intelligence Laboratory, Cambridge, MA (1970).

[5] Neumann J. von: *Theory of Self-Reproducing Automata*, University of Illinois Press, Illinois (1966). Edited and completed by A. W. Burks.

[6] Ulam S. M.: On some mathematical problems connected with patterns of growth of figures; *Proc. Symp. Appl Math., Amer. Math. Soc.* 14, 215–224 (1962).

[7] Wolfram Stephen: *Theory and Applications of Cellular Automata*, World Scientific, Singapore (1986).

[8] Wolfram S.: *A New Kind of Science*, Wolfram Media (2002).

[9] Burks A.: *Essays on Cellular Automata*, Univ. of Illinois Press (1970).

[10] Codd: *Cellular Automata*, Academic Press, New York (1968).

[11] Ilachinski Andrew: Cellular Automata, a Discrete Universe (2001).

[12] Schiff Joel L.: *Cellular Automata – A Discrete View of the World*, John Wiley and Sons (2008).

[13] Ghosh S., Basu S.: Evolution patterns of some boolean cellular automata having atmost one active cell to model simple dynamical systems, *Bulletin of the Calcutta Mathematical Society* 108 (6): 449–464 (2016).

[14] Ghosh S., Basu S.: Evolution patterns of finite celled synchronous cellular automata having atmost one active cell, Proceedings of The 10th International Conference MSAST 2016, pp. 154–164 (Dec. 2016).

[15] Hopcroft, Ullman: *Introduction to Automata Theory, Languages, and Computation*, Addison-Wesley (1979).

[16] Kari J.: Theory of cellular automata: A survey. *Theoretical Computer Science* 334, 3–33 (2005).

[17] Ghosh S., Basu S.: Some algebraic properties of linear synchronous cellular automata, arXiv:1708.09751v1 [nlin CG] (30 Aug. 2017).

[18] Liberti Leo: Structure of the invertible CA transformations group. *Journal of Computer and System Sciences* 59: 521–536 (1999).

[19] Ghosh S.: Evolutions of some one-dimensional homogeneous cellular automata, *Complex Systems*. 30(1), 75–92 (2021). https://doi.org/10.25088/ComplexSystems.30.1.75.

[20] Mizas C., Sirakoulis G. C., Mardiris V. et al.: Reconstruction of DNA sequences using genetic algorithms and cellular automata: Towards mutation prediction? *BioSystems* 92, 61–68 (2008).

[21] Worldometer For COVID-19, url: https://www.worldometers.info (2020).

[22] Basu S., Ghosh S.: Fuzzy cellular automata model for discrete dynamical system representing spread of MERS and COVID-19 virus, *Book Chapter in Internet of Medical Things for Smart Healthcare*, 267-304,Springer Nature, 2020, https://doi.org/10.1007/978-981-15-8097-0_11.

[23] Ning Bin, Li Ke-Ping, Gao Zi-You: Modeling fixed-block railway signaling system using cellular automata model, *International Journal of Modern Physics C* 16(11), 1793–1801 (2005). https://doi.org/10.1142/S0129183105008308.

9

An Efficient Imputation Strategy Based on Adaptive Filter for Large Missing Value Datasets

S. Radhika, A. Chandrasekar, and Felix Albu

CONTENTS

9.1 Introduction

In the recent world, the applications of artificial-intelligence-based algorithms are increasing at a tremendous rate. The various fields of application of these algorithms include medical field, stock market, finance, education, advertising, etc. One of the important parameters required for the efficient operation of any machine learning or deep learning algorithm is the dataset. Even though the dataset is said to be enormously bigger, they often suffer from missing values. The presence of missing or incomplete values in the dataset is one of the unavoidable situations, especially in real time as these data are often collected from a sensor, mobile phone, or in an open environment [1]. In such situations, the effects of environmental, device measurement error, and human error act as major contributors in the incompleteness of the data. Such missing values can significantly degrade the quality of the dataset obtained and they may result in the inefficient model for the machine learning algorithm. Thus data preprocessing or data preparation is done prior to any machine learning algorithm. It is an important task as the efficiency and the reliability of any algorithm depends largely on the data preprocessing. The problem of missing values in the data preparation phase is generally attacked by either removing them or by imputation [2]. The process of discarding or removing the missing values is not an efficient one as they are more prone to more bias and they degrade the efficiency of the algorithm. Moreover, they are not suitable when the dataset is very small, where even a small amount of data may be useful for further processing and when the size of the missing value is considerably larger compared to the data size. Therefore, the missing values are generally imputated. The process of adding a suitable value in the place of missing value is called imputation [3,4].

9.1.1 Motivation

The main advantage of the imputation method is that the bias produced is lower and the efficiency of the machine learning algorithm is improved [5]. Secondly, the imputation method can be applied to any data type and for any percentage of missing values in the dataset [6]. Thirdly, the information content present in the data can be retained [7].

Generally data imputation methods are classified as single and multiple imputation methods. In the single imputation method, the complete dataset is obtained at one time instant, whereas multiple imputation is an iterative procedure where the imputation is done several times before the final result is obtained [8].

The most easy and simple method of imputation of missing values is by the mean of the available data. This method suffers from the biased dataset with less variance, which completely ignores correlation between features. Another well-known method is the Expectation–Maximization method. It is a two-step approach where in E-step, the expectation of the data and parameter of the estimate is obtained from the observed data where in the M-step the updation of the parameters is performed using maximum likelihood approach. The problem with this method is that they are not suitable for all data types and for real data applications [9].

The K-Nearest Neighbor (KNN) algorithm is another widely used method of data imputation where the nearest neighbors are used to compute the missing values. They suffer from the problem of estimating the number of neighbors as the distance measure plays a major role in the performance of the KNN algorithm [10]. Other well-known methods include the singular value decomposition (SVD) method and Least Squares (LS) method [3]. All of the above-mentioned single imputation methods suffer from poor accuracy due to the prediction of missing values in the single run.

The multiple imputation method includes the prediction of missing values based on a function that is suitable for the dataset. It is an iterative procedure where several iterations are performed to achieve the predicted value similar to the actual value [11]. Some of the well-known states of algorithms include the Markov Chain Monte Carlo (MCMC) algorithm, family of stochastic gradient, least square, and linear regression algorithms where multiple iterations are done achieve the imputed data. Many machine learning algorithms and deep learning algorithms fall under the category of data imputation [12]. As they capture the interaction between data, they are more flexible and give more accurate results. Moreover, they are more suitable when the dataset is large, complex, and unsupervised, whereas the single imputation method cannot be used efficiently.

Thus, this chapter deals with the multiple imputation strategy based on adaptive filters. Even though there are several adaptive filters available, the Least Mean Square (LMS) algorithm is found to be most widely used because of its simplicity in nature and faster convergence. In this chapter, a novel adaptive LMS filter called the Data Imputation LMS (DI-LMS) algorithm is proposed. This chapter is described as follows: In Section 2, the state-of-art methods available for data preprocessing are discussed. Also, the adaptive filter used for prediction is also dealt with. Problems with the current approach are also analyzed. In Section 3, the proposed method of imputation using an adaptive filter is described. The new adaptive algorithm called the data imputation LMS adaptive algorithm is proposed. Mathematical illustration and flow process are also described. A detailed experiment setup is explained in Section 4. In Section 5, the description of dataset is included and the results, comparison, and discussion are presented. And in Section 6, the conclusion and future scope are discussed.

9.2 Literature Survey

There are numerous adaptive filtering algorithms [13]. Out of the various algorithms available, the LMS is found to be widely used for its simplicity and easy implementation. The LMS base prediction algorithm is based on the Wiener filtering theory and it has good performance. The general framework of adaptive filters is shown in Figure 9.1 and the application of an adaptive filter for prediction is shown in Figure 9.2. As seen in Figure 9.1, the adaptive filter adapts the filter coefficient in such a way that the error is minimum in the mean square sense. The prediction version of adaptive filter is a modification of the general framework where the delayed version of input is fed as the input. The present input is the desired response. Thus, the adaptive filter predicts the present value of input from the past input such that the error is minimized. After the algorithm converges, the estimated output is the same as the actual output. The earliest proposed one was used to predict the future value in the context of speech processing and control applications [14].

Later on, several adaptive filters were used to predict the data in the context of a Wireless Sensor Network (WSN). Most of the literature was focused on reduction of the energy consumption by transfer of less data packets in situations where the signal received is damaged or when the data is lost. It can be concluded that the use of an adaptive filter results in better prediction accuracy when compared to other stochastic processes [15,16,17]. For truck time missing data prediction, the Recursive Least Square (RLS) algorithm is successfully employed [12]. The experimental results indicated that thee adaptive filters were very successful in missing value imputation of truck travel time. Other papers successfully investigated the prediction of the stock market [18,19,20]. Later, a correlation-based factor is introduced into the LMS prediction algorithm to remove the large error due to weather fluctuations [21].

Thus, from the open literature, it is evident that a LMS-based prediction algorithm is suitable for prediction of data. Also it is found that the conventional one is not suitable and there is a need to incorporate a correlation-based factor in the update recursion. Moreover, very few papers are available for data imputation using an adaptive filter.

Therefore, the main objectives of the paper are as follows:

1. To propose an adaptive filter called a data imputation LMS algorithm that can efficiently impute missing values.

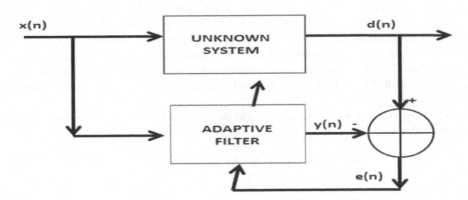

FIGURE 9.1   General framework of adaptive filter.

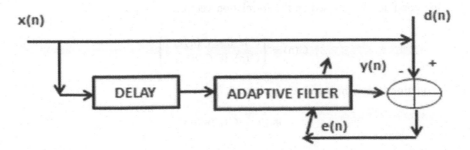

FIGURE 9.2   Adaptive filter as a linear predictor.

2. To propose a new parameter that is based on a correlation factor between the reference and available value to update the coefficients of the adaptive filter.

3. To check the validity of the proposed technique for different types of simulated missing values of varying degrees as well as for a real-time dataset with missing values. Finally, the proposed technique is validated by analyzing the performance with different classifiers.

9.3 Proposed Algorithm

The equations used in our proposed algorithm are introduced in this section. The equation describing the LMS algorithm is described first. Then, the improved version, namely the data imputation LMS algorithm suitable for data imputation is described. All bold fonts indicate vectors. Also, the time index is indicated by n.

Let $x(n)$ be the input for a dataset with n as length and with the desired response given by d(n). The desired response is modeled as $d(n) = w_o x(n) + v(n)$, which is based on the multiple linear regression model. Here, w_o illustrates the optimal weight vector and the noise source is represented as v(n). The noise is assumed as a white Gaussian noise with zero mean and variance σ_v^2. If the estimated output is y $(n) = w^T(n)x(n)$, then the error is the difference between the desired and estimated output given by e(n) = d(n) − y(n). The update equation for LMS [13] is

$$w(n + 1) = w(n) + \mu e(n)x(n) \tag{9.1}$$

where $x(n) = [x(0),\ x(1),\ x(2),\ .....x(n − N + 1)]$ and $w(n) = [w(0),\ w(1),\ w(2),\ ....w(n − n + 1)]$ are input vector and weight vector, respectively, and the step size is given by μ. The first term is the weight at *n* and the next is the gradient term, which is updated based on the value of step size.

Equation (9.1) is the general equation for a LMS adaptive filter. It is evident from equation (9.1) that the prediction of missing values does not require any historical data and the output is obtained by iterative adjustment of weight vector to obtain the expected response which is the imputed value. However, the main problem with the current approach is that the weight update recursion does not take into consideration the correlation between the desired values and the past value of the dataset. Thus, based on the above fact, a correlation factor is introduced into the weight update recursion in order to use only the dataset that has a high correlation and discard the less correlation value dataset with the desired value.

Let *C(n)* be the correlation factor that is defined as the variance between the current value of input that is the desired value and the available input.

$$C(n) = Var\ [d(n),\ x(n)] \tag{9.2}$$

Thus, the correlation vector is given as

$$C(n) = [C(0),\ C(1),\ ....C(N − 1)] \tag{9.3}$$

The following condition is imposed on the correlation vector:

$$C(n) = \begin{cases} 0 & \text{if } 0 < C(n) \leq 1 \\ C(n) & \text{if } C(n) > 1 \end{cases} \tag{9.4}$$

The weight equation is now modified as

$$w_p(n) = C(n)w(n) \tag{9.5}$$

The estimated missing value is given as $y_p(n)$, which is defined as follows

$$y_p(n) = w_p^T(n)x(n) \qquad (9.6)$$

The error and the weight update recursion are given by the following two equations:

$$e(n) = d(n) - y_p(n) \qquad (9.7)$$

$$w_p(n+1) = w_p(n) + \mu e(n)\ x(n) \qquad (9.8)$$

Thus, it can be seen that depending on the correlation vector $C(n)$, the influence of uncorrelated data on the update weight prediction is reduced. The algorithm in the form of flow diagram is given in Figure 9.3.

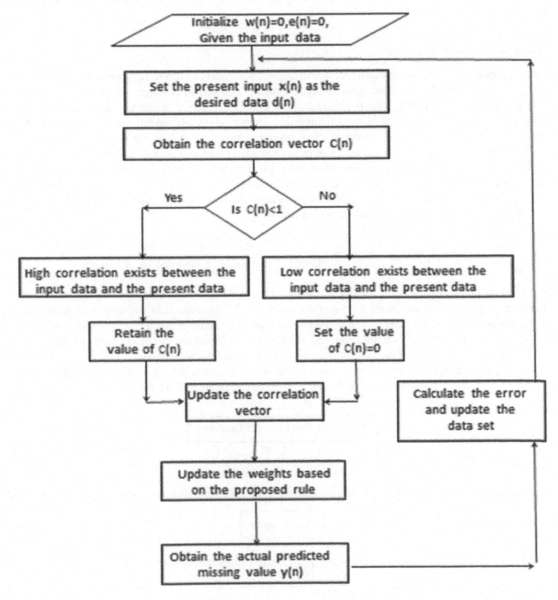

FIGURE 9.3 Proposed data imputation LMS algorithm.

9.4 Experiment Procedure

The procedure for the proposed algorithm is shown in Figure 9.4 [1]. The proposed steps involved in the procedure are explained as follows.

9.4.1 Data Collection

In this step, two types of datasets are collected from the UCI database [22] and KEEL database [23]. The first type consists of a complete dataset without missing values and the second type is the dataset with missing values. In the first experiment, the complete dataset without missing values is taken. The missing values are simulated in order to check the algorithm for different types of missing data and for different percentages of missing values. The second experiment is done for a real dataset that is collected from KEEL that consists of missing values. Therefore, the algorithm is tested for the dataset and performance is analyzed by a fair comparison.

9.4.2 Data Preprocessing

Here, the missing values are artificially created in a complete dataset in order to have good control over the missing values in the dataset. Three types of mechanisms are followed for creating missing values. They are missing at random (MAR), missing not at random (MNAR), and missing completely at random (MCAR) mechanisms. In a MAR mechanism, the missing values are not completely random and they depend on the instance's attribute data and not on the existing missing value [1]. If it does not depend on the present attribute value or the instance or on the existing missing value, then it is said to be MCAR. In a MNAR mechanism, the missing value does depend on the existing missing value and on the instance's attribute data. Five different missing degrees are chosen to validate the proposed algorithm. Here, the improved missing degree is used as the number of instances has an important place in the degree of missingness in a dataset [1]. The improved missing degree is defined as

$$Improved\ missing\ degree = \frac{Number\ of\ missing\ data}{number\ of\ instance\ *\ number\ of\ attributes}$$

In the data preprocessing stage, firstly the datasets are normalized [0-1] to remove the difference between maximum and minimum values of the attributes. In this step, data imputation is performed. For a fair comparison, the general state-of-the-art methods of imputation, namely zero imputation, mean imputation, simple tree, KNN imputation, and Support Vector Machines (SVM) methods of imputation were used for comparison of the proposed method [1]. Then the dataset is divided into two sets, one is an incomplete dataset and the other is a complete dataset. The initial weight vector is calculated based on the correlation between the available inputs and the present input. The missing value after calculation

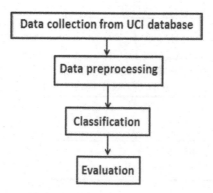

FIGURE 9.4   Procedure for data imputation evaluation.

TABLE 9.1

Dataset Information

Dataset	Number of Class	Number of Attributes	Number of Instances
Heart Disease	2	13	303
Banknote Authentication	2	5	1372
Occupancy Detection Dataset	2	7	20560
Telecom Customer-Churn	2	21	7043
Climate Model Dataset	2	18	540
Horse Colic Dataset	2	23	368

is directly imputed using the proposed method. The proposed algorithm is depicted as pseudo code, as shown in Table 9.1.

9.4.3 Classification

This step involves the classification and evaluation with the imputed datasets. Four different classifiers, namely KNN, SVM, Multilayer Perceptron (MLP), and Random Forests (RF) are used for the classification purpose.

9.4.4 Evaluation

Accuracy and root mean square error (RMSE) are used for evaluation. The accuracy is the ratio between the true value and total instance and RMSE is the square root of the mean of the error square obtained between predicted and actual values.

9.5 Experiment Results and Discussion

This section deals with the experiment setup, the database, and the obtained results. The experimental environment is the Python 2.7 version with Orange tool, version 3.26, on an Intel running the Windows 7 operating system. The proposed method of imputation is verified by comparison of the performance of classifier accuracy. In these experiments, five different classifiers, namely Decision Tree, KNN, Naïve Bayes, Logistic Regression, and SVM are used. In all these experiments, the MAR, MNAR, and MCAR mechanisms were used with five different missing degrees as 10%, 20%, 30%, 40%, and 50%, respectively. All the results are tabulated using the average of 10 iterations. All the datasets are normalized to remove the discrepancy between the minimum and maximum values.

Table 9.2 provides the details of the datasets used. All the completed datasets without missing values are taken from the UCI repository and the real missing value dataset is obtained from the KEEL database. The horse colic dataset consists of 23 attributes out of which 7 attributes consist of no missing values with a total missing percentage of 98% [23].

Table 9.2 illustrates the accuracy percentage of the proposed method of imputation and that of the other selected methods of imputation. The accuracy values are calculated by averaging the accuracy values obtained by five classifiers over 10 independent runs. The chosen missing mechanism is MAR. The degree of missing values is calculated using the proposed formula in Cheng et al. [1]. Table 9.4 illustrates the proposed method of imputation with respect to the MCAR mechanism and Table 9.5 with the MNAR mechanism. From Tables 9.2–9.5, it is confirmed that the proposed method of imputation has a better accuracy for most data types and for different missing degrees. The RMSE analysis for the different imputation strategies is discussed for different missing degrees and is shown in Table 9.6 for the heart disease dataset.

TABLE 9.2

The Dataset with the MAR Missing Mechanism

Heart Disease

Method	Degree of Missing (%)				
	10	20	30	40	50
Zero imputation	85.6	85.53	85.23	85.11	85.10
Mean imputation	85.64	85.2	85.31	83.01	84.87
Simple tree	86.2	86.1	86.00	86.23	**86.56**
KNN imputation	86.55	86.6	86.45	86.24	86.47
SVM	86.32	86.4	86.35	**86.7**	86.21
Proposed DI-LMS	**86.7**	**86.8**	**86.40**	86.4	86.44

Banknote Authentication

Method	Degree of Missing (%)				
	10	20	30	40	50
Zero imputation	99.78	99.8	99.7	99.80	99.75
Mean imputation	99.65	99.70	99.68	99.57	99.60
Simple tree	99.75	99.70	99.64	99.58	99.49
KNN imputation	99.87	99.70	99.68	99.65	99.56
SVM	**99.89**	99.78	99.80	**99.85**	**99.82**
Proposed DI-LMS	**99.89**	**99.9**	**99.87**	99.82	99.81

Occupancy Detection Dataset

Method	Degree of Missing (%)				
	10	20	30	40	50
Zero imputation	90.2	90.1	91.23	91.15	90.50
Mean imputation	91.10	91.8	91.4	91.56	91.25
Simple tree	91.20	91.02	91.40	91.25	91.74
KNN imputation	92.01	**92.04**	**92.06**	**92.51**	**92.14**
SVM	92.02	92.00	91.89	91.87	91.81
Proposed DI-LMS	**92.10**	92.01	92.02	92.15	92.03

Telecom Customer-Churn

Method	Degree of Missing (%)				
	10	20	30	40	50
Zero imputation	89.23	89.20	89.10	88.89	88.90
Mean imputation	89.24	89.26	89.28	89.40	89.20
Simple tree	89.65	**89.74**	89.50	89.40	89.30
KNN imputation	89.66	89.65	89.64	89.20	89.10
SVM	89.67	89.5	89.4	89.5	**89.7**
Proposed DI-LMS	**89.8**	89.7	**89.65**	**89.64**	89.60

Climate Model Dataset

Method	Degree of Missing (%)				
	10	20	30	40	50
Zero imputation	92.71	91.80	91.45	91.47	91.54
Mean imputation	92.31	**93.10**	**93.00**	**92.97**	**92.89**
Simple tree	92.41	92.3	92.21	92.28	92.01
KNN imputation	92.51	92.48	92.47	92.32	92.12
SVM	92.54	92.65	92.47	92.20	92.09
Proposed DI-LMS	**93.00**	92.81	92.74	92.40	92.58

TABLE 9.3

The Dataset with the MCAR Missing Mechanism

Heart Disease

Method	Degree of Missing (%)				
	10	20	30	40	50
Zero imputation	85.40	85.3	85.10	85.01	85.04
Mean imputation	85.52	85.21	85.22	83.20	84.77
Simple tree	86.08	86.17	85.89	86.07	86.14
KNN imputation	86.09	86.12	86.21	86.14	86.24
SVM	**86.65**	86.4	86.35	**86.47**	86.31
Proposed DI-LMS	86.45	**86.63**	**86.40**	86.1	**86.50**

Banknote Authentication

Method	Degree of Missing (%)				
	10	20	30	40	50
Zero imputation	99.64	99.65	99.64	99.70	99.31
Mean imputation	99.35	99.42	99.47	99.27	99.50
Simple tree	99.65	99.63	99.51	99.18	99.62
KNN imputation	99.77	99.55	99.51	99.63	99.45
SVM	99.82	99.78	99.79	99.78	**99.80**
Proposed DI-LMS	**99.87**	**99.90**	**99.88**	**99.84**	**99.80**

Occupancy Detection Dataset

Method	Degree of Missing (%)				
	10	20	30	40	50
Zero imputation	90.19	90.01	91.13	91.17	90.39
Mean imputation	91.09	91.71	91.20	91.45	91.15
Simple tree	91.07	91.04	91.03	91.00	91.05
KNN imputation	92.00	**92.04**	**92.06**	**92.51**	**92.14**
SVM	92.01	91.09	91.69	91.67	91.71
Proposed DI-LMS	**92.09**	92.00	92.01	92.05	92.05

Telecom Customer-Churn

Method	Degree of Missing (%)				
	10	20	30	40	50
Zero imputation	89.15	89.10	89.12	88.68	88.79
Mean imputation	89.17	89.24	89.25	89.30	89.18
Simple tree	89.45	89.34	89.10	89.21	89.25
KNN imputation	89.55	**89.47**	89.35	89.19	89.45
SVM	89.67	89.45	89.34	89.45	89.36
Proposed DI-LMS	**89.91**	89.31	**89.55**	**89.61**	**89.50**

Climate Model Dataset

Method	Degree of Missing (%)				
	10	20	30	40	50
Zero imputation	92.64	91.70	91.25	91.27	91.35
Mean imputation	92.24	**93.00**	**92.97**	**92.77**	**92.89**
Simple tree	92.25	92.30	92.10	92.18	91.99
KNN imputation	92.25	92.38	92.37	92.31	92.10
SVM	92.31	92.45	92.31	92.10	92.05
Proposed DI-LMS	**93.01**	92.81	92.74	92.40	92.58

TABLE 9.4

The Dataset with the MNAR Missing Mechanism

Heart Disease

Method	Degree of Missing (%)				
	10	20	30	40	50
Zero imputation	84.6	84.5	**84.6**	84.10	84.02
Mean imputation	84.64	**84.66**	84.45	84.41	84.11
Simple tree	84.2	84.21	84.12	84.10	84.01
KNN imputation	84.55	84.45	84.44	84.41	84.31
SVM	84.32	84.44	84.51	84.51	84.60
Proposed DI-LMS	**84.7**	84.45	84.56	**84.55**	**84.74**

Banknote Authentication

Method	Degree of Missing (%)				
	10	20	30	40	50
Zero imputation	97.68	97.41	97.53	97.41	97.12
Mean imputation	97.65	97.12	97.54	97.56	97.41
Simple tree	97.75	97.64	97.62	97.21	97.01
KNN imputation	97.87	**97.85**	97.74	97.72	97.62
SVM	**97.89**	97.78	97.84	97.81	97.80
Proposed DI-LMS	97.44	97.41	**97.87**	**97.82**	**97.81**

Occupancy Detection Dataset

Method	Degree of Missing (%)				
	10	20	30	40	50
Zero imputation	88.25	88.02	88.25	88.12	88.03
Mean imputation	89.20	89.18	89.11	89.21	89.74
Simple tree	89.30	89.30	89.27	89.17	89.45
KNN imputation	89.51	89.41	89.21	89.11	89.10
SVM	90.02	90.11	91.00	91.01	**91.00**
Proposed DI-LMS	**91.01**	**91.01**	**91.02**	**91.15**	90.03

Telecom Customer-Churn

Method	Degree of Missing (%)				
	10	20	30	40	50
Zero imputation	87.25	87.20	87.10	86.89	87.90
Mean imputation	87.21	87.26	87.28	87.40	87.20
Simple tree	87.61	**87.74**	87.50	87.51	87.30
KNN imputation	87.61	87.65	87.64	87.20	87.10
SVM	87.62	87.5	87.4	87.05	87.7
Proposed DI-LMS	**87.81**	87.71	**87.65**	**87.64**	**89.60**

Climate Model Dataset

Method	Degree of Missing (%)				
	10	20	30	40	50
Zero imputation	91.62	91.51	91.01	91.00	90.89
Mean imputation	91.02	91.21	91.00	91.01	91.05
Simple tree	90.99	91.01	91.02	91.00	91.04
KNN imputation	91.5	91.45	91.32	91.22	91.12
SVM	91.54	91.45	91.07	91.20	91.05
Proposed DI-LMS	**91.71**	**91.61**	**92.74**	**92.40**	**92.58**

TABLE 9.5

Accuracy Evaluation of Proposed Method of Imputation for Horse Coli Dataset

Method	Classifiers				
	Logistic Regression	**Decision Tree**	**Naïve Bayes**	**KNN**	**SVM**
Zero imputation	78.00	78.24	75.23	79.21	79.54
Mean imputation	77.21	77.45	77.52	78.82	79.56
Simple tree	75.21	76.25	78.10	77.89	80.20
KNN imputation	79.20	80.21	81.24	81.11	81.21
SVM	80.25	80.01	80.12	81.13	82.01
Proposed DI-LMS	**81.21**	**81.65**	**81.78**	**81.99**	**82.20**

TABLE 9.6

RMSE Analysis for Different Imputation Strategies for Heart Disease Dataset

Method	Degree of Missing (%)				
	10	**20**	**30**	**40**	**50**
Zero imputation	1.7014	2.147	3.870	3.924	4.001
Mean imputation	0.6324	0.5247	0.6784	0.7124	0.9983
Simple tree	0.0156	0.064	0.0978	0.9004	0.8142
KNN imputation	0.0056	0.0081	0.0098	0.0917	0.9
SVM	0.0023	0.0030	0.0091	**0.0877**	0.0978
Proposed DI-LMS	**0.0020**	**0.0025**	**0.0071**	0.0899	**0.0910**

Thus, it is evident from Table 9.6 that the zero imputation has the highest RMSE and the proposed imputation has the smallest RMSE (except from the 40% case) when compared to other imputation methods. However, it should be also noted that as the degree of missing value increases, the RMSE also increases for all methods of imputation due to the uncertainty associated with the dataset due to missing values. Further, the additional advantage claimed by the proposed method is that the complexity is lower when compared to conventional LMS as only a highly correlated dataset is used for prediction.

9.6 Conclusions and Future Work

A new missing value imputation strategy based on adaptive filter is proposed. The proposed algorithm takes advantage of the correlation coefficient between the actual value and predicted value. The experiment is done for a simulated missing value dataset from the UCI repository and for a real missing value dataset from the KEEL database proved that proposed work have better performance for different types as well as degrees of missing value and even for real missing values. Further, the results obtained by comparing the proposed method with other imputation models by various classifiers clearly depicted that the proposed method is capable of imputation with better accuracy than other methods. In the future, this work could be extended by using other adaptive filters, hybrid methods, and a variable step size approach.

REFERENCES

[1] Cheng, Ching-Hsue, Jing-Rong Chang, and Hao-Hsuan Huang. "A novel weighted distance threshold method for handling medical missing values." *Computers in Biology and Medicine* 122 (2020): 103824.

[2] Bertsimas, Dimitris, Colin Pawlowski, and Ying Daisy Zhuo. "From predictive methods to missing data imputation: an optimization approach." *The Journal of Machine Learning Research* 18, no. 1 (2017): 7133–7171.

[3] Lin, Wei-Chao, and Chih-Fong Tsai. "Missing value imputation: a review and analysis of the literature (2006–2017)." *Artificial Intelligence Review* 53, no. 2 (2020): 1487–1509.

[4] Wu, Pan, Lunhui Xu, and Zilin Huang. "Imputation methods used in missing traffic data: a literature review." In *International Symposium on Intelligence Computation and Applications*, pp. 662–677. Singapore: Springer, 2019.

[5] Rado, Omesaad, Muna Al Fanah, and Ebtesam Taktek. "Performance analysis of missing values imputation methods using machine learning techniques." In *Intelligent Computing-Proceedings of the Computing Conference*, pp. 738–750. Springer, Cham, 2019.

[6] Baraldi, Amanda N., and Craig K. Enders. "An introduction to modern missing data analyses." *Journal of School Psychology* 48, no. 1 (2010): 5–37.

[7] Chiu, Chia-Chun, Shih-Yao Chan, Chung-Ching Wang, and Wei-Sheng Wu. "Missing value imputation for microarray data: a comprehensive comparison study and a web tool." *BMC Systems Biology* 7, no. Suppl 6 (2013): S12.

[8] Farhangfar, Alireza, Lukasz A. Kurgan, and Witold Pedrycz. "A novel framework for imputation of missing values in databases." *IEEE Transactions on Systems, Man, and Cybernetics-Part A: Systems and Humans* 37, no. 5 (2007): 692–709.

[9] Molenberghs, Geert, and Geert Verbeke. "Multiple imputation and the expectation-maximization algorithm." *Models for Discrete Longitudinal Data* (2005): 511–529.

[10] Zhang, Shichao. "Nearest neighbor selection for iteratively kNN imputation." *Journal of Systems and Software* 85, no. 11 (2012): 2541–2552.

[11] Rubin, Donald B. *Multiple Imputation for Nonresponse in Surveys*. Vol. 81. John Wiley & Sons, 2004.

[12] Karimpour, Abolfazl, Amin Ariannezhad, and Yao-Jan Wu. "Hybrid data-driven approach for truck travel time imputation." *IET Intelligent Transport Systems* 13, no. 10 (2019): 1518–1524.

[13] Haykin, Simon S. *Adaptive-Filter Theory*. Pearson Education India, India, 2008.

[14] Goodwin, Graham C., and Kwai Sang Sin. *Adaptive Filtering Prediction and Control*. Courier Corporation, Mineola, New York, 2014.

[15] Ganjewar, Pramod, Selvaraj Barani, and Sanjeev J. Wagh. "A hierarchical fractional LMS prediction method for data reduction in a wireless sensor network." *Ad Hoc Networks* 87 (2019): 113–127.

[16] Stojkoska, Biljana, Dimitar Solev, and Danco Davcev. "Data prediction in WSN using variable step size LMS algorithm." In *Proceedings of the 5th International Conference on Sensor Technologies and Applications*, 2011.

[17] Dias, Gabriel Martins, Boris Bellalta, and Simon Oechsner. "A survey about prediction-based data reduction in wireless sensor networks." *ACM Computing Surveys (CSUR)* 49, no. 3 (2016): 1–35.

[18] Wesen, J. E., V. Vermehren, and H. M. de Oliveira. "Adaptive filter design for stock market prediction using a correlation-based criterion." *arXiv preprint arXiv:1501.07504* (2015).

[19] Huang, Shian-Chang, Chei-Chang Chiou, Jui-Te Chiang, and Cheng-Feng Wu. "A novel intelligent option price forecasting and trading system by multiple kernel adaptive filters." *Journal of Computational and Applied Mathematics* 369 (2020): 112560.

[20] Garcia-Vega, Sergio, Xiao-Jun Zeng, and John Keane. "Stock returns prediction using kernel adaptive filtering within a stock market interdependence approach." *Expert Systems with Applications* 160 (2020): 113668.

[21] Ma, Dongchao, Chenlei Zhang, and Li Ma. "A C-LMS prediction algorithm for rechargeable sensor networks." *IEEE Access* 8 (2020): 69997–70004.

[22] Dua, D. and Graff, C. *UCI Machine Learning Repository* [http://archive.ics.uci.edu/ml]. Irvine, CA: University of California, School of Information and Computer Science, 2019.

[23] Alcalá-Fdez, Jesús, Alberto Fernández, Julián Luengo, Joaquín Derrac, Salvador García, Luciano Sánchez, and Francisco Herrera. "Keel data-mining software tool: dataset repository, integration of algorithms and experimental analysis framework." *Journal of Multiple-Valued Logic & Soft Computing* 17 (2011): 255–287.

10

An Analysis of Derivative-Based Optimizers on Deep Neural Network Models

Aruna Pavate and Rajesh Bansode

CONTENTS

10.1 Introduction

Deep learning, a subset of machine learning, enables computer systems to solve the problem without being explicitly programmed. Convolutional neural networks are one of the most commonly used techniques with the exponential growth in image data and most of the research showed remarkable results in computer vision domain using the same. To train a deep neural network with high dimensional and non-linear data is the most challenging optimization problem. Most of the applications are designed, considering the goal to design a model. Optimization techniques take in part to improve many deep learning architectures such as VggNet [1], ResNet [2], DenseNet [3] EffieicnetNet [4], GoogleNet [5] and many more with increasing complexity and depth. The convolutional neural network is one of the classes of neural networks, the role of optimization to search global optima by training the model and very speedy convergence using derivative-based optimization techniques like the gradient descent algorithm [6].

Traditional machine learning algorithms outline many problems like a computational bottleneck, prerequisite of domain knowledge, expert understanding, and curse of dimensionality so most of the domains make use of the neural network to design various applications. To train the deep neural network with high dimensional data is very challenging for nonconvex problems and if samples are low in numbers then it leads to the problem of overfitting. Depending upon the problem, experts have to design a model that gives faster and better results by reducing the error loss function with the help of hyperparameter tuning that results in improvement in model prediction. To tune the model, it is necessary to adjust the weights as per error loss and the path selection in the correct direction using optimization techniques and interest in finding the global minima for that loss function. Selection of suitable learning rate is also a challenging task if the learning rate is too small, converge goes too long, and if the learning rate is increased then neural network model will not concentrate. The selection of suitable optimization techniques improves the model performance; selection of an improper technique results in a network to be stuck in local minima while training and that result does not to improve the model. If a model gets the global minima, there is no assurance that the model remains in the global minima. Hence, to deal with these challenges, and to improve the model, an analysis of performance and better understanding of the behavior of optimization techniques is necessary. There are many methods available to deal with these challenges. Hence, this work contributed in the direction of an experimental comparative analysis of the eight most commonly used derivative-based optimization techniques using convolutional neural networks on four different network architectures VGG [1], RestNet [2], DenseNet [3], EffieicnetNetB5 [4] using COVID-19 dataset (https://www.kaggle.com/bachrr/detecting-covid-19-in-x-ray-images-with-tensorflow/) and tried to find out the answers such as how fast, accurate, and stable each algorithm is able to tackle the relevant, optimal minima during the training of the model. The performance of each technique is evaluated using the loss function and accuracy and convergence speed.

The proposed work is organized as follows: Section 2 represents methodology of the proposed system with a detailed explanation of each optimizer and Section 3 gives a brief description of result and analysis of each technique. Table 10.1 represents the different parameters used throughout this work.

10.2 Methodology

At the time of building deep neural networks, there are lots of things that are essential and need to be defined before training the model. Building the model starts with the first thing, which is to provide the input layers succeeded by different dense layers and the last output layer. After completion of building the model, the function of the optimizer is to compile the model using different loss functions and

TABLE 10.1

Notations/Parameters and Their Meaning, Which Are Used in the Methodology

Parameter/Notation	Purpose of Notation
α	Learning rate
W	Weight vector
ΔW	New weight vector
$J(\theta)$	Objective function
$\nabla_\theta J(\theta)$	Gradient of objective function
$(x^{(i)}:y^{(i)})$	Training examples input: corresponding labels
b	Batch size
L	Loss function
ϵ	Very small value added to escape the divide by zero/numerical stability constant
$\beta1,\beta2$	Hyperparameters that are to be tuned
gt	$\frac{df(x,w)}{dw}$: cost gradient with respect to current layer
pt	Exponentially weighted average of past gradients
qt:	Exponentially weighted average of past square of gradients
$\widehat{pt}$, $\widehat{qt}$	Bias correction as first and second averages have bias towards zero
ρ	Damping coefficient in the weighted sum
γ	Momentum
v	Velocity

metrics applied to find out the performance of the model. The role of the loss function/cost function is to compute the error between the desired value and actual value generated by the model and direct the optimizer to move in the correct direction, as mentioned in Equation (10.1), whereas the optimizer helps the model to reduce error and improve the model performance and gives better results. There are several error loss functions [7,8] and optimizers [9] that help the model to improve performance in various situations. Many of the optimization algorithms propose faster convergence, complexity, more parameters, and the performance of the algorithm dependent upon the problem that is to be solved. To select the best method, analyze each parameter and different values of the problem. This process is time consuming. Selecting the correct optimizer for deep neural network models is evaluative to get the best results in a limited time.

$$\text{Error Loss function (L)} = \text{Desired Output} - \text{Actual Output} \qquad (10.1)$$

Figure 10.1 shows the proposed working model trained using the COVID-19 dataset on four different architectures: VGG16, RestNet50, DenseNet201, and EffieicnetNetB5. The dataset is applied on architectures and different optimizers attempted such as SGD, Adam, Adagrad, Adadelta, RMSprop, NDAM, and SGD with Momentum parameter; the performance of the system is evaluated. Here, the dataset has image sizes of 224×224. Head models are trained using the concept of transfer learning and the base model used is Imagenet. The performance of the models is evaluated based on validation loss, training loss, validation accuracy, training accuracy, and computational time. The following section elaborates on the optimizers used in experimental studies.

10.2.1 SGD

SGD is simple and effective, but requires an essential tuning of hyperparameters. Here, learning is complicated as input samples in each layer depend on parameters of all preceding layers [10]. This algorithm in each reiteration randomly selects limited samples and calculates the gradients for those samples instead of all, in order to train the model rather than selecting the whole dataset. Selecting the whole dataset for training helps in getting the minima without noise; for a very large dataset this does

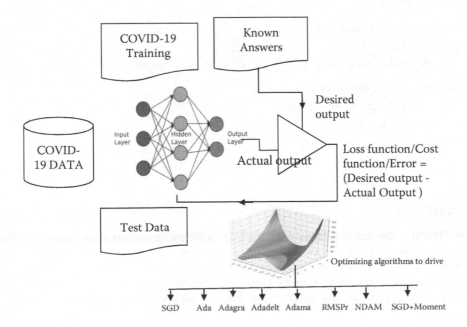

FIGURE 10.1 Blueprint for the proposed work.

not work. SGD helps in selecting random samples and updates the parameters for each training example $(x^{(i)}:y^{(i)})$, which benefits in increasing the convergence speed and also saves the memory [11].

Algorithm 1 **Stochastic Gradient Descent**

Requirement setting: $(x^{(i)}:y^{(i)})$, b,α

    1. *Initialize b, α, W*
    2. *For $\alpha = 1,2,...$*
             Do random sampling on $\{x^{(1)}, ..., x^{(n)}\}$ for corresponding labels $\{y^{(1)}, ..., y^{(n)}\}$
    3. *Update $gt = \frac{1}{n}\nabla\theta\sum_i^n L(f(x^{(i)}, w), y^{(i)})$*
    4. *$w = w - \alpha_k\ gt$*
    5. *End*

10.2.2 SGD with Momentum

In practice, it is necessary to generalize the obscured data. There are many variants of SGD [12,13,14,15,16,17] proposed for working on extensive machine learning models. These methods concentrate on updating the specific models based on some observations. The learning rate affects remarkable performance of the model. During training of the neural network models, selecting the best learning that sets the hyperparameter is a difficult task. SGD with momentum solves this problem but it increases the cost of adding another hyperparameter.

Algorithm 2 **Stochastic Gradient Descent with Momentum**

Requirement setting: $(x^{(i)}:y^{(i)})$,b,α

    1. *Initialize $b,\alpha = 0.0001$, $W,\gamma = 0.9,v$*
    2. *For $\alpha = 1,2,...$*
         a.   *Do random sampling on $\{x^{(1)}, ..., x^{(m)}\}$ for corresponding labels $\{y^{(1)}, ..., y^{(m)}\}$*
    3. *Update $gt = \frac{1}{n}\nabla W\sum_i^n L(f(x^{(i)}, w), y^{(i)})$*
    4. *Compute velocity $v = \gamma w - \alpha_k\ gt$*
    5. *Update $w \leftarrow w + v$*
    6. *End*

10.2.3 RMSprop

RMSprop [18,19] is identical to Adaprop, which helps to solve the limitations of the Adagrad optimizer. It is based on the concept of adaptive learning rate optimization, where learning rate changes over time. Here, the first average of square of the gradient is computed exponentially and then the learning rate decides the direction of the gradient, suggested learning rate 0.0001, and epsilon is set to be 1e-7. The third step includes an update of the step; initially it has been set but needs to be tuned.

Algorithm 3 **RMSprop: Root Mean Square Propagation**

1. *Initialize $\alpha = 0.0001$, $q = 0$, ρ, $\epsilon = 10^{-7}$*
2. *For each parameter w*
   a. *Do random sampling on $\{x^{(1)}, \ldots, x^{(n)}\}$ for corresponding labels $\{y^{(1)}, \ldots, y^{(n)}\}$*
3. *Update $gt = \frac{1}{n}\nabla\theta\sum_i^n L(f(x^{(i)}, w), y^{(i)})$*
4. *Calculate the first moment vector $qt = \rho. \ q_{t-1}(1 - \rho). \ g^2 t$*
5. *Calculate $\Delta\theta = -\frac{\epsilon}{\sqrt{qt + \epsilon}} * gt$*
6. *Return $\theta \ldots = \ldots \theta + \Delta\theta$*
7. *End*

10.2.4 Adagrad

Adagrad [20] is a derivative-based optimization technique to calculate the gradient [21], like other algorithms discussed here. Adagrad works well on a sparse dataset, and learns the individual features by adopting the learning rate in keeping with parameters. If parameters have higher gradients, then it slows the learning rate, whereas if parameters have lower gradients, it increases the learning rate and the model is learned quickly. Learning rate/step size is reciprocally proportional to the sum of the squares of all past gradients of the parameter. This algorithm works on aggregation of squared gradients. As during training, the model aggregate sum that increases the step size is reduced imperceptibly and therefore the model stops learning additional information. This problem is solved with Adadelta. Dean et al. [19] proved that Adagrad improved the limitations of SGD and was more robust than SGD.

Algorithm 4 **Adagrad Adaptive Gradient**

Initialize $\alpha = 0.0001$, $w0$, $\epsilon = 10^{-7}$

1. *For each parameter w*
   a. *Do random sampling on $\{x^{(1)}, \ldots, x^{(n)}\}$ for corresponding labels $\{y^{(1)}, \ldots, y^{(n)}\}$*
2. *Update $gt = \frac{1}{n}\nabla\theta\sum_i^n L(f(x^{(i)}, w), y^{(i)})$*
3. *Calculate the first-moment vector $qt = \beta1. \ q_{t-1}(1 - \beta1). \ g^2 t$*
4. *Calculate $\Delta\theta = -\frac{\epsilon}{\sqrt{qt + \epsilon}} * gt$*
5. *Return $\theta \ldots = \ldots \theta + \Delta\theta$*
6. *End*

10.2.5 Adadelta

This algorithm [22] is similar to SGD and extension for the Adagrad algorithm. Here the term *delta* calculates the variance between the present weights and the updated weights and uninterruptedly learns the weights even after many updates. This algorithm is computationally expensive.

Algorithm 5   Adadelta Adaptive delta

Default setting: Initialize $\alpha = 0.0001$, ρ, b, $w0, \epsilon = 10^{-7}$

1. *Initialize aggregation of variables $E[g2]_0 = 0$, $E[\Delta \theta g^2]_0 = 0$*
2. *Do random sampling on $\{x^{(1)}, \ldots, x^{(n)}\}$ for corresponding labels $\{y^{(1)}, \ldots, y^{(n)}\}$*
3. *For update at time t*
4. *Compute gradient $gt = \frac{1}{n} \nabla \theta \sum_i^n L(f(x^{(i)}, w), y^{(i)})$*
5. *Aggregate gradient $E[g^2]_t = \rho E[g^2]_{t-1} + (1-\rho)gt^2$*
6. *Compute $\Delta \theta t = \frac{-\epsilon}{\sqrt{E[g2]t + \epsilon}} gt$*
7. *Compute $E[\Delta \theta^2]_t = \rho E[\Delta \theta^2]_{t-1} + (1-\rho)\Delta \theta^2$*
8. *Return $\theta t + 1 = \theta t + \Delta \theta t$*
9. *End for*
10. *End*

10.2.6 Adam

Adam, Adaptive Moment Estimation [20,23], is one of the most commonly used optimizers. This algorithm gives better results compared to other optimizers, but recently [23] has been found that it may take different search directions than the original direction. Adam optimizer is derived from RMSProp and AdaGrad [23]. This algorithm works on utilizing the momentum factor to the current gradient to calculate, with the help of previous gradients. This optimizer is most popularly adopted to train the neural network. It includes two steps:

1. Momentum factor is added to RMSprop to rescale the gradients and computes the gradient square and exponential changing average of the gradient.
2. Biases are updated by calculating the first and second moment estimates. The decay rates ($\beta 1$, $\beta 2$) are selected very low close to 1.

Algorithm 6   Adam: Adaptive moment estimation

Default setting: $\alpha = 0.0001$, $\beta 1 = 0.9$, $\beta 2 = 0.999$ and $\epsilon = 10^{-8}$

1. *Initialize parameters $p0, q0, w0$, and $t0 = 0$*
2. *While new weights (ΔW) do not converge, follow the steps from a to f*
    a. *Calculate gradient cost function gt*
    b. *Calculate the first-moment vector $pt = \beta 1. p_{t-1}(1 - \beta 1). gt$*
    c. *Calculate the second-moment vector $qt = \beta 2. q_{t-1}(1 - \beta 2). gt^2$*
    d. *Calculate $\widehat{pt}$ Bias correction as first average $\widehat{pt} = pt(1 - \beta 1^t)$*
    e. *Calculate $\widehat{qt}$ Bias correction as second average $\widehat{qt} = qt(1 - \beta 2^t)$*
    f. *Update parameter $\Delta W = \Delta W - 1 - \alpha. \widehat{pt}/\sqrt{qt + \epsilon}$*
3. *Return ΔW*

10.2.7 AdaMax

AdaMax [18] is the revision of Adam, dependent on the infinity norm as the high value of p norm is mostly unstable so $\ell1$ and $\ell2$ norms are mostly preferred. $\ell\infty$ norm have a stable behavior so the author proposed AdaMax, which simplifies and stabilizes the algorithm. In this algorithm, constrained infinity norm based on max operation and bias are not adjustable toward zero.

Algorithm 7 Adamax

Default setting: $\alpha = 0.0001$, $\beta1 = 0.9$, $\beta2 = 0.999$ and $\epsilon = 10^{-8}$

1. *Initialize parameters $\theta0, pt = 0, qt = 0, t = 0$*
2. *While θt not converged do*
3. *$t = t + 1$*
4. *Do random sampling on $\{x^{(1)}, \ldots, x^{(n)}\}$ for corresponding labels $\{y^{(1)}, \ldots, y^{(n)}\}$*
5. *Update $gt = \nabla\theta$ $(ft(\theta t - 1)$*
6. *$pt = \beta1. pt - 1 + (1 - \beta1). gt$*
7. *$qt = max (\beta\beta2\text{-} qt\text{-}1|gt|)$*
   a. *For $\ell2$ norm $pt = \beta2. pt - 1 + (1 - \beta2) |gt|^2$*
   b. *For $\ell2$ norm $pt = \beta2^p. pt - 1 + (1 - \beta2) |gt|^p$*
   c. *For $\ell\infty$ norm ..// This is considered*
8. *Update parameter $\theta t - 1 = \theta t - 1 - (\alpha. (1 - \beta1)). pt/qt$*
9. *End while*
10. *Return $\theta t - 1$*

10.2.8 NADAM

This algorithm is comprised of the Nesterov accelerated gradient and Adaptive Moment Estimation. To combine ADAM with NAG [24], the momentum term is updated; here the past momentum is replaced with the current momentum vector.

Algorithm 8 **NADAM-Nesterov-Accelerated Adaptive Moment Estimation (Nadam)**

1. *Initialization: $\alpha_0, \ldots, \alpha_T;$ $\mu_0, \ldots, \mu_T; \upsilon; \epsilon$:*
   $p0; q0 = 0(first/second moment vectors)$
2. *while θt not converged do*
3. *$gt = \nabla\theta t - 1ft(\theta t - 1)$*
4. *$pt = \mu t \gamma t\text{-}1+(1\text{-}\mu t)gt$*
5. *$qt = \upsilon qt\text{-}1+(1\text{-}\upsilon)g2t$*
6. *$p = (t+1t/(1\text{-} i=1t+1i))+((1\text{-}t)gt/(1\text{-}i=1ti))$*
7. *$\hat{q} = \upsilon\ qt/(1 - \upsilon^t)$*
8. *$\theta t = \theta t - 1 - \frac{\alpha t}{\sqrt{\hat{q}\ t+\epsilon}}\widehat{p}t$*
9. *End while*
10. *Return θt*

TABLE 10.2

Performance Evaluation (for Epochs=10) of Optimizers Using Training Accuracy and Validation Accuracy under COVID-19 Dataset

Optimizer/ Architectures	SGD		SGDM		RMSProp		AdaGrad		AdaDelta		Adam		Adamax		Nadam	
	Train Acc	Val Acc	Train Acc	Val Acc	Train Acc	Val Acc	Train Acc	Val Acc	Train Acc	Val Acc	Train Acc	Val Acc	Train Acc	Val Acc	Train Acc	Val Acc
VGG16	0.55	0.36	0.53	0.53	0.55	0.49	0.45	0.50	0.36	0.50	0.56	0.49	0.57	0.47	0.55	0.50
ResNet50	0.56	0.48	0.60	0.47	0.60	0.48	0.55	0.54	0.39	0.50	0.62	0.48	0.57	0.51	0.59	0.48
DenseNet201	0.51	0.49	0.78	0.95	0.87	0.95	0.66	0.80	0.54	0.42	0.84	0.93	0.74	0.91	0.85	0.95
Efficient NetB5	0.51	0.50	0.61	0.49	0.60	0.52	0.56	0.51	0.42	0.53	0.61	0.49	0.61	0.48	0.62	0.50

TABLE 10.3

Performance Evaluation (for Epochs=10) of Optimizers Using Training Loss and Validation Loss under COVID-19 Dataset

Optimizer/ Architectures	SGD		SGDM		RMSProp		AdaGrad		AdaDelta		Adam		Adamax		Nadam	
	Train Loss	Val Loss	Train Loss	Val Loss	Train Loss	Val Loss	Train Loss	Val Loss	Train Loss	Val Loss	Train Loss	Val Loss	Train Loss	Val Loss	Train Loss	Val Loss
VGG16	0.70	0.71	0.78	0.74	0.55	0.49	1.17	0.97	1.10	0.86	0.76	0.69	0.70	0.69	0.73	0.67
ResNet50	0.72	0.70	0.67	0.72	0.60	0.48	0.70	0.74	1.47	1.14	0.65	0.69	0.71	0.70	0.67	0.68
DenseNet201	0.79	0.76	0.45	0.23	0.87	0.95	0.62	0.53	0.85	0.85	0.33	0.23	0.51	0.35	0.33	0.22
Efficient NetB5	0.70	0.69	0.67	0.72	0.60	0.52	0.68	0.70	0.42	0.53	0.67	0.71	0.67	0.72	0.67	0.71

10.3 Result and Analysis

In this section, the performance of the SGD, SGD with Momentum, Adam, Adadelta, AdaMax, Adagrad, RMSprop, and NADAM optimizers on four different architectures using convolutional neural networks were evaluated. All the models are trained using the COVID-19 dataset, including three convolutional layers and two fully connected layers. To train the model, a transfer learning concept was applied, where the head model is selected as Imagenet that is placed above the base model. There are four different base models selected: VGG16, ResNet50, DenseNet201, and EfficientNetB5. Table 10.2 presents the classification accuracy during training of the model and validating the model. The generated models were compiled using loss as the binary cross entropy and the models first trained for 10 epochs. As per analysis for 10 epochs, DenseNet201 architecture gave good performance, with more than 74% accuracy for SGDM, RMSProp, Adamax, Adam, and Nadam out of eight optimizers.

Adam optimizer performed well for training accuracy as well as for validation accuracy on DenseNet201 architecture and the second RMSprop gave a good result for the same architecture, whereas the performance of the SGD optimizer is steady on all four models.

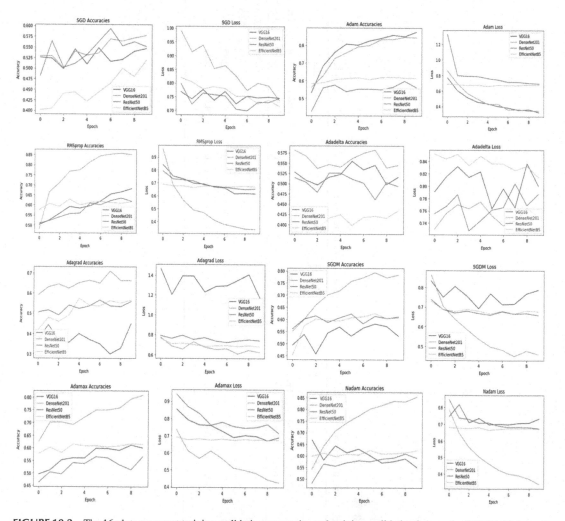

FIGURE 10.2 The 16 plots represent training, validation accuracies and training, validation loss on the COVID-19 dataset by applying eight different optimization algorithms: SGD, SGDM, RMSProp, Adagrad, Adadelta, Adam, Adamax, Nadam, and four different deep neural architectures: VGG16, DenseNet201, ResNet50, and EfficientNetB5, respectively. Parameter setting is considered during the training model as steps_per_epoch = 20, epochs = 10, and learning rate $\alpha = 0.0001$.

TABLE 10.4

Performance Evaluation (for Epochs=100) of Optimizers Using Training Accuracy and Validation Accuracy under COVID-19 Dataset

Optimizer/ Architectures	SGD		SGDM		RMSProp		AdaGrad		AdaDelta		Adam		Adamax		Nadam	
	Train Acc	Val Acc	Train Acc	Val Acc	Train Acc	Val Acc	Train Acc	Val Acc	Train Acc	Val Acc	Train Acc	Val Acc	Train Acc	Val Acc	Train Acc	Val Acc
VGG16	0.77	0.76	0.77	0.76	0.88	0.90	0.52	0.50	0.46	0.50	0.88	0.88	0.82	0.86	0.88	0.88
ResNet50	0.61	0.43	0.61	0.43	0.80	0.85	0.71	0.88	0.56	0.47	0.99	0.95	0.92	0.94	0.71	0.73
DenseNet201	0.90	0.94	0.90	0.94	0.98	0.94	0.54	0.51	0.50	0.46	0.99	0.96	0.71	0.73	0.92	0.94
Efficient NetB5	0.62	0.50	0.62	0.50	0.61	0.49	0.49	0.46	0.52	0.50	0.78	0.87	0.60	0.47	0.60	0.47

TABLE 10.5

Performance Evaluation (for Epochs=100) of Optimizers Using Training Loss and Validation Loss under COVID-19 Dataset

Optimizer/ Architectures	SGD		SGDM		RMSProp		AdaGrad		AdaDelta		Adam		Adamax		Nadam	
	Train Loss	Val Loss	Train Loss	Val Loss	Train Loss	Val Loss	Train Loss	Val Loss	Train Loss	Val Loss	Train Loss	Val Loss	Train Loss	Val Loss	Train Loss	Val Loss
VGG16	0.50	0.86	0.50	0.53	0.29	0.28	0.75	0.69	0.98	0.72	0.31	0.30	0.44	0.45	0.44	0.45
ResNet50	0.64	0.69	0.64	0.69	0.47	0.42	0.58	0.71	0.71	0.74	0.05	0.14	0.20	0.16	0.58	0.56
DenseNet201	0.23	0.18	0.23	0.18	0.05	0.16	0.72	0.67	0.88	0.80	0.05	0.10	0.58	0.56	0.20	0.16
Efficient NetB5	0.66	0.71	0.66	0.71	0.66	0.71	0.69	0.70	0.69	0.69	0.48	0.41	0.66	0.72	0.66	0.72

Table 10.3 represents the model loss during training and validating the system for 10 epochs. It has been observed that there are distinguishable differences between the performance of the optimizers. For training loss and validation loss, RMSProp and Adam again performed uniformly, as did the previous one. From the observation, it is suggested that Adam and RMSProp are well-grounded optimizers.

In this work, the step size and the learning rate of models was constant. As shown in Figure 10.2, a combined plot for all the models represents training, validation accuracy and training, validation loss considering steps_per_epoch = 20, epochs = 10, and learning rate $\alpha = 0.0001$. Figure 10.2 represents the combined plot for accuracy and loss by compiling a model for 10 epochs.

The performance of the model was evaluated after 100 epochs and the results show DenseNet201 architecture performed well for SGD, SGDM, RMSProp, Adam, Adamax, and Nadam optimizers with the highest accuracy of 98% using the Adam optimizer, as shown in Table 10.4.

As shown in Table 10.5, training and validation loss of all the models was observed. The analysis represents the minimum loss for samples achieved using the Adam and RMSProp optimizers with 0.05 with the model compiled for 100 epochs. Though in this work, step size and the learning rate kept constant, elementally the model requires learning rate or step_per_size should change with the number of iterations. As per observations in Figure 10.3, for Adam and RMSProp gradient descent curve inclines flatter towards minima, the more the models leading towards minima considered as the the optimum solution. It has been analysed that the original learning rate may not be sufficient to converge

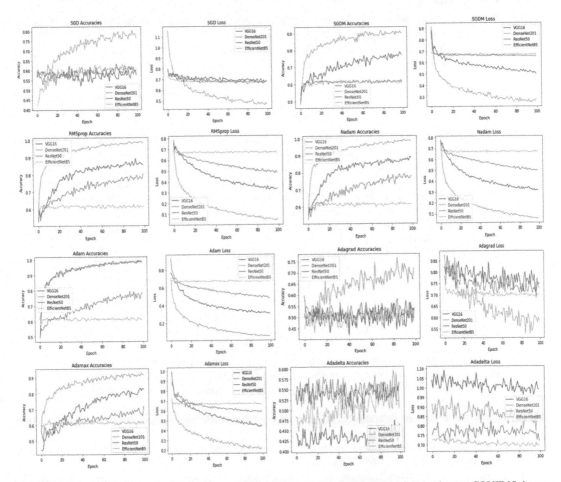

FIGURE 10.3 The 16 plots represent training, validation accuracies and training, and validation loss on COVID19 dataset by applying eight different optimization algorithms: SGD, SGDM, RMSProp, Adadelta, Adam, Adamax, Adagrad, Nadam, and four different deep neural architectures: VGG16, DenseNet201, ResNet50, and EfficientNetB5, respectively. Parameter setting is considered during training model as steps_per_epoch = 20, epochs = 100, and learning rate $\alpha = 0.0001$.

the solution. Hence from above, it has been suggested that the learning rate is dynamic instead of static throughout training the model. Manually changing the learning rate sometimes helps or choosing the scheduler policies.

10.4 Conclusion

In this work, we have made an attempt to determine how the choice of gradient-based optimizers changes the performance of the models by applying different optimizers on the COVID-19 dataset. Selection of the optimizer to train the model is dependent on various parameters like input data, learning rate, and so on. As per observation, the Adam optimizer is the best choice on different types of neural network architectures, as it helps models to train fast. Adam takes optimal steps during initial training but Adam still fails to beat the convergence as compared to SGD. To train network models having more numbers of layers like complex model DenseNet201, adaptive learning rate methods will be a good choice. The future direction of research considers changing the learning rate dynamically during training either manually or by using different schedulers like exponential scheduler or cosine annealing scheduler.

REFERENCES

[1] Simonyan, Karen and Andrew Zisserman, "Very deep convolutional networks for large-scale image recognition," Conference paper at (ICLR 2015), pp. 1–14.

[2] He, K., X. Zhang, S. Ren, and J. Sun, "Deep residual learning for image recognition," in Proceedings of 2016 IEEE Conference on Computer Vision and Pattern Recognition (Las Vegas, NV, USA, 2016), pp. 770–778.

[3] Huang, G., Z. Liu, K. Q. Weinberger, and L. van der Maaten, "Densely connected convolutional networks," in Proceedings of 2017 IEEE Conference on Computer Vision and Pattern Recognition, (Honolulu, HI, USA, 2017), pp. 2261–2269.

[4] Tan, Mingxing and Quoc V. Le, "EfficientNet: Rethinking model scaling for convolutional neural networks," in Proceedings of the 36th International Conference on Machine Learning (Long Beach, California, PMLR 97, 2019).

[5] Szegedy, C., W. Liu, Y. Jia, P. Sermanet, S. Reed, and D. Anguelov et al., "Going deeper with convolutions," in Proceedings of 2015 IEEE Conference on Computer Vision and Pattern Recognition (Boston, MA, USA, 2015), pp. 1–9.

[6] Ruder, S., "An overview of gradient descent optimization algorithms," 2016. Retrieved from http://arxiv.org/abs/1609.04747 (29 October 2020).

[7] Czarnecki Wojciech Marian, "On loss functions for deep neural networks in classification," arXiv:1702.05659v1 [cs.LG] (18 February 2017).

[8] Nie, Feiping, Zhang Xuan Hu, and Xuelong Li, "An investigation for loss functions widely used in machine learning," *Communications in Information and Systems*, 18(1): 37–52 (2018).

[9] Le, Quoc V., Jiquan Ngiam, Adam Coates, Abhik Lahiri, Bobby Prochnow, and Andrew Y. Ng, "On optimization methods for deep learning," Appearing in Proceedings of the 28 th International Conference on Machine Learning (Bellevue, WA, USA, 2011).

[10] Ioffe, Sergey and Christian Szegedy, "Batch normalization: Accelerating deep network training by reducing internal covariate shift," Retrieved arXiv:1502.03167 [cs.LG] (23rd March 2015).

[11] Ruder, Sebastian, "An overview of gradient descent optimization algorithms," arXiv:1609.04747v2 [cs.LG] (15 June 2017).

[12] Polyak, B. T. and A. B. Juditsky, "Acceleration of stochastic approximation by averaging," *SIAM Journal on Control and Optimization*, 30(4): 838–855 (1992).

[13] Lan, Guanghui, "An optimal method for stochastic composite optimization," *Mathematical Programming*, 133(1–2): 365–397 (2012).

[14] Roux, Nicolas L., Mark Schmidt, and Francis Bach, "A stochastic gradient method with an exponential convergence rate for finite training sets," In *Advances in Neural Information Processing Systems (NIPS)* (2012), pp. 2663–2671.

[15] Johnson, Rie and Tong Zhang, "Accelerating stochastic gradient descent using predictive variance reduction," In *Advances in Neural Information Processing Systems* (2013), pp. 315–323.

[16] Defazio, Aaron, Francis Bach, and Simon Lacoste-Julien, "SAGA: A fast incremental gradient method with support for non-strongly convex composite objectives," In *Advances in Neural Information Processing Systems* (2014), pp. 1646–1657.

[17] Bottou, Léon, Frank E. Curtis, and Jorge Nocedal, "Optimization methods for large-scale machine learning," *SIAM Review*, 60(2): 223–311 (2018).

[18] Kingma, Diederik P. and Jimmy Lei Ba, "Adam: A method for stochastic optimization," arXiv:1412.6980v9 [cs.LG] (30 January 2017).

[19] Dean J., G. S. Corrado, R. Monga, A. Y. Chen et al.,, "Large scale distributed deep networks." *NIPS 2012: Neural Information Processing Systems*, 1–11. http://papers.nips.cc/paper/4687-large-scale-distributed-deep-networks.pdf (2012).

[20] Kingma, Diederik and Jimmy Ba, "Adam: A method for stochastic optimization," Published as a conference paper at the 3rd International Conference for Learning Representations (San Diego, pp. 1–13, 2015), arXiv:1412.6980 [cs.LG].

[21] Duchi J., E. Hazan, and Y. Singer, "Adaptive subgradient methods for online learning and stochastic optimization," *Journal of Machine Learning Research*, 12, 2121–2159 (2011). Retrieved from http://jmlr.org/papers/v12/duchi11a.html.

[22] Zeiler M. D., "ADADELTA: An adaptive learning rate method," Retrieved from http://arxiv.org/abs/1212.5701 (22 December 2012).

[23] Reddi, Sashank J., Satyen Kale, and Sanjiv Kumar, "On the convergence of Adam and beyond." In *International Conference on Learning Representations* (2018). arXiv abs/1904.09237.

[24] Dozat, T., "Incorporating Nesterov Momentum into Adam," *ICLR Workshop* 1, 2013–2016 (2016).

Section III

Applications of Data Science and Data Analytics

11

Wheat Rust Disease Detection Using Deep Learning

Sudhir Kumar Mohapatra, Srinivas Prasad, and Sarat Chandra Nayak

CONTENTS

11.1 Introduction

Nowadays, technologies deliver to humankind the ability to produce enough food for billions of people over the world. Even though the world is producing huge amounts of crops to ensure food security of the people, there are a lot of factors that are threats in the process of ensuring food security. The threats that basically occur on crops can be with climate changes, pollinators, and plant diseases. Plant diseases are not only threats to global food security, but they also have devastating consequences on smallholding families in Ethiopia, who are responsible for supporting many in one family. In Ethiopia, this crop is the second most [1] used crop to ensure food security and covers an estimated 17% of Ethiopia's total agricultural land use. It is not only a critical crop to smallholder farmers' livelihood but also a means of ensuring food security for millions of people in Ethiopia.

The outbreak of wheat rust disease is threatening the crop production gain of the country in wheat-producing regions of Ethiopia, following a long period of El-Niño caused by drought across the country. The wheat rust was first spotted in Southern Nations (SNNP) regions and Oromia. The crop-damaging fungus has since spread to different regional states, especially to the northern part of the country, and especially to Amhara and Tigray regions. These diseases basically occur by funguses, well known to bring stunting in plants and cause pre-harvest losses between 50% and 100%. Wheat rusts are known to cause stunting in plants and pre-harvest losses of between 50 and, in severe cases, 100% [2], the diseases have been detected in nearly 2,200 communities and on close to 300,000 hectares of land across the country. The application of machine learning, particularly deep learning in agriculture fields, is showing promising result. Deep learning can be summarized as a sub-field of machine learning [3] that study statistical models called deep neural networks. Early work on deep learning, or rather Cybernetics, as it was called at the time, was done in the 1940s and 1960s, and describes biologically inspired models such as Perceptron, Adaline, or Multi-layer Perceptron. Then, a second wave called Connectionism came in the years 1960–1980 with the invention of "backpropagation." This algorithm persists today and is currently the algorithm of choice for optimizing deep neural networks. The ambition for creating a feasible neural network for detection and recognition of images that have automatic feature extraction and translation invariance promotes a new category of neural networks called Convolution Neural

Network (ConvNet). These networks have special types of processing layers in the extractor module that learns to extract discriminated features from the given input image.

11.2 Literature Review

There are three most common wheat rusts, which are very severe and have the capability of damaging 50 to 100% of the crop unless it is controlled as soon as it occurs on the crop. These rusts are leaf rust, yellow rust, and stem rust. From these rusts, stem and yellow rusts represent the greatest disease threat to Ethiopian wheat farmers, with both diseases capable of causing huge losses. Even though yellow and leaf rusts are both types of leaf rusts, they are treated as different kinds of rust races, but most of the time they are identified in laboratories, because of the similarities they make on the structure and color of the fungus on the crop.

Even though machine learning applications advance in such fields, efficiency from different angles still remains a question. Authors [4] used 15,000 manually cropped RGB images into a single leaf to detect only the infected area of the crop. These images were used to classify three types of cassava leaf diseases, by applying a different set of a train, validate, and test split ranges, in which 10% is used for validating the model, and others are used for train and test of 10/80, 20/70, 40/50 and 50/40%, respectively. They also used Google InceptionV3 and achieved 98% of accuracy, but at the same time, this study cannot achieve good performance when we have random images, which are captured under random conditions, which will not allow the model to be applied in real-world conditions.

The researcher [5] used GoogleNet and AlexNet models to train 54,306 images from the plant village website, in which GoogleNet performs better and consistently with a training accuracy of 99.35%. But in this study, the accuracy degrades to 31.4% when it is tested using images taken under conditions different from images used for training the model. In this study, we have used three train test split distribution of 75/25, 60/40, and 70/30 in percent with three types of image types, which are RGB color images, grayscale images, and segmented images.

Authors [6] used an automated pattern recognition using CNN to detect three types of plants and their diseases, based on simple leaves of the plants, using the five basic CNN models, from pre-trained models. The study uses 70,300 for training and aother 17,458 images for testing, with a standard size of 256 × 256 pixel size. Models fine-tuned [4,7,8] in these studies are AlexNet, AlexNetOWTBN, GoogleNet, OverFeat, and VGG, with the highest accuracy on the training set with 100% and 99.48% on the testing set in VGG model.

Practically, deep learning [9,10] is a subset of machine learning with more power and flexibility than traditional machine learning approaches. The biggest advantage of deep learning algorithms is that they try to learn high-level features from data in an incremental manner. This prevents the need for manual feature extractions, which is done by human intervention in traditional machine learning. Deep learning emulates the human brain [11], and it works with unstructured data, especially for applications like computer vision (image processing) and speech recognition.

TABLE 11.1

Some Selected Work Relevant to This Study

Ref.	Technique	Accuracy	Gaps
Ramcharan et al. (2017) [4]	Applied fine-tuning using pre-trained deep learning models.	99.35%	The study constrained to single leaf images with homogenous background
Mohanty et al. (2016) [5]	Applied different pre-trained networks to train it on laboratory images	99.48%	Accuracy degrades when the model tested on images from real cultivation field
Ferentinos et al. (2018) [6]	Fine-tuned Resnet50 model	87%	Images are segmented manually by expert technicians

11.3 Proposed Model

This is a convolutional neural network architecture and implemented from scratch with 2,113 data of the infected and healthy image classes, with three different training and test split sets, which are categorized as 1,633 for training, 411 for validating the model, and the rest for an explicit singlet test if needed. These train test split distributions are 50%–50%, 75%–25%, and 70%–30% for train and test, respectively. Sigmoid activation function for the output layer is used with the loss function of the binary cross-entropy and the efficient Adam gradient descent algorithm is used to learn the weights using the most common and efficient learning rates of 0.001 and 0.0001.

The first layer is a convolution layer called a Conv2D. The layer has 32 feature maps, which has a size of 3 × 3 and a rectifier activation function. This is the input layer, expecting images shape with (pixels, width, and height) which I fed it with 150 × 150 image sizes. The next layer contains a pooling layer that takes the max called MaxPooling2D. It is configured with a pool size of 2 × 2. The second layer contains a convolutional layer with 32 feature maps with a size of 3 × 3 and a rectifier activation function called ReLU and a pooling layer with a size of 2 × 2. The third layer contains a convolutional layer with 64 feature maps with the size of 3 × 3 and rectifier activation function followed by the max pooling layer with a pool size of 2 × 2. The next layer converts the 2D matrix data to a vector called flatten; it allows the output to be processed by standard fully connected layers flowed by a rectifier activation function. The next layer is a regularization layer using Drop out. It is configured to randomly exclude 30% of neurons in the layer in order to reduce overfitting. The next layer is a fully connected layer with 64 neurons with a rectifier activation function. The output layer has two neurons for the two classes and a sigmoid activation function to output probability-like predictions for each class. The model is trained using a binary cross-entropy as loss function and the ADAM gradient descent algorithm with different learning rates.

11.4 Experiment and Results

11.4.1 Dataset Preparation

There are around 213 original datasets and the data is augmented into around 2,113 images, by applying 10 feature factors, which are rotation, width shift, height shift, rescaling, shear, zoom, horizontal flip, fill mode, data format, and brightness. These features are applied to every single image in the original image, and generated more than 2,000 images from those original images and save it in the same format; in my case, I used a PNG image format. The next thing is to increase the dataset size (amount) by using the 10 feature factors, as described in the above section. Here are the augmented images of the original image.

Figure 11.2 shows images that are generated from one original image by using an augmentation technique to generate 21 different images, which means 20 images are using 10 feature factors for a single image [1 × 10 + 1 original image], which results in 21 total images. Therefore, from 213 images, 2,113 training images are generated for the designed model.

11.4.2 Image Pre-processing

The images in the dataset are sparse in nature with different dimension sizes; thus, we need to normalize to the same image dimension. Therefore, a dimension of 150 × 150 for all images in the training set is used. Here are some samples of distorted data that needs to be pre-processed or resized to the same image dimension, which is a 150 × 150 image size. Figure 11.3 shows sample images that are not pre-processed and resized images of the size 150 × 150.

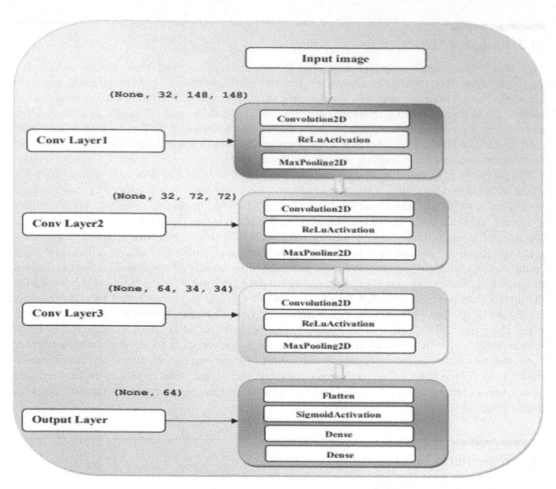

FIGURE 11.1 Schematic diagram of the model.

11.4.3 Image Segmentation

After sorting out our images by performing the pre-processing step through resizing, the next step is to segment the image based on the color code from the infected crop images.

There are two kinds of images, the first row with four images, which are the normal RGB images (before segmentation), and the four images with their respective below are segmented images for their respective original images on the above. Therefore, by segmenting all images in the training set to feed to the model, it can easily classify them by identifying the patterns made in the segmentation part. In this case, the healthy images hold solid black without any pattern and the infected images form a specific pattern, which is totally different from the healthy images and by comparing images with patterns and without patterns it perfectly classifies them into healthy or infected crops.

After performing all the evaluations on the grayscale and color-segmented dataset on the model, experiments with top results are discussed below. The model is evaluated using different parameters that can affect the efficiency of the model. These parameters are a number of epochs; train test split ratio, learning rate, and dropout ratio. Different parameter ratios are used for the evaluation purpose.

Table 11.2 summarizes top results found for the evaluation of the model on three types of dataset types, which are used for the purpose of comparison. These dataset types are the grayscale image type, which is a type of images with only one color channel, the RGB image types, which are images

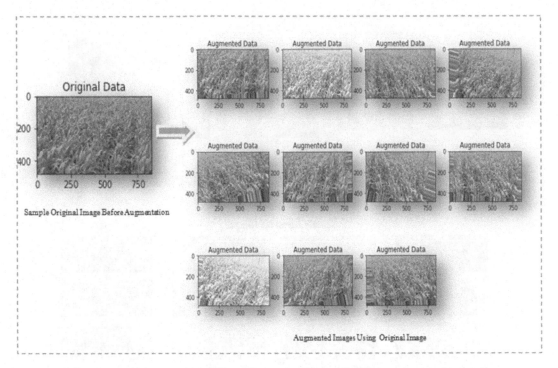

FIGURE 11.2 Sample original image before augmentation and augmented images using original image.

containing more than 16 million colors in one RGB image and the RGB segmented images which are images proposed in this study.

11.4.4 Discussion for the Model on Grayscale Images

Grayscale images are images with only one color channel, which cannot hold enough information to be processed or extracted from the image data. Evaluating the same model on the same dataset in Table 11.3, by changing their parameters that can affect the efficiency of the model, the effect of the learning rate is discussed for results 1 and 2 in the table. The only parameter changed from the two results is their learning rate, in which 0.001 is used for the first result and 0.00001 is used for the second result, which results with an accuracy of 85.89% and 81.63%, respectively. This shows that the learning rate in result 1, which is equal to 0.001, has decreased to 0.00001 in result 2.

This sounds, as the learning rate decreases, the accuracy of the model decreases proportionally, which sounds like decreasing the learning rate means, decreasing in the speed of the learning ability of the model. The model starts to degrade on the 300th epoch and this shows for grayscale images it has nothing more to extract and learn because there is only one channel; this makes it lose more features from the data and that will degrade the efficiency of the model after the 200th epoch. This result will force us to use RGB images, which have three channels and can contain more than 16 million colors. This helps the model to extract and learn from the color nature of images and helps to prevent losing information from the images, which can be extracted from the color of the images since in the case of this study, wheat rusts are identified by their colors from the healthy wheat images.

11.4.5 Evaluating the Model on RGB Images

After evaluating the model on grayscale images, images with only one channel, which results in a model with a lot of misclassified data on both training and validation data, is a needed option to find a new solution to get a better model that can perform in a better way.

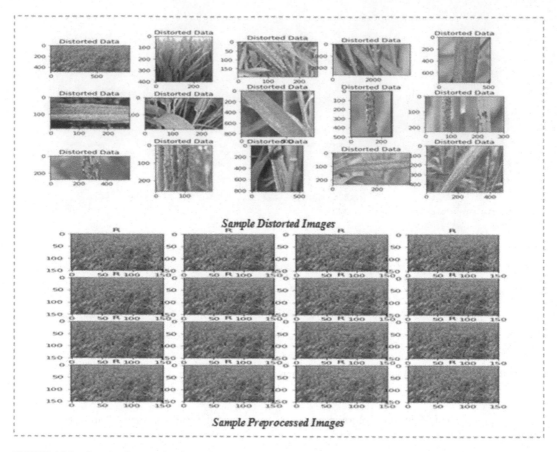

FIGURE 11.3 Sample distorted images and sample preprocessed images.

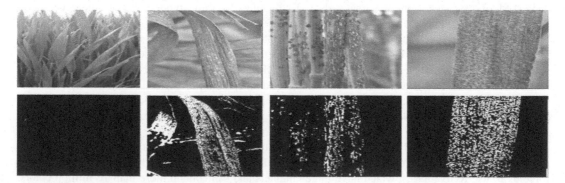

FIGURE 11.4 Image comparison of original with color segmented.

The above table summarizes the top six results found when evaluating the model on RGB images using different learning parameters and their effects on the model. As we can learn from the table, each and every parameter change has its own effect on the result the model is delivering with the training time needed and accuracy of the model.

TABLE 11.2

Summary Table for Model

No	Dataset Type	Epochs	Learning Rate	Test Ratio	Dropout	Training Time	Accuracy	Error
1	Grayscale	100	Adam(0.001)	25%	50%	60.49	85.89%	14.11%
		100	Adam(0.00001)	25%	50%	60.95	81.63%	18.37%
		200	Adam(0.001)	25%	30%	120.77	80.78%	19.22%
		200	Adam(0.001)	25%	50%	120.43	86.62%	13.38%
		300	Adam(0.001)	25%	50%	179.25	79.08%	20.92%
2	RGB	200	Adam(0.001)	25%	50%	110.34	98.78%	1.22%
		200	Adam(0.001)	20%	50%	115.65	98.48%	1.52%
		300	Adam(0.001)	25%	30%	170.9	99.51%	0.49%
		300	Adam(0.001)	25%	50%	196.24	99.27%	0.73%
		300	Adam(0.0001)	25%	50%	176.19	97.57%	2.43%
		300	Adam(0.00001)	25%	50%	169.17	96.84%	3.16%
3	RGB Segmented	300	Adam(0.001)	25%	30%	165.61	99.76%	0.24%
		300	Adam(0.001)	25%	50%	168.14	98.05%	1.95%

11.4.5 Result Comparison of the Model on RGB Images Based on Learning Rate

From Table 11.4, we can take results from rows 4, 5, and 6, which have the same parameters except they differ in their learning rates, in which results in row 4 has a LR of 0.001, results in row 5 with a LR of 0.0001, and results in row 6 with a LR of 0.0001. By comparing the three results with respect to their learning rate, we can conclude the effect of the learning rate on the model. Table 11.4, row 4: Results in row 4 are evaluated using 300 epochs with a test ratio of 25% and dropout ratio of 50%, and LR of 0.001, which results in an accuracy of 99.27% taking a training time of 196.24 minutes.

As we can see from the classification report of Figure 11.6, the model achieves a 100% training accuracy and it has a few misclassifying data which are explained below in the confusion matrix. The above confusion matrix shows that the model works perfectly when tested on the images it already knows or trained on. But it has some misclassifying images on validation data, which are three misclassifying images from the total 411 validation data. The model misclassified two healthy wheat images as infected and one infected wheat image as healthy as stated on the confusion matrix for validation data.

The above classification report shows that by decreasing the learning rate from 0.001 to 0.0001 from the results in row 4, there is little change in the accuracy of the model, which decreases from 99.27% to 97.57%. But it still achieves a training accuracy of 100%, which cannot be an issue of discussion as long as the model knows the training data when we fit the model. What matters is achieving high accuracy on the validation data. It's obvious that as the accuracy of the model decreases, misclassifying data increases inversely, so in order to minimize the number of misclassifying data, we need to increase the accuracy of the model. In Figure 11.8, it is shown that as the accuracy of the results in row 5 decreased, we can figure it out as the numbers of misclassifying images are increased from the previous result.

In Figure 11.8, there are a total of 10 misclassified images that increased from the previous result in Table 11.4, row 4, the one with only three misclassified images. In the results of row 5, there are four healthy wheat images which are classified as infected wheat images and six infected wheat images which are classified as healthy. But here there is no misclassified image for the training data, which means it has achieved a training accuracy of 100%. Results in row 6 are evaluated using 300 epochs with a test ratio of 25% and dropout ratio of 50%, and LR of 0.00001, which results in an accuracy of 96.84%, taking a training time of 165.61 minutes.

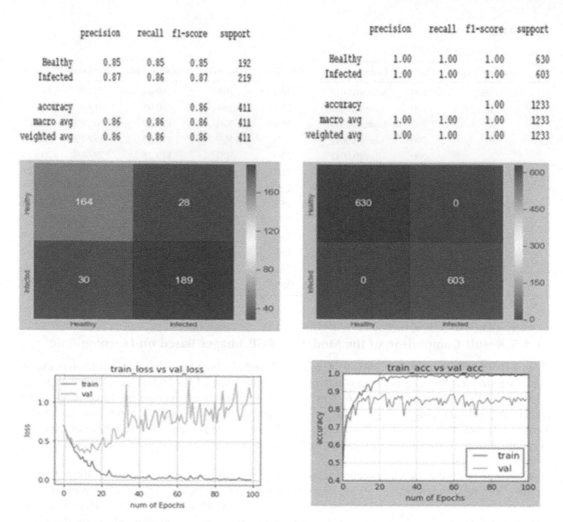

FIGURE 11.5 Model evaluation with parameters, epoch of 100, learning rate Adam (0.001), test data ratio of 25%, and dropout 50%, which results with an accuracy of 85.89%, from Table 11.3, row 1.

TABLE 11.3

Result Summary of the Model on Grayscale Images

No.	Epochs	Learning Rate	Test Ratio	Dropout	Training Time (minutes)	Accuracy	Error
1	100	Adam(0.001)	25%	50%	60.49	85.89%	14.11%
2	100	Adam(0.00001)	25%	50%	60.95	81.63%	18.37%
3	200	Adam(0.001)	25%	30%	120.77	80.78%	19.22%
4	200	Adam(0.001)	25%	50%	179.25	86.62%	13.38%
5	300	Adam(0.001)	25%	50%	120.43	79.08%	20.92%

As the results of the three evaluations are discussed above in detail, we can easily conclude the effect of the learning rate on the model based on the results the model brought. Starting from the results in row 4, the model is trained using LR 0 f 0.001 and achieved an accuracy of 99.27%, whereas with results in row 5, it is evaluated using LR of 0.0001 which is lesser learning

TABLE 11.4

Result Summary of the Model on RGB Images

No.	Epochs	Learning Rate	Test Ratio	Dropout	Training Time (minutes)	Accuracy	Error
1	200	Adam(0.001)	25%	50%	110.34	98.78%	1.22%
2	200	Adam(0.001)	20%	50%	115.65	98.48%	1.52%
3	300	Adam(0.001)	25%	30%	170.9	99.51%	0.49%
4	300	Adam(0.001)	25%	50%	196.24	99.27%	0.73%
5	300	Adam(0.0001)	25%	50%	176.19	97.57%	2.43%
6	300	Adam(0.00001)	25%	50%	165.61	96.84%	3.16%

	precision	recall	f1-score	support
Healthy	1.00	0.99	0.99	219
Infected	0.99	0.99	0.99	192
accuracy			0.99	411
macro avg	0.99	0.99	0.99	411
weighted avg	0.99	0.99	0.99	411

	precision	recall	f1-score	support
Healthy	1.00	1.00	1.00	603
Infected	1.00	1.00	1.00	630
accuracy			1.00	1233
macro avg	1.00	1.00	1.00	1233
weighted avg	1.00	1.00	1.00	1233

```
[[217    2]
 [  1  191]]
```

```
[[603    0]
 [  0  630]]
```

FIGURE 11.6 Classification report of validation and training data for Table 11.4, row 4 and confusion matrix of validation and training data for Table 11.4, row 4.

(a) *For validation data*

	precision	recall	f1-score	support
Healthy	0.97	0.98	0.98	200
Infected	0.98	0.97	0.98	211
accuracy			0.98	411
macro avg	0.98	0.98	0.98	411
weighted avg	0.98	0.98	0.98	411

(b) *For training data*

	precision	recall	f1-score	support
Healthy	1.00	1.00	1.00	603
Infected	1.00	1.00	1.00	630
accuracy			1.00	1233
macro avg	1.00	1.00	1.00	1233
weighted avg	1.00	1.00	1.00	1233

FIGURE 11.7 Classification report of result in Table 11.4, row 5.

(a) *For validation data*

```
[[196    4]
 [  6  205]]
```

(b) *For training data*

```
[[622    0]
 [  0  611]]
```

FIGURE 11.8 Confusion matrix of result in Table 11.4, row 5.

(a) *For validation data*   (b) *For training data*
precision recall f1-score support   precision recall f1-score support

	precision	recall	f1-score	support
Healthy	0.97	0.96	0.96	187
Infected	0.96	0.98	0.97	224
accuracy			0.97	411
macro avg	0.97	0.97	0.97	411
weighted avg	0.97	0.97	0.97	411

	precision	recall	f1-score	support
Healthy	0.98	0.99	0.99	635
Infected	0.99	0.98	0.99	598
accuracy			0.99	1233
macro avg	0.99	0.99	0.99	1233
weighted avg	0.99	0.99	0.99	1233

FIGURE 11.9 Classification report of result in Table 11.4, row 6.

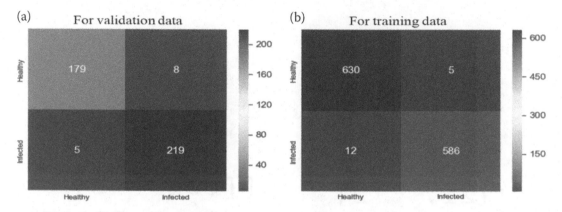

FIGURE 11.10 Confusion matrix of result in Table 11.4, row 6.

rate from the previous model and achieved an accuracy of 97.57%, which has also decreased accuracy from the previous result; finally, we continue decreasing the LR, like the results in row 6, which decreases the LR to 0.00001, it still decreased the accuracy to 96.23%. This clearly shows that decreasing the LR when still other parameters are the same, also decreases the efficiency of the model. Therefore, the model LR value of 0.001 has achieved an efficient model. Bear in mind that we have the same parameters for all three models and the only difference is their learning rate value:

LR = 0.001 → Accuracy of **99. 27%** – ––––––– **Best model**
LR = 0.0001 → Accuracy of **97. 57%**
LR = 0.00001 → Accuracy of **96. 23%**

It helps us to overcome overfitting by setting outputs on previous neurons, so that the model couldn't generalize features which drives it to overfit easily. Dropout drops some neurons from the previously hidden layers, but that doesn't mean we have to drop out all the neurons from the previous layer that affects the model to not learn some features from its preceding layers. In the model, a 30% (0.3) dropout rate has performed best, but it depends on the amount of dataset we have and this dropout rate might not work on other datasets, so we have to bear in mind that the dropout rate performed best on the model doesn't necessarily mean it will perform the same on another dataset type and model.

In Figure 11.11, we can see that the model with a dropout rate 0.3 (30%) has an f1-score of almost 1.00, which means it has a better performance than the model with a dropout rate of 0.5 (50%), both models performing an accuracy of 100% when tested on training data.

As we can see in Figure 11.12, it is clear that the dropout ratio of 0.3 (30%) worked well, with only two misclassified images, but if we see the confusion matrix with a dropout rate of 0.5 (50%), there are three misclassified images.

TABLE 11.5

Comparison Table for Results with Different Dropout Rates

No.	Epochs	Learning Rate	Test Ratio	Dropout	Training Time (minutes)	Accuracy	Error
1	300	Adam(0.001)	25%	30%	170.9	99.51%	0.49%
2	300	Adam(0.001)	25%	50%	196.24	99.27%	0.73%

(a) *Dropout = 0.5*   (b) *Dropout = 0.3*

	precision	recall	f1-score	support		precision	recall	f1-score	support
Healthy	1.00	0.99	0.99	219	Healthy	0.99	0.99	0.99	199
Infected	0.99	0.99	0.99	192	Infected	1.00	1.00	1.00	212
accuracy			0.99	411	accuracy			1.00	411
macro avg	0.99	0.99	0.99	411	macro avg	1.00	1.00	1.00	411
weighted avg	0.99	0.99	0.99	411	weighted avg	1.00	1.00	1.00	411

FIGURE 11.11 Classification report comparison based on dropout rate.

(a) *Dropout = 0.5*   (b) *Dropout = 0.3*

```
[[217    2]        [[198    1]
 [  1 191]]        [  1 211]]
```
FIGURE 11.12 Confusion matrix comparison based on dropout rate.

There is no common standard for splitting the training and test ratio because it depends on the type of data used, the ability of the model to filter information quickly, and the amount of data used to train our model. In this model, the ratio that performs best is a 75% train and 25% test split ratio. After training the model on grayscale images, the model couldn't achieve a satisfying result. So it is needed to try it on RGB images so that the model can extract more features from colored images. As discussed in the above section, we have achieved the highest accuracy level on the model after trying different methods and dataset types on RGB images, achieving 99.51% accuracy. Segmentation helps to get more important and only the needed features from the image, and that will increase the accuracy of the model because the model can get more refined information from the images. Therefore, the wheat dataset is color segmented to increase the accuracy of the model. This increases the accuracy to 99.76%.

11.5 Conclusion

Three dataset types are used in the study to conduct the experiments for the model, and these dataset types are grayscale image dataset, a dataset which only contains one-channel image, RGB dataset, a dataset with three channel images and RGB color-segmented dataset, a dataset which is RGB and segmented with the disease color code. This model has achieved an accuracy of 86.62% with 200 epochs, 0.001 learning rate, and a 50% dropout rate. This result is improved when the model is trained on the RGB image dataset, which climbed to an accuracy of 99.51%. Finally, after segmenting the images using the color of the infected images, the model extracted better information than the previous model and achieved an accuracy of 99.76% with 300 training epochs, the learning rate of 0.001, and the dropout rate of 30%. In the future, we collect a variety of data and a large set will help us to take this study a long way forward to help the agricultural system.

REFERENCES

[1] Tefera, Nigussie. "Technical efficiency of fertilizer-use and farm management practices: evidence from four regions in Ethiopia." (2020). https://www.researchgate.net/publication/344200750_Technical_Efficiency_of_Fertilizer-use_and_Farm_Management_Practices

[2] Sticklen, Mariam. "Transgenic, cisgenic, intragenic and subgenic crops." *Advances in Crop Science and Technology* 3, no. 2 (2015): e123.

[3] Miceli, P. A., W. Dale Blair, and M. M. Brown. "Isolating random and bias covariances in tracks." *In 2018 21st International Conference on Information Fusion (FUSION)*, pp. 2437–2444. IEEE, Cambridge, UK, 2018.

[4] Ramcharan, Amanda, Kelsee Baranowski, Peter McCloskey, Babuali Ahmed, James Legg, and David P. Hughes. "Deep learning for image-based cassava disease detection." *Frontiers in Plant Science* 8 (2017): 1852.

[5] Mohanty, Sharada Prasanna, David Hughes, and Marcel Salathe. "Using deep learning for image-based plant disease detection." arXiv (2016): arXiv-1604.

[6] Ferentinos, Konstantinos P. "Deep learning models for plant disease detection and diagnosis." *Computers and Electronics in Agriculture* 145 (2018): 311–318.

[7] Too, Edna Chebet, Li Yujian, Sam Njuki, and Liu Yingchun. "A comparative study of fine-tuning deep learning models for plant disease identification." *Computers and Electronics in Agriculture* 161 (2019): 272–279.

[8] Picon, Artzai, Aitor Alvarez-Gila, Maximiliam Seitz, Amaia Ortiz-Barredo, Jone Echazarra, and Alexander Johannes. "Deep convolutional neural networks for mobile capture device-based crop disease classification in the wild." *Computers and Electronics in Agriculture* 161 (2019): 280–290.

[9] Mahapatra, Sambit. "Why deep learning over traditional machine learning." *Towards Data Science* (2018).

[10] Singh, Asheesh Kumar, Baskar Ganapathysubramanian, Soumik Sarkar, and Arti Singh. "Deep learning
for plant stress phenotyping: trends and future perspectives." *Trends in Plant Science* 23, no. 10 (2018): 883–898.

[11] Hurwitz, J., and D. Kirsch. *Machine Learning Machine Learning for Dummies*. J. Wiley, June 2018.

12

A Novel Data Analytics and Machine Learning Model Towards Prediction and Classification of Chronic Obstructive Pulmonary Disease

Sridevi U.K., Sophia S., Boselin Prabhu S.R., Zubair Baig, and P. Thamaraiselvi

CONTENTS

12.1 Introduction

COPD is an acute inflammatory lung disease that results in blocked flow of air from lungs. COPD disease is categorized by recurrent respiratory problems and breathing difficulty, due to trachea defects typically triggered by strong connections to toxic pollutants or chemicals. The common indications of COPD include difficulty in breathing, prolonged cough, mucus formation, and occurrence of wheezing. COPD is normally formed by continuous contact with poisonous gases, but maximum occurrence happens by cigarette smoking. Individuals possessing COPD will be in greater danger in attaining heart diseases, lung cancers, etc. Emphysema and chronic bronchitis are the two most prevalent disorders attributed to COPD. These two disorders typically come about all together and may show variation in severity amid patients with COPD. Chronic bronchitis is the occurrence of swelling over the linings of bronchial valves that transport airflow from and to the lungs. The major symptoms include prolonged cough and formation of sputum. Emphysema corresponds to the situation in which alveoli at the terminal of the bronchioles of lungs were damaged owing to the exposure towards cigarette smoking, other poisonous gases, and particulate matters.

Even though COPD is a progressive disorder that gets worse over time, COPD was found to be fully curable. By appropriate management, numerous patients with COPD have achieved better symptom control and improved life quality, and also have attained reduced complications of other related disorders. In today's world, people are facing infectious diseases because of the state of the climate and their changing lifestyles. So, earlier-stage prediction of disease has become an essential task.

Yet, it becomes too difficult for the doctors to determine the diseases precisely based on diagnosis. One of the most difficult objectives is to determine the type of disease correctly. For overcoming these consequences, data mining plays a vital part in predicting the disease. Medical sciences have resulted in increased quantity of medical data for every year. Owing to this increase in data growth towards medical and healthcare field, exact prediction of medical information is a challenging task so as to benefit in the early treatment of patients. Several original issues and considerations associated with interpretation and information extraction with growing accumulation of big data were observed. In an age where everything is tangible, basic statistical study of the past decades is possibly not enough. The healthcare industry will benefit from the recognition of similar patterns in different patients in this setting.

Data mining discovers the secret pattern knowledge in vast number of patient data by using disease data. COPD was identified as a major global public health problem because of its associated impairments and increased death rate. Despite the increasing usefulness and effectiveness of supervised ML algorithms in the modeling of predicting diseases, there still seems to be improvement needed in the range of study. Primarily, we identified few study papers that used various supervised learning processes for predicting diseases to perform a detailed analysis. This work therefore seeks in identifying current findings amid dissimilar techniques for supervised ML strategies, their accuracy of output, and the severe diseases under study. Furthermore, the benefits and drawbacks of various machine learning algorithms under supervision are summarized.

The research findings will allow analysts to identify recent trends and reasons in disease forecasting using machine learning algorithms that are supervised and thereby refine their study goals. Recent findings have demonstrated that numerous patients have acquired COPD without having smoking habits. Additional aspects such as air pollution and lifestyle shall also affect the patients.

The chapter has been structured as follows. A detailed introduction on chronic obstructive pulmonary disease and how data mining impacts COPD is discussed in Section 12.1. A well-organized and state-of-the-art literature review encompassing machine learning models, Bayesian networks, classification methodologies, binary logistic regression algorithms, k-nearest neighbor algorithm, convolutional neural network method, deep learning methods, classification and regression tree approach, etc., and how these methods impact COPD disease prediction are vividly discussed in Section 12.2. The research methodology featuring training/testing data, feature extraction, and ML-based classification algorithm applicable towards COPD patients are elaborated in Section 12.3. Moreover, various disease classification models including logistic regression method, random forest method, etc., are also explained in this section. The experimental results and the derived outcomes from this present investigation are enumerated in Section 12.4. The concluding remarks, along with future scope, are discussed in Section 12.5.

12.2 Literature Review

Ma et al. (2020) [1] provided the design of machine learning methods towards predicting the chronic obstructive pulmonary disease over tobacco smoking individuals and people exposed to higher air pollution environment. COPD patients were saddled with routine risks of increased incidence and loss in control that shall be remedied by successful decision-support services on demand.

Swaminathan et al. (2017) [2] proposed a machine-based learning method towards early prediction and subsequent triage of exacerbations. The program uses doctor's opinions to train a supervised prediction algorithm in clinically rigorous collection of patients. The model's effectiveness is calculated against a group of clinicians in a generic patient testing collection for similar cases.

Cigarette smoke and obesity are significant causes toward etiology of chronic obstructive pulmonary disease and its clinical characteristics. Wytrychiewicz Kinga et al. (2019) [3] published more in-depth analyses of the ties among smoking behavior and body mass index, also relations among important components of Quality of Life (QoL) with patient's compliance towards illness. Their study findings indicate some mechanism towards possible impact of weight loss and smoking habits on QoL. Dangerous habits like smoking and at-risk body mass have severe effects on certain aspects of QoL related to health.

Himes et al. (2009) [4] established medical constraints that control the threat of COPD advancements over the individuals with asthma using information retrieved from electronic medical records, and used Bayesian networks to discover a forecasting model. Accurate diagnosis of people who are at risk for COPD development is crucial to the preventive and control techniques. Matheson et al. (2018) [5] aimed at systematically reviewing and monitoring the effectiveness of all published models that were forecasting COPD growth.

Macaulay et al. (2013) [6] proposed a model for prediction on the basis of assumptions about the frequency of COPD. Organizational statements are a valuable source of data towards COPD investigations but reliable measures of a patient's COPD rigorousness were typically lacking, which is an important necessity of quality of care. The model was formulated using medically assessed COPD difficulty and provides investigators with a method for classifying the individuals with the help of claim data when clinical indicators were inaccessible.

Research by Aramburu et al. (2019) [7] showed the effect of comorbidities on the major COPD rating systems. Cardiovascular diseases like coronary heart disease, irregular heartbeat, and congenital heart disease are typically the comorbidities that have severe effects on mortality rate. It should be noted that COPD was a heterogeneous disease.

Manian (2019) [8] proposed different classification methodologies and their associated phenotypes. Their investigation points out the prevailing classifications of COPD, thereby elaboratating necessary phenotypes and offers a standard framework toward COPD risk assessments. It was observed that several phenotypes/endotypes of COPD would be characteristically defined, thereby offering personalized medicine for COPD patients.

The rapid prediction and analysis of high-cost COPD patients developed by Luo et al. (2019) [9] are essential in driving the financial constraints of COPD. The objective of their research was to employ machine learning techniques for classification and identification of future high-cost patients, thereby to validate important elements of prediction results by comparing variations in forecast results over different features identified.

Logistic regression is one of the most widely employed statistical methodologies for research that involves risk assessments over complex diseases. One recent strategy is the use of binary logistic regressions. Numerous research works and implementations showed that the logistical regression model shall fulfill the category data analysis specifications and is now the traditional modeling approach for categorical predictor variables.

Xu et al. (2018) [10] discussed the significance of managing contributing effects during the study of binary logistic regression. COPD patients face routine dangers of severe exacerbation in controls that were remedied using successful decision-making resources as services. The study presented a ML-based methodology for detection in the initial stages of exacerbations and further treatments.

A predictive model for risk stratification in individuals with COPD has been developed by Bellou et al. (2019) [11]. This research is a systematic analysis and evaluation of the help accelerate for risk prediction in patients with COPD. The results suggest many computational drawbacks and a relatively low acceptance rate in their growth. Future work shall focus on improving current models by updating and quality assessment, as well as assessing the health, quality attributes, and cost-effectiveness of clinical practice implementation of these analyses amid the potential by risk assessments.

Dahiwade et al. (2019) [12] had suggested a general prediction of disease based on patient symptoms. For prediction of the disease, machine learning algorithm, K-Nearest Neighbor (KNN), and Convolutional Neural Network (CNN) were employed. The disease prediction typically requires a valid disease symptoms dataset. Along with usual disease prediction, a system that would be capable of offering lower risk associated with general disease is an important need of the hour.

Recent advancements in acoustics, automated sound processing, and diagnosis in medical technology opened up new possibilities to increase the accuracy of the detection of respiratory illnesses such as COPD. Yogesh Thorat et al. (2019) [13] tried to assess the accuracy of the COPD severity methods which were regarded using machine learning technology and lung signals. Peng J et al. (2020) [14] in their study monitored the patients with COPD and Acute Exacerbations (AEs).

Gonzalex et al. (2018) [15] have developed a deep learning model for better predictive modeling. To evaluate whether deep learning, specifically CNN research, may diagnose and point out COPD and forecast severe Acute Respiratory Disease (ARD) incidents and deaths over smokers, were the core intentions of their research. A deep learning technique that includes information from ultrasound imaging analysis only can classify those smokers with COPD and determine the patients most likely to possess ARD indications and with greatest possibility of death. Analyzing the CNN at the statistical level can be a useful method for evaluating the risk.

ML algorithms help identify and recognize diseases such as heart disease, cardiovascular disease, brain tumor, hypertension, and many more. These tools are effective in many issues of statistics and analysis that enable machines to understand from historical data and identify relevancy in recent findings. Moreover, few ML algorithms assist in the identification of sources and other variables that play an important role towards the origin of the disease.

Mariani et al. (2019) [16] analyzed the prediction methodologies towards cancer and heart disease information with the help of five ML-based approaches. Esteban et al. (2011) [17] conducted a study and validated a novel approach, a Classification and Regression Tree (CART) on the basis of readily available standardization process for death in stable COPD patients. A simple decision-making tree using factors widely collected by doctors may provide a rapid assessment of disease severity as assessed by risk.

12.3 Research Methodology

Supervised ML algorithms were dominant over the data mining field. Accurate prediction of diseases on the basis of medical information has revealed a budding consideration in such approaches. Uddin et al. (2019) [18] in their research made vast critical investigations for identifying the existing studies that have employed more than one supervised ML algorithm over a single disease prediction. This research work aims in describing the foremost tendencies amid dissimilar kinds of supervised ML procedures with their performances, thereby using them for early prediction of the risk of the disease.

The research study focuses on the following research gaps:

1. How to do efficient patients classification based on the extracted features
2. How to apply machine learning techniques to improve the accuracy
3. How the machine learning algorithms helps patients and doctors to predict the disease

Machine-learning methods, such as precision medicine, can identify consistent data trends that can inspire health experts in clinical care. Effective ML techniques used for disease predictions were used in this research. Studies such as classification of pulmonary patient information enable the process to expect distinct metrics in separating either person or group patient details. The feature selection method is implemented using the following algorithm.

Algorithm 1

Pseudo code for feature selection algorithm

Input: Training data (feature vectors with class labels),

Parameter S: number of random training samples out of total samples used to learn the weights of feature, W.

W: weights for each feature

n: total number of training samples

d: number of features (dimensions)

W[A]: 0.0; : Feature weights set

for k: 1 to S do

updating of weights

end for

end for

Return W; : weight vector of features that calculate the quality of features

---

Figure 12.1 shows the articulation of the general classification model and its associated blocks.

Predictive models using machine learning algorithms can give better diagnose chronic diseases. A large portion of global health issues are caused by chronic diseases (CDs). Life-long care is required for individuals suffering from these disorders. The predictive models of machine learning require proper data for training and testing.

Algorithm 2

Classification of COPD Disease

Begin

Apply pre-processing of COPD dataset using pre-processing statistical techniques Min-Max normalization on the dataset.

Feature selection algorithm is applied on the dataset

Train the classifiers using training dataset

Validate using testing dataset

Compute performance evaluation metrics

End

When balanced datasets are used for training and model testing, the quality of the classifier can be enhanced. In addition, the analytical capabilities of the model can be enhanced by using relevant and accurate data features. Therefore, for improving the performance of these models, data modeling and feature selection are essential. Predictive models were also used over the analysis and prediction of these diseases today. This section enumerates a few ML approaches, those would be useful in analyzing the COPD data. Moreover, the regularization techniques for obtaining the best model with significant features in the datasets have been elaborated in detail. Also, the estimation of tuning parameters of these models for obtaining the least mean square error, least misclassification rate, and best predictive accuracy have also been enumerated. The classification algorithm is given in Algorithm 2. Also, Figure 12.2 shows the method of implementation towards COPD disease classification.

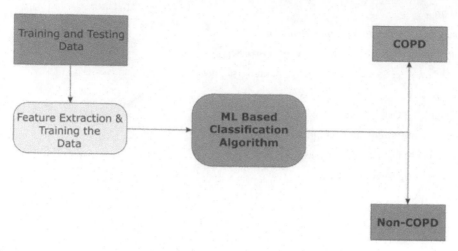

FIGURE 12.1   Classification model for COPD disease.

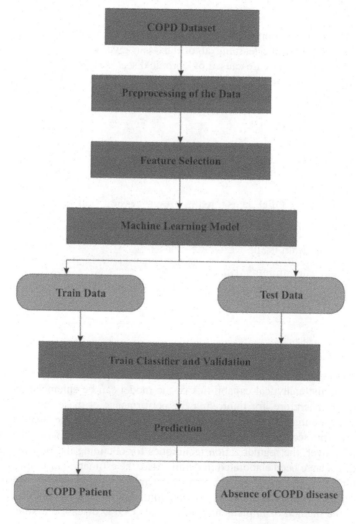

FIGURE 12.2   Method of implementation towards COPD disease classification.

12.3.1 Logistical Regression Model for Disease Classification

Logistical regression is a valid classification method that was employed in predicting the possibility of a categorical variable. Here, it is assumed that the predictors are independent of each other; thereby this model has no multi-collinearity. This model shall be expressed as below in Equation (12.1)

$$logit(p) = \beta_0 + \beta_1 x_1 + \beta_2 x_2 + \beta_3 x_3 + \ldots\ldots + \beta_k x_k \qquad (12.1)$$

where p is the probability of occurrence of characteristics of interest and $\beta_0, \beta_1, \ldots, \beta k$ are the corresponding coefficient parameters. Therefore,

$$logit(p_{COPD}) = -0.15 + (0.045)_{AGE} + (0.015)_{BMI} + (0.056)_{SMOKE} \qquad (12.2)$$

12.3.2 Random Forest (RF) for Disease Classification

The random forest method is an integrated model that is capable of predicting the data by integrating the decisions from a base model sequence. However, it is capable of reducing the variance by preventing over model fit. The base model class shall be mathematically expressed as given below in Equation (12.3)

$$g(x) = f_0(x) + f_1(x) + f_2(x) + \ldots. \qquad (12.3)$$

where last model g is combination of base classifier model f_i. Here, every base classifier is defined as a modest decision tree. Therefore, it is a valuable approach that takes multiple learning algorithms into consideration so as to obtain the best prediction model for the treatment of COPD patients.

12.3.3 SVM for Disease Classification

SVM is a supervised ML method that was typically employed for both classification and regression requirements. As specified by James et al. (2013) [19], it determines the optimal boundary of decision separating datasets from various class, thereby it forecasts the class of test results with the help of boundary of separation. Variables are averaged and scaled to get a decision boundary.

12.3.4 Decision Tree Analyses for Disease Classification

In the classification algorithms, the decision tree was applied to attribute the values and numerical features in various domains. The objective of the research is to gain valuable information through the creation of prediction model between treatment groups and patient characteristics related with the symptoms. Decision tree is amongst the most important ways of managing the data with large dimensions. Trees increasing at a particular node of decision were halted when at most one class had instances equal to or less than the "minimal cases" that prevent the tree from splitting into unnecessarily narrow nodes that have no statistics to support. Briefly, different decision trees with various "minimal cases" were determined, and the ensuing value was selected for the best performing tree.

12.3.5 KNN Algorithm for Disease Classification

A method that would be capable of classifying the diseases on the basis of absence or presence of a specific disease shall be greatly useful in formulating a valid approach towards mass drug administration programs and will be assisting in concentrating on correct patients with effective resource utilization. Moreover, the statistical tools shall tend in compromising over accuracy, speed, and efficiency. Also, implementation is basic and simple. For observed values such as the Euclidean distance, KNN is based on a distance function. The k-Nearest Neighbors of training examples are first evaluated into this classification algorithm. Therefore, the comparisons of one result from test data to neighbors, k-Nearest are collated based on the neighboring class; thereby the test sample shall be allocated to some of the most identical cases. The efficiency of the kNN method is determined with the help of a distance metric that is used for extracting identification and formulating the decision rule.

This algorithm shall be explained using the following steps.

Step 1: From the dataset, separate the records with COPD disease and non-COPD disease.
Step 2: For the new unlabeled record, calculate the Euclidean distance.
Step 3: Calculate the least distance in both the patient's classes.
Step 4: By computing the smallest distance in both classes, assign the query record into the class which possesses the smallest distance.

12.4 Experiment Results

A sum of 441 COPD patients and 192 control subjects have been recruited with five clinical features. The data shared by the research contribution of Ma et al. (2020) [1] was taken as the relevant dataset and the link was assessed from https://github.com/weilan-yuan/COPD_machine-learning. The sample was checked with the program after the desired cleaning and anonymization of data. The pre-processing of data for good representation is typically important. Pre-processing methods, like eliminating missing attribute values, regular scalar, and min-max scalar, were incorporated with the dataset. Using logistic regression, descriptive and inferential statistics of all the variables, correlation amid variables of the study and a foremost forecasting methodology were presented. In addition to data analysis, in order to implement machine learning models for classification, Python library was used. The label count of the participating patients who were considered for this present investigation is shown in Figure 12.3. The figure shows the male count of 461 and female count of 172. The crosstab gives us a simple overview of the distribution of regression model on an independent predictor variable.

As many models affirm the difficulties that are generally associated with early detection of disease and refer to features that must be taken into consideration in their interpretation, the findings obtained thus far have been positive. The model maintains with the highest accuracy after training, as

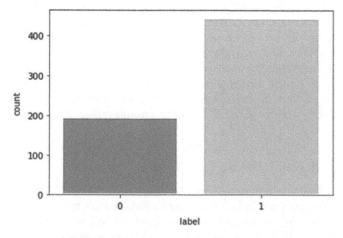

FIGURE 12.3   Label count of the participants.

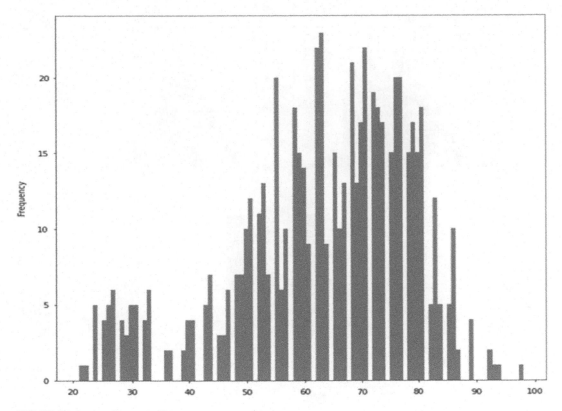

FIGURE 12.4 Age frequency histogram.

well as their hyper-parameter values. The dataset was divided into 20% and 80% for testing them in an unpredictable real-time situation, with 20% as the test set and 80% being the train set. The training algorithms transfer the best classifiers to all of them and test them with the unknown 20% results.

Figure 12.4 shows the age frequency distribution of the participating patients. From the figure, it could be seen that maximum frequency is observed inbetween 60 years to 65 years. Prior to 40 years of age, the frequency is considerably low.

Table 12.1 shows the sample correlations between the features. The parameters including label, sex, age, body mass index, and smoke have been considered for the formulation of this current research.

Figure 12.5 enumerates the feature distributions including parameters like label, sex, age, body mass index, and smoke. Figure 12.6 exhibits the correlation matrix of the features. Alternatively, Figure 12.7 shows the confusion matrix for the COPD dataset for this experimentation.

TABLE 12.1

Correlation between the Features

	Label	Sex	Age	BMI	Smoke
Label	1.000000	−0.323147	0.542443	−0.029823	0.358614
Sex	−0.323147	1.000000	−0.183081	0.067489	−0.513150
Age	0.542443	−0.183081	1.000000	0.005443	0.269636
BMI	−0.029823	0.067489	0.005443	1.000000	−0.095913
Smoke	0.358614	−0.513150	0.269636	−0.095913	1.000000

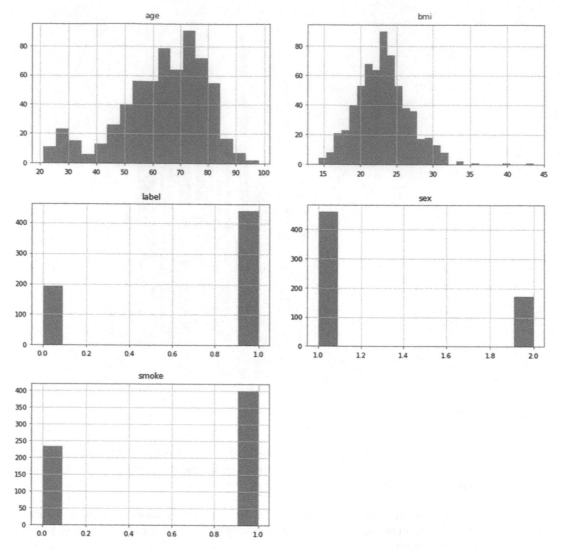

FIGURE 12.5 Feature distribution.

We have divided the dataset into 20% and 80% for testing them in an unpredictable real-time situation, with 20% as the test set and 80% being the train set. The predictive logistical regression accuracy score based on 80 training data and 20 test data is observed as 82%. Model accuracy by using the Jaccard similitude value is 0.832. Figure 12.7 displays the matrix of uncertainty for the real and expected values. Table 12.2, with its results, shall permit us to infer that for training purposes, it is not always appropriate to consider large quantities of data from records and that it shall be relevant to often use the minimum collection of usable data records.

Undoubtedly, a collection of 441 data records will offer entire details and shall render classifications and forecasts as accurate as possible. Support vector machine calculation delivered an accuracy of 73%, logistic regression with 72%, random forest with 74%, decision tree with 74%, and KNN with a highest accuracy of 75%.

However, as per the classification results over COPD, severity level using the K-Nearest Neighbor algorithm, the attained accuracy is 75%, and the corresponding F1 score was 81%, which is higher compared to the accuracy obtained using other algorithms.

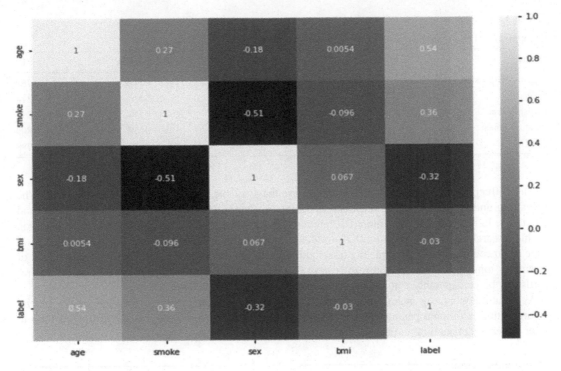

FIGURE 12.6 Correlation matrix.

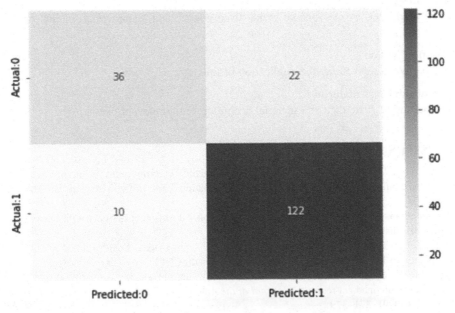

FIGURE 12.7 Confusion matrix for the COPD dataset.

12.5 Concluding Remarks and Future Scope

A methodology that shall classify the diseases based on presence/absence of a particular disease shall assist in the implementation of a consistent plan in mass drug administration systems, which shall aid

TABLE 12.2

Comparison of the Considered Machine Learning Models

Model	Accuracy	Recall	Precision	F1
Logistic Regression	0.72	0.739	0.844	0.788
KNN	0.755	0.77	0.861	0.814
Decision Tree	0.740	0.716	0.887	0.792
Random Forest	0.740	0.796	0.824	0.809
SVM	0.732	0.716	0.875	0.788

towards effective selection of patients as well to use the available resources in an effective manner. The prevailing and well-established statistical models were found to compromise of accuracy, speed, and efficiency. In this chapter, we explored different techniques of machine learning. The foremost intention of this research is to use such algorithms to identify patients with COPD disease. For each method, we have enhanced the model by extracting less-significant parameters over cross-validation with the help of dissimilar tuning parameters. The results have clearly revealed that the data acquired from health records can be considerably employed in formulating effective prediction models.

As a future work, by making considerable enhancements in methods for data extraction and by incorporating additional parameters, these models shall be made to be clinically relevant, thereby to offer better understanding in predicting the disease trends and disease statistics.

12.6 Declarations

Source of funding

This research work received no specific grants from government, commercial, or non-profit funding agencies.

Consent for publication

We declare that we consented for the publication of this research work.

Availability of data and material

Authors are willing to share data and material according to the relevant needs.

REFERENCES

[1] Ma, X., et al. "Comparison and development of machine learning tools for the prediction of chronic obstructive pulmonary disease in the Chinese population." *Journal of Translational Medicine* 18 no. 146 (2020).

[2] Swaminathan, S., et al. "A machine learning approach to triaging patients with chronic obstructive pulmonary disease." *PLoS One* 12 no. 11 (2017).

[3] Wytrychiewicz, Kinga, et al. "Smoking status, body mass index, health-related quality of life, and acceptance of life with illness in stable outpatients with COPD." *Frontiers in Psychology* 10 (2019).

[4] Himes, B. E., et al. "Prediction of chronic obstructive pulmonary disease (COPD) in asthma patients using electronic medical records." *Journal of the American Medical Informatics Association: JAMIA*, 16 no. 3 (2009): 371–379.

[5] Matheson, M. C., et al. "Prediction models for the development of COPD: a systematic review." *International Journal of Chronic Obstructive Pulmonary Disease* 13 (2018): 1927–1935.

[6] Macaulay, Dendy, et al. "Development and validation of a claims-based prediction model for COPD severity." *Respiratory Medicine* 107 (2013): 1568–1577.

[7] Aramburu, A., et al. "COPD classification models and mortality prediction capacity." *International Journal of Chronic Obstructive Pulmonary Disease* 14 (2019): 605–613.

[8] Manian, P. "Chronic obstructive pulmonary disease classification, phenotypes and risk assessment." *Journal of Thoracic Disease*, 11 no. 14 (2019): S1761–S1766.

[9] Luo, L., et al. "Using machine learning approaches to predict high-cost chronic obstructive pulmonary disease patients in China." *Health Informatics Journal*, 26 no. 3 (2019): 1577–1598.

[10] Xu, W., et al. "Differential analysis of disease risk assessment using binary logistic regression with different analysis strategies." *The Journal of International Medical Research* 46 no. 9 (2018): 3656–3664.

[11] Bellou, V., et al. "Prognostic models for outcome prediction in patients with chronic obstructive pulmonary disease: systematic review and critical appraisal." *The BMJ* 367 (2019).

[12] D., Dahiwade, G., Patle, and E., Meshram. "Designing disease prediction model using machine learning approach." *3rd International Conference on Computing Methodologies and Communication (ICCMC)* (2019): pp. 1211–1215.

[13] Yogesh, Thorat, et al. "Diagnostic accuracy of COPD severity grading using machine learning features and lung sounds." *European Respiratory Journal* 54 (2019): PA3992.

[14] Peng, J., et al. "A machine-learning approach to forecast aggravation risk in patients with acute exacerbation of chronic obstructive pulmonary disease with clinical indicators." *Scientific Reports* 10 no. 3118 (2020).

[15] González, G., et al. "Disease staging and prognosis in smokers using deep learning in chest computed tomography." *American Journal of Respiratory and Critical Care Medicine* 197 no. 2 (2018): 193–203.

[16] Mariani, M. C., Tweneboah, O. K., and Bhuiyan, M. "Supervised machine learning models applied to disease diagnosis and prognosis." *AIMS Public Health* 6 no. 4 (2019): 405–423.

[17] Esteban, C., et al. "Development of a decision tree to assess the severity and prognosis of stable COPD." *European Respiratory Journal* 38 no. 6 (2011): 1294–1300.

[18] Uddin, S., et al. "Comparing different supervised machine learning algorithms for disease prediction." *BMC Medical Informatics and Decision Making* 19 no. 281 (2019).

[19] James, G., et al. "An introduction to statistical learning." *Springer Texts in Statistics* (2013): 1–419.

13

A Novel Multimodal Risk Disease Prediction of Coronavirus by Using Hierarchical LSTM Methods

V. Kakulapati, BasavaRaju Kachapuram , Appiah Prince, and P. Shiva Kalyan

CONTENTS

13.1 Introduction

People are currently suffering from the pandemic of coronavirus, an infectious disease; the occurrence activated in Wuhan. This disease is spread by individuals, and healthcare found that many cases were reported in Wuhan. The virus was spread by traveling outside China. This virus spread to 216 countries and territories throughout the world as of May 11, 2020. Around 4.8+ crore people suffer from this pandemic, 3.4+ cr people recovered from this virus, and 1.2 cr patients died due to this virus.

The novel coronavirus was recognized on January 7, 2020, and renamed coronavirus by the World health organization (WHO). As the epidemic was observed and tested in China Laboratories, testing performed on January 5, 2020, Chinese authorities starved of the suspected SARS virus. Since the epidemic was detected in places besides China, Melbourne has confirmed that the virus diagnosis lab

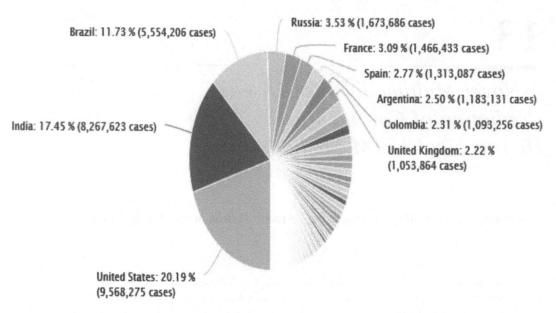

FIGURE 13.1   Total cases of coronavirus throughout world (from world meter).

has effectively brought up the PDIII (Peter Doherty Institute for Infection and Immunity) pathogen cell culture lab on January 5, 2020 [1].

The rapidly increasing statistics for the pandemic [2] clearly show that coronavirus is rapidly spreading worldwide. In struggling to control the spread, the scarcity of diagnostic tests and coronavirus as a novel infection complicated non-symptoms. The raised instances of the epidemic inevitably may overburden the healthcare system, as physicians and hospital staff are overloaded in dealing with new cases and hospitals, particularly the ICU. Studies have focused on medications and epidemic-control vaccines, but clinical trials are a minimum of a one-year-long process (Figure 13.1).

Significant coronavirus symptoms are fever, dry cough, sore throat, muscle pain, and breathing problems are found in infected people (Figure 13.2).

In the field of healthcare, machine learning methods were used extensively. Crucial healthcare management technologies have now become available. These methods helped improve healthcare by predictive approaches for people around the world suffering infectious diseases. The WHO has stepped towards the use of learning and development technologies that enhance healthcare quality. The

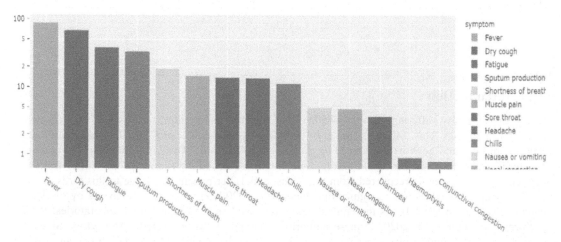

FIGURE 13.2   Coronavirus patient symptoms.

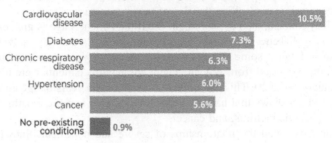

FIGURE 13.3   The percentages of coronavirus patient deaths with underlying chronic diseases.

classification, clustering, and forecasting of machine learning algorithms are used to overcome numerous problems in real-time applications. These provide confirmation of performance and reliability integrity in classification and prediction approaches.

Numerous efficient machine learning algorithms are applied to forecast and analyze serious illnesses such as kidney, diabetes mellitus, cancer, and heart conditions. Those are decision tree (DT), SVM, ANN, linear regression (LR), KNN, NB, and the forecasting models of regression models. A vast amount of data is being generated, leading to fast development and a detailed overview of the field of artificial intelligence. With the execution of a database management system, more possibilities can be generated to improve health services. Obtaining correlations and processing vast volumes of dimension data from such datasets is becoming an effective ensemble learning method. The machine learning approach is utilized to classify health datasets for supporting healthcare providers and communities to learn usefully (Figure 13.3).

The other one was recommended for the adapted Long Short-Term Memory (LSTM) form and is the appropriate treatment system classification. The LSTM networks have been successful ways to determine, analyze, and forecast data since anomalies in data can occur among significant events. LSTMs are shown as a targeted sequencing in situations of sentences. In contrast, in this situation, the context depends on the input sequence, which may be associated effectively with explorative and diminishing regression issues that may arise in the learning of conventional RNNs.

A long-term illness's complexity results in mortality for the individual who suffered from coronavirus and previously established underlying conditions such as cardiac arrest, renal disease, diabetes mellitus, and malignancy. Numerous fatalities based on these medical conditions are involved in this instance. A machine learning approach was utilized to assess the probability of chronically ill patients affected by a coronavirus, including the prevalence and intensity of an epidemic. Controlled pandemics and stochastic models indicate several possible outcomes. Analysis can also facilitate perception for demographic changes, uncertainty in travel patterns, and incorporate epidemic prevention insights. Even if coronavirus has insignificant pathogens in most of the population, a high prevalence of morbidity and mortality for individuals with associated cognitive impairment requires additional care [3].

The rest of the chapter is divided into various sections. The proposed work is discussed in Section 13.1, and literature studies are addressed in Section 13.2. The chapter's theme is explored in Section 13.3, and the methodology of the proposed work is explained in Section 13.4, followed by the outcomes of the relevant experiment described in Section 13.5. Section 13.6 discusses the proposed method and its significance, followed by concluding remarks in Section 13.7, and the future direction in Section 13.8.

13.2   Related Works

Nevertheless, different risk management methods are used for increasing the probability of deep learning models for higher-quality predictions [4–6]. Moreover, in these multitudinous and multimodal research results, forecasts can be produced relatively accurately utilizing evolutionary learning techniques instead of uni-model data [7]. Also, early detection of coronavirus by using the Hybrid MCS (Monte-Carlo simulation) technique [8] was developed for supporting countries in implementing essential steps and decisions on controlling the rise of new coronavirus.

The coronavirus- [9] contaminated person might die if the patient's age is greater than 50 years or if cardiovascular issues or diabetic indications can be confirmed. As per the analysis, as a decision on quarantine liberation or fatality, some patients were infected with coronavirus communicable diseases. The epidemic probably originated from Wuhan, where coronavirus patients were treated and diagnosed in hospitals until January 26, 2020. This risk of death was above 56 years of age and 62% were men out of the total patients, which shows that half of the fatality patients had pre-existing medical conditions such as heart issues, diabetic mellitus, and cancer.

Numerous investigators found the relationships of severe and persistent illnesses with COVID-19. One method is assessing coronavirus patients with detected risks of chronic disorders as of diabetes, cardiovascular, and dementia-related problems and high blood pressure [10]. The existence of such chronic health conditions in ICU is anticipated by healthy patients. In patients suffering from cardiovascular attack (10.5%), high cholesterol (7.3%), and blood glucose levels (6.0%), the fatality rate rises by 2.3% compared to previous investigations about the patient who suffers from chronic diseases. Several experiments have also demonstrated that coronavirus patients with acute conditions are at greater risk. Italy's statistics to be submitted to the dissociative disorders system for comparable death rates and an increased risk of death with underlying pre-existing medical conditions [11]. Demanding data are available as an epidemic outbreak.

The fatality rate of coronavirus patients who have a pre-existing cardiovascular disease is 10.5%. Patients with diabetes havereduced immunity and become rigid to fight against the virus. People with elevated blood sugar levels as in diabetes may gradually provide an environment for infections to flourish. Those with chronic asthma-like breathing problems and lung disease also have a higher risk if they are infected by coronavirus.

Though people may not know the risk aspects of COVID-19, numerous investigations have developed a substantial percentage of enduring pre-existing health conditions. In [12], SARS-Cov pneumonia exhibits that 50.5% of patients had enduring chronic health conditions, heart issues, and brain-related issues 40.4%. Of SARS-CoV-2 patients (1,099), 23.2% had at least one pre-existing disorder, and hypertension was 14.9% and diabetes was 7.4%. Also, coronavirus patients were likely to have comorbidities when compared with non-severe diseases. Similarly, out of 138 SARS-CoV-2 patients with pneumonia, 47% had comorbidities (Figure 13.4).

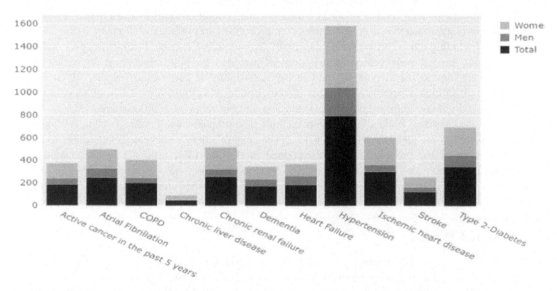

FIGURE 13.4   The coronavirus patient fatalities with underlying pre-existing chronic diseases [13].

Diabetes patients infected by coronavirus can require specialized medical care [14]. In a "public health emergency" situation, several medicines were utilized to cure the coronavirus. These medicines were an antimalarial drug, chloroquine, derived from HCQ (hydroxychloroquine) of another antiviral medication. This HCQ is approved in the diagnosis of diabetes type 2 in India as a third- or fourth-line drug, and it is fascinating to look into its effect in patients with diabetes, tainted with COVID-19.

The treatment of chronic diseases was developed by CNN, LSTM, and hierarchical models [15]. Four machine learning algorithms, such as the SVM, kernel, sparse logistic regression, and random forests [16] described forecasting chronic cardiac and diabetic disorders. The community net algorithm [17] is recommended to predict chronic diseases for a convolution neural network (CNN). The analyses are then carried out utilizing evidence from nearby medical centers and noted that the highest accuracy has been attained by CNN. The deep learning technique [18] has predicted chronic disease of the kidneys.

The CNN-MDRP model utilizes numerical and categorical data from hospitals as the basis of the convolution neural network. A method [19] is established for predicting chronic disease through machine learning algorithms such as Naïve Bayes, decision-making book, SVM, and ANN. The efficiency of algorithms is evaluated in contrast. It is known to be the most reliable rate for predicting diabetic disease with the vector machines and Naïve Bayes. To forecast chronic illness, a deeply learned algorithm was used to develop natural computational algorithms [20] for diagnosing chronic disease [21] and an automatic learning algorithm for developing e-health for diagnosing chronic diseases [22].

A neural network [23] demonstrated hand-foot-mouth diseases in preparation. To forecast pathologic disease wavelets, outbreak spareness was analyzed by using [24] ML algorithms. AI instruments are also suggested to predict coronary disease outbreaks [25], measles, and epidemic diarrhea. A pleasant analysis of AI requests is recorded on such a projection [26]. To classify individual risks, a group learning approach [27] is suggested. Multivariate regression models are used in other health fields such as outbreaks of antibiotic resistance [28] and outbreaks of influenza [29]. Various algorithms are efficiently utilized in multiple predictions, such as the deep neural network [30], LSTM (long-term memory model) [31], GRU (gated recurring unit), and GMU (gated repeating model).

13.3 About Multimodality

Multimodality of risk prediction of coronavirus, a combination of chronic disease modalities may provide a better solution to overcome the independent techniques' limitations. This approach may offer a large amount of information for each pre-existing medical condition associated with coronavirus risk prediction. These proposed models predict the disease based on multimodal (Support Vector Machine, Naive Bayesian, RNN) classifier algorithms with hierarchical LSTM. The proposed model will be beneficial for the medical industry as well as general people. The classifier obtained by supervised machine learning techniques will be very supportive in medical disorders and proper diagnosing.

13.3.1 Risk Factors

While the coronavirus risks are uncertain, numerous studies have demonstrated that a substantial percentage of patients have pre-existing medical conditions. In SARS-CoV influenza respondents, 50.5% of patients have been diagnosed with chronic illnesses, 40.4% cardiac, and cerebrovascular. In 1,099 SARS-CoV-2 patients, 23.2% of the individuals have at least a single coexisting condition and 14.9% of high blood pressure, led by 7.4% of insulin resistance, seem to be the most major illness. Some other significant analyses of various inclination coronavirus cases observed that high blood pressure, accompanied by diabetic 5.4%, and cardiac, was 12.8%, other prevalent diseases. Comorbidities are more likely to happen in acute coronavirus patients than non-severe disease patients [32]. A significant correlation has also been identified in 138 SARS-CoV-2 patients with comorbidity in 46.4% of patients.

COVID-19 cases based on pre-existing conditions

PRE-EXISTING CONDITION	CASES PER CONDITION (Counts are among the 7,162 cases with completed information on pre-existing conditions.)	PERCENT OF THOSE CASES THAT ARE: NON-HOSPITALIZED	NON-ICU	ICU
Chronic liver disease	41	59%	22%	17%
Current smoker	96	64%	23%	5%
Former smoker	165	48%	27%	20%
Chronic renal disease	213	24%	45%	26%
Immunocompromised	264	53%	24%	16%
Cardiovascular disease	647	37%	37%	20%
Chronic lung disease	656	55%	23%	14%
Diabetes mellitus	784	42%	32%	19%
Other chronic disease	1,182	49%	30%	14%
One or more	2,692	52%	27%	13%
None of the above	4,470	84%	7%	2%

FIGURE 13.5 COVID-19 cases based on pre-existing conditions.

While most coronavirus victims were adolescents of middle ages, COVID-19 was also transmitted by aged and infants. Furthermore, males with coronavirus are high in occurrence than women; further investigation is needed to validate this observation. Consequently, SARS-CoV-2 may be contaminated in the clinic by medical professionals and patients with acute. Finally, there were several associated illnesses in at least 20% of COVID-19 cases, and comorbidities seem to be more probable to happen in severe cases [33,34] (Figure 13.5).

Cardiac specialists are generally involved in treating patients with COVID-19 on the relying occurrences of illness. The virus can cause heart diseases directly. Heart disease, which was before, will entitle coronavirus infections. Cardiac-infected patients have a high chance of adverse outcomes, and heart conditions have been correlated with the illness itself [10]. Cardiovascular-related risk factors may also be observed in many scenarios.

The significant proportion of affected who need medication may influence an appropriate therapeutic strategy with severe cardiovascular issues. coronavirus diagnosis has the potential for severe cardiac consequences, and CV practitioners experience having the epidemic and become sources of the outbreak. The heart rhythm of the patients with coronavirus has become a typical heart symptom. In 7.3% of the cases with a population of 137 patients hospitalized with COVID-19, cardiac palpitations were non-specific [35]. Heart attack in the inpatients with coronavirus is severe in the ICU patient and non-ICU patients (44.4% to 6.9%) in 16.7% of 138 patients [36]. Information on the patterns of arrhythmias in such patients is typically not yet documented or shown. The highest arrhythmia rates in patient populations with or without heart disease might be related to metabolic processes, hypotension, neuropsychiatric, or inflammatory stress in the context of viral infection.

Rapidly growing data implies a significant incidence of complications such as deaths in diabetic patients. For instance, the most identifiable comorbidities of non-survivors are 22% diabetes and brainvascular disorders in COVID-19 patients. A recent study revealed a cumulative countrywide death rate of 2.3%. However, this rises to 10.5% in patients with heart disease, and 7.3% and 6% for patients suffering from diabetes or hypertension [37], respectively. These findings lead to previous evidence of respiratory illnesses. For instance, at the age of 75 and above from pneumonia, death rates among adults with diabetes are higher than in this age category from heart and leukemia diseases [38].

The two preceding COVID outbreaks, SARS from 2002 that affected more than 8,000 people, specifically in many countries, has also seen identical risk warnings for diabetes [39] and MERS in 2012, impacting approximately 2,000 people [40]. This allows for enhanced diagnosis and screening of inpatient diabetes and specific doctors' facilities for COVID-19 and a decreased inpatient requirement for such cases. During this respect, a few of the investigators' noticed disturbing observations in that certain people with diabetes are discontinuing their appointments to diabetic hospitals in normal conditions. This advancement and the rise in anxiety based on social separation and moderate exercise include a fertile basis for weakening glycemic regulation and control of blood pressure, which are more susceptible to COVID-19 infections for these vulnerable patients.

Health professionals were often unable to diagnose or immunize pregnant ladies due to maternal protection concerns in earlier outbreaks [41]. If a good reason occurs, pregnant ladies are not denied life-saving intervention against this significant infectious disease threat. Then for all treatment decisions in the context of pregnancies, careful assessment of interventions' effectiveness with possible consequences is essential for maternal and fetal patients. While surveillance processes for coronavirus cases are formed, it is critical to receive and reveal data on pregnancy and pregnant women's effects.

While there is a preliminary investigation on SRAS or MERS, there has been no evidence that pregnant ladies are much more sensitive to the outbreak. However, more males than women have been affected in this novel coronavirus outbreak [34,42], which has been noticed due to detection, sensitivity, diagnosis, prediction, and treatment changes.

One of the central organs of humans is the liver. It allows the body to absorb food, eradicate poisoning, and store fuel. Hepatic disease, a term for liver disease, is damaging. There are several associated liver disorders, including signs of jaundice and lack of weight. Viruses such as hepatitis can cause liver dysfunction. The modifications in intestinal microecology under central nervous system dysfunction is a potential cause for non-medical workers with GI symptoms who are more likely to develop more symptoms and more inadequate liver function. Coronavirus in infection may contribute to GI symptoms such as diarrhea and abdominal pain. Inflation of intestinal tissue is average. Genetic changes improve the absorption of toxic metabolites and stimulate drowsiness and fatigue through the liver system to impair nervous system control. Intestinal metabolic abnormalities often lead to toxic metabolites in the intestinal tissue [43].

Renal disease is a leading cause of mortality. Numerous investigations have been reported to analyze the risk of chronic diseases, and the advancement of kidney failure is usually recognized as directly related to hypertension [44].

13.4 Methodology

The framework of the proposed multimodal coronavirus risk prediction incorporate three aspects: the multimodal extractor, the attention bidirectional recurring neural network, and the diagnosis prediction node will be implemented in this portion. A multimodal convolutional layer integrates several information categories based on three components, detection and treatment extraction feature generated, the spread of infections extraction and classification, and an insightful model combination.

13.4.1 Naïve Bayes (NB)

It is a classification algorithm for data analysis utilized to classify instances of datasets focusing on specific features or characteristics [45]. NB is a deterministic classification that utilizes the probability classification theorem [46].

13.4.2 RNN-Multimodal

The framework integrates normalized text characteristics and diagnostic information in simple RNN instead of using a complicated feature combination and then utilizes standardized RNN performances explicitly to predict the final diagnosis.

Recurring networks have the fundamental concept of having channels. Alliterations are allowed to be using knowledge from previous system passes [47]. The length of the processing is determined by many variables, but it is not unspecified. Information can be regarded as degrading, with even lesser current information [48].

13.4.3 LSTM Model

It may depend on sequences forecasting in the form of recurrent neural networks. In complicated potential problems, including translation software, voice commands, or more, it's an essential behavior. LSTM is a thriving area with in-depth analysis. LSTMs are how bidirectional, and line-to-sequence concepts are relevant in this area, difficult to figure out.

In [49] predicted the LSTM or, in other words, the RNN Special Model and projected LSTM. The model RNN needs to trick the aspects of the current layer concealed in an initially hidden n-level layer to execute LSTM. This result increases the measurement of calculation exponentially, thus increasing the limited resources available of the model. RNN models are never used easily for long and short memory calculations along with the same principles.

13.4.4 Support Vector Machine (SVM)

This is a supervised classification and regression modeling algorithm [50]. Calibration and validation data include several samples of the data [51] for classification problems in the SVM. There are one or more target values in each instance of the training data collection, and thus SVM's main objective is to construct a model that can predict target value or values.

Binary predictions were at least as exact in the SVM and Bayes Classifiers as the recTree Classifier. Classifier Fis varies from the others, as its output estimates the degree to which the input belongs to one of the two groups (positive, negative). This can be a positive thing if the risk factor of patients is expected in practice.

Recurring hierarchical neural networks (HRNNs): These is a class of stacked RNN models modeling hierarchical structures in a sequence of data (texts, video streams, speech, programs, etc.). In documents, these hierarchies may be characteristic at the lowest level, merging terms to form phrases while linking modules naming the submodules in a computer program. The central concept then is to update the neurons' weights from the various stack layers that correspond to the results' hierarchical layers.

13.4.5 Performation Evaluation

Evaluation methods are being used for the assessment of the method proposed. The real, specific, and sensitive assessment matrices, accuracy, recall, and F-score, were used to perform the proposed model. The performance measurements are measured using standard parameters. Those parameters are positive true (TP), negative true (TN), negative false (FP), and false negative (FN).

13.4.5.1 Accuracy

Precision is the number of observations that the algorithm makes for all sorts of predictions. The total number of correct marks (TP + TN) is determined by the total number of datasets (P + N) of chronic disease:

$$\text{Accuracy} = \frac{\text{True Positives} + \text{True Negatives}}{\text{All Samples}}$$

13.4.5.2 Specificity

A metric that tells us about the proportion of patients without chronic diseases that are expected as not chronic diseases (also known as a true negative rate) is the model specificity:

$$\text{Specificity} = \frac{\text{True Negatives}}{\text{True Negatives} + \text{False Positives}}$$

13.4.5.3 Sensitivity

Sensitivity is the metric that says the number of patients who currently have chronic illnesses and who are diagnosed with the classification algorithms of chronic diseases (the true positive rate, reminder, or chance of detection):

$$\text{Sensitivity} = \frac{\text{True Positives}}{\text{True Positives} + \text{False Negatives}}$$

13.4.5.4 Precision

Precision is a measure that tells about the percentage of chronically ill patients diagnosed. The positive predictive value is known as (PPV):

$$\text{Precision} = \frac{\text{True Positive}}{\text{True Positive} + \text{False Positive}}$$

13.4.5.5 F1-Score

The harmonic mean (average) of performance is the F1 score (also called accuracy, F score, F test, and recall):

$$\text{Recall} = \frac{\text{True Positive}}{\text{True Positive} + \text{False Negative}}$$

13.5 Experimental Analysis

The dataset is collected from Kaggle, which is open access, and it is cleaned data. The dataset contains pre-existing medical conditions like diabetic mellitus, heart issues, hypertension, obesity, and other health issues.

Given the data, predict the patient type and probably death in ICU. Build a model to predict how many patients with other ailments tend to be in severe ICU conditions. Identify the most common diseases that lead a patient to join ICU. Compare patients in ICU vs. home quarantined to understand which disease leads to what, home quarantine patient's common ailments vs. ICU patient's common conditions, categorize diseases into lung, heart, liver/stomach, urinal/rectal, and bucket them accordingly. Intubated patients count vs. patients in ICU count should match. Generate synthetic data for the model as 5,000 records is not enough.

Variables are patient_type, intubed, pneumonia, age, pregnancy, diabetes, copd, asthma, inmsupr, hypertension, other_disease, cardiovascular, obesity, renal_chronic, tobacco, contact_other_covid, and covid_res. icu patient_type is 1 is home quarantined patients and patient_type is 2 iis ICU patients (Figures 13.6 and 13.7).

Accuracy: 99%
Precision: 1.0
Recall: 0.9

The model design for diagnosing COVID-19 was based on RNN and LSTM. Each model was designed to detect COVID-19, using the COVID dataset. The detector for COVID-19 was trained and tested on the collected dataset, 70% for training, and 30% as a remainder for testing. To reduce the imbalance of data, the class weight technique was applied. Adjust weight inversely proportional to class

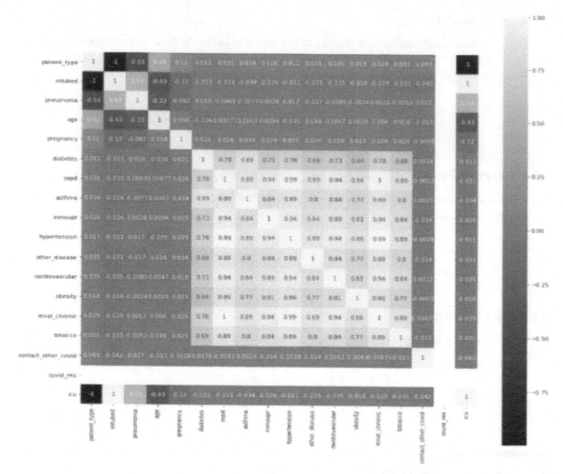

FIGURE 13.6 Heat map of the coronavirus patients with underlying chronic disease.

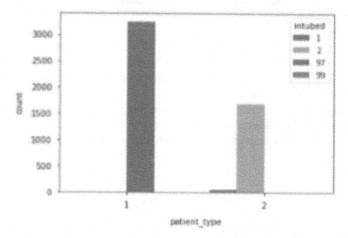

FIGURE 13.7 Home quarantined patients vs ICU patients.

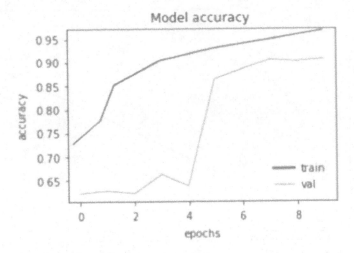

FIGURE 13.8 LSTM training and validating accuracy.

frequencies in the input data. Each model was able to distinguish between data for higher classification accuracy.

The result of the study was very encouraging in the field of diagnosing methods in COVID-19. Multiple epochs were applied to train the model of RNN and LSTM. The use of the machine learning technique was effective. The prediction model for RNN achieved a higher accuracy of 96.6% and an F-measure of 94%. Also, the LSTM attained an accuracy of 94.8% and an F-measure of 92%. The figures show the performance of both neural network models concerning classification accuracy (Figures 13.8 and 13.9).

13.6 Discussion

This analysis shows in many different ways the usefulness of multi-models to evaluate coronavirus-appropriate therapeutic cases. Initially, observations are probably better than in textbooks, and that no other way of working is better. Nevertheless, it can be thoroughly tested since there were

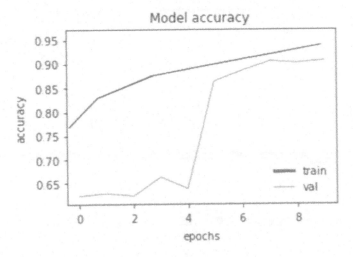

FIGURE 13.9 RNN training and validating accuracy.

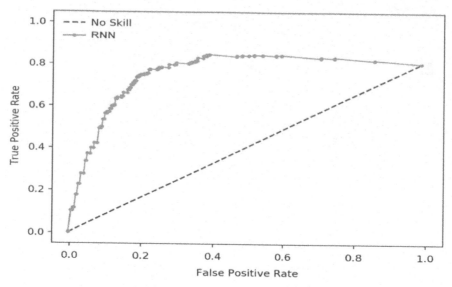

FIGURE 13.10   Area under curve of RNN.

too few learning and actual results. More systematically recorded classification results are usually recommended for some other method instructional strategy on such significant improvements. The framework is straightforward and can be effectively intended to convey via an assessment for a strategic plan. There were no specific optimal solution methods there. Both proposed models obtain a better result. Comparing our model accuracy and precision with other models, the RNN, COVID-19 prediction is best, receiving 96.6% for accuracy and 96.4% for precision. The best training process was gained as the difference between the training and validation became closer. A robust COVID-19 detector built as the F-measure improved to 0.97. The metrics of AUC were impressive as the model achieved 0.9. The figure below shows the result of the metric AUC. Thus, the COVID-19 diagnosis model trained on the x-ray data provides superior performance metrics (Figure 13.10).

Using RNN provided high sensitivity, as seen from the figure, recommend scientists working on COVID-19 to depend on systems with models built using RNN (Figure 13.11).

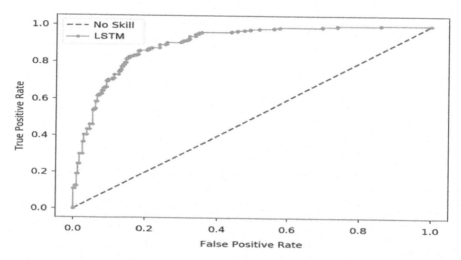

FIGURE 13.11   Area under curve of LSTM.

13.7 Conclusion

The scientific study indicates that a high chronic disease risk of mortality in patients is associated with more than 70% of the patient's total expenditure on chronic illness medication. In developed countries worldwide, treatment is a significant crisis. Serious illness is the primary cause of mortality, as per the clinical report. The long-term illness diagnosis is far more meaningful to prevent the risk of surviving. The results are comparable to the analytical techniques, including Bayes, LSTM Support Vector, and Recurrent Neural Network. The maximum precision of the recurrent neural network is when the recent input loop is recommended for an earlier diagnosis of heart disease through classifiers as a computational model system for LSTM. LSTM models showed better outcomes compared with conventional methods (with and without window duration) in predicting the risk of chronic diseases affected by the COVID-19 diagnosis.

13.8 Future Enhancement

In the future, the research aims at giving framework-based analysis by utilizing diverse techniques to estimate comparisons among the patient symptoms between risk calculation, further innovative designing of an estimate model, and feature extraction approaches and encompassing anticipated framework to forecast other scientific risks with a medical recommendation for avoiding COVID-19 with parameter analysis.

REFERENCES

[1] Nature. Coronavirus latest: Australian lab first to grow virus outside China. Available online: https://www.nature.com/articles/d41586-020-00154-w.

[2] https://www.teradata.com/Blogs/Advanced-Analytics-for-coronavirus-Trends-Patterns-Predictions.

[3] Kakulapati, V., et al., Risk analysis of coronavirus caused death by the probability of patients suffering from chronic diseases – a machine learning perspective. *JCR* 2020;7(14): 2626–2633. doi: 10.31838/jcr.07.14.499.

[4] Mukherjee, H., et al., Shallow convolutional neural network for coronavirus outbreak screening using chest X-rays. (2020). https://doi.org/10.36227/techrxiv.12156522.v1.

[5] Rajinikanth, V., et al., Harmony-search and Otsu based system for coronavirus disease (COVID19) detection using lung CT scan images. arXiv preprint arXiv:2004.03431, 2020.

[6] Das, D., et al., Truncated inception net: coronavirus outbreak screening using chest X-rays. doi: https://doi.org/10.21203/rs.3.rs-20795/v1.

[7] Fong, S., et al., Finding an accurate early forecasting model from small dataset: a case of 2019-ncov novel coronavirus outbreak. arXiv preprint arXiv:2003.10776, 2020.

[8] Fong, S., et al., Composite Monte Carlo decision making under high uncertainty of novel coronavirus epidemic using hybridized deep learning and fuzzy rule induction. *Applied Soft Computing* 2020; 93: 106282.

[9] https://www.newscientist.com/article/2236846-coronavirus-risk-of-death-rises-with-age-diabetes-and-heart-disease/#ixzz6J2szlsdL

[10] Li, B., et al., Prevalence and impact of cardiovascular metabolic diseases on coronavirus in China. *Clinical Research in Cardiology* 2020; 109(3).

[11] Porcheddu, R., et al., Similarity in case fatality rates (CFR) of COVID-19/SARS-COV-2 in Italy and China. *Journal of Infection in Developing Countries* 2020;14: 125–128.

[12] The Novel coronavirus Pneumonia Emergency Response Epidemiology Team. The epidemiological characteristics of an outbreak of 2019 novel coronavirus disease (COVID-19) e China. *China CDC Weekly* 2020; 41(2).

[13] https://www.kaggle.com/virosky/novel-coronavirus-covid-19-italy-dataset

[14] Gupta, R., et al., Clinical considerations for patients with diabetes in times of coronavirus epidemic. *Diabetology & Metabolic Syndrome* 2020 Mar 10;14(3): 211–212.

[15] Liu, J., et al., Deep EHR: chronic disease prediction using medical notes. 2018, https://arxiv.org/abs/1808.04928

[16] Brisimi, T.S., et al., Predicting chronic disease hospitalizations from electronic health records: an interpretable classification approach. *Proceedings of the IEEE* 2018;106(4): 690–707.

[17] Zhang, X., et al., A novel deep neural network model for multi-label chronic disease prediction. *Frontiers in Genetics* 2019;10: 351.

[18] Kriplani, H., et al., Prediction of chronic kidney diseases using deep artificial neural network technique. *Computer Aided Intervention and Diagnostics in Clinical and Medical Images*, Springer, Berlin, Germany, pp. 179–187, 2019.

[19] Deepika, K., et al., Predictive analytics to prevent and control chronic disease, in Proceedings of the International Conference on Applied and Aeoretical Computing and Communication Technology (iCATccT), pp. 381–386, IEEE, Bangalore, India, July 2016.

[20] Kim, C., et al., Chronic disease prediction using character-recurrent neural network in the presence of missing information. *Applied Sciences* 2019;9(10): 2170.

[21] Gautam, R., et al., A comprehensive review on nature inspired computing algorithms for the diagnosis of chronic disorders in human beings. *Progress in Artificial Intelligence* 2019;8(4): 401–424.

[22] Rojas, E.M., et al., Contributions of machine learning in the health area as support in the diagnosis and care of chronic diseases. *Innovation in Medicine and Healthcare Systems, and Multimedia*, Springer, Berlin, Germany, vol. 145, pp. 261–269, 2019.

[23] Jia, W., et al., Predicting the outbreak of the hand-foot-mouth diseases in China using recurrent neural network. 2019 IEEE International Conference on Healthcare Informatics (ICHI). IEEE, pp. 1–4, 2019.

[24] Hamer, W.B., et al., Spatio-Temporal prediction of the epidemic spread of dangerous pathogens using machine learning methods. *ISPRS International Journal of Geo-Information* 2020;9: 44.

[25] Mezzatesta, et al., A machine learning-based approach for predicting the outbreak of cardiovascular diseases in patients on dialysis. *Computer Methods and Programs in Biomedicine* 2019;177: 9–15.

[26] Philemon, M.D., et al., A review of epidemic forecasting using artificial neural networks. *International Journal of Epidemiologic Research* 2019;6: 132–143.

[27] Abdulkareem, et al., Risk perception and behavioral change during epidemics: comparing models of individual and collective learning. *PLoS One* 2020;15(1): e0226483.

[28] Jiménez, F., et al., Feature selection based multivariate time series forecasting: an application to antibiotic resistance outbreaks prediction. *Artificial Intelligence in Medicine* 2020;104:101818.

[29] Ochodek, M., et al., Deep learning model for end-to-end approximation of COSMIC functional size based on use-case names. *Information and Software Technology* 2020;103: 106310.

[30] Wen, S., et al., Real-time identification of power fluctuations based on LSTM recurrent neural network: a case study on Singapore power system. *IEEE Transactions on Industrial Informatics* 2019;15: 5266–5275.

[31] Yuan, J., et al., A novel GRU-RNN network model for dynamic path planning of mobile robot. *IEEE Access* 2019;7: 15140–15151.

[32] Guan, W.J., et al., Clinical characteristics of 2019 novel coronavirus infection in China. *medRxiv* Feb 9, 2020. https://doi.org/10.1101/2020.02.06.20020974.

[33] Chen, N., et al., Epidemiological and clinical characteristics of 99 cases of 2019 novel coronavirus pneumonia in Wuhan, China: a descriptive study. *Lancet* 2020;395: 507e.

[34] Huang, C., et al., Clinical features of patients infected with 2019 novel coronavirus in Wuhan, China. *Lancet* 2020;395: 497e506. https://doi.org/10.1016/S0140-6736(20)30183-5.

[35] Liu, K., et al., Clinical characteristics of novel coronavirus cases in tertiary hospitals in Hubei Province. *Chinese Medical Journal (Engl)* 2020;133(9): 1025–1031.

[36] Wang, D., et al., Clinical characteristics of 138 hospitalized patients with 2019 novel coronavirus-infected pneumonia in Wuhan, China. *JAMA* 2020;323(11): 1061–1069.

[37] Wu, Z., et al., Characteristics of and important lessons from the coronavirus disease 2019 (COVID-19) outbreak in China. Summary of a report of 72 314 cases from the Chinese Center for Disease Control and Prevention. *JAMA* Feb 24, 2020;323(13): 1239–1242. doi: 10.1001/jama.2020.2648.

[38] Wu, H., et al., Secular trends in all-cause and cause-specific mortality rates in people with diabetes in Hong Kong, 2001–2016: a retrospective cohort study. *Diabetologia* 2020 Apr;63(4): 757–766.

[39] Huang, Y.T., et al., Hospitalization for ambulatory-care-sensitive conditions in Taiwan following the SARS outbreak: a population-based interrupted time series study. *Journal of the Formosan Medical Association* 2009;108: 386–394.

[40] Morra, M.E., et al., Clinical outcomes of current medical approaches for Middle East respiratory syndrome: a systematic review and meta- analysis. *Reviews in Medical Virology* 2018;28: e1977. doi: 10.1002/rmv.1977.

[41] Haddad, L.B., et al., Pregnant women and the Ebola crisis. *New England Journal of Medicine* 2018;379: 2492–2493.

[42] Li, Q., et al., Early transmission dynamics in Wuhan, China, of novel coronavirus-infected pneumonia. *New England Journal of Medicine* 2020;382(13): 1199–1207.

[43] Zhou, Z., et al., Effect of gastrointestinal symptoms on patients infected with COVID-19, *Gastroenterology* 2020;158(8): 2294–2297. doi:https://doi.org/10.1053/ j.gastro.2020.03.020.

[44] Assmann, G., et al., Simple scoring scheme for calculating the risk of acute coronary events based on the 10-year follow-up of the prospective cardiovascular Münster (PROCAM) study. *Circulation* 2002;105(3): 310–315.

[45] Gandhi, R. Naive Bayes classier, towards data science. 2018. https://towardsdatascience.com/naive-bayes-classier-81d512f50a7c accessed 25th April, 2020

[46] Mehta, M., et al., SLIQ: A fast scalable classier for data mining. In: Apers, P., Bouzeghoub M., Ardarin G. *Proceedings of the 5th International Conference on Extending Database Technology*, Pringer-Verlag, Berlin, pp. 18–32, 1996.

[47] Sak, Haim, et al., Long short-term memory based recurrent neural network architectures for large vocabulary speech recognition, 2014, arXiv:1402.1128

[48] Zhang, Y.-D., et al., Fractal dimension estimation for developing pathological brain detection system based on Minkowski-Bouligand method. *IEEE Access* 2016;4: 5937–5947.

[49] Gurwitz, J., et al., Contemporary prevalence and correlates of incident heart failure with preserved ejection fraction. *The American Journal of Medicine* 2013;126(5): 393–400. 59. Clinical Classifications Software (CCS).

[50] Islam, M.M., et al., Prediction of breast cancer using support vector machine and K-Nearest neighbors. In: *2017 IEEE Region 10 Humanitarian Technology Conference (R10-HTC)*. IEEE, pp. 226–229, 2017.

[51] Mavroforakis, M.E., et al., A geometric approach to Support Vector Machine (SVM) classification. *IEEE Transactions on Neural Networks* 2006;17(3): 671–682.

14

A Tier-based Educational Analytics Framework

Javed Nazura and Paul Anand

CONTENTS

14.1 Introduction

The digitization of education in recent years has resulted in large volumes of educational data. This voluminous data with high velocity and variety can be harnessed, processed, and analyzed to obtain valuable insights leading to better learning outcomes. The potential influence of data mining analytics on the students' learning processes and outcomes in higher education has been recognized [1]. Many educational institutions have educational databases that are underutilized and could be potentially used for data mining. Educational data mining (EDM) is an important tool that analyzes the data collected from learning and teaching and applies techniques from machine learning for predicting student's future behavior through detailed information such as student's grades, knowledge, achievements, motivation, and attitude [2].

Online learning and digital content which received a fillip during the pandemic-induced lockdown is today at the cusp of transformative changes and educational analytics has a major role to play in this transformation. The multimodal, multidisciplinary, and non-sequential nature of learning today has generated large volumes of structured, semi-structured, and unstructured data requiring multifarious techniques of data analysis. This paper proposes a three-tiered framework for academic data analysis.

The first tier of our model proposes structured data analysis for numerical evaluation and prediction of student performance. Statistical techniques like aggregation, correlations, and regression analysis can be used for data summarization, data correlation, and predictive modeling. Machine learning techniques like association mining, classification, and prediction can reveal patterns, categorize data, and forecast outcomes. Unsupervised learning techniques like clustering yield performance-based clusters and discover outliers which could be students with exceptional learning capabilities or students with learning challenges.

The second tier of our framework is based on semi-structured content. This tier examines the semi-structured data and textual content to perform qualitative analysis. Though textual content is typically considered to be unstructured data, our three-tiered framework includes textual analysis in the second tier. We propose the use of text mining techniques, NLP, and computational linguistics for mining tasks such as student feedback analysis, automated assignment valuation, and valuation of subjective answer scripts. The analysis can be further extended to include the creation of intelligent linguistic models that can auto-generate answers to FAQs.

Online classes, proctored examinations, online tests, and assignments have become a norm today. Still images, audio clips, and video recordings of online classes generate multi-modal content which can be analyzed using multi-modal analysis techniques. The third tier of our framework analyzes multi-modal data to obtain deeper insights relating to student/teacher involvement, instructional strategy and class engagement. The deep learning networks like Convoluted Neural Networks (CNN), Recursive Neural Networks (RNN), and Deep Belief Network (DBN) that have exhibited enhanced machine learning outputs can be leveraged for discovering student interest, participation, effectiveness of teaching-learning process, and overall impact.

This work proposes a framework for educational analysis specifying inputs, techniques, and deliverables at each tier. It follows a use-case based approach depicting the different users, the techniques used, and the resulting outputs. This framework provides implementation guidelines for educational data analysis and advocates a model for phased implementation in the higher education institutes (HEIs) in India. It focuses on analysis for enhanced learning outcomes in the context of higher education and does not include in its scope the analysis of administrative, financial, marketing, or promotional data. It uses the term *educational data analysis* to mean academic data analysis and uses both these terms interchangeably.

To the best of our knowledge, there are no previous works in educational data analysis that propose a modular multi-tiered approach specifying the inputs and techniques at each tier, and this is the distinct contribution of our paper.

This paper is structured as follows. Section 2 examines the related works in the area of educational analytics. Section 3 describes the three-tiered framework with the use cases and the possible challenges. Section 4 discusses the implementation guidelines and challenges with a focus on the Indian context. Section 5 examines the scope and boundaries of the framework and Section 6 concludes the paper by listing possible areas of future research.

14.2 Related Works

The usage of analytics in the higher educational sector holds both promise and challenges. The main applications of learning analytics are tracking and predicting learners' performance as well as identifying potential problematic issues and students at risk [3]. This paper also talks about how analysis of big data can help to identify weaknesses in student learning and comprehension so as to determine whether or not improvements to the curriculum are necessary. Learning analytics (LA) has evolved from a mere score aggregation and predictive platform to the one that also helps identify outliers like underperforming/high-performing students and helps in the process of personalization of content [4]. Although LA is maturing, its overall potential is yet to be realized. This poses the question of how we can facilitate the transfer of this potential into learning and teaching practice [5]. This paper also points out the importance of data as the bedrock for analysis. Data plays a pivotal role in analysis and hence a careful understanding and evaluation of the data required for analysis and the analytic techniques to be adopted is essential. The potential of learning analytics which is yet to be optimally realized is also discussed [6]. Although vast volumes of data are available in Learning Management Systems (LMS), it is only recently that education institutions have begun to dip into the deep waters of data analysis and machine learning to gather insights into teaching quality and student learning experiences. The importance of data for analytics programs also finds mention in this paper. It points out the critical role of data and discusses how data sources employed in learning analytics have evolved from a single source of student learning data (e.g., LMS) to integrating multiple data sources.

Educational data analysis techniques need to go beyond mere counting and aggregation. We recognize that an analysis program is not just about simple quantitative measures, but requires consideration of multiple variables and their interactions. The significance of going beyond mere counting is also mentioned [7]. There is a need for holistic measures which combine variables from multiple sources to arrive at more accurate conclusions. In our paper, we have proposed a three-tiered approach to data analysis which enables multiple measures to be obtained from different and diverse data sources.

Learning analytics is a multidisciplinary subject, which combines advanced statistical techniques, machine learning algorithms, epistemology, and educational policies. Although it may seem promising to automate many measurements and predictions about learning and teaching, the sole focus on outcomes, as the primary target of learning analytics without consideration of teaching-learning processes can have detrimental consequences. It is imperative that all concerned stakeholders are a part of the analytics journey [7]. Learning analysis that does not promote effective learning and teaching is susceptible to the use of trivial measures such as for e.g. increased number of log-ins into an LMS, as a way to evaluate learning progression. In order to avoid such undesirable practices, the involvement of the relevant stakeholders like learners, instructors, instructional designers, information technology support, and institutional administrators is necessary at all stages of development of appropriate measures, their implementation, and evaluation of learning.

Predictive analytic models should not be interpreted in isolation. It is necessary to consider and correlate all relevant factors and parameters that come into play. A study of the cause, effect, and interplay of the parameters can help us benefit from educational analysis. For example, course completion and retention rates of underperforming students should be related to effective intervention strategies so as to help at-risk students succeed [8].

Implementing a learning analytics program is both a complex and a resource-intensive effort. There are a range of implementation considerations and potential barriers to adopting educational data mining and learning analytics, including technical challenges, institutional capacity, legal, and ethical issues [9]. Successful application of educational data mining and learning analytics will not come without effort, cost, and a focus on promoting a data-centric culture in educational institutions.

The various techniques relating to data and learning analytics are discussed [4]. The use of multimodal data in learning analysis is discussed [10,11]. The privacy and ethical issues relating to the usage of data for educational analytics are important [11] and although we have not discussed this in detail in our work, its significance in the overall scheme is acknowledged.

14.3 The Three-Tiered Education Analysis Framework

The education sector is experiencing a transformation in the method of imparting education, mode of delivery, and the method of assessment. This transformation has generated volumes of structured, semi-structured, and unstructured data. The three-tiered framework proposed by us is based on these three categories of data. Structured data is tabular, has a schema, can be organized as rows and columns, and typically includes numeric, alphanumeric, date/time, and Boolean values. Relational databases are generally used to store this data and SQL is used for manipulating/querying this data. Semi-structured data does not have a rigid structure or a schema. However, it contains tags that identify separate semantic elements and enforce hierarchies of records and fields within the data. XML data and JSON are some examples of semi-structured data. Student feedback containing ordinal values as well as textual content is an example of semi-structured data. Unstructured data does not conform to any data model and cannot be stored as rows and columns. It includes streaming data on the WWW like web pages, audio, video, and social media content. NO-SQL databases are generally used to store this data and Application Programming Interface (API) functions are used for manipulation. Machine learning algorithms including deep learning architectures have shown promising results in image processing and multi-modal analysis for better classification and predictive modeling. Figure 14.1 gives an overview of the use cases for educational data analysis. This figure depicts the actors or primary stakeholders contributing to the generation of educational data. The student, faculty, placement officer/cell, management, and the administrator/system *(admin)* are the main actors in an academic institution and the actions taken by them or their interactions with the system results in the generation of data. The data analysis modules use this data as input and generate various aggregative, predictive, and diagnostic models that can be leveraged by faculty, management, and students themselves for informed decision making. The following subsections discuss in detail the three-tiered educational analysis model using a use case approach.

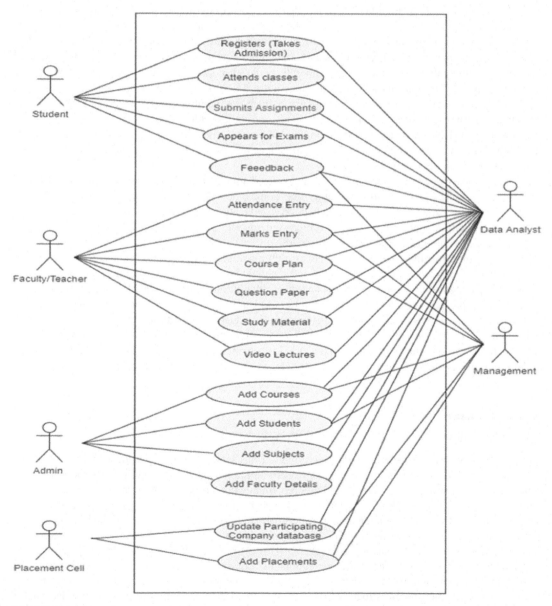

FIGURE 14.1 Educational data analysis.

14.3.1 Structured Data Analysis

In this section, we examine the scope and challenges of structured educational data analysis. We limit the scope of our study to academic data and ignore the financial and operational data of an educational institution. Figure 14.2 depicts the techniques used for analysis of structured educational data. Structured educational data generally comprises:

1. Student-related data which includes enrollment data like name, date of birth, contact details, parent/guardian details, and academic achievements.
2. Student attendance records.
3. Student academic performance like the scores on assignments, scores on tests, and other evaluation parameters.
4. Student performance in co-curricular/extra-curricular activities.
5. Faculty data like profile and academic achievements, courses taught, and research interests.
6. Placement records including internships and field works.

Educational institutions typically generate reports like attendance/attendance shortage reports, results and result analysis reports, subject-wise merit reports, and the like. These are regular MIS reports which may help in decision making. However educational data analysis goes beyond MIS and attempts to investigate and interpret the data, extract patterns, and provide insights. We propose the following techniques for structured data analysis.

14.3.1.1 Techniques for Structured Data Analysis

The following subsections discuss statistical and machine learning techniques that can be applied for analyzing structured data.

14.3.1.1.1 Correlation Analysis

The students who perform well in mathematics are typically good at physics and computer science. Such types of relationships can be discovered using correlation analysis. Correlation analysis is an extensively used technique that identifies interesting relationships between two or more variables. The commonly used correlation analysis involves two variables and measures the positive/negative (inverse) relationship between them. However, the main drawback of correlation is the linear relationship restriction. If the correlation is null between two variables, they may be non-linearly related [12]. Nonetheless, correlation analysis can be employed for preliminary investigation and can reveal

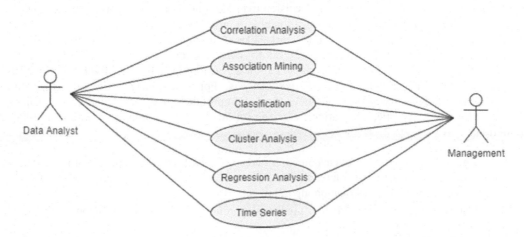

FIGURE 14.2   Techniques for structured data analysis.

relationship between two variables like attendance and marks, marks of one subject vis-à-vis marks of another subject, count of students in the class related to class performance, or correlation between faculty feedback and student performance.

14.3.1.1.2 Association Mining

While correlation analysis measures positive/negative correlation between numerical variables, association rule mining discovers frequently occurring patterns or associations from datasets or databases such as relational databases, transactional databases, and other forms of repositories. Most machine learning algorithms work with numeric datasets but association rule mining is suitable for even non-numeric, categorical data. The market basket analysis [13] which discovers the groups of items that are frequently purchased together can be applied to educational data too. These grouping patterns can be represented as association rules. For example, students who select Artificial Intelligence as a major also tend to select Gaming theory as minor. This can be represented as association rule: Artificial Intelligence → Gaming Theory. Thus, association rule mining or market basket analysis can find frequent patterns like:

1. Frequent/popular major subject and associated minor subject combinations.
2. The faculty and the associated student performance.
3. Course opted and theplacement company combinations like for example:
   CompSc → TCS
   or (CompSc, Google) → Data Scientist

14.3.1.1.3 Predictive Modeling

This section discusses the different machine learning techniques which can be used for predictive analysis of academic data.

   a. Classification

A student wants to learn about the skills or courses in which he is most likely to succeed. The placement cell may need to find the students who would fit a particular role or job description. These data analysis tasks involve classification. Classification is a supervised machine learning technique that requires a training set containing training examples made of database tuples and the associated class labels [13]. Classification algorithms when trained using a training set, predict categorical class labels for the input data. In other words, they map the input data to a specific class label; the classifier maps a tuple X with attributes $x_1, x_2, x_3...x_n$ i.e., $X = (x_1, x_2, x_3...x_n)$ to the class label Y (predicted by the classifier) i.e., $X \rightarrow Y$. Decision tree, Maximum entropy, Naïve Bayes, K-nearest neighbors, SVM are some popular classification algorithms. Artificial Neural Networks (ANN) and the more recently used deep learning networks like Convoluted Neural Networks (CNN) and Recurrent Neural Networks (RNN) are also used for classification.

   In the area of educational analysis, classification algorithms can be effectively employed for categorizing data and performing predictive analysis. For example, classification algorithms can categorize students based on their inclination and aptitude/skills like "Quantitative Ability," "Analytical skills," "Artistic," "Creative," etc. The following are examples of classification-based predictions.

1. Student → Course i.e., the course/courses a student is most likely to succeed in. In this example the *student* is represented as a tuple Student$(x_1, x_2...x_n)$ with *n* attributes and *Course* is the class label predicted by the classification algorithm.
2. Student → Profession. The classifier predicts the profession suitable for Student$(x_1, x_2...x_n)$.

b. Clustering and Outlier Detection

Cluster analysis groups data objects into different clusters such that objects within a cluster exhibit similarities. Thus each cluster is a homogenous unit. Clustering is an unsupervised learning technique and does not require labeled training data. K-means, K-medoids, hierarchical clustering methods like agglomerative and divisive clustering, and density-based methods like DBSCAN are some popular clustering algorithms. Clustering which has applications in the areas of business intelligence, targeted marketing, image processing, and financial analysis can also be applied for educational analysis. Clustering can be effectively used with educational data to discover clusters based on student performance, proficiencies in courses/subjects, performance in co-curricular/extra-curricular activities, etc. Cluster analysis groups data objects into homogeneous clusters and also reveals outliers (objects that do not belong to any cluster). For example, outlier analysis can bring to light students with exceptional learning abilities/learning challenges. We propose the following use cases for clustering education data:

1. Student marks and academic results can yield performance-based/skill-based clusters.
2. Student attendance data can help to derive attendance-based clusters and bring to light the outliers who have extreme attendance shortage.
3. Student data pertaining to participation in co-curricular and extra-curricular activities can cluster students based on inclinations and aptitude.

Cluster analysis provides insights about data object distribution and identifies the different student clusters. For example, students with different learning abilities can be identified and a customized teaching approach can be adopted. Finding targeted solutions based on cluster analysis can help to achieve better learning outcomes.

c. Regression Analysis

While classification algorithms predict categorical labels for a data tuple, regression analysis performs numeric prediction. For example, classification algorithms can predict the grade for a student, while regression analysis can predict the numerical percentage for a student. Regression analysis which has applications in market planning, financial forecasting, and trend analysis can also be employed for forecasting in the educational sector. Simple regression (relationship between two variables) and multiple regression (relationship between multiple variables) techniques can be effectively employed to:

1. Predict student performance in terms of percentage/percentile based on multiple academic parameters.
2. Predict the number of students taking admissions for the various courses based on historical enrolment data, employment trends, and current preferences.

d. Time Series Analysis

Time series data comprises a series of numeric values obtained over particular time periods or intervals. Time series analysis shows trends and is very popular for stock market analysis, sales forecasting, economic forecasting, inventory planning, etc. Box-Jenkins ARIMA models and Box-Jenkins multivariate models are primarily used for time series analysis. Student performance in tests spanning across the semesters of study is an example of time series data. Time series analysis of student marks can reveal the student progress in learning. Comparison of academic data of different students over time intervals can reveal differences in the learning abilities and performance trajectories.

14.3.1.2 Challenges in Structured Data Analysis

The basis of a robust and effective educational analytics program is the underlying data. Data quality refers to the correctness, comprehensiveness, and consistency of the existing datasets including its volume and availability. Since there are multiple touchpoints that generate data, there is a possibility that the data quality is compromised. Bad data can be worse than no data at all. Some of the manifestations of bad data are as below:

1. Data tends to be disparate with data existing in silos across departmental boundaries.
2. Data redundancy due to multiple data sources or inconsistent database design can lead to integrity issues.
3. Missing data values, noisy data, and incomplete data may result in incorrect aggregations and misleading interpretations.

In order to make the data amenable for mining, data cleaning techniques for filling in missing values, smoothing noise, and resolving inconsistencies need to be applied. Data pre-processing, integration, deduplication, and normalization techniques may be essential when data exists in silos. Data reduction or dimensionality reduction using data encoding schemes can help to achieve compact representations i.e., non-lossy data compression.

The steps for data pre-processing are however minimized when educational institutions use an ERP solution for all their interactions. This is because of the built-in validations and error handling routines incorporated in the ERP for ensuring permanent, non-redundant, and consistent data.

14.3.2 Analysis of Semi-Structured Data and Text Analysis

In the previous section, we discussed statistical and data mining techniques that could be applied to structured data stored in databases. Besides quantitative and structured data, educational institutions generate extensive semi-structured and textual content too. Though textual content is typically considered to be unstructured data, our three-tiered framework includes textual analysis in the second tier. The third tier of our framework focuses on non-textual content like images, audio clips, and video content. Analyzing text content can result in better insights. Semantic text classification can help in building efficient information storage and retrieval systems and organizing institutional knowledgebase (KB) leading to optimized search outcomes.

Text mining techniques including computational linguistics, NLP, use of tools and resources like WordNet [14], Sentiwordnet [15], sentiment lexicons (Afinn, LIWC, Sentiment 140, Vader, NRC sentiment lexicon), and emotion lexicons like NRC emotion lexicon along with machine learning algorithms can be used for text interpretations.

Semi-structured data in educational institutions include:

1. Course plans[1]: Course plans stating the date-wise and subject-wise lesson plan for the semester.
2. Student feedback containing ordinal data and descriptive text.
3. Student answer scripts containing Multiple Choice Questions (MCQ), subjective content, and numericals.
4. Subject-wise/topic-wise course material and question banks.
5. Student assignments and projects.
6. Student queries and doubts.

While analysis of *tagged semi-structured* content could provide a preliminary measure of course progress status, feedback etc., analysis of the text content can reveal deeper insights. The following subsections discuss the different analysis techniques that can be applied to text content. The scope of text classification techniques for organizing course material and KB for efficient and precise search and retrieval systems is also examined.

14.3.2.1 Use Cases for Analysis of Semi-Structured and Text Content

Student feedback typically contains ordinal (ranked) data and descriptive text. While ordinal data shows faculty ratings on the different teaching parameters, the textual content in the feedback generally contains student sentiments and opinions. Sentiment mining and emotion detection techniques using supervised learning algorithms and/or sentiment and emotion lexicons can discover the underlying opinions and extract reactions or behavior patterns of students as well as of the teachers. Such interpretive feedback systems can provide valuable guidelines and inputs for student mentoring and faculty improvement.

Text classification techniques can be used for classifying course material, question bank, research material, and KBs. Subject-based, author-based, topic-based, and keyword-based hierarchical classification systems can help to organize the KB and enable semantic, drill-down type of search and information retrieval systems [16]. This enables efficient and effective information retrieval.

Text analysis techniques can be further leveraged for answer script valuation. Answers to the subjective questions can be valued by matching answer keys with answer scripts. However, many challenges with respect to conversion of hand-written answer scripts to digital form or conversion of oral answers to digital documents may have to be addressed. The effectiveness of the proposed system should be verified through experiments. Though implementation of automated valuation may require initial human intervention, its scope should be examined and explored further. Figure 14.3 gives an overview of the process of answer script valuation.

Autonomous user interactions, chatbots have been effectively employed in various areas to answer FAQs and address other queries of the users [17]. Virtual assistants or chatbots are AI agents consisting of modules for NLP, machine learning, Natural Language Generation (NLG), and speech synthesis. These AI-based systems accept textual/verbal user input, perform text processing, and use machine learning algorithms in conjunction with historical/archived queries, responses, and KB to auto-generate responses using NLG techniques. Though these interactive systems are commonly used for telemarketing, customer-support, responding to admission related queries, and similar applications, they have been less utilized for autonomous personalized coaching and doubt solving. These human-machine interaction systems or chatbots/virtual assistants can be employed for tutoring or doubt solving sessions. They can be effectively deployed for addressing queries, reducing the drudgery, and making the academic systems more available as well as responsive. Figure 14.4 depicts the modules of a virtual assistant/teacher.

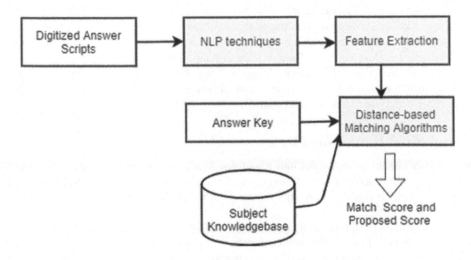

FIGURE 14.3 Answer script valuation using NLP techniques.

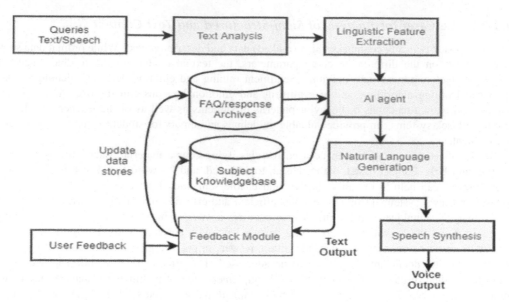

FIGURE 14.4   Virtual assistant/chatbot for student queries and FAQs.

14.3.2.2 *Challenges of Semi-Structured/Textual Data Analysis*

Incorrect spellings, abbreviations, slang, and colloquial terms are very common in text content. Phonetically spelled words and grammatical errors can result in incorrect analysis and interpretations. Hence, special cleaning and pre-processing techniques are required to make the content suitable for machine learning [18].

Text mining techniques include text classification, sentiment and emotion detection, cluster analysis, feature extraction, text summarization, etc. Application of machine learning techniques for text interpretation may require a quantitative representation of text. The bag of words model is the simplest model for text representation. However, this model disregards grammar and word order, is a sparse representation, and may not provide semantic insights. To an extent, this problem is addressed by means of NLP tools like Python NLTK (Natural Language Toolkit), Stanford NLP tools, Montylingua, and lexicons that have exhibited meaningful interpretations and improved classification even on syntactically/grammatically incorrect text content.

The recent years have seen an increased research in deep learning models like CNN and RNN for text analysis. These models use word embedding to represent text [19]. The advantage of using word embeddings for representation is that they are less sparse, capture the semantics, and are very effective for problems like negation and sarcasm. They provide semantic representation because correlated words tend to cluster and hence have similar embeddings. CNN/RNN-based deep learning models which use word embeddings to represent text, are found to yield better machine learning outcomes, when compared with other supervised learning algorithms.

14.3.3 Analysis of Unstructured Data

Unstructured data cannot be organized into a uniform format and is typically stored in NO-SQL databases. Capturing multimodal data can be expensive if the entire gamut of modal data is to be captured. We therefore consider it practical to restrict the scope of multimodal data to include only still images, audio, and video content.

The video recordings from LMS and virtual classrooms (enabled by tools like Zoom, Google Meet, Microsoft teams, WebEx) can yield significant audio-visual content. Multiple *modes* like spoken language, facial expressions, gestures, pictures, or other audio-visual content can be analyzed to reveal deeper insights and helps gauge student understanding, interest, reactions, and effectiveness of teaching methodologies. The following section discusses the different multimodal techniques and use cases in the area of educational analysis.

14.3.3.1 Analysis of Unstructured Data: Study and Use Cases

Analysis of facial expressions, eye and hand movement, gestures and speech prosody are some of the modal data that can be studied using AI-based algorithmic systems. Combining AI-based methods with epistemological frames can help in comprehending student engagement and student understanding of learning content [20]. Most of the work in multimodal analysis is in the area of sentiment and emotion detection. Many of these models process each of the text, audio, and visual content separately. They extract textual, acoustic, and video features and apply an ensemble of machine learning techniques for enhanced sentiment/emotion detection. While individual modal data points can be a good proxy for understanding learning experiences and outcomes, fusing data from different modalities can further enhance the insight that can be gained from multimodal data [10].

Commercial facial expression analysis software is available that measures duration of smiling, nose position, and looking away from the camera for analysis. Poria et al. [21] extracted facial expressions such as distance between eyes and facial landmarks using open-source software. Techniques for facial expression analysis can be applied to student data also. For example, we can capture the facial expressions of a student at different points during a class. We can also capture facial expressions of multiple students at the same point of time in the class. Such studies and comparisons can shed light on the interests, learning capacities, and attention levels of the students. They also reveal the effectiveness of teaching-learning methodologies and scope of improvising.

Analysis of the audio content which includes audio lectures, the chats (interactions), and queries can reveal faculty and student involvement, enthusiasm, student engagement, and the query handling capabilities of the faculty. Lecture delivery by the teacher can be evaluated on the basis of parameters like the pitch of voice, interactions in the session, and the style of delivery. The pitch and interaction speak about the student-faculty involvement and class engagement. Supervised learning techniques use labeled training sets containing annotated/labeled audio clips to train classifiers. These classifiers can classify the teaching session audio clips with the class labels like *Engaging, Interesting, Effective, Boring,* and *Confusing.* Correlation techniques showing association between delivery style and student interest can provide valuable feedback about the effectiveness of the teaching-learning mechanisms.

Video content analysis has applications in various disciplines like sociology, criminology, psychology, surveillance, robotics and education research. Video analysis is best suited for research questions focusing on interactions, emotions, or other aspects of situational dynamics. Visual data offer a quantum leap in access to data on real-life situational dynamics and human interaction [22]. The same video can be analyzed in many different ways, focusing on different analytic dimensions like facial expressions, body posture, interactions, and context [23].

We recognize the possibility and potential of using video recordings of online classes for conducting video content analysis. While audio clipping can only reveal the pitch, expression, and interaction, the video clippings depict the expressions, gestures, and body language of the teacher and students. Video content analysis also sheds light on the instructional strategy of the teachers. Correlating instructional strategy with student performance can provide insights about the effective teaching methodologies. Video content analysis can provide insights for personalization of delivery and content on the basis of the target audience. Video has long been used to help teachers observe, assess, and confront their own actions [24]. This analysis can help teachers to assess themselves, adapt their instructional styles, and change their teaching strategies based on situations and target audience.

Machine learning methodologies can be used for annotation and classification of student and teacher videos. Deep learning networks like CNN and RNN/LSTM (Long Short Term Memory) networks that have exhibited enhanced results in the area of image classification, pattern analysis, speech recognition, computer vision, and NLP can be used for educational video analysis. Videos can be classified based on instructional strategy, student involvement, student engagement, and response.

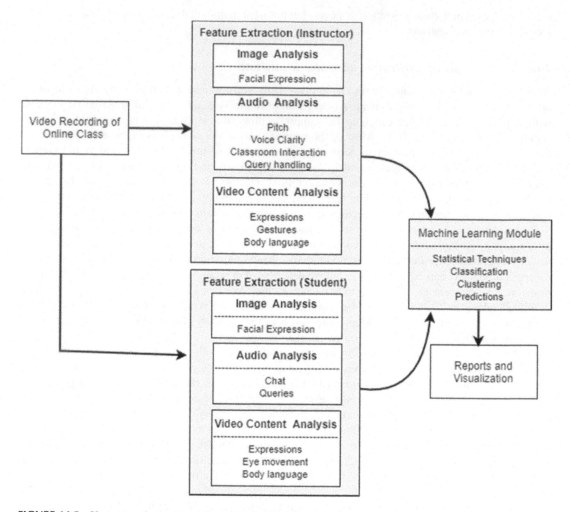

FIGURE 14.5 Unstructured educational data analysis (third tier).

Figure 14.5 illustrates the third tier of educational data analysis, which considers the different modes of input for unstructured data analysis.

14.3.3.2 Challenges in Unstructured and Multimodal Educational Data Analysis

Unstructured educational data analysis primarily involves the classification or captioning of images and audio/video files. Video analysis can help in understanding the classroom dynamics. However, mining unstructured multimodal content has its own challenges. Availability of devices to capture a learner's physiological state can be a challenge. Also, the legal and regulatory framework that governs such data capture must be considered.

The next challenge would be the sheer volume. Supervised machine learning algorithms like ANN, SVM, and AdaBoost are generally employed for such classification. These machine learning algorithms however take extensive computational time and require long training time and cycles. These make them difficult to use for real-time video analysis tasks [25].

The recent experiments in deep learning have exhibited promising results in the areas of image processing, computer vision, speech processing, and NLP. These techniques have received an impetus because of the research and development in the area of High Performance Computing (HPC). The time and computational resources required to train these deep learning networks however cannot be discounted. Experiments are being conducted to reduce the running cost, filter size, and have GPU-based implementation of deep learning networks for higher efficiency.

14.4 Implementation of the Three-Tiered Framework

The significance of the proposed three-tiered framework is that it can be implemented by HEIs in phases, wherein each phase maps to a single tier of the framework. In other words, an institution may in the first phase plan to implement the statistical and/or machine learning modules for only structured data. They may implement semi-structured and unstructured data analysis in the later phases. Each tier has its own set of independent inputs and deliverables (without any inter-dependencies) and hence can be implemented in phases.

We envisage the usage of this framework by aligning to the Ministry of Education, Government of India's National Education Policy (NEP) 2020. The NEP talks about a 360-degree student assessment based on three dimensions viz. self-assessment, peer-level assessment, and an assessment of the student by the teacher. While this policy direction reduces the overemphasis on marks as a means of assessment, it is still subjective and prone to *gaming*. Use of resulting analytics as detailed in our paper can bring in a higher level of objectivity by tracing the *digital footprint* of students and discovering patterns and trends using data-driven statistical and machine learning models.

14.5 Scope and Boundaries of the Framework

This paper has focused on analysis of educational data for enhancing student learning outcomes and improving delivery of learning content by faculty. It takes a pragmatic implementation-oriented approach, keeping in mind practical limitations of effort, data availability, data quality, and the existing analytics culture. The proposed three-tiered framework considers usage of different data types resulting in educational analysis which is holistic and provides multiple and diverse views of analyzed data. HEIs are free to adopt what is required and feasible from the framework. Quantitative measures thus obtained should be combined with inputs from domain experts and epistemological frames to maximize benefit of the framework.

While the scope of learning analytics has increased with online learning, the use of analytics when the mode of learning is offline should not be undermined. The advantage of our framework is that it does not discount the fact that all HEIs may not have an LMS or a matured learning platform and thus proposes different levels of analysis that can be applied in all HEIs across the spectrum.

This paper has dealt with the data aspects and analysis techniques at different tiers of the framework. However, there are other relevant factors like educational policies, theories from learning science, involvement of stakeholders, and the interplay of these factors [26]. Also, the change management process that is required for the success of a technology-intensive initiative in a *human-centric* domain like education is not considered in this work.

Finally, the implementation must also consider ethical and privacy aspects of data usage and its reporting. The personalization focus of an analytics program might come at the cost of privacy. How does one strike a mutually acceptable compromise in this regard? Data privacy and security rules vary from country to country. Also, privacy sensitivities can vary across individuals, groups, and institutions. This has a bearing on what data is available (or not available) when embarking on an educational analytics program. This paper does not get into the specifics of data protection and it is left to the implementing authorities to refer to local laws and practices regarding the same.

14.6 Conclusion and Scope of Future Research

This research work proposes a three-tiered framework for educational data analysis in the context of higher educational institutions. It discusses the use cases, techniques, and deliverables at each level of the framework and examines the machine learning techniques that can be employed for different types of data viz. structured, semi-structured, and unstructured. This three-tiered approach for analysis is easy to implement in phases and can be applied by institutions across demographics. The limitations mentioned in the previous section can become the scope for further research. Also, specific customized measures for various categories of learners are an area for future research. Automated valuation of answer scripts as discussed in Section 3.2.1 requires further explorations and experiments for testing effectiveness. The detailed execution plan for each tier of the framework can create a guideline-based approach for implementation by HEIs and this is the proposed enhancement in the future.

Note

1. Course plans are subject-wise and topic-wise plans devised by the faculty members with an objective of spacing out the topics that need to be taught and ensure timely completion of syllabus. Course plans are typically semi-structured in nature as they contain structured content like the planned_date, completion_date, module, etc. and textual content like topics and remarks.

REFERENCES

[1] Aldowah, Hanan, Hosam Al-Samarraie, and Wan Mohamad Fauzy. "Educational data mining and learning analytics for 21st century higher education: A review and synthesis." *Telematics and Informatics* 37 (2019): 13–49.

[2] Ahuja, Ravinder, Animesh Jha, Rahul Maurya, and Rishabh Srivastava. "Analysis of educational data mining." In *Harmony Search and Nature Inspired Optimization Algorithms*, pp. 897–907. Springer, Singapore, 2019.

[3] Avella, John T., Mansureh Kebritchi, Sandra G. Nunn, and Therese Kanai. "Learning analytics methods, benefits, and challenges in higher education: A systematic literature review." *Online Learning* 20, no. 2 (2016): 13–29.

[4] Bienkowski, Marie, Mingyu Feng, and Barbara Means. "Enhancing teaching and learning through educational data mining and learning analytics: An issue brief." *US Department of Education, Office of Educational Technology* 1 (2012): 1–57.

[5] Viberg, Olga, Mathias Hatakka, Olof Bälter, and Anna Mavroudi. "The current landscape of learning analytics in higher education." *Computers in Human Behavior* 89 (2018): 98–110.

[6] Joksimović, Srećko, Vitomir Kovanović, and Shane Dawson. "The journey of learning analytics." *HERDSA Review of Higher Education* 6 (2019): 27–63.

[7] Gašević, Dragan, Shane Dawson, and George Siemens. "Let's not forget: Learning analytics are about learning." *TechTrends* 59, no. 1 (2015): 64–71.

[8] Jayaprakash, Sandeep M., Erik W. Moody, Eitel JM Lauría, James R. Regan, and Joshua D. Baron. "Early alert of academically at-risk students: An open source analytics initiative." *Journal of Learning Analytics* 1, no. 1 (2014): 6–47.

[9] İnan, Ebru, and Martin Ebner. "Learning analytics and MOOCs." In *International Conference on Human-Computer Interaction*, pp. 241–254. Springer, Cham, 2020.

[10] Giannakos, Michail N., Kshitij Sharma, Ilias O. Pappas, Vassilis Kostakos, and Eduardo Velloso. "Multimodal data as a means to understand the learning experience." *International Journal of Information Management* 48 (2019): 108–119.

[11] Hoel, Tore, Dai Griffiths, and Weiqin Chen. "The influence of data protection and privacy frameworks on the design of learning analytics systems." In *Proceedings of the Seventh International Learning Analytics & Knowledge Conference*, pp. 243–252, 2017.

[12] Tan, Pang-Ning, Michael Steinbach, and Vipin Kumar. "Classification: Basic concepts, decision trees, and model evaluation." *Introduction to Data Mining* 1 (2006): 145–205.

[13] Han, Jiawei, Jian Pei, and Micheline Kamber. *Data Mining: Concepts and Techniques.* Elsevier, 2011.

[14] Miller, George A. "WordNet: A lexical database for English." *Communications of the ACM* 38, no. 11 (1995): 39–41.

[15] Baccianella, Stefano, Andrea Esuli, and Fabrizio Sebastiani. "Sentiwordnet 3.0: An enhanced lexical resource for sentiment analysis and opinion mining." In *LREC* 10, no. 2010 (2010): 2200–2204.

[16] Abdulkarim M. N. *"Classification and Retrieval of Research Classification and Retrieval of Research Papers: A Semantic Hierarchical Approach."* PhD diss., Christ University, 2010.

[17] Winkler Rainer, and Matthias Soellner *Unleashing the potential of chatbots in education:* A state-of-the-art *analysis*(2018).

[18] Javed, Nazura, and B. L. Muralidhara. "Automating corpora generation with semantic cleaning and tagging of tweets for multi-dimensional social media analytics." *International Journal of Computer Applications* 127, no. 12 (2015): 11–16.

[19] Pennington, Jeffrey, Richard Socher, and Christopher D. Manning. "Glove: Global vectors for word representation." In *Proceedings of the 2014 Conference on Empirical Methods in Natural Language Processing (EMNLP)*, pp. 1532–1543, 2014.

[20] Andrade, Alejandro, Ginette Delandshere, and Joshua A. Danish. "Using multimodal learning analytics to model student behaviour: A systematic analysis of behavioural framing." *Journal of Learning Analytics* 3, no. 2 (2016): 282–306.f

[21] Poria, Soujanya, Erik Cambria, Newton Howard, Guang-Bin Huang, and Amir Hussain. "Fusing audio, visual and textual clues for sentiment analysis from multimodal content." *Neurocomputing* 174 (2016): 50–59.

[22] Nassauer, Anne, and Nicolas M. Legewie. "Analyzing 21st century video data on situational dynamics—Issues and challenges in video data analysis." *Social Sciences* 8, no. 3 (2019): 100.

[23] Nassauer, Anne, and Nicolas M. Legewie. "Video data analysis: A methodological frame for a novel research trend." *Sociological Methods & Research* 50 (2018): 0049124118769093. doi: https://doi.org/10.1177/0049124118769093.

[24] Hannafin, Michael, Arthur Recesso, Drew Polly, and J. W. Jung. "Video analysis and teacher assessment: Research, practice and implications." *Digital Video for Teacher Education: Research and Practice*, pp. 164–180. Routledge, Abingdon, 2014.

[25] Abbas, Qaisar, Mostafa EA Ibrahim, and M. Arfan Jaffar. "Video scene analysis: An overview and challenges on deep learning algorithms." *Multimedia Tools and Applications* 77, no. 16 (2018): 20415–20453.

[26] Lee, Lap-Kei, and Simon KS Cheung. "Learning analytics: Current trends and innovative practices." *Journal of Computers in Education* 7, no. 1 (2020): 1–6.

15

Breast Invasive Ductal Carcinoma Classification Based on Deep Transfer Learning Models with Histopathology Images

Saikat Islam Khan, Pulak Kanti Bhowmick, Nazrul Islam, Mostofa Kamal Nasir, and Jia Uddin

CONTENTS

15.1 Introduction

Breast cancer is one of the most prominent reasons for death worldwide. In the United States, cancer is the second prominent reason of death. According to a study [1], most women are diagnosed with breast cancer in the United States, excluding skin cancer. In this study, it is also stated that breast cancer is the

second principal cause of cancer-related death in women. About 12% of women in America are diagnosed with breast cancer at least once in their lifetime. Women from different races and ethnicities
had breast cancer and also died from it [1].

As the mortality rate in breast cancer is pretty high, it is essential to detect the cancer type as early as
possible. To detect breast cancer, one of the most reliable methods is the inspection of histopathological
images. To reduce human error in making critical decisions, machine learning has helped from the last
few years. Especially deep learning models are used for early detection of breast cancer from histopathological images. Even some popular machine learning techniques like random forest, support vector
machine, and Bayesian networks are also used for early detection and diagnosis of breast cancer. But
deep learning models made things easier to classify breast cancer from histopathological images [2].

Machine learning techniques for histopathological image diagnosis has come a long way. Different
types of techniques are used. Computer-aided diagnosis, content-based image collection, and discovering new clinicopathological are included as machine learning applications in modern pathology.
Machine-learning-based methods used in the diagnosis of digital histopathological images contain
extract feature, collection, and classification of features. While performing feature extraction stage,
identical features from the input images are extracted. These identical features result in better classification performance.

Recently, deep learning models have gained much popularity for high availability of pre-trained
models, which are trained with the huge dataset. It made things easier to train a model for new tasks.
Deep learning has a serious data dependency. It usually needs massive data to train a model from
scratch. By definition, transfer learning is a machine learning technique where a model trained for a task
is reused as the beginning point for a model on a different task. Transfer learning has solved this data
dependency problem. It also has the capability to work with fewer data. Transfer learning has gained
high popularity also for its less computation time [3].

Among the pre-trained models, ResNet50 pre-trained on the ImageNet dataset is one of the most
popular. It has gained huge popularity for classification and segmentation tasks. ResNet50 has been
performed better in malaria cell image classification on microscopic cell images [4]. In this study [5],
ResNet-50 pre-trained in architecture has been used to classify malware sample software from byte plot
grayscale images with 98.62% accuracy. In another study [6], only the last layer of the ResNet-50 model
has been trained in performing the classification task. ResNet-50 DNN architecture has also been used
for various tasks, including face recognition, measuring gender and ethnicity bias, and skin lesion
classification [6,7].

VGG19 and DenseNet201 are another two very famous pre-trained models that are often used to
transfer learning. DenseNet201 has been used for diagnosis of multiple skin lesions. These pre-trained
deep learning models are used for early detection of diseases, for different classification tasks, and
segmentation of defect areas in the medical images. In a study [8], transfer learning-based approach
VGG19 pre-trained model is used for detecting computer-generated images in the region of the eyes. In
another study [9], a VGG19 pre-trained model with transfer learning approach is used for fault diagnosis
with a very promising accuracy.

This study proposed a transfer learning-based approach with three popular pre-trained models
ResNet50, VGG19, and DenseNet201 to detect the IDC, which is the most deadly breast cancer type. To
detect IDC from images, we have used ResNet50, VGG19, and DenseNet201 pre-trained models individually. For extracting features from the images, we have used weights for the pre-trained models
and only trained the dense layer with the dataset images. We have got the highest 96.55% accuracy from
the DenseNet201 pre-trained model and achieved 87.27% and 79.61% accuracy from the VGG19 and
ResNet50 pre-trained architectures, respectively.

15.2 Background Study

Researchers are now using a wide range of machine learning and deep learning approaches for analyzing the microscopic breast tissue images due to the advancement of machine learning and deep

learning technique in the medical imaging field. Such techniques can help radiologists and pathologists find tumor size, shape, and color, etc. This section is divided into three subsections, where each subsection presents a detailed description of such techniques in the medical imaging field.

15.2.1 Breast Cancer Detection Based on Machine Learning Approach

Machine learning techniques depend on feature extraction and feature selection techniques, wherein the feature extraction, the distinct features of the input image are extracted. The important features of the input image selected through the feature selection process. Such unique features lead to high classification accuracy [10]. The researchers had used several feature extraction methods, including contour-based, thresholding-based, clustering-based, texture-based, and morphological-based operation. Such operations are mainly aimed at segmenting the cells and nuclei from the breast tissue. For example, Veta et al. Proposed an automated nuclei segmentation approach in histopathology breast images [11]. A morphological operator was used for pre-processing the breast images, and for segmentation, a watershed algorithm was used with different markers. A total of 21 and 18 breast images was used to achieve 87.5% and 85.3% sensitivity in cases 1 and 2. In another work, Basavanhally et al. applied a multifield-of-view classifier for discriminating low, medium, and high grade of the Modified Bloom–Richardson (MBR) [12]. The MBR is a prognosis value that represents whether cancer presents in breast tissue or not. They used a total of 126 breast images and achieved an area under the curve of 0.93, 0.72, and 0.74 for low, medium, and high grades of MBR, respectively. Besides identifying benign and malignant breast tissue, Punitha et al. performed both segmentation and classification methods [13].

For the preprocessing step, the Gaussian filters were used to remove the image noise. Optimized region of growing technique used to segment the nuclei from the tissue, where the threshold value and the initial seed points of such method are optimally produced using a swarm optimization technique. Finally, they performed an artificial feed-forward neural network on 300 images and achieved 97.8% accuracy for classifying benign and malignant breast tissue. Furthermore, Zeebaree et al. extract the region of interest (ROI) from the breast tissue to identify breast cancer abnormality [14]. The local pixel information method was used to extract such a region. A distance transforms method, then identified ROI and non ROI. They performed their method on 250 ultrasound images and achieved 95.4% accuracy. In another work, Badawy et al. proposed a double thresholding based approach for mammogram image segmentation [15]. They added the final segmented image border as a contour, which will easily help the radiologists find the tumor region. Such segmentation-based machine learning methods provide detail and complex information for the breast tissue. However, segmentation-based techniques are time-consuming and costly since such strategies required huge computational power and human interference. Besides, segmentation-based methods worked well with a small amount of data, but more advanced technologies are required when working with many images.

15.2.2 Breast Cancer Detection Based on Deep Convolutional Neural Network Approach

Several studies have used convolutional neural network (CNN) to identify breast abnormalities in the histopathology images. Such a network provides a segmentation-free approach by extracting features using the convolution layer, max-pooling layer, and transition layer [16]. CNN also allows the researchers to work with many images, which ensures the stability of the model. For example, Araújo et al. Proposed a 13-layer-based CNN architecture for classifying the breast tissue images into four classes, including benign tissue, normal tissue, in-situ carcinoma, and invasive carcinoma [17]. In this study, the proposed CNN architecture will extract the features, and a support vector classifier will classify the breast tissue images. Overall, 95.6% sensitivity was achieved during training the model. In another study, Kandel et al. proposed a CNN architecture with 15 convolution layers and 2 fully connected layers [18]. They contrasted different activation functions and eventually found that the exponential linear unit (ELU) activation function performed better rather than using the default activation function like relu. They achieved an AUC of 95.46 percent, which outperformed the other state-of-the-art models.

Furthermore, Rahman et al. proposed a six-layer CNN architecture for identifying the invasive ductal carcinoma (IDC) tumor [19]. A dropout layer is used in this study for solving the overfitting issue. They achieved 89.34% accuracy, and no such overfitting issue occurred during training the model. In similar research, Cruz-Roa et al. detect IDC on a whole slide image [20]. They contrasted the adaptive sampling method with the CNN approach and found that the adaptive sampling method outperformed the CNN approach when dealing with limited data volumes. Guan et al. proposed a CNN architecture to detect breast cancer on a mammogram [21]. They applied a generative adversarial network (GAN) to generate more synthetic mammographic images from the database. An extensive data augmentation technique was also carried out to achieve 85% accuracy. CNN performed well compared to the conventional machine learning approaches when dealing with a large number of images. However, it could be a difficult task to acquire such a large image dataset, particularly in the field of medical imaging. Another disadvantage is that the CNN model faced an overfitting problem when worked with a small number of images.

15.2.3 Breast Cancer Detection Based on Deep Transfer Learning Approach

The transfer learning model solves the CNN model issue by working efficiently on small and large numbers of the image dataset. Since we need to train only the last fully connected layer in the transfer learning model, it requires less computational power than the CNN approach. Many researchers utilized the benefits of a transfer learning model for breast cancer detection. For example, Talo et al. applied two pre-trained models, including ResNet50 and DenseNet161, for classifying the histopathology images [22]. The DenseNet161 model trained on grayscale images and achieved 97.8% accuracy, where the ResNet50 model achieved 98.8% accuracy on color images. Furthermore, Celik et al. applied the ResNet50 and DenseNet161 pre-trained models for invasive ductal carcinoma (IDC) detection [23]. Results indicated that the DenseNet161 model detects IDC with 94.11% accuracy, which outperformed the ResNet50 model. In other research, Khan et al. applied an ensemble technique on three pre-trained models, including VGGNet, GoogLeNet, and ResNet, to identify benign and malignant breast tissue [24]. The ensemble method outperformed all other pre-trained models by showing 97.5% accuracy. They split the dataset three times, including 90–10%, 80–20%, and 70–30% in the training and testing step, and took the average accuracy for making the model more robust. For multi-class breast histology image classification, Vesal et al. used ResNet50 and Inception-V3 pre-trained models [25]. Data augmentation techniques, including rotation and flipping, were also performed to increase the number of images. In this study, the ResNet50 model outperformed the Inception-V3 pre-trained model by showing 97.5% accuracy in four classes. In another study, Kassani et al. used the Xception pre-trained model for extracting the features from the histology images [26]. A global pooling was used to classify the breast tissue. Such a pre-trained model achieved an average accuracy of 92.5%, which shows credible performance compared to conventional machine learning techniques.

15.3 Methodology

Figure 15.1 demonstrates the model architecture used in this study. The architecture starts with the image extraction and label loading from the dataset. Then several pre-processing techniques are performed before splitting the dataset into training, testing, and validation. The data augmentation technique is performed to increase the number of dataset images. Finally, the transfer learning model is built to train the model and for classifying the IDC label. The following subsection presents a detailed description of such a model.

15.3.1 Data Acquisition

This study has used the publicly available BreakHis dataset to evaluate and analyze the transfer learning model performance [27]. The BreakHis dataset contains both benign and malignant microscopic breast tumor images where malignant tumors are cancerous and can spread to the surrounding breast tissue.

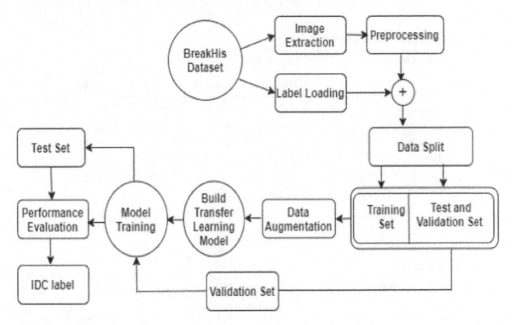

FIGURE 15.1 Model architecture.

This study has used Mucinous Carcinoma and Papillary Carcinoma as IDC (+) since both tumors are the IDC subtype. As IDC (−), we have used Adenosis, Fibroadenoma, Phyllodes, and Tabular Adenona tumors, which are benign. Figure 15.2 presents a sample of the microscopic images used in this study. The IDC (−) and IDC (+) classes include a total of 2,480 and 1,352 microscopic images, respectively, obtained from 82 patients. The images have different magnifiers factor, including 40×, 100×, 200×, and 400×. The additional details of the dataset presented in Table 15.1.

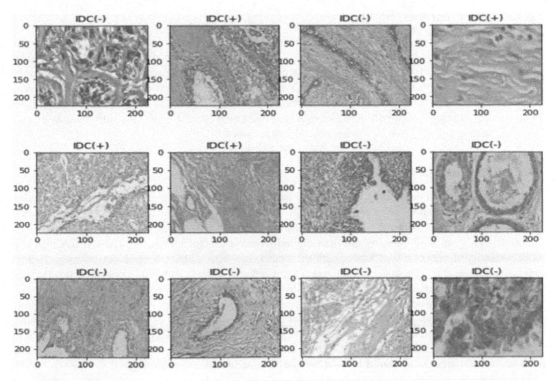

FIGURE 15.2 Images from BreakHis dataset.

TABLE 15.1

Supplementary Description for BreakHis Dataset

Type	Tumor Name	Magnification				Total
		40×	100×	200×	400×	
IDC(−)	Adenosis	114	113	111	106	444
	Fibroadenoma	253	260	264	237	1,014
	Phyllodes	109	121	108	115	453
	Tubular Adenona	149	150	140	130	569
IDC(+)	Mucinous Carcinoma	205	222	196	169	792
	Papillary Carcinoma	145	142	135	138	560
						3,832

TABLE 15.2

Data Augmentation Strategies with Parameter Value

Number	Data Augmentation Parameter	Value
1	zoom_range	2
2	rotation_range	90
3	shear_range	.2
4	width_shift_range	.1
5	height_shift_range	.1
6	horizontal_flip	True
7	vertical_flip	True

15.3.2 Data Preprocessing Stage

The images are in a three-channel RGB PNG format. As per the transfer learning model concept, images reduced from 700 * 460 pixels to 224 * 224 pixels. The images are then converted into a NumPy array so that it can take less space. Different data augmentation strategies like rotation, zooming, shearing, height shift range, width shift range, horizontal, and vertical flip are applied to increase the dataset size (as presented in Table 15.2). The dataset is increased from 3,832 to 26,824 after carrying out the data augmentation strategy, which will help overcome the overfitting issue. Finally, we split the dataset into 75% for training and 25% for validation and testing purposes.

15.3.3 Transfer Learning Model

The conventional machine learning method required a handcrafted feature extractor technique to acquire knowledge from the raw image data. But with large amounts of data, such a technique is time-consuming and difficult to work with. Transfer learning models are segmentation free approach where the model can learn without using any handcrafted feature extractor technique. The transfer learning models consist of convolutional layers with different kernel size and stride; pooling layers including max, min, and average pooling; normalization layers; flatten layers; and fully connected layers. The transfer learning models have been constructed by stacking all the layers together into a network like VggNet and AlexNet. Such layers are used to extract the features, including shapes, colors, borders, and corners from the raw image data. As we go deeper into the model, the model will extract more complex features, including textures, blur, and sharpening. The traditional CNN approach also provides the segmentation free approach to extract such complex features. However, the transfer learning models have several advantages compared to the CNN method, including:

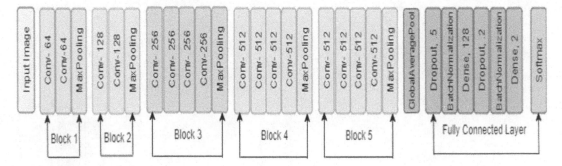

FIGURE 15.3   Fine-tuned VGG19 CNN pre-trained architecture.

- The transfer learning models are deeper than the CNN approach and utilized more dynamic relations among the alternating layers.
- It required less computational power than the traditional CNN method for the model already trained on the ImageNet database containing more than a million images. We need to train only the last fully connected layers.
- CNN performed poorly on a small image dataset and faced the overfitting issue where the transfer learning model limits such an issue by using the pre-trained weights.

This study uses three transfer learning models, including VGG19, ResNet50, and DenseNet201, to find the IDC type in the BreakHis dataset. We use the pre-trained weights from those models, but alter the fully connected layers to integrate such models into our classification method. The following subsections present the description of building the transfer learning models.

15.3.3.1 *Visual Geometry Group Network (VGGNet)*

The VGGNet pre-trained model was first introduced by Simonyan et al., which obtained the second position for image classification and the first position for image localization at the ILSVRC 2014 competition [28]. Figure 15.3 presents the architecture of the fine-tuned VGG19 model used in this study. The VGG19 pre-trained model consists of 16 convolution layers, followed by the three fully connected layers [30]. In this study, we use the pre-trained weights of the 16 convolution layers, but alter the fully connected layers with GlobalAveragePooling2D layer, two batch normalization layers, two dropout layers, and two dense layers. The GlobalAveragePooling2D was used in this study to flatten all the layers into a 1D vector by calculating the average value for each of the input channels. The batch normalization is used to make the computation easier by maintaining the output value close to zero and the outputs standard deviation close to one. During training the model on small datasets, such models tend to face the overfitting issue where the model learns well with training data but negatively impacts the testing data. Regularization techniques like L1 and L2 can help limit the overfitting issue by modifying the cost function. However, the dropout layer can modify the cost function itself and limit the overfitting issue more efficiently. In dropout layers, the model drops some neurons during training, so that the model can train on unordered data. In this study, two dropout layers are used. The first dropout layer drops 50% of the neurons during training right after flattening all the channels. The second dropout layer drops 20% of the neurons before applying the fully connected layer. The final dense layer is used to classify the IDC type using the softmax activation function.

15.3.3.2 *Residual Neural Network (ResNet)*

The ResNet pre-trained model was first introduced by He et al., which obtained the first position at the ILSVRC 2015 competition by obtaining a small error rate of 3.5% [29]. The ResNet architecture consists of 152 deep layers, where a total of 50 layers used as convolution layers. Such a model

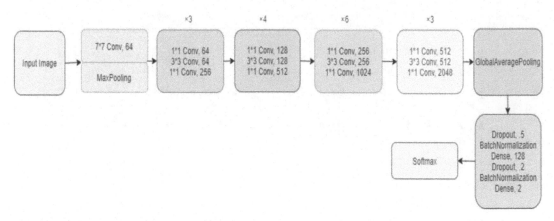

FIGURE 15.4 Fine-tuned ResNet50 CNN pre-trained architecture.

designed for analyzing the large-scale image dataset since deep-layer CNN architecture has been used to build the model compared to the Alex Net and VGGNet models, which consists of 8 and 19 layers, respectively. The ResNet model introduced residual connections, which prevents information loss and the vanishing gradient descent problem during training the model. Such connections increase the network capacity by boosting the performance of the model. Figure 15.4 presents the architecture of the fine-tuned ResNet50 model used in this study. The architecture, mainly composed of residual blocks which are connected among themselves. A total of five residual blocks are used which preserve the gained knowledge and forward it in the fully connected layers. A total of seven fully connected layers are used where the last layer will classify the IDC type using the softmax activation function.

15.3.3.3 Dense Convolutional Networks (DenseNet)

The DenseNet pre-trained model was first introduced by Huang et al. [30], which had the best classification accuracy of CIFAR-10, CIFAR-100, and ImageNet dataset in 2017. The DenseNet model was constructed in such a way that the overfitting problem can be mitigated when dealing with a small dataset. This model was built using a total of 201 deep CNN layers. Compared to the AlexNet, VGGNet, and ResNet architectures, the DenseNet201 pre-trained model will derive more complicated and important features as more deep CNN layers are included in the architecture. However, during training, the DenseNet201 pre-trained model used more training parameters compared to the ResNet and VGGNet architecture, which makes the computation costly. Figure 15.5 presents the architecture of the fine-tuned DenseNet201 model used in this study. In DenseNet201 model, all the layers are densely connected, where each layer is connected to all the other layers. Such a connection gives the network to share important information within the network, which will make the network training more effective and

FIGURE 15.5 Fine-tuned DenseNet201 CNN pre-trained architecture.

boost the network performance [31]. In this study, we use all the feature extractor layers from the DenseNet201 model, but replace the fully connected layers with the GlobalAveragePooling2D layer, two batch normalization layers, two dropout layers, and two dense layers. The final dense layer with neuron two will classify the IDC type.

15.4 Experimental Setup and Results

The section demonstrates the classification results obtained using the transfer learning pre-trained models, including VGG19, ResNet50, and DenseNet201. All the models are performed using Python and trained at the Google Colab, which provides free graphics processing unit (GPU) and supports 25 GB RAM. The performance of the model is evaluated using statistical parameters.

15.4.1 Performance Evaluation Metrics

This section demonstrates a detailed description of the statistical parameters used in this analysis. Parameters like recall, precision, F1-score, True Negative Rate (TNR), and False Positive Rate (FPR) used to evaluate the performance of the transfer learning models. Such parameters calculated by using the confusion matrix outcomes, including True Positive, True Negative, False Positive, and False Negative. The detailed description of such parameters is as follows:

True Positive (TP): refers to an outcome where the transfer learning model correctly identified the IDC (−) class.

True Negative (TN): refers to an outcome where the transfer learning model correctly identified the IDC (+) class.

False Positive (FP): refers to an outcome where the transfer learning model incorrectly identified the IDC (−) class.

False Negative (FN): refers to an outcome where the transfer learning model incorrectly identified the IDC (+) class.

Recall (R): is a ratio of correctly identified IDC (+) class from cases that are actually IDC (+).

$$R = \frac{TP}{TP + FN}$$

Precision (P): is a ratio of correctly identified IDC (+) class from cases that are predicted as IDC (+).

$$P = \frac{TP}{TP + FP}$$

F1-Score: maintains the balance between precision and recall and determine the test accuracy.

$$F1 * Score = 2 * \frac{P * R}{P + R}$$

TNR: is a probability that an actual predicted IDC (−) class will test as IDC (−).

$$TNR = \frac{TN}{TN + FP}$$

FPR: is a probability that an actual predicted IDC (+) class will test as IDC (−).

$$FPR = \frac{FP}{FP + TN}$$

15.4.2 Training Phase

Figure 15.6 demonstrates the simulation result during training the transfer learning models. The parameter values used for the training presented in Table 15.3. Such values used for tuning all the three transfer learning models. As a loss function, binary cross-entropy is used due to the binary classification. A small batch size of 32 has been used, which shows a suitable generalization of the model. During training, selecting the learning rate is tricky since it causes an undesirable effect on the loss function when the learning rate is very high. However, if the learning rate is meagre, the model takes more time to converge. In this method, a learning rate of .0001 used to limit such issues. Adam used as an optimizer function, which is easy to configure and works well on the large dataset. During training the models, DenseNet201 trained well and showed the best validation accuracy of 98.78% at the 19th epoch. The loss value is almost zero, which shows the stability of the model. The overfitting problem is not present in the DenseNet201 model because of the proper tuning. The ResNet50 model achieved 96.61% validation accuracy at the 18th epoch. The loss value started to reduce after training the model only four epochs. Furthermore, the VGG19 model achieved 94.5% validation accuracy at the 11th epoch. However, there are some fluctuations present in the VGG19 loss curve, which is due to the small batch size. Such instability restricts the model for being trained well. But after the 15th epoch, the loss value started to reduce.

15.4.3 Result Analysis

Figure 15.7 presents the confusion matrix and the ROC curve extracted from VGG19, ResNet50, and DenseNet201 models. For testing the models, a total of 145 microscopic images have been used for the dataset. Among them, 75 images were used as an IDC (−) class, and the other 70 images were used as an IDC (+) class. The VGG19 pre-trained model classifies 127 images correctly, but misclassified 18 images. From 127 images, a total of 67 images are classified as IDC (−) (True Positive), and a total of 60 images is classified as IDC (+) (True Negative). The ResNet50 model classified 116 images correctly, but misclassified 29 images. Compared to the VGG19 model, the performance of the ResNet50 model during the classification is poor. This model performance considered inferior since it confused a total of 22 IDC (+) images as IDC (−), which would be a disaster. The DenseNet201 pre-trained model outperformed both VGG19 and ResNet50 models by classifying 140 images correctly. Where only five images misclassified by the DenseNet201 model. In this work, the ROC curve is used to determine the capability of the binary classifier. The best area under the curve (AUC) found for the DenseNet201 pre-trained model is 0.973, indicating its perfect stability. Although VGG19 also performed well with .875 AUC, ResNet50 shows the model is less stable in the ROC curve.

The model's performance is compared by calculating precision, recall, F1-Score, FPR, and FNR. Table 15.4 presents a detailed description of such parameters. The VGG19 pre-trained model achieved an average precision of 87.62%, a recall of 86.93, and 87.27% accuracy. The ResNet50 pre-trained model performed well for IDC(−) images, but negatively impacted IDC(+) images. This model achieved an average precision of 81.41%, a recall of 79.62%, and 79.61% accuracy. Moreover, the DenseNet201 pre-trained model outperformed the other two pre-trained models by demonstrating higher parameter value. The DenseNet201 achieved an average precision of 96.58%, recall of 96.52%, and 96.55% accuracy. The FPR is almost zero, and TNR is close to one, which indicates the model's best performance. A simulation result of the DenseNet201 model classifying IDC images is presented in Figure 15.8, where all the images are classified correctly.

15.4.4 Comparison with Other State of Art Models

Few studies work with the BreakHis dataset to classify the microscopy breast tumor images. These studies include different pre-trained models, CNN models, and feature extractor techniques. For example, Nejad et al. proposed a single-layer CNN model to classify benign and malignant breast tumors [32]. They achieved 77.5% accuracy by using a convolution filter of 5 * 5 size with stride 3, a normalization channel, a ReLU activation function, a max-pooling layer, and a fully connected layer. In the

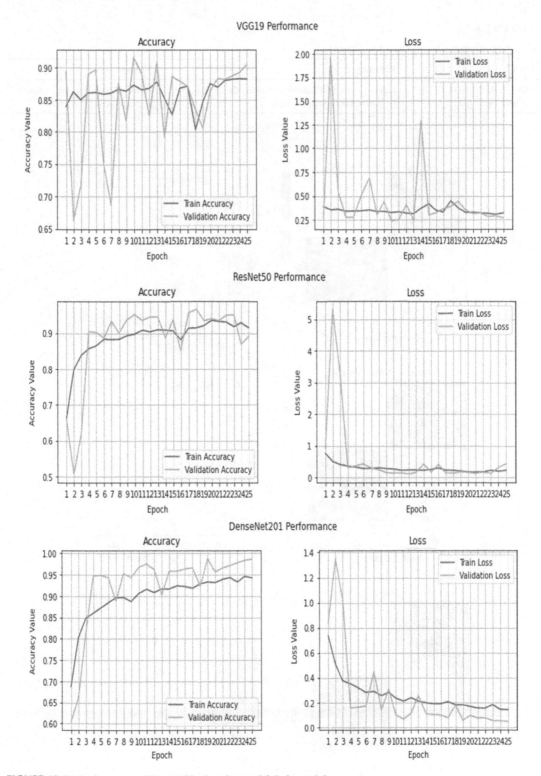

FIGURE 15.6 Performance of the transfer learning model during training.

TABLE 15.3

Hyper-Parameter Values Used for Training

Model	Parameters	Values
VGG19 ResNet50 DenseNet201	Loss Function Optimizer Function Metrics Epochs Batch Size Learning Rate	Binary Cross Entropy Adam Accuracy 2532 .0001

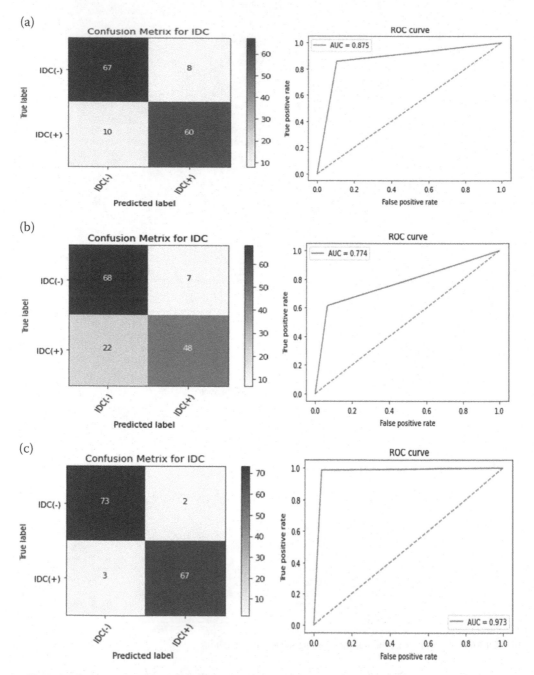

FIGURE 15.7 Confusion matrix and ROC curve for the three transfer learning models. (a) VGG19 model, (b) ResNet50 model, and (c) DenseNet201 model.

TABLE 15.4
Classification Result Obtained from the Three Transfer Learning Models

Metrics	Method	Class	TP	TN	FP	FN	Precision	Recall	F1-Score	FPR	TNR
BreakHish Dataset	VGG19	IDC(−)	67	60	10	8	87.01%	88.15%	87.58%	.14	.86
		IDC(+)	60	67	8	10	88.23%	85.71%	86.95%	.11	.89
	ResNet50	IDC(−)	68	48	22	7	75.55%	90.66%	82.42%	.31	.69
		IDC(+)	48	68	7	22	87.27%	68.57%	76.79%	.09	.91
	DenseNet 201	IDC(−)	73	67	3	2	96.05%	97.33%	96.69%	.04	.96
		IDC(+)	67	73	2	3	97.10%	95.71%	96.40%	.02	.98

same dataset, Zhi et al. applied pre-trained VGGNet architecture [33]. They performed data augmentation techniques like zooming, horizontal, and vertical flip to achieve 92.7% accuracy. Besides, Song et al. represent the microscopy image feature by using the Fisher Vector encoding technique and extract it using the CNN pre-trained model [34]. They also developed a new adaption layer to achieve higher accuracy. Finally, they have reported 86.67% accuracy for the BearkHis dataset. Nahid et al. proposed three models, including CNN, long short term memory (LSTM), and a combination of CNN and LSTM for the breast cancer image classification [35]. As a classifier, they used a softmax and SVM layer. The best accuracy is 91%, which is achieved by the CNN model with the SVM classifier. Mehra et al. compared three pre-trained models, including VGG16, VGG19, and ResNet50, with the logistic regression classifier for breast cancer classification [36]. They split the dataset into three sections (90–10%, 80–20%, and 70–30%) to determine the proposed model's influence. They have obtained an average accuracy of 92.6% for the VGG16 pre-trained model, which outperformed the other models. Celik et al. randomly divided the data into 80% training and 20% testing and validation [23]. They contrasted two CNN pre-trained models, including ResNet50 and DenseNet161, for the IDC detection. The DenseNet161 model outperformed the ResNet50 model by achieving 93.85% accuracy. Table 15.5 compares our proposed model with the previous literature using the same BreakHis dataset. It can be seen from Table 15.5 that our proposed DenseNet201 pre-trained model achieved 96.55% accuracy, which outperformed all other existing literature.

15.5 Discussion with Advantages and Future Work

15.5.1 Discussion

In this study, the Break His dataset is used to detect whether the breast tissues are IDC type or not. The dataset contains a total of 7907 microscopic breast tissue images. Among them, a total of 3,832 microscopic images are used, which contains IDC (−) (benign tissue) and IDC (+) (malignant tissue) breast images. A total of three transfer learning models, including VGG19, ResNet50, and DenseNet201, are used in this study for the early detection of IDC type. The transfer learning model required less computational power of such models are already trained on the ImageNet database containing millions of images. It allows the researcher to use the pre-trained weights for their study. In this study, we use the transfer learning models pre-trained weights, but replace the fully connected layers with the GlobalAveragePooling2D layer, two BatchNormalization layers, and three Dense layers. We only train the replaced fully connected layer in our study.

Several data augmentation techniques, including zooming, rotation, shearing, height, and width shift range, horizontal and vertical flip, are carried out to increase the number of microscopic images. Managing the overfeeding dilemma is one critical activity of designing such models. The overfitting issue makes the model unstable and less effective when it comes to classifying the test images. The model will wrongly predict the breast tissue if such an issue presents in the model. For solving such issues, proper tuning of the model is required. One solution is to introduce the dropout layer in the

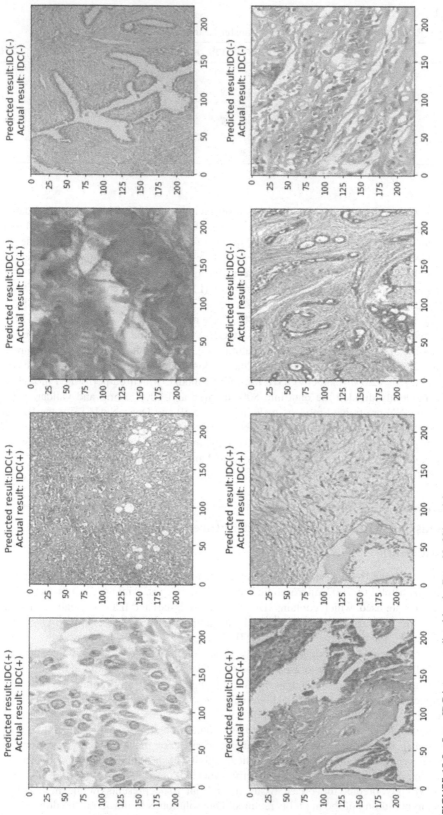

FIGURE 15.8 Some IDC images predicted by the DenseNet201 model.

TABLE 15.5

Comparison of Our Proposed Model with Other State-of-the-Art Models Using BreakHis Dataset

Name	Method	Accuracy
Nejad et al. 2017 [32]	Single-layer CNN	77.5%
Zhi et al. 2017 [33]	VGGNet	92.7%
Song et al. 2017 [34]	Fisher Vector+ CNN	86.67%
Nahid et al. 2018 [35]	CNN+LSTM+Softmax+SVM	91%
Mehra et al. 2018 [36]	VGG16 + Logistic Regression	92.6%
Celik et al. 2020 [23]	DenseNet161	93.85%
Proposed Method	DenseNet201	96.55%

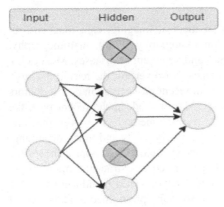

FIGURE 15.9   Dropout layer example.

pre-trained model. The dropout layer will drop some of the neurons, such that the model can train on some unordered data. Figure 15.9 presents an example of the dropout process. In the proposed fine-tuned pre-trained models, we use two dropout layers to handle such an issue. We can observe from Figure 15.6 that the overfitting issue did not occur during training the model. After comparing the models, the DenseNet201 pre-trained model showed 96.55% accuracy, which outperformed all other state-of-the-art models.

15.5.2 Advantages

Nevertheless, the key benefits of this research are summarized as follows:

- Most of the existing literature based on the patchwise breast cancer classification, where our study is based on the subject wise classification, including IDC (+) and IDC (−).
- The transfer learning models provide segmentation free feature extraction strategies that do not require any handcrafted feature extraction approaches relative to the conventional machine learning methods.
- A total of 3,832 microscopic images was used for IDC detection.
- Less computational power and time required during training the model.
- The overfitting issue did not occur during the training of the model.
- Only 25 epochs are required to achieve more than 95% accuracy.
- The fine-tuned DenseNet201 pre-trained model outperformed all the other existing literature by showing great performance.

15.5.3 Future Works

Several future approaches are applied to improve performance.

- We train our model only for 25 epochs. Further training will help the model to achieve higher accuracy.
- More data augmentation strategy, including cropping, translation, color, brightness, and saturation, could be used. Such a strategy will increase the dataset size and help to achieve higher accuracy.
- More layers may be applied to the pre-trained model fine-tuned process, which will expand the number of training parameters.

15.6 Conclusion

From the previous decades, we have observed the necessity of medical imaging, e.g., magnetic resonance (MR), computed tomography (CT), positron emission tomography (PET), mammography, ultrasound, X-ray, and so on, for the early identification, analysis, and treatment of diseases. Most of the methods needed human experts such as radiologists and pathologists. However, for the reason the large fluctuations in pathology and probable fatigue of human experts, in recent past researchers and doctors have started to privilege from the computer-assisted diagnosis (CAD) method. In the recent past, the CAD system has been upgraded using machine learning and deep learning methods. However, machine learning techniques needed a native feature extractor method, which is very costly and time-consuming. A deep-learning-based approach limits such issue by providing a segmentation-free approach. In this study, automated invasive ductal carcinoma (IDC) detection is performed to extract the microscopic images feature using deep transfer learning techniques, including ResNet50, VGG19, and DenseNet201 pre-trained models. For classifying the IDC, the features extracted from the pre-trained models are fed into a fully connected layer. In the experiment, the DenseNet201 model achieved the highest 96.55% accuracy that outperformed all the other state-of-art models, where ResNet50 and VGG19 pre-trained models achieved 79.61% and 87.27% accuracy, respectively. Finally, to detect biomedical solutions and biological samples, the proposed DenseNet201 fine-tuned pre-trained model could be a great candidate.

REFERENCES

[1] DeSantis CE, Fedewa SA, Goding Sauer A, Kramer JL, Smith RA, Jemal A. Breast cancer statistics, 2015: Convergence of incidence rates between black and white women. CA: a cancer journal for clinicians. 2016 Jan;66(1):31–42

[2] Al Bataineh, Ali. "A comparative analysis of nonlinear machine learning algorithms for breast cancer detection." *International Journal of Machine Learning and Computing* 9, no. 3 (2019): 248–254.

[3] Tan, Chuanqi, Fuchun Sun, Tao Kong, Wenchang Zhang, Chao Yang, and Chunfang Liu. "A survey on deep transfer learning." In *International Conference on Artificial Neural Networks*, pp. 270–279. Springer, Cham, 2018.

[4] Reddy, A. Sai Bharadwaj, and D. Sujitha Juliet. "Transfer learning with ResNet-50 for malaria cell-image classification." In *2019 International Conference on Communication and Signal Processing (ICCSP)*, pp. 0945–0949. IEEE, 2019.

[5] Rezende, Edmar, Guilherme Ruppert, Tiago Carvalho, Fabio Ramos, and Paulo De Geus. "Malicious software classification using transfer learning of ResNet-50 deep neural network." In *2017 16th IEEE International Conference on Machine Learning and Applications (ICMLA)*, pp. 1011–1014. IEEE, 2017.

[6] Acien, Alejandro, Aythami Morales, Ruben Vera-Rodriguez, Ivan Bartolome, and Julian Fierrez. "Measuring the gender and ethnicity bias in deep models for face recognition." In *Iberoamerican Congress on Pattern Recognition*, pp. 584–593. Springer, Cham, 2018.

[7] Khan, Muhammad Attique, Muhammad Younus Javed, Muhammad Sharif, Tanzila Saba, and Amjad Rehman. "Multi-model deep neural network based features extraction and optimal selection approach for skin lesion classification." In *2019 International Conference on Computer and Information Sciences (ICCIS)*, pp. 1–7. IEEE, 2019.

[8] Carvalho, Tiago, Edmar RS De Rezende, Matheus TP Alves, Fernanda KC Balieiro, and Ricardo B. Sovat. "Exposing computer generated images by eye's region classification via transfer learning of VGG19 CNN." In *2017 16th IEEE International Conference on Machine Learning and Applications (ICMLA)*, pp. 866–870. IEEE, 2017.

[9] Wen, Long, X. Li, Xinyu Li, and Liang Gao. "A new transfer learning based on VGG-19 network for fault diagnosis." In *2019 IEEE 23rd International Conference on Computer Supported Cooperative Work in Design (CSCWD)*, pp. 205–209. IEEE, 2019.

[10] Komura, Daisuke, and Shumpei Ishikawa. "Machine learning methods for histopathological image analysis." *Computational and Structural Biotechnology Journal* 16 (2018): 34–42.

[11] Veta, Mitko, Paul J. Van Diest, Robert Kornegoor, André Huisman, Max A. Viergever, and Josien PW Pluim. "Automatic nuclei segmentation in H&E stained breast cancer histopathology images." *PLoS One* 8, no. 7 (2013): e70221.

[12] Basavanhally, Ajay, Shridar Ganesan, Michael Feldman, Natalie Shih, Carolyn Mies, John Tomaszewski, and Anant Madabhushi. "Multi-field-of-view framework for distinguishing tumor grade in ER+ breast cancer from entire histopathology slides." *IEEE Transactions on Biomedical Engineering* 60, no. 8 (2013): 2089–2099.

[13] Punitha, S., A. Amuthan, and K. Suresh Joseph. "Benign and malignant breast cancer segmentation using optimized region growing technique." *Future Computing and Informatics Journal* 3, no. 2 (2018): 348–358.

[14] Zeebaree, Diyar Qader, Habibollah Haron, Adnan Mohsin Abdulazeez, and Dilovan Asaad Zebari. "Machine learning and region growing for breast cancer segmentation." In *2019 International Conference on Advanced Science and Engineering (ICOASE)*, pp. 88–93. IEEE, 2019.

[15] Badawy, Samir M., Alaa A. Hefnawy, Hassan E. Zidan, and Mohammed T. GadAllah. "Breast cancer detection with mammogram segmentation: A qualitative study." *International Journal of Advanced Computer Science and Application* 8, no. 10 (2017).

[16] Yildirim, Ozal, Ru San Tan, and U. Rajendra Acharya. "An efficient compression of ECG signals using deep convolutional autoencoders." *Cognitive Systems Research* 52 (2018): 198–211.

[17] Araújo, Teresa, Guilherme Aresta, Eduardo Castro, José Rouco, Paulo Aguiar, Catarina Eloy, António Polónia, and Aurélio Campilho. "Classification of breast cancer histology images using convolutional neural networks." *PLoS One* 12, no. 6 (2017): e0177544.

[18] Kandel, Ibrahem, and Mauro Castelli. "A novel architecture to classify histopathology images using convolutional neural networks." *Applied Sciences* 10, no. 8 (2020): 2929.

[19] Rahman, Md Jamil-Ur, Rafi Ibn Sultan, Firoz Mahmud, Sazid Al Ahsan, and Abdul Matin. "Automatic system for detecting invasive ductal carcinoma using convolutional neural networks." In *TENCON 2018-2018 IEEE Region 10 Conference*, pp. 0673–0678. IEEE, 2018.

[20] Cruz-Roa, Angel, Hannah Gilmore, Ajay Basavanhally, Michael Feldman, Shridar Ganesan, Natalie Shih, John Tomaszewski, Anant Madabhushi, and Fabio González. "High-throughput adaptive sampling for whole-slide histopathology image analysis (HASHI) via convolutional neural networks: Application to invasive breast cancer detection." *PLoS One* 13, no. 5 (2018): e0196828.

[21] Guan, Shuyue, and Murray Loew. "Breast cancer detection using synthetic mammograms from generative adversarial networks in convolutional neural networks." *Journal of Medical Imaging* 6, no. 3 (2019): 031411.

[22] Talo, Muhammed. "Automated classification of histopathology images using transfer learning." *Artificial Intelligence in Medicine* 101 (2019): 101743.

[23] Celik Y, Talo M, Yildirim O, Karabatak M, Acharya UR. Automated invasive ductal carcinoma detection based using deep transfer learning with whole-slide images. *Pattern Recognition Letters*. 2020 May 1;133:232–239.

[24] Khan, SanaUllah, Naveed Islam, Zahoor Jan, Ikram Ud Din, and Joel JPC. Rodrigues. "A novel deep learning based framework for the detection and classification of breast cancer using transfer learning." *Pattern Recognition Letters* 125 (2019): 1–6.

[25] Vesal, Sulaiman, Nishant Ravikumar, AmirAbbas Davari, Stephan Ellmann, and Andreas Maier. "Classification of breast cancer histology images using transfer learning." In *International Conference Image Analysis and Recognition*, pp. 812–819. Springer, Cham, 2018.

[26] Kassani, Sara Hosseinzadeh, Peyman Hosseinzadeh Kassani, Michal J. Wesolowski, Kevin A. Schneider, and Ralph Deters. "Breast cancer diagnosis with transfer learning and global pooling." arXiv preprint arXiv:1909.11839, 2019.

[27] BreakHis dataset. Available at: https://web.inf.ufpr.br/vri/databases/breast-cancer-histopathological-database-breakhis/ [Online Accessed: 30 September, 2020].

[28] Simonyan, Karen, and Andrew Zisserman. "Very deep convolutional networks for large-scale image recognition." arXiv preprint arXiv:1409.1556, 2014.

[29] He, Kaiming, Xiangyu Zhang, Shaoqing Ren, and Jian Sun. "Deep residual learning for image recognition." In *Proceedings of the IEEE Conference on Computer Vision and Pattern Recognition*, pp. 770–778, 2016.

[30] Huang, Gao, Zhuang Liu, Laurens Van Der Maaten, and Kilian Q. Weinberger. "Densely connected convolutional networks." In *Proceedings of the IEEE Conference on Computer Vision and Pattern Recognition*, pp. 4700–4708, 2017.

[31] Hao, Wangli, and Zhaoxiang Zhang. "Spatiotemporal distilled dense-connectivity network for video action recognition." *Pattern Recognition* 92 (2019): 13–24.

[32] Nejad, Elaheh Mahraban, Lilly Suriani Affendey, Rohaya Binti Latip, and Iskandar Bin Ishak. "Classification of histopathology images of breast into benign and malignant using a single-layer convolutional neural network." In *Proceedings of the International Conference on Imaging, Signal Processing and Communication*, pp. 50–53, 2017.

[33] Zhi, Weiming, Henry Wing Fung Yueng, Zhenghao Chen, Seid Miad Zandavi, Zhicheng Lu, and Yuk Ying Chung. "Using transfer learning with convolutional neural networks to diagnose breast cancer from histopathological images." In *International Conference on Neural Information Processing*, pp. 669–676. Springer, Cham, 2017.

[34] Song, Yang, Ju Jia Zou, Hang Chang, and Weidong Cai. "Adapting fisher vectors for histopathology image classification." In *2017 IEEE 14th International Symposium on Biomedical Imaging (ISBI 2017)*, pp. 600–603. IEEE, 2017.

[35] Nahid, Abdullah-Al, Mohamad Ali Mehrabi, and Yinan Kong. "Histopathological breast cancer image classification by deep neural network techniques guided by local clustering." *BioMed Research International* (2018): 1–20.

[36] Mehra, Rajesh. "Breast cancer histology images classification: Training from scratch or transfer learning?" *ICT Express* 4, no. 4 (2018): 247–254.

16

Prediction of Acoustic Performance Using Machine Learning Techniques

Ratnavel Rajalakshmi, S. Jeyanthi, Yuvaraj L., Pradeep M., Jeyakrishna S., and Abhishek Krishnaswami

CONTENTS

16.1 Introduction

In this day and age, noise and vibration can be accounted detrimental in various mechanical systems such as home appliances, automobiles, and in different infrastructures. These harmful effects can be effectively controlled using sound absorbing materials. Such absorptive materials play a vital role in efficiently converting the impinging acoustic energy into heat. Since the vitality contained in sound waves is typically less, the amount of heat produced is also negligible. Hence, the usage of sandwich panels plays a cardinal role in the contraction of noise in different applications. Strengthening acoustics along with mechanical properties is made possible by utilizing numerous natural fiber reinforcements. Overall, it is evident that natural fibers have relatively higher sound absorption capability compared to petro-chemical-based fibers. From the existing literatures [1]. It can be observed that, acoustic properties can be enhanced by employing various macro-sized reinforcement fibers which account for the pore size, number, and porosity [2].

The usage of conventional absorbent materials such as polyurethane foam, mineral fiber composites and glass fiber felts can be used for sound proofing [3]. Poly-Urethane foams (PU) displays high sound and energy absorption which thereby motivated us to prepare the multi-layer sandwich foam for noise control applications [4]. Owing to the fact that open-celled materials are poor absorbers at low-sound frequencies, materials such as fibrous, foam, and granular materials, are preferred as good sound-absorbing materials [5]. Porosity, pore size, pore opening, thickness, static flow resistivity, and so on are few parameters that affects sound absorption coefficient [6]. Furthermore, analysts have made composite materials with common or artificial fibers [7]. While the impedance tube-based transfer function is utilized to evaluate the sound absorption coefficients for a polyurethane foam sample, ASTM E 1050 standard is followed for test setup [8].

Although analytical models have bridged the gap between experimental and theoretical prediction, certain number of studies [9] have shown that soft computing skills played a prominent role in predicting sound absorption coefficients of different materials. Subsequently, the advancements in the field of materials synthesis and characterizations have benefited to a large extent by using machine learning techniques and AI methods for composite materials [10]. These methods help in solving abstruse problems efficiently due to their excellent optimization in addition with their unique algorithms that pave their way for endless possibilities amongst various researchers [11].

In this study, sound absorption coefficient is predicted using Machine Learning Regression models by taking certain parameters including thickness, area density, porosity and pore size as inputs, and estimating sound absorption coefficient of each combination. The various layers of materials include polyurethane foam and wood powder, whose percentages differs between 5% and 15%, respectively.

It will be conceivable to assess the acoustic performance of a material for various arrangements without the need to perform acoustic estimations [12]. Furthermore, numerous regression analysis has been performed on composites. Dong [13] studied on dimension variation prediction for composites with finite element analysis and regression modeling. In other words, MLR is based on a linear least-squares fitting process which requires a trace element or property for determination in each source or source category [14]. Phusavat and Aneksitthisin [15] applied Multiple Linear Regressions (MLR) for establishing the interrelationship among productivity, price recovery, and profitability. By using the multiple-linear regression model, the interrelationships between profitability, productivity, and price-recovery were explicitly demonstrated. On the basis of the results obtained from both ANN and regression analysis, we can predict the various properties of fabric accurately [16]. The most commonly used criterion to evaluate model performance is coefficient of determination (R^2), which is not only robust but also an easy and reliable measure for indicating the performance of a model.

The objective of our work is to estimate the sound absorption coefficient of the composite material by using the most optimal regression model.

16.2 Materials and Methods

The primary ingredient for synthesizing Flexible polyurethane is with the help of Isocyanate—mainly consisting of a material called WANNATE 8018 and Polyol – mainly consists additives such as catalyst, stabilizers, water, chain extenders and surfactants. Before adding to polyol, the isocyanate and sawdust are being treated in an oven for 24 hours at 80°C. Then PU foam is prepared using the free rising method. Varied percentage of chemical (taken by weight) are subsequently added along with saw dust fiber and allowed to mix properly. The mixed material is then added with WANNATE 8018 and then stirred thoroughly at 2000 rpm. After the action is performed, the foam has to be kept in the open environment to get the desired shape and size. After the de-mold time, further testing can then be performed.

The next step is to estimate the pore size in which measuring the viscous and thermal length demand is a completely complex and dedicated setup for accurate measurements. The cell size and structure are measured with the Image-J software using FESEM images. We determine the strut length (l) and the strut thickness (t) using a mathematical relation that connects a cell size and strut dimension for a highly porous material mathematically defined as – l = 0.707*cellsize/A. and t = l/b – "A" can be determined by knowing the value of A = 2 in a tetrakaicehedron unit cell structure. To find the porosity, the perfect gas law principle is used, and the equation is given below.

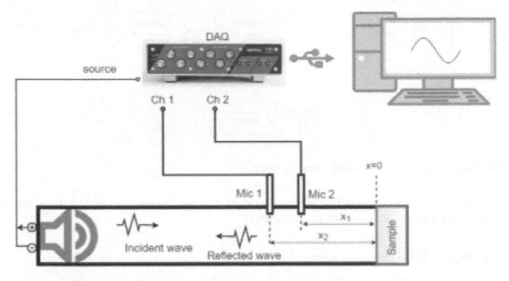

FIGURE 16.1 Schematic diagram of impedance tube.

$$\phi = 1 - \frac{RT}{V_t}\left[\frac{m_2 - m_1}{P_2 - P_1} - \frac{m_4 - m_3}{P_4 - P_3}\right]$$

In the above equation, m_1 and m_3 depict the mass of the low-pressure cylinder while m_2 and m_4 depict the mass of the high pressure cylinder. P_1, P_2, P_3, and P_4 depict the low and high pressures in an empty cylinder when the samples are placed respectively.

The final stage is the measurement of the sound absorption that is done purely on the basis of impedance tube transfer function method. The samples are cut into circular sections of diameters 33 and 100 mm, respectively. The process is carried out from 220–6,300 Hz. After obtaining a suitable M + P signal, it is imported to MATLAB for determining the transfer function. Subsequently as the transfer function is determined, the reflection and absorption coefficient can be estimated.

$$R = \frac{e^{-jks} - H_{12}}{H_{12} - e^{jks}} \times e^{2jk(l+S)}$$
$$(\alpha) = 1 - |R|^2$$

H_{12} is the acoustic transfer function and p1 and p2 are the two measured acoustic pressure of the two microphones See Figure 16.1.

16.3 Proposed Methodology

Soft computing has played a vital role in enhancing the prediction for different models. Although analytical models have played a vital role to bridge the gap in predicting various coefficients, there still lies room for inaccuracies or inconsistencies that can thereby result in inaccurate results. In order to mitigate these errors, machine learning approaches are preferred because of their algorithms and re-duced complexities for result generation. While human effort is required for creating datasets, the estimated outcome can be suitable for any model for real-time situations.

Regression analysis gives an ideal estimate for an output entity when a targeted input parameter is provided. The mechanical properties which have some role in predicting the sound absorption coeffi-cients are considered to be our inputs, which include porosity, pore size, pore opening, bulk density, and static flow resistance.

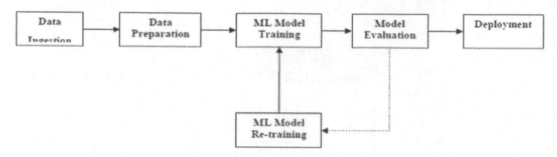

FIGURE 16.2 Steps for building a machine learning model.

The process can be carried out with the following steps: data pre-processing, building the model, and fine-tuning and deployment as shown in Figure 16.2.

16.3.1 Step 1: Data Preprocessing

The dataset is checked for any missing data. Since we had almost all the data needed for the experiment with no categorical features, the data preprocessing data step was simple and did not take much time to process. The dataset was split into training and testing in the ratio of 80/20 to analyze the output for various instances and predict subsequent errors.

16.3.2 Step 2: Fitting Regression Model

A typical multiple regression model can be defined as

$$y = b0X0 + b1X1 + b2X2 + b3X3 + \ldots + bnXn \text{ where } X0 = 1$$

In the above expression, y is the output parameter to be defined and x is the different independent parameters (sound absorption properties) which play a vital role in predicting y (sound absorption coefficients). We have applied two methods viz., backward elimination and forward selection, to select the important features as discussed below.

16.3.3 Building a Backward Elimination Model

In order to evaluate the performance and optimize the model thoroughly, we use the concept backward elimination. By doing the backward elimination, we eliminate certain features that have negligible effects in predicting the output because unnecessary features increase the complexity of the model. The acceptance or rejection of hypothesis depends on the p-value. The model begins with all the predictors and starts comparing each predictor value to the significant value. The predictor is discarded if the p-value is greater than the significant level. While the model immediately scans through the rest of the predictors, it decides the predictor to be effective when the p-value is less than the significant value and rejects the converse.

16.3.4 Building the Model Using Forward Selection Model

Forward selection chooses a subset of predictor values for the final value. This method can be performed as a forward stepwise in context of linear regression with either n greater than or lesser than p, where n is the size of the dataset and p being the dimension of the explanatory variable. Using this approach is feasible because it is both tractable and allows better optimization of models. Initially, the model has a single intercept (over mean) since it has no predictors. Subsequently, predictors are being added on the basis of their importance on the parameter of residual sum of squares.

16.3.5 Step 3: Optimizing the Regressor Model—Mean Squared Error

The Mean Squared Error (MSE) estimates how close the regression line is to the set of points. It calculates the distance of the points from the regression line—the distance being defined as the error. The deviation is then squared to analyze to determine how far the predicted value to the actual value is. After obtaining the line of best fit, the estimated y values obtained from the line of best fit are subtracted from the expected values. The average deviation of the squared values gives the mean squared error. Generally, the errors must be minimalistic as possible to depict the line of fit.

$$SSE = \sum (Y - Y_{pred})^2$$

In the above relation, Y is the original value and Y_{pred} is the estimated value from the line of best fit.

16.3.6 Step 4: Understanding the Results and Cross Validation

The accuracy can be confirmed on the basis of least difference in error or how close the predicted and experimental values converge. To evaluate the efficacy of the model and understand if the model has been overfit, cross validation can be performed. Cross validation was performed on machine learning models to test the accuracy for unseen models. This way we get an estimate of how the model will perform on new data which are never used in the testing model.

16.3.7 Step 5: Deployment and Optimization

The learned model can then be deployed for a real-world problem for a specific issue. The results can then be obtained and stored in a database for inspection. Certain parameters can be altered to ensure a good fit model. If the features have not met the expected standards, the model can again be re-tested with a different model or boost the algorithm used in the previous testing method. The model can be retrained to experience a better prediction and good accuracy. There can also be difference in the correlation coefficient.

16.3.7.1 Structural Parameters of Each Layer Material Is Shown in Table 16.1

See Table 16.1.

Using the mechanical properties of the material, we use the structural parameters as the input to the testing set. Sound absorption coefficients of the samples are estimated for different frequencies using regression models. Further, an average value is estimated for all the sound absorption coefficients to give the best results.

TABLE 16.1

Structural Parameter of Each Layer Material

Material Symbol	Thickness (10^{-3} m)	Area Density (10^{-3} kg/m^3)	Porosity (%)	Pore Size (10^{-6} m)
a	10	48.3	87.28	435
b	10	52.9	93.50	539
c	10	57.5	94.70	694
d	10	68.2	95.13	817

The symbols a, b, c, and d denote the following notations:
a refers to Polyurethane (PU) foam; b refers to PU with 5% wood powder;
c refers to PU with 10% wood powder; d refers to PU with 15% wood powder.

16.4 Results and Discussions

We have conducted various experiments to develop a feasible machine learning model that can be applied to correctly predict the sound absorption coefficients at six different central frequencies (Table 16.2). In the first experiment denoted as "All-in-one approach," we have built a multiple linear regression model in which we assume that each of the 16 independent variables to be equally contributing to the dependent variable and kept all data at six different central frequencies (α_{125}, α_{250}, α_{500}, α_{1000}, α_{2000}, α_{4000}).

It is observed that the models based on the "all-in approach" result in highly negligible errors in case of lower frequencies like α_{125} and α_{250}. Further, the approach is also found to be suitable for predicting the sound absorption coefficients at higher frequencies of α_{2000} and α_{4000}. On the other hand, the "all-in approach" results in marginally higher errors in predicting the sound absorption coefficients at α_{500} and α_{1000}, as observed in Figure 16.3.

This fact is further corroborated by plotting the measured and predicted sound absorption coefficients at different frequencies, for the random samples generated for the test set. One such randomly chosen sample from the test set is *ADBD (Sample Index – 56)*, which is used to cross evaluate our results for this study.

Figure 16.4 clearly depicts the presence of scope in improvement of the results obtained through the "all-in-one approach." Although the scikit learn library used for the study does the necessary job of identifying the significant parameters, feature selection methods like "Backward elimination" and "Forward selection" may further improve the accuracy of predictions.

The significance level assumed for the study is 10%. We have kept all the 16 independent variables first and then eliminated the unimportant features based on its p-value. At different frequencies (α_{125}, α_{250}, α_{500}, α_{1000}, α_{2000}, α_{4000}), the number of relevant features varied and it is reduced to 4, 3, 7, 4, 6, 6 that have p-value above 0.5. We have re-trained the regression model using the relevant features that are found using this backward elimination method and the results are summarized below.

Improvements in prediction and reduction in mean square error (MSE) were observed. Figure 16.5 depicts the improvement in prediction of the sound absorption coefficients for our random sample—ADBD.

TABLE 16.2

Sound Absorption Values

Index	Sample Code	α_{125}	α_{250}	α_{500}	α_{1000}	α_{2000}	α_{4000}	$\bar{\alpha}$
1	aaaa	0.023	0.15	0.533	0.82	0.872727	0.96	0.559843
2	aaab	0.008	0.165	0.413	0.9	0.836364	0.92	0.540449
4	bcac	0.019	0.2	0.493	0.74	0.863636	0.95	0.544328
5	bcad	0.007	0.185	0.347	0.74	0.863636	0.95	0.515384

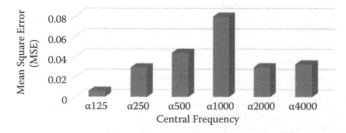

FIGURE 16.3 Mean square error (MSE) at various frequencies for multiple linear regression—"all-in-one approach".

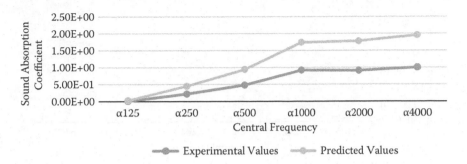

FIGURE 16.4 Measured and predicted sound absorption coefficients for a random test sample—ADBD – "all-in-one approach".

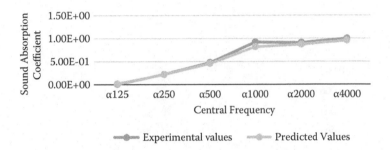

FIGURE 16.5 Measured and predicted sound absorption coefficients for a random test sample—ADBD "Backward Elimination approach".

The second experiment was conducted using the forward selection method, in which we started with most significant feature first and included additional features based on its p-value. Once the first variable is identified, all possible two independent variable combinations of datasets are tried. The combination which corresponds to the lowest p-value (less than 0.1 or 10%) for the newly added feature is now deemed significant and subsequently finalized as the second significant parameter. This process repeats until all the remaining features exhibit p-values in excess of 0.1 or 10%, indicating that all significant variables have already been extracted. We found that, at frequencies $\alpha_{125}, \alpha_{250}, \alpha_{500}, \alpha_{1000}, \alpha_{2000}, \alpha_{4000}$, only 5, 6, 5, 5, 6, 6 variables are most significant using this forward selection approach also.

Figure 16.6 depicts the refinement of the predicted results for our random sample—ADBD by following the forward selection approach.

16.4.1 Error Analysis and Validating Model Performance for All Test Samples

To measure the significance of the proposed approach, we compared the errors in prediction and tried to find the best-suited algorithm for our application. In order to validate the performance and to expand the scope of the model, the prediction of Sound Absorption Coefficients has been done for each of the test samples at all six central frequencies.

The reduction in mean square error (MSE) by using the feature selection methods such as "Backward Elimination" and "Forward Selection" can be observed in Figure 16.7. Although the improvements are only minor at higher frequencies, there is a noticeable drop in errors at the lower and middle frequencies.

Since these metrics conform to our earlier results obtained through random sample prediction, it can be definitively concluded that manual feature selection methods do improve the accuracy of test data predictions.

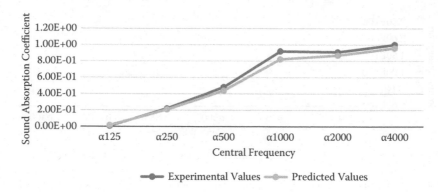

FIGURE 16.6 Measured and predicted sound absorption coefficients for a random test sample—ADBD "Forward Selection approach".

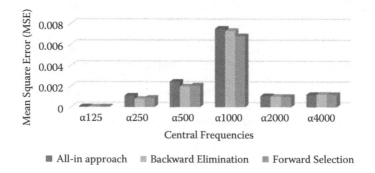

FIGURE 16.7 Mean square error (MSE) at various frequencies for the three multiple linear regression models.

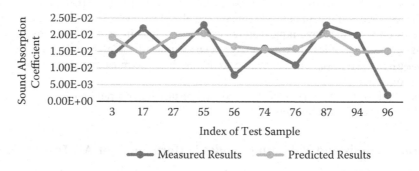

FIGURE 16.8 The measured and predicted sound absorption coefficient at 125 Hz for backward elimination.

Further, the measured and predicted sound absorption coefficients for each of the 10 test samples has been observed. For one test sample, the obtained results at 125 Hz are depicted in Figures 16.8 and 16.9 for backward elimination and forward selection methods, which clearly indicates that applying feature selection on regression models can improve the prediction performance. By applying cross-validation, we have studied the performance of the proposed approach using mean square error as the metric and tabulated the same in Table 16.3.

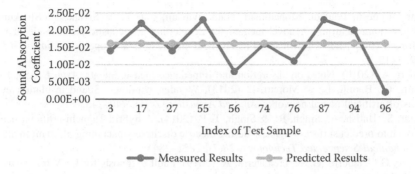

FIGURE 16.9 The measured and predicted sound absorption coefficient at 125 Hz for forward selection.

TABLE 16.3

Average Mean Square Errors of Test Samples at Each Central Frequency

Sound Absorption Coefficient	Average Mean Square Error (MSE)
α_{125}	0.0000675
α_{250}	0.00098
α_{500}	0.0037
α_{1000}	0.0048
α_{2000}	0.000807
α_{4000}	0.0028

16.5 Conclusion

This research work was carried out to study the behavior of different models on the ability to predict sound absorption coefficient values. It was noted that the linear regression-based models are best suited for this. The detailed analysis was performed and it is observed that the prediction results are as good as the experimental results that are carried out in the lab setup. It is also observed that the mean square error is significantly lower and is negligible. This study could be extended with different layers of composites and other techniques will be explored in the future.

REFERENCES

[1] Sung, G., Kim, J. W., & Kim, J. H. (2016). Fabrication of polyurethane composite foams with magnesium hydroxide filler for improved sound absorption. *Journal of Industrial and Engineering Chemistry*, *44*, 99–104.

[2] Agrawal, A., Kaur, R., & Walia, R. S. (2017). PU foam derived from renewable sources: Perspective on properties enhancement: An overview. *European Polymer Journal*, *95*, 255–274.

[3] Liu, J., Bao, W., Shi, L., Zuo, B., & Gao, W. (2014). General regression neural network for prediction of sound absorption coefficients of sandwich structure nonwoven absorbers. *Applied Acoustics*, *76*, 128–137.

[4] Yuvaraj, L., Jeyanthi, S., Thomas, N. S., & Rajeev, V. (2020). An experimental investigation on the mechanical and acoustic properties of silica gel reinforced sustainable foam. *Materials Today: Proceedings*, *27*, 2293–2296.

[5] Lv, Z., Li, X., & Yu, X. (2012). The effect of chain extension method on the properties of polyurethane/SiO$_2$ composites. *Materials & Design*, *35*, 358–362.

[6] Guan, D., Wu, J. H., Wu, J., Li, J., & Zhao, W. (2015). Acoustic performance of aluminum foams with semiopen cells. *Applied Acoustics*, *87*, 103–108.

[7] Sekar, Vignesh, Fouladi, Mohammad, Namasivayam, Satesh, & Sivanesan, Sivakumar. (2019). Additive manufacturing: A novel method for developing an acoustic panel made of natural fiber-reinforced composites with enhanced mechanical and acoustical properties. *Journal of Engineering, 2019*, 1–19.

[8] Seybert, A. (2010). Notes on absorption and impedance measurements. *Astm E1050*, 1–6.

[9] Buratti, C., Barelli, L., & Moretti, E. (2013). Wooden windows: Sound insulation evaluation by means of artificial neural networks. *Applied Acoustics, 74*(5), 740–745.

[10] Kumar, S., Batish, A., Singh, R., & Singh, T. P. (2014). A hybrid Taguchi-artificial neural network approach to predict surface roughness during electric discharge machining of titanium alloys. *Journal of Mechanical Science and Technology, 28*(7), 2831–2844.

[11] Iannace, G., Ciaburro, G., & Trematerra, A. (2019). Fault diagnosis for UAV blades using artificial neural network. *Robotics, 8*(3), 59.

[12] Iannace, G., Ciaburro, G., & Trematerra, A. (2020). Modelling sound absorption properties of broom fibers using artificial neural networks. *Applied Acoustics, 163*, 107239.

[13] Dong, Chensong, Zhang, Chuck, Liang, Zhiyong, & Wang, Ben. (2004). Dimension variation prediction for composites with finite element analysis and regression modeling. *Composites Part A: Applied Science and Manufacturing, 35*(6), 735–746.

[14] Henry, R., Lewis, C., Hopke, P., & Williamson, H. (1984). Review of receptor model fundamentals. *Atmospheric Environment (1967), 18*(8), 1507–1515.

[15] Phusavat, K., & Aneksitthisin, E. (2000). Interrelationship among profitability, productivity and price recovery: Lessons learned from a wood-furniture company. *Proceedings of industrial engineering network*, Petchaburi, Thailand.

[16] Ogulata, S. & Sahin, Cenk & Ogulata, Tugrul & Balci, Onur. (2006). The prediction of elongation and recovery of woven bi-stretch fabric using artificial neural network and linear regression models. *Fibres and Textiles in Eastern Europe*, 14.

Section IV

Issue and Challenges in Data Science and Data Analytics

17

Feedforward Multi-Layer Perceptron Training by Hybridized Method between Genetic Algorithm and Artificial Bee Colony

Aleksa Cuk, Timea Bezdan, Nebojsa Bacanin, Miodrag Zivkovic, K. Venkatachalam, Tarik A. Rashid, and V. Kanchana Devi

CONTENTS

17.1 Introduction

Artificial neural network (ANN) represents the most advanced method in the machine learning domain. Machine learning (ML) is an area of artificial intelligence (AI) that gives facility to the computer system to learn from the data. There is accelerated growth in this field in the last decade because of the increase in training speed effected by GPUs and deep learning. ANNs are biologically inspired algorithms, which mimic the learning process of the human brain. ANNs have broad utilization in different areas, such as regression, classification, pattern recognition, and different forecasting problems [1–5].

ANN's architecture starts with the input layer, and the final layer represents the classification layer that predicts the class. There are one or more hidden layers between the input and output layers. The first layer contains an equal number of nodes (units) as the number of input features, the number of nodes in the hidden layer is a hyperparameter that should be tuned and the output layer represent the classification layer which has an equal number of nodes as the classes to predict. The units between different layers are connected by modifiable connection weights. Bias is an additional parameter for adjusting the weighted sum of the input, and move the activation function result towards the negative or positive side. The output value of one neuron is calculated by applying an activation function to the weighted sum and bias as follows:

$$z = a(Wx + b) \tag{17.1}$$

where z expresses the output value, a is the activation function, the input is denoted by x, W indicates to the weigh, and b is the bias term.

The most popular activation function is sigmoid, other activation functions are tanh, and Rectified Linear Unit (ReLU) [6].

The value of the weights and biases should be determined and it represents an optimization problem. For multi-layer perceptron (MLP) neural networks there are two widely used methods for optimizing the value of the connection weights, gradient-based training, and stochastic optimization algorithms. Backpropagation [7] is a gradient-based algorithm, which has a disadvantage, as it gets trapped in local minima. Other stochastic gradient descent (SGD) optimizations are momentum, rmsprop, adam, adadelta, adamax, and adagrad [8, 9, 10].

To address this issue of getting trapped in the local minima, in this study, we introduce a model for optimizing the value of the connection weights in MLP by the hybridized metaheuristic algorithm. The connection weigh optimization belongs to the NP-hard class, where computing the optimal solution is intractable and cannot be solved by exact optimization techniques. Metaheuristic approaches gives satisfactory resolution in solving NP-hard optimization issues. Thus, in this paper, we develop and present an improved metaheuristic algorithm with the hybridization of artificial bee colony algorithm (ABC) and genetic algorithm (GA).

17.2 Nature-Inspired Metaheuristics

Metaheuristic algorithms are inspired by nature and represent a field of stochastic optimization. Stochastic optimization methods employ some level of randomness and search for optimal or near-optimal solutions. Metaheuristic algorithms are powerful in optimization problems, where the search space is extensive and exact, brute-force search methods would fail. Brute-force methods implicitly explore all the possibilities in the search space, which takes too much time; on the other hand, metaheuristic techniques use randomization to explore the search space. There are two main phases in each metaheuristic algorithm, intensification, and diversification. The diversification (also called exploration) process is responsible for search space exploration globally, while the intensification (also called exploitation) does the local search, around the current fittest solution. For achieving good results, it is very important to make a good balance between intensification and diversification. Two main categories of the metaheuristic algorithms are the swarm intelligence (SI) and the evolutionary algorithms (EAs).

Swarm intelligence algorithms are motivated by group (collective) intelligence developed from nature where the overall population drives to intelligent global action. Numerous swarm-intelligence-based algorithms are introduced with various designs, but all of them have certain common characteristics. First, the population is generated randomly in the initialization phase. Randomization is utilized for search space investigation and avoiding becoming stuck in local optima. The location of each solution is changed after each iteration, and when the algorithm meets the termination condition, outputs the best solution. The position update allows the system to evolve, and to converge toward the global optimum.

Swarm-intelligence-based metaheuristic approaches have successful implementation in various areas, such as convolutional neural network architecture design in deep learning [11], image clustering [12–14], implementation in cloud computing to schedule tasks (user requests) [15], etc.

The biological evolution process motivates the EAsn, and it has three sub-categories, namely, Evolutionary Programming [16], Evolutionary Strategies [17], and Genetic Algorithms [18].

Each evolutionary algorithm incorporates the following elements: solution definition, random initialization of the population, fitness function evaluation, reproduction, selection, replacement strategy, and termination criteria. Metaheuristic hybridization is a very successful category of metaheuristic study. The hybrid algorithm is a parallel or distributed implementation of two or more algorithms. It blends benefits of various metaheuristic algorithms using algorithmic ingredients from distinct optimization methods or a mixture of metaheuristics with various methods from artificial intelligence.

There are many successful implementations of hybridized metaheuristics in different fields. In deep learning, hybrid metaheuristic variations are applied for convolutional neural network architecture

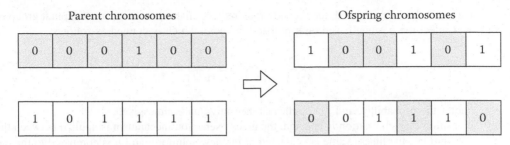

FIGURE 17.1 Crossover operation.

optimizations [19–21], dropout probability estimation in convolutional neural networks [22], different applications in cloud computing [23, 24], and wireless sensor optimization problems [25].

17.3 Genetic Algorithm Overview

Genetic algorithms (GAs) are motivated by the evolution mechanism of nature; the algorithm was developed in the 1970s [26]. GA is a powerful optimization method that employs crossover and mutation operations to create new individuals (chromosomes), which are responsible of search space exploration and to find the optimal solution.

The algorithm has an iterative procedure; in each iteration, new chromosomes are generated by the crossover and mutation operators. From the current population, parents are selected by taking two individuals, and by the crossover operator new offsprings are generated by swapping parts of the parents, then the mutation operator changes the offsprings based on the mutation probability. The crossover operation is visualized in Figure 17.1.

The genetic algorithm has some disadvantages, such as the mutation rate, crossover rate selection, and fast converge could lead to premature convergence.

17.4 Proposed Hybridized GA Metaheuristic

To achieve better performance, we hybridized the GA with the ABC algorithm [27]. ABC is effectively employed in different NP-hard optimization issues [28–31]. The algorithm is inspired by three honey bee groups (the employed bee group, onlookers, and scout bee group), which are responsible for making the exploration/exploitation trade-off.

Similarly to the genetic algorithm or any other metaheuristics, the ABC generates a random population at the beginning of the algorithm, as follows:

$$x_{i,j} = min_j + rand\,(0,\ 1) * (max_j - min_j) \tag{17.2}$$

where an individual's new location is indicated by $x_{i,j}$, max_j, and min_j to define the solutions of the upper and lower bounds.

In the next step, the exploitation and position update is executed according to the following equation:

$$x_{i,j} = \begin{cases} x_{i,j} + a\,(x_{i,j} - x_{k,j}),\ R_j < MR \\ x_{i,j}, \quad otherwise \end{cases} \tag{17.3}$$

where the new position is denoted by $x_{i,j}$, the neighbor solutions are denoted by $x_{k,j}$, $a \in [0,\ 1]$, and the modification rate is denoted by *MR*.

After the exploitation is completed, the second group receives the information from the first group of solutions, and select the position based on a probability value, which is defined as follows:

$$p_i = \frac{f(x_i)}{\sum_{j=1}^{n} f(x_j)}, f(x_i) = \frac{1}{1 + f_i} \tag{17.4}$$

where p denotes the probability, and $f(x)$ indicates the individual's fitness value.

After the position of each solution is updated, the greedy selection mechanism is applied between the old and new solutions, the fitness value is evaluated of the new solutions, and it is compared to the old solutions' fitness. The new individual alters the old one, if its value of the fitness is better; otherwise, the old individual is retained.

If an employed bee is not showing improvement through the course of the iteration, and it reaches the defined number of trials, the scout bee generates a new random solution.

The proposed algorithm is named as a genetically guided enhanced artificial bee colony, in short GGEABC, and Algorithm 17.1 presents the details of the pseudocode.

Algorithm 17.1   Genetically guided enhanced artificial bee colony (GGEABC)

Randomly create the set of the initial population of N solutions.
Evaluate the value of the fitness of each solution.
while $t < MaximumIteration$ **do**
    for $i = 1$ to N **do**
        Parent selection
        Crossover operation
        Mutation operation
        Phase of ABC group I
        Phase of ABC group II
        Phase of ABC group III
        Evaluate the value of the fitness of each solution.
        Sort the population and keep the fittest individual.
    end for
end while
Output x_1

The pictorial representation of the proposed GGEABC is depicted in Figure 17.2.

17.5 MLP Training by GGEABC

The proposed GGEABC is adopted to train the MLP, which has one hidden-layer. The solutions in the GGEABC's populations encode the weights and biases in a one-dimensional vector. The length of the vector is calculated as follows:

$$n_w = (n_x \times n_h + n_h) + (n_h \times n_o + n_o) \tag{17.5}$$

where n_w denotes the length of a solution, the input feature size is denoted by n_x, the hidden unit number is indicated by n_h, and n_o denotes the output layer size.

The solution encoding is presented in Figure 17.3.

As an optimization fitness function, MSE (mean square error) is used and the objective is to minimize its value. The value is calculated as:

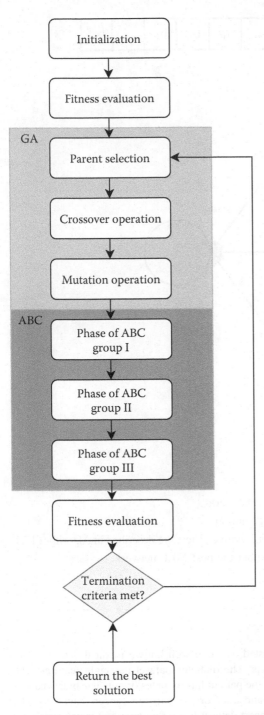

FIGURE 17.2 GGEABC flowchart.

$$MSE = \frac{1}{n} \sum_{i=1}^{n} (y_i - \hat{y}_i)^2 \tag{17.6}$$

where the number of instances are denoted by n, y denotes the actual value, and the predicted value is denoted by $\hat{y}$.

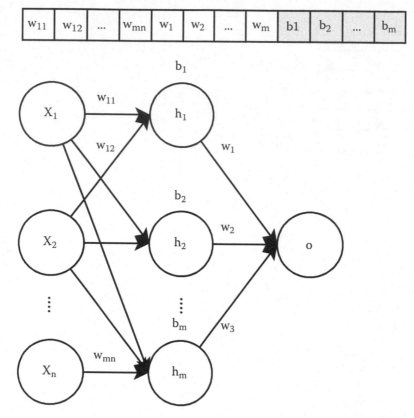

FIGURE 17.3   Solution encoding.

Steps of the algorithm's procedure:

- Step 1: Random solution initialization of N MLP networks.
- Step 2: MSE fitness function evaluation of each solution.
- Step 3: Update the position of each solution by the iterative procedure described in Algorithm 17.1.
- Step 4: After the maximum iteration reached, output the best MLP network.
- Step 5: Test the network on the test dataset.

17.6 Simulation Setup and Results

In this work, the model developed by GGEABC is tested on three well-known medical datasets, diabetes, breast cancer [32, 33], and SAheart [34] datasets. The diabetes dataset has eight features, 768 instances, and two classes; the classes indicate whether the patient has diabetes or not. The breast cancer dataset has two classes; one class indicating benign and another class to the cancer diagnosis. The dataset contains 699 instances and 9 features. The SAheart dataset has 9 features, 462 instances, and 2 classes, the classes indicating if the patient has diseases or not.

The data is normalized by utilizing the following formula:

$$X_{norm} = \frac{X_i - X_{min}}{X_{max} - X_{min}}$$

(17.7)

where X_{norm} denotes the normalized value, the ith input feature us denoted by X_i, and the maximum and minimum value of the corresponding feature is denoted by X_{max}, and X_{min}, respectively.

Two-thirds of the entire dataset is utilized for training purposes, while 1/3 is utilized for testing the model. We used five different metrics to evaluate the proposed approach; the accuracy (*acc.*), specificity (*spec.*), sensitivity (*sens*), geometric mean (g_{mean}), and area under the curve (*AUC*) metrics, which are popular metrics in the field of medicine, and the equations are formulated as:

$$acc = (TP + TN)/(TP + FP + TN + FN) \qquad (17.8)$$

$$spec = (TN)/(TN + FP) \qquad (17.9)$$

$$sens = \frac{TN}{FN + TP} \qquad (17.10)$$

$$g_{mean} = \sqrt{specificity \times sensitivity} \qquad (17.11)$$

$$AUC = 1/(TP + FP)(TN + FN) \int_0^{-1} TP \ d \ FP \qquad (17.12)$$

where *TP* denotes the true positive, *TN* the true negative, *FP* the false positive, and *FN* the false negative values from the confusion matrix.

The configuration setup is done in a similar fashion as in the work [35]. The simulation results are compared to the results of the algorithms reported in [35].

The size of the population is set to 50, and each solution is initialized between −1 and 1. To show consistency, the proposed GGEABC is carried out 30 times; 250 generation in each run. Table 17.1 depicts the control parameters and the corresponding values.

Tables 17.2–Table 17.4 present the best, mean, and worst statistical results and comparisons with other metaheuristic approaches on the same dataset.

Figure 17.4 illustrates the algorithm comparison of the best result on five metrics.

Figure 17.5 visualizes the accuracy convergence graph.

From the obtained simulation results, we can conclude that the GGE-ABC method has high performance and outperformed other metaheuristic methods. Diabetes dataset–GGEABC achieved the best results on the best statistic in accuracy, sensitivity, g-mean, and AUC. Breast cancer achieved the highest accuracy of 98.379%, 100% on the specificity test, and the best AUC of 99.835%. SAheart dataset–GGEABC achieved the best results on best statistic accuracy, g-mean, and AUC. The best accuracy of GGEABC on the diabetes dataset is 80.425%, and 79.215% on the SAheart dataset. The proposed method has the best worst statistical result on all metrics in the case

TABLE 17.1

GGEABC's Control Parameters

Parameter Name	Notation	Value
Size of the population	N	50
Crossover probability	p_c	0.9
Mutation probability	m_p	0.015
Employed bee group size	EB	25
Onlooker bee group size	OB	25
Scout bee	SB	1
Modification rate	MR	0.8
Trial limit	*limit*	5

TABLE 17.2

Results of the Diabetes Dataset

Method	Result	Acc.(%)	Spec.(%)	Sens.(%)	G_{mean}	AUC
GGEABC	best	**80.425**	86.325	**88.915**	**0.79585**	**0.86935**
	worst	**77.861**	81.398	74.069	**0.79825**	0.75609
	mean	**78.301**	83.296	82.878	**0.82673**	0.80797
GOA	best	77.863	89.157	59.375	0.72511	0.86433
	worst	75.191	**87.349**	54.167	0.68785	**0.84682**
	mean	76.489	**88.373**	55.938	0.70303	**0.85528**
ABC	best	80.534	94.578	70.833	0.78115	0.86509
	worst	70.992	72.892	37.500	0.59554	0.78181
	mean	74.822	84.799	57.569	0.69560	0.82251
GA	best	78.244	89.759	63.542	0.73016	0.85950
	worst	72.137	83.133	47.917	0.65582	0.82674
	mean	75.165	85.723	56.910	0.69804	0.83888
PSO	best	78.244	95.181	62.500	0.73887	0.84419
	worst	67.176	79.518	37.500	0.57216	0.77987
	mean	73.104	86.265	50.347	0.65648	0.81890
BAT	best	79.389	90.361	64.583	0.75367	0.86383
	worst	73.282	81.325	48.958	0.66068	0.79744
	mean	76.374	87.289	57.500	0.70779	0.84349
FF	best	77.481	58.333	88.554	0.71873	0.85398
	worst	75.191	56.250	**86.145**	0.69611	0.83967
	mean	76.349	57.153	**87.450**	0.70695	0.84664
FPA	best	78.244	92.169	62.500	0.73376	0.84752
	worst	72.137	82.530	48.958	0.65620	0.81859
	mean	75.242	86.546	55.694	0.69369	0.83299
BBO	best	77.099	89.157	60.417	0.72143	0.85442
	worst	73.282	83.133	53.125	0.67885	0.82649
	mean	75.611	86.325	57.083	0.70183	0.84211
MBO	best	78.626	**95.783**	64.583	0.73802	0.86195
	worst	70.611	78.916	42.708	0.60867	0.77548
	mean	74.733	85.763	55.660	0.68939	0.82938

TABLE 17.3

Breast Cancer Dataset Results

Method	Result	Acc.(%)	Spec.(%)	Sens.(%)	G_{mean}	AUC
GGEABC	best	**98.379**	**100.000**	98.295	0.98021	**0.99835**
	worst	96.251	97.131	97.321	**0.96698**	0.98452
	mean	**97.498**	**98.799**	97.652	**0.97384**	**0.99699**
GOA	best	97.899	97.531	98.726	0.97810	0.99693
	worst	95.798	92.593	96.178	0.94991	0.99229
	mean	97.115	95.309	98.047	0.96665	0.99536
ABC	best	98.319	**100.000**	98.726	**0.98718**	0.99772
	worst	94.958	91.358	94.904	0.94047	0.92593
	mean	96.891	96.214	97.240	0.96713	0.98544
GA	best	97.479	97.531	98.726	0.97492	0.99709
	worst	95.378	90.123	**97.452**	0.94022	0.99418
	mean	96.751	94.362	97.983	0.96151	0.99549

(Continued)

TABLE 17.3 (Continued)

Breast Cancer Dataset Results

Method	Result	Acc.(%)	Spec.(%)	Sens.(%)	G_{mean}	AUC
PSO	best	97.899	98.765	**99.363**	0.98107	0.99756
	worst	95.378	90.123	96.815	0.94022	0.99402
	mean	97.045	94.774	**98.217**	0.96471	0.99558
BAT	best	98.319	98.765	**99.363**	0.98127	0.99568
	worst	92.437	79.012	96.178	0.88605	0.89188
	mean	96.218	93.457	97.643	0.95494	0.97079
FF	best	97.899	98.089	97.531	0.97810	0.99678
	worst	**96.639**	**98.089**	93.827	0.95935	**0.99575**
	mean	97.311	98.089	95.802	0.96938	0.99619
FPA	best	98.319	98.765	98.726	0.98427	0.99670
	worst	95.378	90.123	**97.452**	0.94022	0.99292
	mean	97.241	95.432	98.174	0.96789	0.99511
BBO	best	98.319	97.531	98.726	0.98127	0.99670
	worst	**96.639**	93.827	**97.452**	0.95935	0.99355
	mean	97.255	95.514	98.153	0.96822	0.99550
MBO	best	97.899	98.765	**99.363**	0.98107	0.99693
	worst	94.958	87.654	95.541	0.93026	0.98616
	mean	96.695	94.074	98.047	0.96031	0.99453

TABLE 17.4

Results of the SAheart Dataset

Method	Result	Acc.(%)	Spec.(%)	Sens.(%)	G_{mean}	AUC
GGEABC	best	**79.215**	83.897	87.698	**0.74598**	**0.82499**
	worst	**71.568**	**78.958**	**80.659**	**0.67668**	**0.77523**
	mean	**74.358**	80.032	81.236	0.69385	**0.79415**
GOA	best	79.114	57.407	**91.346**	0.71238	0.78793
	worst	67.722	42.593	79.808	0.58653	0.72685
	mean	73.122	49.383	**85.449**	0.64913	0.75555
ABC	best	76.582	**95.192**	61.111	0.71909	0.81250
	worst	67.722	72.115	29.630	0.53109	0.66560
	mean	71.160	82.276	49.753	0.63644	0.74454
GA	best	75.949	94.231	55.556	0.67792	0.78241
	worst	68.354	75.962	40.741	0.61048	0.73326
	mean	71.814	82.372	51.481	0.65030	0.76671
PSO	best	77.848	**95.192**	61.111	0.68990	0.79897
	worst	64.557	70.192	38.889	0.57689	0.71546
	mean	72.658	**85.096**	48.704	0.64126	0.76022
BAT	best	75.949	89.423	59.259	0.67779	0.78846
	worst	68.987	76.923	42.593	0.61715	0.74252
	mean	72.405	83.654	50.741	0.65086	0.76642
FF	best	74.051	55.556	84.615	0.68172	0.77902
	worst	69.620	48.148	79.808	0.62361	0.76086
	mean	71.730	51.667	82.147	0.65137	0.77276
FPA	best	76.582	93.269	64.815	0.71050	0.80520
	worst	68.354	77.885	38.889	0.59377	0.72489
	mean	72.869	84.231	50.988	0.65336	0.76480
BBO	best	75.316	91.346	61.111	0.69696	0.78775

(*Continued*)

TABLE 17.4 (Continued)

Results of the SAheart Dataset

Method	Result	Acc.(%)	Spec.(%)	Sens.(%)	G_{mean}	AUC
	worst	69.620	78.846	40.741	0.60359	0.75036
	mean	72.911	83.910	51.728	0.65776	0.77369
MBO	best	76.582	89.423	62.963	0.70408	0.79790
	worst	68.354	75.000	40.741	0.59706	0.71599
	mean	72.932	83.782	52.037	0.65881	0.76113

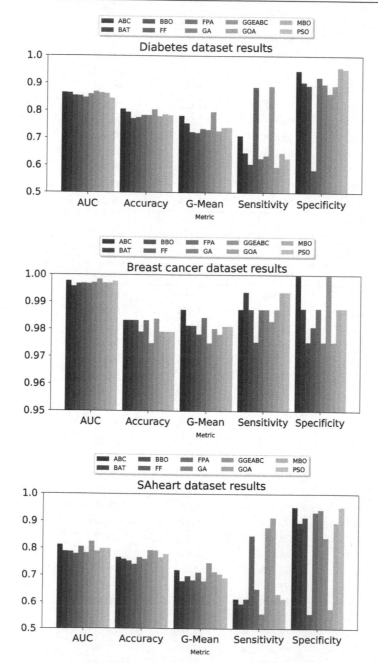

FIGURE 17.4 Algorithm comparison of best results on five metrics.

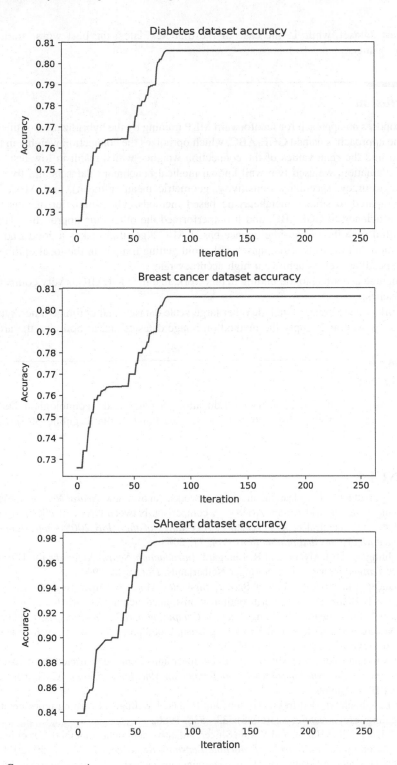

FIGURE 17.5 Convergence graph.

of the SAheart dataset, while in the case of the diabetes dates, the best worst statistic is on the accuracy, and g-mean.

17.7 Conclusion

This study proposes an approach for feedforward MLP training by the hybridization of the GA and ABC algorithm. The approach is named GGE-ABC, which optimizes the connection weights in the MLP. The objective is to find the right values of the connection weights, which result in low test error rate. For performance evaluation, we used two well-known medical benchmark datasets and five different metrics, namely, accuracy, specificity, sensitivity, geometric mean (g-mean), and AUC. The obtained results are compared to similar metaheuristic based methods. The simulation results prove the robustness and efficiency of GGEABC, and it outperformed the other nine approaches. Hybridizing the genetic algorithm with the swarm-intelligence-based ABC algorithm makes a good trade-off between the diversification and intensification phases and avoid getting trapped in the local optima, to have fast convergence speed, as well as achieve a high accuracy rate.

We can conclude according to the finding in this work, that the GGEABC is very competitive over the current approaches.

In future work, we are going to include other large-scale datasets and optimize other hyperparameters in the network, as well as to apply the method on image datasets and to optimize the architecture.

Acknowledgment

The paper is supported by the Ministry of Education, Science and Technological Development of Republic of Serbia, Grant No. III-44006 and the Science Fund of the Republic of Serbia, Grant No. 6524745, AI-DECIDE.

REFERENCES

[1] Jürgen Schmidhuber. Deep learning in neural networks: An overview. *Neural Networks*, 61:85–117, 2015.

[2] M. Braik, A. Sheta, and Amani Arieqat. A comparison between GAs and PSO in training ANN to model the TE chemical process reactor. *Proceedings of the AISB 2008 symposium on swarm intelligence algorithms and applications, Vol. 11,* 2008.

[3] C. Nightingale, D. J. Myers, and R. Linggard. *Introduction Neural Networks for Vision, Speech and Natural Language*, pages 1–4. Springer Netherlands, Dordrecht, 1992.

[4] Sankhadeep Chatterjee, Sarbartha Sarkar, Sirshendu Hore, Nilanjan Dey, Amira S Ashour, and Valentina E Balas. Particle swarm optimization trained neural network for structural failure prediction of multistoried RC buildings. *Neural Computing and Applications*, 28(8):2005–2016, 2017.

[5] Amir Mosavi, Pinar Ozturk, and Kwokwing Chau. Flood prediction using machine learning models: Literature review. *Water*, 10(11):1536, 2018.

[6] Vinod Nair and Geoffrey E. Hinton. Rectified linear units improve restricted Boltzmann machines. In *Proceedings of the 27th International Conference on Machine Learning*, ICML'10, pages 807–814, USA, 2010. Omnipress.

[7] David E. Rumelhart, Geoffrey E Hinton, and Ronald J Williams. Learning representations by back-propagating errors. *Nature*, 323(6088):533– 536, 1986.

[8] John C. Duchi, Elad Hazan, and Yoram Singer. Adaptive subgradient methods for online learning and stochastic optimization. *Journal of Machine Learning Research*, 12:2121–2159, 2011.

[9] Matthew D. Zeiler. Adadelta: An adaptive learning rate method. *arXiv preprint arXiv:1212.5701,* 2012.

[10] Diederik P. Kingma and Jimmy Ba. Adam: A method for stochastic optimization. *arXiv preprint arXiv:1412.6980,* 2014.

[11] Timea Bezdan, Eva Tuba, Ivana Strumberger, Nebojsa Bacanin, and Milan Tuba. Automatically designing convolutional neural network architecture with artificial flora algorithm. In Milan Tuba,

Shyam Akashe, and Amit Joshi, editors, *ICT Systems and Sustainability*, pages 371–378. Springer Singapore, Singapore, 2020.

[12] Eva Tuba, Ivana Strumberger, Nebojsa Bacanin, Timea Bezdan, and Milan Tuba. Image clustering by generative adversarial optimization and advanced clustering criteria. In Ying Tan, Yuhui Shi, and Milan Tuba, editors, *Advances in Swarm Intelligence*, pages 465–475. Springer International Publishing, Cham, 2020.

[13] Eva Tuba, Ivana Strumberger, Timea Bezdan, Nebojsa Bacanin, and Milan Tuba. Classification and feature selection method for medical datasets by brain storm optimization algorithm and support vector machine. *Procedia Computer Science*, 162:307–315, 2019. *7th International Conference on Information Technology and Quantitative Management (ITQM 2019): Information Technology and Quantitative Management Based on Artificial Intelligence.*

[14] Ivana Strumberger, Eva Tuba, Nebojsa Bacanin, Miodrag Zivkovic, Marko Beko, and Milan Tuba. Designing convolutional neural network architecture by the firefly algorithm. In *Proceedings of the 2019 International Young Engineers Forum (YEF-ECE)*, Costa da Caparica, Portugal, pages 59–65, 2019.

[15] Nebojsa Bacanin, Timea Bezdan, Eva Tuba, Ivana Strumberger, Milan Tuba, and Miodrag Zivkovic. Task scheduling in cloud computing environment by grey wolf optimizer. In *2019 27th Telecommunications Forum (TELFOR)*, pages 1–4. IEEE, 2019.

[16] D.B. Fogel and IEEE Computational Intelligence Society. *Evolutionary Computation: Toward a New Philosophy of Machine Intelligence*. IEEE Series on Computational Intelligence. Wiley, 2006.

[17] Hans-Georg Beyer and Hans-Paul Schwefel. Evolution strategies – A comprehensive introduction. *Natural Computing*, 1(1):3–52, Mar 2002.

[18] David E. Goldberg. *Genetic Algorithms in Search, Optimization and Machine Learning*. Addison-Wesley Longman Publishing Co., Inc., Boston, MA, USA, 1st edition, 1989.

[19] Eva Tuba, Ivana Strumberger, Nebojsa Bacanin, Timea Bezdan, and Milan Tuba. Optimizing convolutional neural network hyperparameters by enhanced swarm intelligence metaheuristics. *Algorithms*, 13(3):67, 2020.

[20] Nebojsa Bacanin, Timea Bezdan, Eva Tuba, Ivana Strumberger, and Milan Tuba. Monarch butterfly optimization based convolutional neural network design. *Mathematics*, 8(6):936, 2020.

[21] Timea Bezdan, Miodrag Zivkovic, Eva Tuba, Ivana Strumberger, Nebojsa Bacanin, and Milan Tuba. Glioma brain tumor grade classification from MRI using convolutional neural networks designed by modified FA. In *International Conference on Intelligent and Fuzzy Systems*, pages 955–963. Springer, 2020.

[22] N. Bacanin, E. Tuba, T. Bezdan, I. Strumberger, R. Jovanovic, and M. Tuba. Dropout probability estimation in convolutional neural networks by the enhanced bat algorithm. In *2020 International Joint Conference on Neural Networks (IJCNN)*, pages 1–7, 2020.

[23] Timea Bezdan, Miodrag Zivkovic, Milos Antonijevic, Tamara Zivkovic, and Nebojsa Bacanin. Enhanced flower pollination algorithm for task scheduling in cloud computing environment. In Amit Joshi, Mahdi Khosravy, and Neeraj Gupta, editors, *Machine Learning for Predictive Analysis*, pages 163–171. Springer Singapore, Singapore, 2021.

[24] Timea Bezdan, Miodrag Zivkovic, Eva Tuba, Ivana Strumberger, Nebojsa Bacanin, and Milan Tuba. Multi-objective task scheduling in cloud computing environment by hybridized bat algorithm. In *International Conference on Intelligent and Fuzzy Systems*, pages 718–725. Springer, 2020.

[25] Miodrag Zivkovic, Nebojsa Bacanin, Eva Tuba, Ivana Strumberger, Timea Bezdan, and Milan Tuba. Wireless sensor networks life time optimization based on the improved firefly algorithm. In *2020 International Wireless Communications and Mobile Computing (IWCMC)*, pages 1176–1181. IEEE, 2020.

[26] John Henry Holland et al. *Adaptation in Natural and Artificial Systems: An Introductory Analysis with Applications to Biology, Control, and Artificial Intelligence*. MIT Press, 1992.

[27] Dervis Karaboga and Bahriye Basturk. On the performance of artificial bee colony (abc) algorithm. *Applied Soft Computing*, 8(1):687–697, 2008.

[28] Milan Tuba and Nebojsa Bacanin. Artificial bee colony algorithm hybridized with firefly algorithm for cardinality constrained mean-variance portfolio selection problem. *Applied Mathematics & Information Sciences*, 8(6):2831, 2014.

[29] Nadezda Stanarevic, Milan Tuba, and Nebojsa Bacanin. Modified artificial bee colony algorithm for constrained problems optimization. *Int J Math Models Methods Applied Sci*, 5(3): 644–651, 2011.

[30] Milan Tuba, Nebojsa Bacanin, and Nadezda Stanarevic. Adjusted artificial bee colony (abc) algorithm for engineering problems. *WSEAS Transaction on Computers*, 11(4):111–120, 2012.

[31] Nebojsa Bacanin, Milan Tuba, and Ivona Brajevic. Performance of object-oriented software system for improved artificial bee colony optimizationInt J Math Comput Simul, 5(2): 154–162, 2011.

[32] Olvi L Mangasarian and William H Wolberg. Cancer diagnosis via linear programming. Technical report, University of Wisconsin-Madison Department of Computer Sciences, 1990.

[33] William H Wolberg and Olvi L Mangasarian. Multisurface method of pattern separation for medical diagnosis applied to breast cytology. *Proceedings of the National Academy of Sciences*, 87(23): 9193–9196, 1990.

[34] JE Rossouw, JP Du Plessis, AJ Benadé, PC Jordaan, JP Kotze, PL Jooste, and JJ Ferreira. Coronary risk factor screening in three rural communities. The CORIS baseline study. *South African Medical Journal = Suid-Afrikaanse tydskrif vir geneeskunde*, 64(12):430, 1983.

[35] Ali Asghar Heidari, Hossam Faris, Ibrahim Aljarah, and Seyedali Mirjalili. An efficient hybrid multilayer perceptron neural network with grasshopper optimization. *Soft Computing*, 23(17):7941–7958, 2019.

18

Algorithmic Trading Using Trend Following Strategy: Evidence from Indian Information Technology Stocks

Molla Ramizur Rahman

CONTENTS

18.1 Introduction

The growth of big data is due to rapid progress in this digitalized world, which resulted in an immeasurable increase in data generated and shared in every domain of work, ranging from public administration, non-government organizations, business, academic research, etc. Such data with complex characteristics has become difficult to process with traditional methods and techniques. Big Data is characterized as the seven Vs, namely Volume, Velocity, Variety, Veracity, Valence, Value, and Variability. Volume refers to the large size of data, growing exponentially. As per Dobre and Xhafa [1], 2.5 quintillion bytes of data are produced globally, whereas Gantz and Reinsel [2] predicted that by 2020, 40 zettabytes of data is expected worldwide. Velocity is defined as the speed at which information is processed or retrieved. It is necessary to have sophisticated data processing techniques capable of processing big data at a higher speed. Variety is defined as a type of data varying from textual to multimedia content. Textual data can either be structured, semi-structured, or unstructured. Most data, about 90%, is considered to be unstructured. However, multimedia content may be in the form of video, audio, or images. Variety indicates data complexity due to its existence in different forms, thereby challenging to process. Veracity is defined as the quality of the data, the lack of which affects accuracy [3]. It arises because of data uncertainty, due to inconsistency in large datasets [4]. Valence speaks of data connectivity in the form of a graph [5]. Value refers to the process of transforming data into useful information, capable of generating revenues in business, or provide better insights to marketers in order to better understand customers, etc. Data may change continuously and may be inconsistent over time, and hence is termed as Variability [5]. Variability reduces the meaning of data, and such inconsistency is commonly faced in stock prices [4]. Traditionally big data is characterized with 3 Vs, and therefore, Gartner [6] defines big data as "high-volume, high-velocity, and high-variety information assets that demand cost-effective, innovative forms of information processing for enhanced insight and decision-making."

Development in data analytics has made it possible to capture, measure, and analyze a large amount of unstructured data. This facilitates to process any kind of data generated from any device giving valuable output, which is termed as datafication [7]. Saggi and Jain [4] mention various analytical techniques for processing data, namely classification, regression, clustering, graph analytics, association analyses, and decision trees. However, big data analytical tools include machine learning, artificial neural network, data mining, deep learning, and natural language processing.

In the field of banking and finance, a massive technological transformation has taken place, resulting in generation of petabytes of data, both in structured and unstructured form, giving birth to big data in finance. In this domain, digital evolution has drifted traditional operations to digital in order to handle customers [8]. In the banking sector, big data analytics helps in preventing financial frauds and judicious sanction of big-ticket corporate loans. While disbursing loans, data analytics help bankers to analyze credit risk by segmenting customer profiles. This is done by examining all possible financial networks of probable customers. This facilitates to examine financial nature and solvency of the customer, and helps the banker to take a strong judicious decision. It also helps in monitoring sanctioned loans, thereby reducing non-performing loans in banks. Data analytics is essential in assessing different kinds of financial risks, namely credit risk, operation risk, etc., with robust models. In the stock market, data analytics finds applications in predicting stock price. This helps in making smart investment decisions by relying on historical stock returns and analyzing real-time sentiments, economic and political scenarios, and even micro-level company fundamentals.

However, Sun et al. [9] pointed out significant challenges in financial big data analytics. It may be difficulties associated with organizing heterogeneous financial data effectively, in order to develop efficient business models. There also arises complications in implementing financial data analytics to approach critical topics like risk modeling and hence, requires expertise. Further, it also becomes challenging to provide complete safety, security, and privacy of such massive and confidential financial data.

High-Frequency Trading (HFT) has become an essential subject of study in the stock market, as thousands of orders need to be executed in seconds. HFT generates a massive amount of data, which is processed, and orders are executed swiftly and perfectly using algorithms. This resulted in the requirement of algorithmic trading, involving different kinds of trading strategies. This paper adopts Trend Following Strategy to study Indian Information Technology (IT) stocks featured in NIFTY 50, during FY 2019-20. Moving Averages at 11 and 22 days are computed for each of the respective companies, and the pairwise correlation coefficient is estimated. The efficiency of Trend Following Strategy is assessed for each of the IT stocks, and individually for "BUY-SELL" and "SELL-BUY" trade executions.

The remainder of the paper is organized as follows. Section 2 covers the literature explaining data analytics in various fields of finance. Section 3 discusses the model with a flowchart. Section 4 discusses the results. Section 5 ends up with conclusions and future scope of the study.

18.2 Literature Survey

Research has been carried out in recent times in various domains of finance like auditing [10], accounting [11], banking [12,13], and stock markets [14,15,16] using data analytics.

Earley [10] has enlisted applications of data analytics in auditing. Auditors can examine a large number of financial transactions with analytical tools and hence, improves the quality of audit. It takes leverage of technology to scrutinize, thereby reducing financial frauds. Auditors also have the advantage of providing additional services, serving their clients efficiently. Appelbaum et al. [11] proposed the Managerial Accounting Data Analytics (MADA) framework, which uses a balance scorecard. MADA helps in assessing three types of business analytics, namely descriptive, prescriptive, and normative, implemented in the business for financial, customer, internal process, and learning and growth. Thus, it becomes an important question, whether accountants and auditors face problems to survive in this era of big data. To answer this question, Richins et al. [17] provided a conceptual framework and explains, as an accountant professional has expertise in problem-solving capabilities, they can work together with data scientists, thereby indicating big data is a compliment for the job of accountants.

Data analytics is widely used in the banking sector. In banks, big data is used in supply chain finance to obtain credit reports and to execute e-wiring transactions. It is also reported by Hung et al. [12] that big data analytics has the advantage of better marketing without compromising on risk management. Srivastava et al. [18] claim that analytics will help banks in India to get better accounting information, thereby will have a competitive advantage by making appropriate decisions. Even to analyze banking stability and to answer the fundamental question "Why do banks fail?" data analytics is used. Viviani and Hanh [13] used text analytics to explain that loan and bank management are critical factors responsible for a bank's failure in the United States.

Data analytics has grown its importance in the stock market for predicting real-time stock prices based on the arrival of stock-specific and macro news. With High-Frequency Trading gaining importance, data analytics finds application in algorithmic trading. Lee et al. [14] used big data analytics to analyze stock market reactions for 54 investment announcements in NASDAQ and NYSE listed companies between 2010 and 2015. The study indicated that announcements on investment have a positive impact on the stock market. It was also observed that investors' valuations on big data analytics are higher for larger companies over small companies. The arrival of stock-specific news can impact stock prices. Groß-Klußmann and Hautsch [15] used a high-frequency VAR model to study stock returns, volatility, trading volumes, and bid-ask spreads. The study is conducted by considering stocks in the London Stock Exchange for intraday high-frequency data, where information and news are exploited to identify its effects. It is also observed that sentiments influence stock prices; however, profitability is reduced with an increase in the bid-ask spreads [15].

A data analytic technique was proposed using fuzzy logic, where the effect of a hurricane in the stock market is predicted [19]. Nann et al. [20] aggregated messages from a microblogging platform and segregated such messages for individual stocks. Sentiment analysis is performed on such text to gather information in order to generate buy and sell calls. Such a technique, when applied for S&P 500 stocks, was observed to outperform the index, securing a positive return of 0.49% per trade and 0.24% when adjusted to the market. Pang et al. [16] proposed two models, namely deep long short-term memory neural network with embedded layer and long short-term memory neural network with automatic encoder for forecasting stock prices. It was observed that accuracy is higher for embedded layer deep long short-term memory neural network, with accuracy being 57.2% compared to 56.9% when experimented with Shanghai A-shares composite index. Sigo [21] indicated that machine learning techniques like the artificial neural network have the advantage to predict stock price accurately, if information arising from stocks are efficiently preprocessed, thereby resulting in long-term capital gain.

Algorithmic Trading finds importance to improve an investor's stock return and information efficiency. However, it has a negative impact on slow traders by increasing the selection cost. High correlation is observed among strategies followed by algorithmic traders, though it does not deteriorate the quality of the market [22].

Major Algorithmic Trading includes Mean Reversion, Momentum Strategy, Statistical Arbitrage, and Trend Following Strategy. The mean reversion strategy indicates that the asset price will revert to the asset's long-term mean, hence capitalizing on extreme asset price changes when overbought or oversold. From the name itself, the momentum strategy indicates to buy assets when they are rising and sell them when they lose momentum. Statistical Arbitrage is a group of trading strategies applied on a diversified portfolio constructed using various securities, in order to minimize risk. Trend Following Strategy follows market movement, thereby buying when the prices go up and sell when prices go down. Various indicators are used in Trend Following Strategy, out of which Moving Average is one of the most prominent.

Extant literature has described the different analytical techniques and their applications in various domains of finance. Literature has also outlined the importance of algorithmic trading. However, literature lacks to study the efficiency of Trend Following Strategy, specifically for "BUY-SELL" and "SELL-BUY," particularly in an emerging economy like India. After studying trading algorithms, and having a detailed literature survey, the chapter implements the Trend Following Strategy among Indian Information Technology stocks. In such a context, the following objectives are proposed:

1. To implement the Trend Following Strategy among Indian IT Stocks.
2. To assess the Trend Following Strategy's efficiency for "BUY-SELL," "SELL-BUY," and overall stock.

18.2.1 Data and Period of Study

A sample of five companies in the Information Technology sector, featured in the NIFTY 50 benchmark index have been selected to examine the efficiency of Trend Following Strategies. The companies selected are the top five IT companies in India, on the basis of their market capitalization as of October 19, 2020. The period of the study is Financial Year 2019-20. The closing price of the data is collected from the National Stock Exchange (NSE) website. The R program is used to execute the Trend Following Strategy. The details of the company, along with its description, is depicted in Table 18.1.

It is observed that TCS is traded highest among the studied Information Technology (IT) companies, with the average stock price for the FY-2019-20 being Rs. 2123. Wipro is traded at the lowest price at Rs. 254.

18.3 Methodology

Trend Following Strategy is used to analyze the probability of success for BUY and SELL call, for five Information Technology stocks listed in NIFTY 50. This will assess efficiency of the Trend Following Strategy of algorithmic trading.

Stock return is estimated using daily closing price as formulated in eq. (18.1).

$$Ret_t = \ln \frac{Price_t}{Price_{t-1}} \tag{18.1}$$

Simple moving average at 11 and 22 days is estimated as exhibited in eq. (18.2).

$$SMA_t = \frac{1}{m} \sum_{t-m+1}^{t} Ret_t \tag{18.2}$$

Where t is the trading day and m is the order of moving average. Here, m is 11 and 22.

If Simple Moving Average at 11 days is greater than 22 days, it is a "BUY" call; otherwise, it is a "SELL" call. Pairing of buy and sell, or sell and buy is done for consecutive trading days. This indicates squaring of positions in the market is carried out on successive trading days. A call is considered to be a success if profit is generated while squaring off. Individual probability of success for BUY-SELL,

TABLE 18.1

Descriptive of Sample Data

Company	SCRIP	Trading Days	Market Capitalization (INR cr.)	Average Price (INR)
TCS	TCS	247	1,018,397.21	2123.098
Infosys	INFY	247	479,418.11	741.884
HCL Technologies	HCLTECH	248	229,209.72	910.7401
Wipro	WIPRO	247	196,166.22	254.2522
Tech Mahindra	TECHM	247	80,048.18	735.8692

SELL-BUY, and overall stock is the ratio of number of successful calls to the total calls, and is estimated using eq. (18.3). The workbook representing sample data is represented in Figure 18.1.

$$P = \frac{Number\ of\ Successful\ Calls}{Total\ Calls} \tag{18.3}$$

Pairwise Pearson correlation coefficient is computed between stock returns, Moving Averages at 11 and 22 days as represented in eq. (18.4), to identify the determining parameter for stock price prediction.

$$\rho_{x-y} = \frac{\sum_{i=1}^{n}(x_i - \bar{x})(y_i - \bar{y})}{\sqrt{\sum_{i=1}^{n}(x_i - \bar{x})^2(y_i - \bar{y})^2}} \tag{18.4}$$

Symbol	Date	Close Price	Return	SMA-11	SMA-22	Buy/Sale
TCS	8-May-19	2152.85	0.04%	0.09%	0.26%	Sale
TCS	9-May-19	2172.55	0.91%	0.01%	0.16%	Sale
TCS	10-May-19	2135.8	-1.71%	0.05%	0.20%	Sale
TCS	13-May-19	2128.75	-0.33%	-0.08%	0.27%	Sale
TCS	14-May-19	2092.35	-1.72%	-0.23%	0.18%	Sale
TCS	15-May-19	2095.4	0.15%	-0.44%	0.05%	Sale
TCS	16-May-19	2108.75	0.64%	-0.60%	0.01%	Sale
TCS	17-May-19	2095.45	-0.63%	-0.63%	0.15%	Sale
TCS	20-May-19	2143.95	2.29%	-0.51%	0.17%	Sale
TCS	21-May-19	2109.75	-1.61%	0.05%	0.28%	Sale
TCS	22-May-19	2081.75	-1.34%	-0.20%	-0.01%	Sale
TCS	23-May-19	2054.05	-1.34%	-0.30%	-0.11%	Sale
TCS	24-May-19	2048	-0.29%	-0.43%	-0.21%	Sale
TCS	27-May-19	2055.15	0.35%	-0.54%	-0.25%	Sale
TCS	28-May-19	2073.75	0.90%	-0.35%	-0.22%	Sale
TCS	29-May-19	2107.55	1.62%	-0.24%	-0.23%	Sale
TCS	30-May-19	2146.3	1.82%	0.07%	-0.18%	Buy
TCS	31-May-19	2196.55	2.31%	0.22%	-0.19%	Buy
TCS	3-Jun-19	2242.3	2.06%	0.37%	-0.13%	Buy
TCS	4-Jun-19	2183.1	-2.68%	0.62%	0.05%	Buy
TCS	6-Jun-19	2166.1	-0.78%	0.16%	0.11%	Buy
TCS	7-Jun-19	2181.75	0.72%	0.24%	0.02%	Buy
TCS	10-Jun-19	2231.5	2.25%	0.43%	0.06%	Buy
TCS	11-Jun-19	2252.8	0.95%	0.75%	0.16%	Buy
TCS	12-Jun-19	2260.9	0.36%	0.87%	0.16%	Buy
TCS	13-Jun-19	2254.1	-0.30%	0.87%	0.26%	Buy
TCS	14-Jun-19	2254.5	0.02%	0.76%	0.26%	Buy
TCS	17-Jun-19	2249.2	-0.24%	0.61%	0.34%	Buy
TCS	18-Jun-19	2250.85	0.07%	0.43%	0.32%	Buy

FIGURE 18.1 Workbook of Trend Following Strategy.

Where x and y are pairwise combinations of stock returns, simple moving average at 11 and 22 days, to compute correlation coefficient ρ_{x-y}, n represents number of trading days.

The flowchart in Figure 18.2 represents the implemented Trend Following Strategy in this chapter.

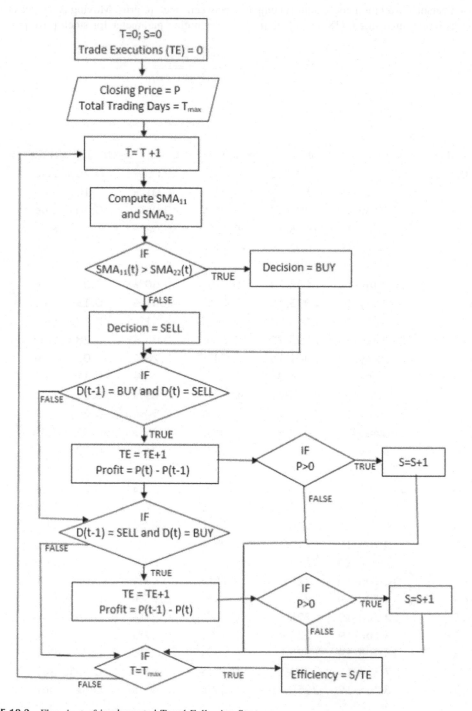

FIGURE 18.2   Flowchart of implemented Trend Following Strategy.

18.4 Results and Discussions

Table 18.2 depicts returns of IT stocks along with the average returns of SMA at 11 days and 22 days. It is observed that all companies experience a negative return due to the bearish period in the Indian stock market for the year 2019-20. Among the five studied stocks, Infosys has the least negative return, and HCL Technology yields the highest negative return. It is also observed that SMA at 22 days gives a higher return as compared to SMA at 11 days, indicating the more time an investor holds the stock in the market, the more possibility of return. The average returns of SMA at 11 days and 22 days are consistent with their respective stock returns.

Table 18.3 depicts pairwise Pearson correlation between stock return and SMA at 11 days and 22 days. Weak correlation is observed between the return of stock and SMA at 11 days and 22 days. This indicates it is difficult for an investor to make a decision by computing correlation with stock return. However, a strong positive correlation is found between SMA at 11 days and 22 days, thus becoming a parameter for an investor to make a decision.

Table 18.4 depicts the total number of possible trade executions for consecutive trading days with Trend Following Strategy, for both "Sale-Buy" and "Buy-Sell." It is observed that Infosys has the

TABLE 18.2

Stock Return along with SMA at 11 Days and 22 Days

Company	Return	SMA-11	SMA-22
HCL Technologies	−0.42%	−0.42%	−0.37%
Infosys	−0.05%	−0.10%	−0.06%
TCS	−0.07%	−0.11%	−0.06%
Tech Mahindra	−0.16%	−0.18%	−0.11%
Wipro	−0.18%	−0.22%	−0.16%

TABLE 18.3

Correlation between Return and Simple Moving Average at 11 and 22 Days for IT Companies

Companies	Return and SMA-11	SMA-11 and SMA-22	Return and SMA 22
HCL Technologies	−0.02	0.70	−0.03
Infosys	−0.05	0.79	−0.07
TCS	−0.04	0.76	−0.1
Tech Mahindra	0.08	0.92	0.03
Wipro	0.05	0.84	−0.07

TABLE 18.4

Efficiency of Trend Following Strategy along with the Number of Trade Executions

Company	Number of Trade Executions		Efficiency		
	Sale-Buy	Buy-Sale	Sale-Buy	Buy-Sale	Overall
HCL Technologies	17	17	41.18%	41.18%	41.18%
Infosys	20	20	35%	60%	47.50%
TCS	14	13	64.29%	46.15%	55.56%
Tech Mahindra	16	17	50%	58.82%	54.55%
Wipro	10	9	50%	33.33%	42.11%

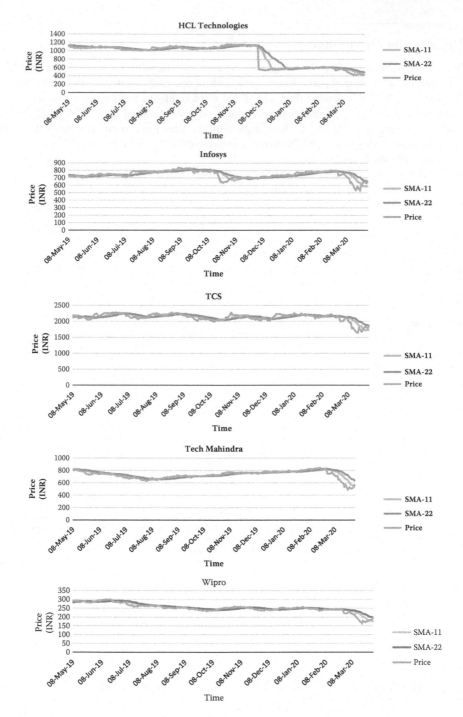

FIGURE 18.3 Time-varying graph of price, long and short moving average for five IT stocks.

highest trade executions while Wipro has the lowest trade executions. Among the efficiency, TCS has the highest efficiency in order to book profit, whereas HCL Technologies finds its place at the bottom. Among "Sale-Buy," TCS exhibits the highest efficiency at 64.29%, and the lowest is observed for Infosys at 35%. For "Buy-Sale," Infosys has the highest efficiency to book profit at 60%, whereas Wipro exhibits the lowest efficiency at 33.33%.

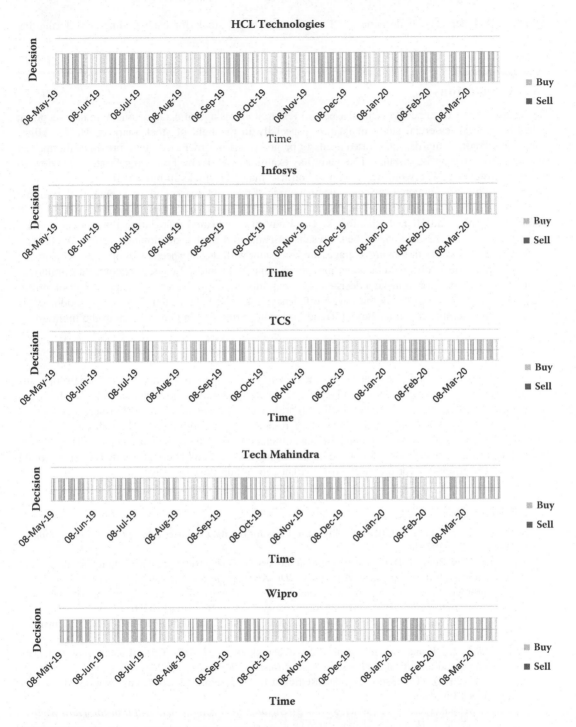

FIGURE 18.4 Decision to "BUY" or "SELL" IT stocks.

Figure 18.3 depicts a time-varying graph of stock price along with Moving Averages at 11 and 22 days for HCL Technologies, Infosys, TCS, Tech Mahindra, and Wipro, to identify positions to BUY and SELL stocks.

Figure 18.4 depicts the decision to "BUY" and "SELL" stock for each trading day during FY 2019-20.

18.5 Conclusions

Data analytics has become an essential aspect of research in this age of datafication. With no exception, it has become an essential study in finance, especially in the field of stock markets. Due to High-Frequency Trading, big data generated needs to be processed in order to execute orders in the market with effective trading algorithms. The study has examined the Trend Following Strategy in view to assess its efficiency. The work was conducted on five major IT stocks in NIFTY50.

As the study was conducted during the bearish phase of the stock market, all companies in the sample resulted in negative returns, with Infosys having the least negative returns followed by TCS, Tech Mahindra, Wipro, and HCL Technologies. The study also indicated that during the bearish market, moving average for 22 days yields better results as compared to that of moving average at 11 days. However, returns and both moving averages are consistent with their respective companies. As a strong positive correlation is observed between moving average at 11 and 22 days, it becomes an important parameter for an investor to make a decision. TCS exhibits the highest overall efficiency to book profit, whereas HCL Technology bears the lowest efficiency. The study conducted with this methodology is significant in assessing the efficiency of Trend Following Strategy, and contributes to the literature.

18.5.1 Future Scope

The study is conducted for one year during the down-cycle of the stock market, and hence scope lies among researchers to experiment with a larger time duration, including both bullish and bearish phases of the stock market, where efficiency of the algorithm is expected to improve. Further, the study is carried with five stocks in one sector. In the future, researchers are expected to work with a large sample of companies from different sectors, and estimate efficiency for both sector and company. The study is conducted for the Indian Stock Market (NSE) (Emerging Nation), and hence it can be further extended to examine the efficiency for different stock markets, including developed nations.

REFERENCES

[1] Dobre, C., & Xhafa, F. (2014). Intelligent services for big data science. *Future Generation Computer Systems*, *37*, 267–281.

[2] Gantz, J., & Reinsel, D. (2012). The digital universe in 2020: Big data, bigger digital shadows, and biggest growth in the Far East. *IDC iView: IDC Analyze the Future*, *2007*(2012), 1–16.

[3] Vasarhelyi, M. A., Kogan, A., & Tuttle, B. M. (2015). Big Data in accounting: An overview. *Accounting Horizons*, *29*(2), 381–396. doi: 10.1080/10864415.2018.1512270.

[4] Saggi, M. K., & Jain, S. (2018). A survey towards an integration of big data analytics to big insights for value-creation. Information Processing & Management, 54(5), 758–790.

[5] Sivarajah, U., Kamal, M. M., Irani, Z., & Weerakkody, V. (2017). Critical analysis of Big Data challenges and analytical methods. *Journal of Business Research*, *70*, 263–286.

[6] Gartner. (2013). IT glossary: Big data.Retrieved from December 1, 2014, http://www.gartner.com/it-glossary/big-data

[7] Mayer-Schönberger, V., & Cukier, K. (2013). *Big data: A revolution that will transform how we live, work, and think*. Houghton Mifflin Harcourt, Boston.

[8] Ravi, V., & Kamaruddin, S. (2017, December). Big data analytics enabled smart financial services: Opportunities and challenges. In *International Conference on Big Data Analytics* (pp. 15–39). Springer, Cham.

[9] Sun, Y., Shi, Y., & Zhang, Z. (2019). Finance big data: Management, analysis, and applications. *International Journal Of Electronic Commerce*, 23(1), 9–11.

[10] Earley, C. E. (2015). Data analytics in auditing: Opportunities and challenges. *Business Horizons*, *58*(5), 493–500.

[11] Appelbaum, D., Kogan, A., Vasarhelyi, M., & Yan, Z. (2017). Impact of business analytics and enterprise systems on managerial accounting. *International Journal of Accounting Information Systems*, *25*, 29–44.

[12] Hung, J. L., He, W., & Shen, J. (2020). Big data analytics for supply chain relationship in banking. *Industrial Marketing Management*, *86*, 144–153.

[13] Viviani, J. L., & LE Hanh, H. (2018). Why Do banks fail? – The explanation from text analytics technique. *SSRN Electronic Journal*. https://doi.org/10.2139/ssrn.3220163.

[14] Lee, H., Kweon, E., Kim, M., & Chai, S. (2017). Does implementation of big data analytics improve firms' market value? Investors' reaction in stock market. *Sustainability*, *9*(6), 978.

[15] Groß-Klußmann, A., & Hautsch, N. (2011). When machines read the news: Using automated text analytics to quantify high frequency news-implied market reactions. *Journal of Empirical Finance*, *18*(2), 321–340.

[16] Pang, X., Zhou, Y., Wang, P., Lin, W., & Chang, V. (2020). An innovative neural network approach for stock market prediction. *The Journal of Supercomputing*, *76*(3), 2098–2118.

[17] Richins, G., Stapleton, A., Stratopoulos, T. C., & Wong, C. (2017). Big data analytics: Opportunity or threat for the accounting profession? *Journal of Information Systems*, *31*(3), 63–79.

[18] Srivastava, A., Singh, S. K., Tanwar, S., & Tyagi, S. (2017, September). Suitability of big data analytics in Indian banking sector to increase revenue and profitability. In *2017 3rd International Conference on Advances in Computing, Communication & Automation (ICACCA) (Fall)* (pp. 1–6). IEEE.

[19] Camara, R. C., Cuzzocrea, A., Grasso, G. M., Leung, C. K., Powell, S. B., Souza, J., & Tang, B. (2018, July). Fuzzy logic-based data analytics on predicting the effect of hurricanes on the stock market. In *2018 IEEE International Conference on Fuzzy Systems (FUZZ-IEEE)* (pp. 1–8). IEEE.

[20] Nann, S., Krauss, J., & Schoder, D. (2013). Predictive analytics on public data-the case of stock markets. ECIS 2013 Completed Research. 102. http://aisel.aisnet.org/ecis2013_cr/102

[21] Sigo, M. O. (2018). Big data analytics-application of artificial neural network in forecasting stock price trends in India. *Academy of Accounting and Financial Studies*, *22*(3). Available at SSRN: https://ssrn.com/abstract=36653

[22] Chaboud, A. P., Chiquoine, B., Hjalmarsson, E., & Vega, C. (2014). Rise of the machines: Algorithmic trading in the foreign exchange market. *The Journal of Finance*, *69*(5), 2045–2084.

19

A Novel Data Science Approach for Business and Decision Making for Prediction of Stock Market Movement Using Twitter Data and News Sentiments

S. Kumar Chandar, Hitesh Punjabi, Mahesh Kumar Sharda, and Jehan Murugadhas

CONTENTS

19.1 Introduction

Stock market prediction is a thriving topic in the field of the financial world and has received greater consideration over stockholders, experts, and investigators. Prediction is the strategy in which the future price or stock market shift may be expected. This includes the process of taking historical stock prices and technical indicators and collecting data patterns seen through certain techniques. Then the model is employed to make predictions about the future direction or price of stock market. A precise forecast of the future movement or price of a stock market may yield a high profit.

Stock market research encapsulates three elemental trading philosophies: (i) fundamental investigation, (ii) technical investigation, and (iii) time series prediction. Fundamental analysis is a method of estimating share value of a company by analyzing some factors such as sales, profits, earnings, and other economic factors [1]. In order to identify the potential movement or price, technical analysis uses historical stock prices. Fundamental analysis is a long-term investment approach, while short-term methodology is far more known as quantitative analysis. Time series forecasting involves two basic models: (i) linear models and (ii) non-linear models. Autoregressive moving average (ARMA) and autoregressive integrated moving average (ARIMA) were extensively accepted linear models used to make predictions about the stock market. Linear models use some predefined assumptions such as normality and postulates to fit a mathematical model [2].

These models need more historical prices to meet these assumptions. Because of this, the trends present in the stock data cannot be established. Since stock markets are considered non-linear systems, it is important to increase the prediction accuracy of more versatile methods that can learn hidden information in stock data. Artificial Neural Networks (ANNs) have strong advantages in this regard because they can derive nonlinear data relationships without prior knowledge of input data through the training process. Several studies have showed that the ANN technique outperforms the linear models [3].

Sentiment analysis is a contextual text mining aimed at detecting and extracting subjective knowledge from source content and helping a company understand the social feelings of its brand, product, or service by analyzing online conversations. In addition, sentiment analysis helps businesses evaluate what customers want or dislike and therefore take action to enhance their service, thus enhancing their credibility. Businesses must also be aware of what is written about them in the public domain, as it can have a positive or negative effect on them and have a direct impact on their stock market values, affecting either earnings or losses of their investment value [4].

For both traders and analysts, predicting stock market movements by analyzing historical stock data has always been a fascinating subject. Researchers have used numerous machine learning models, such as ANN and historical data deep learning models, to forecast stock market movements. Many methods have been developed, and ANN-based prediction models are popular and widely used due to their ability to identify stock movement from the massive amount of stock data that can capture the underlying patterns through training process. Twitter details and both financial news/social media, are exterior influences which shall influence the movement of stock market.

In literature, the use of news and Twitter data for forecasting stock movements is very unusual. Adding social media data and news data with historical data is relevant because unusual events on both Twitter and news information can also influence the stock market. Twitter is a modern medium of web content for social media. A significant aspect of social media data is the appropriate availability of original data and the quick interface between the customers. Those correspondences were seen as an indicator towards the interest of customers to many topics, including stock market issues. However, Twitter data alone does not affect the stock market movement.

For individuals or investors who try to invest in capital markets, the trend of equity markets is unclear. They shall not identify the exact share to buy and which share to sell so as to get high returns for their invested money. Such investors recognize that the conduct of the stock market relies on financial news. They also need to be more precise and appropriate listing data on stock markets, thereby their trade decisions were made with timely and reliable information. Also, traders' expectations focused only on financial news because the trading approach cannot be adequate. Numerous methods have been developed for predicting the stock market trend on the basis of historical information or combination of historical data and media data or historical data and news data. However, little research is done to investigate the impact of social media and economic bulletin on improving correctness in predictions. Stock sentiment score may be positive or negative, making investors bullish or bearish about a particular stock. Utilizing unique types of information might not provide high prediction accurateness. Social media information and news data together can affect investors' decisions, so both sources and historical data should be considered when designing a model to forecast behavior of stock markets. The prediction accuracy of the prediction model will increase, taking into account three types of historical data, social media data, and financial news information.

A new approach to machine learning based on the above analysis is proposed in the chapter to forecast the path of the stock market price by analyzing Twitter data, financial news data, and historical data.

For this research, historical data are collected from Yahoo finance and financial news is collected from Bloomberg terminal (https://www.bloomberg.com).

The main focus of the analysis is to examine the influence of the Twitter sentiment and news sentiment score in enhancing accurateness of stock market prediction by means of artificial neural network movements.

Major contributions in this research are as follows:

- Proposed a blend of historical data, Twitter data, and financial news data to predict stock market movements.
- Designed a machine learning approach, Probabilistic Neural Network (PNN) for predicting stock market trends.
- Evaluated performance of the developed model by computing prediction accuracy.
- Analyzed the efficacy of the designed model by using only historical data and combined data (historical and sentiment score).
- Compared the performance of the established model with previous models to prove its superiority with respect to prediction accuracy.

As follows, remaining sections of this chapter are structured. A brief overview of relevant work in this domain is provided in Section 19.2. The research approach used is explained in Section 19.3. Numerical results and analysis are provided in Section 19.4. Section 19.5 gives a detailed description about the comparative analysis over existing and proposed decision-making methods. Finally, Section 19.6 concludes the chapter.

19.2 Review of Literature

The stock market movement prediction is a very tricky and highly challenging task in finance since the stock market is complicated, volatile, dynamic, and non-linear. Moreover, the factors affecting stock market include trader's expectations, political events, psychology, economic conditions, and other stock market movements [1].

Dang and Duong [2] forecasted the future movement of stock market using the news article dataset. An accuracy of 73% was achieved by linear SVM. Sheta et al. [3] suggested a stock prediction model by means of ANN and Support Vector Machine (SVM). As input to the established models, 27 possible financial and economic variables are used. In comparison with regression and ANN models, the built SVM approach with RBF kernel strategy delivered decent prediction abilities.

Ondieki et al. [4] combined Twitter sentiment score with the historical prices to improve the prediction accuracy. For regular sentiment scores, WordNet and Sentiwordnet lexicons were used to classify and score. Non-Linear Autoregressive Neural Network using Exogenous Inputs (NARX) approaches fitted with Levenberg-Marquart (LM) back propagation to predict stock movement. The findings showed that the inclusion of Twitter sentiment scores as additional inputs to historical prices contributed to a more precise forecast. Schumaker et al. [5] evaluated the strength of news sentiment in predicting future movement of stock market. A prediction model was developed using SVM; 53.2% accuracy was obtained.

Kordonis et al. [6] identified the correlation between Twitter sentiment score and the stock market and predicted the future behavior of the stock market. Two prediction models, namely Naïve Bayes Bernoulli (NBB) and SVM, were developed using investor sentiment and stock market data. Feature vectors such as Positive Sentiment Score (PSS), Negative Sentiment Score (NSS), closing price, High-Low Percentage (HLPCT), percentage change, and volume are employed to predict the future movement of stock price. Eighty-seven percent prediction accuracy was obtained by applying SVM. Ho and Wang [7] PNN was used for forecasting the movement of the stock market based on the news sentiment score and obtained a mean accuracy of 54.47%.

Das et al. [8] tried to predict the pattern of the stock market opening price on the basis of Twitter streaming results. Each Twitter data represents the state of the user about a particular theme. Twitter data is collected through an elemental HTTP authentication and a Twitter account and then analysis of the sentiments related to each tweet is done by Recurrent Neural Network (RNN). Empirical findings showed that the sentiment analysis of Twitter data can be used for forecasting the behavior of the stock market more precisely.

TABLE 19.1

A Summary of Reviewed Chapters

Researchers	Features	Model	Accuracy (%)
Dang and Duong [2]	News sentiment	Linear SVM	73
Ondieki et al. [4]	Historical prices and Twitter sentiment	NARX	85
Schumaker et al. [5]	News sentiment	SVM	53.2
Kordonis et al. [6]	PSS, NSS, closing price, HLPCT, percentage change, volume, and Twitter sentiment	NBB, SVM	87
Ho and Wang [7]	News sentiment	PNN	54.47
Shastri et al. [9]	News sentiment and historical data	MLP	91
Khan et al. [10]	Social media and financial news	Hybrid algorithm	80.53

Shastri et al. [9] proposed an approach for forecasting the movement of stock prices using historical data and news data. News headlines are made based upon statistical facts and different events, which have a direct implication on the trend of stock price. The collected data is preprocessed by the Hive ecosystem and passed to the Naïve Bayes classifier to get a sentiment score. The obtained sentiment score and historical data are used as input to a Multilayer Perceptron (MLP) to make predictions about the movement of stock price. Prediction ability of the developed model is analyzed in two ways (i) longer period of data (three years' data) considered for training and (ii) shorter period of data (one-year data) taken for training. A prediction accuracy of 91% and 98% were obtained for longer periods and shorter periods, respectively, which indicates that the proposed model is good for shorter period of data.

Khan et al. [10] combined machine learning, social media data, and financial news classifiers in 2020 for forecasting the direction of stock market closing price value. In order to find positive and negative information, Natural Language Processing (NLP) is employed for pre-processing the social media and financial news on the basis of content. After computational sentiment score, Principal Component Analysis (PCA) is used for decreasing the dimension of the characteristics. Ten machine learning systems were employed for learning and finding the association between sentimental analysis and stock market behavior. Table 19.1 presents the summary of reviewed chapters.

Many analysts have attempted to forecast the potential actions of the stock market in literature using various techniques. Each method has their own merits and demerits. Most of the researchers have used either Twitter or news sentiment score as an input to their models. Some researchers combined historical price and Twitter sentiment. No one integrated historical data, news sentiment score, and Twitter sentiment score to make predictions about stock prices.

This study seeks to establish a model of stock prediction using PNN. Initially, only historical prices are taken as feature vectors and applied to PNN to make prediction about future price. Day Twitter sentiment score, day news sentiment score, and historical prices are applied to PNN to test if there would be development over prediction accuracy or not.

19.3 Proposed Methodology

The foremost objective of this work is towards developing a model for predicting stock market movements using the machine learning model. The suggested model forecasts the stock market trend based on historical prices, tweet sentiment score, and financial news sentiment score.

The proposed prediction model's structure is shown in Figure 19.1. The forecast model is developed using the PNN. Typically, PNN is a type of feed forward neural network that is commonly used in pattern recognition and problem classification. The method applied in the research work involves gathering Twitter and news sentiment score and historical prices. A prediction model is developed and accuracies compared when there is tweet and news sentiments score versus when there is no tweet and news sentiment score as inputs. The proposed stock prediction method involves the following processes:

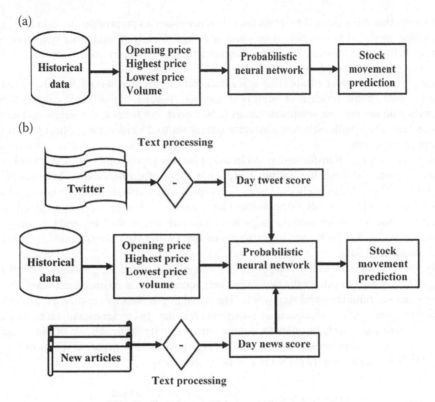

(a)

(b)

Text processing

Text processing

FIGURE 19.1 Proposed method for stock prediction: (a) prediction without investor sentiment scores; (b) prediction with sentiment scores.

1. Preprocessing
2. Computation of daily sentiment score
3. Labelling
4. Creature of feature matrix
5. Prediction of stock movement using PNN
6. Historical Data Preprocessing

Historical stock prices are collected using Yahoo Finance API (http://Yahoo.fianance.com). The dataset consists of the opening, closing, highest, lowest, and volume prices for each day. To become more acceptable for further process, stock market data had to be preprocessed. We were presented with the key issue of missing stock values. For weekends and other holidays when the stock market is closed, stock value was lacking. To fill the missing values, we used simple statistical function and can be computed as

$$y_i = \frac{(x_{i-1} + x_{i+1})}{2} \tag{19.1}$$

where y_i is the missing value on ith day and x_{i+1} and x_{i-1} represent the previous value and next value, respectively.

19.3.1 Sentiment Score

To investigate the relationship between stock market trend, news, and Twitter, a series of Twitter sentiment is collected from the Twitter API. Positive sentiment score and negative sentiment scores are computed from the collected tweets using the method presented by [4]. Each tweet's text has a larger number of works that are unrelated to its feelings. It is necessary to preprocess the data before applying machine learning models. For instance, some tweet hash tags, @, URLS, and other symbols that have no correlation with the stock market. To compute sentiment score, tweeter data is processed with some techniques to remove unwanted information.

Tokenization is the method of splitting a sentence into terms that would later be saved as word vectors to be used in the process of sentiment scoring. Tokens like @keny_care and @sdfe are removed as they do not possess sentiment values to be stored. For tokens, the minimum character size is set to three and the lengthiest token character size is set to 25 since those short text components have no sentiment values.

Uppercase characters are transformed to lowercase to prevent repetition of the same words in feature. Stop words are removed from the Twitter body since they were observed to be unusable towards sentiment scores. The wordnet body dictionary is accepted to acquire the nouns, verbs, and adjectives since they would be vital towards safeguarding that accurate sentiment score is acquired from senti-wordnet corpus. The stemming method helps in minimizing terms with common meanings that are derivationally associated. Finally, sentiment scores of the Twitter data are obtained by using wordnet 3.0 and sentiwordnet 3.0.0.

Similarly, daily news of selected companies is gathered and stored in database. Natural Language Processing (NLP) is used to extract the news sentiment score from the unstructured news. We removed number, punctuation, html tags, and stop words. The remaining sentences are then used to calculate the news sentiment score. After calculating sentiment scores, day tweet sentiment score and day news sentiment score are calculated. In order to measure the positivity or negativity of the complete daily tweets, a regular tweet score is calculated by the average positive and negative scores of the company tweets [4]. Mathematically, day tweet score can be expressed as

$$Day\ tweet\ score = \frac{Sum\ of\ scores\ for\ sentence}{Total\ number\ of\ day\ tweets} \tag{19.2}$$

Similarly, day news score is defined as

$$Day\ news\ score = \frac{Sum\ of\ scores\ for\ sentence}{Total\ number\ of\ news\ publication} \tag{19.3}$$

The calculated values were then applied to the PNN as additional feature vectors to test for any improvement in the accuracy.

19.3.2 Labeling

After collecting the stock data for the intended period, all the daily closing prices are labeled as up or down using Equation (19.4)

$$Stock\ market\ movement = \begin{Bmatrix} \text{``up''} & if\ closing\ price_i > opening\ price_i \\ \text{``down''} & Otherwise \end{Bmatrix} \tag{19.4}$$

The proposed model uses "up and down" stock price changes as training patterns.

19.3.3 Feature Matrix

The pre-processed historical data and sentiment scores are used to form a feature matrix. In this work, two features matrices are created using historical data and sentiment score. Historically, each sample consists of opening price, closing price, highest price, lowest price, and volume. For each sample, opening price, highest price, lowest price, and volume are considered as input and closing price as output. Let H and SS represents the historical data and sentiment score, respectively. N is the quantity of samples.

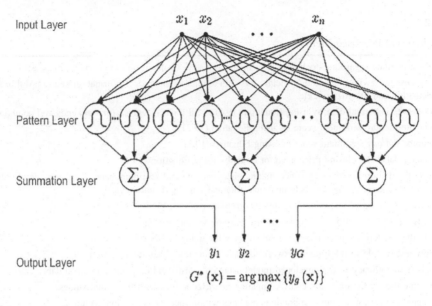

FIGURE 19.2 Articulation of PNN.

H = [D1, D2, D3... Di, ...DN] 0>i<N
Di= {Opening price, Highest price, Lowest price, Volume}
SS= [SC1, SC2, ...Scj,....SN] 0>j<N
SCj= {Day tweet score Day news score}
Feature matrix 1 = [H]= [D1, D2, D3... Di, ...DN]
Feature matrix 2 = [H SS] = [D1, D2, D3... Di, ...DN SC1, SC2, ...Scj,....SN]
The above formed matrices are taken as feature vectors to be trained by PNN.

19.3.4 Probabilistic Neural Network

PNN is a complex organized feed forward network possessing a complex structure. Figure 19.2 depicts the structure of a typical PNN. There are four layers in the network, namely an input, a pattern, a summation, and an output layer. As shown in Figure 19.2, the input layer receives the external data and is then moved to pattern layer. A radial base layer is the pattern layer. Every neuron has their own core in the pattern layer.

The pattern layer receives the data from the input layer, and subsequently calculates the distance amid the center, and the input data obtained. The resulting value will be moved to the next sheet. The summation layer calculates the weighted average of the similar types of neuron node from pattern layer.

After measuring every neuron's node at the summation layer, the higher possibility as the end node has been evaluated, and transports it towards output layer. The PNN is implemented in the study work by means of MATLAB Neural Network Toolbox, possessing network architectures identified by default settings. Maximum likelihood was selected as the result node after measuring each neuron node in the summation layer, and transports it towards the output layer. Based on features in test samples, the qualified network was employed for forecasting the stock market trends. The detailed procedure of proposed method is given in Table 19.2.

19.4 Numerical Results and Discussion

The details of stock data used for implementation are presented here in this section. It also discusses the numerical results obtained using the proposed model.

TABLE 19.2

Pseudo Code of the Proposed Method

Step 1: Collect the data regarding stock market from social media, financial news and yahoo finance.
Step 2: Preprocess the Twitter data and financial news data to remove unwanted information i.e., removal of stop words, punctuation and tokenization etc.
Step 3: Process the historical data by using Equation (19.1) to fill missing values for weekends and holidays
Step 4: Calculate the day sentiment score by using Equation (19.2)
Step 5: Compute the day sentiment score by using Equation (19.3)
Step 6: Manually label the closing price as up or down by using Equation (19.4)
Step 7: Create two feature matrices by concatenating historical data and sentiment score. One consists of only historical data whereas another one has both historical data and sentiment score
Step 8: Design a PNN using MATLAB neural network toolbox
Step 9: Divide the feature matrices into two groups: training set and testing set
Step 10: Train the network using training sample and save the trained PNN for future use
Step 11: Apply test sample to the trained network to make prediction about stock movement
Step 12: Analyze the efficacy of the developed model using only historical data and combined data
Step 13: Compute the prediction accuracy by comparing predicted values with the actual values
Step 14: Compare the outcomes with the previous methods with respect to prediction accuracy

19.4.1 Data Description

Two stock companies, namely Infosys and Bharti Airtel Limited, are selected. The dataset used in the research work are from three sources: historical data, Twitter sentiments, and news sentiments. For the experiment, daily news for the selected stocks is gathered over a period of three years from January 2016 to December 2018. Twitter sentiments are downloaded from Twitter API conforming over the period from January 2016 to December 2018.

Similarly, historical prices for selected stocks are obtained from Yahoo Finance over a period of three years. Table 19.3 shows the list of companies and duration used in this research work.

19.4.2 Statistical Measure

Performance of the developed stock prediction method is evaluated by computing classification accuracy. Since the work is a classification problem, therefore we have used prediction accuracy to measure the efficacy of the proposed method. Mathematically, prediction accuracy can be expressed as

$$\text{Prediction accuracy (PA)} = \frac{\text{Number of correct predictions}}{\text{Total number of predictions}} \times 100 \tag{19.5}$$

19.5 Simulation Results and Validation

The major intention of this investigation is to assess the effects of investor sentiments on stock movement forecasting. After collecting data, a feature matrix is created with the following attributes:

TABLE 19.3

List of Companies

Stock Name	Stock ID	Start Date	End Date
Bharti Airtel Limited	BHARTIARTL.NS	01/01/2016	31/12/2018
Infosys	INFY.NS	01/01/2016	31/12/2018

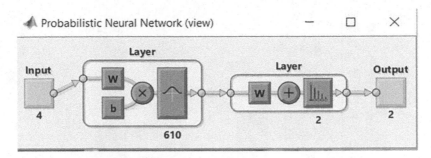

FIGURE 19.3 Proposed PNN in a MATLAB environment.

opening price of the day, highest price of the day, lowest price of the day, volume, day tweet score, and day news score. The PNN is designed with m input neurons and n output neurons. The number of features is expressed by m and the number of classes by n. In this work, m is 4 (historical data) and 6 (with additional inputs) and n is 2 (up and down). Figure 19.3 shows the developed PNN in a MATLAB environment.

Performance of the proposed model is assessed in two cases:

CASE 1: Predict the stock market movement using stock indicators.

CASE 2: Predict the direction of stock market movement with stock indicators and Twitter features.

For the PNN procedure, the MATLAB 2018a neural network toolbox is employed. The entire data is broken down into the following ratio: 80% of the samples used for network training and 20% of the samples used for model output testing. The training sample is used to design and train a prediction model, while the test sample is used to validate the model created. The proposed PNN is trained with a training pattern and validated with testing samples to assess the prediction capability of this method. The method of training helps the network for assessing the correct weights by minimizing the error amid actual and predicted values.

Initially, the network is trained with historical prices. Several experiments are accompanied for determining optimum values of spreading factor. The network is trained with historical prices along with sentiment scores after finding the optimal value of the spread factor. For forecasting the future course of the stock market, a qualified network was used. The effectiveness of the model is measured in accordance with the prediction accuracy. The results of the simulation are collected and displayed in bar graph form, as shown in Figure 19.4.

As in Figure 19.4, results showed that for the selected stocks, higher prediction accuracy was the one that had news and tweet scores as additional inputs to the PNN. It strongly indicates that the PNN is reliable in determining future movement of stocks if addition of investor sentiments as inputs to PNN.

19.5.1 Comparative Analysis over Existing and Proposed Decision-Making Methods

The performance of the proposed PNN method is assessed with other earlier models, such as NARX [4], SVM [6], linear SVM [2], SVM [5], and PNN [7], in order to demonstrate the predictive potential of the proposed method in terms of predictive accuracy recorded in the literature. Dang and Duong [2] used the news sentiment score to forecast the market trend as an input to the SVM. Ondieki et al. [4] predicted the stock market movement by combining historical prices with Twitter sentiment score. An accuracy of 85% was obtained by combining historical prices with sentiment score. Schumaker et al. [5] used SVM and Kordonis et al. [6] forecasted the stock market trend using Twitter sentiment score along with stock data and achieved an accuracy of 87%. Ho and Wang [7] used PNN to predict the stock market trend with news sentiment score. Most of the researchers used historical prices or historical price with Twitter or news sentiment as an input.

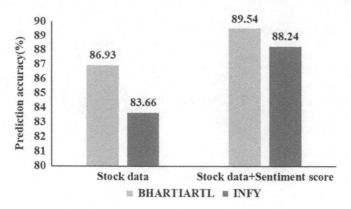

FIGURE 19.4 Prediction accuracy before and after addition of sentiment scores as an input to PNN.

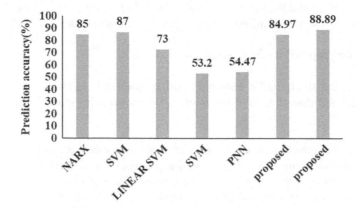

FIGURE 19.5 Performance comparison in terms of mean accuracy.

No one considered combined features (historical prices, news sentiment score, and Twitter sentiment score) as an input. The proposed approach incorporates historical prices and sentiment score (both news and Twitter) to check whether or not prediction accuracy would increase.

As in Figure 19.5, it is noted that with an accuracy of 84.97% for historical input data and 88.89% for additional input data (historical data and sentiment score), the proposed model can forecast the stock market). Further to this, it is obvious that prediction accuracy of the proposed PNN is higher when compared to other methods taken for comparison since the proposed model uses historical data, Twitter sentiment score, and news sentiment score to make a prediction about stock market movement.

19.6 Conclusion and Future Enhancement

This chapter has presented an ANN model for stock movement prediction and uses input of a combination of historical data and public sentiment, as measured from Twitter and news. The proposed method used PNN to make a prediction about the future direction of the stock market. Two stock data such as Infosys and Bharti Airtel Limited have been considered for implementation. Historical data, Twitter data, and financial news of the selected stocks have been collected over the period of three years from 2016 to 2018. Initially, historical data, media data, and news information have been preprocessed to make it fit for further processes. Subsequently, sentiment scores of media and news data have been computed. Two sets of features have formed: one has the historical data of the selected stocks and another one consists of both historical data and sentiment score.

The obtained features are taken as input variables. Closing prices have been labeled as either up or down based on the results obtained by comparing opening price with the closing value. The target value is set to decrease elsewhere if the closing price is greater than the opening price. The labeled values are considered as targets. Finally, a PNN was developed and trained with the training sample to tune PNN parameters. The designed PNN is trained with historical data and then the trained network is employed to make prediction about the future trend of stock market. The prediction efficiency of the system developed is calculated in terms of prediction accuracy.

In combination with historical values, news, and Twitter sentiment score are used in the probabilistic neural network to assess its effect on prediction accuracy. PNN is trained with combined data and then used by the trained network to forecast the potential direction of the stock market. Prediction ability of the proposed method is evaluated by calculating prediction accuracy. In order to find an acceptable one, the output of the proposed method is compared. The findings have shown that the proposed neural network model can predict stock market movement with high predictive accuracy when adding public sentiment score, news, and Twitter score as inputs to the network. Furthermore, by marking up(down) in day I as the closing price is greater (lower) than the opening price in day I, the proposed probabilistic neural network model provides better results than other models. From the empirical findings, it is concluded that ups and downs in stock price of a company are affected by public emotions on media data, Twitter, and news data. More sophisticated methods are required to make an accurate prediction about the trend of the stock market.

In the future, we focus on improving prediction accuracy by collecting more public sentiment and analyzing different combinations to find out the best model. Metaheuristics algorithms and deep learning networks will be explored to enhance prediction accuracy.

REFERENCES

[1] Chandar, S.K. "Fusion model of wavelet transform and adaptive neuro fuzzy interference system for stock market prediction." *Journal of Ambient Intelligence and Humanized Computing* (2019): 1–9. https://doi.org/10.1007/s12652-019-01224-2

[2] Dang, M., and Duong, D. "Improvement methods for stock market prediction using financial news articles." *Proceedings of the 3rd National Foundation for Science and Technology Development Conference on Information and Computer Science (NICS), Danang, Vietnam* (2016).

[3] Sheta, A.F., Ahmed, S.E., and Faris, H. "A comparison between regression, artificial neural networks and support vector machines for predicting stock market index." *International Journal of Advanced Research in Artificial Intelligence* 4, no. 7 (2015): 1–7.

[4] Ondieki, A.R., Keyo, G.O., and Kibe, A. "Stock price prediction using neural network models based on tweets sentiment scores." *Journal of Computer Sciences and Applications* 5, no. 2 (2017): 64–75.

[5] Schumaker, R.P., Zhang, Y., Huang, C., and Chen, H. "Evaluating sentiment in financial news articles." *Decision Support Systems* 53, (2012): 458–464.

[6] Kordonis, J., Symenonidis, S., and Arampatzis, A. "Stock price forecasting via sentiment analysis on Twitter." *Proceedings of the 20th Panhellenic Conference on Informatics (PCI '16), Greece* (2016).

[7] Ho, K.Y., and Wang, W. "Predicting stock price movements with news sentiment: An artificial neural network approach." *Studies in Computational Intelligence* (2016): 395–403. doi: 10.1007/978-3-319-28495-8_18.

[8] Das, A., Behera, R.K., Kumar, M., and Rath, S.K. "Real time sentiment analysis of Twitter data for stock prediction." *Proceedings of the International Conference on Computational Intelligence and Data Science* (2018).

[9] Shastri, M., Roy, S., and Mittal, M. "Stock price prediction using artificial neural network: An application of big data." *EAI Endorsed Transactions on Scalable Information Systems* 6, no. 20 (2019): 1–8.

[10] Khan, W., Ghazanfar, M.A., Azam, M.A., Karami, A., Alyoubi, K.H., and Alfakeeh, A.S. "Stock market prediction using machine learning classifiers and social media, news." *Journal of Ambient Intelligence and Humanized Computing* (2020).

20

Churn Prediction in the Banking Sector

Shreyas Hingmire, Jawwad Khan, Ashutosh andPandey Aruna Pavate

CONTENTS

20.1 Introduction

20.1.1 Problem Statement

In the banking industry, customers can easily switch between banks due to public policies. This results in a competitive market. Identifying customers who are likely to discontinue from the service is a remunerative concern of the banking industry. When a customer leaves a bank or any organization, it's detrimental to the bank/company. Our proposed system will help the bank to be in the competition and act accordingly to handle the churn of customers, by recognizing the customers who are likely to churn using past information and behavior.

20.1.2 Current Scenario

Nowadays, to reduce customer churn, banks focus more on customer experience. The churn rate is 25–30% for companies which do not hold any contract with its customers, whereas for companies with some type of contract it is 5–8%. After market research, companies have come to a conclusion that the retention of the customers is also as important as acquiring new customers for the growth of the company's business as the cost involved in customer retention is less. So for long-term sustainability, it is important that the banks reduce the churn rate by analyzing the behavior of their customers. In order to get a solution for this problem, the companies are coming forward with unique solutions to forecast customer preferences and behaviors, to ensure a minimization in their customer churn figure. Some of the major user experiences factors contributing to customer churn are:

1. Fees – Customers leave the bank if they are charged higher fees. Poor customer service is also a reason for leaving.
2. Rates – Many customers look around for other banks which may provide them higher rates, even if they have an account in a particular bank.
3. Poor customer service and on-hold times – Customers don't like to wait for a longer duration of time, specifically with financial risk involved.
4. Online services – Customers also leave the bank if mobile or online experiences are slow or too complex.

20.1.3 Motivation

The banking industry is humongous, making customer retention essential concerns for its survival and good long-term profitability. Significant research in the field of churn prediction is being carried out using various statistical and data mining techniques for a decade. Very few studies have addressed churn prediction with the use of Artificial Neural Network models in the banking sector. This thesis aims to predict customer churn using the Artificial Neural Network technique like backpropagation and optimization technique stochastic gradient descent algorithm. During the process of customer churn prediction, bank operators would often need to analyze the steps to figure out the probable cause and rationale instigating customers to churn. This could be possible with Artificial Neural Network models as they generate accurate results.

20.1.4 Objective

To build the customer churn model which helps the bank to:

- Predict the customers who will churn.
- Finding factors which influence customers to churn.
- Retain churn customers by applying strategy and providing offers based on influencing factors.
- Control churn rate and improve their image in the market.

20.2 Related Work

P. K. Dalvi et al. (2016) proposed a model using R programming with the help of the decision tree and logistic regression algorithms. It uses feature extraction. The paper stated that selecting correct attributes and fixing the proper threshold values may produce more accurate results.

Karvana et al. (2019) proposed an efficient model which compared SVM with other Machine Learning algorithms. The results demonstrated that SVM had high fitting accuracy and simple classification surface, etc. as SVM has high precision.

Spider and Azzopardi (2018) proposed a model for predicting customers who are going to leave a motor insurance company. A random forest algorithm was used and it obtained an accuracy of 91.18%. To find the most relevant features, feature analysis was done. Though this model focuses on a different sector, their approach can be used in the banking sector as well.

Cao et al. (2019) proposed a model using the SAE (Sparse Autoencoder) network. Multiple autoencoders were stacked together. Logistic regression was used along with SAE (Sparse Autoencoder) to perform customer churn classification. Less accuracy was obtained even if the model was trained on a large dataset and the highest accuracy achieved was 80%.

Irfan Ullah et al. (2019) proposed a model using K-Means clustering. It explained distinguished cluster problems very substantially, but it was found to be only desirable with less diverse and huge datasets. Precision obtained was 80%; improvements on data modeling and accuracy are required in this research.

As per the above discussion, there are many systems designed, but each has some limitations, most of which have average accuracy and very few of the papers have identified the features affecting the customer churn.

20.3 Methodology

ANN (Artificial Neural networks) typically consists of thousands of artificial neurons called units that work in coordination for mathematical processing and derive relevant and purposeful conclusions from it. Some of the advantages of Artificial Neural Networks over other algorithms are that they are fault tolerant and have parallel processing capability. Missing a few pieces of information does not affect the network as information is stored on the entire network and not just on the database. The hidden layer filters some of the important patterns. Neural Networks have the capability to learn from events by themselves and apply them when a similar event arises. In the proposed system, Keras, Sklearn, and Pandas libraries were used and analysis was done in Tableau software.

20.3.1 Dataset

Figure 20.1 represents a dataset used in the model which was taken from the kaggle website (https://www.kaggle.com/santoshd3/bank-customers, 2018). It consists of 13 parameters and a final class column which shows the supervised outcome of the given parameters. RowNumber, CustomerID, and Surname parameters were ignored in the model as they have no impact on output.

Data preprocessing was done on the dataset to convert raw data into well-structured data, which will be more useful for the model. It is an important step as it directly impacts the accuracy of the model. The following steps were done in data preprocessing:

1. Handling missing values: In a particular row, if many values were missing then the entire row was deleted. Sometimes if a particular value was missing then the mean of the entire column was taken to fill that value, whereas sometimes mode was taken. Sometimes the mean of only particular rows was taken, which match some other values for that particular row.

	A	B	C	D	E	F	G	H	I	J	K	L	M	N
1	RowNumb	Customer	Surname	CreditScor	Geography	Gender	Age	Tenure	Balance	NumOfPrc	HasCrCard	IsActiveMe	Estimated:	Exited
2	1	15634602	Hargrave	619	France	Female	42	2	0	1	1	1	101348.9	1
3	2	15647311	Hill	608	Spain	Female	41	1	83807.86	1	0	1	112542.6	0
4	3	15619304	Onio	502	France	Female	42	8	159660.8	3	1	0	113931.6	1
5	4	15701354	Boni	699	France	Female	39	1	0	2	0	0	93826.63	0
6	5	15737888	Mitchell	850	Spain	Female	43	2	125510.8	1	1	1	79084.1	0
7	6	15574012	Chu	645	Spain	Male	44	8	113755.8	2	1	0	149756.7	1
8	7	15592531	Bartlett	822	France	Male	50	7	0	2	1	1	10062.8	0
9	8	15656148	Obinna	376	Germany	Female	29	4	115046.7	4	1	0	119346.9	1
10	9	15792365	He	501	France	Male	44	4	142051.1	2	0	1	74940.5	0
11	10	15592389	H?	684	France	Male	27	2	134603.9	1	1	1	71725.73	0
12	11	15767821	Bearce	528	France	Male	31	6	102016.7	2	0	0	80181.12	0
13	12	15737173	Andrews	497	Spain	Male	24	3	0	2	1	0	76390.01	0
14	13	15632264	Kay	476	France	Female	34	10	0	2	1	0	26260.98	0
15	14	15691483	Chin	549	France	Female	25	5	0	2	0	0	190857.8	0

FIGURE 20.1 Sample dataset for customer churn analysis.

2. Handling categorical columns: Label encoding was applied on the gender column which consists of 2 values, female and male. Then one hot encoding was applied in the Geography column which consists of three values, France, Spain, and Germany.

3. Feature scaling: It helps to normalize the data within a particular range and is also useful in speeding up the calculations in an algorithm.

Figure 20.2 shows the dataset before and after applying data preprocessing.

20.3.2 Proposed System for Customer Churn Prediction

Figure 20.3 represents the block diagram of the model where initially the data is collected from the dataset. Then data-preprocessing is applied, which converts raw data into a desirable form. This data is provided as input for the ANN (Artificial Neural Network), which would be employed for the classification of the dataset to estimate whether the customer would churn or not. After this, analysis is done on the churn and loyal customers to find factors which influence the customers to churn. Then clustering is applied among churn customers to segregate churn customers into different clusters, after which through exploratory data analysis a reason for churning is found for all clusters.

Following are the steps to build the customer churn model:

Step 1: Initialization of weights

The weights are initialized very close to zero, but randomly. When the system randomly initializes the weights, it gives much better accuracy as every neuron is no longer performing the same computation.

Step 2: All feature values are entered in input layer

Step 3: Weight calculation using forward propagation

Figure 20.4 shows forward propagation i.e., moving in one direction in a neural network.

Following are the notations used in the paper:

Input Features $= x_1, x_2, \ldots\ldots, x_{11}$

Bias Unit (always equal to one) $= x_0$

Weights $= \theta_{11}, \theta_{12}, \theta_{13}$

Sigmoid activation function $= g$

Activation of unit i in layer j $= a_i^{(j)}$

$$a_1^{(2)} = g\,(\theta_{10}^{(1)}x_0 + \theta_{11}^{(1)}x_1 + \theta_{12}^{(1)}x_2 + \theta_{111}^{(1)}x_{11}) \tag{20.1}$$

$$a_2^{(2)} = g\,(\theta_{20}^{(1)}x_0 + \theta_{21}^{(1)}x_1 + \theta_{22}^{(1)}x_2 + \theta_{211}^{(1)}x_{11}) \tag{20.2}$$

$$a_3^{(2)} = g\,(\theta_{30}^{(1)}x_0 + \theta_{31}^{(1)}x_1 + \theta_{32}^{(1)}x_2 + \theta_{311}^{(1)}x_{11}) \tag{20.3}$$

$$h_\theta\,(x) = a_1^{(3)} = g\,(\theta_{10}^{(2)}a_0^{(2)} + \theta_{11}^{(2)}a_1^{(2)} + \theta_{12}^{(2)}a_2^{(2)} + \theta_{13}^{(2)}a_3^{(2)}) \tag{20.4}$$

predicted output obtained from forward propagation

Step 4: Error Calculation

Error of cost for $a_i^{(l)} = \delta_j^i$ (unit j in layer l)

Actual value $= y_i$

Value found by model $= a_i^{(4)}$

$$\delta_1^{(4)} = \frac{1}{2}(y_j - a_i^{(4)})^2 \tag{20.5}$$

Figure 20.5 represents backpropagation and calculating error. The aim of the training is to minimize the difference between actual value and predicted value. Weights directly affect the prediction value, hence to change the prediction value, the value of the weights are updated so that the error is reduced.

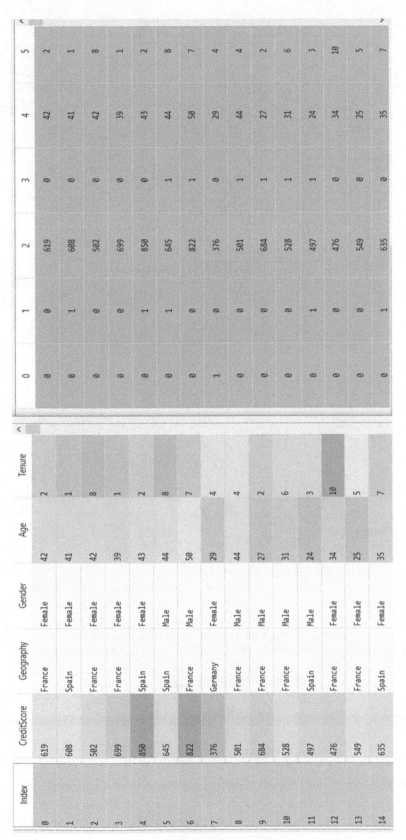

FIGURE 20.2   (Left) Before data preprocessing; (right) after data preprocessing.

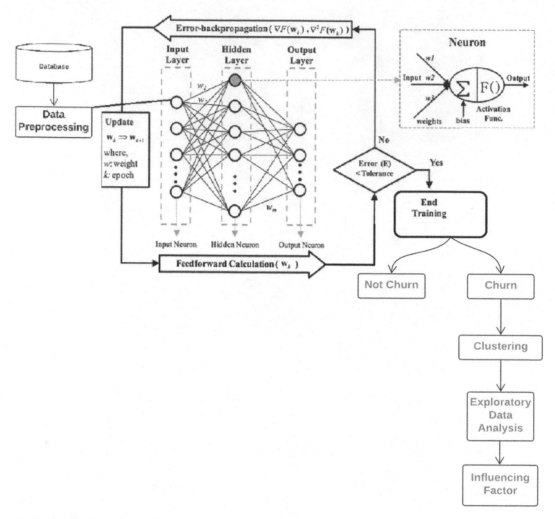

FIGURE 20.3 Block diagram of model.

Step 5: Backpropagation and Applying Optimization

Backpropagation is known as the backward propagation of errors as it updates the weights using gradient descent, which is an optimization algorithm which locates the minimum of the function. Backpropagation calculates the gradient of the error function with respect to weights. Backpropagation distributes these errors backward through the network so that the neurons can use them for adjusting individual weights. The error terms for the previous layers are calculated as follows:

$$\delta^{(l)} = ((\theta^{(l)})^T \delta^{(l+1)}) \cdot_* g'(z^{(l)}) \tag{20.6}$$

$$\delta^{(l)} = ((\theta^{(l)})^T \delta^{(l+1)}) \cdot_* a^{(l)} \cdot_* (1 - a^{(l)}) \tag{20.7}$$

$$\delta_2^{(3)} = \delta_1^{(4)} \cdot \theta_{12}^{(3)} \tag{20.8}$$

$$\delta_2^{(2)} = \delta_2^{(3)} \cdot \theta_{22}^{(2)} + \delta_1^{(3)} \cdot \theta_{12}^{(2)} \tag{20.9}$$

This backward propagation stops at l = 2 as l = 1 is the input layer and there is no need to update weights there.

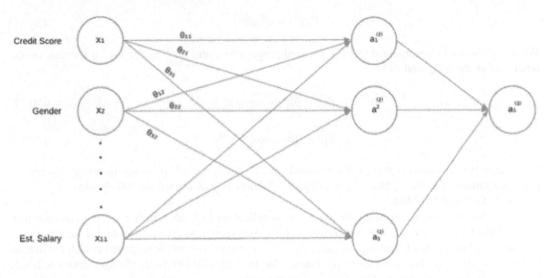

FIGURE 20.4 Forward propagation.

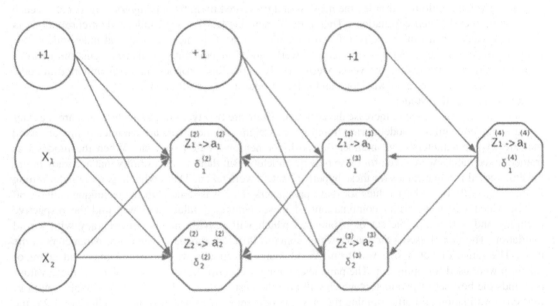

FIGURE 20.5 Backpropagation and calculating error.

Step 6: Weight Updation

The gradient of the loss is calculated with respect to the weights once the loss is calculated. The weights are updated in a direction opposite to the gradient which will decrease the loss function which is the goal. Over the training process, the goal is to minimize the loss function so the weights which were initialized randomly keep on updating.

$$*W: = W - \alpha \cdot j'(W) \tag{20.10}$$

Where W is the weight at hand, $*W$ is new weight α is the learning rate (i.e., 0.1 in our example), and $J'(W)$ is the partial derivative of the cost function $J(W)$ with respect to W.

$$J'(W) = a_j^{(l)} \cdot \delta^{(l+1)} \tag{20.11}$$

Where $a_j^{(l)}$ is the value obtained through forward-propagation, and $\delta^{(l+1)}$ is the loss at the unit on the other end of the weighted link:

$$\theta_{22}^{(1)} = \theta_{22}^{(1)} - \alpha \cdot x_{(2)} \cdot \delta_2^{(2)} \tag{20.12}$$

$$\theta_{22}^{(2)} = \theta_{22}^{(2)} - \alpha \cdot a_2^{(2)} \cdot \delta_2^{(3)} \tag{20.13}$$

Mini-batch gradient descent was used in the model with a batch size of 10. When the whole training set is passed through the ANN, that makes an epoch. The model was trained on 100 epochs.

Step 7: Evaluate the Model

The model was optimized using the k-fold cross-validation method, which fixed the variance problem. Cross-validation is a statistical method to see how a model performs on unseen data. k refers to the number of groups/folds that a given data sample is to be split into. In the proposed model, the dataset is split into 10 folds. Ten accuracies are obtained for 10 folds and the mean of those values is taken, which results in the accuracy of the model as 83.5% and variance as 0.9%.

Step 8: Improving the Model

Even though the model had a low variance of 0.9%, dropout regularization was used to avoid overfitting which randomly disabled the neurons and prevented them from being too dependent on each other while they learned correlations. Therefore the neurons learn several independent correlations in the data because each time there is a different configuration of the neurons. Several independent correlations of data were found because neurons work more independently, which prevents the neurons from learning too much which prevents overfitting. To apply this, dropout class was imported in code. Dropout at each hidden layer was done and 0.1% of neurons were disabled.

Step 9: Tuning the Model

Parameter tuning is used to increase the accuracy. There are two types of parameters, first are the ones that are learned from the model during training e.g., weight and the others are parameters that are fixed that are hyperparameters, e.g., number of epochs or neurons, batch size, etc. When the model was trained, fixed values were taken for these hyperparameters. But there is a possibility that accuracy might have increased if other values for these hyperparameters were taken. That's what hyperparameter tuning is all about. It finds the best values for these parameters. This was done with the technique called grid search which will test several combinations of these parameter values and will find the respective accuracy and will return the set of parameters which will provide maximum accuracy with k-fold validation. The model used a dictionary which contains different ranges of values for parameters in the code. The range of batch size was from 25–32; range of epochs was from 100–500; and adam or rmsprop were used for optimizer. The parameter tuning uses a different combination of all these values and finds the best set of parameters which will give the best accuracy. This model was applied with k-fold cross-validation and after running the code the best set of parameters were a batch size of 25; the number of epochs was 500 and the optimizer was rmsprop; and the model obtained an accuracy of 86.4% on these parameters.

20.4 Results

Figure 20.6 represents the confusion matrix. The system is evaluated using accuracy, precision, recall, and F1 score as mentioned below:

1. Accuracy = (TP + TN/TP + FP + FN + TN) = 86.4%
2. Precision = (TP/TP + FP) = 95.48%
   Of all the customers which the model predicted will stay, 95.48% actually stayed.

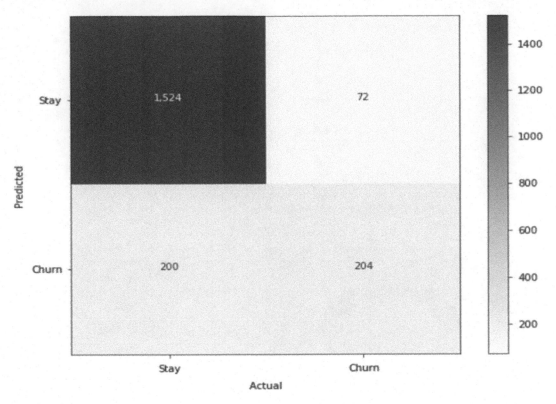

FIGURE 20.6 Confusion matrix.

3. Recall = (TP / TP + FN) = 88.39%
   Of all the stayed customers, we predicted 88.39% correctly.
4. F1 Score = (2*P*R / P + R) = 91.8%

After running the model, analysis was done on the entire output i.e., churn/loyal customers. The aim of this analysis was to find the features which showed a major impact on churn customers. The dataset consists of 10,000 rows of which 2,000 are churn customers and 8,000 are loyal customers. It has 5,500 male customers and 4,500 female customers. After analysis, it was found that 25% of female customers churned, whereas only 16.5% of the males churned. Hence, female customers are 60% more likely to churn as compared to male customers (Figure 20.7).

   Other meaningful insights:

- Average age of customers who left – 45; who stayed – 37.5
- Average balance of customers who left – 91,000; who stayed – 73,000
- Among those who left only 36% were active, whereas among those who stayed 55% were active.
- In the dataset: 5,000 are from France, 2,500 are from Germany and Spain. From France and Spain, 16% people churned while 32.5% people from Germany churned. Hence, people from Germany are twice as likely to churn as compared to France and Spain.
- Even if people from Germany are more likely to churn, balance is not the factor that determines if they will churn or not. However, this is not the case for people from Spain or France. Churn customers have an average balance of 72,000 compared to 60,000 for those who stayed.
- 37.5% females in Germany are churn customers, whereas only 13% of males from Spain and France churn.

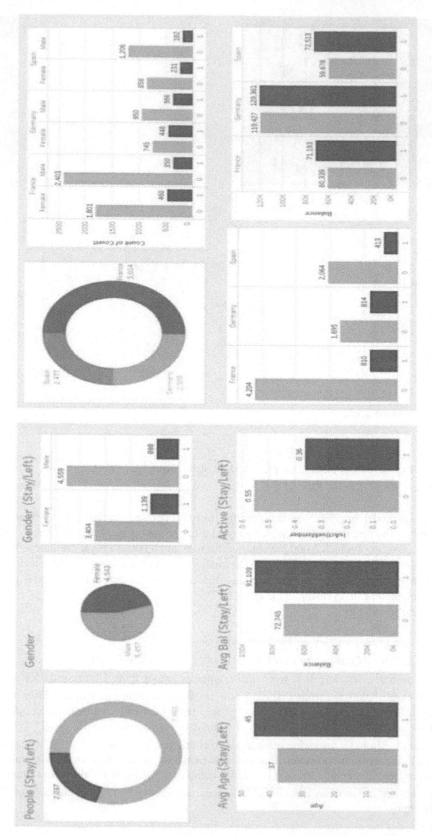

FIGURE 20.7   Analysis of churn and loyal customers.

20.4.1 Analysis of Clustering of Churned Customers

After applying ANN, a clustering algorithm was applied on churn customers so that churn customers could be segregated into different clusters. Clustering can be used to find common aspects within customers to find groups and focus on services or improvement. In the proposed system, K-Means clustering algorithm is used and churn customers are segregated into four clusters. After applying clustering, patterns or reasons for the churn of customers for different clusters were found. It will be different for each cluster and this information can be used to stop these customers from leaving the bank by providing them appropriate offers with the help of this information (Figure 20.8).

Cluster 0:Total 750 customers	Cluster 2:Total 280 customers
60% of them are from Germany	None from Germany
Avg Balance is 121,000	Avg Balance is 4,700
Est Salary 150,000	Est Salary 53,000
Cluster 1:Total 720 customers	Cluster 3:Total 280 customers
60% of them are from	Germany None from Germany
Avg Balance is 121,000	Avg Balance is 5,500
Est Salary 50,000	Est Salary 150,000

20.5 Conclusion

The issue of customer churn is increasingly pressing by the day. The proposed models help to control customer churn. The multi-layered ANN (Artificial Neural Network) model is designed to solve this problem, which produced an accuracy of 86.4%. The proposed model will help the bank to identify which customers will leave the bank and hence the bank can retain those customers, saving a lot of money which would rather had been used for replacing the churn customers and also save the money

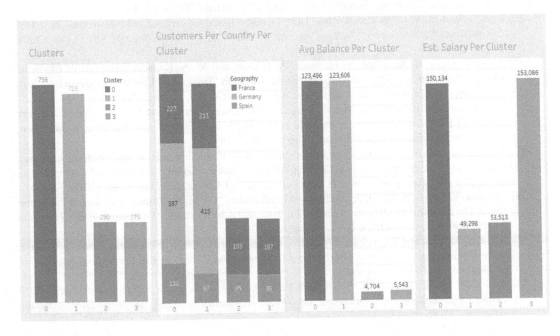

FIGURE 20.8 Analysis on clusters.

which would be used for retaining already loyal customers. The proposed model not only provides high accuracy but also provides with the best insights to further prevent churn behavior. With the help of influencing factors obtained through clustering and analysis, it will be easy to design retention policies to retain the customers as these methods provide the reasons for their churn along with the list of customers with high probability to churn.

20.6 Future Work

In the future, clustering will be implemented on the customers based on their likelihood of churning, i.e., customers which are more likely to churn can be kept in one cluster (i.e., chances of leaving are greater than 0.85), those that are likely to leave the bank by $0.65 < x < 0.85$ can be kept in one cluster and those that are less likely to leave the bank can be kept in another cluster and analysis can be done accordingly. Those that are more likely to leave will be on a high-priority list and attempts will be made to stop them first by taking necessary steps. The model can be deployed on the cloud, where frontend will be implemented for interaction, using azure/gcp cloud model by implementing an API to pipeline the data into the cloud datastore followed by the model implementation on the cloud. To use the pipelined data for analysis, this model can be used to scale the application by using the API for different banks across the country to analyze their data, and generate the monthly or quarterly churn values of the customers. The implementation of cloud deployment using MLOps would be beneficial for continuous monitoring of the ML model and analyzing its performance. The frontend can be made using latest cutting-edge technological advancements like material design and trending design patterns which will help the manager, admin, or appointed authority to easily maneuver the website so that they can check details of customers, their chances of leaving and analysis and graphs which will highlight the reason for their churn. Additionally, a chatbot could be added that will make the website more efficient.

REFERENCES

[1] Agrawal, S., A. Das, A. Gaikwad, and S. Dhage, "Customer Churn Prediction Modelling Based on Behavioural Patterns Analysis using Deep Learning," *2018 International Conference on Smart Computing and Electronic Enterprise (ICSCEE)*, (Shah Alam, 2018), pp. 1–6.

[2] Cao, S., W. Liu, Y. Chen, and X. Zhu, "Deep Learning Based Customer Churn Analysis," *2019 11th International Conference on Wireless Communication and Signal Processing (WCSP)*, (Xi'an, China, 2019), pp. 1–6.

[3] Dalvi, P. K., S. K. Khandge, A. Deomore, A. Bankar, and V. A. Kanade, "Analysis of Customer Churn Prediction in Telecom Industry Using Decision Trees and Logistic Regression," *2016 Symposium on Colossal Data Analysis and Networking (CDAN)*, (Indore, 2016), pp. 1–4.

[4] Hegde, Sandeep Kumar, and Monica Mundada, "Enhanced Deep Feed Forward Neural Network Model for the Customer Attrition Analysis in Banking Sector," *International Journal of Intelligent Systems and Applications*, vol. 11, no. 7, pp. 10–19 (2019).

[5] Hemalatha, Putta, and Geetha Mary Amalanathan, "A Hybrid Classification Approach for Customer Churn Prediction using Supervised Learning Methods Banking Sector," *International Conference on Vision Towards Emerging Trends in Communication and Networking (ViTECoN)* (2019).

[6] Karvana, K. G. M., S. Yazid, A. Syalim, and P. Mursanto, "Customer Churn Analysis and Prediction Using Data Mining Models in Banking Industry," *2019 International Workshop on Big Data and Information Security (IWBIS)*, (Bali, Indonesia, 2019), pp. 33–38.

[7] Sai, B.N. Krishna and T. Sasikala, "Predictive Analysis and Modeling of Customer Churn in Telecom using Machine Learning," *3rd International Conference on Trends in Electronics and Information (ICOEI)*. ISBN: 978-1-5386–9439-8 (2019).

[8] Spider, M., and G. Azzopardi, "Customer Churn Prediction for a Motor Insurance Company," *2018 Thirteenth International Conference on Digital Information Management (ICDIM)*, (Berlin, Germany, 2018), pp. 172–178.

[9] Ullah, I., B. Raza, A. K. Malik, et al., "A Churn Prediction Model Using Random Forest: Analysis of Machine Learning Techniques for Churn Prediction and Factor Identification in Telecom Sector," in IEEE Access, vol. 7, pp. 60134–60149 (2019).

[10] Ullah, I., H. Hussain, I. Ali, and A. Liaquat, "Churn Prediction in Banking System using K-Means, LOF, and CBLOF," *2019 International Conference on Electrical, Communication, and Computer Engineering (ICECCE)*, (Swat, Pakistan, 2019), pp. 1–6.

[11] Wadikar, Deepshika, "Customer Churn Analysis," Masters Dissertation. Technological University, Dublin. DOI: 10.21427/KPSZ-X829, Corpus ID: 211547276 (2020).

21

Machine and Deep Learning Techniques for Internet of Things Based Cloud Systems

Raswitha Bandi and K. Tejaswini

CONTENTS

21.1 Introduction

Nowadays IoT plays an important role to make everyone's life easier in complex tasks. As technology is growing and thus around the United States has become connected more than before. So, a net of things hatched a network with interconnected devices and sensors which they administered everyday tasks simply [1]. The IoT applications like smart cities, smart health care, smart automobiles, smart retails, smart homes, etc. will give information on how connected devices are and disturbing the norm prompting the assembly of an efficient and automatic planet. Over the years, these devices are becoming very smart and affect vast amounts of knowledge to transfer between different machines. Over time, IoT devices are capable of affecting real-time data like sensor data, images, and audio and video data [1]. The IoT generates quantities of knowledge and in turn puts a burden on network infrastructure. Because it puts a huge strain on network infrastructure, it becomes very difficult for the clients to affect big data to transfer from one place to another. To agitate this instance, cloud computing has entered into data technology and provides different services for the end users according to their needs. These IoT devices alone will not give benefits to the progression of infrastructure, instead they combine with other technologies like cloud services that will give massive advantages to the clients [1]. Distributed computing administrations encourage moment, on-request conveyance of registering foundation, information bases, stockpiling, and applications needed for the cycle and examination of data focuses produced through a few IoT devices. At present, 96 of the associations received cloud administrations and with the rise of Amazon Internet providers, Google cloud stage, Microsoft Azure, and IBM cloud, the broadening possibilities of the snare of things appear to be much more brilliant. In lightweight of the guidelines of capacity and availability, the cloud is hailed as reformist advancement over the planet. Here are some key reasons the cloud is prime to the achievement of the Internet of Things [1].

21.1.1 Power of Remote Computing

The technology is increasing along with the improvements in speed of Internet; cloud applications are rapidly increasing to provide solutions to the client needs. By this it will increase the remote computing power to produce solutions at one click [1].

21.1.2 Security and Privacy Policies

Proliferation of IoT devices might enable organizations to modify their tasks; however, some security issues are in addition poses. For this, a viable resolution is also a cloud with a decent variety of controls [1]. Cloud arrangements can facilitate the execution of reliable safety efforts, with top-quality cloud arrangements, it's feasible to oversee and provide security to the users those who are accessing IoT devices.

21.1.3 Integration of Data

As IoT keeps on appreciating the significance of the perspectives, foundations have started exploring different avenues regarding associating devices to extricate timeframe information on key business measures. Using these devices, it increases the operational speed and it enhance the prices; likewise they produce huge info that is too large to even process in any event. Cloud frameworks with their strong information coordination abilities handle monstrous volumes of data radiating from various sources.

21.1.4 For Hosting, Providers Remove Entry Barrier

Innovations in the field of IoT request problem-free solutions. In such a scenario, cloud solutions square measure is quite acceptable. Using these cloud services, Internet of Things uses the power of remote knowledge centers from the Asian country. On the other hand, these cloud services are working on the principle called on demand [1]. So, the corporations measure giant direct prices. So, introduced innovative cloud solutions and become an entry point for several IoT-based businesses and allow them to implement large-scale IoT applications.

21.1.5 Improves Business Continuity

Cloud computing solutions are better known for responsibility. The services of cloud are placed on the top of the best network servers and used in multiple locations. These types of systems store copies of our knowledge and places in multiple data centers in India [1]. Because of this duplication, IoT-based activities actually perform perfectly, but one of the systems may disconnect for certain reasons or the other option. In addition, there isn't any danger of data misfortune.

21.1.6 Facilitates Inter-device Communication

Notwithstanding human action with us, IoT gadgets and administrations should associate with one another. Cloud arrangements encourage consistent correspondence between IoT gadgets [1]. They license a few tough class Apis like Cloud flare and Drop str and grant communication between associated gadgets and great telephones there by clearing the methods for the development of associated innovations.

21.1.7 Pairing with Edge Computing

To decrease the response time and to increase the speed of processing Internet of Things paired up with new technology called edge computing.

21.1.8 How IoT and Cloud Complement Each Other?

Now a day's distributed computing plays an important role to expand the effectiveness of computing power just like IoT and cloud devices. IoT devices produce lots of information while these distributed computing clears the route to travel or to pass enormous amount of information. On the other hand cloud devices use pay as you utilize model based upon the assets utilized by the clients. Here, Table 21.1 shows the difference between Internet of Things and cloud computing [1,2].

21.1.9 Cloud and IoT: Which Is Better?

With the rising reception of multi-cloud and hybrid cloud conditions, organizations are arousing to the essentialness of cloud arrangements. The IoT display is additionally seeing a captivating movement. Inside the wake of those turns of events, it's secured to presume that distributed computing will offer roads for the Internet of Things (IoT). Network, dependability, and registering quality from the cloud will initiate unrest inside the IoT house [1,2]. It might possibly be truthful to means that cloud can speed up the expansion of IoT.

TABLE 21.1

Comparison between IoT and Cloud Computing

IoT vs Cloud Computing
• IoT act as a source for large amount of data sets whereas cloud will manage the large amounts of data.
• Reachability of IoT devices are very limited whereas cloud systems can be far and widespread over the network.
• Storage capacity of IoT devices are limited in other words we can say there is no storage whereas cloud systems will have large capacity virtually it is endless.
• The computing capability of IoT devices is very limited whereas cloud systems will have more computing power.
• IoT devices will run on hardware whereas cloud systems runs on virtual machines.

21.1.10 The Challenges Posed by the Cloud and IoT Together?

21.1.10.1 Handling an Outsized Amount of Knowledge

Taking care of a lot of information can be overpowering particularly when there are a huge number of devices in the image. Henceforth, following the No SQL development could be advantageous, yet it isn't attempted and tried since quite a while ago run. This is the reason there exists no stable or secure technique for the cloud to oversee large information [1].

21.1.10.2 Networking and Communication Protocols

Cloud and IoT include machine-to-machine correspondences among a wide range of devices having different conventions. Dealing with this sort of variety could be extreme since a larger part of utilization zones don't include versatility. Starting at now Wi-Fi and Bluetooth are utilized as a makeshift answer for encouraging versatility partially [1,2].

21.1.10.3 Sensor Networks

Sensor networks have intensified the advantages of IoT. These organizations have permitted clients to remain to construe and perceive unobtrusive signs from the climate. Notwithstanding, the very much coordinated preparation of an outsized amount of this sensor data has been a genuine test. One essential task it really is confronted by way of cloud IoT is the processing of an outsized quantity of sensor records which successively consists of safety and privateness problems [1,2].

21.1.10.4 Security Challenges

Security risks incorporate unstable passage focuses and abuse of individual data and encouraging assaults on different frameworks. A genuine case of this is the Dyn cyber attack which occurred on October 21, 2016. It included numerous disseminated disavowals of administration assaults focusing on DNS supplier Dyn. The conveyed refusal of administration assaults was executed through an enormous number of associated devices, for example, printers, IP cameras, and child screens that were contaminated with malware. A portion of the administrations influenced by this assault included Amazon, Airbnb, Grubhub, HBO, Netflix, Overstock.com, PayPal, Twitter, Visa, and Walgreens. Clinics are one of the weakest business areas to cyber attacks by the method of IoT clinical gadgets. Clinical gadgets and embedded clinical gadgets including heart pacemakers, drug organization gadgets, checking gadgets, just as mixture siphons, defibrillators, and glucometers can effectively affect wellbeing whenever messed with by programmers. This is particularly inconvenient since the strategy for conveyance or checking is by an associated gadget. The danger of cyber attacks is that they can disturb a working medical clinic by decimating a whole data innovation framework leaving destroying results to patients.

21.2 Security Issues in IoT-Based Cloud Systems

Another huge empowering device for IoT is that the dispensed computing which is employed for coping with big records created by way of the IoT subsystems. Security in IoT is of high importance from cloud inhabitant's factor of view. It deserves referencing that cloud are frequently an indispensable component of the IoT basis thanks to a couple of overlap reasons: managing extensive information, inserting away and making ready colossal measure of facts from IoT, and handing over last merchandise to the man or woman functions in IoT climate [3]. Furthermore, cloud stage likewise offers a scope of administrations, for occasion, Management of devices, Management of resources, records preparing, examination, etc. the dimensions of IoT units represents an actual venture for carrying out the required safety and safety goals for IoT. Besides, the IoT purposes are deliberate from a solitary location as pinnacle precedence and hence ahead do not envelop the total scope of a number area which will make use of the information started out from one unique IoT area [4]. Along these lines, the range of units brought to IoT companies and consequently the statistics delivered via these devices, and in a while put away prepared, and examined through the cloud want feasible, productive, and adaptable safety and safety contemplations.

21.2.1 Attacks in IoT

From the previous few years, the IoT framework has been confronting quite a number assaults which make the Manufacturers and customers are very mindful with reference to growing and making use of IoT units [4]. IoT assaults are regularly often divided into two kinds: 1) cyber-attacks and 2) bodily attacks. Cyber assaults ask a hazard that ambitions unique IoT unit at some point of a Wi-Fi community by means of hacking the machine so as to change the user's information. On the contrary, bodily assaults ask the assaults that bodily injury IoT device. Here, the attackers do not want any community to assault the system. The following gives you the information regarding two most important attack types [5].

21.2.1.1 Active Attack

An active attack happens when an intruder gets to the organization and its related data to control the setup of the framework and interfere with specific administrations. There are various approaches to assault IoT device security, including interruption, intercessions, and changes under dynamic assaults. Figure 21.1 explains about various active attacks.

21.2.1.2 Passive Attack

Passive attacks attempt to assemble the client's data without their assent and endeavor this data to decode their private information. Snooping and traffic analysis are the two different ways to play out an uninvolved assault through an IoT network. Snooping basically sends the client's IoT device as a sensor to gather and abuse their classified data and area [6,7]. Figure 21.2 explains various passive attacks.

21.3 Machine Learning and Deep Learning: A Solution to Cyber Security Challenges in IoT-Based Cloud Systems

ML and DL algorithms are carried out in several applications of internet of things packages and frameworks. These strategies have the functionality to find out from revel in and these techniques are utilized for kind of assaults in Internet of Things n/w's [8,9]. ML and DL methods stop up more well-known due to the fact of numerous algorithms with new capabilities, generation and processing of huge volume of information, and espresso computational price [9]. From the past decade, ML and DL techniques demonstrated improvement in appearing precise lookup of various packages [9]. This financial ruin examines ML and DL techniques or algorithms utilized for the identification and kind of assaults in IoT n/w. In ML techniques, attribute extraction is employed to retrieve suitable skills for appearing kind of assaults in IoT networks. A DL machine makes use of wonderful pre-skilled fashions for abstracting discriminative or generative skills to rise out assessment of patterns [10]. The motivation at the lower back of inspecting ML and DL methods is to grant a pinnacle to bottom consider of these techniques wont to steady IoT mainly based totally definitely cloud structures. ML is interdisciplinary in nature and acquires its foundations from Science and engineering that consist of AI, improvement hypothesis, records hypothesis, and technological know-how and so forth [11]. Machine analyzing is employed whilst human understanding each do no longer exist or on the different hand cannot be applied, as an instance, exploring an antagonistic place whereby human beings can now not make use of their intelligence, as an instance robotics, speech recognition then on. It's likewise carried out in situations whereby account a few specific concern changes vain to say

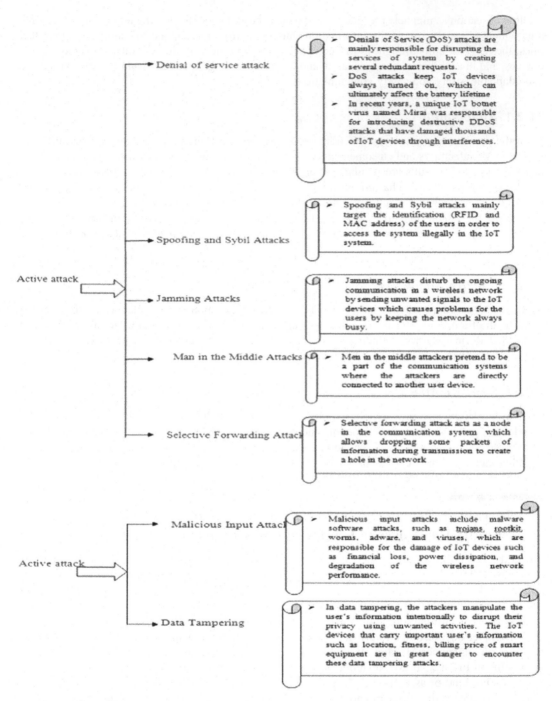

FIGURE 21.1 Types of active attacks.

(routing at some stage in a neighborhood at some stage in a product or application). Besides, it is utilized in lower-priced savvy frameworks, as an instance. It's moreover utilized for distinguishing and disposing of malware from contaminated handsets. Amazon makes use of ML to type and signify records saved on cloud garage. In spite of the very reality that ML techniques lift out proper in several areas on the other hand there is an opportunity of going on faux positives and actual negatives. There are various traditional methods used for numerous factors of IoT like programs,

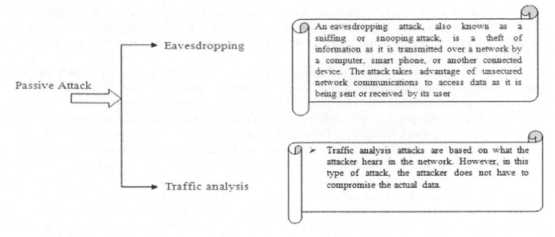

FIGURE 21.2 Types of passive attacks.

services, architectures, protocols, records aggregation, resource allocation, clustering, analytics, and of these consists of security issues [11]. Machine analyzing and deep analyzing techniques are promising one for IoT notably based totally absolutely cloud constructions way to various causes as an instance IoT specifically primarily based absolutely cloud constructions produce substantial volume of facts that is required via machine and deep analyzing techniques to deliver brain to the structures. These machine and deep reading techniques are in giant section used for safety, privacy, assault type, malware detection, and evaluation. Deep analyzing techniques moreover may also be utilized in IoT especially primarily based definitely cloud buildings to elevate out intricate obligations like sensing and reputation in genuine time environment. Using these system analyzing and deep analyzing techniques it is very challenging task to create fabulous model to gadget the data this is coming from various IoT specially based totally completely cloud system programs. Another challenging assignment is to label the enter record efficaciously and accurately [12]. Another mission consists of minimization of categorized data in analyzing machine and one of a kind worrying conditions consist of deployment of the version, processing and storage of information, necessary infrastructure maintenance.

21.3.1 Machine Learning and Deep Learning Techniques Introduction

ML and DL is that the most unexpectedly developing technological know-how and steady with researchers we are inside the golden yr of AI and ML [13]. It is wont to resolve many real-world complicated troubles which cannot be solved with the normal approach. Following are some real-world functions of ML and DL—Figure 21.3 depicts various applications of Machine Learning and Deep Learning techniques.

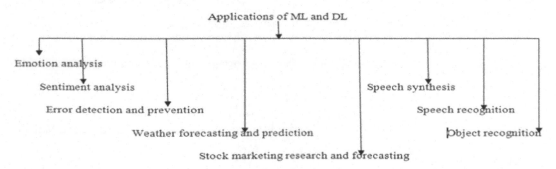

FIGURE 21.3 ML and DL application areas.

In this phase we speak diverse Machine learning and deep learning strategies in IoT primarily based totally cloud systems [14]. Basic Machine learning algorithms are categorized into four categories: supervised, unsupervised learning, semi-supervised learning, and reinforcement learning algorithms.

In supervised learning, first label the information and from that one it attempts to pick out the one of a kind lesson and through education the categorized information expect the very last factors to a given class. In Un Supervised Learning, it does now no longer require labeled information and look at similarity amongst unlabeled information and classify the information into one of a kind group. In semi-supervised learning, it falls among each supervised and unsupervised getting to know and the price for labeling could be very excessive so, it wishes human professional to label the information. So, in those conditions the semi supervised getting to know could be very beneficial to pick out and classify information into one of a kind groups [15]. In reinforcement learning, no results are described and on this agent research from the remarks interacting with the environment. Basic Deep Learning algorithms are categorized into categories: Deep Learning and Deep Reinforcement Learning algorithms. In Deep, it is thought for Distributed computing and its miles used for classify unlabeled information, uncategorized information, and unsupervised information [16]. In Deep Reinforcement Learning, its miles a mixture of Reinforcement Learning and Deep Learning and its miles used to clear up complicated studies problems. Deep Reinforcement getting to know is broadly utilized in domain names known as fitness care, clever grids, Robotics, recreation playing, finance, and plenty of more. Figures 21.4 and 21.5 explain classification of ML and DL algorithms.

The following list will give you the information regarding different classes of machine learning and deep learning algorithms.

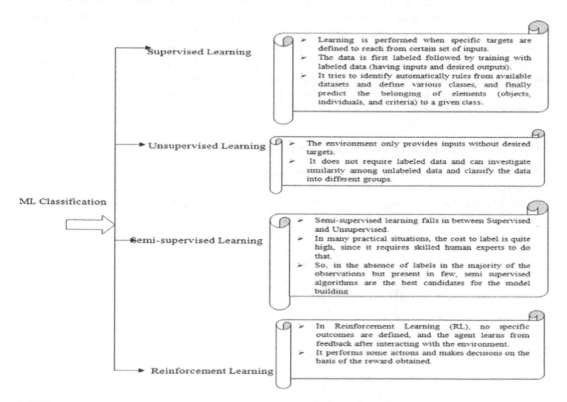

FIGURE 21.4 ML classification.

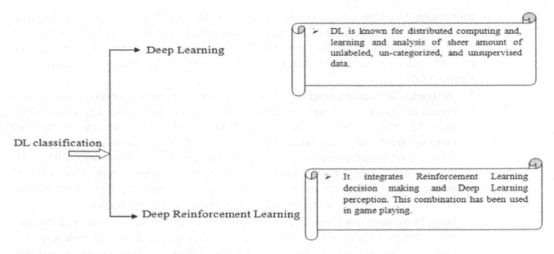

FIGURE 21.5   DL classification.

- **Deep Learning**
  - **Supervised Models**
    - **Classic Neural Networks (Multilayer Perceptions):** A classic neural networks are class of artificial neural networks. An MLP comprises of three layers: information or input, a shrouded or hidden, and a yield or output layer [23].
      - Ex: Fitness approximation, speech recognition, image recognition, and machine translation, etc…
    - **Convolution Neural Networks (CNNs):** In DL, a convolution neural n/w (CNN or ConvNet) is a class of deep neural associations or organizations, generally used for perception. They are generally called move invariant or space invariant ANN or organizations (SIANN) [24].
      - Ex: Decoding Facial Recognition, Historic and Environmental Collections, Analyzing Documents, Grey Areas, Advertising, etc…
    - **Recurrent Neural Networks (RNNs):** An RNN is a class of ANN where the hubs are associated with a graph along with a sequence. Thus, it acts progressively and these are gotten from feed forward neural n/w; RNNs can use their internal state (memory) to deal with variable-length plans of data sources. The articulation "redundant neural n/w's" is used unusually to imply two extensive classes of associations with a tantamount general structure, where one is a restricted inspiration and the other is perpetual drive. The two classes of associations show transitory dynamic behavior [6]. A restricted drive irregular association is a planned non-cyclic graph that can be unrolled and superseded with a cautiously feed-forward neural association, while an unending inspiration redundant association is an organized cyclic outline that can't be unrolled. Both restricted drive and unlimited inspiration dull associations can have additionally taken care of states [25].
      - Ex: Language Modeling and Generating Text, Machine Translation, Video Tagging, Text Summarization, etc…
  - **Unsupervised Models**
    - **Self-Organizing Maps (SOMs):** A SOM is one variant of artificial neural network it is used to deliver two dimensional representation of input space using the training samples called a chart, and is accordingly a strategy to do dimensionality reduction [26].
      - Ex: Project prioritization and selection, Seismic facies analysis for oil and gas exploration, Failure mode and effects analysis, Creation of artwork, etc…

- **Boltzmann Machines:** A Boltzmann machine (additionally called stochastic Hopfield network with shrouded units or Sherrington–Kirkpatrick model with outside field or stochastic Ising-Lenz-Little model) is a kind of stochastic intermittent neural organization. It is based upon the model called spin glass and The Boltzmann Machines are partitioned into various kinds they are

  a **Restricted Boltzmann machine**: Restricted Boltzmann machine (RBM) which doesn't permit intralayer associations between shrouded (hidden)units and noticeable(visible) units, for example, there is no association between noticeable to obvious and covered up to shrouded units. Subsequent to preparing one RBM, the exercises of its shrouded units can be treated as information for preparing a more significant level RBM. This strategy for stacking RBMs makes it conceivable to prepare numerous layers of shrouded units effectively and is one of the most widely recognized profound learning procedures. As each new layer is added the generative model improves.

  b **Deep Boltzmann machine:** A deep Boltzmann machine (DBM) is a sort of double pair wise Markov arbitrary field (undirected probabilistic graphical model) with numerous layers of concealed irregular factors. Like DBNs, DBMs can learn perplexing and conceptual inner portrayals of the contribution to assignments, for example, article or discourse acknowledgment, utilizing restricted, named information to adjust the portrayals constructed utilizing an enormous arrangement of unlabeled tangible info information. Notwithstanding, dissimilar to DBNs and profound convolution neural organizations, they seek after the induction and preparing methodology in the two ways, base up and top-down, which permit the DBM to more readily reveal the portrayals of the info structures [27].

    - Ex: linguistics, robotics, computer vision, etc…

- **Auto Encoders:** An auto encoder is a sort of ANN used to learn effective information codings in a solo way. The point of an auto encoder is to get familiar with a portrayal (encoding) for a bunch of information, ordinarily for dimensionality reduction, via preparing the organization to overlook signal "commotion." Along with that reduction, a remaking side is found out, where the auto encoder attempts to produce from the diminished encoding a portrayal as close as conceivable to its unique info, consequently its name. A few variations exist to the essential model, with the point of constraining the scholarly portrayals of the contribution to accept valuable properties. Models are the regularized auto encoders (Sparse, Denoising, and Contractive auto encoders), demonstrated power in learning portrayals for ensuing order undertakings, and Variation auto encoders, with their ongoing applications as generative models. Auto encoders are adequately utilized for taking care of many applied issues, from face acknowledgment to gaining the semantic significance of words [28].

  - Ex: Image Denoising, Dimensionality Reduction, Sequence to sequence prediction, Recommendation system, etc…

- **Machine Learning**
  - **Supervised Learning**
    - **Regression:** this algorithm is used when you want to predict a continuous variable from a range of discrete variables. If the variable is dichotomous then use the logistic regression. The unbiased variables used in regression can be both non-stop and dichotomous. One factor to hold in thought with regression evaluation is that causal relationships amongst the variables can't be determined. While the terminology is such that we say that X "predicts" Y, we can't say that X "causes" Y [17].

      - Ex: Prediction, Forecasting, estimating expectancy of life, etc…

    - **Classification:** Classification can also be described as the manner of predicting category or class from found values or given information points. The classified output can have the shape such as "Black" or "White" or "spam" or "no spam." Mathematically, classification is the venture of approximating a mapping characteristic (f) from enters variables (X) to output variables (Y). It is essentially belongs to the supervised desktop getting to know in which objectives are additionally furnished alongside with the enter records set. An instance of classification trouble can be the unsolicited mail detection in emails. There can be solely two classes of output, "spam" and "no spam"; therefore this is a binary kind classification [18].

- Ex: Classification of images, Customer Retention, Fraud Detection, etc...

- **Unsupervised Learning**
  - **Clustering:** clustering is used to group the information according to similar characteristics. Assume you are the top of a rental store and wish to comprehend the inclinations of your clients to scale up your business. Is it feasible for you to take a gander at the subtleties of every customer and devise an interesting business system for every single one of them? Unquestionably not. In any case, what you can do is to bunch the entirety of your customers into state 10 gatherings dependent on their buying propensities and utilize a different methodology for costumers in every one of these 10 gatherings [19].
    - Ex: Segmentation Targeted Marketing, etc...

  - **Dimensionality Reduction:** Dimensionality reduction alludes to strategies for lessening the number of information factors in preparing information. High-dimensionality may mean hundreds, thousands, or even a large number of info factors. Fewer info measurements frequently mean correspondingly fewer boundaries or a less complex structure in the AI model, alluded to as levels of opportunity. A model with an excessive number of levels of opportunity is probably going to overfit the preparation dataset and accordingly may not perform well on new information. It is attractive to have straightforward models that sum up well, and thusly, input information with scarcely any info factors. This is especially valid for direct models where the number of sources of info and the levels of the opportunity of the model is frequently firmly related [20].
    - Ex: Structure Discovery, Compression, Visualization, etc...

- **Semi-Supervised Learning**
  - **Semi-Supervised Clustering**: In the real world, there is more unlabelled information at that point marked information, however, there is still some named information. We need to utilize all accessible data for generally strong and best-performing models. Semi-directed bunching encourages us there. Creating names may not be simple or modest, and subsequently, because of restricted assets, we may have names for just a couple of perceptions. For instance, researching extortion is costly so we may think about affirmed misrepresentation or affirmed non-misrepresentation just for restricted protection claims. However, not knowing doesn't imply that those cases can't be misrepresented. A few instances of semi-managed grouping can be news class order, as you have seen on Google News[21]. There might be some data about a news thing being identified with "legislative issues" or "sports" however no one can filter through a huge number of things consistently to make completely named information. Essentially, picture acknowledgment utilizes the comparable strategy as you may encounter now on Google Photos.
    - Ex: Speech analysis, DNA Sequence Classification, etc...

  - **Semi-Supervised Classification**: The semi-supervised algorithm dependent on agreeable preparation understands the use of unlabeled information by utilizing different classifiers. In the learning cycle, the unlabeled information is utilized as a stage for data association between different classifiers. The contrasts between numerous classifiers are basic to the viability of such realizing, which is named as semi-directed learning dependent on disparity. Semi-regulated characterization calculation dependent on different classifier cooperation just uses marked examples to improve the variety of classifiers and doesn't utilize the bountiful data of an enormous number of unlabeled examples to upgrade the variety of classifiers [22].

- Ex: Speech analysis, DNA Sequence Classification etc…

- **Reinforcement Learning**
  - **Positive Reinforcement Learning**: It is characterized as a function, which happens on account of explicit conduct. It builds the quality and the recurrence of the conduct and effects emphatically on the activity taken by the specialist. This sort of Reinforcement encourages you to expand execution and support change for a more broadened period. Be that as it may, an excessive amount of Reinforcement may prompt over-enhancement of state, which can influence the outcomes.
    - Ex: Resource Management, Traffic light control, robotics, etc…

  - **Negative Reinforcement Learning:** Negative Reinforcement is characterized as fortifying of conduct that happens in light of a negative condition which ought to have halted or maintained a strategic distance from. It causes you to characterize the base remain of execution. Notwithstanding, the disadvantage of this strategy is that it gives enough to get together the base conduct.
    - Ex: Resource Management, Traffic light control, robotics, etc…

21.3.1.1 A Tour of Machine Learning Algorithms

While crunching the information to demonstrate business choices, you're mostly used supervised and unsupervised learning algorithms.

Algorithms according to similarity:

Algorithms are often gathered by utilizing comparability in expressions of their component (how they work). For example, tree-based strategies, and neural n/w enlivened techniques. During this segment, we list a large number of the supported AI calculations assembled the manner in which we expect is that the most instinctive. The rundown isn't comprehensive in either the gatherings or the calculations [28,29].

21.3.1.1.1 Regression Algorithms

Regression cares with demonstrating the association between factors that are iteratively refined utilizing a proportion of mistake inside the forecasts made by the model. Figure 2.1.6 explains about various regression algorithms.

21.3.1.1.2 Instance-Based Algorithms

An instance-based learning model could likewise be a decision issue with occurrences or tests of in-structing information that are regarded significant or needed to the model. Such techniques regularly

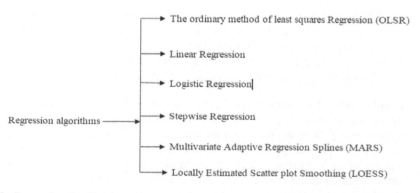

FIGURE 21.6 Regression algorithms.

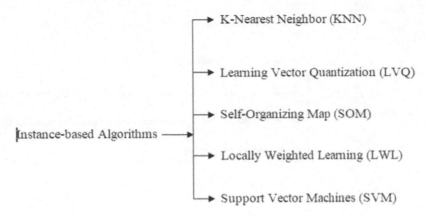

FIGURE 21.7 Instance-based algorithms.

develop an information base of model information and contrast new information with the information base utilizing a comparability measure in order to search out the least difficult match and make a forecast. Figure 21.7 explains about various instance-based algorithms.

21.3.1.1.3 Regularization Algorithms

An expansion made to an alternate strategy (normally relapse strategies) that punishes models upheld their intricacy, preferring less difficult models that likewise are better at summing up. Figure 21.8 explains about various Regularization algorithms [29].

21.3.1.1.4 Decision Tree Algorithms

Decision tree strategies gather a mannequin of decisions made upheld legitimate estimations of properties inside the information. Decision fork in tree structures till an expectation decision is molded for a given record [29]. Decision timber is taught on records for grouping and regression issues. Decision trees are routinely snappy and right and a tremendous courtesy in AI [23,24]. Figure 21.9 explains various Decision Tree algorithms.

21.3.1.1.5 Bayesian Algorithms

Bayesian procedures are these that expressly notices Bayes' Theorem for issues, for example, grouping and regression [30]. Figure 21.10 explains about various Bayesian algorithms.

21.3.1.1.6 Clustering Algorithms

Clustering is the same as regression and it explains about type of problem and method of category. These techniques are usually maintained by means of modeling algorithms like centroid-based and hierarchical [30]. Figure 21.11 explains various clustering algorithms.

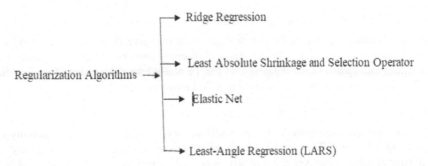

FIGURE 21.8 Regularization algorithms.

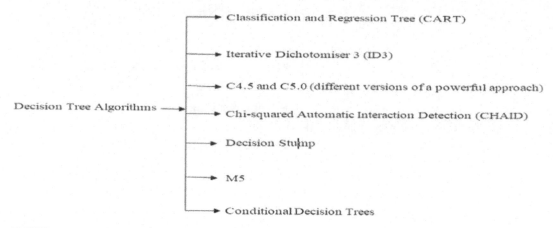

FIGURE 21.9   Decision tree algorithms.

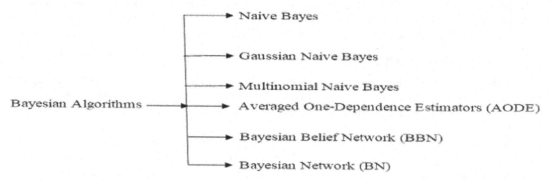

FIGURE 21.10   Bayesian algorithms.

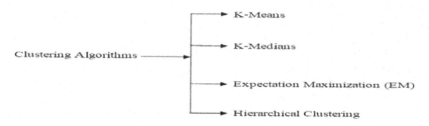

FIGURE 21.11   Clustering algorithms.

21.3.1.1.7 Association Rule Learning Algorithms

Association rule learning techniques extract strategies that fine give clarification to found connections between factors in the information. These rules can discover the crucial and financially valuable relationship in giant multidimensional datasets that can be abused with the guide of an association [30]. Figure 21.12 explains about various Association Rule Learning algorithms.

21.3.1.1.8 Artificial Neural Network Algorithms

Artificial Neural Networks are models that are motivated by the structure and additionally capacity of natural neural organizations. They are a class of example coordinating that are generally utilized for relapse and arrangement issues yet are actually a colossal subfield included many calculations and varieties for all way of issue types. Note that I have isolated out Deep Learning from neural

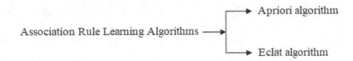

FIGURE 21.12 Association rule learning algorithms.

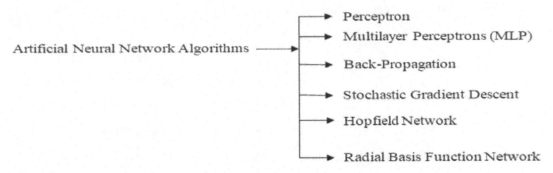

FIGURE 21.13 Artificial neural network algorithms.

organizations due to the gigantic development and ubiquity in the field [30]. Figure 21.13 explains various artificial neural network algorithms [25,26].

Deep Learning Algorithms according to similarity:

21.3.1.1.9 Deep Learning Algorithms

Deep Learning techniques are an advanced update to Artificial Neural Networks that misuse bountiful modest calculation. They are worried about building a lot bigger and more perplexing neural organizations and, as remarked on above, numerous techniques are worried about enormous datasets of named simple information, for example, picture, text, sound, and video [30]. Figure 21.14 explains about various Deep learning algorithms.

21.3.1.1.10 Dimensionality Reduction Algorithms

Like clustering techniques, dimensionality reduction looks for and misuses the intrinsic structure in the information, yet for this situation in an unaided way or to sum up or depict information utilizing fewer data. This can be valuable to envision dimensional information or to rearrange information which would then be able to be utilized in a managed learning strategy. A huge number of these techniques can be adjusted for use in grouping and relapse [30]. Figure 21.15 explains various Dimensionality Reduction algorithms.

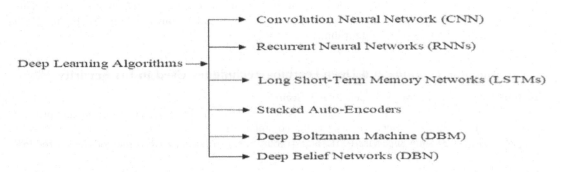

FIGURE 21.14 Deep learning algorithms.

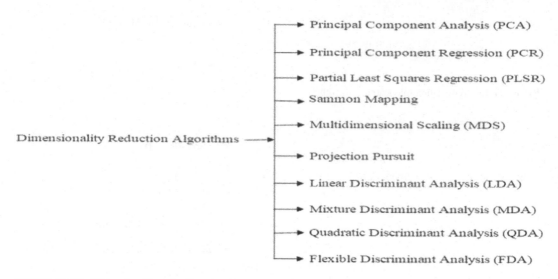

FIGURE 21.15 Dimensionality reduction algorithms.

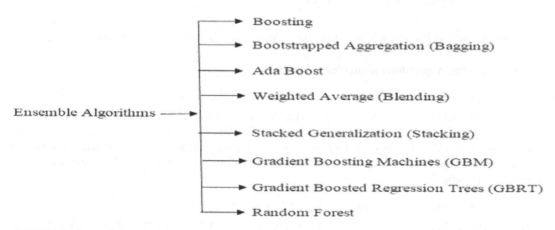

FIGURE 21.16 Ensemble algorithms.

21.3.1.1.11 Ensemble Algorithms

Ensemble strategies are models made out of various more vulnerable models that are freely prepared and whose forecasts are joined somehow or another to make the general expectation. Much exertion is placed into what kinds of powerless students to consolidate and the manners by which to join them. This is an exceptionally amazing class of methods and as such is extremely mainstream [26,30]. Figure 21.16 explains about various Ensemble algorithms.

21.3.2 Machine Learning and Deep Learning Techniques Used in IoT Security

Machine Learning Techniques Used in IoT Security

This section briefs about various ML algorithms that specialize in the underlying security and privacy problems in IoT networks. Here we discuss the common ML algorithms (i.e., 1) supervised ML, 2) unsupervised ML, 3) semi supervised ML, and 4) reinforcement learning (RL) methods) used for IoT security [24,25].

21.3.2.1 Supervised Machine Learning

In this segment we discuss about various supervised learning approaches used for IoT security.

21.3.2.1.1 Decision Trees

In Decision trees, the information is constantly divided as per the particular boundary. The Decision tree can be clarified by utilizing two certifiable articles one is a hub and another is leaves. The leaves are the ultimate results and the hubs are part focuses as indicated by the condition. Choice trees are on a very basic level separated by orchestrating the examples as indicated by their component esteems. Every hub in a tree speaks to a component, and each branch means a worth that the hub can have in an example to be grouped. Countless strategies are utilized to distinguish the highlights that are ideal to part the preparation information that incorporates data gain and Gini record esteem [27].

The vast majority of the decision tree-based methodologies comprise two sorts of cycles one is enlistment and another is a derivation. In enlistment measure, at first, the choice tree is developed with vacant hubs and leaves. In the induction cycle after the development of trees, the new examples with a bunch of highlights and obscure classes are characterized during the preparation cycle. In Decision tree-based methodologies there are two sorts of pruning strategies that are utilized they are pre pruning and post pruning. These strategies are applied for different reasons right off the bat, to decrease the size of the tree. Furthermore, to change the state search space. Thirdly, to improve the calculation speed. Fourth, to lessen the information includes eliminating repetitive highlights through the inquiry cycle. At last, to change over the structure of the tree into a set of rules. The primary weakness of choice tree-based methodologies is the enormous space expected to build the tree, it is exceptionally straightforward if less choice trees are included, the computational intricacy is high if a huge number of choice trees are included, and technique is perplexing in certain applications. A Decision tree is going about as one significant classifier alongside different classifiers to give security and to distinguish interruptions in applications, thusly to identify the conduct of forswearing of administration assaults [27].

21.3.2.1.2 Support Vector Machines (SVMs)

SVMs are used for partitioning a hyper plane in to at any rate two classes and SVMs are exceptional for their theory limit and expressly sensible for datasets with more number of highlight credits however less number of tests focuses. Theoretically, SVMs were set up from measurable learning, for that it uses various possible hyper planes. Hyper planes are having choice limits utilizing that it is extremely simple to group the information focuses. Data centers falling around either side of the hyper plane can be credited to different classes. The points of interest of help vector machines are It is amazing in high dimensional spaces, It is incredible in circumstances where the amount of information highlights is more significant than the amount of tests, It uses a subset of planning centers in the choice capacity (called maintain vectors), so it is memory viable. The Disadvantages of Support vector machines are It doesn't perform well when we have gigantic informational collection, it requires higher preparing time, It doesn't perform very well, when the informational index is having more clamor all things considered the objective classes are covering, one more disservice is it utilizes cross overlay approval to appraise likelihood it is pricey. Backing vector machines are broadly utilized in numerous security applications like identification of interruption, location of malware, and so on... The examination gives the data that Support vector machines performed very much contrasted with other AI calculations like innocent bayes, arbitrary woodland, and choice trees. In late investigation it gives the data that help vector machines are utilized as an instrument to give the security [26,27].

21.3.2.1.3 Bayesian Theorem-Based Algorithms

These algorithms are based on past data and find the likelihood of hypothesis. For example, a DoS assault location is related to network traffic data. Thusly, contrasted and surveying network traffic without information on past organization traffic, utilizing Bayes' hypothesis can assess the likelihood of organization traffic being an assault (related or not) by utilizing past traffic data. NB has been utilized for network interruption identification and oddity recognition. The principle favorable circumstances of NB classifiers incorporate effortlessness, the simplicity of usage, appropriateness to paired and multiclass characterization, low preparing test prerequisite, and power to insignificant highlights (The highlights are safeguarded autonomously.) [20,21].

21.3.2.1.4 K-Nearest Neighbor (KNN)

KNN is a nonparametric procedure. KNN classifiers routinely use the Euclidean separation as the measurement, and the KNN classifier sorts the new model dependent on the votes of the picked number of its nearest neighbors'. KNN is predominantly used to recognize two sorts of assaults in IoT gadgets they are U2R and R2L. It utilizes two-level arrangement model to upgrade effectiveness and it shows great outcomes for both the assaults. It displays great outcomes in location of interruptions in IoT systems [22].

21.3.2.1.5 Random Forest (RF)

In a Random forest, many numbers of choice trees are developed and they are joined to obtain a decent forecast model to improve the general consequences of calculation. In RF from the number of developed choice trees classes are distinguished and votes will be given to every single class, the class which is having most elevated votes will be chosen as conclusive arrangement yield. In RF to give votes in favor of classes set of rules are planned to take care of the preparation information in to the organization and these arrangement of rules are utilized group the new input. RF is all the more impressive against over fitting, it sidesteps include choice and it requires just not many boundaries. Generally, RF calculations are utilized for the location of abnormalities and interruptions in the framework. Progressively arrangement RF calculations give better outcomes over other ML grouping calculations if the restricted capabilities were utilized and it will keep away from computational overhead. It is best appropriate to accurately recognize unapproved IoT devices [22,23].

21.3.2.1.6 Association Rule (AR) Algorithms

Association rule techniques are utilized to look at the relationship among known factors from the preparation informational index to distinguish the obscure variable and to find the connections among the factors and accordingly it used to develop a model. Utilizing this model we can anticipate the new example classes. It utilizes mixes of factors that every now and again exist in assaults. This calculation shows great execution in the identification of interruptions. Ordinarily, we can't utilize these calculations alone in IoT security however the mix of these calculations with different calculations will give compelling answers for IoT security. The primary disservices of these calculations are right off the bat, time intricacy is more; besides, these calculations are not compelling in all the circumstances; at last, these calculations are relying on straightforward presumptions among factors, due to this explanation at times like security applications these suspicions are invariant and in applicable [22,23].

21.3.2.1.7 Ensemble Learning (EL)

It is one of the best classification algorithms among all ML algorithms to improve performance of a system. To obtain the final result these algorithms combine both heterogeneous and homogeneous multi classifiers. Alone these algorithms are also not effective in the context of performance but if we combine these algorithms with multi class classifiers will give good results. According to the problem it uses several learning methods and it will adapt the problem easily and find the solution to the problem. However the time complexity of these algorithms is more rather than single classifier because it comprises of various multi class classifiers. It is best suitable for detection of anomalies and intrusions and also used detect anomalies in online IoT environment [23].

21.3.2.2 Unsupervised ML

In this segment we discuss about various unsupervised learning techniques.

21.3.2.2.1 K-Means Clustering

It is an Iterative algorithm and it divides the dataset into different set of partitions called clusters they are also called it as non-overlapping partitions. It is used to provide secure to wireless sensor networks to detect intrusions [23,24]. These algorithms are used mainly to provide security while exchange of data happens in the network.

21.3.2.2.2 Principal Component Analysis (PCA)

PCA might be a component decrease method which will be applied to improve an outsized arrangement of factors into a diminished set that jelly the majority of the information spoke to inside the huge set. This framework changes over assortment of likely related highlights into a decreased number of un-correlated highlights, which are called head segments. In this manner, the most working guideline of PCA are frequently used for highlight determination to see continuous interruption recognition for IoT frameworks; The creator revealed that the combination of PCA with these classifiers gave a period and registering productive framework which will be used progressively in IoT conditions. Figure 21.17 shows Potential ML techniques for making sure about IoT systems [25].

Classification Type	ML Method	Functional principle of algorithm	Role of algorithm in IoT based cloud systems Security
Supervised Learning	Decision trees	Decision trees learn from data to approximate a sine curve with a set of if-then-else decision rules. The deeper the tree, the more complex the decision rules and the fitter the model.	Intrusion Detection, To detect Distributed Denial of Service attacks, To detect Wormhole attacks, Detecting suspicious traffic sources.
	Support Vector Machines	The SVM accomplishes the classification task by constructing, in a higher dimensional space, the hyper plane that optimally separates the data into two categories.	Detection of attacks, mitigation of attacks, To detect Distributed Denial of Service attacks, Analysis of Malware.
	Naïve Bayes classifier	A Naïve Bayes classifier assumes that the presence of a particular feature in a class is unrelated to the presence of any other feature.	Anomaly and intrusion detection, Detection of Phishing attack, To detect spam,
	K-Nearest neighbor classifier	KNN works on a principle assuming every data point falling in near to each other is falling in the same class. That means similar things are near to each other.	Detection of attacks, mitigation of attacks, To detect Distributed Denial of Service attacks
	Random Forest	Random Forests are an ensemble learning method (also thought of as a form of nearest neighbor predictor) for classification and regression that construct a number of decision trees at training time and outputting the class that is the mode of the classes output by individual trees	To detect Distributed Denial of Service attacks, Analysis of Malware, To detect unauthorized IoT Devices.
	Association rule algorithms	Association rule learning is a rule-based machine learning method for discovering interesting relations between variables in large databases. It is intended to identify strong rules discovered in databases using some measures of interestingness	Intrusion Detection
	Ensemble Learning	Ensemble algorithms are used to combine the predictions of several base estimators built with a given learning algorithm in order to improve robustness over a single estimator.	Intrusion Detection, Anomaly detection, detection of malware.
Unsupervised Learning	K-Means Clustering algorithm	It uses Expectation-maximization principle; The E-step is assigning the data points to the closest cluster. The M-step is computing the centroid of each cluster.	Anomaly and Intrusion detection, securing WSNs by detecting intrusions, Sybil detection in industrial WSNs, preserve private data anonymisation in an IoT system.
	Principle component Analysis	Principal Component Analysis, or PCA, is a dimensionality-reduction method that is often used to reduce the dimensionality of large data sets, by transforming a large set of variables into a smaller one that still contains most of the information in the large set.	real-time intrusion detection for IoT systems, detection of malware

FIGURE 21.17 Role of ML methods in IoT security.

21.3.2.3 Deep Learning (DL) Methods for IoT Security

As of late, the chief fascinating exploration point is that the uses of DL to IoT frameworks. The most essential favorable position of DL over conventional ML is its boss exhibition in enormous datasets. A few IoT frameworks produce an outsized measure of information; consequently, DL techniques are reasonable for such frameworks. DL is regularly wont to remove complex portrayals from information consequently. It utilizes one extraordinary convention i.e. Deep connecting wont to allow the IoT based frameworks and their applications cooperate with one another without the contribution of human [26]. For instance, the IoT gadgets during a shrewd home can naturally interface to make a thoroughly brilliant home. DL techniques give a computational design that blends a few handling levels (layers) to discover information portrayals with a few degrees of deliberation. Contrasted and customary ML techniques, DL strategies have significantly improved cutting edge applications. DL might be a ML sub-field that uses a few non-direct preparing layers for discriminative or generative component reflection and change for design examination. The fundamental hidden idea driving the DL is enlivened by human cerebrum and neurons for signal processing [27]. There are two models for DL techniques: one is convolution neural organizations and the other is intermittent neural organizations.

21.3.2.3.1 Convolution Neural Networks (CNNs)

CNN's were acquainted with diminishing the information boundaries utilized in a conventional artificial neural organization (ANN). The information boundaries are decreased by using three ideas, to be a specific, meager collaboration, boundary sharing, and equivariant portrayal [28]. The advancement of CNNs is primarily coordinated towards image acknowledgment progression. Appropriately, CNNs have become broadly utilized, prompting creating fruitful and compelling models for picture arrangement and acknowledgment with the utilization of huge public picture sources, for example, Image Net. Moreover, CNN shows power in various other applications. With the utilization of CNN, the huge highlights identified with malware recognition are found out naturally from the crude information, consequently killing the requirement for manual element designing [27,28]. A CNN can break cryptographic executions effectively.

21.3.2.3.2 Recurrent Neural Networks (RNNs)

A RNN could likewise be a significant class of DL calculations. RNNs were proposed to deal with successive information. In a few applications, anticipating this yield depends on the investigation of the relationship from a few past examples. Accordingly, the yield of the neural organization relies upon this and past sources of info. In such a gathering, a feed-forward NN is wrong in light of the fact that the relationship between the info and yield layers is protected with no reliance. Subsequently, utilizing intermittent associations can improve neural organizations and uncover significant personal conduct standards. The premier disadvantage of RNNs, nonetheless, is that the trouble of evaporating or detonating slopes [28]. RNNs and their variations have accomplished incredible execution in numerous applications with successive information, similar to MT and discourse acknowledgment. Besides, RNNs are frequently utilized for IoT security. IoT gadgets produce a lot of successive information from a few sources, similar to arrange traffic streams, which are among the critical highlights for distinguishing a few potential organization assaults. For instance, a past report talked about the achievability of a RNN in analyzing network traffic conduct to identify expected assaults (noxious conduct) and affirmed the value of the RNN in arranging network traffic for exact pernicious conduct recognition.

21.3.2.4 Unsupervised DL (Generative Learning)

In this segment, we discuss various Generative Learning algorithms.

21.3.2.4.1 Deep Auto Encoders (AEs)

A deep AE is a solo learning neural organization prepared to replicate its contribution to its yield. An AE has a shrouded layer h, which characterizes a code used to speak to the information. An AE neural organization is separated into two sections: the encoder work h = f(x) and the decoder work, which endeavors to repeat the info r = g(h). The encoder gets the info and converts it into a deliberation, which is commonly named a code. Thusly, the decoder obtains the developed code, which was at first delivered to speak to the contribution, to revamp the first information. The preparation cycle in AEs ought to be cultivated with a base recreation blunder. Be that as it may, AEs can't learn to repeat the info consummately. AEs are likewise limited on the grounds that they can deliver an inexact duplicate, in particular, simply replicating the sources of info that are like the preparation information. The model is needed to organize which qualities of the sources of info ought to be duplicated; in this manner, it oftentimes learns helpful attributes of the information. AEs are conceivably significant for the extraction of information [27,28]. AEs can be effectively utilized for portrayal figuring out how to learn highlights (instead of the physically designed highlights utilized in conventional ML) and lessen dimensionality with no earlier information. AEs, in any case, devour high computational time. Despite the fact that AEs can adequately figure out how to catch the qualities of the preparation information, they may just confound the learning cycle instead of speaking to the qualities of the dataset if the preparation dataset isn't illustrative of the testing dataset. The DBN learning calculation was prepared to identify vindictive code.

21.3.2.4.2 Restricted Boltzmann Machines (RBMs)

A RBM could even be a totally undirected model with no connection between any two hubs inside a similar layer. RBMs contain two kinds of layers: obvious and concealed layers. The noticeable layer holds the known info, while the shrouded layer comprises of various layers that incorporate the inactive factors. RBMs progressively comprehend highlights from information, and hence the highlights caught inside the underlying layer are utilized as inert factors inside the following layer. The test is that the consistent development of peculiarity conducts with time. Accordingly, the model ought to be powerfully adjusted to identify any new very assaults and summed up to recognize the abnormality in a few organization conditions. To disentangle these difficulties, the specialists proposed a learning model that is upheld a discriminative RBM; to identify network oddity during a semi-directed design even with fragmented preparing information. The highlights portrayal capacity of 1 RBM is limited. Notwithstanding, RBM is regularly considerably applied by stacking at least two RBMs to make a DBN [29].

21.3.2.4.3 Deep Belief Networks (DBNs)

DBNs are generative techniques. A DBN comprises stacked RBMs that execute layer-wise and preparing to achieve vigorous execution in an unaided climate. In the pre-preparing stage, the introductory highlights are prepared through a voracious layer-wise solo methodology, while a soft max layer is applied in the adjusting stage to the top layer to calibrate the highlights with regard to the marked examples. DBNs are successfully utilized in detection of malware and it best suitable for feature representation and it is shows significant results in the detection malicious attacks in IoT devices.

21.3.2.5 Semi-Supervised or Hybrid DL

In this segment we discussed about various hybrids deep learning algorithms.

21.3.2.5.1 Generative Adversarial Networks (GANs)

GANs are promising DL systems. It trains two models at the same time utilizing the system, in particular generative and discriminative models, by means of an ill-disposed cycle. The generative model learns the information dispersion and creates information tests [27,28]. GANs are as of late executed in IoT security. For instance, the examination for making sure about the internet of IoT frameworks, and accordingly the design includes preparing DL calculations to group the framework conduct as typical or strange. since they'll learn distinctive assault situations to ask tests nearly kind of a zero-day assault and give calculations a gaggle of tests past the predominant assaults. GANs can produce tests before can completely obvious DBNs on the grounds that the past isn't needed to ask various passages inside the examples successively. Be that as it may, GAN preparation is insecure and troublesome. Figuring out how to encourage discrete information, similar to the message, by utilizing a GAN could likewise be a difficult assignment.

Classification Type	DL Method	Functional principle of algorithm	Role of algorithm in IoT based cloud systems Security
Supervised Learning	Convolution neural networks	A Convolution neural network (CNN) is a neural network that has one or more convolution layers and are used mainly for image processing, classification, segmentation and also for other auto correlated data	Malware detection, can break cryptographic implementations, automatically learn features from IoT security data, construct end to end model for IoT security.
	Recurrent neural networks	In this algorithm it remembers its input, due to an internal memory, which makes it perfectly suited for machine learning problems that involve sequential data	Authentication, For analysis of malware, for detecting malicious behavior in networks, Detecting time series based threats in IoT devices.
	Auto encoders	Auto encoders (AE) are a neural network that aims to copy their inputs to their outputs. They work by compressing the input into a latent-space representation, and then reconstructing the output from this representation.	Detection of malware
	Restricted Boltzmann machines	Boltzmann machines are stochastic and generative neural networks capable of learning internal representations and are able to represent and (given sufficient time) solve difficult combinatory problems.	To detect network anomalies
	Deep belief networks	Deep belief networks are algorithms that use probabilities and unsupervised learning to produce outputs. They are composed of binary latent variables, and they contain both undirected layers and directed layers.	To detect malicious attacks
Unsupervised Learning	Generative adversarial networks	Unlike auto encoders, generative models can create new meaningful outputs given arbitrary encodings.	For securing the cyberspace of IoT systems.
	Ensemble of DL networks	Ensemble learning combines the predictions from multiple neural network models to reduce the variance of predictions and reduce generalization error.	To improve the accuracy and performance of Distributed environment
	Deep Reinforcement Learning	Deep reinforcement learning is a category of machine learning and artificial intelligence where intelligent machines can learn from their actions similar to the way humans learn from experience	To detect malware, Denial of service attacks, Distributed denial service attacks, brute force attack.

FIGURE 21.18 DL methods for IoT security.

21.3.2.5.2 *Ensemble of DL Networks (EDLNs)*

EDLNs are frequently refined by combining generative, discriminative or half breed models. EDLNs are frequently wont to deal with complex issues with vulnerabilities and high-dimensional highlights. The investigation showed that our semi-directed for interruption location approach are prepared to accomplish more precise assault recognition rate contrasted with the prior work. In spite of the fact that EDLNs have made striking progress in numerous applications, similar to act acknowledgment, EDLNs application in IoT security needs further examination, especially the probability of actualizing light homogenous or heterogeneous classifiers during a disseminated climate to fortify the exactness and execution of an IoT security framework and illuminate difficulties identified with computational complexity [29].

21.3.2.5.3 *Deep Reinforcement Learning (DRL)*

Reinforcement Learning (RL) has created to turn into an effective strategy that allows a learning specialist to direct its approach and infer an ideal arrangement by means of experimentation. Profound Reinforcement Learning (DRL) strategies like profound Q-organization (DQN) are acquainted as a strong option with disentangle the high-dimensional issues and build up adaptability and offloading productivity in different portable edge processing based applications. One among the ongoing fruitful RL strategies is that the profound Q organization. Augmentations of profound Q networks are recommended, including twofold Q-learning, ceaseless control with profound RL, and organized experience replay. In another exploration bearing, DLR has been applied to make sure about digital protection; creators have examined a few DRL approaches to set up for network safety, including DRL-based security techniques for digital actual frameworks, self-sufficient interruption identification methods, and multi-specialist DRL-based hypothesis of games reenactments for safeguard methodologies against digital assaults. Investigating these methodologies inside the IoT eco-framework holds likely future course. Figure 21.18 presents the Functional rule and part of every DL calculation in IoT security [29,31].

21.4 Conclusion

Here, I examined rudiments of Internet of Things devices and the function of distributed computing in IoT climate and after that; I present essential AI and ML learning algorithms. The rundown of all AI and ML algorithms clarified the function of AI and M/c learning calculations in the IoT security. These calculations assume a significant part in the field of security for IoT based cloud frameworks. In this chapter, gave the information regarding the IoT security and how the machine learning and deep learning algorithms are used to identify the different attacks like Distributed Denial of service attack, Detecting malware, Detection of Malicious software, Detection malicious attacks, provide security to IoT devices in IoT based cloud systems. In future chapters will concentrate on attacks that lead to more damage to IoT devices.

REFERENCES

[1] Aaron Chichioco, "What-is-the-role-of-cloud-computing-in-IoT," https://blog.resellerclub.com/what-is-the-role-of-cloud-computing-in-iot/.
[2] K. Sravanthi, Kavitha Agarwal, A. K. Tyagi, "Beyond things: A systematic study of internet of everything," In: Abraham A., Panda M., Pradhan S., Garcia-Hernandez L., Ma K. (eds) Innovations in Bio-Inspired Computing and Applications. IBICA 2019. Advances in Intelligent Systems and Computing, vol. 1180. Springer, Cham. https://doi.org/10.1007/978-3-030-49339-4_23, 2020.
[3] D. Evans, "The internet of things: How the next evolution of the internet is changing everything," CISCO White Paper, vol. 1, no. 2011, pp. 1–11, 2011.
[4] S. Ray, Y. Jin, and A. Ray Chowdhury, "The changing computing paradigm with internet of things: A tutorial introduction," IEEE Design & Test, vol. 33, no. 2, pp. 76–96, 2016.
[5] A. R. Sfar, E. Natalizio, Y. Challal, and Z. Chtourou, "A roadmap for security challenges in the Internet of things," Digital Communications and Networks, vol. 4, no. 2018, 118–137, 2018.
[6] M. K. Saggi and S. Jain, "A survey towards an integration of big data analytics to big insights for value-creation," Information Processing & Management, 54(5) DOI: 10.1016/j.ipm.2018.01.010, 2018.
[7] D.Li, Z. Cai, L.Deng, X. Yao, and H. H. Wang, "Information security model of block chain based on intrusion sensing in the IoT environment."Cluster Comput, vol. 22, pp. 451–468. doi: 10.1007/s10586-018-2516-1.
[8] F. Restuccia, S. D. Oro, and T. Melodia, "Securing the internet of things in the age of machine learning and software-defined networking," IEEE Internet of Things Journal, vol. 5, pp. 4829–4842, Dec. 2018.
[9] A. Thakkar and R. Lohiya, "A review on machine learning and deep learning perspectives of IDS for IoT: Recent updates, security issues, and challenges." Arch Computat Methods Eng, vol. 4, pp. 234-237, 2020. https://doi.org/10.1007/s11831-020-09496-0.

[10] T. Hothorn. "CRAN task view: Machine learning and statistical learning," Version:2017-01-06 URL:https://CRAN.R-project.org/view=MachineLearning, 2019.

[11] R. Bandi and G. Anitha, "Machine learning based Oozie workflow for hive query schedule mechanism," 2018 International Conference on Smart Systems and Inventive Technology (ICSSIT), Tirunelveli, India, 2018, pp. 513–517, doi: 10.1109/ICSSIT.2018.8748711.

[12] R. Bandi and J. Amudhavel, "Object recognition using Keras with backend tensor flow." International Journal of Engineering and Technology (UAE), 7, no. 3.6, pp. 229–233, 2018.

[13] Raswitha Bandi, J. Amudhavel, and R. Karthik, "Machine learning with PySpark–Review," Indonesian Journal of Electrical Engineering and Computer Science, vol. 12, no. 1, pp. 102–106, 2018.

[14] K. A. da Costa, J. P. Papa, C. O. Lisboa, R. Munoz, and V. H. C. de Albuquerque, "Internet of things: A survey on machine learning-based intrusion detection approaches," Computer Networks, vol. 151, pp. 147–157, 2019.

[15] J. Hou, L. Qu, and W. Shi, "A survey on internet of things security from data perspectives," Computer Networks, vol. 148, pp. 295–306, 2019.

[16] M. binti Mohamad Noor and W. H. Hassan, "Current research on internet of things (IoT) security: A survey," Computer Networks, vol. 148, pp. 283–294, 2019.

[17] S. Zhang, L. Yao, A. Sun, and Y. Tay, "Deep learning based recommender system: A survey and new perspectives," ACM Computing Surveys vol. 52, no. 1, p. 5, 2019.

[18] S.-G. Leem, I.-C. Yoo, and D. Yook, "Multitask learning of deep neural network-based keyword spotting for IoT devices," IEEE Trans. Consum. Electron., vol. 65, no. 2, pp. 188–194, May 2019.

[19] W. Z. Khan, M. Y. Aalsalem, and M. K. Khan, "Communal acts of IoT consumers: A potential threat to security and privacy," IEEE Trans. Consum. Electron., vol. 65, no. 1, pp. 64–72, Feb. 2019.

[20] H. H. Pajouh, R. Javidan, R. Khayami, D. Ali, and K.-K. R. Choo, "A two-layer dimension reduction and two-tier classification model for anomaly-based intrusion detection in IoT backbone networks," IEEE Trans. Emerg. Topics Comput., vol. 7, no. 2, pp. 314–323, Apr–Jun 2019.

[21] G. Dulac-Arnold, D. Mankowitz, and T. Hester, "Challenges of real-world reinforcement learning," 2019. [Online]. Available: arXiv: 1904.12901.

[22] P. Asghari, A. M. Rahmani, and H. H. S. Javadi, "Internet of things applications: A systematic review," Computer Networks, vol. 148, pp. 241–261, 2019.

[23] L. Xiao, X. Wan, and Z. Han, "Phy-layer authentication with multiple landmarks with reduced overhead," IEEE Transactions on Wireless Communications, vol. 17, pp. 1676–1687, Mar. 2018.

[24] D. Li, Z. Cai, L. Deng, X. Yao, and H. H. Wang, "Information security model of block chain based on intrusion sensing in the iot environment," Cluster Computing, Mar. Special Issue 1, 2018.

[25] J. F. Colom, D. Gil, H. Mora, B. Volckaert, and A. M. Jimeno, "Scheduling framework for distributed intrusion detection systems over heterogeneous network architectures," Journal of Network and Computer Applications, vol. 108, pp. 76 –86, 2018.

[26] I. Makhdoom, M. Abolhasan, J. Lipman, R. P. Liu, and W. Ni, "Anatomy of threats to the internet of things," IEEE Communications Surveys Tutorials, vol. 21, no. 2, pp. 1636–1675, 2018.

[27] D. E. Kouicem, A. Bouabdallah, and H. Lakhlef, "Internet of things security: A top-down survey," Computer Networks, vol. 141, pp. 199–221, Aug. 2018.

[28] I. Yaqoob et al., "The rise of ransom ware and emerging security challenges in the Internet of Things," Computer Networks, vol. 129, pp. 444–458, Dec. 2017.

[29] L. Xiao, X. Wan, X. Lu, Y. Zhang, and D. Wu, "IoT security techniques based on machine learning," 2018. [Online]. Available: arXiv:1801.06275.

[30] Jason Brownlee, "A tour of Machine learning algorithms," https://machinelearningmastery.com/a-tour-of-machine-learning-algorithms/.

[31] A. Oussous, F.-Z. Benjelloun, A. A. Lahcen, and S. Belfkih, "Big data technologies: A survey," J. King Saud Univ. Comput. Inf. Sci., vol. 30, no. 4, pp. 431–448, 2018.

Section V

Future Research Opportunities towards Data Science and Data Analytics

22

Dialect Identification of the Bengali Language

Elizabeth Behrman, Arijit Santra, Siladitya Sarkar, Prantik Roy, Ritika Yadav, Soumi Dutta and Arijit Ghosal

CONTENTS

22.1 Introduction

India is a vast country with huge diversity of languages. People of India speak in many languages. As per the constitution of India, there are many languages in India. There are also several languages in India which are being spoken by different tribes and they are not recognized. Even it is also observed that several languages of India do not have any written format, they are only vocal. Every language pronunciation styles vary from one geographic region to other geographic region, though people of these two geographic positions are speaking in the same language. This type of variation within the same language is termed a dialect of that language. A single language will have many dialects as people speaking in a particular language are not restricted within a geographical boundary, rather they are spread in different geographic regions.

Classification of Indian languages is a very fascinating investigation area because of the colossal assortment of Indian languages. As there are lots of languages in India, as well as lots of regional variation in India, all the languages of India contain several dialects within it. Dialect is not a new language, rather it is a sub-language. Dialect is nothing but a distinguishable form within a single language which is totally specific to a geographic region or social group. Geographic region creates a deep impact on languages because variations of geographic regions will create cultural variations also which will generate a dialect. Pronunciation style of a language gets changed according to geographic region. The way people of West Bengal speaks Bengali, people of Tripura of Jharkhand or any other geographic localities do not speak in the same way—pronunciation style is changed although they are speaking the same language—Bengali. Though dialect is mainly a pronunciation variation of a language, still it is found that the dialect of a language is deviated from the main language in such a way that sometimes it becomes very tough to understand that it is a variation of that language and not a new separate language.

Dialect identification plays an important role in automated speaker recognition. If the system is well trained with different dialects of languages, performance of the system will increase. More types of dialects will be considered in the dataset, the versatility of dataset will increase, and as a result system performance will increase. Basically dialect identification task will support the language identification task.

Among the languages in India, Bengali language is one of the largest languages in the world also. Bengali is also spoken in Bangladesh which is a neighboring country of India. Bengali is the national language of Bangladesh also. Bengali is seventh most spoken language in the world [1, 2]; 3.4% [1] of the population of the whole world speaks Bengali. In India, Bengali is largely spoken by Bengalis residing in West Bengal, Tripura, Jharkhand, Chhattisgarh along with other states also. Even in Andaman and Nicobar Islands, Bengali is widely spoken. Moreover national anthems of both Bangladesh and India are sung in Bengali which was written by the great Bengali Nobel laureate Rabindranath Tagore. Even the national song of India is also written and sung in Bengali, which was written Bankim Chandra Chatterjee. Among the Indian languages, Bengali is globally acknowledged. Also, Bengali language itself is a famous research domain. Lots of research work is going on in Bengali language. But when the question of dialect identification comes, unfortunately it is found that most of the works were done either on European languages or other Indian languages like Hindi, etc. Very few works are identified on Bengali dialects which were based on Bengali dialects of Bangladesh. Surprisingly research works on Bengali language dialects of India remains unexplored for unknown reasons. These have motivated to identify dialects of Bengali language as a whole.

In Bengali language, there exists lots of dialects but among them three major dialects are considered in this work—Bangali (pronounced as "Bongaali"), Manbhumi (Jharkhandi), and Rarhi. These dialects are major because lots of people who speak in Bengali follow this dialect as well as they are prominent. These dialects are being spoken in western, southern, and eastern regions of West Bengal.

In this work, previous efforts related to dialect identification and its related exertions are discussed in Section 22.2. Proposed approach for dialect identification of Bengali language is placed in Section 22.3. Section 22.4 describes the experimental results along with the comparative analysis with other work. Section 22.5 concludes the whole work.

22.2 Previous Works

Automatic Dialect Identification is a topic which has attracted many researchers in the field of speech signal processing. Previously researchers have put their endeavors with different kinds of facets for working with different dialects of a language. Past work reveals that less work has been carried out for dialect identification of Bengali language, whereas Bengali is the seventh-largest spoken language in the world [1,2].

Torres-Carrasquillo et al. [3] have used Gaussian Mixture Models to identify the dialects. They proposed the model with the help of shifted-delta-cepstral features and yield an average of 30% and 13% equal error rate for the dialects in the Miami and Call Friend corpus, respectively. Bangla Phoneme production and perception is discussed by Hossain et al. [4] for computational approaches. They have proposed speech production mechanism along with the linguistics classification on Bangla phoneme processing and analysis of Bangla speech. The dominance of region of origin and the usefulness of experience in case of dialect identification is discussed by Baker et al. [5]. They have said that the dialect can be identified more accurately if the native has some amount of experience on that particular language.

Automatic Speech Recognition work for Bangla digits has been carried by Muhammad et al. [6]. They have used Mel Frequency Cepstral Coefficients (MFCCs) based features and Hidden Markov Model for classification purpose. Das Mandal et al. [7] defined the prosodic units of Bangla with the help of F_0 contour analysis using the command-response model. The role of neural network models for the purpose of developing speech systems is discussed by Rao [8]. He explained the use of neural networks to model the prosodic parameters of the syllables from their positional, contextual, and phonological features.

The phonological analysis of Chatkhil Dialect of Noakhali District (Bangladesh) is done by Rashel [9]. He analyzed the consonants of the Chatkhil dialect according to the place and manner of origin. The comparison between declarative and interrogative utterance in standard colloquial Bangla is done by Warsi et al. [10]. They have presented a comparative study of prosodic features of utterances of declarative type and interrogative type, where the textual data are same except for the punctuation marks in Bangla. The dialect identification work in Hindi language has been done by Rao and Koolaagudi [11]. They proposed the identification model with the help of spectral and prosodic features of speech.

Saxena and Borin [12] have done the classification work of the dialects of the Himalaya region. They have examined the generic relationships among nine Tibeto-Burman varieties spoken in the Kinnaur region of India with the help of semi-automatic computational approach. Classification of speech varieties in the Bangla language is done by Faquire [13]. According to him, classification of varieties will help in further language planning. The analysis and synthesis of declarative, interrogative, and imperative utterances of Bangla with the help of F_0 contour are done by Warsi et al. [14]. They examined the differences in the gross features of the fundamental frequency contour, which is responsible for the discriminating utterances of these three sentence types.

Das et al. [15] had discussed the effect of aging on the speech features and that too in phoneme recognition. They have analyzed MFCC of different sounding Bengali vowels and noted the phoneme dissimilarities between the two age groups of 20–40 years and 60–80 years. A survey on language and dialect identification has been carried by Etman and Beex [16]. They have discussed what works have been already done in this field and they also provided a brief idea about what can be achieved in near future.

Mehrabani and Hansen [17] have done the automatic analysis of dialect/language sets. They proposed a method to capture the spectral acoustic differences between dialects and then text-independent prosody features are used to study the excitation structure differences between the dialects. Dialect identification of Bangladeshi language using MFCC, Delta, Delta-Delta, and GMM is done by Das and Rahman et al. [18]. Sarma and Sarma [19] have identified the Assamese dialects using Prosodic Features. They have used a Neuro Fuzzy classifier for the classification task.

The detection and classification of phonological features, which are based on place and manner of articulation from Bengali continuous speech, have been done by Bhowmik et al. [20]. They have used deep-structured models to classify and the C-DAC speech corpus for continuous spoken Bengali speech data. The role of Acoustic distance and the sociolinguistic knowledge in the purpose of dialect identification task is discussed by Ruch [21]. She examined that how different segments, acoustic between dialect distance, and the listeners' knowledge about dialect play important roles in the dialect identification process.

A comprehensive study to show the differences and uniqueness of Bhairab dialects has been carried forward by Khan [22]. His objective was to bring out the traditionalism and pastoral of a same language in any other dialect, which is differing from its standard version. A survey in the field of language and dialect identification system is done by Ismail [23]. The requirements of automation in the field of dialect and language identification are described here. Mamun et al. [24] have also applied MFCC but for detection of accent variation in Bengali.

22.3 Proposed Methodology

Previous research works were mostly related with dialect identification of either European languages or other Indian languages like Hindi. Being one of the largest speaking languages of the world [1,2], dialect identification of Bengali language remains ignored for some unknown reason. As geographically India is a vast country, lots of languages are there as well as lots of dialects are also there due to geographic variation. So, it is very normal to be able to identify lots of dialects in the Bengali language. Several languages exist in Bengali language in India. Among them there are three major dialects are noted in Bengali language in India. These dialects are Bangali (pronounced as "Bongaali"), Manbhumi (Jharkhandi), and Rarhi. As India is the main source of Bengali language in the world, more or less the same major dialects are also observed in the rest of the world too as Bengali-speaking people are spread through the globe.

While designing a machine learning based automated dialect identification system, it must be kept in mind that it should be able to recognize the components which have the capacity of recognizing linguistic contents from the input audio signal. Also at the same time another aspect should also need to be considered, that the number of facets should not be so large that it will increase the complexity of the intended system. Thus, the process of dialect identification task should have to follow some steps—initially the audio signal that is pronounced in Bengali language needs to be supplied to the system. Then facets need to be selected through suitable feature selection system from each of the input audio data. Once the facets are selected, they need be fed to the classifier for the classification task. Supervised classifiers are preferred to be used in this exertion. The classifier then tags the data with its category based on the training provided through the facet set. All these steps are rendered through Figure 22.1.

This exertion aims to put forward a simple acoustic facet group which is computationally simple as well as stumpy dimensional.

22.3.1 Computation of Features

Dialect is actually a sub-language of any language which can be better observed during the speaking style. It is a fact that any dialect is mainly identifiable based on phonemes and the pronunciation style of the native speakers because these are the main causes of a generation of dialects of a certain language. Apart from phonemes and the pronunciation style, there are certain characteristics of audio which play a significant role to identify recognizing different dialects of a certain language. These characteristics may be loudness, tonality, and nasality. Time domain along with frequency domain aural features can be employed to measure these characteristics.

22.3.1.1 Feature Selection

During this phase, identification of possible facets which will be able to identify dialects of Bengali language need to be carried out. It means the facets which have discriminating power those will be extracted during this phase. Feature selection task is considered as an imperative phase of preprocessing. It is the first step towards the formation of final facet vector. At the end of this phase final feature set gets formed after applying proper facet assortment procedure.

There are several techniques that exist for feature selection like Sequential Forward Selection (SFS), Sequential Backward Selection (SBS), Plus l-take away r Selection, Sequential Floating Forward Search (SFFS), Sequential Floating Backward Search (SFBS), and Max-Min approach.

In case of SFS if a facet is chosen that facet cannot be deleted, causing nesting effect. In SFS if after choosing a facet classification accuracy decreases then also it cannot be deleted. Similarly in case of SBS if a facet is rejected that facet cannot be taken again, creating nesting effect.

Plus l-take away r selection method adds l number of facets and to eradicate r number of facets at every step of feature selection. This is very much a time-consuming process and takes a long time to form the final feature vector. In case of SFFS, initial feature vector starts with an bare set and then the most noteworthy facet is added first. At every juncture, a new facet can be added and at the same time a facet which is deemed to be a least one can be removed. But the best thing of SFFS is that if after removing a facet classification accuracy reduces that facet can be added back again.

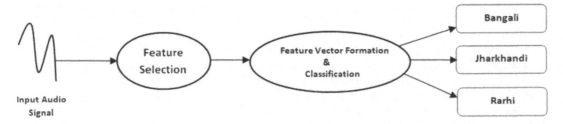

FIGURE 22.1   Process of dialect identification of Bengali language.

SFBS is just opposite to SFFS where the feature vector is formed with all possible facets which is really tough to start with as there may be huge number of facets applicable for a particular categorization task. If all possible facets to be put into the initial feature vector, calculation complexity of the system may get affected. Comparatively identification of most noteworthy facet is an easy task. Even if the first facet which is supposed to be the most noteworthy facet, does not come out as really the most noteworthy facet, at any future step it is possible to remove that facet.

Max-Min approach starts with two facets at the beginning but in future steps also it considers two facets at a time. The hitch of Max-Min approach is that it cannot be applied in multi-dimensional space as it does the calculations in two-dimensional space.

SFFS technique is applied in this work as among these facet assortment techniques SFFS appears to be the most practical approach. Mel Frequency Cepstral Coefficients (MFCC) is known to be able to capture human auditory system's response very well, along with phonemes and the pronunciation style of the native speakers. These are key elements to discriminate one dialect from dialect. Consequently Mel Frequency Cepstral Coefficients (MFCC) appears to be the most noteworthy facet. Therefore according to SFFS procedure MFCC gets added into the feature vector first.

The facets are chosen in this phase keeping in mind that they should not be affected by irrelevant elements like noise as well as they must be able to discriminate these three dialects properly. The length of the total facet set also should not be large enough.

Zero Crossing Rate (ZCR) as a time domain feature along with Mel Frequency Cepstral Coefficients (MFCCs), Skewness, and Spectral Flux as frequency domain aural facets have been extracted in this phase because they are able to capture the differences among the three dialects of Bengali language. All these three features are well used in different research works.

While facets are identified or chosen, the fact of "Curse of Dimensionality" is always given much importance. "Curse of Dimensionality" says that classification accuracy will increase with respect to increase in the number of facets up to some extent. After some optimal number of facets, classification accuracy may start to decrease instead of increase in the number of facets. This scenario is depicted in Figure 22.2.

Decrement in classification accuracy may arise because those facets which were added later may not have good discrimination characteristics. In this work facet vector, is chosen with flexibility.

Initially all the possible as well as suitable facets for identification of dialects in Bengali language is selected. Then gradually the facets are added in the facet vector and its corresponding classification accuracy has been monitored. Whenever the classification accuracy drops down even after adding a new facet in the facet vector, then it can be concluded that the facet vector has reached to its optimal dimension and no further facet addition will be fruitful. This principle has been adopted in this work to shorten the length of the facet set to avoid computational complexity as well as to avoid the "Curse of Dimensionality."

22.3.1.1.1 Zero Crossing Rate (ZCR) Based Feature Computation

Zero Crossing Rate (ZCR) is an important parameter in speech processing as it is computationally very simple. Task of dialect identification comes under speech processing as dialect of a specific language is

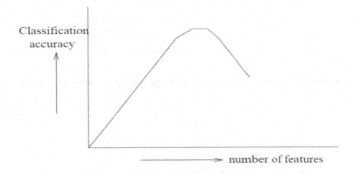

FIGURE 22.2 Curse of dimensionality.

identified from speech. Zero Crossing Rate (ZCR) captures how many times a signal changes its sign from positive to negative and vice versa with respect to the zero axis. Actually ZCR is said to occur when two successive samples of an audio signal have different algebraic signs—one is positive and another is negative. ZCR is a time domain facet as it measures sign changing of signals with respect to time. When people speak in different dialects of a certain language, certain differences among them are observed. Generally this speaking style or dialect creates a difference on the grounds of loudness and nasality. When loudness and nasality vary, sign changing characteristics of signals also vary. Hence Zero Crossing Rate (ZCR) is used in this work.

ZCR is a very good as well as popular audio feature. Many researchers have used this facet in their different research work. To measure the sign changing of a signal, the entire signal needs to be broken into several small duration frames (20–30 ms duration). Duration of frames is short because audio signal is dynamic; they are constantly changing. The sign change is measured against each of these frames. ZCR is computed using equations (22.1) and (22.2):

Input audio signal is detached into Q number of frames {x_i(m): $1 \leq i \leq Q$}. Then, for ith frame, zero crossing rates are computed using equation number 1:

$$zcr_n = \sum_{m=1}^{n-1} sign \ [x_i(m-1) \ * \ x_i(m)] \tag{22.1}$$

where n is a sign of quantity of samples in the ith framing and

$$sign \ [v] = \begin{cases} 1, & if \ v > 0 \\ 0, & otherwise \end{cases} \tag{22.2}$$

Mean and standard deviation is observed to be the most common statistical properties estimated from any distribution. It is known from the statistical property of any distribution that mean and standard deviation provide an overall idea of that distribution. Here, to acquire the overall idea of distribution of ZCR mean and standard deviation of ZCR has been considered in this work. Hence, Zero Crossing Rate (ZCR) based two facets are taken into consideration for extraction for dialect identification task.

If ZCR distribution of a dialect of language is plotted, dissimilarities among them will be identified.

ZCR plots of three dialects of Bengali—Bangali, Manbhumi (Jharkhandi), and Rarhi—are depicted in Figures 22.3, 22.4, and 22.5, respectively.

If Figures 22.3, 22.4, and 22.5 are watched minutely, it will be found that the rate of crossing the zero axis is quite different for the three dialects of Bengali language.

22.3.1.1.2 Mel Frequency Cepstral Coefficients (MFCCs) Based Feature Computation

Mel Frequency Cepstral Coefficients (MFCCs) are frequency domain facets. Short-term power spectrum of a sound is represented by Mel Frequency Cepstral Coefficients (MFCCs). This facet is specific to audio. Originally Mel Frequency Cepstral Coefficients (MFCCs) were advocated for recognizing monosyllabic words from uninterruptedly spoken sentences.

The coefficients are derived from cepstral representation of the audio clip. This facet can measure human auditory system's response. Aim of MFCC is to reflect the dynamics of phones of speech signal. MFCC actually tries to find out human perception compassion with respect to frequencies of the speech signal. MFCC is mostly used in speech recognition system because of this nature of MFCC. Nowadays MFCC is found to be used in music information salvage purposes; also like genre classification etc.

It is known as dialect identification is a part of speech recognition. Therefore MFCC is employed in the dialect identification task also. In case of processing of audio signal, Mel Frequency Cepstrum (MFC) is considered as an illustration of short period power spectrum of the audio signal in frequency domain. MFCCs are the coefficients that jointly form a Mel Frequency Cepstrum (MFC). MFC is judged as the cepstral representation of acoustic signal. Spectrum of log of the spectrum of the input speech signal is termed as cepstrum. Cepstrum indicates the information of rate of alteration in spectral bands of a speech signal.

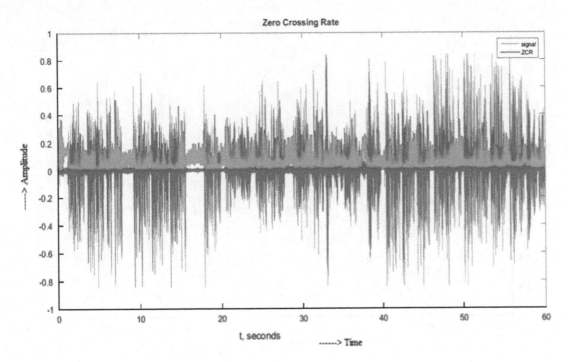

FIGURE 22.3   ZCR plot of Bangali dialect.

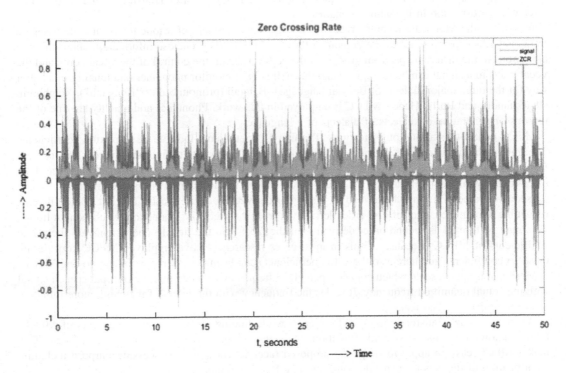

FIGURE 22.4   ZCR plot of Manbhumi dialect.

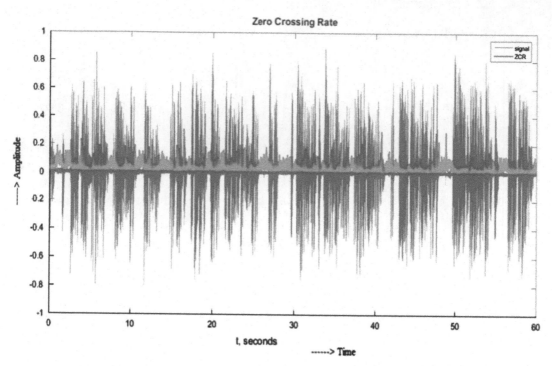

FIGURE 22.5   ZCR plot of Rarhi dialect.

MFCC also captures information in frequency domain. Discrete Fourier Transform (DFT) is executed to capture information in frequency domain.

In MFCC, the Mel scale recounts recognized frequency, or pitch, of a tone to its tangible assessed frequency. As cepstral features are computed through MFCC, they enclose information about the rate alterations in the different spectrum groups. In the cepstral realm, the control of the vocal cords and the vocal tracts in a signal can be segregated and this will help to monitor phonemes and tonality in a better way for the three major dialects of Bengali language—Bangali (pronounced as "Bongaali"), Manbhumi (Jharkhandi), and Rarhi. Hence, MFCC is employed in this work. Phonemes and tonality are one of the reasons of generation of dialects of dialects of a language.

MFCC contributes a total of 39 features. The first 12 coefficients indicate 12 Cepstrum coefficients. The thirteenth coefficient indicates energy of each frame. This assists to find out phones. Phones vary from one dialect to another dialect for a single language. The next 13 coefficients calculate the delta assessments which actually assess the alteration of values in facets from the preceding frame to the subsequent frame. This may be termed as first-order derivatives of the facets. The last 13 coefficients reflect the dynamic changes of first-order derivatives from the preceding frame to the subsequent frame. This may be termed as second-order derivative of the facets. So the first 13 coefficients are the prime coefficients of MFCC. Because of this in most cases researchers have employed MFCC considering these 13 coefficients and here also these 13 coefficients have been considered while employing MFCC.

Mel scale is such a scale which connects perceived frequency of a certain tone of input speech signal with the actual quantified frequency. It scales the frequency with the intent of matching more minutely what the human ear can listen to.

Discrete Cosine Transformation (DCT) is done while finding the values of coefficients of MFCC. DCT is known to be an orthogonal revolution. Thus, the outputs of DCT are unassociated facets. This makes MFCC easy to apply to shape the proposed facet set for speech processing purpose including identification of dialects of a specific language like Bengali language.

MFCC is computed in Figure 22.6¾

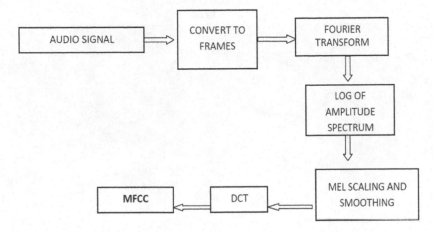

FIGURE 22.6 Process of MFCC computation.

Steps for Computing MFCC:

1. Input audio signal is segregated into number of frames of fixed duration (20–30 ms). These frames are preferred to be 50% overlapped with its adjacent frames.
2. Amplitude spectrum for each of these frames is achieved by employing DFT and subsequently logarithm of amplitudes is acquired.
3. The spectrum is then smoothened to craft it perceptually momentous using Mel frequency (f_m) which is calculated using equation (22.3):

$$f_m = 2595 \ * \ log_{10}\left(1 + \frac{f}{100}\right) \tag{22.3}$$

where f is frequency (in Hertz) of the input audio signal.

4. The components in the smoothened Mel-spectra vector are vastly interrelated. To de-associate and to diminish the number of parameters DCT is carried out to acquire MFCCs and first 13 coefficients are considered as facets for the frame.
5. After calculating the MFCCs for all frames, the vector encompasses the average value corresponding to each coefficient shapes the facet descriptor.

MFCC plots of Bangali, Jharkhandi, and Rarhi are depicted in Figures 22.7, 22.8, and 22.9, respectively. From these plots it is very clear that MFCCs of the three dialects of Bengali language are not the same.

22.3.1.1.3 Skewness-Based Feature Computation

Skewness is basically a frequency domain feature. It quantifies the disproportion within different categories. It also helps to identify dissimilarities within different categories of dataset. Bangali, Jharkhandi, and Rarhi, the three major dialects of Bengali language, exhibit certain amounts of dissimilarities as well as disproportions among them due to different pronunciation styles. This can be perceived during hearings of these three major dialects. This way skewness is capable to capture pronunciation style differences of Bangali, Jharkhandi, and Rahi dialects. Therefore skewness-based feature is considered in this work. To compute skewness, every input audio signal is segregated into number of frames of fixed duration (20–30 ms). These frames are preferred to be 50% overlapped with its adjacent frames. Then skewness *skw* for each frame is computed using equation (22.4):

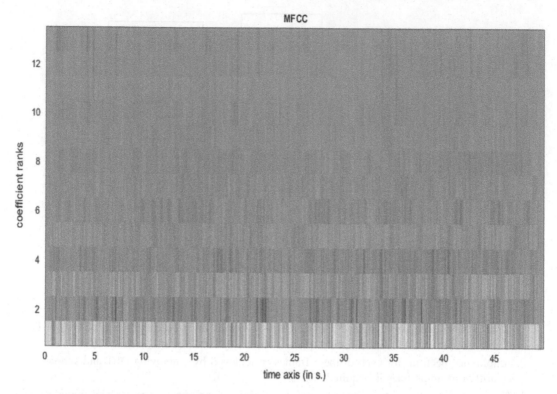

FIGURE 22.7 MFCC plot of Bangali dialect.

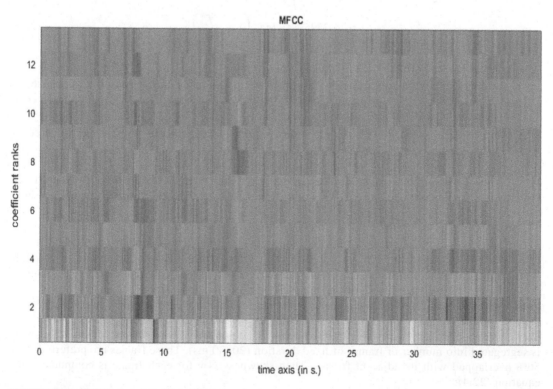

FIGURE 22.8 MFCC plot of Jharkhandi dialect.

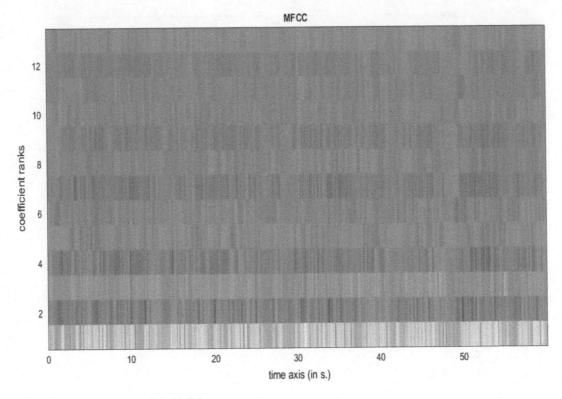

FIGURE 22.9 MFCC plot of Rarhi dialect.

$$skw = \frac{E(d - \mu)}{\sigma^3} \tag{22.4}$$

where μ points to mean of exemplar information d, standard variation of d is referred by σ, and the expected evaluation of magnitude h is indicated by $E(h)$.

After calculating the skewness for all frames, the vector encompasses the average value corresponding to each coefficient shapes the facet descriptor. Therefore, the skewness-based feature contributes only a single facet value to the facet set used to discriminate dialects of Bengali language.

22.3.1.1.4 Spectral Flux Based Feature Computation

Spectral flux first and foremost indicates spectral distinctions of input audio signal. Rate of alteration of power spectrum of that signal is incarcerated through spectral flux.

Spectral flux calculates rate of alteration of power spectrum by judging the power spectrum of a certain frame of short duration (20–30 ms) against the power spectrum of its successive frame. Spectral flux is a good facet for gender discrimination from speech signal because it is able to capture the pronunciation style difference from input audio signal. Based on this observation, spectral flux is applied in this work to capture the pronunciation style difference within a language which is actually a dialect of that language. Spectral Flux spec_f is computed using equation (22.5):

$$spec\_f(Y) = \sum_{j=0}^{t-1} s(Y, j) - s(Y - 1, j) \tag{22.5}$$

where t indicates overall frame number. *spec_f* represents spectral flux for Y^{th} spectrum of the signal. If $s(Y,j)$ is the value of jth bin for Y^{th} spectrum then $s(Y-1,j)$ is the value of j-1th bin. Like ZCR only mean and standard deviation of spectral flux is considered.

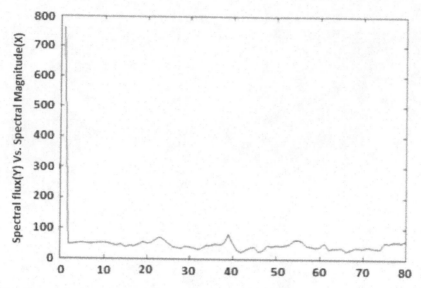

FIGURE 22.10   Spectral flux plot of Bangali dialect.

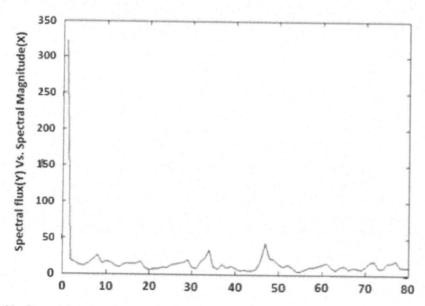

FIGURE 22.11   Spectral flux plot of Jharkhandi dialect.

Spectral flux plots of Bangali, Jharkhandi, and Rarhi are depicted in Figures 22.10, 22.11, and 22.12, respectively.

22.3.2 Formation of Feature Vector and Classification

After computation of all possible facets, the feature selection procedure needs to be applied to form the final facet vector. Obviously different standard classifiers will assist feature selection procedure in this matter. Sequential Floating Forward Search (SFFS) technique is used in this work to form the final facet vector. This technique starts with adding MFCC in the probable facet set first. After adding MFCC in the initial facet set which is termed F_1. As per SFFS technique mean and standard deviation of ZCR is added in the facet set

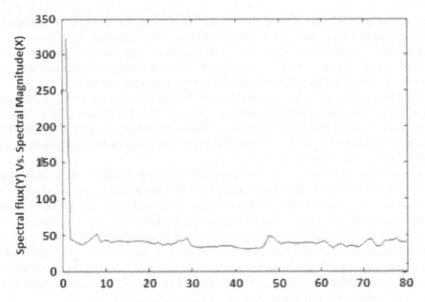

FIGURE 22.12   Spectral flux plot of Rarhi dialect.

which is termed F_2. Next skewness is added with the facet set and the extended facet set is termed F_3. Lastly spectral flux based facets are added in the facet set and the extended facet set is termed F_4.

Classifier is an important tool in any machine learning work. Its task is to distinguish various categories of data of a machine learning work using the feature set generated during the feature extraction phase. The differentiating power of the recommended F_1, F_2, F_3, and F_4 facet set is assessed through Neural Network (NN), Naïve Bayes, Random Forest, and K-Nearest Neighbor classifiers. MLP (Multi Layer Perceptron) model of Neural Network has been applied in this work. An audio dataset is prepared for carrying out this work.

The dataset contains 600 audio files. This dataset has equal contribution of all three categories of Bengali dialects (Bangali, Jharkhandi, and Rahi) which specifies 200 files for each of three dialects (Bangali, Jharkhandi, and Rahi). This dataset is applied for testing and training roles by setting apart the entire dataset into two indistinguishable divisions. Among these two indistinguishable divisions, one division is used for training purposes and the other division is used for testing purposes.

MLP or Multi Layer Perceptron model of Neural Network (NN) is applied in this work considering the number of neurons in the input stratum equal to the dimension of facet set. In this Multi Layer Perceptron (MLP) model, there are three neurons in the output stratum which points to three categories of Bengali dialects (Bangali, Jharkhandi, and Rahi). In the concealed stratum of this MLP model, the number neurons is equal to the half of neuron in input stratum + 1. A tenfold cross-validation is applied in this work to enforce the Naïve Bayes classifier. The Random Forest classifier has been enforced through the conception of the decision tree classifier. K-Nearest Neighbor or K-NN is one of the trouble-free supervised classifiers. It is very easy to employ. This classifier is employed with k=3 as there are three categories of Bengali dialects (Bangali, Jharkhandi, and Rahi). City Block distance metric has been considered here for measurement of distance between two sample elements. Random rule and nearest rule have been used in this classifier to break the tie to label a data with a tag of any three categories of the dialects.

22.4 Experimental Results

All the audio files in the dataset are of monophonic category. The question may arise that why monophonic sound is considered instead of stereophonic sound whereas whatever sounds we, human beings hear, all are stereophonic type in most of the cases. Actually monophonic sounds have some advantages over stereo sounds. Monophonic sounds appear in the same way for every user. This means that all the listeners will have the same sense of hearing against a single sound signal. This characteristic is not observed in case of stereophonic sounds. Apart from this, there is another fact that monophonic sounds are less expensive for reproduction compared to stereophonic sounds.

All the sound files in the dataset are 90 seconds long. To maintain diverse nature of the dataset so that it can reflect the real-world scenario in a better way, speech of both female and male is considered. Also to add more assortments in the dataset, speech of different-aged people was also considered. These sound files are accumulated from various sources like CD/DVD soundtrack, records of various live shows, alongside from the Internet.

Each of the sound files is segregated into many frames. Every frame inside a single sound file is generated in such a way with the intention that they get 50% overlapped with its adjacent frame. This overlapping is done intentionally so that no border nature of any frame get missed out. Half of the sound files in the data set have been used to train the supervised classifiers used in this work. Rest sound files have been used for testing by applying the trained supervised classifiers. After the completion of discrimination task using these training dataset and testing dataset, this training dataset and testing dataset got reversed and the same discrimination task is repeated once more. Average of these two discrimination tasks is considered as the final discrimination conclusion of the three categories of Bengali dialects (Bangali, Jharkhandi, and Rahi) for each of F_1, F_2, F_3, and F_4.

This final discrimination conclusion is put into Tables 22.1, 22.2, 22.3, and 22.4, respectively.

From these tables (Tables 22.1–22.4) it is observed that inclusion of spectral flux decreases classification accuracy (in Table 22.4). Hence applying Sequential Floating Forward Search (SFFS) technique

TABLE 22.1

Accuracy of Dialect Identification of Bengali Language (Using F_1)

Classifier	Discrimination Exactness (in %) Meant for Suggested Feature Set
Neural Network (NN)	78.28
Naïve Bayes	79.81
Random Forest	75.77
K-Nearest Neighbor	77.05

TABLE 22.2

Accuracy of Dialect Identification of Bengali Language (Using F_2)

Classifier	Discrimination Exactness (in %) Meant for Suggested Feature Set
Neural Network (NN)	80.17
Naïve Bayes	83.23
Random Forest	77.51
K-Nearest Neighbor	79.82

TABLE 22.3

Accuracy of Dialect Identification of Bengali Language (Using F_3)

Classifier	Discrimination Exactness (in %) Meant for Suggested Feature Set
Neural Network (NN)	83.81
Naïve Bayes	86.67
Random Forest	79.14
K-Nearest Neighbor	80.95

TABLE 22.4

Accuracy of Dialect Identification of Bengali Language (Using F_4)

Classifier	Discrimination Exactness (in %) Meant for Suggested Feature Set
Neural Network (NN)	81.81
Naïve Bayes	85.67
Random Forest	77.14
K-Nearest Neighbor	79.95

TABLE 22.5

Relative Analysis of Intended Facet Set with Other Work

Erstwhile Technique	Classification Accuracy (in %)
Mamun et al. [24] (Naïve Bayes)	79.81
Proposed Method (Naïve Bayes)	86.67

for facet selection spectral flux based facets are discarded and F_3 is considered as final facet set, which is of 16 dimensional (13 coefficients of MFCC, mean and standard deviation of ZCR and skewness).

22.4.1 Relative Analysis

Discrimination supremacy of the advised facet set is weighed up against earlier exertion done in this domain. The dataset which is used in this work was kept unaffected while performing comparative investigation.Khan [22] has worked with Bengali speaker accent variation. They have employed Mel frequency cepstral coefficient (MFCC) based features in their work. Their facet set has been applied in the current dataset just to perform a comparative investigation on a common platform. From Table 22.5 it is very much apparent that suggested facet set performs better than the approach suggested by Khan [22]. Mel frequency cepstral coefficient (MFCC) is also employed in this work along with some other facets. Table 22.5 clearly says that Mel frequency cepstral coefficient (MFCC) alone is not sufficient to identify accent variation or dialects of Bengali language.

22.5 Conclusion

This work indicates that suggested facet set is able to identify three major categories of Bengali dialects (Bangali, Jharkhandi, and Rahi) with 86.67% success rate using the Naïve Bayes classifier. This work also establishes the fact that MFCC along with mean and standard deviation of ZCR and skewness is capable of identifying dialects of Bengali language.

Sequential Floating Forward Search (SFFS) facet selection technique is applied in this venture to find the best possible facet set to identify dialects of Bengali language. Through this facet selection technique the most significant facet is added first in the plausible facet set and gradually the other facets. If a facet is found to be a low discriminating facet, that facet will be discarded in the subsequent phase. In this work, MFCC is added the plausible facet set first as MFCC is the most significant facet for speech processing related activities. Next, mean and standard deviation of ZCR is added in the plausible facet set. After that skewness based facet is included. Gradually classification accuracy is observed to be increasing whenever a new facet is attached in the plausible facet set. But whenever spectral flux based facet is added in the plausible facet set, classification accuracy of the system is observed to be decreased. From this observation it is concluded that spectral flux based facets are not able to identify dialects of

Bengali language very well, rather the combination of MFCC, mean and standard deviation of ZCR with skewness produces better classification accuracy.

In the future, other facets may be explored to improve the classification accuracy. Also other non-major dialects of Bengali language will also be explored. Also, sub-classification of these dialects may also be explored in future endeavours also. Through comparative analysis of previous efforts it is also clear that Mel frequency cepstral coefficient (MFCC) alone is not sufficient to identify different dialects of Bengali language. Zero Crossing Rate (ZCR) and skewness-based aural facets are also required to be considered along with the Mel frequency cepstral coefficient (MFCC) as these dialects diverge both in time domain as well as in frequency domain.

REFERENCES

[1] "The World Factbook" (https://www.cia.gov/library/publications/the-world-factbook/geos/xx.html). www.cia.gov. Central Intelligence Agency. Archived (https://web.archive.org/web/20080213004843/https://www.cia.gov/library/publications/the-world-factbook/geos/xx.html) from the original on 13 February 2008. Retrieved 21 February 2018.

[2] "Summary by language size" (https://www.ethnologue.com/statistics/size). *Ethnologue*. 3 October 2018. Archived (https://web.archive.org/web/20130911104311/http://www.ethnologue.com/statistics/size) from the original on 11 September 2013. Retrieved 21 February 2019.

[3] Torres-Carrasquillo, P. A., Gleason, T. P., & Reynolds, D. A. (2004). Dialect identification using Gaussian mixture models. In *ODYSSEY04-The Speaker and Language Recognition Workshop* (pp. 297–300).

[4] Hossain, S. A., Rahman, M. L., & Ahmed, F. (2005, October). A review on Bangla phoneme production and perception for computational approaches. In *7th WSEAS International Conference on Mathematical Methods and Computational Techniques in Electrical Engineering* (pp. 69–89).

[5] Baker, W., Eddington, D., & Nay, L. (2009). Dialect identification: The effects of region of origin and amount of experience. *American Speech*, *84*(1), 48–71.

[6] Muhammad, G., Alotaibi, Y. A., & Huda, M. N. (2009, December). Automatic speech recognition for Bangla digits. In *2009 12th International Conference on Computers and Information Technology* (pp. 379–383). IEEE.

[7] Mandal, S. D., Warsi, A. H., Basu, T., Hirose, K., & Fujisaki, H. (2010, November). Analysis and synthesis of F0 contours for Bangla readout speech. In *Proc. of Oriental COCOSDA*.

[8] Rao, K. S. (2011). Role of neural network models for developing speech systems. *Sadhana*, *36*(5), 783–836.

[9] Rashel, M. M. (2011). Phonological analysis of Chatkhil Dialect in Noakhali District, Bangladesh. *Theory and Practice in Language Studies*, *1*(9), 1051–1061.

[10] Warsi, A. H., Basu, T., Hirose, K., & Fujisaki, H. (2011, October). Prosodic comparison of declarative and interrogative utterances in Standard Colloquial Bangla. In *2011 International Conference on Speech Database and Assessments (Oriental COCOSDA)* (pp. 56–61). IEEE.

[11] Rao, K. S., & Koolagudi, S. G. (2011). Identification of Hindi dialects and emotions using spectral and prosodic features of speech. *IJSCI: International Journal of Systemics, Cybernetics and Informatics*, *9*(4), 24–33.

[12] Saxena, A., & Borin, L. (2011, May). Dialect classification in the Himalayas: A computational approach. In *Proceedings of the 18th Nordic Conference of Computational Linguistics (NODALIDA 2011)* (pp. 307–310).

[13] Faquire, A. B. M. R. K. (2012). On the classification of varieties of Bangla spoken in Bangladesh. *Bup Journal*, *1*(1), 136.

[14] Warsi, A. H., Basu, T., Hirose, K., & Fujisaki, H. (2012, December). Analysis and synthesis of F 0 contours of declarative, interrogative, and imperative utterances of Bangla. In *2012 International Conference on Speech Database and Assessments* (pp. 56–61). IEEE.

[15] Das, B., Mandal, S., Mitra, P., & Basu, A. (2013). Effect of aging on speech features and phoneme recognition: A study on Bengali voicing vowels. *International Journal of Speech Technology*, *16*(1), 19–31.

[16] Etman, A., & Beex, A. L. (2015, November). Language and dialect identification: A survey. In *2015 SAI Intelligent Systems Conference (IntelliSys)* (pp. 220–231). IEEE.

[17] Mehrabani, M., & Hansen, J. H. (2015). Automatic analysis of dialect/language sets. *International Journal of Speech Technology*, *18*(3), 277–286.

[18] Das, P. P., Allayear, S. M., Amin, R., & Rahman, Z. (2016, February). Bangladeshi dialect recognition using Mel frequency cepstral coefficient, delta, delta-delta and Gaussian mixture model. In *2016 Eighth International Conference on Advanced Computational Intelligence (ICACI)* (pp. 359–364). IEEE.

[19] Sarma, M., & Sarma, K. K. (2016, February). Dialect identification from Assamese speech using prosodic features and a neuro fuzzy classifier. In *2016 3rd International Conference on Signal Processing and Integrated Networks (SPIN)* (pp. 127–132). IEEE.

[20] Bhowmik, T., Chowdhury, A., & Mandal, S. K. D. (2018). Deep neural network based place and manner of articulation detection and classification for Bengali continuous speech. *Procedia Computer Science*, *125*, 895–901.

[21] Ruch, H. (2018). The role of acoustic distance and sociolinguistic knowledge in dialect identification. *Frontiers in Psychology*, *9*, 818.

[22] Khan, M. E. I. (2019). Exploring Bhairab dialect vis-à-vis standard Bangla. *Journal of ELT and Education*, *2*(1), 14–18.

[23] Ismail, T. A Survey of Language and Dialect Identification Systems.

[24] Mamun, R. K., Abujar, S., Islam, R., Badruzzaman, K. B. M., & Hasan, M. (2020). Bangla speaker accent variation detection by MFCC using recurrent neural network algorithm: A distinct approach. In *Innovations in Computer Science and Engineering* (pp. 545–553). Springer, Singapore.

23

Real-Time Security Using Computer Vision

Bijoy Kumar Mandal and Niloy Sarkar

CONTENTS

23.1 Introduction

The real-time security system is developed for the computers. The security system has the potential to recognize its owner this will prevent anyone to misuse the computer. The system has face recognition [1,2], which is able to recognize its owner and only provide access to its owner. The main user, which can be denoted as the primary user, can limit the access of other users to the computer. This will prevent others from misusing the computer. This system is better than other security systems in the sense that it has the capability to watch its owner and then provide only him/her full access to the computer. Other systems use an authentication process which is based on rules or protocols which will provide security for only once until the protocol is checked and sometimes it may happen that someone else has other means to check [3] and validate the protocols and the rules; these protocols and rules do not check the person who is using the data or the system. At that point, a computer vision based security system will prove to be an effective means of protection.

23.1.1 Biometric

Biometric login systems use the face recognition [3,4], fingerprint matching, and other means but they are just for login into the system; once the user has somehow logged into the system there will be no cross check until the system or the computer has been logged out. These are the areas where computer vision based security system will prove to be effective. Biometric is used to refer to measurement and calculation. Examples of biometrics are as follows

- Fingerprint
- Palm Veins
- Face Recognition
- DNA
- Palm Print
- Hand Geometry
- Iris Recognition
- Retina

23.1.2 Computer Vision

Computer vision is a technology which uses computer algorithm to carry out human vision like work. The computer takes the image either still or in motion and applies different algorithms on them to produce meaningful data. Computer vision algorithms are time and processor consuming algorithms but there are certain libraries which provide optimized and fast processing algorithms that consume lesser amounts of memory [5]. Computer vision is a field of computer study that tries to mimic the natural vision of living for providing power of vision to computer, robot, etc. Computer vision used a list of algorithms to take, process, and analyze an image [6,7] (still or moving). Computer vision provides the machine the power of sight like humans. Computer vision is also used for the extraction of useful information from images [8], which can later be used for doing different work. Computer vision study began in the late 1960s as an agent for artificial intelligence work. The different field in which computer vision works are

- Face Detection
- Face Recognition
- Depth Map
- Image Processing
- Image Repainting
- 3D Construction and a lot more

23.1.3 Opencv Library

The library used here is opencv, computer vision library, which has large number of functions for image and video processing as well as for computer vision. Opencv is largely useful for real-time computer vision [9,10]. It also supports machine learning. OpenCV comes under BSD license. It is written c/c++. Initial release June 2000, original authors are Intel Corporation, Willow Garage, Itseez. Stable release date 4.0, 22 December 2018; 4 months ago. It supports cross the platform of size 200MB.

23.2 Data Security

Data security is a major issue which we are facing today in this digital world of communication. As we know that today hackers are almost at every corner in search of our useful data, which can be hacked by them for their different purposes [11]. Even the risk gets doubled when come to the data of any country's government. Data is central to calculate, and now a day's data security is biggest concern for customers [12]. Everywhere data needs to be handled securely in all stages, from transmission to computation and persistence. Data security can be used in a range of techniques and many kinds of technologies, physical security, organizational standards logical controls, and using other techniques that protect the data and limit access to unauthorized users and unwanted access [13].

Data security is very essential because any kind of business is dealing with data, and we need to secure our data because if it leaked then it can be a disaster for any person or any organizations. It doesn't matter which type of technology, device, or which type of process we use nowadays for storing or collect the precious data, at first the data must be secured all the time from unwanted access [14]. Data security comes in many types and forms and we have to protect this data from many types of threats. Many types of threats are from external sources, but every organization should be focused on safeguarding their valuable data from the inside too. There are many ways for securing data [15].

- **Data encryption:** In data encryption we create a line of programs or lines of codes to individual pieces of data and this coding helps to not access encrypted data without the particular key or password.
- **Data masking:** Data masking means hiding the original data with any type of modified content; the purpose of data masking is to protect the information or personal data from unauthorized persons.
- **Data erasure:** Data erasure means which type of information or data is not active since many times then this has to be erased for organizational purposes. Example: A customer has requested for their details to be removed from his old workplace, the details should be deleted permanently.
- **Data resilience:** It means if any organizational data is erased for some issue like storage hardware corrupted accidentally or stolen during process, after that this data can restore via backup. It is also a data security process.

A. Security Goal

It is the most common aspect of the information security. It allows authorized users to access sensitive and protected data. The data sent over the network should not be accessed by unauthorized users. Attackers will try to capture data. To avoid this, various encryption techniques are used to safeguard our data. So that even if anattacker get access they will not decrypt it to the original message. In banks when we deposit and withdraw money, the balance needs to be maintained. Change needs to be done by only authorized persons. Nobody else should modify the data. Data must be available to authorized users. Info is useless if we can't not use it.

B. Security Services

i. Data confidentiality
ii. Data integrity
iii. Authentication
iv. Non repudiation
v. Access control

C. Data Confidentiality

Data confidentiality means secure or protect the data from unauthorized access from unauthorized users. Ensure that data can only be used by the authorized persons only. Because data encryption and decryption are the part of cryptography so, in cryptography data security is the main purpose that's why data confidentiality is the main thing or main purpose for this project. Data confidentiality can only be achieved by using strong algorithms for high security of the data that cannot be stolen or broken by anyone; that's the main purpose of cryptography or data encryption or decryption. Confidentiality is the main purpose or main thing for data encryption and decryption. We have to achieve the security by using the encryption technique. Data that secure that much, if anyone can read or steal the data is can't read by anyone means data is jumbled up with thousands of characters, data is only read by the authorized users when use the password or passkey for read the data, this time jumbled up data is decrypted. Otherwise if anyone wants to break the passkey, then the data is deleted automatically and the machine is protected on high security alert in this time due to unauthorized access.

D. Data Integrity

Data integrity means the data which is in digital format in web or computers; it can be online or offline mode we have to protect the data which is in digital format.

We have to protect the data by using strong passwords or by using encryption techniques using strong algorithms. Data integrity can follow through in this matter:

    i. If the error is occurred by not any bad intension.
    ii. Error is occurred during the time of transfer the data from one device to another device.
    iii. If any threat is occurred by a virus or something.
    iv. If any hardware issue is confirmed in this time it can be compromised.

Two types of integrity can happen. One is passive and another one is active. In passive there can be held any changes in data by accidentally, data fault is not created by any intension. But active means the data is changed by manipulating this by any unauthorized users; it means data is accessed by unauthorized person.

E. Authentication

Authentication means only authorized users can access the data by proper authentication, by using any strong password or strong encrypted technique, but if the users do not have any proper authentication then the user can't use the data and it is called malicious access by unauthorized users. Authentication means the proper key or proper way for using the data. In authentication, we verify the user's identity by verifying the data that they used for access the data. Such as in our mobile phone, we use a password or pin for access. Or nowadays we use biometric authentication techniques for access on our mobile; our mobile cannot be used by anyone other than us. In this way we protect our online account or our laptop, computers by using login by generating user id and password; that's why our data is always protected from unauthorized users and it's secure all the time. Only we can use our precious digital data by using proper authentication. The main thing about authentication is the data can only be accessed by a verified user.

F. Non-repudiation

Non-repudiation is a method in this area or a place is protected with a security if the security key is lost then it is reported as soon as possible at that time. In cyber security or cryptography, it is used in many places. Example: An area or an office is master key protected, if anyone wants to enter there then the card is required; if it is not theirs then they don't access that area, if the card is lost then it is reported at this time due to security purposes.

G. Access Control

Access control means if you have the proper password or technique for using the data then you only access the data; otherwise you can't access the data. Access control is a very vital part in data security.

Example: In our Facebook account, without having proper id and password we can't login in our account; it's called access control. We have the full access of our account and data.

H. Security Attack
    ○ **Passive Attack**

The passive attack attempts to learn or make use of information from the system but does not affect system resource. Passive attacks are in the nature of eavesdropping on transmission. The purpose of the opponent is to gain information being transmitted [16].

i. The release of message content

Mobile conversation and electronic message or a transferred file might contain sensitive information. We will prevent an attacker from learning the information of these transmissions.

ii. Traffic analysis

Let's assume we had a way of encryption of info so that if the attacker captured the message they could not get any information from the message. The attacker could find the location and identity of communicating host and could observe the frequency and length of messages. This info might be useful in assuming the nature of the communication that occurs [17].

- **Active attacks:** Active attacks try to change the system info or affect their operation. Active attacks involve some changes of the data or creation of false statements.
- **Masquerade:** Masquerade attacks occur when one entity pretends to be a different entity. A masquerade is one of the other forms of active attacks.

iii. Python

Python is high-level language. And it is interpreted, interactive, and object-oriented scripting language. There are many places where we are using Python programming like web development software development and system scripting. It is a language we can code easily in a short type manner and for when we reconstruct the code or create any changes this time it is easy to understand and easy to read for the programmers.

iv. Python uses:
    ○ It is used on a server to create web applications.
    ○ It is also used to connect a database system.
    ○ It is used to handle big data and perform complex mathematics.
    ○ It is used for Data Analysis.
    ○ Machine Learning is also implemented by Python.
    ○ Through the Python, architecture of Deep Learning has been designed.
    ○ Application of Artificial Intelligence has been introduced.
    ○ Python can be work on different platforms like Windows, Mac, Linux etc.
    ○ Python is used as in procedural way and object-oriented way or functional way.
    ○ In Python Programming, we don't use semicolons or parentheses.
    ○ Python has huge library other than other programming language.
    ○ Most of the data scientists and software engineers use is Python to research and coding.

Nowadays it more popular in Artificial (AI) and data science. When it comes to cybersecurity, it is more powerful than other languages. Python responses to security threats faster than other languages.

In Python, there are no type declarations of variables, parameters, functions, or methods in source code. Most of the organizations are used for scripting for web applications.

Google, Facebook, Quora, and Instagram are using Python.

Python is more productive than other programming languages because it requires less time, effort, and lines of code to perform any operations.

After learning of Python we can be a:

- Web Developer
- Desktop Application Developer
- Apps Developer
- Software Developer
- Data Analyst
- Data Scientist

v. Editors for Python:

Editor: The term editors usually refers to source code editors that include many special features for writing and editing source code.

Eclipse
Pycharm
Emacs
Notepad++
Visual studio
Spyder
Thonny

vi. Eclipse

It is most popular IDE for Windows and Linux. Eclipse contains many features. We can code many programming languages in it like Java, C, C++, Python, etc.

vii. Pycharm

Most of the programmers are using this IDE for development. It's available for both paid and open source. Pycharm installs quickly and works on Windows, Mac, and Linux platforms.

viii. Spyder

It is also an open-source Python IDE which contains many great features included with the Anaconda package manager. Spyder integrates well with common Python data science libraries. It has robust syntax highlighting and variable explorer.

23.3 Technology

The project is a real-time security project in which the camera of the computer keeps constantly looking at the owner. The authentication process is done at regular intervals, which ensures that the system is protected. When the user moves from its place or a new user can in front of the computer the system will recognize the user as an invalid user and stop the system access to the user.

On finding an unknown person, the system will continue to freeze or inactivate the keyboard and display a notification of not the user and access denied sequentially. The system will keep doing this until a known person uses the computer. The keyboard will keep locking again and again inspite of unlocking it. If a known person of the primary user of the computer is found, the computer will stop doing the same. Moreover, the valid person can use the computer without any interruption. The technology used in this project is computer vision.

23.3.1 Face Detection

Face detection is a technique, which is used to detect human faces in an image or a video. Haar cascade are used for this purpose which can be considered as predefined or pre-trained model for face detection. The Haar cascade is based on the work of viola-jones, it is created by superimposing positive i.e., image containing those objects which we need to find also called as positive image and those that do not contain the target images known as the negative images [18,19].

23.3.2 Face Recognition

Face recognition identifies the person in the image or video. The algorithm used here is LBPH i.e., local binary patterns histogram. LBPH uses its surrounding pixel as a reference for matching purpose [20]. The algorithm chooses a matrix of $n * n$ dimension and then take the central pixel and compare it with the neighbors and then assign binary 0 and 1 to it surrounding pixel based on the fact whether the central pixel is greater than itself then it is assigned 1; otherwise 0. Image Processing is the use of computer algorithms to process image and videos and extract useful information [21]. With the help of image processing we can recognize images and objects in the image. We are combining image recognition and speech synthesis in real time with a portable device which can be helpful for a blind person to know their surroundings [22,23]. In this project we will be taking the help of Digital Image Processing (DIP) and speech synthesis technology [24,25].

23.3.3 Haar Cascade Classifier

Haar cascade is an object detection technique. It was proposed by Viola and Michael Jones in their paper. It is a machine learning based method for object detection [26]. It can detect objects both in images and in videos. It consists of different stages, each having weak learners' collection and these weak learners are called decision stumps, and each stage is trained using a technique called boosting. Training a cascade classifier needs a large number of positive images which means those images that contain the target object and negative images that do not contain the required image set (Figures 23.1–23.4).

FIGURE 23.1 Process of capturing image for database.

FIGURE 23.2   Reorganization of face.

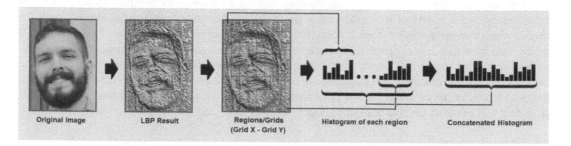

FIGURE 23.3   Local binary pattern histogram.

23.4 Algorithm

23.4.1 Algorithm to Capture the Image for Database

1. Create connection to the camera using cap=cv2.VideoCapture ()
2. Open the camera
3. Read each frame using cap.read()
4. Detect face inside the frame using the haar cascade classifier for face
5. If a face is detected then store the frame in jpg format
6. Otherwise display the message to come in front of the frame.

23.4.2 Algorithm to Recognize the Face

1. Activate the camera using cap=cv2.VideoCapture ()
2. Read each frame
3. Detect a face inside the frame using the haar cascade classifier
4. Compare the data inside the pre-trained database with the face in the live footage
5. If a match is found then find the label associated with the face
6. Then find the name associated with the label and display it

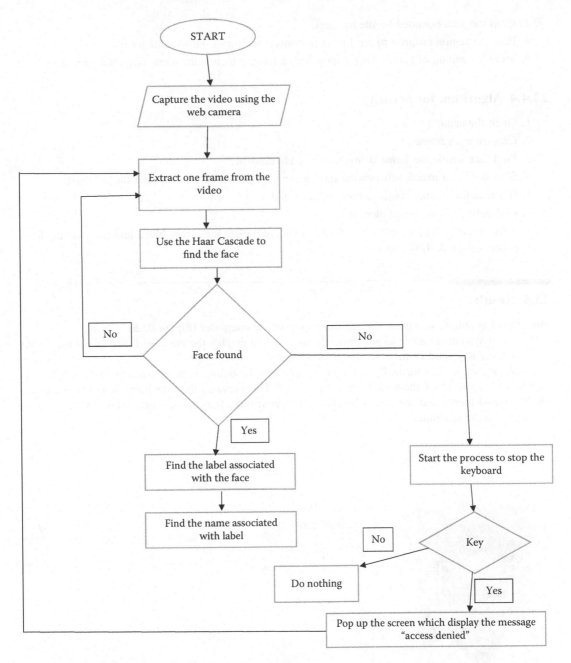

FIGURE 23.4 Flowchart.

7. If a face is not detected then give the message that the person is unknown
8. If the area of the bounding rectangle on the face is smaller then set threshold area and print the person is far from the computer

23.4.3 Algorithm to Train the Face Recognizer

1. Pass an image containing the face, which can be detected by haar cascade classifier
2. Create a bounding rectangle around the detected face

3. Crop the area bounded by the rectangle
4. Pass the region cropped to the LBPH to convert the image into vector form
5. Store the region of face in vector form with a label, which is the name of the face in an yml file

23.4.4 Algorithm for Security

1. Open the camera
2. Capture each frame
3. Find face inside the frame using haar cascade classifier
4. Start finding a match between the face detected in the frame and those in the database
5. If a match is found, continue the process 3 and 4
6. Else active the keyboard blocking
7. And then the user manually unlocks the keyboard initiate the screen block and continue the from process from 3, 4, 6, and 7

23.5 Result

The system is able to recognize the rightful owner of the computer (Figure 23.5).

When the system is unable to recognize the user, it will display the message that it is not the owner and block the keyboard of the computer (Figure 23.6).

When the key lock is manually unlocked by clicking the button then a screen as in Figure 23.7 is shown, which will block the back view of the screen. This prevents the user from using the computer. The keyboard locker and the screen blocker will appear one after another, preventing the user to effectively use the computer.

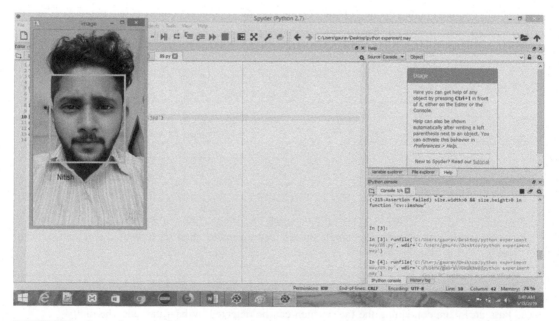

FIGURE 23.5   Owner face recognition.

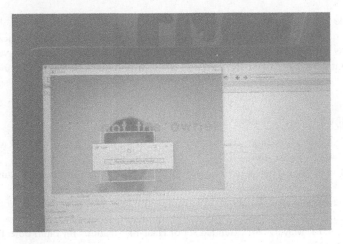

FIGURE 23.6 When user is not owner.

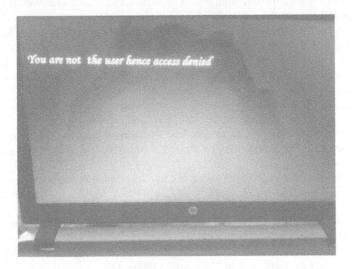

FIGURE 23.7 System locked due to unauthorized user.

23.6 Conclusion

Using biometrics, a security system will prove to be effective in the long run of this cyber security field and this will help to cope with a lot of attacks and using the person as the security key will make it less vulnerable as anyone can mimic the key that is mathematically generated but mimicking a person is a difficult job and doing it for always at certain interval of time makes it frustrating. Image spoofing can be effectively removed, as one has to always show the image in front of the camera and the program will always track the same person after a certain interval of time.

23.7 Future Scope

At this time, this program is working for just the laptop or desktop security purpose; later on with advancement it will work for secure connections also. This system can be used for any device. Presently it is able to provide access to one person but with advancement of technology, it will provide different levels of access to different persons on the same computer. This will work as a barrier for those who are restricted to access only some parts of the computer i.e., if someone is not provided the access of notepad the computer will not open the notepad for him and keep blocking the same as per the settings made.

REFERENCE

[1] F. Crow, "Summed-area tables for texture mapping", Proceedings of SIGGRAPH, vol. 18, no. 3 (1984): 207–212.

[2] Viola and Jones, "Rapid object detection using a boosted cascade of simple features", Computer cool Vision and Pattern Recognition, 2001.

[3] Oren Papageorgiou and Poggio, "A general framework for object detection", International Conference on Computer Vision, 1998.

[4] R. Lienhart and J. Maydt, "An extended set of Haar-like features for rapid object detection", ICIP02 (2002): 900–903.

[5] C. H. Messom and A. L. C. Barczak, "Fast and efficient rotated haar-like features using rotated integral images", Australian Conference on Robotics and Automation (ACRA 2006): 1–6.

[6] D. C. He and L. Wang, "Texture unit, texture spectrum, and texture analysis", IEEE Transactions on Geoscience and Remote Sensing, vol. 28 (1990): 509–512.

[7] L. Wang and D. C. He, "Texture Classification using texture spectrum", Pattern Recognition, vol. 23, no. 8 (1990): 905–910.

[8] T. Ojala, M. Pietikäinen and D. Harwood, "Performance evaluation of texture measures with classification based on Kullback discrimination of distributions", Proceedings of the 12th IAPR International Conference on Pattern Recognition (ICPR 1994), vol. 1 (1994): 582–585.

[9] T. Ojala, M. Pietikäinen and D. Harwood, "A comparative study of texture measures with classification based on feature distributions", Pattern Recognition, vol. 29 (1996): 51–59.

[10] M. Heikkilä and M. Pietikäinen, "A texture-based method for modeling the background and detecting moving objects", IEEE Transactions on Pattern Analysis and Machine Intelligence, vol. 28, no. 4 (2006): 657–662.

[11] L. Scripcariu, A. Alistar and M. D. Frunza, "JAVA implemented encryption algorithm", Proceedings of the 8th Int. Conference "Development and Application Systems", Suceava, DAS 2006 (2006): 424–429.

[12] H. Gilbert and M. Minier, "A collision attack on seven rounds of Rijndael", Proceedings of the 3rd AES Candidate Conference (2000): 230–241.

[13] D. J. Wheeler and R. Needham, "TEA, A tiny encryption algorithm", Technical Report 355, Computer Laboratory, University of Cambridge (1994): 1–3.

[14] B. Schneier, "The GOST encryption algorithm", Dr. Dobb's Journal, vol. 20, no. 1 (1995): 123–124.

[15] L. Scripcariu and S. Ciornei, "Improving the encryption algorithms using multidimensional data structures", Proceedings of the Third European Conference on the Use of Modern Information and Communication Technologies, ECUMICT 2008, Gent (Belgium) (2008): 375–384.

[16] M. E. Hellman and W. Diffie, "New directions in cryptography", IEEE Transactions on Information Theory, vol. 22, no. 6 (1976): 644–654.

[17] F. Ballardin, "A calculus for the analysis of wireless network security protocols", Formal Aspects of Security and Trust. Springer: Berlin Heidelberg; (2011): 206–222.

[18] Guoying Zhao and Pietikainen Matti, "Dynamic texture recognition using local binary patterns with an application to facial expressions", IEEE Transactions on Pattern Analysis and Machine Intelligence vol. 29, no. 6 (2007): 915–928.

[19] Kertész, "Texture-based foreground detection", International Journal of Signal Processing, Image Processing and Pattern Recognition (IJSIP), vol. 4, no. 4 (2011).

[20] Sally Cole, "U.S. Army's AI facial recognition works in the dark", Military Embedded Systems (2018): 1–8.

[21] Joy Buolamwini and Timnit Gebru, "Gender shades: intersectional accuracy disparities in commercial gender classification", Proceedings of Machine Learning Research, vol. 81 (2018): 1–15.

[22] L. C. Chen, G. Papandreou, I. Kokkinos, K. Murphy, et al., "Deeplab: semantic image segmentation with deep convolutional nets, atrous convolution, and fully connected CRFs", EEE Transactions on Pattern Analysis and Machine Intelligence vol. 40, no. 4 (2018): 834–848.

[23] Kaushal M., Khehra B. and Sharma A., "Soft computing based object detection and tracking approaches: state-of-the-art survey", Applied Soft Computing, vol. 70 (2018): 423–464.

[24] Z. H. Peric and J. Nikolic, "An adaptive waveform coding algorithm and its application in speech coding," Digital Signal Processing, vol. 22, no. 1 (2012): 199–209.

[25] R. K. Moore, "Cognitive informatics: the future of spoken language processing?" in Proceedings of the 10th International Conference on Speech and Computer (SPECOM), Patras, Greece, October 2005.

[26] J. Nikolic and Z. H. Peric, "Lloyd-Max's algorithm implementation in speech coding algorithm based on forward adaptive technique," Informatics (Lithuanian Academy of Sciences), vol. 19, no. 2 (2008): 255–270.

24

Data Analytics for Detecting DDoS Attacks in Network Traffic

Ciza Thomas and Rejimol Robinson R.R.

CONTENTS

24.1 Introduction

Distributed Denial of Service (DDoS) attack is usually launched to make an online service, a network, or even a website, unavailable by flooding it with traffic from many sources. DDoS attacks are becoming bigger, more frequent, and more sophisticated and advanced. They are very common and its impact is most devastating that network defenders and analysts must watch out for. According to Helpnetsecurity, a featured news blog, the average bandwidth of DDoS attacks are increasing and low and slow attacks targeting layer 7 are also increasing. In Q1 2020 the biggest attack stopped was 406 Gbps, but in Q1 2019 the maximum bandwidth peaked to 224 Gbps. The share of multi-vector attacks rose to 64% in Q1 2020 from 47% in Q1 2019. The attack techniques are also fast evolving. The low rate, slow attacks, multi-vector and layer 7 attacks, are prevalent today. They do have the common characteristic that they are decoys and their similarity to benign traffic is large. A memcached DDoS attack is a type of modern day cyber attack which comes under the category of amplification attack. The attacker spoofs requests to a vulnerable UDP memcached server, which then floods a targeted victim server with Internet traffic, ultimately causing saturation of its resources. Memcached is a database caching system for speeding up websites and networks. Here the main attacking vector is UDP. Similarly the sophisticated DDoS attacks are all different only in their attacking strategies, but their attacking vectors mainly fall under the category of UDP flooding, TCP SYN flooding, HTTP low and slow rate attacks, etc.

Intrusion Detection Systems (IDS) are usually used to detect network attacks, but the different traditional detection strategies are incapable of identifying novel attacks or evolving attacks. Hence, we need intelligent IDS system to detect the more sophisticated attacks. Researchers are now using machine learning algorithms in this area.

Important consequences of the digitally connected world are the collecting and managing of raw data. Managing needs attention, because the data is valuable and come in different sizes and formats. Big data in the form of network traffic is very powerful and it affects all parts of society from social aspects to almost all other areas. As the amount of data increases, big data analytic based processing involving experimentation, data analysis and monitoring get more importance. Machine learning is one of the very important tools and works in supervised and unsupervised models. The power of machine learning analytics depends on data input. The more exact and representative the data input, the more effective will be the analytical performance. To gauge and improve the effectiveness of detection algorithms, we need large and representative datasets of Internet traffic consisting of the combination of benign and attack network traffic patterns.

The large variety of attacks demands case specific approach to hinder the attack. There exists no such single system which can perform well to detect and mitigate attacks. Hence, we have to choose the appropriate method to handle the attack. There exist certain factors that need thorough analysis and attention. As thousands of packets are passing by a particular point at any given instance on any computer network, it is very difficult to gather a set of balanced data instances. The attack instances are comparatively very less compared to the instances of normal packets. According to Thomas et al., this skewness in distribution of real-world network traffic data is known as an imbalanced dataset problem.[1] This scenario will affect training, model designing, and finally causes misclassification. Moreover, it is very hard to get all possible situations of normal and attack traffic to train a machine learning algorithm.

The second important factor which affects the performance of the machine learning algorithm is the stealthy nature of attack instances. Majority of supervised learning algorithms fail to detect a marginal percentage of attacks even if their features are very distinguishable. According to Feistein et al., stealthy traffic means the traffic flood launched by sophisticated attackers that mimic the legitimate traffic expected to evade detection. Many advanced attacking tools are available today that can determine typical entropy levels seen at the detector end and tune the attacking parameters to match. Hence an attacker who is equipped with the kind of knowledge that could produce attack traffic that would produce not even a slight change in the entropy observed at the detector.[2] Normally, the attack traffic coming at the victim end in the network has very prominent features, unless otherwise the attackers use guesswork, penetration, or trial and error to mimic the behavior of normal traffic.

The proposed system improves the performance of the machine learning algorithms by considering the aspects such as imbalanced dataset problem and the stealthiness of DDoS attacks. It starts with dataset preparation by extracting features from the network traffic available in pcap format. The marginal percentage of attack misclassification is mainly due to the disproportional number of instances of attack and normal traffic. Based on this, it is proposed to analyse the performance of machine learning algorithms in attack detection by doing preprocessing such as oversampling and synthetic oversampling of attack instances. Then, we address the problem of misclassification of attack that happens due to its similarity to normal traffic. The features that can be used for attack detection are not that much sharp enough to take the decision confidently. Hence, we have computed the similarity index based on Hellinger distance (HD) and it is taken as a measure to represent the stealthiness of attack and this information can be exploited to detect stealthy layer seven attacks.

The contributions of this chapter are as follows.

1. We describe how an analysis of data related to its imbalance in distribution and the stealthy nature can be used to choose the proper preprocessing method such as oversampling, synthetic oversampling or feature engineering based on distributional similarity of attack and benign instances to have a proper model that correctly fits the data.
2. Ranking of machine learning algorithms in detecting DDoS attacks while addressing the

contradictory constraints such as maximising the recall and precision and minimizing false positives and negatives using multi criteria decision aid system called PROMETHEE.

3. A performance evaluation of this framework is conducted on bench mark datasets: LLS DDoS scenario specific dataset, CAIDA dataset, and CICIDS 2017, and comparing the proposed system with the existing systems to assess its effectiveness in detecting DDoS attacks.

The rest of this chapter is organized as follows. The background on DDoS detection is presented in Section 24.2. Section 24.3 describes related work, especially covering the areas on machine learning based DDoS detection, the importance of flow-based approach, and the various preprocessing experiments to prepare the data. The proposed methodology is presented in Section 24.4 and results are discussed in Section 24.5. Finally the conclusion and future works are given in Section 24.6.

24.2 Background

DDoS attacks can be classified into volumetric attack, protocol attack and application layer attack. The specific focus of volumetric attack is to congest the network by sending large volume of data packets over the network and utilising the network bandwidth. This kind of attack is usually executed by botnets. The protocol attack targets actual web/DNS/FTP servers, routers, switch, firewall devices, and load balancers to disrupt the network services and will cause resource exhaustion. Application layer attacks are also termed as layer 7 attacks which mainly target the layer 7 protocols and exploit them to cause resource exhaustion. These attacks are very sophisticated with low traffic rate, which appears to be legitimate for the victim system. UDP flood, HTTP flood, and slowloris are some of the sophisticated attacks worth mentioning and considered in this work as well. These attacking vectors are very stealthy in nature and are part of multi-vector attacks. UDP flood targets the opened UDP ports on the victim network and start the flood by simply sending UDP packets. HTTP flood targets the web applications and use legitimate HTTP GET and POST requests to launch the attack. These are simply legitimate requests and the main aim is to bring down the server. Slowloris is entirely different from the attacks mentioned. It is a perfect benign HTTP traffic and is launched by making use of a software called slowloris.

The DDoS defence challenges are mentioned in the work of Mirkovic et al.[3] The seriousness of the DDoS attack demands distributed response from the network. Most of the defence systems are meant for a specific kind of DDoS attack. There is no such single system which can resist all the attacking strategies. Hence, there is a need for such a system which can combine the approaches effectively to solve the problem.

24.3 Related Work

As the number of packets per unit time is huge to be processed and for having global perspective of handling network traffic, it is desirable to aggregate packets into flows. Many of the services and web applications available today are based on application layer protocols such as FTP, HTTP, DNS, Hadoop etc. and their working is controlled by data centers. The work of Xiao et al. is mainly on aggregated flow data that comes from data centers. The features specifically related to flows such as flow duration, flow size, etc. are selected and applied CKNN (K-nearest neighbors traffic classification with correlation analysis) as the detection algorithm. This work is based on the fact that there exists a high correlation among the flows of traffic from the same application.[4]

The work of Wagner et al. also considers attributes of Netflow records and projects data points into a higher dimension, before the classification. They modelled one class SVM classifier, which is capable of identifying outliers and anomalies.[5]

The work of Qin et al. do the aggregation of packets into flows with five tuples such as source and destination addresses, source and destination ports, and protocol type. Then the features of such flow data namely, packet size, source address, destination address, destination port, and flow duration are derived. Then constructed entropy vectors of these five features are using Shannon entropy. The information distance so formed can measure the deviation of probability distribution between attack traffic and normal traffic.[6]

As this chapter proposes the effectiveness of data analytics in DDoS detection, it is necessary to look at the challenges of machine learning in DDoS attack detection. The work of Sommer et al., lists the challenges of machine learning algorithm for implementing systems in large-scale and operational environments.[7] Fundamentally, machine-learning algorithms are meant for classification problems because it works by finding similarities rather than identifying activities that deviates from normal profile. So, in order to get a reliable classification, it is required to train them with sufficient numbers of instances from all the categories. The important factor is the high cost of false positives. Another challenge is the system should adapt to the diversity in network traffic properties such as bandwidth, duration of connections, and application mix etc. It is very challenging to get such a network traffic to build a proper model. The primary reason for the lack of publicly available datasets is its sensitive nature. The recommendation of their work is to obtain insight into the operation of an anomaly detection system in terms of its capabilities and limitations from an operational point of view.

There are so many seminal works giving importance to supervised learning, unsupervised learning, soft computing techniques, and most importantly deep learning techniques as well. Rather than simply detecting attacks at the destination point, certain works investigate machine learning methods that enable the network to stop these attacks early and close to the sources. The work of Berral et al. explains an adaptive learning where a learning component lets the system create, adjust, and renew the behavior models. Network learns from its neighborhood and shares the local traffic patterns, so the information is collected in a local model or classifier.[8]

The work done by Robinson et al.[9] rank machine learning algorithms detecting DDoS attacks based on some criteria. Their paper gives an evaluation and ranking of some of the supervised machine learning algorithms with the aim of reducing type I and type II errors, increasing precision and recall while maintaining detection accuracy. Random forest algorithm gives a much better performance and the ensemble classifiers with random forest as the base classifier tops the rank list. Usually decision tree based algorithms perform much better than other traditional machine learning algorithms.

There are works in the field of machine learning especially with features of packet level data. Saied et al.[10] use an Artificial Neural Network (ANN) to segregate attack traffic from genuine traffic based on features specific to packet-level data. They have compared the features of benign packets generated by normal applications with the features of malicious packets generated by DDoS advanced attacking tools. Then, they extracted discriminating features as input variables to train ANN structures, involving source IP address, source and destination port number, packet size, the number of packets, etc. The trained model can detect known and unknown DDoS flooding attacks with high accuracy.

Vijayasarathy et al.[11] propose an anomaly-based system to detect DoS attacks using a Naive Bayes classifier approach, together with some methods to work in real time. The main focus of the work is on transport/transmission layer protocols such as TCP and UDP. The training phase takes features namely TCP flags, the amount of source and destination addresses, the number of packets, source and destination ports, packet size, and packet arrival time as inputs and trains them using the Naive Bayes algorithm. Windowing is the special technique used in this work, where time windows and packet windows are experimented and they found that packet windows provide smaller reaction time during the attack and it provides more accurate modeling.

Su[12] proposes a detection method using a weighted k-nearest neighbor (KNN) classifier to detect large-scale attacks. They have given importance to good feature selection policy involving genetic algorithms combined with KNN. For known attacks, an accuracy rate of 97.42% was obtained with only 19 features and for unknown attacks the accuracy of 78% was obtained with 28 features.

Kong et al.[13] identify the features such as the number of unique source addresses, the number of increased source addresses, the average of the number of packets sent by source addresses, and the standard of the number of packets sent by source addresses to discriminate DDoS flooding attacks from flash crowds. They have given importance to preprocessing methods and data mining algorithms like logistic, multilayer perceptron, J48, and PART to obtain optimal discrimination.

Lee et al.[14] propose a proactive detection method for DDoS flooding attacks by exploiting the communication between an attacker and victims. The entropy of source and destination ports, the entropy of source and destination addresses, the entropy of packet types, and the number of packets and the occurrence of packet types (TCP, UDP, and ICMP) are taken as the features and follow a packet-based detection approach. Then a hierarchical clustering algorithm was applied to form clusters using these feature vectors.

Casa et al.[15] propose a big data analytics framework specifically for network monitoring applications. In this work they employ machine learning based algorithms for network security using off-the-shelf machine learning libraries. This method is used to detect different types of network attacks on top of real network measurements collected at the WIDE backbone network. They also explore and identify novel features for better and faster detection of common network attacks. Feature selection techniques are also analysed to further reduce the execution time and it is useful to keep the required features only. The significant and noteworthy solutions to classify the skewed data can be broadly classified into two. Data pre-processing and algorithmic procedure. In the former level, methods can be adopted to change the distribution of data to make it somehow balanced and then present to the learning algorithm to improve the performance. Algorithmic way of enhancement tries to develop new algorithms and make the algorithm suit the classification of skewed data. Innovative research and development works are flourishing in these areas and several seminal works are there to guide further improvements.[16] SMOTE (Synthetic Minority Oversampling Technique)[17] comes under the intelligent oversampling strategy and is the most used enhancement methods in combination with other machine learning algorithms. Synthetic samples are being generated along the line between the randomly selected minority sample and its selected nearest neighbors. Random sample selection is based on oversampling rate. By taking the k nearest neighbors, where $k = 5$ of the randomly selected minority sample, new synthetic examples are created.

The work of Japkowicz et al. explore the question of when class imbalance really matters. This work showed the evidence of the fact such that sensitivity of standard multilayer perceptron closely related to complexity of the domain but not the size of the training set.[18] The work of Jo and Japkowicz, analyze the random resampling methods for tackling the within class imbalance. It is found to be very simple, beneficial, and addresses both within class and between class imbalance problems. After verifying the fact that the small disjunct problem is more unpredictable as compared to between class imbalance, cluster based oversampling method is suggested to alleviate the small disjunct problem and finally established that addressing both imbalance problems simultaneously has an added advantage.[19]

Towards Data Science is a blog sharing concepts, ideas, and codes states that according to a survey in Forbes, data scientists spend 80% of their time on data preparation. Data preparation mainly involves feature engineering why because machine learning algorithms require features with some specific characteristic to work properly. It is an essential step to extract optimal information about datasets, so that we can present proper data to the algorithms. As variety of attacks emerges everyday, it is very difficult to identify the features relevant to each case and detect them efficiently. Exploring more and more features relevant to the attack vector may help the machine learning algorithms to reach up to the required performance level. Preprocessing methods such as oversampling, undersampling, and synthetic oversampling techniques can also contribute to improve the performance of machine learning algorithms. What we have to do is exploit the knowledge that we can infer from the data. The first step of the proposed methodology is to infer the knowledge from data and then evaluate the performance of algorithms.

Some research works investigate on data preprocessing methods and different kinds of feature selection techniques to improve the performance of detection algorithms. An ensemble of multi-filter feature selection involving CFS (Correlation-based Feature Selection), IG (Information Gain), Chi-squared, and ReliefF applied on Decision tree algorithm (J48) is mentioned in the work of Osanaiye et al.[20] Feature engineering methods such as backward elimination, chi2, and information gain scores are employed to obtain significant features according to the work of Aamir et al.[21]

Table 24.1 shows the details of recent research works on DDoS detection and mitigation that are used for comparison with the approach proposed in this work.

TABLE 24.1

Summary of Literature Used for Comparison

Reference	Topic Discussed	Remarks
[22]Singh et al.	Multilayer Perceptron with a Genetic Algorithm (MLP-GA). Layer 7 HTTP attack using slowloris attacking tool is addressed.	Accuracy of 98.04% for detecting the layer seven DDoS attacks and false positives are less compared to Naive Bayes, Radial Basis Function (RBF) Network, MLP, J48, and C45 (2017).
[23]Lima et al.	Machine learning DoS detection system and makes inferences based on signatures previously extracted from samples of network traffic.	Four datasets namely CIC-DoS, CICIDS2017, CSE-CIC-IDS2018, CICIDS2017 and customized dataset. Acquired detection rate and precision higher than 93% with FAR less than 1.8%.
[24]Shone et al.	Non-symmetric deep auto-encoder (NDAE) for unsupervised feature learning and deep learning classification model constructed using stacked NDAE.	KDD Cup'99 and NSL-KDD datasets used.
[25]Ahmed et al	New structures called application fingerprints are generated using transport layer packet-level and flow-level features.	Accuracy of over 97% is achieved with the misclassification rate of 2.5%.
[26]Alsirhani et al.	A dynamic DDoS attack detection system framework uses fuzzy logic to dynamically select an algorithm from a set of prepared classification algorithms that detect different DDoS patterns.	Trade-off exists in the classification algorithm's accuracy and its delay.

24.4 Methodology

The machine learning based DDoS detection system is depicted in Figure 24.1. The initial part of DDoS detection system is the collection of network traffic in pcap format. Specific application programming interface called packet capture (pcap) is used to collect network traffic. Software like Libpcap of Unix and Winpcap of Windows are the libraries used to collect data in pcap format. This kind of software can be used to do additional statistical functionalities related to packets. TCPdump and Wireshark are the free software which aids packet sniffing and monitoring along with statistical analysis. Wireshark is actually the GUI version of TCPdump.

In high-speed connections having rates up to hundreds of Gigabits per second (Gbps), it is very costly to do packet level data analysis. Moreover, it leads to poor performance of the detection system as well. Hence, it is more convenient and efficient to aggregate packet level data into flow level data and it greatly supports big data analytic of network traffic to a large extent. According to RFC 3697A, a flow can be defined as a sequence of packets sent from a particular source to a particular unicast, anycast, multicast destination that the source desires to label as a flow. It is more logical to consider a flow as an instance which can be malicious or benign. Hence, it is desirable to extract features related to each flow. We have selected the features mentioned in the work of Karimazad and Faraahi, which hold the information very specific to represent DDoS attack.[27] We have defined these features in relation to the flows. The features are Average packet size, Number of packets, Time interval variance, Packet size variance, Number of bytes, Packet rate, and Bitrate. Average packet size is the sum of size of each packet of a flow averaged over total number of packets and is given in (24.1), where N is the total number of packets in a flow and P_i is the size of the ith packet. Time interval variance quantifies the variance in the inter arrival time of packets in a flow and is given in (24.2), where t_i is the arrival time of ith packet. Packet size variance quantifies the size difference of adjacent packets averaged over total number of packets and is given in (24.3). Packet rate is expressed in (24.4), where t_{end} is the arrival time of last packet and t_{start} is the arrival time of first packet related to a particular flow.

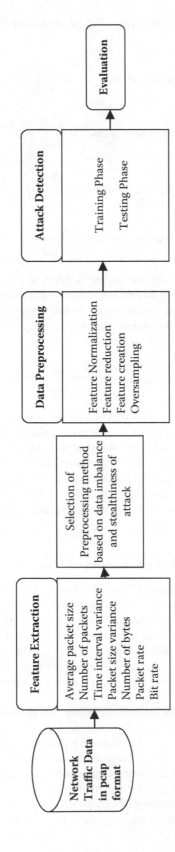

FIGURE 24.1 Organization of machine learning based DDoS detection system.

Number of packets, Number of bytes, and bitrate can be computed directly from the packet features exported by Wireshark.

$$Average\_Packet\_size = \frac{1}{N} \sum_{i=0}^{N} P_i \tag{24.1}$$

$$Time\_interval\_variance = \frac{1}{N} \sum_{i=0}^{N} t_{i+1} - t_i \tag{24.2}$$

$$Packet\_size\_variance = \frac{1}{N} \sum_{i=0}^{N} P_{i+1} - P_i \tag{24.3}$$

$$Packet\_rate = \frac{N}{t_{end} - t_{start}} \tag{24.4}$$

Feature normalization is an essential step for scaling features to fit into a particular range, and will eliminate the bias from data without modifying the statistical nature of the features. Minmax normalisation is being employed to scale the feature values in the range [0 1] and is given in (24.5). The normalized features are stacked to form feature vectors and they are shuffled to have a proper distribution of the instances across the sample space.

$$x_{norm\_i} = \frac{x_i - x_{max}}{x_{max} - x_{min}} \tag{24.5}$$

DDoS attack detection is subsequently done by considering two different situations that affects the algorithm performance. The DDoS attack traffic is inherently imbalanced in nature because the presence of attack instances is very low compared to the benign traffic. Hence it is proposed to do the random oversampling or synthetic sampling to make the data appropriate to build the model. The stealthy layer 7 attacks are handled by creating a new feature which represents the similarity of attack traffic to benign traffic. Then the analysis of machine learning algorithms are done based on multiple criteria like improving the True Positive (TP) rate and True Negative (TN) rate and reducing the False Positive (FP) rate and False Negative (FN) rate.

24.4.1 Oversampling and Synthetic Sampling of Data

The direct approach for handling imbalanced dataset problem is by having equal number of samples in each class. This simple method of generating more number of minority instances just by repeating the randomly sampled instances is called oversampling. The disadvantage of oversampling is over-fitting. Hence this approach is less desirable as it affects the generalization capability of machine learning algorithms. However, as far as DDoS detection is concerned, misclassification of attacks is very costly and we want to reduce the FN rate. It is desirable to repeat the rarer attack vectors as it encourages the proper learning of certain variants of rarer DDoS attacks. Hence it is proposed to do the oversampling of rarer DDoS attack events.

The attack instances distributed in the range [0 S], where S is the total number of instances in attack class and are randomly selected. The algorithm simply repeats the attack instances based on the parameter i expressed in percentage which determines the percentage of attack class instances selected to do the oversampling. According to this experimental setup, we can do the oversampling by varying the percentage parameter and can update training data with the oversampled instances. Then the whole dataset is shuffled to get the attack instances distributed in the dataset.

SMOTE (Synthetic Minority Oversampling Technique) is an intelligent oversampling strategy and it is used with other machine learning algorithms to enhance the performance. According to SMOTE, the synthetic samples are generated along the line of randomly selected instances. This kind of over-sampling may lead to the generation of spurious samples and it will affect the performance of the model. In the case of DDoS attacks, feature vector associated to a particular attack can be regarded as the signature of that attack. Hence, it is proposed to generate attack instances inside the attack class distribution rather than generating samples based on SMOTE.[28]

The proposed methodology begins with a prior classification phase, which splits the training data into 60% train and 40% test. The attack instances misclassified in this phase are further used for oversampling. It selects the maximum of all feature values and creates a feature vector named *Max_attack*. Then the minimum of all feature values is selected and created a feature vector named *Min_attack*. These two feature vectors are formed from the correctly classified attack class. Then the synthetic samples are created based on equations (24.6) and (24.7).

$$Syn\_sample\_\min = randn\,(0-1) * [FN\_ins\tan ce\,(i) + Min\_attack] \tag{24.6}$$

$$Syn\_sample\_\max = randn\,(0-1) * [FN\_ins\tan ce\,(i) + Max\_attack] \tag{24.7}$$

Syn_sample_min and *Syn_sample_max* are the two synthetic samples created. *FN_ instance(i)* represents the ith misclassified attack sample, *i* can vary from *1* to *N*, where *N* is the total number of misclassified attacks. *randn(0 -1)* is the function used to generate a number in the interval [0 1]. For *N* number of misclassified attack instances only *2N* number of synthetic samples is created. These synthetic samples are added to the original train data and shuffled to get an evenly distributed dataset.

24.4.2 Detection of Stealthy DDoS attacks

Stealthy attacks do have the property that they are similar to benign traffic. This same information can be exploited to detect low rate layer 7 attacks such as slowloris and slowHTTPtest. Hellinger Distance (HD) metric is mainly used to capture the similarity because it is used to compute the distance between two distributions. There exists a marginal similarity between stealthy attacks and benign traffic, because most of the stealthy attacks are launched by fabricating the parameter guessed to have a match with benign traffic. Hence, according to the proposed work, a subset of normal and attack traffic is randomly selected. The Hellinger distance between attack samples with randomly selected benign traffic is calculated and is named as HD_A. The HD between attack samples and randomly selected attack samples are represented as HD_B. The difference between these two calculated entries carries the information related to the similarity of attack with benign traffic and is termed as *Sim_index* and is given in (24.8) where *i* denote the ith instance. Then the instances are updated with the newly created feature and then the instances are shuffled.

$$Sim\_index\,(i) = |HD_A\,(i) - HD_B\,(i)| \tag{24.8}$$

24.4.3 Performance Evaluation by Ranking Machine Learning Algorithms

The performance of machine learning algorithms can be evaluated and ranked based on the decision of Multi Criteria Decision Aid (MCDA) software called Visual PROMETHEE. Maximising Precision and Recall, while minimizing FP rate and TP rate are mutually conflicting criteria selected to do the evaluation. Mathematical representation of this statement can be written as *maximize $f_1(a)$, $f_2(a)$ and minimize $f_3(a)$, $f_4(a)$* where $a \in A$ and set *A* is the finite set of four algorithms selected for evaluation. They are called actions in Visual PROMETHEE and f_1, f_2, f_3, and f_4 are criteria namely Precision, Recall, FN rate, and FP rate, respectively. When two actions *a* and *b* are compared, the multicriteria preference index is computed:

$$f(a, b) = \sum_{j=1}^{k} w_j P_j(a, b) \tag{24.9}$$

It involves the values taken by the preference functions associated to the criteria and not directly the evaluations of the actions themselves. The advantage of the PROMETHEE is that, it does the pairwise comparisons of actions. Two actions a and b are compared by computing the multicriteria preference index as given in (24.9), where $P_j(a, b)$ is defined as the preference function and non negative weights that represent the relative importance of the criteria can also be defined. Then the preference flows are computed to consolidate the results of the pairwise comparisons of the actions and rank all the actions from the best to the worst. The mathematical expressions to compute preference flows are given in equations (24.10) and (24.11).

$$\varphi^+ = \frac{1}{N-1} \sum_{b \neq a} f(a, b) \tag{24.10}$$

$$\varphi^- = \frac{1}{N-1} \sum_{b \neq a} f(b, a) \tag{24.11}$$

Φ^+ is the positive preference flow which measures how much an action a is preferred to the other $n-1$ actions. It is a global measurement of the strength of action a and larger the Φ^+, better the action. Similarly Φ^- measures how much the other $n-1$ actions are preferred to action a. It is global measure of weaknesses of action a and smaller the Φ^- the better the action. We make use of PROMETHEE Complete ranking as we are dealing with strong conflicting criteria and it is given by net preference flow as shown in (24.12).

$$\varphi(a) = \varphi^+(a) - \varphi^-(a) \tag{24.12}$$

It aggregates both the strengths and the weaknesses of the action into a single score. Hence, the proposition is *aPb if and only if $\Phi(a) > \Phi(b)$*. The action a is preferred over action b if and only if it is preferred to b according to the net preference flow.

24.5 Result and Discussion

The results are evaluated based on three different datasets. The following subsections will illustrate the datasets that are used, the metrics selected for evaluation, and the discussion of results.

24.5.1 Datasets Used for Evaluation

CICIDS2017 dataset contains most of the modern-day attacks along with benign traffic, which resembles the real-world data in pcap and CSV formats. Realistic background traffic is the notable feature of this dataset. The dataset used here is the July 5, 2017, samples comprising four different attacks generated by modern attacking tools, namely, slowloris, Slowhttptest, Hulk, and GoldenEye.

The CAIDA attack 2007 is one hour of anonymized traffic traces from a DDoS attack on August 4, 2007 (20:50:08 UTC to 21:56:16 UTC). It is a collection of several different types of data at geographically and topologically diverse locations, and makes this data available to the research community while preserving the privacy of data.

LLS DDoS scenario specific dataset is the DARPA Lincoln labs packet traces. The criticism regarding the DARPA dataset about collected traffic data, attack taxonomy, and evaluation criteria are well explained in the literature of McHugh.[29] Irregularities in the attributes of the DARPA dataset are addressed by Mahoney and Chan.[30] However, the usefulness of the DARPA dataset was brought out with the work of Thomas et al. It is demonstrated using signature-based IDSs and anomaly-based IDSs.[31]

2000 DARPA LLS-DDoS 1.0-Scenario One dataset contains attack and the normal data of week one. So this mixture comprises DDoS run by a novice attacker and a collection of packets with majority of normal traffic. The attacker is using the Mstream DDoS tool, one of the less sophisticated DDoS tools. It does not make use of encryption and does not offer as wide a range of attack options as other tools. Mstream server software that actually generates and sends the DDoS attack packets, is installed on each of the three victim hosts, while an Mstream master software that provides a user-interface and controls the servers, is installed on one of the victims.

24.5.2 Evaluation Metrics Used

The algorithms heavily depend on instance distribution and the statistics of features. Hence, it is required to choose proper performance metrics giving certain preferences. As the network data itself is skewed, it is less important to get better accuracy as accuracy is not indicative of the performance with skewed data. In this work, accuracy metric is only used to compare the proposed method with some of the recent literature on DDoS detection. For the better performance analysis of algorithms, it is required to give more importance to recall and precision. It is very difficult to set a crisp boundary for attacks because its presence is less in number in the dataset and obviously detection will be difficult.[32]

All the relevant metrics for doing performance evaluation can be derived from the confusion matrix shown in Table 24.2. This 2 × 2 matrix has the following four cell contents. The True Positive (TP) is the number of truly classified attacks, False negatives (FN) are the number of attacks that are wrongly classified, True negative (TN) is the number of benign instances classified as benign, and False positive (FP) is the number of benign instances misclassified as attack. Precision is the fraction of test data predicted as attacks truly belonging to attack class and Recall is the fraction of attacks that are truly classified as attack. So, these two metrics are obviously conflicting criteria and there exists a trade-off between precision and recall when classifiers are evaluated. Hence, we have used PROMETHEE II complete ranking to evaluate the algorithms, in which the Precision, Recall, FN rate, and FP rate are used as criteria for evaluation.

As far as DDoS detection is concerned, our interest lies in TP rate of attack class rather than the overall accuracy as sparing the attacks undetected is considered as very costly. Moreover, an imbalanced data cannot be evaluated by using accuracy parameter only. The equation for TP rate metric is

TABLE 24.2

Confusion Matrix

Predicted Actual	Attack	Normal
Attack	TP	FN
Normal	FP	TN

TABLE 24.3

LLS-DDoS Scenario Specific Dataset

TP Rate Algorithm	Synthetic Sampling Normal	Attack	Similarity Based Normal	Attack	SMOTE Normal	Attack
Random forest	0.995	0.993	0.991	0.981	0.992	0.99
J48	0.993	0.955	0.994	0.992	0.981	0.958
Adaboost	0.995	0.992	0.991	0.981	0.993	0.991
KNN	0.983	0.972	0.964	0.952	0.982	0.991

TABLE 24.4

CAIDA 2007 Dataset

TP Rate Algorithm	Synthetic Sampling Normal Attack		Similarity Based Normal Attack		SMOTE Normal Attack	
Random forest	1	0.997	0.994	0.992	0.991	0.983
J48	0.997	0.983	0.991	0.982	0.989	0.97
Adaboost	1	0.996	0.996	0.992	0.991	0.983
KNN	0.98	0.974	0.991	0.98	0.99	0.987

TABLE 24.5

CICIDS 2017 Dataset

TP Rate Algorithm	Synthetic Sampling Normal Attack		Similarity Based Normal Attack		SMOTE Normal Attack	
Random forest	0.982	0.953	1	0.995	1	0.992
J48	0.980	0.9323	0.993	0.987	0.991	0.988
Adaboost	0.989	0.962	0.991	0.998	1	0.992
KNN	0.953	0.948	0.982	0.973	0.992	0.951

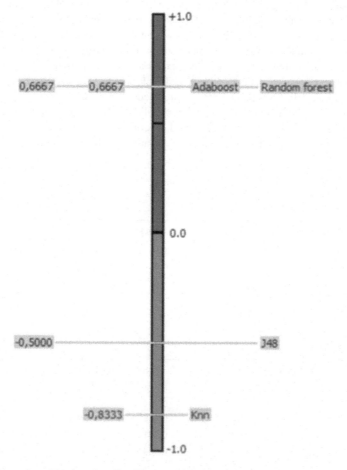

FIGURE 24.2 Ranking of machine learning algorithms on LLS-DDoS dataset.

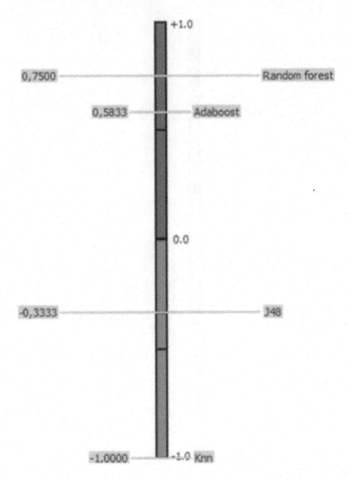

FIGURE 24.3 Ranking of machine learning algorithms on CAIDA 2007 dataset.

given in (24.13), where TP is the number of positives correctly predicted as positives and FN is number of positives wrongly predicted as negative.

$$TPR = \frac{TP}{TP + FN} \tag{24.13}$$

24.5.3 Observations

The results based on TP rate of attack class is shown in Tables 24.3–24.5. In the situations where there exists high imbalance in distribution of attack and benign instances, we simply do the oversampling of attack instances. We have experimented the random oversampling of attack instances and the synthetic oversampling of instances as proposed in the methodology and SMOTE. Random oversampling of attacks has been conducted by varying the percentage of attack instances selected for oversampling. To get a better performance of algorithm it is observed to select 75% of instances to do random over-sampling. However, in synthetic sampling, we have generated double the misclassified attack instances as the synthetic samples. The performance achieved is far better than the simple random oversampling and the results are shown in the column labeled "Synthetic sampling" in Tables 24.3–24.5.

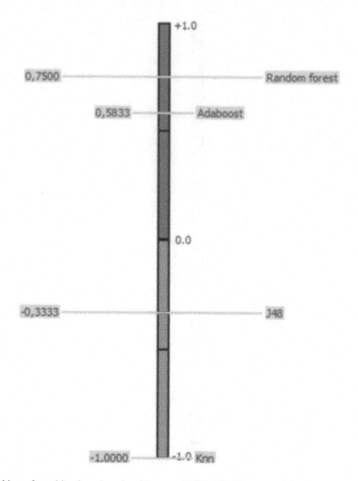

FIGURE 24.4   Ranking of machine learning algorithms on CICIDS 2017.

The existence of hard-to-detect attacks in the network traffic are the stealthier attacks. Their distribution parameters are very similar to benign traffic, smartly fabricated by attackers and used as a technique to evade attack detection.

Even then, there exists a marginal difference in distribution of attack and benign traffic. The difference in HD of instances with the true class and the opposite class is represented as a new feature. Hence, a positive value shows the similarity of samples to the opposite class. Zero and negative value indicates its similarity to true class instances. The *sim_index* feature effectively capture the difference and hence the TP rate obtained for CICIDS 2017 data using this preprocessing step is far better than oversampling and SMOTE based preprocessing. The best TP rate obtained by doing oversampling is 0.962 for Adaboost, 0.992 by SMOTE and 0.998 by similarity-based approach. Slowhttptest and slowloris attack instances in CICIDS2017 are hard to detect, because of their similarity towards benign traffic and their presence is competitively very low in train data. The TP rate obtained for these three attacks by similarity-based Adaboost algorithm demonstrate the effectiveness of approach in detecting stealthy attacks.

PROMETHEE complete ranking gives the performance evaluation of algorithms in terms of conflicting criteria related to the performance metrics extracted from the confusion matrix and are shown in Figures 24.2–24.4. Two pairs of conflicting criteria are used here. Precision and Recall forms one pair of conflicting criteria whose values are to be maximised. FN rate and FP rate constitutes the second pair, which are to be minimised. The results of PROMETHEE Complete ranking demonstrate the fact that Adaboost and Random forest algorithms perform better in detecting DDoS attacks than KNN and J48 algorithms, as KNN and J48 algorithms are marked towards the negative

TABLE 24.6

Comparison of Accuracy Obtained

Accuracy (%)	LLS-DDoS			CAIDA 2007			CICIDS 2017		
Algorithm	Synthetic Sampling	Sim Index	SMOTE	Synthetic Sampling	Sim Index	SMOTE	Synthetic Sampling	Sim Index	SMOTE
Random forest	**99.43**	98.75	99.13	**99.88**	99.32	98.79	97.14	99.82	99.71
J48	97.97	99.33	97.29	99.15	98.75	98.16	96.25	99.08	98.99
Adaboost	99.39	98.75	99.23	99.84	99.44	98.79	97.91	99.36	99.71
Knn	97.91	95.98	98.52	97.77	98.67	98.88	95.12	97.87	97.70

side of preference flow. Adaboost and Random forest algorithms are towards the positive side of preference flow.

The results can be compared with some of the existing research works in this area. The literature summarized in Table 24.1 is selected for comparison, as these are the recent works. The work of Singh et al.[33] and Lima et al.[34] used the modern benchmark dataset called CICIDS 2017. The results shown in these literatures give detection accuracy as the performance metric. Our result on CICIDS 2017 gives TP rate of 0.998 by Adaboost algorithm. The observed accuracy of the proposed method is 99.82% on CICIDS 2017 dataset. The observed accuracy of various methods on three datasets are given in Table 24.6.

The proposed methodology in our system is less complex and it is evaluated using the default settings of algorithms. Moreover the experiments are conducted by supplying test data separately rather than using cross validation. The works of Shone et al.,[35] Ahmed et al.,[36] Lima et al.,[37] and Alsirhani et al.[38] are done mainly on modern attacks and NSL-KDD benchmark dataset and the results can be compared for the complexity of the method and their effectiveness. The works explained in these literatures demonstrate the results obtained from cross-validated data. Ahmed et al. actually experimented five real-world datasets and DDoS flooding using IRC botnet or Slowloris attack is also one among them. The experimental results claim an accuracy of 97%. These comparisons show that our model is very promising and can perform with an average accuracy of 99.8%.

The most important advantage of synthetic sampling is that the number of synthetic samples generated is considerably low as compared to random oversampling and SMOTE. The generation of spurious samples is also reduced, since the new synthetic samples are produced along the line of misclassified attack instances and the extreme samples selected from the correctly classified attack class distribution.

24.6 Conclusion

This chapter discussed the methodologies which cause the performance improvement of machine learning algorithms while dealing with imbalanced dataset and stealthy layer 7 attacks. The solution proposed for the imbalanced dataset problem was random oversampling and synthetic sampling. The empirical results proved that the synthetic sampling is the best choice compared to random sampling and SMOTE. The number of synthetic samples generated was less compared to 1:1 sampling in SMOTE. Only double the number of attacks misclassified in the prior learning phase was selected for synthetic sampling. The stealthy layer 7 attacks were handled by a new feature created, which could hold the information of similarity of attack instances to normal instances. TP rate of detection of stealthy attacks present in CICIDS 2017 data was 0.998 by Adaboost algorithm and the proposed model can ensure an average accuracy of 99.8%. The performance evaluation of algorithms was done using a multi-criteria decision aid system called PROMETHEE Complete ranking where Random forest and Adaboost were proved to be the best algorithms in detecting DDoS attacks. In the future, we can use the newly introduced feature to further reduce the dimension of the training data. We can also extend this study to apply more statistical analysis to bring out the best performance of machine learning algorithms in detecting DDoS attacks.

Notes

1 Ciza Thomas, "Improving intrusion detection for imbalanced network traffic," *Security and Communication Networks* 6, no. 3 (2013): 309–324.
2 Laura Feinstein et al., "Statistical approaches to DDoS attack detection and response," in *Proceedings DARPA information survivability conference and exposition*, vol. 1 (IEEE, 2003), 303–314.
3 Jelena Mirkovic and Peter Reiher, "A taxonomy of DDoS attack and DDoS defense mechanisms," *ACM SIGCOMM Computer Communication Review* 34, no. 2 (2004): 39–53.
4 Peng Xiao et al., "Detecting DDoS attacks against data center with correlation analysis," *Computer Communications* 67 (2015): 66–74.
5 Cynthia Wagner, Jérôme François, Thomas Engel, et al., "Machine learning approach for ip-flow record anomaly detection," in *International Conference on Research in Networking* (Springer, 2011), 28–39.

6 Xi Qin, Tongge Xu, and Chao Wang, "DDoS attack detection using flow entropy and clustering technique," in *2015 11th International Conference on Computational Intelligence and Security (CIS)* (IEEE, 2015), 412–415.

7 Robin Sommer and Vern Paxson, "Outside the closed world: On using machine learning for network intrusion detection," in *2010 IEEE Symposium on Security and Privacy* (IEEE, 2010), 305–316.

8 Josep L Berral et al., "Adaptive distributed mechanism against flooding network attacks based on machine learning," in *Proceedings of the 1st ACM Workshop on AISec* (2008), 43–50.

9 9. RR Rejimol Robinson and Ciza Thomas, "Ranking of machine learning algorithms based on the performance in classifying DDoS attacks," in *2015 IEEE Recent Advances in Intelligent Computational Systems (RAICS)* (IEEE, 2015), 185–190.

10 Alan Saied, Richard E Overill, and Tomasz Radzik, "Detection of known and unknown DDoS attacks using Artificial Neural Networks," *Neurocomputing* 172 (2016: 385–393.

11 Rajagopalan Vijayasarathy, Serugudi Venkataraman Raghavan, and Balaraman Ravindran, "A system approach to network modeling for DDoS detection using a Naive Bayesian classifier," in *2011 Third International Conference on Communication Systems and Networks (COMSNETS 2011)* (IEEE, 2011), 1–10.

12 Ming-Yang Su, "Rcal-timc anomaly detection systems for Denial-of-Service attacks by weighted k-nearest-neighbor classifiers," *Expert Systems with Applications* 38, no. 4 (2011): 3492–3498.

13 Bin Kong et al., "Distinguishing flooding distributed denial of service from flash crowds using four data mining approaches," *Computer Science and Information Systems* 14, no. 3 (2017): 839–856.

14 Keunsoo Lee et al., "DDoS attack detection method using cluster analysis," *Expert systems with applications* 34, no. 3 (2008): 1659–1665.

15 Pedro Casas et al., "Network security and anomaly detection with Big-DAMA, a big data analytics framework," in *2017 IEEE 6th International Conference on Cloud Networking (CloudNet)* (IEEE, 2017), 1–7.

16 Hui Han, Wen-yuan Wang, and Bing-huan Mao, "Borderline-SMOTE: A new over-sampling method in," 2005, 878–887, https://doi.org/10.1007/1153805991.

17 Nv Chawla and Kw Bowyer, "SMOTE: Synthetic minority over-sampling technique," *Journal of Artificial Intelligence Research* 16: 321–357, issn: 10769757, https://doi.org/10.1613/jair.953, arXiv: 1106.1813, http://arxiv.org/abs/1106.1813.

18 N Japkowicz, "Learning from imbalanced datasets.," *Papers from AAAI Workshop* 21, no. 9 (2000): 10–15, issn: 1041–4347, https://doi.org/10.1109/TKDE.2008.239, arXiv: arXiv:1011.1669v3, http://www.aaai.org/Papers/Workshops/2000/WS-00-05/WS00-05-003.pdf.

19 Taeho Jo and Nathalie Japkowicz, "Class imbalances versus small disjuncts," *ACM Sigkdd Explorations Newsletter* 6, no. 1 (2004): 40–49.

20 Opeyemi Osanaiye et al., "Ensemble-based multi-filter feature selection method for DDoS detection in cloud computing," *EURASIP Journal on Wireless Communications and Networking* 2016, no. 1 (2016): 130.

21 Muhammad Aamir and Syed Mustafa Ali Zaidi, "DDoS attack detection with feature engineering and machine learning: the framework and performance evaluation," *International Journal of Information Security* 18, no. 6 (2019): 761–785.

22 Khundrakpam Johnson Singh and Tanmay De, "MLP-GA based algorithm to detect application layer DDoS attack," *Journal of information security and applications* 36 (2017): 145–153.

23 Francisco Sales de Lima Filho et al., "Smart detection: an online approach for DoS/DDoS attack detection using machine learning," *Security and Communication Networks* 2019 (2019).

24 Nathan Shone et al., "A deep learning approach to network intrusion detection," *IEEE Transactions on Emerging Topics in Computational Intelligence* 2, no. 1 (2018): 41–50.

25 Muhammad Ejaz Ahmed, Saeed Ullah, and Hyoungshick Kim, "Statistical application fingerprinting for DDoS attack mitigation," *IEEE Transactions on Information Forensics and Security* 14, no. 6 (2018): 1471–1484.

26 Amjad Alsirhani, Srinivas Sampalli, and Peter Bodorik, "DDoS detection system: using a set of classification algorithms controlled by fuzzy logic system in apache spark," *IEEE Transactions on Network and Service Management* 16, no. 3 (2019): 936–949.

27 Reyhaneh Karimazad and Ahmad Faraahi, "An anomaly-based method for DDoS attacks detection using RBF neural networks," in *Proceedings of the International Conference on Network and Electronics Engineering*, vol. 11 (2011).

28 Chawla and Bowyer, "SMOTE: Synthetic Minority Over-sampling Technique."

29 John McHugh, "Testing intrusion detection systems: a critique of the 1998 and 1999 darpa intrusion detection system evaluations as performed by Lincoln Laboratory," *ACM Transactions on Information and System Security (TISSEC)* 3, no. 4 (2000): 262–294.

30 Matthew V Mahoney and Philip K Chan, "An analysis of the 1999 DARPA/Lincoln Laboratory

evaluation data for network anomaly detection," in *International Workshop on Recent Advances in Intrusion Detection* (Springer, 2003), 220–237.

31 Ciza Thomas, Vishwas Sharma, and N Balakrishnan, "Usefulness of DARPA dataset for intrusion detection system evaluation," in *Data Mining, Intrusion Detection, Information Assurance, and Data Networks Security 2008*, vol. 6973 (International Society for Optics and Photonics, 2008), 69730G.

32 Ciza Thomas and N Balakrishnan, "Improvement in intrusion detection with advances in sensor fusion," vol. 4, 3 (IEEE, 2009), 542–551.

33 Khundrakpam Johnson Singh and Tanmay De, "MLP-GA based algorithm to detect application layer DDoS attack," *Journal of Information Security and Applications* 36 (2017): 145–153.

34 Francisco Sales de Lima Filho et al., "Smart detection: an online approach for DoS/DDoS attack detection using machine learning," *Security and Communication Networks* 2019 (2019).

35 Nathan Shone et al., "A deep learning approach to network intrusion detection," *IEEE Transactions on Emerging Topics In Computational Intelligence* 2, no. 1 (2018): 41–50.

36 Muhammad Ejaz Ahmed, Saeed Ullah, and Hyoungshick Kim, "Statistical application fingerprinting for DDoS attack mitigation," *IEEE Trans-actions on Information Forensics and Security* 14, no. 6 (2018): 1471–1484.

37 Lima Filho et al., "Smart detection: an online approach for DoS/DDoS attack detection using machine learning."

38 Amjad Alsirhani, Srinivas Sampalli, and Peter Bodorik, "DDoS detection system: using a set of classification algorithms controlled by fuzzy logic system in apache spark," *IEEE Transactions on Network and Service Management* 16, no. 3 (2019): 936–949.

REFERENCES

[1] Aamir, Muhammad, and Syed Mustafa Ali Zaidi. "DDoS attack detection with feature engineering and machine learn-ing: the framework and performance evaluation." *International Journal of Information Security* 18, no. 6 (2019): 761–785.

[2] Ahmed, Muhammad Ejaz, Saeed Ullah, and Hyoungshick Kim. "Statistical application fingerprinting for DDoS attack mitigation." *IEEE Transactions on Information Forensics and Security* 14, no. 6 (2018): 1471–1484.

[3] Alsirhani, Amjad, Srinivas Sampalli, and Peter Bodorik. "DDoS detection system: using a set of classification algorithms controlled by fuzzy logic system in apache spark." *IEEE Transactions on Network and Service Management* 16, no. 3 (2019): 936–949.

[4] Berral, Josep L, Nicolas Poggi, Javier Alonso, Ricard Gavalda, Jordi Torres, and Manish Parashar. "Adaptive distributed mechanism against flooding network attacks based on machine learning." In *Proceedings of the 1st ACM workshop on Workshop on AISec*, 43–50, 2008.

[5] Casas, Pedro, Francesca Soro, Juan Vanerio, Giuseppe Settanni, and Alessandro D'Alconzo. "Network security and anomaly detection with Big-DAMA, a big data analytics framework." In *2017 IEEE 6th International Conference on Cloud Networking (CloudNet)*, 1–7. IEEE, 2017.

[6] Chawla, Nv, and Kw Bowyer. "SMOTE: synthetic minority over-sampling technique." *Journal of Artificial Intelligence Research* 16 (2002): 321–357. issn: 10769757. https://doi.org/10.1613/jair.953. arXiv:1106.1813. http://arxiv.org/abs/1106.1813.

[7] Feinstein, Laura, Dan Schnackenberg, Ravindra Balupari, and Darrell Kindred. "Statistical approaches to DDoS attack detection and response." In *Proceedings DARPA Information Survivability Conference and Exposition*, 1: 303–314. IEEE, 2003.

[8] Han, Hui, Wen-yuan Wang, and Bing-huan Mao. "Borderline-SMOTE: a new over-sampling method in imbalanced datasets learning." In *Proceedings International Conference on Intelligent Computing*, pp. 878–887, 2005. https://doi.org/10.1007/1153805991.

[9] Japkowicz, N. "Learning from imbalanced datasets." *Papers from AAAI Workshop* 21, no. 9 (2000): 10–15. issn: 1041-4347. https://doi.org/10.1109/TKDE.2008.239. arXiv: arXiv:1011.1669v3. http://www.aaai.org/Papers/Workshops/2000/WS-00-05/WS00-05-003.pdf.

[10] Jo, Taeho, and Nathalie Japkowicz. "Class imbalances versus small disjuncts." *ACM Sigkdd Explorations Newsletter* 6, no. 1 (2004): 40–49.

[11] Karimazad, Reyhaneh, and Ahmad Faraahi. "An anomaly-based method for DDoS attacks detection using RBF neural networks." In *Proceedings of the International Conference on Network and Electronics Engineering*, vol. 11, 2011.

[12] Kong, Bin, Kun Yang, Degang Sun, Meimei Li, and Zhixin Shi. "Distinguishing flooding distributed denial of service from flash crowds using four data mining approaches." *Computer Science and Information Systems* 14, no. 3 (2017): 839–856.

[13] Lee, Keunsoo, Juhyun Kim, Ki Hoon Kwon, Younggoo Han, and Sehun Kim. "DDoS attack detection method using cluster analysis." *Expert Systems with Applications* 34, no. 3 (2008): 1659–1665.

[14] Lima Filho, Francisco Sales de, Frederico AF Silveira, Agostinho de Medeiros Brito Junior, Genoveva Vargas-Solar, and Luiz F Silveira. "Smart detection: an online approach for DoS/DDoS attack detection using machine learning." *Security and Communication Networks* 2019 (2019).

[15] Mahoney, Matthew V, and Philip K Chan. "An analysis of the 1999 DARPA/Lincoln Laboratory evaluation data for network anomaly detection." In *International Workshop on Recent Advances in Intrusion Detection*, 220–237. Springer, 2003.

[16] McHugh, John. "Testing intrusion detection systems: a critique of the 1998 and 1999 DARPA intrusion detection system evaluations as performed by Lincoln Laboratory." *ACM Transactions on Information and System Security (TISSEC)* 3, no. 4 (2000): 262–294.

[17] Mirkovic, Jelena, and Peter Reiher. "A taxonomy of DDoS attack and DDoS defense mechanisms." *ACM SIGCOMM Computer Communication Review* 34, no. 2 (2004): 39–53.

[18] Osanaiye, Opeyemi, Haibin Cai, Kim-Kwang Raymond Choo, Ali Dehghantanha, Zheng Xu, and Mqhele Dlodlo. "Ensemble-based multi-filter feature selection method for DDoS detection in cloud computing." *EURASIP Journal on Wireless Communications and Networking* 2016, no. 1 (2016): 130.

[19] Qin, Xi, Tongge Xu, and Chao Wang. "DDoS attack detection using flow entropy and clustering technique." In *2015 11th International Conference on Computational Intelligence and Security (CIS)*, 412–415. IEEE, 2015.

[20] Robinson, R. R. Rejimol, and Ciza Thomas. "Ranking of machine learning algorithms based on the performance in classifying DDoS attacks." In *2015 IEEE Recent Advances in Intelligent Computational Systems (RAICS)*, 185– 190. IEEE, 2015.

[21] Saied, Alan, Richard E Overill, and Tomasz Radzik. "Detection of known and unknown DDoS attacks using Artificial Neural Networks." *Neurocomputing* 172 (2016): 385–393.

[22] Shone, Nathan, Tran Nguyen Ngoc, Vu Dinh Phai, and Qi Shi. "A deep learning approach to network intrusion detection." *IEEE Transactions on Emerging Topics in Computational Intelligence* 2, no. 1 (2018): 41–50.

[23] Singh, Khundrakpam Johnson, and Tanmay De. "MLP-GA based algorithm to detect application layer DDoS attack." *Journal of Information Security and Applications* 36 (2017): 145–153.

[24] Sommer, Robin, and Vern Paxson. "Outside the closed world: on using machine learning for network intrusion detection." In *2010 IEEE Symposium on Security and Privacy*, 305–316. IEEE, 2010.

[25] Su, Ming-Yang. "Real-time anomaly detection systems for Denial-of-Service attacks by weighted k-nearest-neighbor classifiers." *Expert Systems with Applications* 38, no. 4 (2011): 3492–3498.

[26] Thomas, Ciza. "Improving intrusion detection for imbalanced network traffic." *Security and Communication Networks* 6, no. 3 (2013): 309–324.

[27] Thomas, Ciza, and N. Balakrishnan. "Improvement in intrusion detection with advances in sensor fusion." *IEEE Transactions on Information Forensics and Security* 4, no. 3 (2009): 542–551.

[28] Thomas, Ciza, Vishwas Sharma, and N. Balakrishnan. "Usefulness of DARPA dataset for intrusion detection system evaluation." In *Data Mining, Intrusion Detection, Information Assurance, and Data Networks Security 2008*, vol. 6973, 69730G. International Society for Optics and Photonics, 2008.

[29] Vijayasarathy, Rajagopalan, Serugudi Venkataraman Raghavan, and Balaraman Ravindran. "A system approach to network modeling for DDoS detection using a Naive Bayesian classifier." In *2011 Third International Conference on Communication Systems and Networks (COMSNETS 2011)*, 1–10. IEEE, 2011.

[30] Wagner, Cynthia, Jérôme François, Thomas Engel, et al., "Machine learning approach for IP-flow record anomaly detection." In *International Conference on Research in Networking*, 28–39. Springer, 2011.

[31] Xiao, Peng, Wenyu Qu, Heng Qi, and Zhiyang Li. "Detecting DDoS attacks against data center with correlation analysis." *Computer Communications* 67 (2015): 66–74.

25

Detection of Patterns in Attributed Graph Using Graph Mining

Bapuji Rao

CONTENTS

25.1 Introduction

The real-life graph has a finite number of nodes or vertices. The relationship among the nodes or vertices is created with the help of the edges. The attributes associated with nodes or vertices represent node or vertex properties. But in a social graph, the node or vertex attributes are used to model the personal characteristics. Similarly, in a web graph, the node or vertex attributes are assigned with the contents such as keywords and tags related to a particular page on the web. This type of extended graph representation is considered as the attributed graph. It is possible to detect the hidden patterns from the attributed graph that provides the relevant knowledge related to various applications. The University Attributed Graph could be treated as one kind of social attributed graph. The attributes of the nodes of University Attributed Graph are some kind of "Job Title." The "Job Title" of nodes may be Vice-Chancellor, Dean, Associate Dean, etc.

25.2 Research Background

Graph matching and graph mining are two typical areas in artificial intelligence. The large-scale collections of network data are due to the growth of the internet has been using by the online services to encourage social interactions such as Facebook and Twitter as well as encourages business communications related to email and LinkedIn. The researchers have studied the structures and attributes of large-scale relational data, and have discovered that data frequently shows a correlation among the attributes of linked individuals. Further research has considered the root cause of the correlation and the noble appearance between the social influences, where the linked individuals by adopting the characteristics of their neighbors as well as homophily (the tendency for people to seek out or be attracted to those who are similar to themselves). So that the links are formed based on the similar attributes of the individuals proposed by Joseph J et al [1].

Attributed graphs are classified into two i.e., Edge-Attributed Graphs and Node-Attributed Graphs proposed by C. Bothorel et al [2]. The edge-attributed graph again is divided into two such as multi-relational edge-attributed graph and multi-layer edge-attributed graph.

From one graph, one node can correspond to multiple nodes in another graph. For instance, in online social media, the same user can open multiple accounts on some services has been proposed by Matio Magnani et al [3]. In the case of non-social networks which consists of different kinds of nodes. For instance, in a power grid and in a control network, where one node in a network can be related to the multiple nodes in another network proposed by Jianxi Gao et al [4]. Similarly, the model introduced by Mikko Kivelä et al. [5] has attributes on nodes and edges respectively.

Stanley Wasserman et al. [6] described that the multiple dimensions can be represented in a social network model: "astructural dimension" is a kind of relationships among actors, "acompositional dimension" is a kind of attributes of the single actors, and "anaffiliation dimension" is a kind of group memberships. So the attributed graph can be expressed as a triple G = (V, E, F). For each node "*v*" is associated with a set of "*a*" attributes. Here "*a*" is a feature vector that can be represented as $[f_1(v), \dots f_a(v)]$ which stores its compositional dimension. In the same way, the affiliation information can be stored by adding dedicated attributes of the memberships.

An attributed graph is the combination of nodes and edges, where nodes may be objects of different kinds such as persons or publications, the attributes of the node are their properties, the edges are the relationship between the objects and the attributes of the edge enable more meaningful of these relations. In a given graph, one may query like "find all the co-authors of Jack" or "people known by Jack or by someone Jack knows". These reachability queries for the existence of paths from a source node here it is "Jack" to other nodes. The current languages unable to request such as "find papers authored by someone related to Jack that published at CIKM but prefer Jack's co-authors to persons only known by Jack." These kinds of requests can be solved by GuLP (Graph Query Language with Preferences) proposed by Valeria Fionda et al [7].

25.3 Literature Survey

The authors propose G-Ray, which detects sub-graphs that may match exactly the query pattern, or not. It provides a framework and a method for the detection of the best-effort sub-graphs quickly that matches exactly with the given pattern query in the large attributed graphs proposed by H. Tong et al [8].

The structural correlation pattern mining is the correlation between all the attribute sets and the occurrence of dense sub-graphs in large attributed graphs. A structural correlation pattern is a dense sub-graph caused to form by correlated attribute sets. The structural correlation pattern mining combines frequent item-set and quasi-clique mining problems. The authors A. Silva et al. [9] propose a statistical method that compares the attribute sets of the structural correlation against the null model's expected values.

The heavyweight pattern mining discovers patterns that have sets of attributes associated with their nodes in attributed flow graphs. The authors propose a new algorithm, AFG Miner which detects heavyweight patterns in a dataset of attributed flow graphs proposed by C. S. Gomes et al [10]. The authors propose a method that modifies the graph template into the common sub-graph pattern among the attributed relational graphs with the maximum size of the graph. Later on, it discovers all the missing nodes, deletes the redundant nodes, and trains the attributes proposed by Q. Zhang et al [11].

The authors Bapuji Rao et al. [12] proposed an algorithm for the detection of line and loop patterns with three numbers of attributes. This extended version of Bapuji Rao et al. [12] proposes an algorithm that can detect line patterns, loop patterns, and star patterns with four numbers of attributes as well as elongated star patterns with five numbers of attributes, respectively.

25.4 General Definitions

25.4.1 Multi-relational Edge-attributed Graph

For N set of nodes and L set of label, the edge-attributed graph is a triple and can be defined as $G = (V, E, l)$ where V is the total vertices i.e., $V \subseteq N$, E is the total edges i.e., (V, E) is a multi-graph, and l is the total labels i.e., $l: E \to L$. Here edge $e \in E$ in the edge-attributed graph has an associated label $l(e)$.

25.4.2 Multi-layer Edge-attributed Graph

For N set of nodes and L set of labels, the edge-attributed graph can be defined as a set of graphs $G_i = (V_i, E_i)$ where V_i is the total "i" number of vertices i.e., $V_i \subseteq N$ and E_i is the total "i" number of edges i.e., $E_i \subseteq V_i \times V_i$. Each graph G_i has an associated unique name l_i i.e., $l_i \in L$.

25.4.3 Attributed Graph

A graph G is said to be an attributed graph that has an n-node $\times$ n-node matrix and n-node $\times$ m-attribute matrix can be represented as $G = \{V = [v_{i,j}], A = [a_{i,k}]\}$ where (i, j) is a pair of nodes with value 1 if there is an edge between them. For every node "i" which is associated with an attributed vector can be represented as $a_i = [a_{i,1}, a_{i,2}, a_{i,3}, \ldots\ldots, a_{i,n}]$, $a_{i,k} = 1$ i.e., the ith node is labeled with the value of the kth attribute; otherwise 0 proposed by Z. Jorgensen et al. [13], H. Tong et al. [8], and A. Silva et al [9].

25.5 Problem Definition

Given:

    i. An attributed graph G whose nodes have unique attributes. In the proposed attributed graph, the attributes are treated as "Job Titles".

    ii. A pattern or sub-graph P shows the desirable configuration of professionals (e.g., "Dean", "Associate Dean" etc.) depicted in "Figure 25.3".

Output: The number of detected patterns or sub-graphs from the attributed graph G.

25.6 Proposed Approach

The author proposes a University Attributed Graph as a social graph by D. J. Cook et al. [14] and Bapuji Rao et al. [15] depicted in "Figure 25.1". This graph has 20 numbers nodes that associate with a unique attribute i.e. "Job Title". In this proposed graph, the attributes of nodes are "Dean", "Associate Dean", "Professor", and "Associate Professor", respectively. These attributes are assigned with a unique ID ranging from 1 to 4 depicted in "Figure 25.2(i)". The 20 numbers of nodes are assigned with a unique ID ranging from 1 to 20. The "Job Title" for the node IDs 1, 2, and 8 is "Dean". The "Job Title" for the node IDs 3, 4, 5, 6, 7, and 9 is "Associate Dean". The "Job Title" for the node IDs 11, 12, 13, 14, 15, and 16 is 'Professor.' Finally, the 'Job Title' for the node IDs 10, 17, 18, 19, and 20 is "Associate Professor" depicted in "Figure 25.2(ii)".

The proposed algorithm, PDAGraph345, first finds the length of the pattern, PAT[ ]. Here the accepted length of the patterns is 4, 5, and 6, respectively.

25.6.1 Pattern Length of 4, 5, and 6

25.6.1.1 For Length = 4

If the length of the pattern is 4 then its actual length will be considered as 3 i.e., Plen: = 3. When the pattern has a loop i.e., the first and the last attribute Id of PAT[ ] is the same, then loop: = 1 and is considered as a 3-attributed loop pattern. Otherwise, loop: = 0 is considered as a 3-attributed line pattern.

25.6.1.2 For Length = 5

The pattern with length 5 has three possible numbers of patterns viz., line, loop, and star. When the pattern has a loop i.e., the first and the last attribute Id of PAT[ ] is the same, then loop: = 1 is considered as the 4-attributed loop pattern and its actual length will be considered as 4 i.e., Plen: = 4. If the last

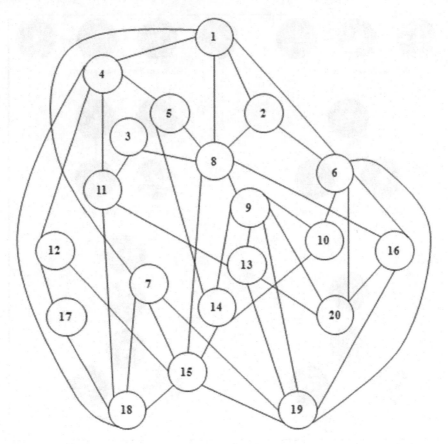

FIGURE 25.1 University attributed graph.

Attributes ID	Attributes		Attributes ID	Nodes ID					
1	Dean		1	1	2	8			
2	Associate Dean		2	3	4	5	6	7	9
3	Professor		3	11	12	13	14	15	16
4	Associate Professor		4	10	17	18	19	20	

(i) Attributes ID and Attributes   (ii) Attributes ID and Nodes ID

FIGURE 25.2 Nodes ID, attributes ID, and attributes of university attributed graph.

attribute Id of PAT[ ] is equal to 0, then the value of the loop will be 0 i.e., loop: = 0, and is considered as the 4-attributed line pattern. If the first and last attribute Id of PAT[ ] are different, then the value of Plen will be 5 i.e., Plen: = 5 which is considered as the 4-attributed star pattern. In the star pattern, the value of the "loop" will not be considered since it is a special case.

25.6.1.3 For Length = 6

If the length of the pattern is 6 then the value of Plen will be 6 i.e., Plen: = 6, and is considered as the 5-attributed elongated star pattern.

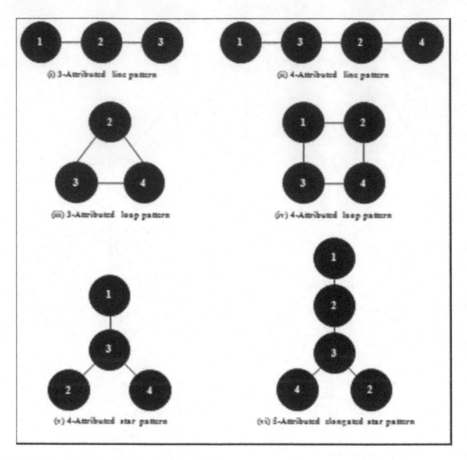

FIGURE 25.3 Line, loop, star, and elongated star patterns.

After finding the values of "Plen" and "loop", the algorithm starts counting the frequency of the attributes belonging to the nodes present in the pattern, PAT[ ] by comparing the Node-Attribute Matrix, NAM[n][m] and the result stores in the matrix, MAT[Plen][ ]. Using the matrix, MAT[Plen][ ], the algorithm starts generating all the possible node-pairs and stores the resultant node-pairs in the matrix, RMAT[ ][2]. There are four possible ways of node-pair generations.

25.6.2 Node-Pair Generations

25.6.2.1 Node-Pair Generation for Three Attributed Line and Loop Patterns

If Len = 4 and Plen = 3, then there will be a node-pairs generation for the 3-attributed line and loop patterns. The possible numbers of node-pairs are generated by calling the procedure, NodePair-Generation() which in turn calls another procedure, NodePairAssignment( ), and the resultant node-pairs are stored in the matrix, RMAT[][2]. Then the procedure, CreatePatterns3(r) is called for the detection of possible numbers of node-pairs from the matrix, RMAT[][2], and those node-pairs are displayed as a 3-attributed line or loop by calling the procedure, DisplayPatterns3( ).

25.6.2.2 Node-Pair Generation for Four Attributed Line and Loop Patterns

If Len = 5 and Plen = 4, then it will generate node-pairs for the 4-attributed line and loop patterns. The possible numbers of node-pairs are generated by calling the procedure, NodePairGeneration() which in turn calls another procedure, NodePairAssignment( ), and the resultant node-pairs are stored in the matrix, RMAT[][2]. Then the procedure, CreatePatterns4(r) is called for the detection of possible numbers of node-pairs from the matrix, RMAT[][2], and those node-pairs are displayed as a 4-attributed line or loop patterns by calling the procedure, DisplayPatterns4( ).

25.6.2.3 Node-Pair Generation for Four Attributed Star Patterns

If Len = 5 and Plen = 5, then the generation of node-pairs will be the 4-attributed star patterns. The possible numbers of node-pairs are generated by calling the procedure, NodePairGeneration() which in turn calls another procedure, NodePairAssignment( ), and the resultant node-pairs are stored in the matrix, RMAT[][2]. Then the procedure, CreatePatterns5(r) is called for the detection of possible numbers of node-pairs from the matrix, RMAT[][2], and starts displaying as 4-attributed star patterns by calling the procedure, DisplayPatterns5( ).

25.6.2.4 Node-Pair Generation for Five Attributed Elongated Star Patterns

If Len = 6 and Plen = 6, then it will generate node-pairs for the 5-attributed elongated star patterns. The possible numbers of node-pairs are generated by calling the procedure, NodePairGeneration() which in turn calls another procedure, NodePairAssignment( ), and the resultant node-pairs are stored in the matrix, RMAT[][2]. Then the procedure, CreatePatterns6(r) is called for the detection of possible numbers of node-pairs from the matrix, RMAT[][2] which in turn calls another procedure, AssignPattern6( ) and assigns the possible numbers of node-pairs in the matrix, Result[][6]. Finally, the procedure, DisplayPatterns6(Result) is called for displaying all the possible 5-attributed elongated star patterns.

The author wants to detect all the six patterns depicted in "Figure 25.3" from the University Attributed Graph.

25.6.3 Pattern Detections

25.6.3.1 Three-Attributed Line Pattern

The 3-attributed pattern "Dean-AssociateDean-Professor" can be coded as attribute's ID way i.e., 1-2-3 depicted in "Figure 25.3(i)". The pattern 1-2-3 is assigned in PAT as PAT[] = {1, 2, 3, 0}. Here Len: = 4, Plen: = 3, and PAT[4] = 0 i.e., loop: = 0, is considered as 3-attributed line pattern. The algorithm detects nine numbers of 3-attributed line patterns and depicted in "Figure 25.4(i)".

25.6.3.2 Three-Attributed Loop Pattern

The 3-attributed pattern "AssociateDean-Professor-AssociateProfessor- AssociateDean" can be coded as attribute's ID way i.e., 2-3-4-2 depicted in "Figure 25.3(iii)". The pattern 2-3-4-2 is assigned in PAT as PAT[] = {2, 3, 4, 2}. Here, Len: = 4, Plen: = 3, and PAT[1] = PAT[4] i.e., loop: = 1, is the indication of a loop and is considered as 3-attributed loop pattern. The algorithm successfully detects eight numbers of 3-attributed loop patterns and depicted in "Figure 25.4(ii)".

25.6.3.3 Four-Attributed Line Pattern

The 4-attributed pattern "Dean-Professor-AssociateDean-Professor" can be coded with the attribute's ID as 1-3-2-4 depicted in "Figure 25.3(iv)". The pattern 1-3-4-2-1 is assigned in PAT as PAT[] = {1, 3, 4, 2, 1}. Here Len: = 5, Plen: = 4, and PAT[1] = PAT[5] i.e. loop: = 1, is the indication of the loop and is considered as a 4-attributed loop pattern. There are 3 numbers of 4-attributed loop patterns detected and depicted in "Figure 25.5(ii)".

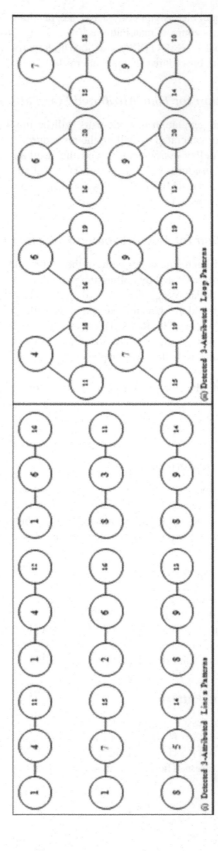

FIGURE 25.4   (i) Detected 3-attributed line patterns (ii) Detected 3-attributed loop patterns.

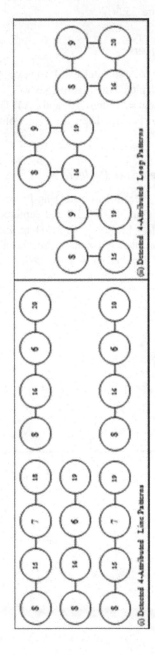

FIGURE 25.5 (i) Detected 4-attributed line patterns (ii) Detected 4-attributed loop patterns.

25.6.3.4 Four-Attributed Loop Pattern

The 4-attributed pattern "Dean-Professor-AssociateProfessor-AssociateDean-Dean" can be coded with the attribute's ID as 1-3-4-2-1 depicted in "Figure 25.3(ii)". The pattern 1-3-2-4 is assigned in PAT as PAT[] = {1, 3, 2, 4, 0}. Here Len: = 5, Plen: = 4, and PAT[5] = 0 i.e., loop: = 0, is the indication of no-loop which is considered as a 4-attributed line pattern. There are five numbers of 4-attributed line patterns detected and depicted in "Figure 25.5(i)".

25.6.3.5 Four-Attributed Star Pattern

The 4-attributed pattern "Dean-Professor-AssociateDean-Professor-AssociateProfessor" can be coded as an attribute's ID way i.e., 1-3-2-3-4 depicted in "Figure 25.3(v)". The pattern 1-3-2-3-4 is assigned in PAT as PAT[] = {1, 3, 2, 3, 4}. Here, Len: = 5, Plen: = 5, and PAT[1]≠PAT[5] is the indication of a star which is considered as a 4-attributed star pattern. There are a total of four number patterns detected and depicted in "Figure 25.6".

25.6.3.6 Five-Attributed Elongated Star Pattern

Finally, the 5-attributed pattern "Dean-AssociateDean-Professor-AssociateProfessor-Professor-AssociateDean" is coded in attribute's ID as 1-2-3-4-3-2 and depicted in "Figure 25.3(vi)". The pattern 1-2-3-4-3-2 is assigned in PAT as PAT[] = {1, 2, 3, 4, 3, 2}. Here, Len: = 6 which does not require any further condition to ascertain as an elongated star pattern. So, the algorithm successfully detects four numbers of elongated star patterns and depicted in "Figure 25.7".

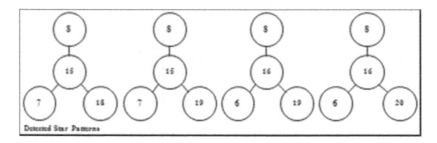

FIGURE 25.6   Detected star patterns.

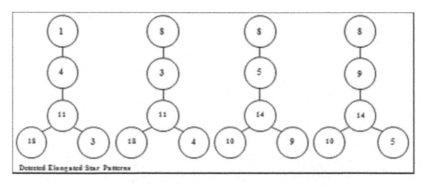

FIGURE 25.7   Detected elongated star patterns.

25.7 Proposed Algorithm for Detection of Patterns – Line, Loop, Star, and Elongated Star

25.7.1 Algorithm PDAGraph345( )

n: Total number of nodes in the attributed graph.

NM[n+1][n+1]: Node-Node adjacency matrix of the attributed graph.

m: Total number of attributes of the attributed graph.

NAM[n+1][m+1]: Node-Attribute adjacency matrix of the attributed graph.

PAT[10]: Pattern to be detected in the attributed graph.

Plen: Pattern length i.e., number of attributes used in the pattern.

loop: To assign the flag value of the pattern to have a loop or not in the pattern.

MAT[Plen][ ]: Matrix to hold the attributes frequency and the node IDs belonging to the respected attribute.

r: Total number of node-pairs of the pattern.

RMAT[r][2]: Matrix to have the node pairs of the patterns.

```
{
 Len: = Length(PAT); // get the length of the pattern
 if(Len = 4) // for 3-attributed line and loop patterns
  {
   Plen: = 3;
 // to check the pattern has loop or not
   if(PAT[1] = PAT[4]) loop: = 1; else loop: = 0;
  }
 if(Len = 5) // for 4-attributed line, loop and star patterns
 {
   if(PAT[1] = PAT[5]) { loop: = 1; Plen: = 4; } // to check for loop pattern
   if(PAT[5] = 0) { loop: = 0; Plen: = 4; } // to check for line pattern
   if(PAT[1]! = PAT[5]) { Plen: = 5; } // to check for star pattern
 }
   if(Len = 6) Plen: = 6; // for 5-attributed elongated star pattern
 // to get and count all attributes node from NAM[][] and store in MAT[ ][ ]
   repeat for i: = 1 to Plen do
   {
    ci: = 2;
    repeat for j: = 1 to m do // 'm' is the number of attributes
     if(PAT[i] = NAM[1][ j+1])
     {
      repeat for k : =  1 to n do
      if(NAM[k+1][ j+1] = 1)
      {
       MAT[i][ ci]: = NAM[k+1][1];
       ci: = ci+1;
      }
       MAT[i][1]: = ci-1; // total number of nodes of ith attribute present in PAT[i]
     }
   }
 // node-pairs creation using MAT[Plen][ ] and storing in RMAT[ ][2]
   r: = 0;
   if(Len = 4 and Plen = 3) // node-pair creations for 3-attributed line and loop pattern
   {
    // 1st row and 2nd row combinations of MAT[Plen][ ]
```

```
    NodePairGeneration(MAT[1][1], 1, MAT[2][1], 2);
 // 2nd row and 3rd row combinations of MAT[Plen][ ]
    NodePairGeneration(MAT[2][1], 2, MAT[3][1], 3);
 // 3-attributed pattern creation
    CreatePatterns3(r);
}
if(Len = 5 and Plen = 4) // node-pair creations for 4-attributed line and loop pattern
{
 // 1st row and 2nd row combinations of MAT[Plen][ ]
    NodePairGeneration(MAT[1][1], 1, MAT[2][1], 2);
 // 2nd row and 3rd row combinations of MAT[Plen][ ]
    NodePairGeneration(MAT[2][1], 2, MAT[3][1], 3);
 // 3rd row and 4th row combinations of MAT[Plen][ ]
    NodePairGeneration(MAT[3][1], 3, MAT[4][1], 4);
 // 4-attributed pattern creation
    CreatePatterns4(r);
}
if(Len = 5 and Plen = 5) // node-pair creations for 4 attributed star pattern
{
 // 1st row and 2nd row combinations of MAT[Plen][ ]
    NodePairGeneration(MAT[1][1], 1, MAT[2][1], 2);
 // 2nd row and 3rd row combinations of MAT[Plen][ ]
    NodePairGeneration(MAT[2][1], 2, MAT[3][1], 3);
 // 4th row and 5th row combinations of MAT[Plen][ ]
    NodePairGeneration(MAT[4][1], 4, MAT[5][1], 5);
 // 4-attributed star pattern creation
    CreatePatterns5(r);
}
if(Len = 6 and Plen = 6) // node-pair creations for 5-attributed elongated star pattern
{
 // 1st row and 2nd row combinations of MAT[Plen][ ]
    NodePairGeneration(MAT[1][1], 1, MAT[2][1], 2);
 // 2nd row and 3rd row combinations of MAT[Plen][ ]
    NodePairGeneration(MAT[2][1], 2, MAT[3][1], 3);
 // 3rd row and 4th row combinations of MAT[Plen][ ]
    NodePairGeneration(MAT[3][1], 3, MAT[4][1], 4);
 // 5th row and 6th row combinations of MAT[Plen][ ]
    NodePairGeneration(MAT[5][1], 5, MAT[6][1], 6);
 // 5-attributed elongated star pattern creation
    CreatePatterns6(r);
 // elongated star pattern display
    DisplayPatterns6(Result);
}
}
```

25.7.2 Procedure for Node-Pair Assignment

```
Procedure NodePairAssignment(r, node1, node2)
{
 RMAT[r][1]: = node1;
 RMAT[r][2]: = node2;
}
```

25.7.3 Procedure to Create Three-Attributed Line and Loop Patterns

Procedure CreatePatterns3(rows)
   rows: Total number of node pairs of the patterns.
{
  a: = MAT[1][1];
  b: = MAT[2][1];
 repeat for i : = 1 to (a*b) do
repeat for j : = (a*b)+1 to rows do
  if(RMAT[i][2] = RMAT[j][1])
  if(NM[RMAT[i][1]][RMAT[i][2]] = 1)
  if(NM[RMAT[j][1]][RMAT[j][2]] = 1)
   DisplayPatterns3(RMAT[i][1], RMAT[i] [2], RMAT[j][2]);
}

25.7.4 Procedure to Display Three-Attributed Line and Loop Patterns

Procedure DisplayPatterns3(a, b, c)
{
  if(loop = 0 and NM[a][c] = 0) display(a, b, c);
  if(loop = 1 and NM[a][c] = 1) display(a, b, c, a);
}

25.7.5 Procedure to Create Four-Attributed Line and Loop Patterns

Procedure CreatePatterns4(rows)
   rows: Total number of node pairs of the patterns.
{
a : = MAT[1][1];
b : = MAT[2][1];
c : = MAT[3][1];
 repeat for i : = 1 to (a*b) do
  repeat for j : = (a*b)+1 to (a*b)+(b*c) do
   if(RMAT[i][2] = RMAT[j][1])
  repeat for k: = (a*b)+(b*c)+1 to rows do
   if(RMAT[j][2] = RMAT[k][1])
   if(NM[RMAT[i][1]][RMAT[i][2]] = 1)
   if(NM[RMAT[j][1]][RMAT[j][2]] = 1)
   if(NM[RMAT[k][1]][RMAT[k][2]] = 1)
    DisplayPatterns4(RMAT[i][1], RMAT[i][2], RMAT[j][2], RMAT[k][2]);
}

25.7.6 Procedure to Display Four-Attributed Line and Loop Patterns

Procedure DisplayPatterns4(a, b, c, d)
{
  if (loop = 0 and NM[a][d] = 0) display(a, b, c, d);
  if (loop = 1 and NM[a][d] = 1) display(a, b, c, d, a);
}

25.7.7 Procedure to Create Four-Attributed Star Patterns

Procedure CreatePatterns5(rows)

```
{
a : =  MAT[1][1];
b : =  MAT[2][1];
c : =  MAT[3][1];
 repeat for i : =  1 to (a*b) do
  repeat for j : =  (a*b)+1 to (a*b)+(b*c) do
   if(RMAT[i][2] = RMAT[j][1])
    repeat for k: = (a*b)+(b*c)+1 to rows do
    if(RMAT[j][1] = RMAT[k][1])
     if(NM[RMAT[i][1]][RMAT[i][2]] = 1)
      if(NM[RMAT[j][1]][RMAT[j][2]] = 1)
       if(NM[RMAT[k][1]][RMAT[k][2]] = 1)
          DisplayPatterns5(RMAT[i][1], RMAT[i][2], RMAT[j][2], RMAT[k][1], RMAT[k][2]);
}
```

25.7.8 Procedure to Display Four-Attributed Star Patterns

```
Procedure DisplayPatterns5(a, b, c, d, e)
{
  display (a, b, c, d, e);
}
```

25.7.9 Procedure to Create Five-Attributed Elongated Star Patterns

```
Procedure CreatePatterns6(rows)
{
a : =  MAT[1][1];
b : =  MAT[2][1];
c : =  MAT[3][1];
d : =  MAT[4][1];
 repeat for i : =  1 to (a*b) do
  repeat for j : =  (a*b) + 1 to (a*b) + (b*c) do
   if(RMAT[i][2] = RMAT[j][1])
    repeat for k : =  (a*b) + (b*c) + 1 to (a*b) + (b*c) + (c*d) do
    if(RMAT[j][2] = RMAT[k][1])
     repeat for m : =  (a*b) + (b*c) + (c*d) + 1 to rows do
     if(RMAT[j][2] = RMAT[m][1])
      if(NM[RMAT[i][1]][RMAT[i][2]] = 1)
       if(NM[RMAT[j][1]][RMAT[j][2]] = 1)
        if(NM[RMAT[k][1]][RMAT[k][2]] = 1)
         if(NM[RMAT[m][1]][RMAT[m][2]] = 1)
     AssignPattern6(RMAT[i][1], RMAT[i][2], RMAT[j][2], RMAT[k][2], RMAT[m][1], RMAT[m][2]);
}
```

25.7.10 Procedure to Assign Node IDs of Five-Attributed Elongated Star Patterns

```
Procedure AssignPattern6(a, b, c, d, e, f)
   Result[][6]: Matrix to hold all the possible patterns node IDs. // global declaration
   rows: = 0; // global declaration
{
 if(d ≠ f)
  {
```

```
    rows: = rows+1;
    Result[rows][1]: = a;
    Result[rows][2]: = b;
    Result[rows][3]: = c;
    Result[rows][4]: = d;
    Result[rows][5]: = e;
    Result[rows][6]: = f;
    }
}
```

25.7.11 Procedure to Display Five-Attributed Elongated Star Patterns

Procedure DisplayPatterns6(Result)
    Result[rows][6]: Matrix to hold all the possible patterns node IDs.
    rows: Total possible number of patterns.

```
{
 repeat for i: =  1 to rows do
   {
   if(Result[i][4] =  Result [i+1][6] and Result[i+1][4] = Result [i][6]) i: = i+1;
   a : =  Result[i][1];
   b : =  Result[i][2];
   c : =  Result[i][3];
   d : =  Result[i][4];
   e : =  Result[i][5];
   f : =  Result[i][6];
   if(b ≠ d and b ≠ f and d ≠ f) display (a, b, c, d, e, f);
   }
}
```

25.7.12 Procedure to Generate Node-Pairs

Procedure NodePairGeneration(Ele1, Row1, Ele2, Row2)

```
{
 repeat for i: = 2 to Ele1 do
 repeat for j: = 2 to Ele2 do
 {
  r : =  r+1;
  NodePairAssignment(r, MAT[Row1][ i], MAT[Row2][ j]);
 }
}
```

25.7.13 Explanation of PDAGraph345( )

The function, Length(PAT), finds the length of the pattern, *PAT*, and assigned to the variable, Len. If the pattern, *PAT* has a loop then a value 1; otherwise 0 is assigned to the variable, *loop*.

When Len = 4, then it is considered as a 3-attributed line or loop pattern. If it has a loop then the variable, the *loop* is assigned with a value 1; otherwise assigned with a value 0 to the variable, *loop,* and a value 3 to the variable, *Plen*. After the variables, *loop,* and *Plen* are assigned with proper values, then it starts the creation of node-pairs and is assigned to the matrix, RMAT[][2].

When Plen = 3, then the procedure, NodePairGeneration() is called two times for detection of valid node-pairs which forms the actual 3-attributed line or loop patterns, and the total numbers of valid node-pairs are counted and assigned to the variable, *r*. Then the procedure, CreatePatterns3(r) is called for the construction of 3-attributed line or loop patterns and displays those patterns by calling the procedure, DisplayPatterns3().

When Plen = 4, then the procedure, NodePairGeneration() is called three times for detection of valid node-pairs which forms the actual 4-attributed line or loop patterns, and the total numbers of valid node-pairs are counted and assigned to the variable, r. Then the function, CreatePatterns4(r) is called for the construction of 4-attributed line or loop patterns and displays those patterns by calling the procedure, DisplayPatterns4().

When Plen = 5, then the procedure, NodePairGeneration() is called three times for detection of valid node-pairs which forms the actual 4-attributed star patterns and the total numbers of valid node-pairs are counted and assigned to the variable, r. Then the procedure, CreatePatterns5(r) is called for the construction of 4-attributed star patterns and displays those 4-attributed star patterns by calling the procedure, DisplayPatterns5().

When Plen = 6, then the procedure, NodePairGeneration() is called four times for detection of valid node-pairs which forms the actual 5-attributed elongated star patterns and the total numbers of valid node-pairs are counted and assigned to the variable, r. Then the procedure, CreatePatterns6(r) is called for the construction of 4-attributed star patterns and displays those 5-attributed elongated star patterns by calling the procedure, DisplayPatterns6(Result). Here, the matrix, Result[ ][ ] holds all the valid node-pairs from which the detected 5-attributed elongated star patterns are to be formed and displayed as results.

The procedure, NodePairGeneration(*Ele1*, *Row1*, *Ele2*, *Row2*) where *Ele1* and *Ele2* are assigned with the total numbers of unique attributes whose attribute IDs depicted in "Figure 25.2" of the attributed graph which is ranging from 1 to 20 from the matrix, MAT[ ][ ], respectively. So that a nested loop is executed *Ele1* × *Ele2* times to count the possible numbers of node-pairs and assigned to the variable, r and calls the procedure, NodePairAssignment(r, MAT[Row1][i], MAT[Row2][j]). The procedure, NodePairAssignment(r, *node1*, *node2*) where r is the row index for the matrix, RMAT[ ][ ] which holds all the possible node-pairs *node1* and *node2*, respectively.

The procedure, CreatePatterns3(*rows*) where, *rows* are the total numbers of possible node-pairs available in the matrix, RMAT[ ][ ]. The nested loop is used to detect the actual node-pair by using the condition (RMAT[i][2] = RMAT[j][1]). If the condition is true, then verifies the actual edge between the node-pairs in the adjacency matrix, NM[ ][ ] of the attributed graph depicted in "Figure 25.9". If both the above conditions are true then it calls the procedure, DisplayPattern3(RMAT[i][1], RMAT[i][2], RMAT[j][2]). So the procedure, DisplayPattern3(*a*, *b*, *c*) where, *a*, *b*, and *c* are the IDs of the node of the attributed graph. If the 3-attributed pattern is a line pattern, then it displays *a-b-c* as a 3-attributed line pattern. Similarly, if the 3-attributed pattern is a loop pattern, then it displays *a-b-c-a* as a 3-attributed loop pattern.

Similarly, the procedures, CreatePatterns4(rows), DisplayPattern4(*a*, *b*, *c*, *d*), CreatePatterns5(*rows*), and DisplayPatterns5(*a*, *b*, *c*, *d*, *e*) execute its loop and displays the desired 4-attributed line and loop patterns and 4-attributed star patterns, respectively.

The procedure, CreatePatterns6(*rows*) where *rows* is the total numbers of possible node-pairs available in the matrix, RMAT[ ][ ]. The nested loop is used to detect the actual node-pairs by using three conditions, (RMAT[i][2] = RMAT[j][1]), (RMAT[j][2] = RMAT[k][1]), and (RMAT[j][2] = RMAT[m][1]). When these three conditions are true then there is a possibility of a pattern. To make the above pattern as the valid pattern, the procedure checks four conditions such as (NM[RMAT[i][1]] [RMAT[i][2]] = 1), (NM[RMAT[j][1]][RMAT[j][2]] = 1), (NM[RMAT[k][1]][RMAT[k][2]] = 1), and (NM[RMAT[m][1]][RMAT[m][2]] = 1) for availability of edges in the adjacency matrix, NM[][] of the attributed graph depicted in "Figure 25.9". Once it is successful, then the valid patterns are assigned to the matrix, Result[][] by calling the procedure, AssignPattern(RMAT[i][1], RMAT[i][2], RMAT[j][2], RMAT[k][2], RMAT[m][1], RMAT[m][2]). So the procedure, AssignPattern(*a*, *b*, *c*, *d*, *e*, *f*) where, *a* and *b* is the first node-pair, *c* and *d* is the second node-pair, and *e* and *f* is the third node-pair, respectively. If the second node ID of second node-pair is not equal to the second node ID of third node-pair then there will be a 5-attributed elongated star pattern and such valid patterns are assigned to the matrix, Result[ ][ ]. Here the variable, *rows* is the total possible numbers of node-pairs for creation of elongated star patterns. Finally, the procedure, DisplayPatterns6(Result) where, the matrix, Result[ ][ ] holds all the valid 5-attributed elongated star patterns. The running time complexity of the algorithm, PDAGraph345 is $O(m \times n \times o \times p)$.

25.8 Experimental Results

25.8.1 Using C++ Programming Language

The author has created two dataset files, namely (i) Attributed Graph Dataset and (ii) Node-Attribute Dataset depicted in "Figure 25.8". The first dataset comprises the total numbers of nodes and the node-pairs where the node edge is formed in the University Attributed Graph. The second dataset comprises the Node-Attribute pairs which are the actual relationship between the node and its attribute. By taking the help of these two datasets, the author has represented the adjacency matrix, NM[n+1][n+1] as well as the node-attribute matrix, NAM[n+1][m+1] in the memory and depicted in "Figure 25.9" and "Figure 25.10," respectively.

Upon inputting the patterns 1-2-3 (3-attributed line pattern), 2-3-4-2 (3-attributed loop pattern), 1-3-2-4 (4-attributed line pattern), 1-3-4-2-1 (4-attributed loop pattern), 1-3-2-3-4 (4-attributed star pattern), and 1-2-3-4-3-2 (5-attributed elongated star pattern) to the algorithm, it has successfully detected nine numbers of 3-attributed line patterns, eight numbers of 3-attributed loop patterns, five numbers of 4-attributed line patterns, three numbers of 4-attributed loop patterns, four numbers of 4-attributed star patterns, and four numbers of 5-attributed elongated star patterns and depicted from "Figure 25.11" to "Figure 25.16," respectively.

The following six patterns have been detected by the proposed algorithm.

25.8.1.1 Three-Attributed Line Pattern (1-2-3)

There are nine numbers of line patterns that have been detected successfully in the University Attributed Graph. So, the detected line patterns are 1-4-11, 1-4-12, 1-6-16, 1-7-15, 2-6-16, 8-3-11, 8-5-14, 8-9-13, and 8-9-14, respectively and depicted in "Figure 25.11". The detected patterns of graphical representation have been depicted in "Figure 25.4(i)".

25.8.1.2 Three-Attributed Loop Pattern (2-3-4-2)

There are eight numbers of loop patterns that have been detected successfully in the University Attributed Graph and the detected loop patterns are 4-11-18-4, 6-16-19-6, 6-16-20-6, 7-15-18-7, 7-15-19-7, 9-13-19-9, 9-13-20-9, and 9-14-10-9 respectively and depicted in "Figure 25.12". Its graphical representation has been depicted in "Figure 25.4(ii)".

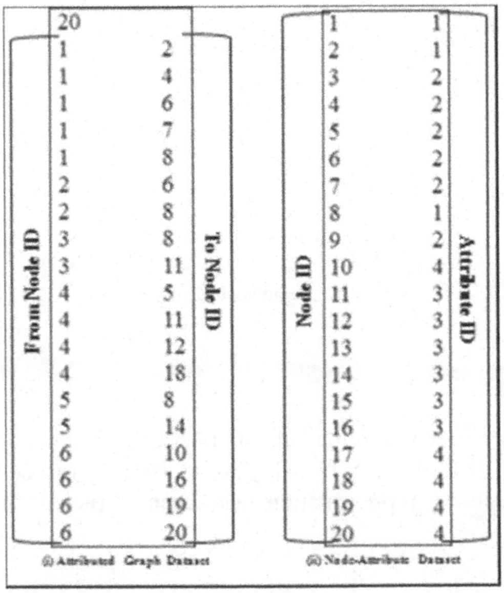

From Node ID	To Node ID		Node ID	Attribute ID
20			1	1
1	2		2	1
1	4		3	2
1	6		4	2
1	7		5	2
1	8		6	2
2	6		7	2
2	8		8	1
3	8		9	2
3	11		10	4
4	5		11	3
4	11		12	3
4	12		13	3
4	18		14	3
5	8		15	3
5	14		16	3
6	10		17	4
6	16		18	4
6	19		19	4
6	20		20	4

(i) Attributed Graph Dataset   (ii) Node-Attribute Dataset

FIGURE 25.8 Datasets.

The Adjacency Matrix of the Attributed Graph

ID	1	2	3	4	5	6	7	8	9	10	11	12	13	14	15	16	17	18	19	20
1	0	1	0	1	0	1	1	1	0	0	0	0	0	0	0	0	0	0	0	0
2	1	0	0	0	0	1	0	1	0	0	0	0	0	0	0	0	0	0	0	0
3	0	0	0	0	0	0	0	0	1	0	0	1	0	0	0	0	0	0	0	0
4	1	0	0	0	1	0	0	0	0	0	1	1	0	0	0	0	0	1	0	0
5	0	0	0	1	0	0	0	1	0	0	0	0	0	1	0	0	0	0	0	0
6	1	1	0	0	0	0	0	0	0	0	1	0	0	0	0	1	0	0	1	1
7	1	0	0	0	0	0	0	0	0	0	0	0	0	0	1	0	0	1	1	0
8	1	1	1	0	1	0	0	0	0	0	0	0	0	0	1	1	0	0	0	0
9	0	0	0	0	0	0	0	0	0	0	0	0	1	1	0	0	0	0	1	1
10	0	0	0	0	0	1	0	0	1	0	0	0	0	0	1	0	0	0	0	0
11	0	0	1	1	0	0	0	0	0	0	0	0	0	0	1	0	0	0	1	0
12	0	0	0	1	0	0	0	0	0	0	0	0	0	0	1	0	1	0	0	0
13	0	0	0	0	0	0	0	0	1	0	1	0	0	0	0	0	0	0	1	1
14	0	0	0	0	0	1	0	0	0	1	1	0	0	0	1	0	0	0	0	0
15	0	0	0	0	0	0	1	1	0	0	0	0	1	0	1	0	0	0	1	1
16	0	0	0	0	0	0	1	0	1	0	0	0	0	0	0	0	0	0	1	1
17	0	0	0	0	0	0	0	0	0	0	0	1	0	0	0	0	0	0	1	0
18	0	0	0	1	0	0	1	0	0	0	0	1	0	1	0	1	0	0	0	0
19	0	0	0	0	0	1	1	0	0	1	0	0	1	0	1	1	0	0	0	0
20	0	0	0	0	0	1	0	0	1	0	0	0	1	0	1	0	0	0	0	0

FIGURE 25.9 Adjacency matrix of the attributed graph.

The Node-Attribute Adjacency Matrix

ID	1	2	3	4
1	1	0	0	0
2	1	0	0	0
3	0	1	0	0
4	0	1	0	0
5	0	1	0	0
6	0	1	0	0
7	0	1	0	0
8	1	0	0	0
9	0	1	0	0
10	0	0	0	1
11	0	0	1	0
12	0	0	1	0
13	0	0	1	0
14	0	0	1	0
15	0	0	1	0
16	0	0	1	0
17	0	0	0	1
18	0	0	0	1
19	0	0	0	1
20	0	0	0	1

FIGURE 25.10 Node-attribute adjacency matrix.

25.8.1.3 Four-Attributed Line Pattern (1-3-2-4)

There is a total of five numbers of line patterns have been detected in the University Attributed Graph. So, the detected line patterns are 8-15-7-18, 8-15-7-19, 8-16-6-10, 8-16-6-19, and 8-16-6-20 respectively, and depicted in "Figure 25.13" and its graphical representation has been depicted in "Figure 25.5(i)".

```
The Line Pattern to Detect.....
1 - 2 - 3
The Detected Line Patterns.....
1 - 4 - 11
1 - 4 - 12
1 - 6 - 16
1 - 7 - 15
2 - 6 - 16
8 - 3 - 11
8 - 5 - 14
8 - 9 - 13
8 - 9 - 14
```

FIGURE 25.11 Detected 3-attributed line patterns.

```
The Loop Pattern to Detect.....
2 - 3 - 4 - 2
The Detected Loop Patterns.....
4 - 11 - 18 - 4
6 - 16 - 19 - 6
6 - 16 - 20 - 6
7 - 15 - 18 - 7
7 - 15 - 19 - 7
9 - 13 - 19 - 9
9 - 13 - 20 - 9
9 - 14 - 10 - 9
```

FIGURE 25.12 Detected 3-attributed loop patterns.

```
The Line Pattern to Detect.....
1 - 3 - 2 - 4
The Detected Line Patterns.....
8 - 15 - 7 - 18
8 - 15 - 7 - 19
8 - 16 - 6 - 10
8 - 16 - 6 - 19
8 - 16 - 6 - 20
```

FIGURE 25.13 Detected 4-attributed line patterns.

25.8.1.4 Four-Attributed Loop Pattern (1-3-4-2-1)

Three numbers of loop patterns with four attributes have been detected successfully in the University Attributed Graph. Here the detected loop patterns are 8-15-19-9-8, 8-16-19-9-8, and 8-16-20-9-8, respectively, and depicted in "Figure 25.14" and its graphical representation has been depicted in "Figure 25.5(ii)".

25.8.1.5 Four Attributed Star Pattern (1-3-2-3-4)

There are four numbers of star patterns that have been detected in the University Attributed Graph. Here the detected star patterns are 8-15-7-15-18, 8-15-7-15-19, 8-16-6-16-19, and 8-16-6-16-20 depicted in "Figure 25.15" and its graphical view has been depicted in "Figure 25.6".

```
The Loop Pattern to Detect.....
1 - 3 - 4 - 2 - 1
The Detected Loop Patterns.....
8 - 15 - 19 - 9 - 8
8 - 16 - 19 - 9 - 8
8 - 16 - 20 - 9 - 8
```

FIGURE 25.14 Detected 4-attributed loop patterns.

```
The Star Pattern to Detect.....
1 - 3 - 2 - 3 - 4
The Detected Star Patterns.....
8 - 15 - 7 - 15 - 18
8 - 15 - 7 - 15 - 19
8 - 16 - 6 - 16 - 19
8 - 16 - 6 - 16 - 20
```

FIGURE 25.15 Detected 4-attributed star patterns.

25.8.1.6 Five-Attributed Elongated Star Pattern (1-2-3-4-3-2)

```
The Elongated Star Pattern to Detect.....
1 - 2 - 3 - 4 - 3 - 2
The Detected Elongated Star Patterns.....
1 - 4 - 11 - 18 - 11 - 3
8 - 3 - 11 - 18 - 11 - 4
8 - 5 - 14 - 10 - 14 - 9
8 - 9 - 14 - 10 - 14 - 5
```

FIGURE 25.16 Detected 5-attributed elongated star patterns.

There are four numbers of elongated star patterns that have been detected in the University Attributed Graph. Here the detected patterns are 1-4-11-18-11-3, 8-3-11-18-11-4, 8-5-14-10-14-9, and 8-9-14-10-14-5 depicted in "Figure 25.16" and its graphical view has been depicted in "Figure 25.7".

The proposed algorithm was implemented in TurboC++ programming language. The experiment was run on Intel Core I5–3230M CPU + 2.60 GHz laptop with 4 GB memory running MS-Windows 7.

25.8.2 Using Python Programming Language

The University Attributed Graph has a total of twenty numbers of nodes and its ID is ranging from 1 to 20. There are four types of unique attributes for these total 20 nodes such as "Dean", "Associate Dean", "Professor", and "Associate Professor", respectively. The node IDs, attribute IDs, and attributes are depicted in "Figure 25.2". The attributed graph is drawn by using the function, **Graph(),** and assigned to the variable, **G**. Then the node IDs and the attributes are assigned to the graph, G by using the ID property and the attribute property of function, **add_node()**. Now graph, G has been set up with its node IDs and attributes but yet to set up the links among the nodes of the graph. The **edge_list** is the list that contains the entire edge list between the node pairs. By using the function, **add_edges_from(edge_list)** to form the actual edges in the graph, **G**. Finally, the University Attributed Graph, G, is written in a graph file **"University-Attributed-Graph.gexp"** and depicted in "Figure 25.17".

To detect all six patterns such as (i) 3-attributed line pattern ("Dean"-"AssociateDean"-"Professor"), (ii) 3-attributed loop pattern ("Associate Dean"-"Professor"-"AssociateProfessor"-"AssociateDean"), (iii) 4-attributed line pattern ("Dean"-"Professor"-"AssociateDean"-"Associate Professor"), (iv) 4-attributed loop pattern ("Dean"-"AssociateDean"-"AssociateProfessor"-"Professor"-"Dean"), (v) 4-attributed star pattern ("Dean"-"Professor"-"AssociateDean"-"Professor"-"AssociateProfessor"), and (vi) 5-attributed elongated star pattern ("Dean"-"AssociateDean"-"Professor"-"AssociateProfessor"-"Professor"-"AssociateDean"), the author has created six individual sub-graphs (patterns) for detection in the University Attributed Graph.

For drawing the individual sub-graph(pattern), the author use functions – **Graph()**, **add_node()**, and **add_edges_from(edge_list)** which draws a sub-graph and assigned to the variable, **P**. The **edge_list** is the list that contains the entire edge list between the node-pairs of the sub-graph. Finally, **P** is to be written in an image file using the function, **write_gexp()** with the respected pattern's name as a file name. The following graph files **"3-Attributed-Line-Pattern.gexp"**, **"3-Attributed-Loop-Pattern.gexp"**, **"4-Attributed-Line-Pattern.gexp"**, **"4-Attributed-Loop-Pattern.gexp"**, **"4-Attributed-Star-Pattern.gexp"**, and **"5-Attributed-Elongated-Star-Pattern.gexp"** were created respectively and depicted in "Figure 25.18". The University Attributed Graph, **G,** and the pattern, **P** which

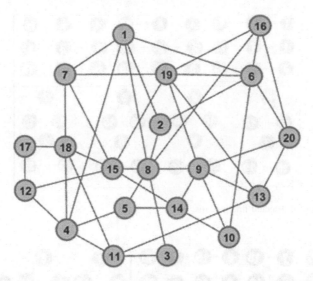

FIGURE 25.17 University attributed graph.

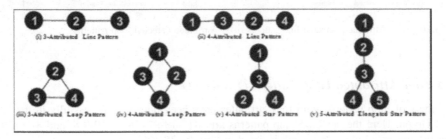

FIGURE 25.18 Patterns to detect in university attributed graph.

holds the data of the graph and sub-graph respectively. The respected pattern, **P** start detection on the graph, **G,** and the following six patterns have been detected successfully.

25.8.2.1 Three-Attributed Line Pattern (1-2-3)

There are nine numbers of line patterns that have been detected successfully in the University Attributed Graph. So, the detected line patterns are 1-4-11, 1-4-12, 1-6-16, 1-7-15, 2-6-16, 8-3-11, 8-5-14, 8-9-13, and 8-9-14 and written in the respected graph files and depicted in "Figure 25.19(i)".

25.8.2.2 Three-Attributed Loop Pattern (2-3-4-2)

There are eight numbers of loop patterns that have been detected successfully in the University Attributed Graph and the detected loop patterns are 4-11-18-4, 6-16-19-6, 6-16-20-6, 7-15-18-7, 7-15-19-7, 9-13-19-9, 9-13-20-9, and 9-14-10-9 and written in the respected graph files and depicted in "Figure 25.19(ii)".

25.8.2.3 Four-Attributed Line Pattern (1-3-2-4)

There is a total of five numbers of line patterns have been detected in the University Attributed Graph. So, the detected line patterns are 8-15-7-18, 8-15-7-19, 8-16-6-10, 8-16-6-19, and 8-16-6-20 and written in the respected graph files and depicted in "Figure 25.20(i)".

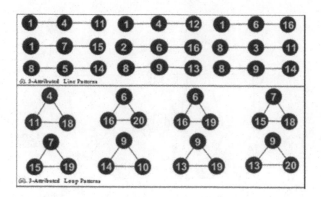

FIGURE 25.19   3-Attributed detected line patterns.

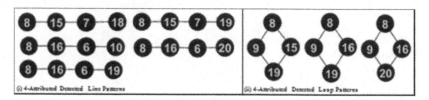

FIGURE 25.20   (i) 4-Attributed detected line patterns (ii) 4-Attributed detected loop patterns.

25.8.2.4 *Four Attributed Loop Pattern (1-3-4-2-1)*

Three numbers of loop patterns with four attributes have been detected successfully in the University Attributed Graph. Here the detected loop patterns are 8-15-19-9-8, 8-16-19-9-8, and 8-16-20-9-8 and written in the respected graph files and depicted in "Figure 25.20(ii)".

25.8.2.5 *Four-Attributed Star Pattern (1-3-2-3-4)*

There are four numbers of star patterns that have been detected in the University Attributed Graph. Here the detected star patterns are 8-15-7-15-18, 8-15-7-15-19, 8-16-6-16-19, and 8-16-6-16-20 and written in the respected graph files and depicted in "Figure 25.21".

25.8.2.6 *Five-Attributed Elongated Star Pattern (1-2-3-4-3-2)*

There are four numbers of elongated star patterns that have been detected in the University Attributed Graph. Here the detected patterns are 1-4-11-18-11-3, 8-3-11-18-11-4, 8-5-14-10-14-9, and 8-9-14-10-14-5 and written in the respected graph files and depicted in "Figure 25.22".

The proposed algorithm was implemented in Python 3.7.3 programming language. The experiment was run on Intel Core I5–3230M CPU + 2.60 GHz laptop with 4 GB memory running MS-Windows 7.

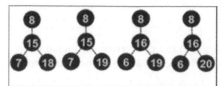

FIGURE 25.21   (i) 4-Attributed detected star patterns (ii) 5-Attributed detected elongated star patterns.

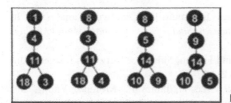

FIGURE 25.22   5-Attributed detected elongated star patterns.

25.9 Analysis of Experimental Results

Before implementing the algorithm, PDAGraph345() in Turbo C++ programming, the author has created two dataset text files namely "Attributed Graph Dataset" and "Node-Attribute Dataset" depicted in "Figure 25.8". During the run-time of the program, it asks to input the above two dataset text files name. After input those dataset file names, two matrices, NM[$n+1$][$n+1$] and NAM[$n+1$][$m+1$] are represented in the memory. Here variable, n is the total number of nodes i.e., it is 20, and the variable, m the total number of attributes i.e., here it is 4 (i.e. designations such as Dean, Associate Dean, Professor, and Associate Professor). The adjacency matrix, NM[$n+1$][$n+1$] holds the edge details of all the twenty node IDs. Similarly, the matrix, NAM[$n+1$][$m+1$] holds the edge details of node IDs and the attribute IDs.

To implement the algorithm, PDAGraph345() in Python programming, no datasets are created in text files externally. The datasets of the attributed graph and the pattern (sub-graph) for detection are available in the code itself. The attributed graph and the pattern (sub-graph) for detection are represented in the memory with the help of these following functions – (i) Graph(), (ii) add_node(), and (iii) add_edges_from(). The function, add_node() has arguments such as node number, node ID, and the node attribute together are the dataset of attributed graph and pattern (sub-graph). This is the first advantage over implementation using Turbo C++ programming. The attributed graph, the pattern to detect, and the detected patterns can be displayed in Turbo C++ way as well as can be written on to the respected image files with extension "**.gexf**". This is the second advantage over implementation using Turbo C++ programming.

In general, the procedure, CreatePatternsN(*rows*) for the creation of an *N*-attributed pattern (line, loop, star, and elongated star) uses a nested loop of (*N*-1) ladders. Here, *N* is the number of attributes. For example, the procedure CreatePatterns5(rows) is used for the creation of 5-attributed elongated star patterns, which uses a nested loop of 4-ladders.

25.10 Conclusion

The author has extended the algorithm of the article Bapuji Rao et al [12]. which only detects the line and loop patterns with three numbers of attributes and named the proposed algorithm, **PDAGraph345** which able to detect patterns with four and five numbers of attributes. The proposed algorithm has been implemented on the proposed University Attributed Graph and successfully detected three-attributed and four-attributed line patterns, three-attributed and four-attributed loop patterns, four-attributed star pattern, and five-attributed elongated star pattern, respectively. The experiment was carried out using C++ and Python programming languages and the results were satisfactory.

REFERENCES

[1] Pfeiffer III, Joseph J., Moreno, Sebastian, Fond, Timothy La, Neville, Jennifer, and Gallagher, Brian. "Attributed graph models: Modeling network structure with correlated attributes." WWW'14, April 7–11, Seoul, Korea. ACM, 2014.

[2] Bothorel, C., Cruz, J. D., Magnani, M., and B. Micenkova, B. "Clustering attributed graphs - Models, measures and methods." *Network Science* 3, no. 3 (2015): 408–444.

[3] Magnani, Matteo, and Rossi, Luca. "The ML-model for multi-layer network analysis." In *Proceedings of IEEE International Conference on Advances in Social Network Analysis and Mining. IEEE Computer Society*, Los Alamitos, 2011.

[4] Gao, Jianxi, Buldyrev, Sergey V., Stanley, H. Eugene, and Havlin, Shlomo. "Networks formed from interdependent networks." *Nature Physics* 1, no. 8 (2012): 40–48.

[5] Kivelä, Mikko, Arenas, Alexandre, Barthelemy, Marc, Gleeson, James P., Moreno, Yamir, and Porter, Mason A. "Multilayer networks." *Journal of Complex Networks* 2 (2014): 1–59.

[6] Wasserman, Stanley, and Faust, Katherine. "Social network analysis: Methods and applications." *Structural Analysis in the Social Sciences*. Cambridge University Press, 1994.

[7] Fionda, Valeria, and Pirrò, Giuseppe. "Querying graphs with preferences." In *Proceedings of CIKM'13*, Oct. 27–Nov. 1, San Francisco, CA, USA, 2013.

[8] Tong, H., Faloutsos, C., Gallagher, B., and Eliassi-Rad, T. "Fast best-effort pattern matching in large attributed graphs." In *Proceedings of the 13th ACM SIGKDD International Conference on Knowledge Discovery and Data Mining*, August 12–15, 2007, ACM, San Jose, California, USA (2007): 737–746.

[9] Silva, A., Meira Jr, W., and Zaki, M. J. "Mining attribute-structure correlated patterns in large attributed graphs." In *Proceedings of VLDW Endowment*, no. 5 (2012): 466–477.

[10] Gomes, C. S., Amaral, J. N., Sander, J., Siu, J., and Ding, L. "Heavyweight pattern mining in attributed flow graphs." In *Proceedings of the IEEE International Conference on Data Mining (ICDM)*, December 14–17, Shenzhen, China (2014): 827–832.

[11] Zhang, Q., Song, X., Saho, X., Zaho, H., and Shibasaki, R. "Attributed graph mining and matching: An attempt to define and extract soft attributed patterns." In *Proceedings of the IEEE Conference on Computer Vision and Pattern Recognition*, June 23–28, Columbus, Ohio, USA (2014): 1394–1401.

[12] Rao, Bapuji, Mishra, Sarojananda, and Kumar, T. Kartik. "An Approach to detect patterns in a social attributed graph using graph mining techniques." *Journal of Engineering and Applied Sciences (JEAS)* 5, no. 13 (2018): 4753–4760.

[13] Jorgensen, Z., Yu, T., and Cormode, G. "Publishing attributed social graphs with formal privacy guarantees." In *Proceedings of the 2016 International Conference on Management of Data*, June 26-July 1, ACM, San Francisco, California, USA (2016): 107–122.

[14] Cook, D. J., and Holder, L. B. *Mining Graph Data*. John Wiley & Sons, Hoboken, New Jersey, USA, 2007.

[15] Rao, Bapuji, Mitra, A., and Narayana, U. "An approach to study properties and behaviour of social network using graph mining techniques." In *DIGNATE 2014: ETEECT 2014* (2014): 1–6.

26

Analysis and Prediction of the Update of Mobile Android Version

Aparna Mohan and R. Maheswari

CONTENTS

26.1 Introduction

26.1.1 Mobile Fragmentation

The world is jeopardized by Android for more than a decade. Mobile fragmentation occurs when few users are making use of the earlier versions of an operating system, while other users are working with the newly released versions. Most of the Android users are observed to have reported an increased number of issues which occurred as a result of Mobile Fragmentation in the past years. Though the cause can be due to the incompatibility of the base hardware provided by Original Equipment Manufacturer (OEM) or the delay in updating the hardware features, the software developers are also responsible for mobile fragmentation confronted by the users across the globe. The software developers are also affected and as a result this group of people should develop different versions of the same application in order for it to be compatible with different operating systems.

26.1.2 Treble – Google

Treble, developed by Google in the year 2019, resolved the issue of Android fragmentation but was not able to successfully eradicate it completely. Treble proposed a new technique of having a base hardware for all OEMs which is a challenging task but a great solution for the rising issue. It failed to address the issue of software compatibility which users report even after the usage of Treble. This project of Google paved the way for faster updates of the Android versions. Any device with Android 8.0 and higher can take advantage of the new architecture. Vendor Test Suite (VTS) is helpful in validating the vendor implementations which ensures forward compatibility. VTS is observed to be similar to the Compatibility Test Suite (CTS). This not just paved way for faster updates of Android versions but also enhanced security features. Thus, the Android users are able to work seamlessly with Treble.

26.1.3 Security Fix Support and Android Update

Securing the Android device is highly significant to prevent the data from getting tampered or getting lost. Updating the Android version will significantly improve the security and also improves the overall performance of the device. The security fixing support which comes with each updated version of Android will help to prevent malwares and from several third-party software penetrations. Thus, updating the Android version of a mobile phone accelerated the security fixes to ensure a safe and user-friendly environment and it is essential for better performance of the device.

26.2 Systematic Literature Survey

26.2.1 API Compatibility Issues and Android Updates

Each version of Android has several features pertaining to a set of APIs provided by the software developers. The APIs provided can be modified or updated to include new features. Hence, this gave rise to several compatibility problems from the user end. The authors Scalabrino et al. [1], have proposed a technique as a solution for the issue of API compatibility with updates in Android. An alternative efficient data-driven approach, named ACRYL was proposed. This system termed ACRYL learns using the significant changes applied in the applications in retort to the changes in API. It was concluded that about 13% of the issues are related to external sources like build and distribution and dependencies. To accomplish this, an intuitive study was done to comprehend the competences and restrictions of existing detectors [2] which helped to progress the state of the art.

26.2.2 Android Updates and Software Aging

Android devices in the current scenario is loaded with a number of applications. This is often leading to software reliability and problems related to performance. The authors D. Cotroneo et al. [3], proposes that as the software is used for a long duration in Android mobile OS, results in poor response and finally causes the system to fail. Several factors such as resource utilization jobs and device arrangement metrics that are linked with this problem are considered. An efficient analysis of Android devices, helped to find the means through which software aging affected the Android updates. Through intuitive study, it was concluded that several components in the OS are affected if the software is used for a long duration. Metrics were used as pointers of software aging to list software upgrading tasks.

26.2.3 Android Updates and Google Play Store

The application store in Android devices are flooded with new apps every day. App store serves as a podium for software developers in the globe to deploy and update their apps. According to authors, McIlroy et al. [4], the frequency of updates pertaining to Android users using 10,713 mobile apps was observed that a small subcategory of these applications is updated at a high frequency rate (i.e.) often updated on a bi-weekly basis. In the proposed technique, it was also found that the end-users are left with no information regarding the rationale of the updates. This paper throws light on the strategies employed for updating by the top mobile apps. The proposed system helped to draw conclusions that the applications in the play store should be updated though the frequency of update is different when compared with applications belonging to different categories. Developers of these applications should focus on new updates in the Android compatibility instead of being tenacious about the details and features of the new update.

26.2.4 Security Standards Hardware Rooted in Mobile Phones

Security of information in computers is of principal concern in today's world. As the number of cyber rates increase due to lack of software security, hardware rooted security standards were proposed as Trusted Platform Module (TPM) 1.0. According to the authors, Ashraf et al. [5], a comparative examination of various security standards was done hence this paper proposes mTPM (modifications in TPM), a comprehensive security standard. The proposed standard also considers several physical constraints apart from dealing with only addresses predominant information security requirements of mobile devices. This also helps to draw conclusions for the implementation of a security processor integrated within existing CPU as inefficient with regard to mobile devices. The proposed model of mTPM has also been counted in as guidelines for highly secure standardization. mTPM is found to be advantageous over the existing models after intuitive comparative study of various techniques for security implementation in mobile phones.

26.2.5 Security Fixes and Android Update

One of the prevailing problems in the Android world is security issues. These bugs when ignored or go unnoticed will lead to severe system and economic problems. Coming up with a security fix is indeed challenging and the harder task would be to ensure that the existing system or version works without any issues with the new security fix. In this paper the authors, have proposed an automated approach [6] for discovering and repairing bugs based on security patterns, to find a solution to vulnerabilities due to security. To detect and fix security bugs, security patterns are used. It comprises of large amounts of software designs. During the discovery of this work, 2,800 Android app repositories that implement javax.crypto APIs were used. Thus, the burden on software maintenance was reduced. This prolific design of new security patterns created a positive impact in the software quality. This also helped to find a new way to locate and find solutions to security bugs in Android which no other earlier proposed techniques were able to achieve.

26.2.6 Machine Learning and Android Antivirus Updates

To escalate the process of updating, the proposed system introduces "ALDROID" and active learning (AL) methods on which ALDROID [7] is based. The proposed system focuses on choosing certain malevolent applications, thus plummeting the labelling or classification methods, and enable a frequent and efficient process of improving the model for identification of hazardous applications and Android's anti-virus software. The proposed active learning algorithms performed better than the existing AL method and experiential engine. While preserving the existing capabilities, the new algorithm was able to detect higher rate of malwares. In comparison with the existing methods, the proposed system was able to acquire double the number of new malwares and 6.5 times greater in amount than the other AL methods.

26.2.7 Smells Detection in Android Using Machine Learning

The number of Android applications is increasing in comparison with the consistent applications. According to the needs of the user it changes often. The changes in the source code while updating involves some bad designs called bad smells [8] which can result in malfunctioning of a particular software and the Android device. To date, the existing systems did not propose a mechanism to efficiently detect these bad smells and provide a solution. This work detects such bad smells and the solution is computed using three different machine learning algorithms. The Android code smells MIM, LIC, DTWC, and SL are measured here for cross-validation method. Out of all the algorithms used, JRip the machine learning algorithm, gave an efficient result for the Android smells up to 90% overall precision. Hence the model proposed in this work serves best for further processing.

26.2.8 Android Malicious Classification Using Various ML Algorithms

Along with the updates of Android version several malicious software are accompanied. An infected application can easily penetrate into an Android device and may result in data theft. In this proposed work [9], detection of malicious applications is done using the fundamental idea of the system call feature. It is implemented using algorithms such as Support Vector Machine (SVM), Naïve Bayes, Decision Tree, Random Forest, Log Regression, and K-nearest Neighbor (KNN). Using system calls in Android, the proposed system aimed at solving the malware detection and classification. It was concluded that Random Forest algorithm provided the greatest accuracy of 76% compared to the other ML algorithms. It was verified that the classification using Random Forest was faster and took an upper hand over the rest in terms of computational time and efficient performance.

26.3 Existing Techniques

Android has distinct features which have made it a widespread platform for mobile. Properties of the Android like openness and extensibility have made it vulnerable. This has led the attackers to penetrate and steal sensitive data. To alleviate these threats, several effective solutions have been proposed. One such technique is to methodically check the security structure of Android and other functionalities followed for security. To get a clear perspective, it was divided two groups namely the stack of software and the system environment. The proposed technique provided an enhanced Android user-friendly ecosystem. Modifications between Android versions affect not only application developers but also makes securing the Android difficult. Keeping track of the updated and non-updated version is even more of a nightmare. A new technique was proposed to handle this issue. The Android framework comprising of several APIs is systematically analyzed. The inconsistency between the updated versions and the currently exists in the OS. To analysis was done using machine learning-based classifiers. The dataset used were malicious-benign datasets to perform the detection. Multiple feature vectors in machine learning were used to target various levels of API. As a consequence, choosing an optimal learning features was more effective to avoid complicating the machine learning model. Top features

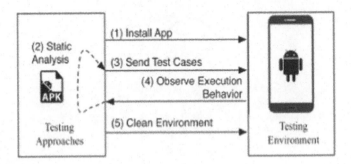

FIGURE 26.1   Existing methodology of Android testing.

obtained show how significant each of them was to particular Android versions. Fine-grained classifiers gave better outcomes than the single classifiers to detect malwares. Three fine-grain classifiers against 3,500 Android applications to realize that there are noteworthy apprises between levels of API, which led to fragmented OS.

26.4 Methodology and Tools Used in Existing Techniques

In one of the proposed techniques, observing the consistency and authorizations the API levels in each Android version was carried out. It not only adds on new APIs but also many would be depreciated. This results in a complicated security audit process. The APK datasets were trained using multiple features ensuring heavy fragmentation of Android OS. The accuracy of prediction is also observed for the proposed classifiers. In another proposed methodology, categorisation was done based on stack and ecosystem. In each of the category limitations, solutions and future work in the research field is discussed.

An innovative approach was also proposed to combat the issues which resulted due to failed updates of Android. In this methodology, a standard system was used to identify the part of the Android application affected due to updates automatically [8]. A statistical overview of the impact of the update is discussed through the methodology. A series of scripts comprising of Bash script along with a group of Python scripts that makes use of the source code of an application is observed to give accurate results. The user-defined classes were found using a recursive approach. From these user-defined classes, Android libraries were traced. After the completion of a particular process, which level of API the application is being updated to is displayed. Then, the proposed methodology involves displaying Android Differences Report to obscure the changes or updates made from the existing packages. If this is the case, then a deep search is employed to that particular class to find out if the code used was removed or changed. For each class that is observed to have been modified the output would be the changed and removed functions and fields used in the code.

Several methodologies were also proposed with regard to the testing of the Android applications in order to improve the overall performance [9]. The approaches proposed aimed to clear issues not just with regard to functional requirements but also non-functional. The schematic diagram as shown in Figure 26.1, gives a clear perspective of the proposed methodology [8][10][31].

26.5 Proposed System

26.5.1 Schematic Overview of Mobile Android Update Prediction and Analysis

The schematic diagram, as shown in Figure 26.2, gives a clear perspective of the proposed system of updating and prediction of Android version. Initially as depicted, the process starts with the collection of the required dataset. The dataset of various mobile manufacturers and the days of release of each version of Android in the past decade is considered here. The dataset is then split as training and test dataset for

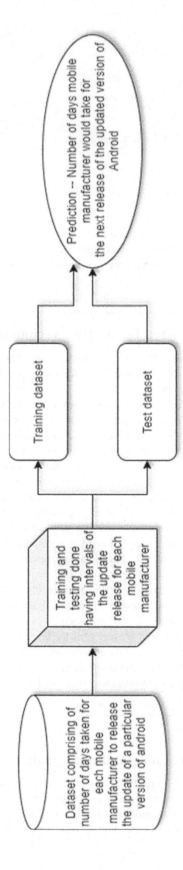

FIGURE 26.2 Overview of mobile Android update prediction and analysis.

applying machine learning algorithm. The regression model is trained and tested considering, the intervals (number of days) between the release of each updated Android version by various mobile manufacturers like Samsung, Huawei, One Plus, HTC, Nokia, Sony Xperia, Motorola, XIOAMI MI and LG. By analyzing the days taken by each manufacturer to release a particular version of Android using the model prediction is done. The final prediction produced as result shows the expected number of days the mobile company would take for the next release. Further analysis is also done by implementing Logistic regression and Decision Tree algorithm. The result of the logistic regression will help to draw conclusions regarding the updates in Android released by Google and security fixes and API (Application Programming Interface) levels in each updated version. The Decision Tree algorithm would give the accuracy of the predicted Decision Tree model with the confusion matrix and Gini Index is also displayed which gives a clear perspective of how often the chosen value may be incorrectly predicted.

26.5.2 Flow Chart Depicting Mobile Android Update Prediction and Analysis

The flow chart as depicted in Figure 26.3 describes the workflow of the proposed technique. The process begins with collected the dataset comprising of various update release days of Android for each mobile phone

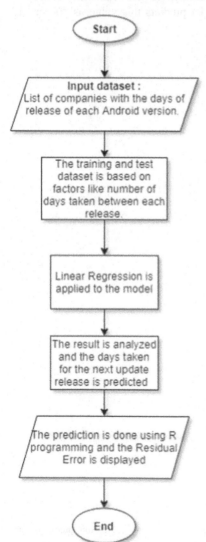

FIGURE 26.3 Flow chart depicting mobile Android update prediction and analysis.

manufacturer. The linear regression model is applied on the training and test data set. The graph obtained from the linear regression model gives a clear idea of the trend followed by each manufacturer (i.e.) the number of days taken for each Android update release is observed in the form of graphical representation. The same prediction is also using another data analytical tool, R programming. The results obtained from R programming not only gives the prediction model but also the Residual error in prediction. The flowchart depicted in Figure 26.4 gives a clear perspective of the Logistic model that is implemented. The model was used to predict the availability of security fixes in different versions of Android. The dataset used comprises of the version history of Google's Android update, API (Application Programming Interface), release date and year of each version of Android, security fix support availability, and the names of each Android version. The dataset is split as training and test dataset (25%) then the input and target features from the dataset is chosen. Logistic regression model is initialized and the target variable (i.e.) the availability of security fix support is predicted. The availability is denoted as "1" and non-availability is denoted as "0." The predicted model is also evaluated using Confusion Matrix. The accuracy of the predicted logistic model is obtained and it is plotted in the form of graphs using matplot library package in Python.

The Decision Tree model represented in Figure 26.5 gives a clear perspective of the algorithm used. The dataset used to train the model consists of Google's Android updated version History with API levels. The target variable or the value to be predicted is the availability and non-availability of security fix. For a particular version of Android, the Decision Tree model predicts this value as "0" or "1,"

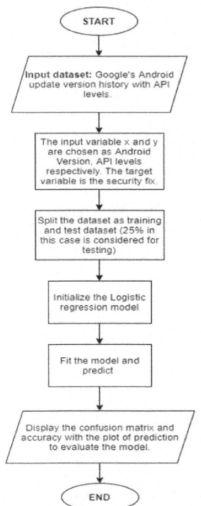

FIGURE 26.4 Flow chart depicting logistic regression prediction and analysis.

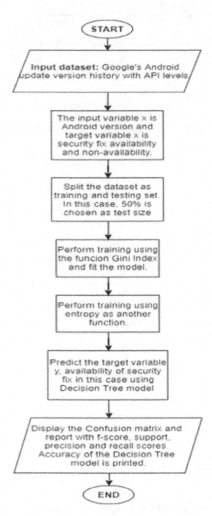

FIGURE 26.5 Flowchart depicting decision tree model.

indicating the availability and non-availability of security fix. The dataset is split into training and testing with test size as 50%. The next process is carried on with the training of model using Gini index and entropy functions. The Confusion Matrix is then displayed with the correct and falsely predicted values by the Decision Tree model. This Confusion Matrix is further used to calculate and display the values for each of the two categories (i.e.) "0" and "1." The values displayed for each category are precision score, f-score, recall score, and support. The resultant scores are obtained from the Confusion Matrix. The accuracy of the predicted Decision Tree model is also printed. The scores obtained suggest the extent to which the actual values are predicted correctly and the values which are incorrectly predicted. Thus, the target variable (i.e.) availability or non-availability of security fix for a specific updated version of Android is experimentally predicted using Decision-Tree model with high accuracy.

26.5.3 Algorithm for the Prediction and Analysis

26.5.3.1 Algorithm for Linear Regression Model and R Programming

Input: Dataset containing the release days between each version of Android. Here the input dataset contains data for like Samsung, Huawei, One Plus, HTC, Nokia, Sony Xperia, Motorola, XIOAMI MI and LG.

Output: Scatter plot with predicted values using ML, using R programming rating of the mobile manufacturers on a scale of 10 as x-intercept and number of days as y-intercept and statistical results like mean median mode is also obtained.

Algorithm 1   bestfit_slope_intercept(xs, ys)

$m = (((np.mean(xs)*np.mean(ys)) - np.mean (xs*ys))/$

$((np.mean(xs)^2)-np.mean(xs^2)))$

$b = np.mean(ys) - m*np.mean(xs)$

$m,b = best\_fit\_slope\_intercept(xs,ys)$

$y\_predicted = m*xs + b$

Plot xs, ys and y_predicted using scatter plot

for i in range 0 to len(xs[0]):

$m1,b1 = best\_fit\_slope\_intercept(xs[:,i],ys)$

Append m1 with a

Append b1 with b

Give legend to the graph for better understanding during analysis using plt.legend(loc = 'best')

Save the graph in the notebook folder as png file using plt.savefig()

plt.show() to display the graph

Print m and b

26.5.3.2 *Algorithm for Logistic Regression Model*

Input: The dataset comprising features like API level, security fix support availability, version name, release date, and year is read as a csv file. Here, input variable x = dataset.iloc[:, [1,4]].values and target variable: y = dataset.iloc[:, 3].values.

Output: Graph with the version number along the abscissa and Android API level along the ordinate and the accuracy of prediction is displayed.

Algorithm 2   logistics_function()

---

xtrain, xtest, ytrain, ytest = train_test_split (x, y, test_size = 0.25, random_state = 0) where xtrain, xtest, ytrain, ytest are the input variable(x) used for training and testing, the target variable (y) used for training and testing respectively.

classifier = LogisticRegression (random_state = 0) Initialise Logistic regression

Fit the logistic regression classifier.fit (xtrain, ytrain)

Predict using y_pred = classifier.predict (xtest)

cm = confusion_matrix(ytest, y_pred) to get the confusion matrix

Print cm (confusion matrix) and accuracy

Plot the predicted values with x and y labels."0": no security fixes for the particular Android version and "1": availability of security fixes.

26.5.3.3 Algorithm for Decision Tree Model

Input: Android update version History with API levels and security fixes.

Output: Accuracy, confusion matrix, and the classification report with precision core, f1 score, recall score, and support value.

Print accuracy, confusion matrix, and the classification report with precision core, f1 score, recall score, and support value.

Algorithm 3   decision_tree_function()

Import the dataset.

Separate input and target variable, X = data_set.iloc[:,1].values.reshape(-1,1)

Y = data_set.iloc[:, 3].values

X_train, X_test, y_train, y_test = train_test_split(X, Y, test_size = 0.5, random_state = 100) Separate training and test dataset where test size is 50% and random_state is 100

clf_gini = DecisionTreeClassifier(criterion = "gini," random_state = 100,max_depth=3, min_samples_leaf=5) for training the dataset using Gini Index.
Equation 3.4: $H(x) = -\sum_{i=1}^{N} p(xi)\log 2\ p(xi)$ where x can take N different values from 1 and p(xi) is the probability value and H(x) is the entropy value.

clf_gini.fit(X_train, y_train), fit the decision tree model.

clf_entropy = DecisionTreeClassifier (criterion = "entropy," random_state = 100, max_depth = 3, min_samples_leaf = 5) for training the dataset using entropy.

clf_entropy.fit(X_train, y_train), fit the decision tree model.

y_pred = clf_object.predict(X_test) Predict the values using Decision tree model.

26.5.4 Methodology

To begin with, the process starts with collecting the dataset comprising of release days between each version of Android. Here the input dataset contains data for like Samsung, Huawei, One Plus, HTC, Nokia, Sony Xperia, Motorola, XIOAMI MI and LG. Four versions of Android are considered in this analysis and for prediction namely Android versions considered are 7.0 NOUGAT, 8.0 OREO,9.0 PIE and Android 9. The data is analyzed and predicted using data analytical tools like Machine learning Regression technique and R programming. Linear Regression is used to accurately predict and with the residual error the correctness is also observed. The data set is trained and tested using the regression model. The best fit line is found, the slope and y-intercept of the line is found by using the formula in equation 3.1. The prediction is done using the known equation of line as shown in equation 3.3. Once the weight and bias are found, these values are used to find the predicted point for any x.

Scatter is used to scatter the points given in the x and y arrays where x is the list of the x-coordinates of all the points and y is the list of the y-coordinates of all the points. This plots a continuous line graph on the plot. Since all y_predicted values are calculated using the formula of line on corresponding x values all the points (x,y_predicted) have to be colinear and hence a line is plotted. Using the prediction function the values are predicted and the respective graphs are plotted. The same analytical approach is followed in R programming and the predicted values are printed which displays the days of the next release. The model is also analyzed statistically by obtaining their mean, median and mode values. The graph for the rating of the users and the number of days is also visualized in the form of a graph. Security assurance during the updating of any version of Android becomes an essential process. The lack of security results in several software problems and the data would be highly insecure This means that with the Android updates if the security fix support is not provided or is unavailable then the user's data is prone to hacking. Any third-party software can easily obtain the confidential files and other resources stored in an Android device. To solve this, the proposed technique of Logistic regression is helpful. Logistic regression is generally used to predict values in the form of binary which serves the purpose here. This basic idea, is used to identify if the updated version of Android has the support of security fixes or not. The dataset used comprises of the version history of Google Android release from Android version 1 to Android 11. API levels of security is also considered. The model is then trained and tested. The prediction of the availability and non-availability of security fix support for a particular version of Android is done and is plotted in the form of graph. The predicted model is also evaluated using Confusion matrix to observe the true and false predictions. The accuracy score is also displayed as percentage for the predicted logistic model. Decision Tree model is a powerful algorithm to predict the target variable with great accuracy. The structure of the Decision Tree model is such that every internal node clearly depicts the test on a specific variable (i.e.) the target variable. In the algorithms used, the process is divided as building phase, training phase, testing phase and prediction phase. The leaf node is considered to depict a class label (i.e.) after initialising the Decision Tree classifier and computing the target variables and the tree branches depicts concurrences of variable or features that results in class labels. Gini index function and entropy functions are invoked. The Gini index and entropy functions using equation 3.4 are used to precisely find out which values are predicted as true variables and the falsely predicted values. The target variable here is the availability and non-availability of security fix in each updated version of Android. The Decision Tree Classifier is initialised and the test size during dataset split up is given as 50%. The values are predicted. Confusion Matrix, precision, recall, f1-score, and support values are displayed. The accuracy of the predicted model is also found by using the calc_accuracy function.

Equation 3.1: $m = (((np.mean(xs)*np.mean(ys)) - np.mean (xs*ys))/$
$((np.mean(xs)^2)-np.mean(xs^2)))$ where xs and ys are the x and y coordinates and np here denotes the numpy library, respectively.

Equation 3.2: $b = np.mean(ys) - m*np.mean(xs)$

Equation 3.3: $y = mx + b$ where m is the slope and b is considered as the y intercept.

Equation 3.4: $H(x) = -\sum_{i=1}^{N} p(xi)\log 2 \ p(xi)$ where x can take N different values from 1 and p(xi) is the probability value and H(x) is the entropy value.

26.5.5 Software Packages Used

1. **sklearn:**
   - The package sklearn in python helps in implementing many ML algorithms.
   - In this work modules like train_test_split, DecisionTreeClassifier, and accuracy_score are used.
2. **NumPy:**
   - For faster and efficient arithmetic calculations, the numeric python module NumPy is used.
   - Large number of numpy arrays can be read and manipulations are also performed using this package.
3. **Pandas:**
   - This package is used for the purpose of reading from and writing to different files.
   - Data frames are helpful in performing manipulations.
4. **RStudio – Scatterplot:**
   - Tovisualize a scatterplot, this package is used implementing using the function plot (x, y).

26.5.6 Dataset Description

26.5.6.1 Attribute and Values Information

1. Dataset 1:
   - Android Version name, Android version number, Month date and year of release of each version of Android, Security fix availability and non-availability, API levels for each version
2. Dataset 2:
   - Manufacturer: Displays the names of each mobile manufacturer.
     The following are the other attributes used with values as the number of days taken by each manufacturer to make the Android compatible for the next release.
   - Android 10, 9.0 Pie, 8.0 Oreo, 7.0 Noughat

26.5.6.2 Missing Attribute Values: None

Further information of the dataset can be found in Tables 26.1 and Table 26.2 in Appendix.

26.6 Experimental Results and Discussions

26.6.1 Graphical Representation

Figure 26.6 depicts a continuous straight-line graph to show that the selected points are collinear. Figures 26.7 and 26.8 give a graphical visualisation of the predicted values by considering the number of days between each release of the updated Android version for each mobile manufacturer. Thus, a scatter plot is obtained in Python with the slope and intercept values. Figure 26.9 as shown below gives a clear idea about the impact of the rating of users depending on the number of days taken to release the updated version for the mobile manufacturers. The output depicted in Figures 26.10 and 26.11 gives a clear perspective of the statistical results like mean, median values, and the predicted values. The standard error value also obtained for the prediction is also found as 1.215 on 34 degrees of freedom.

Figure 26.12 gives a clear perspective of the results obtained from Lasso regression. The model predicted using Lasso regression is evaluated using the Confusion matrix as shown. The true negative value is displayed as 3 and true positive value is displayed as 1. The accuracy of the predicted model is 100% as all the values given for the test dataset were predicted accurately. In Figure 26.12, a plot of

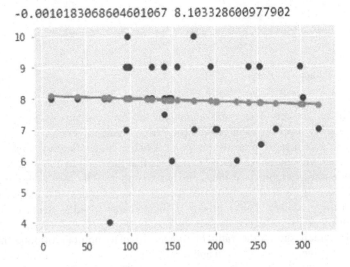

FIGURE 26.6 Straight line graph denoting collinear.

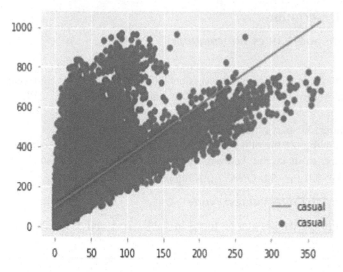

FIGURE 26.7   Best-fit line, collinear points.

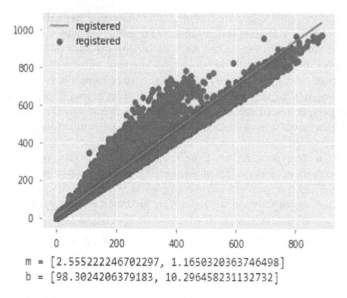

m = [2.555222246702297, 1.1650320363746498]
b = [98.3024206379183, 10.296458231132732]

FIGURE 26.8   Regression line with slope.

the predicted result can be seen. The abscissa contains the Android version number and the ordinate displays the API security level for each version (i.e.) from Android version 1 to the recently released version, Android 11. Lasso regression results gives a better understanding about the security fixes which comes with each version of Android. "1" denotes that the version contains security fix supports and "0" denotes the non-availability of the security fix support. The results obtained from Decision Tree is shown in Figure 26.13. The decision tree predicted model gives an accuracy of 75% which the model has successfully predicted. The results of "1" being categorised as Security fix availability and "0" as non-availability is also obtained as Entropy results with precision for each of the categories 1 and 0, recall score which shows the ratio of true positive to number of false negative, f1 score depicting the weighted average of precision and recall, support values which shows the number of true values in each category "0" and "1." These results are obtained from the confusion matrix. Using the

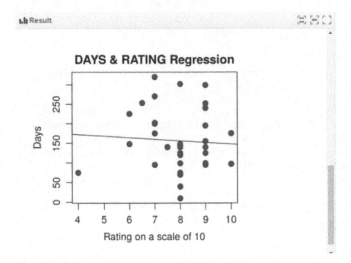

FIGURE 26.9 Graph depicting the user's rating vs days taken.

```
Result

$Rscript main.r

Call:
lm(formula = ys ~ xs)

Coefficients:
(Intercept)          xs
   8.103329    -0.001018


Call:
lm(formula = ys ~ xs)

Residuals:
    Min      1Q  Median      3Q     Max
-4.0270 -0.7902  0.0240  1.0041  2.0749

Coefficients:
             Estimate Std. Error t value Pr(>|t|)
(Intercept)  8.103329   0.469942  17.243   <2e-16 ***
xs          -0.001018   0.002718  -0.375     0.71
```

FIGURE 26.10 Linear regression model using R.

highly accurate results obtained from Decision Tree, Lasso and Linear Regression models, conclusions of the usage of a particular updated version of Android and the security fixes availability is experimentally proved.

26.7 Conclusions and Future Work

The nightmares of security issues faced in mobile phones have resulted in augmentation of cyber rates. The significant reason is the lack of frequent updates of the Android version. With new updates come new features and additional security. Hence this analysis and prediction serves as a

```
---
Signif. codes:  0 '***' 0.001 '**' 0.01 '*' 0.05 '.' 0.1 ' ' 1

Residual standard error: 1.215 on 34 degrees of freedom
Multiple R-squared:  0.004111,  Adjusted R-squared:  -0.02518
F-statistic: 0.1404 on 1 and 34 DF,  p-value: 0.7102

        1        2        3        4        5        6        7        8
8.006589 7.955674 7.874210 7.845697 8.026956 7.960766 7.897631 7.846715
        9       10       11       12       13       14       15       16
8.093146 8.026956 7.952619 7.960766 7.904759 7.798855 7.952619 7.925125
       17       18       19       20       21       22       23       24
8.062596 7.955674 8.003535 7.858935 8.004553 8.032047 8.002516 7.981132
       25       26       27       28       29       30       31       32
8.002516 7.945491 7.976040 8.006589 7.976040 7.976040 7.925125 7.899667
       33       34       35       36
7.960766 7.795800 7.777470 7.828386
```

FIGURE 26.11   Residual standard error and statistical results.

```
Confusion Matrix :
 [[3 0]
 [0 1]]
Accuracy :  1.0
0 ---> No Security Fixes for the particular Android
1 ---> Security Fixes are available for the particul
```

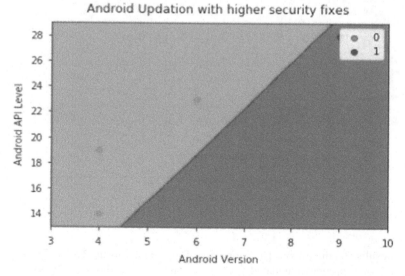

FIGURE 26.12   Lasso regression plot and confusion matrix.

solution for the mobile manufacturers across the globe to gauge the next update release of Android. This would enable the companies to plan and restructure the hardware and software accordingly, thus, improving efficiency, security, and compatibility of the mobile phones. The developers in the long run can extend these results to procure solutions for the existing mobile fragmentation and also to other operating systems like iOS by Apple. Hence, the proposed system helps to solve the

```
Results Using Gini Index:
Confusion Matrix:  [[6 0]
 [2 0]]
Accuracy :  75.0
Report :                 precision    recall  f1-score   support

           0        0.75      1.00      0.86         6
           1        0.00      0.00      0.00         2

avg / total         0.56      0.75      0.64         8

Results Using Entropy:
Confusion Matrix:  [[6 0]
 [2 0]]
Accuracy :  75.0
Report :                 precision    recall  f1-score   support

           0        0.75      1.00      0.86         6
           1        0.00      0.00      0.00         2

avg / total         0.56      0.75      0.64         8
```

FIGURE 26.13 Decision tree results.

problem of delay in Android updates, which not just improves the overall performance of the system but also provides security against cyber threats. In a nutshell, the Android devices and updates may be used to uplift the human race or dig a cave for destruction. It is up to us.

REFERENCES

[1] S. Scalabrino, G. Bavota, M. Linares-Vásquez, *et al.,* "API compatibility issues in Android: Causes and effectiveness of data-driven detection techniques." *Empir. Softw. Eng.* 25, 5006–5046 (2020).
[2] S. Amann, H. A. Nguyen, S. Nadi, T. N. Nguyen, and M. Mezini, "A systematic evaluation of static API-misuse detectors." *IEEE Trans. Softw. Eng.* 45(12), 1170–1188 (1 Dec. 2019), doi: 10.1109/TSE.2018.2827384.
[3] D. Cotroneo, F. Fucci, A. K. Iannillo, R. Natella, and R. Pietrantuono, "Software aging analysis of the Android mobile OS." *IEEE 27th Int. Symp. Softw. Reliab. Eng. (ISSRE)*, Ottawa, ON, 2016, pp. 478–489, doi: 10.1109/ISSRE.2016.25.
[4] S. McIlroy, N. Ali, and A.E. Hassan, "Fresh apps: An empirical study of frequently-updated mobile apps in the Google play store." *Empir. Softw. Eng.* 21, 1346–1370 (2016).
[5] N. Ashraf, A. Masood, H. Abbas, *et al.,* "Analytical study of hardware-rooted security standards and their implementation techniques in mobile." *Telecommun. Syst.* 74, 379–403 (2020).
[6] L. Singleton, R. Zhao, M. Song, and H. Siy, "FireBugs: Finding and repairing bugs with security patterns." *IEEE/ACM 6th Int. Conf. on Mob. Softw. Eng. and Syst. (MOBILESoft)*, Montreal, QC, Canada, 2019, pp. 30–34, doi: 10.1109/MOBILESoft.2019.00014.
[7] N. Nissim, R. Moskovitch, O. BarAd, *et al.,* "ALDROID: Efficient update of Android anti-virus software using designated active learning methods." *Knowl. Inf. Syst.* 49, 795–833 (2016).
[8] A. Gupta, B. Suri, V. Bhat, "Android smells detection using ML algorithms with static code metrics." In: Batra U., Roy N., Panda B. (eds) Data Science and Analytics. REDSET 2019. Communications in Computer and Information Science, vol. 1229, 2020. Springer, Singapore.
[9] M. Anshori, F. Mar'i, and F. A. Bachtiar, "Comparison of machine learning methods for Android malicious software classification based on system call." *Int. Conf. Sustainable Inf. Eng. and Technol. (SIET)*, Lombok, Indonesia, 2019, pp. 343–348, doi: 10.1109/SIET48054.2019.8985998.

[10] Z. Guo, Z. Lv, B. Zhou, and C. Chen, "Feature detection and security evaluation of mobile phone based on decision tree." *14th Int. Comput. Conf. Wavelet Active Media Technol. Inf. Process. (ICCWAMTIP)*, Chengdu, 2017, pp. 89–92, doi: 10.1109/ICCWAMTIP.2017.8301455.

[11] M. Xu, C. Song, Y. Ji, M.-W. Shih, K. Lu, C. Zheng, R. Duan, Y. Jang, B. Lee, C. Qian, S. Lee and T. Kim, "Toward engineering a secure Android ecosystem: A survey of existing techniques." *ACM Comput. Surv.* 49, 2 (2016), Article 38 (November 2016).

[12] N.-V. Long, J. Ahn, and S. Jung, "Android fragmentation in malware detection." *Comput. Secur.* 87 (2019101573).

[13] G. Yang, J. Jones, A. Moninger, and M. Che, "How do Android operating system updates impact apps?" *IEEE/ACM 5th Int. Conf. Mob. Softw. Eng. Syst. (MOBILESoft)*, Gothenburg, 2018, pp. 156–160.

[14] P. Kong, L. Li, J. Gao, K. Liu, T. F. Bissyandé, and J. Klein, "Automated testing of Android apps: A systematic literature review." *IEEE Trans. Reliab.* 68(1), 45–66 (March 2019), doi: 10.1109/TR.2018.2865733.

[15] J. DeLoach, D. Caragea, X. Ou, "Android malware detection with weak ground truth data." Proc. of the *Thirty-First AAAI Conf. Artif. Intell.*, AAAI Press, 2017, p. 4915.

[16] K. Aggarwal, A. Hindle, and E. Stroulia, "GreenAdvisor: A tool for analyzing the impact of software evolution on energy consumption." *IEEE Int. Conf. on Softw. Maintenance and Evolution, ICSME 2015*, 2015, pp. 311–320.

[17] Q. Do, G. Yang, M. Che, D. Hui, and J. Ridgeway, "Redroid: A regression test selection approach for Android applications." *The 28th Int. Conf. Softw. Eng. Knowledge Eng. SEKE 2016*, 2016.

[18] Y. Aafer, G. Tao, J. Huang, X. Zhang, N. Li, "Precise Android API protection mapping derivation and reasoning." Proc. *ACM SIGSAC Conf. Comput. Commun. Secur.*, ACM, 2018, pp. 1151–1164.

[19] R. Mahmood, N. Mirzaei, and S. Malek, "EvoDroid: Segmented evolutionary testing of Android apps." *Proc. ACM SIGSOFT Int. Symp. Found. Softw. Eng.*, 2014, pp. 599–609.

[20] L. Li, "Mining androzoo: A retrospect." *Proc. Doctoral Symp. 33rd Int. Conf. Softw. Maintenance Evolution*, 2017, pp. 675–680.

[21] L. Li, T. F. Bissyande, Y. Le Traon, and J. Klein, "Accessing inaccessible Android APIs: An empirical study." *Proc. 32nd Int. Conf. Softw. Maintenance Evolution*, 2016, pp. 411–422.

[22] N. Mirzaei, J. Garcia, H. Bagheri, A. Sadeghi, and S. Malek, "Reducing combinatorics in GUI testing of Android applications." *Proc. Int. Conf. Softw. Eng.*, 2016, pp. 559–570.

[23] Y. Hu, I. Neamtiu, and A. Alavi, "Automatically verifying and reproducing event-based races in Android apps." *Proc. Int. Symp. Softw. Testing Anal.*, 2016, pp. 377–388.

[24] L. Li, T. F. Bissyande, H. Wang, and J. Klein, "CiD: Automating the detection of API-related compatibility issues in Android apps." *Proc. ACM SIGSOFT Int. Symp. Softw. Testing Anal.*, 2018, pp. 153–163.

[25] L. Wei, Y. Liu, and S. Cheung, "Taming Android fragmentation: Characterizing and detecting compatibility issues for Android apps." *Proc. 31st IEEE/ACM Int. Conf. Automated Softw. Eng.*, 2016, pp. 226–237.

[26] N. Mirzaei, S. Malek, C. S. Psreanu, N. Esfahani, and R. Mahmood, "Testing Android apps through symbolic execution." *Proc. ACM SIGSOFT Softw. Eng. Notes*, 2012, pp. 1–5.

[27] R. Hay, O. Tripp, and M. Pistoia, "Dynamic detection of inter-application communication vulnerabilities in Android." *Proc. Int. Symp. Softw. Testing Anal.*, 2015, pp. 118–128.

[28] G. d. C. Farto and A. T. Endo, "Evaluating the model-based testing approach in the context of mobile applications," *Electron. Notes Theor. Comput. Sci.* 314, 3–21 (2015).

[29] P. Bielik, V. Raychev, and M. T. Vechev, "Scalable race detection for Android applications." *Proc. ACM SIGPLAN Int. Conf. Object-Oriented Program., Syst., Lang. Appl.*, 2015, pp. 332–348.

[30] S. Packevicius, A. Usaniov, S. Stanskis, and E. Bareisa, "The testing method based on image analysis for automated detection of UI defects intended for mobile applications." *Proc. Int. Conf. Inf. Softw. Technol.*, 2015, pp. 560–576.

[31] H. Cai, N. Meng, B. Ryder, D. Yao, "Droidcat: Effective Android malware detection and categorization via app-level profiling." *IEEE Trans. Inf. Forensics Secur.* 14 (6), 1455–1470 (2018).

Appendix: Datasets Sample Attachments

This is a sample dataset used for the prediction of models like Linear, Lasso regression, and Decision Tree model.

TABLE 26.1

Prediction Model Sample Dataset1

S. No	Android Version Name	Android Version No	Release Date	Security Fix Availability	Security Level API
1.	Donut 1	1	September 15, 2009	0	4
2.	Eclair	2	October 26, 2009	0	5
3.	Froyo	2	May 20, 2010	0	8
4.	Gingerbread	2	December 6, 2010	0	9
5.	Honeycomb	3	February 22, 2011	0	11
6.	Ice Cream Sandwich	4	October 18, 2011	0	14
7.	Jelly Bean	4	July 9, 2012	0	16
8.	KitKat	4	October 31, 2013	0	19
9.	Lollipop	5	November 12, 2014	0	21
10.	Marshmallow	6	October 5, 2015	0	23
11.	Nougat	7	August 22, 2016	0	24
12.	Oreo	8	August 21, 2017	1	26
13.	Pie	9	August 6, 2018	1	28
14.	Android 10	10	September 3, 2019	1	29
15.	Android 11	11	September 8, 2020	1	30

TABLE 26.2

Prediction Model Sample Dataset2

S. No	Manufacturers	Android 10	9.0 Pie	8.0 Oreo	7.0 Nougat
1.	Samsung Galaxy S	95	145	225	253
2.	Huawei	75	140	202	252
3.	One Plus	10	75	148	140
4.	HTC	195	299	148	175
5.	Nokia	40	145	98	240
6.	Sony Xperia	97	70	99	120
7.	Motorola Moto	99	155	125	95
8.	Xiaomi MI	125	125	175	200
9.	LG	140	302	320	270

Index

Note: *Italicized* page numbers refer to figures, **bold** page numbers refer to tables